The Western European Union

D1662595

This full-term study of the Western European Union (WEU) brings to life the history of Europe's search for a co-operative security and defence order, from its post-World War II origins to the present day. Establishing the WEU as a support organization, designed to promote the two security 'ideas' of collective defence and integration through the primary organizations of alliance and community, this book offers a window onto the challenges faced in the development and management of NATO and the evolving European Communities/European Union (EC/EU) over time. As the WEU's historical journey unfolds, the frequently competing visions of the future organization of the European security space are exposed in the fluctuating nature of its own functional evolution and devolution. A hybrid organization driven by its dual support role, the constructively ambiguous and conveniently autonomous WEU was to provide a mechanism through which divergent interests could converge and inherent tensions be relieved, preventing NATO and EC/EU stagnation. This book offers fresh insight into the means by which the gradual transformation of the institutional framework of European security was enabled, and it stakes the WEU's claim as a fundamental and life-long contributor to the stability of the European security system.

Sally Rohan is a European Security specialist and Senior Lecturer with King's College, London. Based at the UK's Defence Academy, she has presented widely on European Security issues, has served as UK faculty member of the European Security and Defence College and is a life-member of the Central European Academy of Science and Art.

British Politics and Society

Social change impacts not just upon voting behaviour and party identity but also the formulation of policy. But how do social changes and political developments interact? Which shapes which? Reflecting a belief that social and political structures cannot be understood either in isolation from each other or from the historical processes that form them, this series examines the forces that have shaped British society.

The Western European Union
International Politics between Alliance and Integration

Sally Rohan

Routledge
Taylor & Francis Group

NEW YORK AND LONDON

First published 2014
by Routledge
711 Third Avenue, New York, NY 10017

and by Routledge
2 Park Square, Milton Park, Abingdon, Oxon OX14 4RN

*Routledge is an imprint of the Taylor & Francis Group,
an informa business*

© 2014 Taylor & Francis

Library of Congress Cataloging-in-Publication Data

Rohan, Sally.
The Western European Union : international politics between alliance and
    integration / Sally Rohan.
        pages cm. — (British politics and society)
    Includes bibliographical references and index.
    1. Western European Union.   2. National security—Europe.
3. Europe—Defenses.   4. European Union.   5. North Atlantic Treaty
Organization.   I. Title.
    JN94.A58R63 2014
    341.242′2—dc23
    2014005748

ISBN: 978-0-714-65613-7 (hbk)
ISBN: 978-0-203-34185-8 (ebk)

Typeset in Sabon
by Apex CoVantage, LLC

Printed and bound in the United States of America by Publishers Graphics,
LLC on sustainably sourced paper.

Contents

Abbreviations

ABC	Atomic, biological and chemical
ACA	Agency for the Control of Armaments
AFSOUTH	Allied Forces Southern Europe (NATO)
ARRC	Allied Rapid Reaction Corps
AWAC	Airborne Warning and Control System
CEE	Central and Eastern Europe
CESDP	Common European Security and Defence Policy
CFE	Conventional Forces Europe
CFSP	Common Foreign and Security Policy
CJTF	Combined Joint Task Force
CNAD	Council of National Armaments Directors
CSCE	Conference on Security and Co-operation in Europe
CSDP	Common Security and Defence Policy
DCI	Defence Co-operation Initiative
DQAC	Defence Questions and Armaments Committee
DSACEUR	Deputy Supreme Allied Commander Europe
EAA	European Armaments Agency
EC	European Community/European Communities
ECSC	European Coal and Steel Community
EDA	European Defence Agency
EDC	European Defence Community
EEC	European Economic Community
EFTA	European Free Trade Area
EMU	Economic and Monetary Union
EP	European Parliament
EPC	European Political Co-operation
EPU	European Political Union
ERP	European Recovery Programme

ERRC/ERRF	European Rapid Reaction Corps/Force
ESDA	European Security and Defence Assembly
ESDI	European Security and Defence Identity
ESDP	European Security and Defence Policy
ESS	European Security Strategy
EU	European Union
EUFOR	European Rapid Operational Force
Euratom	European Atomic Energy Community
EUROFOR	European Rapid Deployment Force
EUROMARFOR	European Maritime Force
FAWEU	Forces Answerable to the Western European Union
FCO	Foreign and Commonwealth Office (UK)
FIG	French-Italian-German Arms Pool
FRUS	*Foreign Relations of the United States*
GAC	General Affairs Committee (WEU)
IEPG	Independent European Programme Group
IFOR	Implementation Force (NATO)
IGC	Intergovernmental Conference
INF	Intermediate-range Nuclear Forces
IRBM	Intermediate Range Ballistic Missile
ISS	Institute for Security Studies
KLA	Kosovan Liberation Army
MAPE	Multinational Advisory Police Element
MBFR	Mutual and Balanced Force Reductions
MBT	Modified Brussels Treaty
MCM	Mine Counter Measures
MLF	Multilateral (nuclear) Force
MOD	Ministry of Defence
NAA	North Atlantic Assembly
NAC	North Atlantic Council
NACC	North Atlantic Co-operation Council
NAD	National Armaments Director
NATO	North Atlantic Treaty Organization
NRF	NATO Response Force
OCCAR	Organisation Conjointe de Cooperation en matière d'Armaments
OEEC	Organization of European Economic Co-operation
OSCE	Organisation for Security and Co-operation in Europe
PCA	Partnership and Cooperation Agreement

PfP	Partnership for Peace
PoCo	Political Committee
PSC	Political and Security Committee
QMV	Qualified Majority Voting
ROE	Rules of Engagement
RUSI	Royal United Services Institute
SAC	Standing Armaments Committee
SACEUR	Supreme Allied Commander Europe
SACLANT	Supreme Allied Commander Atlantic
SDI	Strategic Defense Initiative
SDR	Strategic Defence Review
SEA	Single European Act
SHAPE	Strategic Headquarters Allied Powers Europe
SWG	Special Working Group
TEC	Treaty Establishing the European Community
TEU	Treaty on European Union
TFEU	Treaty on the Functioning of the European Union
TNA	The National Archives (London, UK)
TOA	Treaty of Amsterdam
UN	United Nations
UNSC	United Nations Security Council
WEAG	Western European Armaments Group
WEAO	Western European Armaments Organisation
WEU	Western European Union
WEUCOM	WEU communications network
WU	Western Union
WUCOS	Western Union Chiefs of Staff Committee

Acknowledgements

I would like to thank all of those family, friends and colleagues who have supported me through the production of this 'labour of love'. Their constant encouragement and good-natured critique have kept me on track during the long hours during which the WEU became a part of all of our lives! I would also like to salute all of those officer-students at the UK's Joint Services Command and Staff College from whom I have learned so much over the years and pay tribute to their boundless enthusiasm and intellectual curiosity.

This story of the WEU is one for the 'little guy'—for the unassuming supporters of the great and the good, the anonymous and unspoken heroes who silently change the world.

For Nick, Sam, Anna, Charlie and Pip—with love.

Introduction

On 30 June 2011, the Western European Union (WEU), the oldest of the post-war European security organizations, quietly 'shut up shop' for the last time. Its passing was without fanfare and, just as in its quiet existence, it attracted little public attention. Its 10 full member states appeared barely to register its going, their attention drawn by the requirements of maintaining security through other organizations, the promotion of which had been the 'life-long commitment' of the WEU itself. For some, the WEU's historically consistent low profile and its ultimate demise were simply reflections of its limited function or utility. Indeed, Gordon, one of the limited number of academics to take any real interest in the WEU, suggested back in 1997 that 'of all the organizations currently existing in the world, the Western European Union (WEU) must be one of those whose length of existence is the most inversely proportionate to the actual functions that it has fulfilled'.[1] Some simply dismissed the WEU as an institutional aberration[2] or explained its persistence as a consequence of a residual institutional momentum of its own.[3] However, its longevity and staggered development do suggest that it had, in some way, both served and been responsive to the changing requirements and interests of member states within the system in which it functioned. The actual purpose of the WEU, given the apparent limitations of its substantive functions, has been a perennial matter of contention. Indeed, the historiography of the WEU is replete with policy-makers and academics asking the same question: 'What *is* the role of WEU?'[4] The answer to that question is the purpose of this study. As the WEU has reached the end of its institutional life, this birth-to-death historical examination casts new light on the nature and purpose of this modest organization. In doing so, it is an unashamed vote for the 'small guy' and a challenge to the assumptions of those who see greatness only in large and showy packages. The contention of this study is that the WEU has been an unassuming but indispensable element of the story of post-war European security co-operation and that, through its narrative, the complexities of that story and the relationship between its key players may also be better revealed.

This study takes as its explanatory lens the hypothesis that the WEU's development was determined by its duality of function, as articulated in its founding treaty, and that its subsequent contribution to European security can be understood only with reference to its resultant hybrid nature. With its roots in the early post-World War II enthusiasm for collective European behaviour, the Brussels Treaty of 1948, modified in 1954 to establish the WEU, set out a broad remit for the organization encompassing 'Economic, Social and Cultural Collaboration and Collective Self-Defence'. As a collective defence organization with a commitment to 'progressive integration', the WEU was a representation of two 'big ideas' regarding the organization of European security in the post-war world.[5] On the one hand, there was collective defence; a traditional idea, although new in terms of peacetime organization, where the purpose of collective engagement was essentially externally focused, defined in terms of relative power and directed against an existential threat.[6] On the other hand, there was integration, where communities of common interest constructed internally focused co-operative security through policies of mutual reassurance and enhanced interdependence.[7] That these ideas were taken up by other institutions may be seen as an expression of the WEU's limitations. Indeed, from the outset, the WEU may be identified as a 'second-best' alternative, in contrast with the co-operative arrangements established under the North Atlantic Treaty Organization (NATO) and the evolving Communities of Europe. As a defence alliance the WEU remained reliant on the external power of the United States (US), provided through NATO, to whom it was to transfer its defence competency. As a vehicle for European integration, the WEU was kept at a polite distance from a European integration process that has shied away from defence in its gradual evolution from European Communities (EC) to European Union (EU). And yet the story of the WEU is inherently tied up with that of these two primary organizations of security: as an element of the Atlantic Alliance (NATO) mandated with the role of 'promoting unity and encouraging the progressive integration of Europe', the WEU's support status made it often a shadowy figure behind the machinations of these more impressive actors. This study contends that it is in this support role that the contribution of the WEU to the wider European security environment must be assessed.

This raises a number of other issues regarding the nature of the WEU's role. If the WEU was established as a support organization to these dual processes, then its role may be understood only in the context of the broader international security environment in which other organizations were to take the lead. But why was it that this support was required, and what was the nature of that support to be? The central contention of this study is that the WEU played a fundamental role in the management of the tensions inherent within and between the primary European security structures of alliance and community. Through its support of NATO and the EC/EU, the WEU provided a mechanism for compromise between divergent national interests in the pursuit of the core requirements of the security order. Given its broad institutional mandate and 'crossroads' position between the transatlantic and European constituencies,[8] the WEU had a unique role to play in satisfying what were potentially contradictory security priorities and definitions, the management of which had been the WEU's essential raison d'être. The WEU was an institution of only 'secondary' importance when compared with the two 'big players' of collective defence and European integration, NATO and the EC/EU. However, in providing for the management of tensions inherent in the process of developing a coherent European security and defence architecture, the WEU was fundamental to the maintenance of the European security order, and its role has been consistently understated.

A cursory examination of the evolving security architecture of post-World War II Europe begins to illuminate those tensions that it was to be the WEU's role to overcome. In the early post-war years, as structural realities drove NATO to become the institutional hub of transatlantic defence, the EC developed to become the home of 'low politics'—commerce, trade and agriculture—providing 'soft' security as a consequence of an internal market and economic strength, made possible by reliance on the US for 'hard' security or defence. As the constituencies of collective defence and European integration became separated, a number of tensions arose both within each arena and between them. For NATO, US hegemony carried its own challenges, most notably in terms of burden-sharing, and acceptance of the terms and conditions of US leadership. Attempts to devise burden-sharing schemes that could create something approximating a two-pillar structure foundered on the twin reefs of European divisions and American ambivalence. European nations were also divided in their responses to the political dilemmas posed by the emerging structures of integration. The scope of integration in terms of membership and functional area was a matter of much contention as states sought to satisfy national concerns rather than develop any grand vision of co-operation. In terms of a European security dimension for the integrating space, the lack of any institutional blueprint for development reflected diverse ideas as to the desired 'end-state' of the integrative process. Tensions emerged between those who sought to match the Community's developing economic power with the hard power coercive capabilities of defence and those who sought to develop a 'civilian-power' Europe based on a strong economy and the persuasive and co-optive attributes of soft-power.[9]

The requirements of both alliance and community carried costs as well as benefits, leading to tensions within each organisational environment as states sought to mitigate the worst aspects of that particular form of collectivism, whilst driving development in terms of national perceptions of interests. At the same time, that the two security constituencies, transatlantic and European, would conflict was inherent in the uneven nature of their relations. As the relative-power relationship between Europe and the US altered, and integrating Europe became less dependent on its American 'protector', efforts to assert greater authority served to undermine the US leadership position. The central paradox to emerge in the management of European security was that, whilst US policy used the language of partnership to describe the desired transatlantic 'front' against the Soviets, there was no US acceptance of the loss of leadership that this 'partnership' would require. As Europeans sought increasing influence over the security environment, tensions emerged between 'partners', who were frustrated and resentful of each other's 'unreasonable' demands. Distinct strategic visions of Europe's future security order, one European and one Atlantic, were to further complicate the relationship between these two dual imperatives of collective defence and European integration.

Given its dual mandate, the WEU was to encompass the two distinct sets of interests that sat more or less uncomfortably side by side for states as well as institutions. The compromises that states made were possible because they held both sets of interests in mind in seeking to satisfy their security needs. Indeed, the WEU Treaty was in many ways an expression of the basic fact that states could hold building both Europe and Atlantic solidarity as central interests. That these interests were frequently at odds with each other has become something of a truism and has been the subject of a debate well played out in both policy and academic literature. The extent to which states sought compromise between these interests depended on both parochial self-interest and the prevailing conditions of the international environment. This study demonstrates that, for the WEU, providing that compromise was its core business.

If the WEU's role was essentially to support the processes of alliance and integration taking form elsewhere, the nature of that support may be identified, at least in part, by an examination of its formal function, which can also provide insight into the drivers of development. The historical examination of the development of the WEU makes clear that the functions of the institution evolved and devolved over time. The original arms control function of the WEU was to be dropped in 1984, its political function was to evolve and devolve between 1955 and 1970, and its operational function was to develop from the 1980s. Rees identified the multifunctional nature of the WEU and, whilst focusing essentially on the early post-Maastricht environment, recognized that these functions changed 'according to the demand of the time'.[10] Analyses of the WEU in the 1980s reflected on the causes of the WEU's revitalization after a period of somnolence, determining that its development was driven by the frustrated collective and individual interests of states in the primary security apparatus. Pijpers pursued the idea of functional evolution and devolution when he suggested that, in responding to the 'internal' problems of inter-state relations, the WEU had acted as a 'first aid' organization, emerging only to provide the 'crutches to get Europe back on its feet again', evolving when NATO or the EC was unhealthy, devolving when they were not.[11] Schmidt noted that the WEU's functions were 'upgraded only when the desired progress in the preferred organization failed to materialise or when problems and difficulties occurred which could not (initially) be settled within the framework of that organisation'.[12] In this sense, the WEU was a 'forum of convenience',[13] and the extent to which it enabled other alliances and integrative developments to take place largely determined the pace and nature of its development. Its uncomfortable cross-roads position between NATO and the EC/EU often made the WEU something of a 'political football' between the two primary organizations,[14] given its uneasy task of fulfilling a range of frequently competing or contradictory interests. Rees describes the WEU as an institution 'caught in the ebb and flow of a debate' between these two primary organizations, and the history of the WEU serves to demonstrate the challenges that this position posed.[15] However, the WEU's contribution to the European security order lay precisely in this awkward juxtaposition and its subsequent ability to influence both the Alliance and the Community-development processes. In this sense, the WEU had not 'suffered' but had thrived on that very 'ebb and flow', within which this historical examination of its development is placed.

This study examines the development of the WEU from its wartime origins to its recent demise. Its purpose is to assess the role played by the WEU in the European institutional environment and to identify the impact of multilevel factors on its development. From the vantage point of 2013, the study provides an original full-life history, enabling the identification of patterns of development through time and the consistency, or otherwise, of those factors that influenced its development. The history of the WEU is explored over given periods through an examination of the formal declaratory or treaty-based provisions, its institutional development in terms of structures and mechanisms, the definition of its functional scope, and its range of activity, its membership, and its capabilities. Such an examination, however, provides little more than a 'snapshot' and requires contextualization within a broader picture of international structural and strategic change; of national perceptions, priorities and imperatives; and, most particularly given the WEU's dual role, of factors of alliance and integration, which represent the developmental environment.

In this empirical study of the life of a security institution a range of broader analytical problems are explored. Through the examination of how, when and why the WEU was utilized by states, the tensions that existed both for and between states in the management of their security interests, tensions most evident in balancing their approach to European construction with their interests in transatlantic co-operation for defence, will be highlighted. Consideration is given to the constraining and motivating factors influencing states' security preferences. The compromises they sought through the WEU will illuminate the challenges that existed in the management of their often conflicting (internally inconsistent) and contested (by others) security interests. In its broadest sense this study provides insight into the influences on institutional development and the complexity of the interplay between state-based, organizational and systemic factors. Although touching lightly on theoretical models in offering perspective to the historical evidence, this analysis self-consciously avoids any one theoretical approach. In this, it is intended that the broad historical canvas may illustrate the range of factors of change, and provide a panoramic view of the European security landscape that might otherwise be distorted by an interpretative over-emphasis on any single theoretical approach. The WEU's development was a response to the compromises made between both competing national priorities and inter-state interests. This, in turn, was influenced by the WEU's own institutional 'form' and its relationship to the prevailing security architecture and by environmental or external/structural change. And this development itself fed back into the complex interplay of interests from which the present European security architecture was to emerge.

This study has drawn on a broad range of literature; the contemporaneous nature of many of these sources, both primary and secondary, provides a contextualized understanding of the relevant issues. Throughout its lifetime, the WEU received only scant attention from the academic press. Despite some noticeable exceptions (for example on the occasion of the WEU's revitalization in 1984), there has been little in the way of detailed and focused academic scrutiny, with the WEU featuring only at times of Alliance or Community crisis, as an appendage to the consideration of NATO and/or the EC/EU. A brief period of academic activity was ignited during the 1990s as debates regarding European and Atlantic futures identified the WEU as an object of intellectual interest, despite limited 'exclusive' analysis in the secondary literature.[16] As the WEU prepared for dissolution at the turn of the decade, the emphasis was firmly on NATO and the EU's Security and Defence Policy (ESDP) and off the organization that had aided their transition to the new order.[17] Given this general dearth of specific secondary analyses, and the significance of the wider European security context for a full understanding of the WEU's role, this study has drawn on the extensive literature regarding the relationship between security and integration in Europe, the nature of alliance and the development of NATO, and the challenges of maintaining the transatlantic relationship. A wide range of primary sources have been used to support the historical examination, with the UK National Archives (TNA) providing evidence of policy attitudes and direction, whilst access to the restricted files on the WEU's predecessor, the Western Union (WU), was particularly informative for the early debates. Documentation from national governments and departments, NATO, the EC/EU and the WEU has also been utilized widely throughout this study.[18] Most notable amongst these sources have been the WEU Assembly Reports, which throughout the lifetime of the WEU served consistently to articulate the various interests of member states in the organization, its activities and wider security concerns.[19] Newsprint commentary and analysis has been used selectively to offer further evidence of issues in their contemporary setting. The author would also like to thank all those who enhanced this study through their extensive practitioner knowledge and insight, offered to the author through personal interviews, including national and organizational representatives at the highest level.

The development of the WEU has been examined within the time periods representative of significant institutional change. In Chapter 1, 'Birth of the Union', the WEU's contribution to the establishment of the post-war security order for Europe is examined. The origins of the WEU are traced from the Dunkirk Treaty of 1947, to the Brussels Treaty of 1948, through the European Defence Community (EDC) debates of the early 1950s and on to the establishment of the WEU in 1954. This examination demonstrates that the WEU was the product of a debate on the nature of the future security order for Europe. The dominance of the two central strategic 'ideas' of collective defence and European integration are illustrated through the WU debates. The chapter explores how the structural realities of the period led to an acceptance of defence dependency through NATO, although the lack of shared perspective on the nature of threat, the leadership role of the US in the Alliance and the desired scope of European integration were to lead to significant tensions between the participant states. French fears of German rearmament, demanded by the US in light of the Soviet threat, drove Paris to explore the possibilities of European defence integration, an idea that foundered on the supranationalism inherent in the EDC project. The eventual WEU compromise provided a workable solution to the rearmament challenge; the commitment of UK forces to continental defence and the institution of Germany-focused arms control arrangements enabled the establishment of a security order for Europe that was based on the dominance of the Atlantic defence structure whilst conducive to future integrative development largely unanticipated by the WEU's British architects.

Chapter 2, 'From Activity to Dormancy', covers the period from the WEU's inception in 1954 to its retreat into Ministerial hibernation in 1973. It examines how, given the primacy of NATO in defence and the emergence of the evolving Communities in 'low politics', the WEU began its existence in support of the primary organizations of security. It identifies how the tensions resulting from differing national perspectives regarding the efficacy of the NATO alliance and the preferred scope of European integration determined the *ad hoc* nature of the WEU's functional development during this period. Transatlantic tensions emerged as European states questioned the acceptable level of defence dependence: their lack of control and influence over Alliance nuclear strategy led to proposals for WEU-based alternatives for nuclear sharing and at the same time undermined the WEU's arms control function as states sought to develop independent capabilities. The pragmatic British efforts to restrict WEU development where it might challenge NATO primacy, but to utilize it where national interests might be satisfied, are evidenced in Britain's promotion of WEU-based arms co-operation, largely in response to more exclusive European initiatives taking place elsewhere. The British Government's resistance to a defence role for the WEU is also contrasted with its encouragement of the WEU's political role as a lever to further British interests in accession to the European Economic Community in the light of Gaullist resistance. Persistent British Atlanticism limited the possibilities for the WEU to contribute directly, however, to the development of a more balanced Alliance partnership. In 1966, rejecting the WEU as a 'Anglo-Saxon' organization, the French withdrew from NATO's military structures. With British accession to the Communities in 1973, and the transfer of the WEU's political function to the EC's Political Co-operation mechanism, a lack of main-player interest condemned the WEU to a period of Ministerial somnolence, with only its Assembly holding the torch for a future organizational role.

In Chapter 3, 'The Path to Revitalization', an examination of the tensions emerging within the Alliance and Community context during the 1970s illustrates the motivations behind the revitalization of the WEU which began with its reactivation in 1984 and led to the codification of its rebirth in the Hague Platform of 1987. During the 1970s satisfaction with American leadership had declined as European foreign policy perspectives increasingly diverged from those of their American ally, and by the 1980s, Ronald Reagan's arms control unilateralism and Strategic Defense Initiative had contributed to a sense of strategic incoherence within the Alliance. Fearful, on the one hand, that the US might entangle Europe in unnecessary conflicts and, on the other, that US strategy might decouple the Europeans from their American ally, the Europeans sought a vehicle for articulating their concerns in order to influence American policy without further undermining NATO cohesion. At the same time, French and German efforts to develop a European security dimension within the EC had come up against significant resistance from those who sought to maintain Europe's soft-power status. Consequently, the interests of European states converged on the WEU as a vehicle for influencing NATO strategy and enhancing European defence dialogue in the absence of a Community-based alternative. For Atlanticists, for whom the maintenance of the transatlantic relationship in defence (and hence NATO) was the core priority, the WEU's revitalization was a contribution to Alliance management, reflected in an agenda largely composed of areas of transatlantic contention. It also served the purpose of limiting Community 'defence' development by promoting an alternative multinational forum for 'high politics', one that would sit comfortably within the Alliance framework. For Europeanists, who favoured a Eurocentric approach to satisfying European security concerns, the WEU was to serve the diametrically opposed purpose of representing a constituency of European states 'serious' about defence, and serving as a 'staging post' for a nascent European security dimension, whilst taking the unhealthy pressure of division off the Community itself. The discussion in Chapter 3 points up most clearly the manner in which the WEU could satisfy opposing interests, its development being the product of a convergence of ideas as to the method of achieving quite disparate and, indeed, contradictory objectives. Subsequently, during the revitalization process, the WEU was to represent both an enhanced contribution to the primary vehicle of collective defence, the NATO alliance, and an embryonic autonomous EDC. As a bridge between Community and Alliance interests, the WEU provided for a wide span of possible interpretations of its nature, and as such, the debates could be 'sold' as contributing to both the Atlanticist and Europeanist visions. This ambiguity enabled a compromise to be reached and allowed the WEU to serve as a symbol for both Atlanticist co-operation and a nascent European security identity.

In Chapter 4, 'Post Cold-War Challenges and Opportunities', WEU development is examined in the period following revitalization, leading to the Maastricht agreements of 1991 and concluding with the Amsterdam Treaty of 1997. The end of the Cold War broadened the security agenda and called into question the continuing efficacy of the NATO alliance and the potential security role for an ascendant EC. Concerns regarding the potential de-linking of the US-European defence relationship coincided with an increased interest among Europeans in taking a more assertive role in the management of European security issues. The perennial dilemma for Atlanticists was how to provide an enhanced European contribution to allied defence without undermining US commitment. For the Europeanists, the issue was rather how to overcome the constraints on the development of a European security competence within the Community context. Once again, as the discussion in Chapter 4 illustrates, the WEU provided the vehicle for meeting a range of diverse interests regarding the balance within the Alliance, the scope for integration, and the nature of the relationship between the two. The Maastricht compromise of 1991 tied the WEU to the development of the EU and its new Common Foreign and Security Policy, establishing it as an integral part of that Union and as the external 'sub-contractor' for Europe's embryonic defence identity. As an autonomous institution, bridging the European Union and the NATO alliance, the WEU was also able to demonstrate that European security and defence co-operation did not have to be at odds with Atlantic Alliance interests. Through the development of its operational function, the WEU demonstrated the potential contribution of a European defence capability to the resolution of common Alliance concerns, whilst the possibility of European-only operations in the management of European crises resonated with a US administration that was re-addressing its foreign policy direction. The limitations on WEU operations also underlined the realities of Europe's continuing dependence on US capabilities and encouraged both a desire for greater capability (and less dependence) and a more pragmatic acceptance of the limits of European defence aspirations, particularly for the French. Following acceptance of the Combined Joint Task Force concept and the implied level of subordination of the European Security and Defence Identity to the NATO alliance, a major hurdle to the development of a rebalanced security architecture for Europe was overcome. With the WEU's Petersberg Tasks accepted as areas of EU competence in the 1997 Amsterdam Treaty, a small but significant next step had been taken in developing a strategic consensus on the scope of 'defence' integration within the EU. Through its differentiated membership structure, the WEU drew together the range of present and future EU and European NATO states, offering mechanisms for consultation, confidence-building and practical co-operation to former adversaries and valuable experience for the future political and operational relationship between NATO and the EU. The aspirations behind the continuing development of the WEU's operational capabilities remained diverse, but the desire for an enhanced European pillar of the Alliance had become a common objective that the WEU might satisfy, at least in the short term.

Chapter 5, 'The Final Compromise', examines the events leading to the eventual demise of the WEU, beginning with the shift in British policy that led to the 'Blair Initiative' of October 1998. Keen to reinstate Britain as a European as well as a world player, even though it was outside of the evolving Monetary Union, and concerned by European failings in Kosovo, Blair indicated his Government's enthusiasm for a stronger European foreign and security policy role. Rejecting the WEU as 'less than ideal', Blair's acceptance, articulated in the Anglo-French Declaration following the St Malo Summit in December 1998, of an autonomous European crisis-management capability under the EU's intergovernmental second pillar cleared the way for a Common European Security and Defence Policy (CESDP). British acceptance of this European defence competence, although primarily viewed as a European contribution to the NATO alliance, signified the resolution of the final major tension obstructing the transition of the European security order to reflect Europeanist aspirations and consequently signified the beginning of the end for the WEU. Initially ambivalent towards CESDP plans, US support was forthcoming at the NATO Washington Summit of April 1999, where the emphasis shifted from the WEU to support for EU-led operations. By June, the European Council had set the objectives of establishing 'the modalities for the inclusion of those functions of the WEU which will be necessary for the EU to fulfil its new responsibilities in the area of the Petersberg Tasks', after which 'the WEU as an organization would have completed its purpose'.[20] This chapter goes on to trace the gradual dissolution of the WEU's organizational structures, following the Helsinki and Nice agreements on the new crisis-management mechanisms of the EU. In planning for its own demise, the WEU prepared the way for an effective European defence capability, initially within the EU's second pillar. Suspending its consultation mechanisms with the EU and NATO, the WEU facilitated the adoption of its Institute and its Satellite Centre as Agencies of the EU, and disbanded its military staff. With its Council largely 'on ice', the WEU retained those residual functions related to the Article V commitment of the Modified Brussels Treaty and Assembly oversight for which there was no agreed replacement in the EU structures, whilst the role of its Western European Armaments Group for arms co-operation was subsumed within the EU's European Defence Agency. With the coming into force of the Lisbon 'reform' Treaty in 2010, the WEU's two remaining functions were formally replaced by satisficing arrangements, light on defence and democracy but sufficient to meet the requirements of consensus and enable the WEU's final closure.

The study concludes by identifying the general themes that emerge from the historical analysis. The role of the WEU as a support organization to the two primary institutions of alliance and integration is established, and the consistent nature of this role is identified. The functional evolution and devolution of the WEU are explained in terms of this support role, with the WEU responding to meet the challenges presented by changing national and structural imperatives. The benefits of the WEU's broad mandate and key-state membership are identified as significant in its ability to carry out its important support function. However, the study contends that, in light of the historical evidence, the WEU's ambiguity was its main strength, enabling ostensibly divergent interests to converge and inherent tensions to be relieved. In this way, the WEU facilitated the gradual transformation of the institutional frameworks of European security. It satisfied its core role as a support organization to the processes of collective defence and European integration and provided a fundamental and life-long contribution to the stability of the European security system. Ultimately, the WEU's demise was a consequence of this success.

NOTES

1. P. Gordon, 'Does the WEU have a role?', *Washington Quarterly*, vol. 20, no. 1, winter 1997, p. 125.
2. See for example E. Mahant, *Western European Union—or the Reactivation of a Platitude,* St Louis: International Studies Association (mimeo), 1988.
3. Forster notes the relevance of these institutional factors when he comments that WEU survived only 'because it was based on an international treaty, it was a relatively inexpensive institution, and undoubtedly its death would have reopened painful debates about how defence issues fitted into the process of European integration'. A. Forster, 'The ratchet of European defence: Britain and the re-activation of Western European Union, 1984–1991', in A. Deighton (ed.) *Western European Union 1954–1997: Defence, Security, Integration,* Oxford: European Interdependence Research Unit, 1997, p. 29.
4. P. Schmidt, 'The Western European Union in the 1990's: searching for a role', *Strategic Outreach Roundtable Paper and Conference Report,* Washington, 1993; R. Haslach, 'The Western European Union: a defence organisation in search of a new role', *Europe,* January–February 1991, pp. 17–19.
5. A. J. K. Bailes, Political Director of the WEU, 'WEU between the EU and NATO', transcript of speech delivered in Helsinki, 9 December 1998.
6. Alliances are traditionally formed on the basis of external threat, predicated on the necessities of national units and managed on the basis of costs/gains analysis of reaching objectives. Cohesion is maintained by addressing the abandonment/entrapment dilemma, which is itself complicated by adversary/ally relations.
7. The integrative process is characterized variously by formal constitutional developments towards co-operation, functional mutual capability enhancement and attitudinal shift towards community behaviour and loyalties.
8. W. van Eekelen, 'The WEU is a crossroads institution', *International Defense Review,* vol. 23, no. 3, March 1990, pp. 261–2.

9. See J. Nye, *Soft Power: The Means to Success in World Politics*, New York: Public Affairs, 2004, for a discussion of hard and soft power.

10. G. W. Rees, *The Western European Union at the Crossroads: Between Trans-Atlantic Solidarity and European Integration,* Oxford: Westview, 1998, p. 131.

11. A. Pijpers, 'Western European Union and European political co-operation: competition or complementarity', in P. Tsakaloyannis (ed.) *The Reactivation of the WEU: The Effects on the European Community and its Institutions,* Maastricht: European Institute of Public Administration, 1985, p. 78. P. Borcier, *The Political Role of the Assembly of WEU,* Paris: WEU Assembly, 1963, p. 49, refers to the WEU as a 'duty doctor on call'.

12. P. Schmidt, 'The WEU—a Union without perspective?', *Aussenpolitik,* vol. 37, no. 4, 1986, p. 389.

13. I. Gambles, 'Prospects for West European security cooperation', *Adelphi Paper,* no. 244, autumn 1989, p. 11.

14. M. Clarke, book review, *Contemporary Security Policy,* vol. 18, no. 1, April 1997, p. 199.

15. Rees, *The Western European at the Crossroads,* p. 130.

16. See for example S. Duke, 'The second death (or the second coming?) of the WEU', *Journal of Common Market Studies,* vol. 34, no. 2, June 1996, pp. 167–90. Later studies include W. van Eekelen's *Debating European Security 1945–1998,* The Hague: SDU Publishers, 1998, a fascinating portrayal of his years as WEU Secretary General which provides an insider's view of the organization's development between 1989 and 1998, and his 'sequel', *From Words to Deed: The Continuing Debate on European Security,* Brussels and Geneva: Centre for European Policy Studies and Geneva Centre for the Democratic Control of the Armed Forces, 2006. Also see Rees, *The Western European Union at the Crossroads,* and Deighton (ed.) *Western European Union 1954–1997,* for useful analysis of the WEU's post-Maastricht relevance, and A. Dumoulin, *Union de l'Europe Occidentale: La Déstructuration (1998–2006),* Paris: Éditions Brylant, 2005.

17. A notable exception is the excellent final 'obituary' for the WEU by the 'insiders' A. J. K. Bailes, and G. Messervy-Whiting, 'Death of an institution: the end for Western European Union, a future for European defence?', *Egmont Paper,* no. 46, Gent: Academia Press (for Egmont—the Royal Institute for International Relations, Brussels), May 2011, online at http://www.egmontinstitute.be/paperegm/ep46.pdf.

18. The British National Archives sources, used extensively in the early chapters, have been referenced using the TNA prefix and using their original cataloguing system to ensure continuity throughout.

19. The adoption by the Assembly of a number of name changes during the course of its existence are noted in the text, but as these were not recognized by the WEU Council, 'WEU Assembly' is used throughout the references in this book and, for brevity, the specific Assembly Committee is omitted, although the rapporteur is acknowledged throughout.

20. European Council, *Declaration on Strengthening the Common European Policy on Security and Defence* (including the Presidency Report), Annex III, Presidency Conclusions, Cologne, 3–4 June 1999.

1 Birth of the Union
1945–55

The WEU has its roots in the security debate of the final years of the Second World War. Weakened and demoralized by this second major conflict of the century, the European allies sought to find a better means of managing future European relations. The continuing American presence in Europe provided immediate reassurance, but fears of a resurgent Germany and a potential Soviet threat, combined with recognition of general European decline, led many to seek alternative solutions to the seemingly intractable problem of constructing a stable Europe. Whilst talks on the development of a collective security regime under a 'United Nations' began amongst the major Allied Powers as early as 1941, the conflict-preventing potential of co-operative and integrated behaviour in the European arena was beginning to foster interest in elite European circles. The route to the WEU lies along the path leading from these initial debates regarding the very nature of post-war security and the appropriate mechanisms for its management.

This chapter traces the development of these debates from the Dunkirk Treaty of 1947, to the Brussels Treaty of 1948 and on through the failed EDC negotiations of 1950 to 1954. In 1955, as a consequence of the signing of the Modified Brussels Treaty in October 1954, the WEU emerged as an element of the institutional order of post-war Europe. Although the WEU's ascendance was to be short-lived, as it was quickly outshone by NATO and the emerging EC, the WEU was to have a significant influence on these institutional developments. Through an examination of the central influences and interests at play in the emergence of the final post-war compromise, as articulated and institutionalized through the WEU, this chapter explores the significance of the WEU for the management of the emerging European security order.

THE EARLY YEARS

Discussions regarding West European peacetime security arrangements had taken place consistently between the French and the British since the Declaration of London proposals of June 1940, which had envisaged the possibility of a Franco-British Union covering defence, foreign, finance and economic policy as well as joint citizenship.[1] These discussions had been encouraged by the smaller West European governments in exile, with the primarily economic Benelux alliance between Belgium, the Netherlands and Luxembourg emerging in September 1944 following approaches to Britain regarding the establishment of a broader-based custom union.[2] Within the British establishment, consideration of a possible West European security arrangement had accompanied the ongoing allied talks on a world security organization that would eventually lead to the signing of the United Nations Charter in October 1945. Most notable amongst the plans emerging from the British Foreign Office in the final years of the war was the report by Gladwyn Jebb, Head of the Economic and Reconstruction Department, in June 1944, which considered the advantages and disadvantages of UK involvement in a peace-time West European Security Grouping. Conscious of the risk that such a grouping might undermine Britain's important relations with the Americans, the Soviets and her Dominions, Jebb concluded that some form of West European arrangement would nevertheless be in Britain's strategic interests if a dangerous political vacuum was not be left on the continent.[3] Under his plan, Jebb proposed a regional security tier, possibly in the form of a 'United Nations Commission for Europe', subordinated to the envisaged world organization. The tier would involve a West European system of mutual bilateral or multilateral defence pacts that would balance a parallel Soviet arrangement to form a wider 'dumbbell' balance of power in Europe that would prevent future German aggression. Based initially on an Anglo-French arrangement, the report went so far as to envisage common military planning and the standardization of armaments. The alternative view held by Prime Minister Winston Churchill, along with the War and Colonial Offices, was that an alliance with the West Europeans could act as the wartime *cordon sanitaire* against the Soviets, whilst the continuation of the alliance with the US would be the key to meeting the Soviet threat.[4] Rising concerns about this threat and the potential requirement for a German contribution to meet West European security needs were recognized in the response of the Chiefs of Staff to the Jebb proposals and in the following plans drawn up by the interdepartmental Post Hostilities Planning Staff (PHPS). The PHPS concluded that, whatever the outcome of the discussions on a United Nations organization, it was vital that Britain form a West European Security Group, including the French, the Benelux and Scandinavian countries and possibly even Germany, and that this organization should co-operate with the Commonwealth and the US with the intention of eventually establishing a North Atlantic organization to counter the Soviet threat to Western Europe.[5]

The election of Prime Minister Clement Atlee's Labour Government in July 1945 led to the appointment of a new British Foreign Secretary, Ernest Bevin, who was sympathetic to the Foreign Office concept of a 'Western Union' based on close Anglo-French co-operation.[6] Although Bevin was a keen supporter of the Anglo-American relationship, he foresaw the possibility of a 'fortress America', protected economically by a high tariff wall, and thus the need for some level of European economic independence from Washington. The British Labour Party's support, during wartime 'opposition', for federal union had largely dissipated on election in July 1945, when Britain's great-power role and great-power interests excluded her from Euro-centric integration. Nevertheless, Bevin did maintain some real enthusiasm for economic, commercial and political co-operation between Britain and other Europeans. By turning the Foreign Office 'defence first' approach on its head, Bevin sought an economic partnership as the basis of an Anglo-French relationship in which military co-operation would be an indirect result.[7] He was to write to the French socialist Leon Blum, in September 1945, that his policy was 'aiming at increasing economic and cultural co-operation in the hope that out of such co-operation should arise a common outlook in defence matters'.[8] Thus Bevin's view of a Western Union was based on economic co-operation and an Anglo-French axis, supported by the development of an internationally controlled Ruhr, severing from Germany its economic potential for aggression, and the 'long term objective [was] to make the Ruhr industries the central pivot in the economy of an eventual "western union"'.[9]

A partnership with the US may have been Bevin's preferred option, but this compromise solution of WU was further promoted by Soviet antagonism and American unilateralism at the London Council of Foreign Ministers in September–October 1945, which did much to increase Bevin's interest in establishing a strong Anglo-French axis as a potential 'third force' between the emerging superpowers.[10] He approached the French Foreign Minister, Georges Bidault, on the day after the Council meeting to propose opening negotiations on an Anglo-French treaty.[11]

The foreign policy of the French Fourth Republic had been inherited largely from Charles de Gaulle's provisional government of 1944 to 1945.[12] The containment of Germany was central in French deliberations, and it was recognized that this could only be achieved by a combination of political, economic and military factors. The internationalization of the industrial Ruhr and the return to France of the coal-rich Saar region[13] would be a central plank in the policy of denial of German economic and military capabilities; alliance formation, the benefits of which had been mobilized too slowly to secure immediate French interests, remained of secondary relevance. De Gaulle believed that the future security of Europe would require economic and military co-operation between France, the Benelux states and possibly Britain. However, he sought an essentially economic association through a customs union of West European states which 'would seem to constitute a central pillar in a world organization of production, trade and security'.[14] The persistence of a strong colonial orientation in French foreign policy in the immediate post-war years was a reflection of the benefits seen to accrue from French overseas possessions during the war and the foothold that these might provide for the status of France between the two emergent superpowers.[15]

Following the elections to the French National Assembly in October 1945, de Gaulle, formally confirmed President in November, sought to establish a tripartite government representative of the popular vote split between the three main political groups—the Communists, the Christian Democrats and the Socialists. Recognizing British and American concerns at the communists' strength in French politics, de Gaulle presented his foreign and domestic economic agenda as the alternative to a Communist France.[16] However, by 20 January 1946, his inability to garner international support combined with internal political divisions led to the President's resignation from his weak coalition government. The apparent political instability of France did little to reassure the British Government. British rejection of the removal of the Ruhr from Germany on 17 April 1946, acceptance of which had been a precondition of French participation in any alliance, was at least in part a response to these increasing concerns which had served to undermine British enthusiasm for an Anglo-French alliance.[17] The offer, made by US Secretary of State Byrnes in the same month, of a 25-year Four Power treaty for the demilitarization of Germany, suggested a level of American engagement with Europe that would be preferable to any Anglo-French arrangement.[18] Bevin's interest in a customs union for Europe did result in some minor agreements with France on the removal of destructive economic practices in the autumn of 1946, but the notion of an Anglo-French cornerstone to a WU had been all but abandoned.[19] Consequently, the negotiations that followed the Anglo-French Communiqué of 16 January 1947 focused specifically on the development of a treaty against German aggression.[20]

THE DUNKIRK TREATY

Signed on 4 March 1947, the Anglo-French Treaty of Alliance and Mutual Assistance, known as the Dunkirk Treaty, consisted of a bilateral agreement to provide for each signatory 'all the military and other support and assistance' possible and was specifically aimed at the containment of any future German revanchism.[21] In the absence of an Anglo-French consensus on a still prostrate Germany, the Dunkirk Treaty may seem to have offered little more than the 'gilding for the pill that no coal was available', the offer of alliance simply shoring up the French Government at a time of instability and persuading it to give up its plans for the Ruhr as the Moscow Foreign Ministers Conference on Germany began.[22] Certainly, Bevin was keen to reassure the Russians in his speech at the signing of the Dunkirk Treaty that this did not represent the formation of an exclusive 'Western bloc', but rather that it should be seen as 'an attempt to make one contribution, woven into the fabric of Europe and the world, to a pattern of universal peace', a peace in which the Soviets might equally play a part.[23]

The Dunkirk Treaty has been presented by some as the first tentative step by the UK towards alliance creation with the US, resulting in the Brussels Treaty and NATO as a natural consequence of post-war Foreign Office planning.[24] However, it is clear that neither direction nor path was so clearly determined. The Dunkirk Treaty may rather be regarded as a pragmatic response to an uncertain future, meeting immediate needs whilst leaving options open.[25] Not least, as Larres notes, it 'would allow Britain to either take the road to reliance on a Western European Union or to opt for pursuing the path of Atlantic Alliance' dependent upon whether US support would be forthcoming.[26]

The elucidation of the Truman Doctrine on 11 March 1947 and the concomitant US acceptance of responsibility for Greece, Turkey and Iran served to convince the British Government that the US was indeed prepared to tie itself, if loosely, to a defensive system with Western Europe against the Soviet threat. When this was followed in June by the Marshall Plan for economic aid to Europe,[27] US commitment seemed assured and became central to British policy planning thereafter. Thus, it may be argued that, although the Marshall Plan appeared to enhance European unity by requiring Western co-operation in the economic field, leading in turn to the formation of the Organization of European Economic Co-operation (OEEC), the European Payments Union and the European Recovery Programme (ERP), it actually cut short any further developments along the path of true European independence in defence as the British moved solidly down the Churchill 'Atlantic defence' line, tying the UK as closely as possible to the US.

In fact, despite his Atlanticist leanings, Churchill, as leader of the opposition, had lent his support to the continental integrationists such as the Belgian Foreign Minister, Paul Henri Spaak, and the Italian federalists Alcide de Gasperi and Altiero Spinelli. In September 1946 he had called for a United States of Europe, a rousing cry that was to lead to the establishment of a United Europe Committee in London by January 1947.[28] Talks on closer Anglo-French economic co-operation during August 1947 had stumbled as Bevin rejected the integration favoured by both the French and Americans,[29] but by the end of that year an International Committee had formed, and the ideas of a United Europe were later to be reinforced at the 1948 Hague meeting of the International Committee of Movements for European Unity that was effectively to launch the European movement. Just as the potential for peace through integration was the object of elite discourse throughout much of post-war Europe, US promotion of European federalist ideas, explicit in the Marshall Plan and in ongoing diplomatic exchange, encouraged at least a veneer of integrative intent in the management of European affairs.[30]

Equally, relations with the Soviets continued to sour over the course of 1947. In their opposition to the ERP and subsequent creation of 'Cominform', the Soviets were clearly rejecting the path chosen by the British and the rest of the states of Western Europe. The collapse of the Four Power London talks on Germany's future held in December served only to reinforce the breach between East and West. It was during these talks that Bevin aired his concept of Two Circles of Defence; the first represented by a tight inner core of West European states and the second by a looser arrangement including the US and Canada.[31] There followed further discussions in Washington on the consolidation of a Western position on the German question and on the future security order of Europe more generally.

In his landmark 'Western Union' speech in the Commons on 22 January 1948, Bevin's position on the 'necessity of crystallizing Europe into separate blocs' had clearly hardened in the light of Soviet efforts to divide Europe. Having 'striven for the closer consolidation and economic development, and eventually for the spiritual unity, of Europe as a whole', Bevin argued, Britain had been presented by the Soviets with a 'fait accompli', an Eastern Europe of 'handicapped' sovereignties where 'no one [there] is free to speak or think or to enter into other arrangements of his own free will'.[32] The British Government would continue to seek to co-operate with the peoples of Eastern Europe, but it would 'not be diverted, by threats, propaganda or fifth column methods, from our [sic] aim of uniting by trade, social, cultural and all other contacts those nations of Europe and of the world who are ready and able to co-operate'.[33] In his summary of the 'revised' WU plan, presented to US Secretary of State George Marshall by the British Ambassador to Washington in advance of Bevin's speech, the proposed WU was to be dual purpose, offering the French security against any future German revanchism and laying the foundations for a future Atlantic agreement aimed against the rising Soviet threat. 'We shall be hard put to it to stem the further encroachment of the Soviet tide', he stated. 'This in my view can only be done by creating some form of union in Western Europe, whether of a formal or informal character, backed by the Americas and the Dominions . . . This need not take the shape of a formal alliance . . . It does, however, mean close consultation with each of the Western European countries, beginning with economic questions'.[34]

Bevin's apparent enthusiasm for the economic elements of the WU plan may have been at least partially driven by a desire to 'sweeten the pill' of collective defence. In a conversation with the French Ambassador in February, he was to note the British Government's wish 'to present the whole WU project in all its aspects of economic, cultural and overseas co-operation, as well as defence. We wanted to show people that there was a positive reorganization of the West, and not give any impression that we were simply preparing for defence, which in its turn might have an unfortunate effect upon the Soviet Union'.[35] Equally, US reactions to Bevin's proposals, although broadly positive, emphasized that 'the defense aspects, although of vital importance in the question of a Western European Union, are in a sense negative aspects, and only part of a political, economic and spiritual union', which it was hoped Bevin would elaborate on in due course.[36]

Nevertheless, it was the defence elements that dominated Foreign Office and Cabinet discussions following Bevin's Commons speech.[37] His preference was not for a formal regional grouping as was to emerge in the Brussels Pact, but rather a series of bilateral treaties based on the Dunkirk model. Pressure from the Benelux countries and the US persuaded him, by February 1948, to accept a wider multilateral framework of defence guarantees that would leave the way clear for eventual German inclusion and the development of a broad European security system which might be directed against the Soviet threat.[38] However, the British Ambassador to Washington, Lord Inverchapel, was to make it clear that 'without assurances of security, which can only be given with some degree of American participation, the British Government are unlikely to be successful in making the Western Union a going concern. But it appears . . . until this is done, the United States Government for their part does not feel able to discuss participation'.[39] In what was to amount to a British catch-22 the UK Government sought to achieve that which was unachievable without American commitment in order to gain the American commitment that was required in order to make it happen.

At the London Four Power Conference of 19 February to 6 March 1948, the full association of Germany's western zones in the ERP was agreed, having been previously resisted by the French, who sought national economic recovery in advance of any support for German redevelopment. As major communist-led domestic unrest erupted in France, the Prague coup of February 1948 had provided the impetus for agreement between the French and Anglo-American positions by illustrating the linkage between the American presence in Germany and the Soviet threat.[40] Although continuing to harbour concerns about the Atlantic idea, not least that it might exasperate the Russians and had implicit in it a concession on German reconstruction and eventual rearmament, the French Administration were moved to recognize the benefits to be accrued by an alliance with the developing Western bloc.[41]

During the Brussels Conference that followed (6–17 March 1948) the US Administration 'warmly welcomed Mr Bevin's initiative' toward the formation of a WU. However, it was made clear that only 'when there is evidence of unity with a firm determination to effect an arrangement under which the various European countries are prepared to act in concert to defend themselves, the US will carefully consider the part it might appropriately play in support of such a Western European Union'.[42] Inverchapel was acutely aware that acceptance of the ERP by Congress resulted from its presentation as a means of creating a 'climate of peace' in which countries could build up their own economic and defensive structures. Asking Congress for a military guarantee of West European security at the same time could mean that the arguments for the ERP 'would be blown to bits'.[43] However, the British Ambassador was informed that it was 'virtually unthinkable' that the 'de facto guarantee' provided by occupying American forces in Europe would be withdrawn before January 1949, 'when the incoming Administration and Congress should be in a position to consider a more permanent and formal type of guarantee'.[44] Thus, the Americans were seeking a holding measure—offering the potential of American involvement in European defence if the

Europeans could demonstrate their own collective capabilities, when the ERP issue had been resolved and after the forthcoming US elections.[45]

As negotiations on the WU proposals continued, Norway approached the British and American governments seeking reassurances of support, following Soviet demands for the negotiation of a bilateral non-aggression pact. This led Bevin to propose a three-system framework of security: the forthcoming Brussels Treaty system consisting of Britain, France and the Benelux states; a broader Atlantic system with close US involvement; and a Mediterranean system including Italy.[46] The US continued to insist on WU agreement as an 'essential prerequisite to any wider arrangement in which other countries including the United States might play a part', encouraging a speedy and productive conclusion to the negotiations.[47]

THE BRUSSELS TREATY

Britain, France and the Benelux states signed the Treaty of Economic, Social and Cultural Collaboration and Collective Self-Defence in Brussels on 17 March 1948.[48] Article IV of the treaty provided a substantive and definite collective defence commitment whereby signatories were obliged, in the case of an armed attack in Europe on any member, to 'afford the Party so attacked all the military and other aid and assistance in their power'. Whilst specifically identifying the potential German threat,[49] the treaty was to provide for mutual assistance against any antagonist in the European arena. The title and content of the treaty also suggest a wide-based role in terms of the promotion of European co-operation. Identifying the 'common heritage' of signatories, and 'convinced of the close community of their interests and of the necessity of uniting in order to promote the economic recovery of Europe', the treaty committed member states to 'strengthen the economic, social and cultural ties by which they are already united'.[50]

What is clear in the treaty provision of the Brussels Pact is the identity of interest between military defence and the broader context of regional security. Military provision may secure external borders, but co-operation and cohesion, promoted at both the military and non-military levels, ensured the structural basis for effective collective defence and the functional and psychological conditions of security. At the level of treaty declaration and institutional form, the Brussels Treaty articulated a broad remit for security, where defence guarantees were to be accompanied by community-building activities in the areas of 'low politics'. However, that the Brussels Treaty was ever intended to establish the institutional hub for the satisfaction of either of these interests is contentious.

At an institutional level, the Brussels Treaty offered little in terms of organizational direction, being a statement of obligation rather than a structural blueprint. The treaty provided for the establishment of an intergovernmental Consultative Council of Foreign Ministers, which was to meet successively in the capital cities of the five members (meeting for the first time in Paris on 17 April 1948). The rest of the organizational development, however, would seem to have been a response to the requirements of the treaty's broad agenda.[51] A Permanent Commission of Ambassadors of the member states in London was established to act on behalf of the Consultative Council when it was not in session, along with committees of experts on economic, social and cultural issues. Provision was also made for the close association of the US and Canada with the treaty organization as observers.[52]

The Russian blockade of Berlin, which began on 24 June 1948, helped to convince the British Government of the requirement for a defence organization under the direction of the WU Consultative Council, given the clear military incapacity of the member states and the need for some collective defence planning beyond simple mutual guarantees.[53] In September, the Five Power Military Committee, which had been established in London in May 1948, began the task of developing a comprehensive military organization, headed by the WU Defence Committee of Defence Ministers, which was to provide the higher direction for the defence organization. The committee was to be assisted by the first peacetime WU Chiefs of Staff Committee (WUCOS), consisting of the Service Chiefs of Staff of the five nations, which in turn was to be serviced by a Permanent Military Committee of supporting staff in London. A Military Supply Board was to provide the Defence Ministers with advice on the best means of production of military requirements. Directed by the Defence Committee, through WUCOS, a WU Command Organization, headed by a Commanders in Chief Committee, was established in October at Fontainebleau 'to study tactical and technical problems of Western European defence'[54] and to provide the Command of approved forces in the event of an armed aggression in Western Europe. Provision was made for US and Canadian representation across the activities of the defence organization of the WU, including participation in the work of WUCOS and the Military Supply Board.[55]

There was clearly some genuine British interest in establishing the WU as a 'third force' between the emerging superpowers, with US aid being sought only as a short-term imperative.[56] In the secret conclusions of a Cabinet meeting held days before the signing of the Brussels Treaty it was stated that 'We should use United States aid to gain time but our ultimate aim should be to attain a position in which the countries of Western Europe should be independent both of the United States and of the Soviet Union'.[57] However, the evidence does suggest that the Marshall Plan had done much to reassure the British about US commitment to Europe, and Bevin's Brussels Treaty initiative was a reflection of his overriding interest in securing an American responsibility for European defence. Indeed, Larres has argued that for the British, the 'third force' perspective of the WU was never more than 'a contingency plan to face the problems of the post-war world without being able to rely on Washington'.[58]

Nevertheless, it was as a means of engaging the US that the Brussels Treaty would seem to have been most successful. It is no coincidence that on the very day on which the Brussels Treaty was signed, President Harry Truman addressed the US Congress, stating that 'I am sure that the determination of the free countries of Europe to protect themselves will be matched by an equal determination on our part to help them protect themselves'.[59] In fact, even before the Brussels Treaty had been signed, a date was fixed for the secret 'Pentagon Talks' between the US, Canada and the UK.[60] Much against the advice of the US military establishment, which feared entanglement with a militarily weak and arsenal-depleting Europe, the Administration began talks that resulted in NSC 9,[61] the National Security Council paper that opened the way for a 'Collective Defence Agreement for the North Atlantic'.

Initially, the US Administration's interests had lain in the development and expansion of the WU as an organization with which the North Americans could develop a closer defence relationship. In support of this position, a report by the US Policy Planning Staff, on 23 March 1948, recommended that the US offer an immediate 'assurance of armed support' to WU states until such time as a mutual defence agreement could be reached.[62] However, there was considerable resistance from the Europeans both to a broader European membership of the WU and to its further development without the US already firmly on board. British and French resistance to US calls for the inclusion in the WU of strategically important 'stepping stone' states such as Iceland, Denmark and Portugal was largely driven by concerns about sharing the military aid 'pie'.[63]

It was clear that neither the British nor the French believed that the WU was, in itself, a viable organization, and both proved reluctant to develop the Brussels Treaty arrangements for fear of undermining US support by appearing to develop an alternative system. US Under Secretary of State, Robert Lovett, was to note the irony in this position when he stated that in fact 'the more tightly the treaty could be implemented, the better the United States would like it'.[64] Nevertheless, during the tripartite Security Conversations between the US, UK and Canada in late March, the principle was accepted that whilst an enlarged Brussels Treaty was desirable, extension to the North Americans was not. Clearly, the US had plans for the WU, identifying it as the 'hard core' of an eventual United States of Western Europe and believing that 'it would lose its utility for this purpose were the US to join'.[65] Therefore, the establishment of a broader Western Defence Pact including the North Americans, alongside an extended Brussels Treaty, would be the object of US policy in the ongoing negotiations.

At the first meeting of the Defence Ministers and Chiefs of Staff of the WU powers on 30 April 1948, it had been agreed to draw up strategic plans and aims on the basis of available forces and weapons so as to co-ordinate rearmament.[66] However, there was continuous controversy between the Brussels Treaty powers about their respective contributions to the WU, not least because of national concerns that US-stipulated defence spending would undermine economic reconstruction, the importance of which was also clearly recognized by the Americans.[67] In a reply to the US Secretary of

State's questions on the role of the WU in May, the Military Committee's replies made clear the limitations of European capabilities. Establishing the WU's key roles as the pooling of equipment and resources, the standardization of equipment, the harmonization of military organization, the establishment of a 'balance sheet' of available and maintainable forces, and the development of a plan of action in the event of attack, the Military Committee would seem to have set out an impressive range of activity. However, the caveated language in which the prescribed roles are articulated suggests a significant level of dependency, combined with a resistance to act until the US position with regard to engagement was clear.[68] Despite US pressure for high visibility of European collective defence efforts, and the increased European perception of the Soviet threat in light of the 'Prague Putsch' and the Soviet blockade of Berlin,[69] the five Brussels powers proved reluctant to undertake major military efforts. Each maintained individual, national and imperial interests which, it was assumed, US involvement would enable them to develop and maintain.[70] The adoption of NSC 14 (1 July 1948), facilitating US military aid for Europe, resulted in WU concerns focusing on 'the filling of its needs by American aid, rather than implementing or seriously formulating plans for pooling its own resources, standardising weapons, or expanding military production'.[71] As early as September 1948, the WU's dependence on Washington had been acknowledged and effectively institutionalized when it had been agreed that military planners could work on the assumption that, following Presidential approval, US occupation forces would be placed under WU command in time of war, at which time Field Marshall Sir Bernard Montgomery, as Chairman of the Commanders in Chief Committee of the WU, was to be replaced by an American.[72]

The reluctant acceptance of the limited 'strategic plan' of the WU in November 1948 reflected the growing desire within the US Administration to get military aid to Europe as quickly as possible to meet the growing Soviet threat, and in a manner acceptable to Congress and the American people. This 'plan' involved a summary of forces available for mobilization in 1949 if the equipment could be obtained, a position which the US Joint Chiefs of Staff accepted as if these were real achievements. It was to take significant pressure by the Americans to persuade the member states of the WU to pool any resources, organize a level of weapons transfer and put forward a comprehensive Short Term Strategic Plan by the end of March 1949.[73] By this time, it had become increasingly clear that the lack of military power at the disposal of the five nations in terms of manpower, equipment and resources would prevent the Brussels Treaty Organisation from developing into an independently effective military shield.[74] As Montgomery was to note in his memoirs, despite WU plans to defend the West, 'none of the plans could be carried out because the nations were unwilling to produce the necessary forces—properly trained, with a sound command structure and a reliable communication system . . . there was no true unity, and no nation was willing to make any sacrifice of sovereignty for the common good'.[75]

It was the failure of collective European power that would largely necessitate, Gaddis proposes, the development of a US 'sphere of influence', despite Washington's preference for a more pluralistic system of equilibrium.[76]

The Vandenberg Resolution of 11 June 1948[77] having removed much of the constitutional difficulties for US participation in any defence alliance, agreement was finally reached on the principles of a defensive North Atlantic pact to include the Brussels Treaty powers, the US and Canada, and in addition Norway, Denmark, Italy, Iceland and Portugal.[78] The Washington Treaty, a simple, short and non-discriminatory agreement, was signed on 4 April 1949. Replete with an Article 5 commitment by signatories to take such action as they 'deem necessary, including the use of armed force', in the case of armed attack against any other signatories, the treaty was to fall short of the full military commitment offered under the Brussels Treaty's Article IV. Nevertheless, it represented as far as any Administration could go in committing the US to a 25-year peacetime defence pact and to the establishment of NATO as a substantive representation of that commitment. As an element of the broader framework of Atlantic Alliance, the WU was to serve as a regional planning group for NATO, and its Supply Board and Finance and Economic Committee were to be absorbed by the organization. In succeeding in 'entangling' the Americans in an alliance that Osgood has referred to as creating 'an obvious profitable balance of assets over liabilities for all its signatories',[79] the WU powers had effectively 'subverted the stated goal of a self-reliant European Union' implicit in European notions of a 'third force'.[80]

Nevertheless, as a vehicle for 'economic, social and cultural collaboration' the Brussels Treaty represented something of a first step on the path towards a greater European unity. Indeed, Bevin recognized the potential for a WU contribution towards the incremental development of a federal state or political union in his House of Commons speech in May 1948 in which he stated that 'in the world of international politics one is forced to proceed step by step'.[81] However, Bevin's apparent encouragement of European co-operation should not be mistaken for enthusiasm for the federalist cause. In his WU speech he had been damning of the premature and 'ambitious schemes' of the European federalists, seeking European co-operation rather as a pragmatic, incremental approach to British policy interests in ensuring Franco-German rapprochement, securing American support and enhancing Britain's role in the world.[82]

Providing for a level of intergovernmental consultation and co-operation in the areas of low politics, the Brussels Treaty did serve to acknowledge some level of integrative aspiration amongst the European powers. Article II of the treaty had provided for co-operation in social affairs, and the four social committees (Social Committee, Public Health Committee, War Pensions Committee, and Joint Committee for the Rehabilitation and Resettlement of the Disabled) established by the Consultative Council in 1948 were active in promoting a high degree of beneficial interaction. Joint European courses and information exchange were developed and facilitated, the various committees seeking to harmonize activity and legislation, including in their remit aspects of civil defence and the use of atomic energy. In line with the Article III commitment to 'make every effort in common to lead their people towards a better understanding of the principles which form the basis of their common civilization and to promote cultural exchanges by conventions between themselves or by other means' the member states promoted cultural co-operation through bilateral cultural convention and cross-cultural contact, particularly aimed at the young and government officials.[83]

However, the lack of political consensus regarding the nature, purpose and scope of co-operation, most particularly between the British and the others, was also reflected in the treaty provisions. The Brussels Treaty's Article I stipulated that co-operative endeavours carried out under the treaty were not to 'involve any duplication of, or prejudice to, the work of other economic organizations in which the High Contracting Parties are or may be represented but shall on the contrary assist the work of those organizations', thus explicitly establishing the WU's role as a support for alternative European collaborative ventures. Just as the WU Defence Organisation of the Brussels Pact was to serve as a 'preparatory move toward NATO',[84] its social and cultural activities were to provide an example for the establishment of the Council of Europe in Strasbourg in 1949.

In October 1948 the WU's Ministerial Council had established a Committee on European Unity tasked with the establishment of a European Assembly to promote the unification of Europe. British resistance to French federalist leanings in the construction of an autonomous parliamentary assembly led to an eventual compromise agreement, reached by January 1949, on the establishment of a Council of Europe, consisting of a Council of Foreign Ministers and a Consultative Assembly, where decisions would be taken on the basis of Council unanimity. The five WU states were to be joined by Denmark, Ireland, Italy, Norway and Sweden in setting up the Statute of the Council of Europe on 5 May. However, the aim of the Council was vague, seeking 'to achieve a greater unity between its members for the purpose of safeguarding and realising the ideals and principles which are their common heritage and facilitating their economic and social progress'.[85]

It is true that the British had most fervently resisted any 'federal' powers for the Council of Europe, but Elizabeth Baker, in her examination of the negotiations, notes that 'how much further other West European governments would really have been prepared to go if Britain had not acted as a brake and an alibi, is not at all certain'.[86] Nevertheless, the Council of Europe was to provide an arena in which much of the debate regarding the future integration of Europe would be articulated. Consequently, it might be argued that the Brussels Treaty Organisation contributed to its own relative decline. Once it had established itself with the dual aims of promoting low-politics collaboration and collective defence, the establishment of NATO and the Council of Europe helped to push the Brussels Treaty to the periphery of international relations.

THE GERMAN REARMAMENT ISSUE

By the London Foreign Ministers Conference of May 1950, divergent national interests and perceptions were already beginning to produce signs of strain as competitive forces reasserted themselves in Europe.[87] The Soviets had broken the US nuclear monopoly in September 1949, and the communist invasion of South Korea in June 1950 had demonstrated Europe's potential vulnerability to conventional Soviet attack. The US President sought to further increase US troop deployment and military assistance for Europe through the Mutual Defence Aid Program, but the limitations of the NATO position had become clear. As Lord Ismay, NATO's first Secretary General, was to note at the time of the Alliance's first Medium-Term Defence Plan of April 1950, NATO was sorely under-resourced in conventional terms: a total of 14 divisions without adequate reserves, deployed without regard for their operational role, facing 175 Soviet divisions, with a 20:1 disadvantage in aircraft.[88] Without a coherent and co-operative West European effort the Alliance's future, and indeed the future security of Western Europe itself, looked increasingly bleak. As the issue of German participation in the European security system became a central focus of the debate, conflicting national preferences became increasingly evident.

In the UK, Foreign Secretary Bevin had come to see the development of a closer Atlantic community of North American and European states as the only sure basis for the integration of Western democracies, enabling them 'to withstand the great concentration of power now stretching from China to the Oder'.[89] As a recognised great-power, Britain was keen to promote her 'special relationship' with the US, a relationship that would require 'a sustained political, military and economic effort'. NATO was seen as central to both Anglo-American relations and American policy in Europe, hence the importance of ensuring the viability of the Alliance, especially given the belief that 'the Americans do not hesitate to scrap ruthlessly something which is not working well'.[90] At the same time, Britain would offer paternalistic encouragement to a European process from which it was geographically, historically and politically removed. Increasingly at odds with Europe's continental socialists, the British Labour Government rejected supranational integration in Europe, maintaining that national economic controls and the preservation of Commonwealth and US relations were paramount in meeting the broad range of British commercial, resource and security interests.[91] Whilst there were still those within the British establishment who were sympathetic to the idea of British leadership of a purely West European partnership to counter the weight of both Soviet and American power,[92] the dominant view within government had swung towards Atlanticism. The problem of Germany's position in the new Europe could be managed within this new US-led order, wherein a 'rehabilitated' Germany could contribute to the security interests of the Western world. At the same time, West German rearmament would have the positive effect of diverting capital away from the West German economy, benefiting British industry, which was unable to compete whilst committed to rearmament itself.[93]

Within the French Administration, a significant degree of sympathy had emerged for the concept of a united federal Europe, and many had been disappointed by the purely consultative, rather than parliamentary, nature of the Council of Europe in 1949.[94] Inspired by such enthusiastic integrationists as the French technocrat Jean Monnet, and enhanced by the perceived ineffectuality of a French political process that was hampered by communist and Gaullist interests, the idea of a new form of European government had substantial support within the French political elite. Concerns regarding the Soviet threat and the limits of European capability had led the French to accept the necessity of the North Atlantic Alliance, but the search for a European answer to French concerns had become a central plank of French policy debate.

Consequently, when, at the Three Power meeting in Washington in September 1949, Secretary of State Dean Acheson tasked the French Foreign Minister with finding a solution to the thorny problem of German participation in Europe, the resultant 'Schuman Plan' reflected the French predilection for integrative answers to broader political and security problems.[95] By the establishment of an organization for the common production of coal and steel, governed by a supranational authority, the states of Europe could not only contribute to the redevelopment of these essential industries but, in turn, make war between France and Germany 'not merely unthinkable but materially impossible'.[96] 'Sympathetic' to the concept, the British Government rejected participation in the French proposals on constitutional grounds,[97] as great-power and Commonwealth interests combined with a resistance to the integrative model, leading to the separation of Britain from what was to become the core 'Six' of European community-building.[98] Meeting on 18 April 1951, the Foreign Ministers representing France, Germany, Italy and the Benelux states signed the agreement establishing the European Coal and Steel Community (ECSC). Ratified in June 1952, the ECSC was to become the next step in a movement towards a level of European unity consistently encouraged by the US and formerly expressed through official co-operation within the OEEC.

In terms of Europe's defence role, the French's preferred vision was of a future Europe as a 'third world power' that could act independently of both superpowers, rejecting the perceived British preference for subsuming Europe within a transatlantic defence force dominated by the superpower relationship.[99] Lack of enthusiasm for the WU and encouragement of US engagement were a reflection of French limitations in the short term rather than a long-term policy choice. For the French, still smarting from the last bout of German occupation, West German rearmament needed to be prevented at all costs, particularly while the French Army was so highly committed in South-east Asia. However, France was inextricably dependent on American aid in support of its military campaign, support that the Americans were initially prepared to give only as a means of bringing the French forces home so that they might participate more fully in an integrated defence strategy for Western Europe.

Despite French reticence with regard to their allies' proposals for the rehabilitation of Germany, the British and Americans succeeded in promoting Three Power agreement on the establishment of a new German Federal Republic with limited powers under the Basic Law of 23 May 1949. This agreement paved the way for the election of Chancellor Konrad Adenauer's Government and the creation of the Federal Republic of Germany (FRG) on 20 September 1949. Following the Bundestag vote of 26 July 1950, the Federal Government was directed to follow a policy aimed at creating a European federal state,[100] with European integration providing the vehicle for the rehabilitation of Germany by accommodating the sensitivities of its European neighbours. As the new Chancellor was to emphasize, 'above all, other countries' trust in Germany must be restored. That is the task which cannot be completed in three or six or even ten years. To win that trust we must have great patience, great tenacity, we must try to advance step by step'.[101]

From 1950 onwards Chancellor Adenauer was harassed by socialist opposition that saw too close a relationship with the 'West', particularly in defence, as creating unnecessary tensions with the Soviet Union, undermining the central interest of reunification by deepening German divisions and permitting the growth of militarism. Some on the political right urged abandonment of the Western orientation in German policy in order to play East against West.[102] However, the Korean invasion had provided an uncomfortable parallel with a divided Germany, helping to focus German minds on the best means of ensuring their security, resulting in a general consensus on rearmament within the governing coalition. Despite this elite consensus, West German public opinion was essentially pro-neutral and anti-rearmament.[103] Even those in favour of rearmament were not prepared either to put economic recovery at risk or to contribute to European defence simply in terms of immediate Alliance manpower requirements.[104]

During the September 1950 meeting of NATO's governing body, the North Atlantic Council (NAC), in New York the 'package proposal' was presented by the Americans. This made US implementation of its promised troop reinforcement in Europe, and the establishment of an integrated defence force under an American NATO Supreme Commander in Europe, dependent on allied agreement to the formation of German divisions within NATO. Although the issue of how this was to be achieved was left open, it was clear that, as far as the Americans were concerned, the principle was not debatable. The resultant Three Power Communiqué began the process of West German 'rehabilitation', including a defence commitment to the Federal Republic in the case of attack.[105] It also signalled ongoing revision of occupation status and the granting of new powers to the Federal Government, including the acceptance in principle of a level of German military development, although it was noted that the constitution of a German national army would serve no one's interests.[106] Thus the East-West rift had resulted in a significant change from the Potsdam position, which had envisaged the complete disarmament and demilitarization of Germany, including the elimination of any military production facility.[107] Despite the implications of the Communiqué, the French, increasingly isolated within NATO, refused to accept the principle of German contributions under the Supreme Allied Commander Europe (SACEUR).

THE EDC

As debates continued within the NATO context as to the future role of Germany within the Alliance, the possibilities of a European initiative in defence had begun to take shape. During debate in the Consultative Assembly of the Council of Europe in August 1950,[108] the UK Leader of the Opposition, Churchill, was to surprise his audience by suggesting 'the immediate creation of a European Army under a unified command and in which we [UK] should bear a worthy and honourable part'. Churchill went on to accept the Assembly's resolution calling for this army's creation 'under the authority of a European Minister of Defence, subject to proper European democratic control', although it was to act 'in full co-operation with the United States and Canada'.[109]

The French Government had sought assurances that German rearmament would not constitute a threat to France and that the benefits laid out by the US 'package proposals' would be gained. In the absence of a French alternative to the proposed European Army, Monnet suggested that 'our resistance will have proved futile. We shall lose face, and lose the political initiative'.[110] The subsequent Pleven Plan, drafted by Monnet and named after the French Prime Minister, was laid before the French Assembly on 24 October 1950 and envisaged the creation of a European Army of a supranational character by merging military forces 'at the level of the smallest possible unit', financed by a common budget, under the leadership of a European Minister of Defence responsible to a Council of Ministers and a Common Assembly.[111] The Army would initially consist of around 100,000 men and would include West German units. At the same time, NATO members would retain their national forces, integrated under NATO, to which would eventually be added the 'federal unit' of the European Army. This would retain national forces for all NATO members except Germany, whilst allowing for a German contribution to the defence of Europe.

For France, the plan would not present the problems inherent in the US proposals for placing West German forces directly into NATO. A possible resurgence of German military power under the NATO plan would mean that the US presence would be indispensable for the future security of Europe, a scenario not favoured by the French. The French alternative could, on the other hand, lead to the creation of a European 'third force', at the same time stimulating the US to fulfil some of the promises in the 'package proposals'. For Monnet, the notion of a European Army was in itself premature; defence integration would 'force' the pace of community-building beyond its politically acceptable limits, whilst the resultant rehabilitation of the FRG through rearmament could potentially blunt German interest in the more achievable integration envisaged within the ECSC.[112] However, for the French, a European answer to the German problem was the better of two evils, and so, despite some resistance within the French Government, Monnet sought to make the best of it by influencing the decision towards a political project.[113] The Pleven Plan can thus be seen as heavily motivated by a recognition of immediate defence dependency on the US. It was essentially a 'negative contrivance', in that, like the Schuman Plan before it, it was an attempt to deal with the immediate problem of Germany and was driven by fears of an unacceptable NATO alternative.[114]

The Pleven Plan for a German contribution to the defence of the West was received with some scepticism in the US, President Truman sympathizing with the then Secretary of State Acheson's view of the plan as 'hopeless' given its unequal treatment of Germany.[115] Equally, Adenauer noted that, given the perceived urgency of German rearmament, there were concerns in Washington that the European response would almost certainly be at 'snail pace'.[116] Nevertheless, Pleven, during his visit to Washington in December 1950, succeeded in persuading Truman to hold off on any final decision on the German issue until negotiations on a European option had a chance to succeed. The compromise reached in NATO in the same month, known as the Spofford Plan, found agreement on the principle that Pleven's plan could be adapted so as to permit German troops in combat groups of less than 6,000 men, on the basis of one German group to five from other participating countries, and that the European Army should have German units within it from the outset, although there would be no German War or Armaments Ministry.

In the early months of 1951 two sets of negotiations were inaugurated, those on the European Army, held in Paris, and those on the direct remilitarization of Germany within NATO, to be held in the offices of the Allied High Commission in Petersberg, near Bonn. As a consequence of this compromise the US had agreed to implement the 'package proposals', thus separating the German question from the immediate issue of establishing an integrated NATO force under General Dwight D. Eisenhower as the Supreme Commander. With the appointment of SACEUR, and the establishment of the Supreme Headquarters Allied Powers in Europe (SHAPE), modelled on the WU's Headquarters in Fontainebleau, the Brussels Treaty states agreed that 'the continued existence of the Western Union defence organisation is no longer necessary'.[117] The defence planning and military functions of the Brussels Treaty Organisation were effectively subsumed into NATO; the Brussels Treaty powers authorizing SACEUR to take over the responsibilities of the WU Commanders in Chief Committee, with all the staff and facilities of the WU command put at his disposal. It was noted that 'the reorganisation of the military machinery shall not affect the right of the Western Union Defence Ministers and Chiefs of Staff to meet as they please to consider matters of mutual concern to the Brussels Treaty Powers'.[118] Whatever was to be agreed within the ongoing negotiations, however, NATO's position as policy-maker and organizer of common defence was assured, with forces deployed under agreement in NATO.

As the Conference pour l'Organisation de l'Armee Europeenne took place in Paris, the Petersberg Conference on direct West German entry into NATO was to come to an early impasse. The FRG would accept participation within the NATO framework only on the basis of equality of treatment for German forces, the substantial reinforcement of allied forces in West Germany and the end of occupation status, with the 'equality' demand representing a major sticking point for the French. Monnet succeeded in persuading the influential Eisenhower of the merits of European integration, and given the lack of progress in Petersberg, he was to add his support to the Paris talks.[119]

The British Government had tentatively encouraged French attempts to secure support for the EDC from other West European states, although it had made it clear that it would not accept the supranational principle involved in the French proposals and refused to take an active part in the Paris discussions.[120] Britain's immediate interest in the proceedings was more in terms of the likely effect on the American 'package', and thus the level of US commitment to European defence. Bevin feared the federalist leaning of the French proposals as potentially damaging to the Atlantic Alliance, an alliance that had become the mainstay of British defence policy. Bevin noted his opposition to the EDC project in his report to the Defence Committee in November 1950: 'If we are ever to break down this antipathy [to the United States and NATO] and to make the French good members of NATO, we cannot afford to allow the European federal concept to gain a foothold within NATO and thus weaken instead of strengthen the ties between the countries on the two sides of the Atlantic. We must nip it in the bud!'[121] However, the Atlee Government was becoming increasingly keen to deflect UK defence burdens, and the defence spending issue was causing serious splits within the British Labour Party, as defence expenditure was seen to undermine social and economic improvements which in themselves might prove the most effective defence against communism.[122] With the unlikelihood of French agreement on any direct German provision to NATO, desires for early German rearmament contributed to a reassessment of UK preferences for the 'NATO Option'. Equally, given German demands for sovereignty and equality within the Alliance and the tight integration of West German forces within the proposed EDC, itself within the NATO framework, the French proposals began to appear to offer the safer option.[123]

The British and Americans, persuaded that the Paris talks on the EDC must be the way ahead, supported the abandonment of the Petersberg discussions in June 1951. Realizing that Germany might well leave the Paris talks if France did not concede the equality point, the French accepted the principle that *all* member states' forces for the defence of Europe would be included in the European Army from the outset, giving the Paris talks another boost.[124] Following their Washington meeting in September 1951, the Foreign Ministers of Britain, the US and France welcomed both the Schuman and the Paris Plans, the declared aims of which were 'the inclusion of a democratic Germany, on a basis of equality, in a Continental European Community, which itself will form a part of a constantly developing Atlantic Community'.[125]

Britain was to have a significant role in the EDC ratification process as not only the French but also the smaller participating states sought close British co-operation and involvement with the Community as a counterbalance to German power. With the return of the Conservative Government in October 1951 it soon became clear to the Europeans that the new Prime Minister Churchill's earlier rhetoric had been nothing more than an 'empty vessel', supporting defence integration 'for them, not for us'.[126] Indeed, Churchill maintained a clear preference for the NATO route to resolving the German rearmament problem. Eisenhower recalls in his memoirs that he used 'every resource at my [sic] command, including argument, cajolery, and sheer prayer, to get Winston to say a single kind word about EDC'.[127] As negotiations proceeded in Paris, the new British Foreign Minister, Anthony Eden, had become acutely aware of the mounting criticisms of the British Government's 'unhelpful attitude' in both the US and Europe. Eden feared that 'the failure of the Paris Conference would be blamed on us and we should incur, however unjustly, much odium'.[128] Consequently, on the basis of a draft plan agreed following the December Six Power Conference in Paris,[129] agreements were reached on reciprocal guarantees to be offered on ratification of the EDC Treaty, effectively providing for a 'collective defence' association with NATO's Article 5 and with Article IV of the Brussels Treaty, and for a Tripartite Agreement with France offering the US and UK equivalent to a NATO Article 4 commitment to consult together whenever, in the opinion of any of them, 'the territorial integrity, political independence, or security of any of the Parties is threatened'.[130]

In March 1952, despite the continued UK rejection of direct involvement in the EDC, Eden proposed that the Council of Europe might carry out the function of a European Political Community with oversight of all European collective activity. Thus, European unity would be promoted in an environment of 'friendly cohabitation between "integrationists" and "associators"'.[131] Clearly designed to offer the UK influence over the EDC and ECSC whilst ensuring the intergovernmentalism of any future Europe, the outright rejection of the Eden Plan was indicative of the view that 'since nothing more than benevolent non-intervention may be expected from Great Britain, European federation can be reached only by the dynamic methods of the planners of the Six'.[132]

With the British economy in crisis, the strategic realities of a long-haul Cold War called into question the ability of NATO to meet the Soviet threat through the conventional force build-up required by the February 1952 Lisbon Force goals. The British Government's Global Strategy Paper of June 1952 may be identified as the beginning of the nuclearization of British defence policy, with the development of British nuclear capabilities contributing to the 'main deterrent' of the US-led Alliance, providing strategic coherence and UK influence at an affordable cost.[133] Whilst British conventional cutbacks would be needed to facilitate this new policy, it was clear that Europe would also require a significant conventional force presence if the Soviet threat was to be met.[134] This provided further incentive for UK promotion of a successful EDC outcome.

The Truman Administration, having initially advocated British participation in the EDC project, recognized that in the short term it might be more expedient for Britain to maintain a supportive distance. The creation of an effective European Army would free British and American forces for the larger role of global containment of international communism, Britain's global connections giving it a special role in the peripheries of the world stage. Additionally, it was feared that the inclusion of a nuclear-capable Britain into an EDC might promote calls for an increasingly unacceptable 'third force' or neutrality in Europe. In the immediate term, British intervention in negotiations would almost certainly slow down progress towards German rearmament.[135] Nevertheless, Eden's original concept of Britain acting as a 'third pillar', or 'binding link', between the US and Western Europe[136] was seen as only a temporary expedient by the Truman Administration, until such time as Britain could be fully integrated into mainland Europe.[137]

The Paris Treaty establishing 'La Communaute Europeene de Defence' (the EDC) and the associated documents were signed by the six participating states—France, West Germany, Italy and the Benelux three—on 27 May 1952. With a massive 132 Articles and 12 Associated Protocols, the complexity of the EDC agreement is evident. Uncompromising in its language, the treaty stated that 'the High Contracting Parties establish between them a European Defence Community of supranational character, comprising common institutions, common armed forces and a common budget'. Whilst naval forces were to be excluded, the European Army was to include all national land and air forces, except police forces and those required for overseas defence or in the event of serious internal crises.[138] It was to be accountable to a permanent Council whose approval would be required for some decisions of the executive Defence Commission, which in turn was to wield broad executive and supervisory powers over the training, equipment and supply of the European forces, gradually developing powers over recruitment, the determination of rank and advancement, and the conduct of unified training.[139] Although all major decisions would be taken on the basis of unanimous voting, the Commissioners were bound to 'refrain from any action inconsistent with the supra-national character of their duties' (Article 107). The EDC Military Protocol (Article 16) goes on to assert that 'Members of the European Defence Force have the same obligations toward the Community and its command echelons as military personnel of national armies normally have toward their Government and their own command'.

A provisional Defence Assembly of national parliamentarians would be tasked with the examination of budget estimates, approval of Defence Commission reports and the preparation of plans for a directly elected Assembly as part of an eventual EU. Article 38 of the EDC treaty also provided for the establishment of an Ad Hoc Assembly, consisting of the Assembly of the ECSC enlarged by three additional members from each of the big powers, tasked with establishing the requirements for a constitution of a future political federation that might preside over both the EDC and ECSC and that would be the basis for a European Political Community.[140] Thus, it was stressed, the EDC was to be an essential step towards the creation of a United Europe. However, the treaty also made clear that the Community defence effort was placed within the framework of NATO. The NATO Commander in Chief was to supervise the 'organisation, equipment and training of the Community forces' and was to assume command of them in time of war.[141]

The signing of the Paris Treaty was to be the high point of the EDC 'chapter'. The progress towards ratification was to be tortuous, marked by procrastination and backsliding as national governments sought to reconcile domestic and external interests.[142]

THE EDC RATIFICATION PROCESS

French disillusionment with the EDC treaty had set in even before its signing. The swing to the right in the French legislative elections in June 1951 had significantly enlarged the constituency within the Administration who rejected the loss of French national independence implied in the moves to create a supranational entity, and a 'motion of confidence' was passed by the French Assembly on 19 February 1952 on the basis that the Government take a more 'conditional' approach to the EDC.[143] Whilst European defence may have become an increasingly significant US foreign policy priority, the French remained heavily committed in support of their colonial interests, reaffirmed in the French Union established under the new Constitution of 1946. The future of the French presence in Indo-China, which was seen as central to French status and to the maintenance of the French empire, was dependent on a significant commitment of French economic and military assets. In calling for US support of French colonial interests, represented to the Americans in anti-communist terms, the French argued that the burden of communist containment in Indo-China prevented full French support for European defence.[144] The defence burdens of the Indo-China War had necessitated, it was argued, a reduction in French defence targets for the EDC, which could result in a marginal and unacceptable superiority for German forces within the European Army,[145] and the French National Assembly would never accept the EDC with so many of its forces deployed overseas.[146] At the same time, the limited duration of the Washington Treaty could result in an American withdrawal well before the 50-year EDC agreement matured, whilst the limited British association with the EDC provided neither a balance against German forces nor a parity of great-power status for France.[147] The EDC project was increasingly offering less to satisfy French interests in terms of either promoting the level of autonomy from the US or securing French status in the Atlantic Alliance. Consequently, the French representatives deliberating within the Ad Hoc Assembly increasingly resisted the loss of sovereignty implied by the draft treaty on the EDC. As one commentator notes, 'For France military and foreign policy makers, the EDC was no longer about German rearmament *per se* but about the future of France as an independent actor'.[148]

In the Federal Republic, opposition to the EDC was a reflection of a larger debate about the benefits of Adenauer's West-facing policy. The Chancellor remained convinced that the Soviets could be managed only through a policy of 'negotiation from strength', determined by a building-up of Western defence. Equally, European integration could provide the vehicle for the rehabilitation of West Germany both within Europe and within the broader Atlantic community. The EDC would be part of this broader integration project, with Adenauer stating, 'Joint action in the field of heavy industry and of defence will certainly necessitate joint political action also. The men who designed the bold plans for the coal and steel organisation and for the EDC knew this. They were and are convinced that their work would find a political culmination . . . We are putting all our energies into the unification of Europe'.[149] However, amongst the opposition, fears regarding the Soviet response to the EDC agreement added to concerns that the division of Germany might become permanent. On 7 February 1952 the German Federal Parliament passed a resolution approving a German defence contribution to the EDC on the condition that the Federal Republic would be accepted into it as a full and equal partner and that reunification would be sought for Germany. The connection between a German contribution to Western defence and the future sovereignty of the Federal Republic was made clear by the Bonn Contractual Agreements of 26 May 1952. These provided for the ending of occupation status in the FRG on the establishment of the EDC, but overtures from East Germany and the Soviets during the preceding negotiations further mobilized opposition in the Federal Republic.[150]

Given the political situation prevailing over the winter of 1952, the final report of the Ad Hoc Assembly on a European Political Community (6 March 1953) had retreated 'from the idea of a widely-drawn centralised federation'.[151] The report envisaged a single European political authority for the ECSC and EDC, which would have far-reaching responsibilities over a range of economic and external affairs. The planned constitution for this European Political Community offered a combination of federal and inter-governmental solutions, a form of integration that could prove acceptable to the national parliaments of the Six and to which it was intended Britain could be closely associated.

With the draft proposals at the negotiating table, the inauguration of President Eisenhower and the Republican Administration in January 1953 witnessed a reappraisal of the scope of American interests. In what Michael Smith refers to as the 'globalisation of Cold War activities',[152] the dying throes of European colonialism had drawn the US into expanding objectives, internationalizing areas of colonial struggle. Concerns about a potential 'domino effect' elicited by the Korean conflict had led the US to see Indo-China as imperative to the future of Asia, where US strategic interests were seen to be threatened. Eisenhower's 'New Look', introduced in 1953, envisaged heavy reliance on European conventional forces for 'forward defence' in Europe, backed up by the deterrent capacity of the American nuclear arsenal, rationalized under the concept of Massive Retaliation. The singular decline in American defence budgets initiated in 1953 had 'inevitable' implications for Europeans.[153] The New Look was clearly an attempt to meet expanding objectives at a bearable cost.[154] The US, determined to shift the burden of continental defence onto the Europeans, was now prepared to 'bulldoze' Europe into ratifying the EDC Treaty as a means of freeing up US efforts for the pursuit of its 'roll-back' policies against communism in Asia.[155]

Throughout 1953, Secretary of State John Foster Dulles reiterated US support for the EDC[156] but increasingly raised the spectre of American withdrawal from Europe if an acceptable agreement was not soon in the offing.[157] Soviet proposals for Four Power negotiations over the intractable problem of Indo-China were seen as simply an opportunity for 'sabotage', designed to further upset West European solidarity and delay plans for the EDC and NATO, whilst 'time was running out' if Congressional support was to be maintained.[158] Dulles' threats, by the end of the year, of an 'agonising reappraisal' if agreement on the EDC was not forthcoming reflected growing concerns in the US that the European defence project was proving unrealizable and that the essential transatlantic consensus was faltering.[159]

As perceptions of the Soviet threat softened amongst European publics following the death of Premier Joseph Stalin in March 1953,[160] the 'aggressive' shift in American rhetoric towards the Soviet Union and threats towards China over Korea had raised European concerns regarding their partner's escalatory behaviour. As pressure mounted for the acceptance of the EDC, the assumptions of the New Look raised further concerns regarding the ongoing transatlantic relationship. Whilst a united Western Europe 'satellite' of the US might be a 'condition precedent' for the pursuit of US global interests, the imposition of deterrence doctrine established a West European dependency that put all earlier illusions of Atlantic equality and interdependence to rest.[161] A commentator at the time was moved to note that 'American policy and attitude have appeared wittingly or unwittingly to ride roughshod over vital European interests and sentiments. At their worst, they have seemed to treat the Western European nations as expendable pawns in an American-Soviet feud carried on over the heads of all other nations. The sense of partnership in the western world has been offended and neutralism strengthened'.[162] As Acheson was to note, 'the bloom was off NATO'.[163]

The Eisenhower-Dulles period was to mark a significant chilling of Anglo-American relations. Dulles' preference for a 'continental' relationship was evidenced by his strong links with Adenauer and Monnet. He had little regard for British Commonwealth ties, which he saw as surmountable given the necessity for a united Europe in which the British role was imperative.[164] Without Britain, Benelux fears of Franco-German domination and French concerns regarding Germany would almost certainly scupper the EDC ship. The Dullesian concept of defence was rigidly 'two pillar', with Britain as simply another European ally. For Eden, Dulles was insufferable.[165] However, in the light of American persistence, it had become increasingly clear to the British that, if anything was to be salvaged from the increasingly precarious Anglo-American relationship, the UK must be seen to exercise its influence to promote EDC ratification. The seriousness of the situation was brought home to the British Government by Montgomery, NATO Deputy Supreme Allied Commander, in December, when, in a reversal of his previous position, he stated, 'Unless the British will . . . join in the European Army, the European Army ship will crash on the rocks . . . I can see no justification why the British should not come in. They can make any reservations they like'.[166] If Eden had any doubts as to the extent of the US Secretary of State's commitment to the EDC, Dulles was quick to disperse them. In recalling a meeting with Dulles in early 1953, Eden states:

> He [Dulles] had been speaking to M. Jean Monnet and had reached the conclusion that it was probably not possible to find a French Government which could put through EDC and govern France, since the majorities required for these two purposes were different . . . [and therefore] it might be necessary to work for a French Government which could take office solely for the purpose of putting through EDC . . . Mr Dulles then told me that we, by which he meant the United States and Britain, were approaching a parting of the ways with regard to American policy. If things went wrong, the United States might swing over to a policy of western hemispheric defence, with the emphasis on the Far East . . . Mr Dulles pointed out that the consequences of a swing of American policy towards hemispheric defence were of obvious concern to Great Britain. He hoped, therefore, that I might find occasion to underline the warnings which he had issued in his statement, and make some appeal to France.[167]

It was clear that British policy must ensure that, given the likely non-ratification of the EDC Treaty by France, Britain appeared to have had nothing to do with its downfall.

By October 1953 the French were refusing to submit to foreign pressure to sign the EDC without certain preconditions being met, notably the resolution of the Saar problem and the establishment of the political organs to control the proposed European Army. By the spring of 1954, with the negotiations on the Constitution put on hold until ratification of the EDC, concerns that German influence might be increased by the level of supranationality suggested in the draft Constitution led to a cooling of French interest in both projects.[168] Given French ambivalence Eden was to take two steps in March to encourage French ratification, proposing the inclusion of British Army formations within EDC forces and vice versa if requested by SACEUR and, as a gesture of goodwill, the placing of an armoured division within an EDC corps on formation. Committing to the maintenance of such forces on the mainland of Europe so as to contribute its fair share to the defence of the North Atlantic Area, the UK also offered not to alter the level of its armed forces on the continent without consulting the EDC. Symbolically significant as these 'offerings' were, it was privately noted that the proposed force levels would be necessary anyway for British defence for the immediate future and that an agreement did not preclude longer-term reductions.[169] Alongside these proposed force 'commitments', in the association agreement between the UK and EDC signed on 13 April 1954, the British Government further responded to French demands by agreeing to representation on the EDC Board of Commissioners and *ad hoc* Ministerial attendance at EDC Council meetings.[170] This would supplement the November 1953 agreement on military relations drawn up by the EDC Interim Military Committee in Paris, which allowed for the development of 'a common military outlook' in 'harmonising tactical doctrine and logistics, in standardising equipment and methods of training', and in providing for the 'inclusion' of Royal Air Force squadrons within EDC formations and vice versa.[171] This statement of relations represented the furthest point of concessions that the British were prepared to tolerate to satisfy the French over the EDC.[172] The US was to offer further inducements, including consultation with NATO over EDC force levels, integration of NATO and EDC forces where possible and the sharing of information between organizations. At the same time it was made clear that any state that had not ratified the EDC Treaty by 31 December 1954 would get no more aid under the US Mutual Security Act. With the FRG and Benelux states having ratified by 7 April, and the Italian Government waiting on a French decision, resistance to the EDC in France continued to grow.

The politics of Indo-China continued to exercise the French. The fall of the French fort at Dien Bien Phu in May had served to further undermine French-American relations given the US refusal to respond to desperate French calls for direct military support.[173] The subsequent collapse of the

Laniel Government and the investiture of the radical-Gaullist government of Pierre Mendès France on 17 June 1954 altered the complexion of French politics. Committed to the resolution of the Indo-China problem, the new Prime Minister argued that the French negotiating position with the Soviets could only be undermined by seeking a parliamentary agreement on the EDC that could not be guaranteed while the French remained committed in Vietnam. Ignoring Anglo-American calls for an end to French procrastination, and refusing the Benelux invitation to a conference on the EDC, the French cancelled Franco-German talks on the subject.

During the negotiations at the Geneva Conference, which had convened in April, the French had come under significant pressure from the Communists to reject the EDC proposals in order to attain favourable terms from Moscow over Indo-China,[174] and the lack of US support for a diplomatic settlement had served only to further undermine Alliance cohesion.[175] On 14 July, fearing French prevarication on, or even rejection of, the EDC in the light of its ongoing negotiations, Dulles and Churchill informed their respective legislatures that the US and UK would propose immediate sovereignty for West Germany if France failed to ratify the EDC by 15 August 1954, the expected date of the French National Assembly recess.[176] On 21 July, agreement was reached between the French and the Vietminh resulting in the partition of Vietnam, with elections to be held within two years in both the French South and the communist North to determine the governance of a reunited and independent Vietnam. The 'favourable terms' offered to Mendès France by the Communists may not have amounted to a 'deal' in terms of its linkage with the French rejection of the EDC,[177] but clearly these 'sweeteners' may have paved the way for a Soviet political push in Europe 'to destroy the Western Defence community'.[178] It was certainly feared that France may have effectively rung the death knell of the EDC, and the implications of the foreseeable failure of French ratification of the EDC Treaty became the main topic of Anglo-American discussion.[179] Not least, the Bonn agreement on the end of occupation status for the Federal Republic would require untangling from the Paris EDC agreement in the event of French failure to ratify, given that the legal basis of these treaties procured German sovereignty only once the FRG had taken on its responsibilities under the EDC.[180]

At the Brussels Conference on the EDC, beginning 19 August, Mendès France put forward a new Protocol of EDC Treaty Amendments, which he presented as essential in order to procure the support of the French National Assembly. These proposed amendments effectively removed the supranational elements from the treaty by introducing a veto, downgrading the Board of Commissioners to technical manager status, removing Article 38 provisions on Political Community and reintroducing national armies at least for France.[181] The counter-proposals of the Five Powers were summarily rejected, and on 30 August 1954 the French National Assembly threw out EDC ratification on a matter of procedure and without debate.

The consequences of this were equally damning to the contractual accords between the US, UK and EDC. Clearly French fears of Soviet aggression and German rearmament did not exceed those which accompanied the loss of national identity and status implied by European unity.[182] As Duchin states, 'the tide of European unification seemed by this time to have turned. Once a powerful force in continental politics, post-war federalism was ebbing away'.[183]

Responses to the failure of the EDC plan were varied. As noted in a report by the Royal Institute of International Affairs, Chatham House in London, 'Dr Adenauer gave an interview to the correspondent of The Times in which he said harsh words about French inconsistency; US opinion, which had hoped until the last for ratification, took on a strongly anti-French bias and British spokesmen emitted the distant cluckings and tut-tuttings of a reproachful but not altogether unsympathetic governess'.[184] As another commentator was to note at the time, there were widespread concerns that not only was the future of the Atlantic Alliance undermined, but 'worst of all, perhaps, the idealism which had supported the European defence community as a step in the direction of a truly united Europe, was in danger of giving way to disillusion'.[185]

THE EDEN PROPOSALS

For the British, the French failure to ratify had not been altogether unexpected, and although alternative plans had not been openly aired during the ratification process so as to avoid any criticism of British 'sabotage' of the EDC, Eden's biographer notes that Eden 'had long given thought, together with his officials, to what alternative might be appropriate'.[186] On 1 September 1954 the Foreign Office had set out its 'Alternatives to the European Defence Community', the two military options being direct German entry into NATO or a looser non-supranational EDC with UK participation. As it was envisaged that the second option would take the same tortuous route as the EDC, the first option seemed most favourable and was consistent with Churchill's preference.[187] Foreign Minister Eden was to suggest in his memoirs a 'Eureka' experience, as the final solution came to him 'in the bath on Sunday morning',[188] but Cabinet records suggest otherwise. In fact, it was the then Housing Minister, Harold Macmillan, who first 'suggested that a NATO solution might be made more palatable both to French opinion and to the Labour Party in this country if, for this purpose, NATO could be made at least to appear to have been modified in the direction of the European idea. Was it possible for example, for Germany formally to adhere to the Brussels Treaty which continued to subsist within the North Atlantic Treaty?'[189]

During his tour of European capitals from 11 to 17 September 1954, Eden presented 'his' plan for resolving the impasse on European defence organization. An effective compromise could be reached through the expansion of the Brussels Treaty Organisation as a 'political instrument to keep alive the idea of European unity'[190] and through the direct entry of Germany into NATO as the organization in which all military arrangements would be concentrated.[191] The 'new' European defence arrangement, lacking the supranational elements of the EDC, would have Britain as a full member, a commitment that could secure the German contribution to Western defence. Whilst Eden's proposals met with a level of support in Europe,[192] the reaction of the US Administration was guarded. Disappointed by the failure of the Europeans to realize the integrationist expectations that had become the dominant thesis in the Dullesian approach to European security organization, the US Secretary of State was suspicious of any attempts by the British to 'water down' the EDC idea.[193] As the US joined the UK, Canada and the EDC Six in the commencement of the London Nine Power Conference on Eden's proposals (28 September–3 October 1954), Dulles made clear that Congressional support for Eden's plan could not be assumed. In dramatic terms, Dulles was to note that 'a great wave of disillusionment' had swept over the United States and that it was 'particularly manifest in the Congress . . . a feeling that after all the situation in Europe is pretty hopeless and the United States had better not make any long term commitments to be part of it'.[194] Thus, the continuance of American aid was to remain under review given the failure of Europe to fulfil the expected united role that the US had laid out for it on the continent.

As a consequence of Dulles' inferences it had become clear to Eden that in order to keep the US in Europe it was imperative that the London Conference succeed. If France was to accept his proposals, Eden had to be prepared to offer a British commitment to European defence well beyond that offered to the EDC. As Eden was to remark to Churchill, 'the hard fact is that it is impossible to organize an effective defence system in Western Europe, which in turn is essential for the security of the United Kingdom, without a major British contribution . . . By recognising this fact and giving new commitment, we may succeed in bringing the Germans and the French together, and keeping the Americans in Europe'.[195] This 'new commitment' was skilfully played by Eden as discussions progressed.[196] The British 'ace' consisted of an offer to deploy British forces on mainland Europe, to be withdrawn only on agreement of the majority of the Brussels Treaty members.[197] These forces were to consist of four divisions and the Second Tactical Air Force under the caveats that this would not be binding in cases of 'acute overseas emergency' or if they became 'too great a strain on the external finances of the United Kingdom'. Given these caveats and the fact that UK military planning had been based on retaining this level under SACEUR, this 'unprecedented' offer may be seen as nothing 'exceptional' in terms of commitment. Indeed, for Churchill, the British offer was essentially meaningless; as he was to state, 'It can be cancelled at any time . . . It does not mean anything. All words . . . No one in their senses thought we would bring our troops home from the Continent . . . We have always been better than our word . . . Never . . . was the leadership of Europe so cheaply won'.[198] However, as a treaty-based peacetime UK commitment to the Continent it did represent, as Eden was to suggest, a 'formidable step' for an 'island people'[199] and could be seen to mark a significant Europeanization of British foreign policy.

With the British offer on the table, the negotiations moved surprisingly swiftly. Agreement was quickly reached on the modification of the Brussels Treaty, which was to be enlarged to include Italy and the FRG. Lacking the supranational elements of the EDC proposals, the newly named Western European Union was to have a significantly altered institutional framework to that of its predecessor, the Brussels Treaty Organisation. In order to facilitate the participation of the UK in the political movement towards European integration, the new WEU was to be developed on the lines of intergovernmental co-operation, rather than the federative course that Britain felt unable to take. The institution was to be bi-located, with its primary organ, the Council of (Foreign) Ministers, having its seat in London so as to 'symbolize the step taken by Britain towards common European activity and cooperation, if not integration'.[200] Essentially intergovernmental in nature, unanimity being required on areas where voting procedure was not otherwise established, the Council was to be entrusted with the power of decision, unlike the purely consultative Council of the old Brussels Treaty. Significantly, however, the WEU Council was to have provision for majority voting in some prescribed areas for potentially major policy decisions that would be binding on all members, for example those questions submitted by the Agency for the Control of Armaments (ACA). Although not as far-reaching as the supranational powers of the proposed EDC arrangement, the WEU Council's powers eclipsed those of the committee of Ministers of the Council of Europe, which made recommendations to governments on the basis of unanimity, and those of the Council of the OEEC, which could take binding decisions but only with unanimous consent. In this sense the Modified Brussels Treaty (MBT) was to be 'a more effective focus of European integration'.[201] All specific reference to German aggression was to be removed, and the potential threat of German aggression was to be mollified by the Council objective of 'strengthening peace and security' and 'promoting the unity and encouraging the progressive integration of Europe' (MBT, Protocol I, Article IV, Appendix II).[202] Supported by a Permanent Council of Ambassadors and its Secretariat, headed by a Secretary General, the new Council was to be balanced by a consultative parliamentary Assembly, composed of representatives of the Brussels Treaty powers to the Consultative Assembly of the Council of Europe, to which the Council was to make its Annual Report. With an initial task of establishing its own brief and status, the Assembly of the WEU was created 'laconically, and with so simple and general a formula', largely as a consequence of the 'haste with which it was necessary to fill the gap in the European defences' following the failure of the EDC.[203]

Significantly, although the WEU was not to fix levels of total national forces, and the execution of defence programmes was to remain purely a national affair, it was to be given real powers of decision over military provision. This was to include the determination of the maximum strength of national forces to be placed under SACEUR command on mainland Europe during peacetime (MBT, Protocol II, Articles I and III), the most significant and extensive controls being placed on West Germany, which was limited to a maximum of 12 divisions.[204] The Federal Republic was also to be most severely restricted under the treaty's Protocol III provisions, which provided for WEU Council majority voting on permissible atomic, biological and chemical (ABC) weapon stocks by the continental members states. The FRG was prohibited to manufacture on its territory any ABC weapons, large warships, submarines or strategic bomber aircraft without the consent of SACEUR and a two-thirds majority of the WEU Council. (Notably, the UK was not covered by the ABC commitments of the treaty.) To be managed through the Paris-based ACA, these qualitative and quantitative restrictions could be reconsidered at the call of NATO, but revised only on agreement of the WEU powers, ensuring a level of visibility and restraint on future military development.

Retaining the Article IV collective defence provisions of the original treaty (to become Article V under the MBT), Article VII of the MBT committed signatories to not 'conclude any alliance or participate in any coalition directed against any other of the High Contracting Parties', a significant 'internal' security condition given the broadened membership.[205] Member states of the WEU would be commended to 'consult with regard to any situation which may constitute a threat to peace, in whatever area this threat should arise' (MBT, Protocol I, Article VIII), indicating a broad remit beyond the 'in area' provisions of the NATO Treaty. However, NATO primacy was to be accepted in the provisions of the new treaty, where it was to be stated that, 'recognizing the undesirability of duplicating the military staffs of NATO, the Council and its Agency will rely on the appropriate military authorities of NATO for information and advice on military matters' (MBT, Protocol I, Article IV, Appendix II). Consequently, with the NAC accepted as the proper place to discuss strategic planning and defence policy, and the avoidance of any duplication of military staffs, the defence implications of the new organization were to be significantly limited, with the national forces of WEU member states stationed within the area of SACEUR command contributing to a unified military formation under SACEUR authority.[206]

As a consequence of the success of the London negotiations, a range of documents, known collectively as the Paris Agreements, were signed between 20 and 23 October 1954.[207] These agreements covered four key areas. The first included those amending the Bonn Contractual Agreements of May 1952 and providing for the ending of occupation status for Germany, restoring to West Germany 'the full authority of a sovereign State over its internal and external affairs'. Consequently, the Allied High Commission and

Land Commissioners were to be terminated, although the Three Powers' forces stationed in West Germany were to 'retain the rights and responsibilities . . . relating to Berlin and to Germany as a whole, including the reunification of Germany and a peace settlement'.[208] The second area covered by the Paris Agreements was that of West Germany's accession to NATO, to which the West German Army was to be assigned in its totality.[209] Thirdly, the Paris Agreements provided for the resolution of the contentious issue of 'ownership' of the resource-rich Saar region through the original construct of a 'European Statute within the framework of WEU'; this international status was to be the subject of a referendum that would determine the future of the region.[210] And, finally, agreements were signed which were to provide for the modification of the Brussels Treaty and its 'enlargement' to include Germany and Italy. Incredibly, less than five weeks after the French rejection of the EDC, a significant step had been taken towards the construction of a security structure that was to satisfy the Europeans and their American NATO ally.

The passage towards ratification of the Paris Agreements was not, however, without some difficulties. Adenauer's persuasive skills were well exercised in establishing West German support for ratification of the Paris Agreements and most particularly the provisions for the inclusion of the Federal Republic in NATO. Led by the Social Democrats, domestic opposition had a broad base that included trade unions, churches, youth movements, socialists and communists, who feared, following Soviet threats, that ratification might undermine the possibility of Four Power talks on reunification.[211] Even Adenauer's principal allies, the Free Democratic Party, reacted against the restrictions envisaged by the Paris proposals on Germany's military manufacturing, the confirmation of the legal status of the allied troops in Germany, and Adenauer's promise to support the autonomy of the Saar under WEU supervision in the referendum provided for under the agreements. However, Adenauer's diplomatic skills triumphed; the Soviets, he insisted, were offering only propaganda—only under NATO pressure could the Soviets be brought to the negotiating table and the unification of Germany be achieved.[212] Although recognizing the shortcomings of the MBT, not least in terms of its intergovernmental nature, Adenauer argued that, while he was not 'giving up on European integration', the failure of the French EDC vote required the pragmatic compromise offered by the WEU until such time as further European integration might be possible.[213] Following volatile debates in the Bundestag the treaty was finally accepted on 27 February 1955, with ratification taking place on 18 March.

It was clear that the Agreements offered much to satisfy the French, most particularly the new British commitment to continental force deployment, a commitment that, if made earlier, might have 'saved' the EDC.[214] Lacking the supranational elements of the EDC, which would, most significantly, have deprived France of its national army, the MBT secured French sovereignty and appeared far less threatening to France's hold over her overseas territories, the perceived key to the recovery of French grandeur. However, even though many former supporters of the EDC had come to see the Eden Plan as the best possible compromise, initial euphoria regarding the British commitments began to subside as a consequence of what has been referred to as 'the instability of desire after consummation'.[215] Having approved the London Agreements without qualification on 12 October, the view held by all other capitals was that the French Assembly was committed to pass the Paris Agreements. This was rejected by the French, who saw the original vote as one on principal, not practice. Domestic political hostility towards Mendès France led to the rejection of the Paris Agreements by the French National Assembly on 24 December 1954, although it was to pass as a matter of confidence on 30 December. As the Paris Agreements awaited Senate approval, Soviet pressure to dissuade the French from ratification was intense, with Moscow threatening the annulment of the Franco-Russian treaty of friendship of 1944. Most significantly, the Soviets made clear that, in the event of the successful ratification of the Paris Agreements, a treaty of friendship and aid and a unified military command would be established among the communist powers. However, allied insistence on all-party ratification of the Paris Agreements in order to, on the one hand, secure British force deployment and, on the other, prevent exclusive bilateral arrangements between the US and Germany proved most persuasive.[216] On 27 March 1955, following the fall of Mendès France, the French Senate approved the Agreements by 184 to 110 votes.

By 5 May 1955 the ratification of the Paris Agreements was complete and had been achieved with higher parliamentary majorities than those for EDC ratification.[217] The WEU of the MBT came into force the following day, the same day that the occupation status of West Germany was officially ended, and on 9 May the FRG became the 15th member of NATO. On 12 May 1955, the Soviet Union, along with the seven satellite states of Romania, Bulgaria, Albania, Hungary, Poland, Czechoslovakia and the German Democratic Republic, signed the treaty establishing the Warsaw Pact. The Paris Agreements, facilitated by the establishment of the WEU, were consequently a significant factor in the institutionalization of the Cold War, with the architecture of defence providing for a bipolar balance of power as the dominant overlay of the European security environment.

REFLECTIONS

In what has been described as 'one of the most significant milestones of post World War II European Defence history',[218] the Paris Agreements were to mark the high point of almost four years of intense Atlantic diplomacy. Perhaps the most significant amongst these agreements was that which modified the Brussels Treaty and provided for the establishment of the WEU, for it was this agreement that was to be the facilitating element of an enduring Cold War transatlantic security architecture. This chapter has traced the stages of development leading to the eventual establishment of the WEU from the first pragmatic steps towards European defence co-operation in the Dunkirk Treaty, through the complexities of the Western Union debates resulting in the Brussels Treaty, and on through the EDC debacle to the eventual 1954 compromise. The evidence of these early developments suggests that, in the search for a new post-war European security order, two distinct security 'images' emerged; one structurally dependent on a transatlantic constituency for a defence alliance predicated on external threat, the other reflecting the promise of internal security through European integration. The WU concept was to reflect both of these 'images', each of which raised contentious issues as to the acceptable nature of transatlantic relations and the scope and extent of desired European integration.

The Brussels Treaty had taken up the challenge of collective defence in a European context. With its Article IV commitment and its WU Command structures, the treaty provided for the establishment of the first peacetime collective defence organization. Whether this organization was ever intended as anything more than a precursor, if a very necessary one, to a broader collective defence arrangement with the US is contestable. What is clear is that the Brussels Treaty did facilitate an American commitment to the defence of Europe through NATO. As an exercise in 'smoke and mirrors', the Brussels Treaty Organisation created an impression for the American public of European commitment to co-operative action in providing for their own defence. The failure of these efforts to adequately meet the growing Soviet threat was to provide the rationale for an American engagement with Europe.

Whilst the WU may appear on the surface to have been at best a convenient tool for meeting immediate interests through the engagement with American power, the 'evolutionary' potential of the WU had also been recognized. Field Marshall Montgomery, Chair of the Commanders in Chief Committee of the WU, acknowledged the organization's potentially 'great significance in the history of attempts by mankind to organize and guarantee World peace'. The organization had been 'activated by a common fear', but Montgomery was to note the co-operative dynamics whereby 'the requirements of military cooperation at once involved supply and financial questions. Political co-operation at all levels inevitably followed'. Thus the requirements of defence had served to promote wider co-operation that could in turn enhance that unity which could close the door on Europe's bloody past. 'In this organisation, therefore, there is an element of evolution, and it is by the evolutionary process that the affairs of mankind, and of nations, are most readily settled'.[219]

In support of the broader commitment to the promotion of European 'common interests', the Brussels Treaty had invested within it more than just a defence role. As well as a commitment of enhancing social and cultural collaboration, the 'necessity of uniting in order to promote the economic recovery of Europe' had established an economic role for the Brussels Treaty Organization. Its work in these areas was constrained by the commitment not to 'involve any duplication of, or prejudice to, the work of other economic organizations in which the High Contracting Parties are or may be represented but shall on the contrary assist the work of those organizations'. Given the British resistance to closer integration with the European mainland, European economic integration began to develop amongst the 'Six' in the alternative forum of the ECSC, whilst the foundation of the Council of Europe established a broader forum for the continuing development of social and cultural ties being pursued under WU auspices.

Given the lack of a clear vision on the future order of Europe, the Brussels Treaty was established as an 'ambiguous' arrangement. In its provision for collective defence, the treaty established an Article IV defence commitment between European states but did not prescribe the manner in which that defence should be organized. Likewise, in providing for broad-ranging European co-operation as the means of promoting European unity, the treaty did not prescribe supranational integration as the favoured process, nor determine that this integration should include defence. This ambiguity, whilst failing to provide a blueprint for future developments in either area, represented one of the strengths of the treaty in that it enabled the emergent WEU to be 'all things to all people', shifting its functional focus as a range of tensions arose in the European security arena and providing a compromise between alternative visions and interests.

The examination of the EDC debacle serves to further point up the tensions that existed between states with regard to the future organization of European security. Indeed, the satisfaction of these tensions underlay the development of the WEU as a vehicle for promoting both collective defence and European integration as responses to the security conundrum. Most notable amongst these tensions were those related to the absence of a common threat perception, the level of leadership acceptance with regards to the US and diverse national conceptions of the desirable extent and nature of integration for the European area.

In terms of threat perception, concerns in Europe over a resurgent Germany were a 'natural' response to the post-war environment, with the Brussels Treaty, and the Dunkirk Treaty that preceded it, specifically identifying Germany as a primary concern. The Soviet 'threat' had been recognized by all of the NATO allies by the end of the decade, but French concerns regarding the 'uncontrolled' development of German power had led them to resist US calls for the remilitarization of Germany as a member of the Alliance. The French EDC alternative was seen as a means of facilitating a 'controlled' German contribution to defence, and as such had more to do with maintaining national power than any grand federal vision for Europe. The failure of the French option to satisfy US requirements that Europe combine to meet the 'primary' Soviet threat, resulting from the collapse of the EDC project, had led the US to posit the potential for an 'agonising reappraisal' of US engagement with Europe, an engagement which all recognized as a necessary condition for a viable European defence order.

The role of the US in the post-war order had been a matter of some contention. The 'third force' ideas which had emerged in the early post-war years had proposed that Europe develop as a power between the Soviets and Americans, with the pursuit of US aid being only a short-term expedient in the light of Europe's post-war weakness. US defence engagement with Europe, facilitated through the Brussels Treaty and the emergence of NATO, had convinced the British of the essential nature of the Atlantic commitment. This ended British pretensions towards any alternative European model and tied the UK to an Atlanticist view of its interests that was to dominate British thinking throughout the Cold War period. French interests in limiting US power, as a means of ensuring French independence, made the acceptance of defence dependence problematic, and the EDC negotiations focused on French resistance to a US-dominated Atlantic system in offering the potential for an emergent European alternative. The failure of the EDC presented France with something of a dilemma in terms of strategic realities and politically acceptable options.

The US had not perceived the EDC as a challenge to its primacy in the new Atlantic system. Indeed, examination of post-war developments suggests that, for the Americans, European integration could complement the interest of the US in establishing a wider Atlantic system of economic and strategic co-operation. Despite the US' early preference for a more direct route to German inclusion, the integration of European defence through the EDC could have strengthened the transatlantic Alliance by providing for an 'essential' West German contribution in a manner acceptable to the continentals. Furthermore, the EDC could have provided the basis for a uniting Europe, where integration at the level of low politics could create conditions of stability and growth in the European and Atlantic areas. However, US perceptions of the purpose of integration were somewhat at odds with those of the Europeans, for whom European unity was either an end in itself or a means of satisfying national interests, rather than a vehicle for serving a larger Atlantic purpose. Integration might provide the means of creating a balance against the power of the both the US and the Soviets, but for the French it was to prove a step too far in the abrogation of national sovereignty. US policy served to undermine the defence-first integrationist policy encapsulated in the EDC by underestimating the national concerns of participant governments.[220] For the British, resistance to European federalism had grown along with their Atlantic preference. Potentially dangerous for NATO, European integration might well undermine Atlantic relations by creating a 'competitive identity'.[221] Whilst Atlantic interests had led the British to offer 'reluctant' support to the EDC process, the absence of Britain as an internal stabilizer for that process led to the rejection of the EDC on the grounds that it was 'too much integration—too little England'.[222] The WEU was to provide the compromise solution to these central tensions of the post-war era, and in so doing, it was also to facilitate the development of an enduring Cold War European security order.

The WEU supported the continued viability and development of collective defence for Europe by providing the reassurances required by Europeans as to the internal security of the European area, offering guarantees against resurgent German power through a 'secured' British force commitment to the mainland and through the arms control arrangements established under the treaty. In so doing it ensured the dominance of the Alliance as the provider of collective defence, restricting itself to a position of 'subordination' through its new Article IV agreement not to duplicate the work of NATO.[223] In recognition of the structural necessities of the decade, the WEU enabled defence co-operation to develop in an alliance context, facilitating NATO's ascendance and firmly establishing the dominance of the Atlantic constituency for defence. Just as the Brussels Treaty had been the means of getting the US involved in European defence, the WEU was the means of keeping the Americans engaged by 'satisficing' national differences.[224] In providing an acceptable compromise in the form of the WEU, Eden prevented a more significant 'reappraisal' of the US commitment and helped to tie the Americans into the defence of Europe for the foreseeable future.

Rees concludes that the WEU was 'a facilitating mechanism to enable NATO to play the leading defence role in Europe',[225] but it had also been constructed so as to 'emphasise the objective of European unity', being 'strengthened and extended to make it a more effective focus of European integration'.[226] The WEU was to represent the furthest acceptable point of compromise in terms of an integrative process for Europe to which Britain could be committed. It had provided for the rapprochement between France and Germany so necessary for the broader integration process, while at the same time taking the first faltering steps towards a level of political and military integration in Europe, which, Duchin argues, 'Eisenhower felt so crucial to the future of the Free World'.[227] Whilst the EDC had proven a step too far and too fast in terms of any functional imperative for integrative development, the WEU was able to provide the palliative for this failure, preventing any negative 'spill-back' from damaging the prospects of further integration in other, less contentious spheres. The WEU provided for a level of European co-operation which fell well short of the integrative interests of the federalists but which provided an institutional arrangement in which a European Assembly could discuss defence issues; a European Council could develop joint decisions, not always on the basis of unanimity; and a commitment to promoting 'progressive integration' was clearly articulated. And in facilitating the development of NATO, an important element in providing the structural requirements for European economic development, the WEU facilitated a level of potential co-operation that left the door open for a slower pace of European defence integration in the future.[228]

The WEU was thus a product of the post-war debate on the nature and scope of integration, and the requirements of, and for, alliance.[229] As the product of intergovernmental bargaining on the basis of national preferences and interests, influenced by environmental or structural variants, the

WEU was to represent something of a compromise between these two primary security constituencies, reflecting the areas of tension that existed both within and between them. With the potential for development in either direction, and indeed as a facilitator of both approaches, the WEU was clearly developed as a consequence of these dual imperatives. The evidence suggests that, given its ambiguous nature, the WEU was never intended to be anything more than a support organization, enabling the development of collective defence and European integration in other, more suitable organizations. However, as a hybrid organization, the WEU could be, and was, different things to different people—an embryonic EDC or a simple device of Alliance management. Indeed, whilst it was designed to provide for some level of co-operation, its real success was simply in 'being there' as a representation of various and distinct aspirations, a chimera to be selectively and partially viewed according to taste. Perhaps most significantly, in articulating a European identity in defence and a commitment to progressive integration, the WEU was to provide the 'balm' that enabled an acceptance of defence dependency, thus facilitating the establishment of a security architecture that was to provide the basis of the new European security order.

NOTES

1. See A. Shlaim, 'Prelude to downfall: the British offer of Union to France, June 1940', *Journal of Contemporary History,* vol. 9, no. 3, July 1974, pp. 27–63.
2. See The National Archive (TNA): CAB 66/48: WP (44) 181, Anthony Eden, 'The Future of Europe', 3 April 1944. Belgium's Foreign Minister Paul-Henri Spaak had also confirmed Belgian and Dutch keenness, at the conclusion of the war, to develop European military agreements that would include Britain.
3. For Jebb's report see his memorandum to the UK Foreign Secretary and Chief of Staff at TNA: CAB 80/44: Secret COS (44) 113, 'British policy towards Western Europe', 3 June 1944. For discussion see J. Baylis, 'Britain, the Brussels Pact and the continental commitment', *International Affairs,* vol. 60, no. 4, autumn 1984, p. 616.
4. The struggle between Churchill's 'overcurrent' and the Foreign Office's 'undercurrent' raged even after the change in government in 1945. See C. Wiebes and B. Zeeman, 'The Pentagon negotiations March 1948: the launching of the North Atlantic Treaty', *International Affairs,* vol. 59, no. 3, summer 1983, pp. 351–63. Clearly, Churchill had fully prioritized the Soviet threat by the time of famous 'Iron Curtain' speech in Fulton, Missouri, of 11 March 1946.
5. TNA: CAB 81/45: PHP (44) 27 (0), Final, 'Security in Western Europe and the North Atlantic', 9 November 1944. For a detailed study of the machinations of UK strategic defence planning during this period see J. Lewis, *Changing Direction: British Military Planning for Post-war Strategic Defence 1942–47,* 2nd edition, Abingdon: Routledge, 2003.
6. For Bevin's views expressed during discussions within the Foreign Office and Cabinet see TNA: FO 371/49069: Z 9595/13/17, 13 August 1945. For the history of the Western bloc idea up to this point see TNA: FO 371/49069: Z 9639/13/17, 13 August 1945.

7. S. Greenwood, 'Ernest Bevin and "Western Union", August 1945–February 1946', *European History Quarterly*, vol. 14, no. 3, July 1984, p. 325. Also see V. Rothwell, *Britain and the Cold War, 1941–47*, London: Cape, 1982.

8. TNA: FO 371/49069: Z 11077/13/17, 21 September 1945.

9. Bevin's ideas about the Ruhr were welcomed by the French, but not shared by the British Foreign Office, who saw the potential for a German nationalist backlash at any attempt at dismemberment. See TNA: FO 371/46723: C 6134/22/18, 16 September 1945.

10. On Bevin's views on a 'third force' see F. Williams, *Ernest Bevin: Portrait of a Great Englishman*, London: Hutchinson, 1952, p. 262. Also see K. Larres, 'A search for order: Britain and the origins of a WEU, 1944–55', in B. Brivati and H. Jones (eds) *From Reconstruction to Integration: Britain and Europe since 1945*, Leicester: Leicester University Press, 1993, p. 72.

11. The 'Harvey minute' of 9 January 1946 represents the high point of Bevin's WU plans, outlining his policy to 'work steadily towards the closest co-operation and integration economically, socially and militarily with our Western neighbours without, at this stage, creating any formal regional group'. TNA: FO 371/59911: Z 2410/120/72. See A. Deighton, *The Impossible Peace: Britain, the Division of Germany and the Origins of the Cold War*, Oxford: Clarendon Press, 1990, pp. 37–46.

12. See J. Frémeaux and A. Martel, 'French defence policy 1947–1949', in O. Riste (ed.) *Western Security: The Formative Years*, Oslo: Norwegian University, 1985, p. 92.

13. Ceded to France in 1919 as war compensation, the Saar had been administered by the League of Nations until it was returned to Germany under the plebiscite of 1935. The French gave the area autonomy from Germany as well as economic union with France after the Second World War, creating significant Franco-German tension. For French interest in the Ruhr and Saar region see J. S. Hill, 'De Gaulle's strategy for economic reconstruction', in R. O. Paxton and N. Wahl (eds), *De Gaulle and the United States: A Centennial Reappraisal*, Oxford: Berg, 1994, pp. 109–14.

14. De Gaulle to the Consultative Assembly in Algiers, March 1944, in J. W. Young, *Britain, France and the Unity of Europe 1945–1951*, Leicester: Leicester University Press, 1990, p. 13.

15. For French post-war interests see A. W. DePorte, *De Gaulle's Foreign Policy 1944–46*, Cambridge: Harvard University Press, 1968, pp. 126–52.

16. J. W. Young, *France, the Cold War and the Western Alliance, 1944–1949*, Leicester: Leicester University Press, 1990, p. 90.

17. TNA: CAB 128/5: CM (46) 36, 17 April 1946. British occupation of the Ruhr had left them with control over much of Germany's coal supplies.

18. See TNA: FO 371/67670: Z 1215/25/17 and TNA: FO 371/67671: Z 2190/25/17. Also see A. Bullock, *Ernest Bevin: Foreign Secretary, 1945–1951*, London: Heinemann, 1983, p. 359.

19. See TNA: FO 371/599 11: Z 10754/120/72, Ronald Memorandum, 13 March 1946.

20. Blum's caretaker administration, which was to hold power from mid December 1946 until the Constitution of the Fourth Republic became operative in January 1947, had expressed a wish to establish further co-operation with Britain at the unauthorized prompting of the British Ambassador in Paris, Duff Cooper. J. Charmley, 'Duff Cooper and WEU 1944–47', *Review of International Studies*, vol. 11, no. 1, January 1985, pp. 53–64.

21. *Treaty of Alliance and Mutual Assistance, Dunkirk*, Cmd. 7217, London: HMSO, 1947, signed 4 March 1947.

22. See TNA: FO 371/67686: Z 269/119/17, 'Hall-Patch minute', 4 January 1947. Also see S. Greenwood, 'Return to Dunkirk: the origins of the Anglo-French Treaty of March 1947', *Journal of Strategic Studies,* vol. 6, no. 4, December 1983, pp. 49–55.
23. Bevin cited in A. and F. Boyd, *Western Union: UNA's Guide to European Recovery,* London: Hutchinson, 1949, p. 60.
24. J. Baylis, 'Britain and the Dunkirk Treaty: the origins of NATO', *Journal of Strategic Studies,* vol. 5, no. 2, June 1982, pp. 236–47.
25. W. Krieger, 'Foundation and history of the Treaty of Brussels, 1948–1950', in N. Wiggershaus and R. Foerster (eds) *The Western Security Community: Common Problems and Conflicting National Interests during the Foundation Phase of the North Atlantic Alliance,* Oxford: Berg, 1993, p. 231.
26. Larres, 'A search for order', p. 83.
27. For Secretary of State George C. Marshall's speech at Harvard University, 5 June 1947, see *Department of State Bulletin,* vol. 16, no. 415, 15 June 1947, p. 1159–60.
28. See R. S. Churchill (ed.) *The Sinews of Peace: Post-war Speeches by Winston S. Churchill,* London: Cassell, 1948, p. 199, for Churchill's Zurich speech.
29. See S. Newton, 'Britain, the Sterling Area and European integration', *Journal of Imperial and Commonwealth History,* vol. 13, no. 3, May 1985, pp. 163–8. Also see B. Zeeman, 'Britain and the Cold War: an alternative approach; the Treaty of Dunkirk example', *European History Quarterly,* vol. 16, no. 3, July 1986, pp. 343–67.
30. For a contemporaneous discussion of the federal movement in Europe see Boyd and Boyd, *Western Union,* pp. 69–94. Also see D. W. Urwin, *The Community of Europe: A History of European Integration since 1945,* Harlow: Longman, 1996, pp. 1–12; P. Murray and P. Rich (eds) *Visions of European Unity,* Boulder: Westview, 1996.
31. See R. H. Ferrel, 'The formation of the Alliance, 1948–1949', in L. S. Kaplan (ed.) *American Historians and the Atlantic Alliance,* Kent: Kent State University Press, 1991, pp. 22–3.
32. House of Commons, *Hansard,* (official report of debates in the British Parliament), vol. 446, 22 January 1948, cols. 390 and 407.
33. House of Commons, *Hansard,* vol. 446, 22 January 1948, col. 409.
34. The British Ambassador Archibald Clark Kerr, 1st Baron Inverchapel to the Secretary of State Marshall, Telegram including enclosure, 'Summary of a memorandum representing Mr Bevin's views on the formation of a Western Union', 13 January 1948, United States Department of State, *Foreign Relations of the United States (FRUS)1948.* Western Europe (1948), vol. 3, pp. 3–6.
35. TNA: FO 371/73047: Z 1308, 16 February 1948. This document identifies a continuing interest in strengthening Europe's position *vis-à-vis* the US, with Bevin going on to state, 'I was convinced that we should be able to deal with other parts of the world including America better if the western world were more united and did not operate in separate units'.
36. John D. Hickerson (Director of the Office of European Affairs) with Inverchapel present, Memorandum of conversation, 21 January 1948, in *FRUS 1948. Western Europe,* vol. 3, p. 10. In his promotion of the 'soft' aspects of European union Hickerson seems to have drawn on the ideas (and words) of the Director of the US Policy Planning Staff, George F. Kennan, although Kennan takes a more negative line in his rejection of a Dunkirk model defence pact. Kennan to Marshall, 20 January 1948, in *FRUS 1948. Western Europe,* vol. 3, pp. 7–8.
37. See Bullock, *Ernest Bevin,* pp. 516–17.
38. See Hickerson memo, 21 January 1948, p. 11. For Benelux views see the report of Luxembourg's Foreign Minister, Mr Beech's, meeting at the Foreign

Office, TNA: FO 371/73047: Z 1116, 10 February 1948; and reports to the Foreign Office on Spaak's views, TNA: FO 371/73046: Z 894, 3 February 1948 and TNA: FO 371/73047: Z 1250, 13 February 1948.

39. Inverchapel to Robert A. Lovett (US Under Secretary of State), 6 February 1948, in *FRUS 1948. Western Europe*, vol. 3, p. 19.

40. See the communiqué issued at the recess of the London Conference, *FRUS 1948. Germany and Austria*, vol. 2, pp. 142–3.

41. P. Melandri, 'France and the Atlantic Alliance 1950–1953: between great power policy and European integration', in Riste (ed.) *Western Security*, p. 268.

42. TNA: FO 371/73046: Z 896G, Lovett to Inverchapel, 2 February 1948.

43. See TNA: FO 371/73046: Z 1060/G, Inverchapel to Foreign Office, 7 February 1948. Note the Memorandum of Conversation, Lovett with Inverchapel present, 27 January 1948, in which the Under Secretary states that Congressional consideration of the ERP 'would be affected if attention were now directed towards military arrangements'. *FRUS 1948. Western Europe*, vol. 3, p. 13.

44. TNA: FO 371/73047: Z 1210, Washington to Foreign Office, 13 February 1948.

45. For further discussion of the details of the process towards agreement on the Brussels Treaty see T. P. Ireland, *Creating the Entangling Alliance: The Origins of the North Atlantic Treaty*, London: Aldwych Press, 1981, pp. 48–79.

46. British Embassy to Department of State, 11 March 1948, in *FRUS 1948, Western Europe*, vol. 3, p. 47.

47. US Secretary of State to French Embassy, 12 March 1948, in *FRUS 1948, Western Europe*, vol. 3, p. 50.

48. *Treaty of Economic, Social and Cultural Collaboration and Collective Self-Defence*, Cmd. 7599, London: HMSO, 1948, commonly referred to as the Brussels Treaty.

49. Brussels Treaty Preamble—'take such steps as may be necessary in the event of a renewal by Germany of a policy of aggression' and Article VII—'the Council shall be immediately convened . . . with regard to the . . . steps to be taken in case of the renewal by Germany of an aggressive policy'.

50. Brussels Treaty Preamble and Article I.

51. Robertson argues that, whilst 'the authors of the treaty evidently did not intend to create a new international organisation . . . the measures of international co-operation resulting from the treaty could not be realised without the necessary international machinery'. A. H. Robertson, *European Institutions: Co-operation, Integration, Unification*, New York: Praeger, 1959, p. 127.

52. See C. I., 'Western Union: political aspects', *The World Today*, vol. 5, no. 4, April 1949, pp. 170–8.

53. Field Marshal Bernard Montgomery, *The Memoirs of Field-Marshal Montgomery*, Barnsley: Pen and Sword, 2005, p. 503.

54. The combined headquarters was to be known as UNIFORCE. For institutional details see M. Palmer and J. Lambert, *European Unity: A Survey of the European Organisations*, London: Allen and Unwin, 1968, pp. 321–46.

55. For organizational detail see Field Marshal, The Viscount Montgomery of Alemein, 'The Western Union and its defence organisation', originally printed in November 1949 issue of *RUSI Journal*, reproduced in *RUSI Journal*, vol. 138, no. 4, August 1993, pp. 52–7.

56. For an examination of different approaches to the 'third force' idea, and its significance for British policy in the period, see J. Kent and J. W. Young, 'British policy overseas: the "Third Force" and the origins of NATO—in search of a new perspective', in B. Heuser and R. O'Neill (eds) *Securing Peace in Europe 1945–1962*, London: Macmillan, 1992, pp. 41–61.

57. Cabinet Meeting conclusions of 5 March 1948, cited in J. L. Gaddis, 'The United States and the question of a sphere of influence in Europe 1945–49', in Riste (ed.) *Western Security*, p. 78.
58. For Larres, the Dunkirk Treaty represents the high point or 'decisive junction' in the development of a truly European co-operative perspective in defence. Larres, 'A search for order', p. 85.
59. *Public Papers of the Presidents of the United States*, Washington, DC: Office of the Federal Register, National Archives and Records Service, 1953, p. 184.
60. Marshall was to inform Inverchapel on 12 March of US willingness to 'proceed at once in the joint discussions on the establishment of an Atlantic security system'. *FRUS 1948. Western Europe*, vol. 3, p. 48.
61. For the three versions of NSC 9 on 'The position of the United States with respect to support for Western Union and other related countries', see *FRUS 1948. Western Europe* vol. 3, pp. 85–8 (13 April), pp. 100–1 (23 April) and pp. 140–1 (28 June).
62. Policy Planning Staff 27 Memorandum in *FRUS 1948, Western Europe*, vol. 3, p. 62.
63. Krieger, 'Foundation and history of the Treaty of Brussels', p. 244.
64. Memorandum of conversation, Chief of Division of Western European Affairs, Achilles, 5 April 1948, in *FRUS 1948. Western Europe*, vol. 3, pp. 76–8.
65. Minutes of Second Meeting, Washington, 23 March 1948, in *FRUS 1948. Western Europe*, vol. 3, p. 64. Indeed, it should be noted that the concept of a European 'third force' would not have been at odds with much of the thinking within US foreign policy circles at the time, where independent centres of power within a multipolar international system could contribute to both regional and global stability. See Gaddis, 'The United States and the question of a sphere of influence in Europe 1945–49', pp. 70–1.
66. TNA: DG 1/5, Defence Ministers and Chiefs of Staff Meeting, 30 April 1948.
67. In a reply to their Special Representative in Europe's questions on US policy positions, the Acting Secretary of State replied, on 3 December 1948, that 'we feel strongly that economic recovery must not be sacrificed to rearmament and must continue to be given a clear priority'. *FRUS 1948. Western Europe*, vol. 3, p. 305. Nevertheless, the Five Powers had to approve a defence budget of $325m for 1949–50 in order to get US support. TNA: DG 1/9/52, Jebb to Lewis W. Douglas (US Ambassador to the UK), 14 May 1948; TNA: DG 1/1, Permanent Consultative Council with Finance and Defence Ministers present, 14–15 March 1948.
68. Douglas to Secretary of State, 14 May 1948, in *FRUS 1948. Western Europe*, vol. 3, pp. 123–6.
69. These two events served to demonstrate the danger of communist expansion and the possibilities of combined Western action to meet it, Bevin having been influential in engaging the Americans in the Berlin airlift. See F. Roberts, *Dealing with Dictators: The Destruction and Revival of Europe 1930–1970*, London: Weidenfeld and Nicolson, 1991, pp. 127 and 131–7.
70. See G. Lundestad, 'Empire by invitation: the United States and Western Europe, 1945–1952', *Society for Historians of American Foreign Relations Newsletter*, vol. 15, no. 3, June 1984, pp. 1–21.
71. L. S. Kaplan, 'An unequal triad: the United States, Western Union, and NATO', in Riste (ed.) *Western Security*, p. 113. Also see J. Chauvel, *Commentaire d'Alger a Berne (1944–1952)*, Paris: Fayard, 1972, p. 267.
72. TNA: DG1/5/30, Record of Meeting Defence Ministers and Chiefs of Staff, 27 September 1948. Also see TNA: DG 1/9/52, Draft directive with Annex I FP (48) 41, 30 September 1948.
73. See TNA: DG 1/5/32, Memorandum by the Defence Committee 23/3/49; MD (49) 7, 28 March 1949.

74. As Montgomery was moved to report in a secret telegram to the War Office in London, 'My present instructions are to hold the line at the Rhine. Presently available allied forces might enable me to hold the tip of the Brittany peninsula for three days. Please instruct further'. Cited in Ferrel, 'The formation of the Alliance', p. 14.
75. Montgomery, *The Memoirs,* p. 508.
76. Gaddis, 'The United States and the question of a sphere of influence in Europe 1945–49', p. 73.
77. Joint Resolution 239, *Congressional Record,* vol. 94, 80th Congress, 2nd Session, 11 June 1948, p. 7791.
78. For minutes of the Washington Exploratory Talks, which began on 6 July 1948, see *FRUS 1948. Western Europe,* vol. 3.
79. R. E. Osgood, *NATO: The Entangling Alliance,* Chicago: University of Chicago Press, 1962, p. 31.
80. Kaplan, 'An unequal triad', p. 122.
81. Cited in E. Barker, *Britain in a Divided Europe: 1945–1970,* London: Weidenfeld and Nicolson, 1971, p. 81.
82. See discussion in J. W. Young, *Britain and European Unity 1945–1999,* 2nd edn, Basingstoke: Macmillan, 2000, pp. 17–18.
83. See WEU Central Office of Information, *Western Co-operation—a Handbook,* Paris: WEU, 1955, pp. 73–81; also WEU Assembly, *Third Report of the Council to the WEU Assembly,* doc. 79, 21 February 1958.
84. H. Holborn, 'American foreign policy and European integration', *World Politics,* vol. 3, no. 1, October 1953, p. 15.
85. 'The Statute of the Council of Europe, London, 5 May 1949', http://www.conventions.coe.int/Treaty/en/Treaties/Html/001.htm. Also see NA:DG1/3/13, French Prime Minister Bidault's speech at the 2nd Session of the Consultative Council, 'Federation of Europe', The Hague, 20 July 1948.
86. Barker, *Britain in a Divided Europe,* p. 84.
87. See TNA: DEFE 7/529 36B, R. L. Speaight, Head of the Foreign Office Information Policy Department to A. J. Newling, Ministry of Defence, 7 January 1950.
88. Lord H. L. Ismay, *NATO: The First Five Years,* Utrecht: Bosch-Utrecht, 1955, p. 29.
89. TNA: CAB 128/17: CM (50) 29th Cabinet Conclusions, 8 May 1950.
90. Cited from a study prepared by the Permanent Under Secretary at the Foreign Office, William Strang, for Bevin. TNA: FO 371/76385: W 4707: PUSC (51) Final, 'Anglo-American Relations—Present and Future', 24 August 1949, para. 22.
91. See Labour Party Publication (LPP), *Cards on the Table: An Interpretation of Labour's Foreign Policy,* London, 1947; LPP, *European Unity,* Statement by the N.E.C. of the Labour Party, London, 1950; LPP, *Problems of Foreign Policy,* London, 1952; 'The Socialist parties and European unity: a British Labour Party view', *The World Today,* vol. 6, no. 10, October 1950, pp. 415–23.
92. Perhaps most notable amongst these was the British Ambassador in Paris, who saw a European alliance as 'so mighty that no power on earth would have dared to challenge it'. A. D. Cooper, *Old Men Forget,* London: Rupert Hart-Davis, 1954, pp. 344–7.
93. Bevin managed to obtain Cabinet acceptance of the principle of German participation in Western defence, but there was a great deal of opposition within government. See TNA: CAB 128/18: CM (50), 59th Cabinet Minutes, 15 September 1950.
94. G. Hendriks and A. Morgan, *The Franco-German Axis in European Integration,* Cheltenham: Edward Elgar, 2001, p. 23.

95. See D. Acheson, *Present at the Creation,* New York: Norton, 1969, p. 326; J. Pinder, *European Community: The Building of a Union,* Oxford: Oxford University Press, 1991, p. 1.
96. 'The Schuman Declaration', 9 May 1950, online at europa.eu/about-eu/ basic-information/symbols/europe-day/schuman-declaration/.
97. For the debate over the British Government's response to the Schuman Plan see the House of Commons, *Hansard,* vol. 476, 26 June 1950, col. 1907–2056.
98. Dell argues that the decisions of the Atlee Government with regard to the Schuman Plan represent a significant policy failure in terms of broader and longer-term British interests. See E. Dell, *The Schuman Plan and the British Abdication of Leadership in Europe,* Oxford: Clarendon Press, 1995. For a more sympathetic analysis see F. Roberts, 'Ernest Bevin as Foreign Secretary', in R. Ovendale (ed.) *The Foreign Policy of the British Labour Governments 1945–51,* Leicester: Leicester University Press, 1984, pp. 34–5; D. Gowland and A. Turner, *Reluctant Europeans: Britain and European Integration 1945–1998,* London: Longmans, 2000, p. 53.
99. See G. Warner, 'The British Labour Government and the Atlantic Alliance, 1949–1951', in Wiggershaus and Foerster (eds) *The Western Security Community,* p. 152.
100. 'A resolution shall be submitted to the Council of Europe demanding that a supra-national federal organisation be created in Europe, which is to base itself on universal, free elections and which shall possess legislative, executive and judicial powers'. Cited in W. Hallstein, 'Germany's dual aim: unity and integration', *Foreign Affairs,* vol. 31, no. 1, October 1952, pp. 58–66.
101. K. Adenauer, *World Indivisible,* London: Allen and Unwin, 1956, p. 34.
102. See C. Craig, *From Bismarck to Adenauer: Aspects of German State-craft,* Baltimore: John Hopkins Press, 1958, p. 142.
103. See W. Hanreider, *West German Foreign Policy 1949–1963: International Pressure and Domestic Response,* Stanford: Stanford University Press, 1967, p. 105.
104. For a discussion of West German popular anti-militarism and resistance to the 'new army' proposals see G. A. Craig, 'NATO and the new German army', in W. W. Kaufmann (ed.) *Military Policy and National Security,* Princeton: Princeton University Press, 1956, pp. 194–232.
105. 'Communiqué of the Foreign Ministers of the United Kingdom, France, and the US, New York', *Department of State Bulletin,* vol. 23, no. 587, 19 September 1950, pp. 530–1.
106. See G. Bebr, 'The European Defence Community and the WEU—an agonising dilemma', *Stanford Law Review,* 1955, pp. 169–236. The Occupation Statutes were to be officially revised 6 March 1951.
107. See 'Germany 1947–1949: the story in documents', vol. 48, Department of State, Publication no. 3556, *European and British Commonwealth Series,* no. 9, 1950.
108. This was the first time that representatives from West Germany and the Saar attended the Council of Europe as associate members, the first significant engagement of Germany with the emerging European architecture of security and integration. H.G.L., 'The European Defence Community', *The World Today,* vol. 8, no. 6, June 1952, p. 236.
109. Council of Europe, Consultative Assembly, 2nd Session, 1950, *Official Report,* pt. 1, p. 228.
110. J. Monnet, *Memoirs,* London: Collins, 1978, p. 345.
111. For the Pleven Plan see *Journal Officiel,* Debates, 25 October 1950, pp. 7118–19.
112. F. Duchêne, *Jean Monnet: The First Statesman of Independence,* New York: Norton, 1994, p. 229.

113. R. Dwan, 'Jean Monnet and the European Defence Community, 1950–54', *Cold War History*, vol. 1, no. 1, August 2000, p. 149.

114. 'Before the United States Government insisted that there should be German troops to defend Germany and Europe nobody had thought seriously of an integrated European army'. Royal Institute of International Affairs (RIIA), *Britain in Western Europe: WEU and Atlantic Alliance*, London: Chatham House, 1956, p. 30.

115. Acheson, *Present at the Creation*, p. 443.

116. See K. Adenauer, *Konrad Adenauer: Memoirs. 1945–1953*, London: Weidenfeld and Nicolson, 1966, pp. 345–7.

117. See 'Resolution of Consultative Council on the Future of Western Union's Defence Organisation after the establishment of SHAPE' in TNA: DG 1/1/2, Record of the 10th Session of the Consultative Council, Brussels, 20 December 1950.

118. 'Resolution of Consultative Council', 20 December 1950.

119. 'Success [in the EDC] would be a step also toward the unification of Europe. This is the central goal and the only possible way of creating reasonable security, and insuring, at the same time, the improvement in living standards that characterises western civilisations'. SACEUR, 'First Annual Report to the Standing Committee', NATO, Paris, 1952.

120. See TNA: CAB 128/18, CM (50), 69th Cabinet Minutes, 30 October 1950.

121. See TNA: PREM 8/1429/1: DO (50) 100, Bevin Paper for the Defence Committee, 24 November 1950.

122. See M. Newman, *Socialism and European Unity: The Dilemma of the Left in Britain and France*, London: Junction Books, 1983, pp. 140–2.

123. See House of Commons, *Hansard*, vol. 485, 12 February 1951, col. 65–6.

124. Thus national armies in Europe would all but 'cease to exist' upon EDC ratification. S. Dockrill, 'The evolution of Britain's policy towards a European Army, 1950–1954', *Journal of Strategic Studies*, vol. 12, no. 1, March 1989, p. 46.

125. *Three Power Washington Declaration*, Cmd. 8626, London: HMSO, 14 September 1951, p. 134.

126. The Rt. Hon. Anthony Nutting cited in E. Fursdon, 'The role of the European Defence Community in European integration', in F. H. Heller and J. R. Gillingham (eds) *NATO: The Founding of the Atlantic Alliance and the Integration of Europe*, New York: St Martin's Press, 1992, p. 219. See 'European unity: a Conservative Party view', *The World Today*, vol. 7, no. 1, January 1951, pp. 21–30.

127. D. D. Eisenhower, *The White House Years: Mandate for Change 1953–1961*, London: Heinemann, 1963, p. 246.

128. TNA: DEFE 5/35: COS (51) 733, 8 December 1951. For a detailed discussion of British attitudes towards EDC, see S. Dockrill, *Britain's Policy for West German Rearmament 1950–1955*, Cambridge: Cambridge University Press, 1991.

129. For reports see *The Times,* 8 and 23 February 1952.

130. See 'Protocol to the North Atlantic Treaty', Misc. no. 9 (1952), in *Memorandum regarding Western support for the European Defence Community'*, Cmd. 8562, London: HMSO, 27 May 1952, Annex B; *Treaty between the United Kingdom and the Member States of the European Defence Community*, Misc. no. 5, Cmd. 8512, London: HMSO, April 1952.

131. C. J., 'The Schuman Plan and the Council of Europe', *The World Today*, vol. 8, no. 11, November 1952, p. 479. Also see R. A. Eden, *The Memoirs of the Rt. Hon. Sir Anthony Eden, K.G., PP.C., M.C.—Full Circle*, London: Cassell, 1960, pp. 47–8.

132. C. J., 'The Schuman Plan and the Council of Europe', p. 480; E. Fursdon, *The European Defence Community: A History,* London: Macmillan, 1980, pp. 212–14.
133. TNA: CAB 131/12, D (52) 26, 'Defence Policy and Global Strategy', report by the Chiefs of Staff, 17 June 1952. See J. Baylis and A. Macmillan, 'The British Global Strategy Paper of 1952', *Journal of Strategic Studies,* vol. 16, no. 2, June 1993, pp. 200–26.
134. See S. Twigge and A. Macmillan, 'Britain, the United States, and the development of NATO strategy, 1950–1964', *Journal of Strategic Studies,* vol. 19, no. 2, June 1996, pp. 260–81.
135. C. J., 'The Schuman Plan and the Council of Europe', p. 477.
136. See pamphlet for the National Planning Association's Committee on International Policy by T. Geiger and H. van B. Cleveland, 'Making Western Europe defensible—an appraisal of the effectiveness of United States policy in Western Europe', *NPA Planning Pamphlets,* no. 74, August 1951.
137. R. B. Manderson-Jones, *The Special Relationship: Anglo-American Relations and Western European Unity 1947–1956,* London: Weidenfeld and Nicolson, 1972, pp. 101–2.
138. For a discussion of force structures see Dockrill, 'The evolution of Britain's policy towards a European Army', p. 45.
139. See EDC Treaty Article 73(1) and 74(1), EDC Military Protocol Article 12 and 15.
140. Dwan argues that 'Monnet's efforts to construct a European political community on the basis of the defence project may well have contributed to its demise'. Dwan, 'Jean Monnet and the European Defence Community', p. 143.
141. B. Burrows and C. Irwin, *The Security of Western Europe,* London: Charles Knight, 1972, p. 35.
142. Federalists see that these negotiations reflect the need for a political authority as a prerequisite—without it 'a point will always be reached when it is in the interests of some State to do one thing and in the interests of others to do the opposite'. H. G. L., 'The European Defence Community', p. 248.
143. See E. De Larminat, *L'Armee Europeene,* Paris: Berger-Levrault, 1952; and J. C. N., 'The European Defence Community: problems of ratification', *The World Today,* vol. 10, no. 8, August 1954, pp. 326–39.
144. See discussion in J. Aimaq, 'Rethinking the EDC: failed attempt at integration and strategic leverage', in M. Dumoulin (ed.) *The European Defence Community: Lessons for the Future,* Brussels: Peter Lang, 2000, pp. 90–135.
145. Ironically, 'the French wanted a German army which would be both stronger than the Soviet one and yet smaller than the French one!' Melandri, 'France and the Atlantic Alliance 1950–1953', p. 276.
146. Aimaq, 'Rethinking the EDC', p. 124.
147. Hanreider notes the prevailing 'dilemma' for France, which was 'deeply suspicious' of the Anglo-American relationship and yet 'obliged to commit both the United States and the United Kingdom to involvement in Europe to make up for French weakness'. Hanreider, *West German Foreign Policy 1949–1963,* p. 40.
148. Dwan, 'Jean Monnet and the European Defence Community', p. 151.
149. K. Adenauer, 'Germany and Europe', *Foreign Affairs,* vol. 31, no. 3, April 1953, pp. 365–6.
150. See Soviet Premier Joseph Stalin's note of 10 March 1952, in which he offered negotiations on German reunification providing the principle of German neutrality was accepted. TNA: PREM 11/168.
151. A. Layton, 'Little Europe and Britain', *International Affairs,* vol. 29, no. 3, July 1953, p. 293. *Draft Treaty embodying the Statute of the European Community,* Strasbourg: Service des Publications de la Communaute Europeene, 1953.

152. M. Smith, *Western Europe and the United States: The Uncertain Alliance*, London: Allen and Unwin, 1984, p. 40.
153. The US defence budget fell from $50.4b in 1953 to $40.6b in 1955. See J. and G. Kolko, *The Limits of Power: The World and the United States Foreign Policy 1945–1954*, New York: Harper and Row, 1972, p. 695.
154. For Eisenhower's New Look see G. Snyder, 'The "New Look" of 1953', in W. R. Schilling, P. Y. Hammond, and G. Snyder (eds) *Strategy, Politics, and Defence Budgets*, New York: Praeger, 1962, pp. 383–524; J. L. Gaddis, *Strategies of Containment: A Critical Appraisal of Post-war American National Security Policy*, Oxford: Oxford University Press, 1982, pp. 127–63.
155. See NSC 5405 (16 January 1954), in *FRUS 1952–1954. Indochina*, vol. 13, part 1, pp. 971–6, which was the first US National Security Council policy statement on South-east Asia and which identified the conflict as one between the communist and non-communist world. E. R. May, 'The American commitment to Germany, 1949–1955', *Diplomatic History*, vol. 13, no. 4, October 1989, pp. 431–60. Eisenhower, *The White House Years*, p. 141.
156. For example see 'McBride minutes' of the Tripartite Foreign Ministers Meeting, 11 July 1953, in *FRUS 1952–1954. Western European Security*, vol. 5, part 2, pp. 1622–3.
157. See 'United States Delegation to the Tripartite Foreign Ministers Meeting to Department of State', 18 October 1953, *FRUS 1952–1954. Western European Security*, vol. 5, part 1, pp. 826–8.
158. See 'Knight minutes' of the Tripartite Foreign Ministers Meeting, 6 December 1953, in *FRUS, 1952–1954. Western European Security*, vol. 5, part 2, p. 1764. The Richardson Amendment (*Congressional Record*, 83rd Congress, 1st Session, 1953, pp. 8689–93) had provided that half of US aid to Europe would be conditional on ratification of the EDC Treaty.
159. Dulles's statement to the NAC, 14 December 1953, in *FRUS 1952–1954. Western European Security*, vol. 5, part 1, pp. 462–3.
160. Armstrong suggests that the post-Stalin Soviet strategy of 'peaceful coexistence' contributed to altering the post-war Grand Alliance 'from something hard into something soft'. H. F. Armstrong, 'Postscript to EDC', *Foreign Affairs*, vol. 33, no. 1, October 1954, p. 17.
161. See Manderson-Jones, *The Special Relationship*, p. 112.
162. Holborn, 'American foreign policy and European integration', p. 23.
163. Acheson, *Present at the Creation*, pp. 569–70.
164. Although meeting the Soviet threat through German engagement in West European defence remained a key concern of the US, its enthusiasm for integration as a means of overcoming traditional intra-European conflict was also an influential motivation of US policy towards the EDC. See R. W. Pruessen, 'Cold War threats and America's commitment to the European Defense Community: one corner of a triangle', *Journal of European Integration History*, vol. 2, no. 1, 1996, pp. 51–69.
165. See Eisenhower, *The White House Years*, pp. 99 and 142.
166. Montgomery cited in N. Hamilton, *Monty, the Field Marshal*, London: Macmillan, 1978, pp. 826–7.
167. Eden, *The Memoirs*, pp. 57–8.
168. See RIIA, *Britain in Western Europe*, p. 43. It was noted that there was a French 'tendency to be paralysed rather than activated by foreign pressure'. J. C. N., 'The European Defence Community', p. 329.
169. See TNA: CAB 129/66: C (54) 93, 'United Kingdom Association with the European Defence Community', 3 March 1954.
170. *Memorandum Regarding United Kingdom Association with the European Defence Community, with Annexes*, Cmd. 9126, London: HMSO, 1954.

171. See TNA: CAB129/64: C (53) 332, Annex to 'Eden minute', 26 November 1953; and 'Britain and EDC', *The World Today*, vol. 10, no. 5, May 1954, p. 183, for discussion.

172. *Statement of Common Policy on Military Association*, Cmd. 9126, London: HMSO, 1954, Annex B.

173. Aimaq, 'Rethinking the EDC', p. 123. Ruane argues that the lack of international support for Eisenhower's proposal of an armed intervention in Vietnam, given fears of an escalation of the conflict with the potential drawing in of the Chinese, had left the Eisenhower Administration with 'no alternative but to await the outcome at Geneva'. K. Ruane, *The Rise and Fall of the European Defence Community: Anglo-American Relations and the Crisis of European Defence, 1950–55,* Basingstoke: Macmillan, 2000, p. 86.

174. See N. Khrushchev, *Khrushchev Remembers*, Boston: Strobe Talbott, 1970, pp. 481–2. For the British view see TNA: CAB 129/70: C (54) 254, Eden, 'The Geneva Conference', 24 July 1954.

175. R. H. Immerman, 'The United States and the Geneva Conference of 1954: a new look', *Diplomatic History*, vol. 14, no. 1, winter 1990, p. 50.

176. See Churchill's statement in which he argued that some limits on the rearmament of a restored sovereign West Germany would be required in order to maintain standards of fair play. House of Commons, *Hansard*, vol. 530, 14 July 1954, col. 498–502 and his earlier comments on the Anglo-American talks, 12 July 1954, col. 38 and 43.

177. Cable disputes the 'conspiracy theory' explanation, arguing that the Soviets had little to gain from concessions on Indo-China given the small probability of French ratification of the EDC; the inclusion of Indo-China in the Five Power Talks was rather the 'price paid by the *Americans* for the prospect of French ratification of the EDC', an unlikely prospect given the lack of a French majority in favour of it. J. Cable, *The Geneva Conference of 1954 on Indochina*, Basingstoke: Macmillan, 2000, pp. 129–32.

178. Armstrong, 'Postscript to EDC', p. 19.

179. See TNA: CAB 129/69: C (54) 226, Eden, 'European Defence Community', 7 July 1954. For discussion see R. F. Randle, *Geneva 1954: The Settlement of the Indo-Chinese War*, Princeton: Princeton University Press, 1969.

180. See K. Loewenstein, 'The Bonn Constitution and the EDC Treaties', *Yale Law Journal*, 1955, pp. 805–39.

181. For the text of the Joint Communiqué of the Brussels Conference, together with the draft protocol submitted by the French Government (known as the Mendès France Proposals) and the reply proposals (known as the Spaak Declaration) see NATO, Information Division, *NATO Letter*, 1 September 1954, pp. 21–7.

182. Dwan notes the failure of the elite group of US and French pro-integrationists, meeting in Paris to expedite EDC ratification, to recognize the political and practical constraints on achieving French Government approval; the group became 'slaves to an opaque vision shared by few and rejected by many'. R. Dwan, 'The European Defence Community and the role of French-American elite relations—1950–1954', in Dumoulin (ed.) *The European Defence Community*, p. 89.

183. R. B. Duchin, 'The "Agonising Reappraisal": Eisenhower, Dulles, and the European Defence Community', *Diplomatic History*, vol. 16, no. 2, spring 1992, p. 212.

184. RIIA, *Britain in Western Europe*, p. 50.

185. Lester B. Pearson, Canadian Secretary of State for External Affairs and representative at the Nine Power Conferences in London and Paris and NATO Ministerial in Paris, 'WEU: implications for Canada and NATO', *International Journal*, vol. 10, no. 1, 1954, p. 1.

186. D. Carlton, *Anthony Eden: A Biography*, London: Allen Lane, 1981, p. 361.
187. See TNA: CAB 129/70: C (54) 280, Eden, 'Alternatives to the European Defence Community', 1 September 1954. Also see TNA: CAB 128/27: CC 59 (54), Cabinet Conclusions, 8 September 1954, pp. 446–9 for ongoing discussion of alternatives; and TNA: PREM 11/843, Churchill to Eden, 9 September 1954, for Churchill's views.
188. Eden, *The Memoirs*, p. 151.
189. TNA: CAB 128/27: CC 57 (54), Cabinet Conclusions, 27 August 1954 (and thus before French rejection); and TNA: CAB 129/70: C (54) 276, Eden, 'Alternatives to the European Defence Community', 27 August 1954, pp. 70–5.
190. Eden, *The Memoirs*, p. 163.
191. Thorpe notes the 'crucial' nature of Eden's tour in gaining support for the new security arrangements and distancing a cynical Churchill from the process. D. R. Thorpe, *Eden: The Life and Times of Anthony Eden First Earl of Avon, 1897–1977*, London: Pimlico, 2004, pp. 413–14.
192. See TNA: CAB 128/27: CC 60 (54), Cabinet Conclusions, 17 September 1954, pp. 456–8, for the Foreign Secretary's report on the trips to Brussels, Bonn, Paris and Rome.
193. 'The prevention of war between neighbouring nations which have a long record of fighting cannot be dependably achieved merely by national promises or threats, but only by merging certain functions of their government into supra-national institutions'. 'Statement by John Foster Dulles on the rejection of the EDC by the French Parliament (31 August 1954)', *FRUS 1952–1954. Western European Security*, vol. 5, part 2, pp. 1120–2.
194. For the text of Dulles's speech on 29 September 1954, see *Final Act of the Nine-Power Conference held in London, September 28th to October 3rd 1954*, Misc. no. 28, Cmd. 9289, London: HMSO, 1954, Annex IIA, p. 15. For supporting documents see *FRUS 1952–1954. Western European Security*, vol. 5, part 2, pp. 1294–366. For the UK view of proceedings see TNA: CAB 128/27: CC 62 (54), Cabinet Conclusions, 1 October 1954, pp. 467–9.
195. Eden, *The Memoirs*, p. 166.
196. Frank Roberts, a senior Foreign Office Advisor at the time, has depicted the securing of the WEU agreement as Eden's finest hour. *Dealing with Dictators*, pp. 170–2. For Eden's role in securing agreement also see A. Deighton, 'The last piece of the jigsaw: Britain and the creation of the Western European Union', *Contemporary European History*, vol. 7, no. 2, July 1998, pp. 181–96.
197. For a summary of the discussions of 28 September 1954 in Cabinet which led to agreement on the offer of British force deployment see NA:CAB 129/71: C.(54)302. This commitment was to find form in Protocol II on 'Forces of Western European Union', Article VI, modifying the Brussels Treaty. For the full text of the Treaty of Economic, Social and Cultural Collaboration and Collective Self-Defence as amended by the Protocol Modifying and Completing the Brussels Treaty (the MBT) and relevant protocols, see *Protocols to the Treaty signed at Brussels on March 17, 1948 between the United Kingdom of Great Britain and Northern Ireland, Belgium, France, Luxembourg and the Netherlands, Modifying and Extending that Treaty to include the Federal Republic of Germany and Italy. Paris, 23 October 1954*, Treaty Series no. 39 (1955), Cmd. 9498, London: HMSO, 1955.
198. Churchill cited in Carlton, *Anthony Eden*, p. 363.
199. Eden, *The Memoirs*, p. 168.
200. M. Curtis, *West European Integration*, New York: Harper Rowe, 1965, p. 105.

201. *Final Act of Nine-Power Conference,* Cmd. 9289, p. 4. Also see A. H. Robertson, 'The creation of WEU', *European Yearbook,* vol. 2, 1956, pp. 126–9; and Bebr, 'The European Defence Community and the WEU', pp. 169–236, for discussion.

202. US and Canadian requests for permanent observer status on the WEU Council were rejected; the WEU Working Group noted that US observers to the EDC had 'failed to restrict themselves to [the] role of observers', and the UK Foreign Office argued that this would provide an 'in' for the Turks. The US Embassy in London was to note that the 'WEU is an essentially European enterprise which does not cross vital lines of U.S. policy and which would not benefit from an excess of U.S. presence'. 'Ambassador to the United Kingdom (Aldrich) to the Department of State, London, 2 November 1954', *FRUS 1952–1954. Western European Security,* vol. 5, part 2, p. 1468.

203. Robertson, *European Institutions,* p. 138. See statement by the Chairman of the Council, Paul-Henri Spaak, at the Assembly's inaugural meeting: WEU Assembly, *Proceedings of the First Session,* July 1955, p. 24.

204. French, Belgian, Italian, Dutch and West German land and air force maxima in peacetime were to be as fixed by the Special Agreements annexed to the treaty on the Establishment of the EDC (signed 27 May 1952). British continental deployments were only fixed at its commitment of four divisions and the Second Tactical Air Force, and Luxembourg forces at one regimental combat team. Increases to these maxima required unanimous Council approval.

205. The Article X provisions for pacific settlement of disputes and the role of the International Court of Justice in this regard are equally significant 'internal security' elements. See A. Bloed and R. A. Wessels (eds) *The Changing Functions of the Western European Union (WEU),* Dordrecht: Martinus Nijhoff, 1994, p. xvii.

206. See MBT, Protocol 1, Article IV and *Resolution of the NAC Implementing Section IV of the Final Act of the London Conference,* Cmd. 9304, London: HMSO, 1954.

207. Paris Conference held 20–22 October 1954, and the NAC meeting of 22–23 October 1954. For the text see 'Documents relating to the accession to the Treaty of the Federal Republic of Germany', *NATO: Facts and Figures,* 1971, appendix 10, pp. 306–34.

208. See *Resolution of the NAC,* Cmd. 9304, p. 3.

209. Italy was a signatory of the Washington Treaty and was therefore already an ally of the Brussels Treaty powers. See TNA: CAB 129/70: C (54) 298, Eden, 'London Conference', 27 September 1954.

210. This agreement had been based on the study undertaken by the Consultative Assembly of the Council of Europe on the Saar problem. See Council of Europe, *Documents of the Consultative Assembly,* doc. 225, May 1954.

211. RIIA, *Survey of International Affairs 1955–1956,* London: Oxford University Press, 1960, p. 37.

212. See L. S. Kaplan, 'NATO and Adenauer's Germany: uneasy partnership', *International Organisations,* vol. 15, no. 4, autumn 1961, pp. 618–29, for discussion.

213. See discussion in Ruane, *The Rise and Fall of the European Defence Community,* pp. 115–23.

214. Young acknowledges the 'continental criticism' that Eden's support of the EDC had been 'too grudging', and that he had appeared 'anti-European', although his policy was 'coherent, logical and (in September 1954 at least) successful'. J. W. Young, 'German rearmament and the European Defence Community', in J. W. Young (ed.) *The Foreign Policy of Churchill's Peacetime Administration 1951–1955,* Leicester: Leicester University Press, 1988, pp. 101–2.

215. N. Leites and C. De La Malene, 'Paris from EDC to WEU', *World Politics,* vol. 9, no. 2, January 1957, p. 211.
216. RIIA, *Survey of International Affairs 1955–1956,* p. 39.
217. Parliamentary consensus had been achieved in the UK, although there was some resistance by 'Bevanites, pacifists, Crypto-Communists and cranks on party fringes, as well as pressure from constituencies', which resulted in the Labour opposition directing its members to abstain, but not vote against the agreements. 'Ambassador in the UK (Aldrich) to Department of State', 19 November 1954, *FRUS 1952–1954. Western European Security,* vol. 5, part 2, pp. 1485–6.
218. Fursdon, *The European Defence Community,* p. 323.
219. Montgomery, *The Western Union and its Defence Organisation,* p. 57.
220. Burrows and Irwin, *The Security of Western Europe,* p. 37, suggest that the EDC failed because of the 'departure from the logical order of things'.
221. Warner notes that the view that Britain could not cope without the Americans 'led to an exaggerated Atlanticism in British policy' which made them suspicious of anything that might threaten that idea. Warner, 'The British Labour Government and the Atlantic Alliance', p. 152.
222. Mendès France in correspondence with Fursdon, 'The role of the European Defence Community in European integration', p. 238.
223. Hence, Duke suggests that the WEU was 'destined to be NATO's junior sibling from conception'. S. Duke, *The Elusive Quest for European Security,* London: Macmillan, 2000, p. 39.
224. Fursdon quotes Sir Frank Roberts, who states that 'a most unhappy France, an unenthusiastic Britain and an even more unhappy Germany had to accept United States logic'. Fursdon, 'The role of the European Defence Community in European integration', p. 237.
225. G. W. Rees, *The Western European Union at the Crossroads: Between Trans-Atlantic Solidarity and European Integration,* Oxford: Westview, 1998, p. 9.
226. *Final Act of Nine-Power Conference,* Cmd. 9289, p. 4.
227. Duchin, 'The "Agonising Reappraisal"', p. 219.
228. Deighton suggests that, rather than marking the end of European supranational integration, the WEU was to provide the '*sine qua non* of subsequent integration', a 'unwelcome advance' that was to 'dog Conservative (and Labour) governments for generations to come'. Deighton, 'The last piece of the jigsaw', p. 182.
229. As a Chatham House Group identified in 1956, the WEU 'represents a compromise between two schools of European thought: that which looks to an Atlantic framework for the solution of Europe's problems, and that which stresses the need for a much closer European unity in order to strengthen Europe and the whole Western world'. Chatham House, *Britain in Western Europe,* p. 2.

2 From Activity to Dormancy
1955–73

In the period immediately following the signature of the MBT in 1954, the WEU was to develop its institutional competencies in the setting of a new post-war order. Reliance on American security guarantees through NATO had created a level of West European defence dependence that was broadly acceptable to the major European powers in the light of the perceived Soviet threat. However, satisfaction with institutional arrangements was seldom more than grudgingly temporary. What had begun to develop by the mid 1950s was a realization of the limits of alliance, as it became clear that in the important areas of threat perception and burden-sharing, and in the degree and scope of obligation, NATO members often had divergent interests and values.

As early as 1956, the Soviet suppression of the Hungarian Uprising, whilst serving to reinforce the realities of the Soviet threat, had demonstrated what Grosser has referred to as 'a tacit *modus vivendi*', whereby each superpower was compelled, through mutual fear, not to intervene in the other's sphere of influence.[1] In the same year and even more far-reaching in its implications for future Alliance relationships was US condemnation of Anglo-French action in Suez in support of what were seen as vital interests in the Middle East. Implied Soviet nuclear threats in response to the Suez assault were met by the suggestion of American economic sanctions against its two fellow NATO members if they failed to withdraw their forces.[2] What events in Hungary and Suez had demonstrated to all three major European allies was that their interests, however imperative, would not be allowed to prevail over those of their stronger 'partner'.

As the limitations of the NATO alliance became increasingly evident to the Europeans, Soviet technological advances, symbolized by the launch of Sputnik in 1957, called into question the credibility of the US extended-deterrence strategy. In a situation of emerging nuclear parity, mutual interest in the avoidance of superpower confrontation led to increasing European fears of 'peripheralism', under the belligerent partnership of superpower condominium. Perennial concerns about the cost of American leadership led the Europeans to seek increased influence, whether through the development of 'independent' capabilities or through greater involvement in the development and management of Alliance nuclear strategy.

Given the failure of the EDC and the realization of the requirements of, and indeed for, US hegemony,[3] the ECSC Six had adopted a 'defence-last' approach to European integration, whilst taking strides towards economic integration with their promotion of a European customs union. From 1957 the European Economic Community (EEC) was to provide for the re-emergence of Europe as an economic power, and the European Atomic Energy Community (Euratom) for co-operation on the peaceful use of nuclear technology represented one more step in the direction of eventual European unity. The exclusion of the UK from the evolving Communities, first through British resistance and then by French rejection, was to provide a further point of contention in a cooperative Europe where integrationist tendencies were already in conflict with Gaullist nationalism.

Early US post-war policy towards Europe had been guided by the desire to establish strong bonds both within Western Europe and between the US and its 'natural' allies amongst the liberal democracies of Europe. The encouragement of European unity and the establishment of an Atlantic 'Community' were thought of as elements in harmony; short-term economic sacrifices would be acceptable for the US in the pursuit of a strong and prosperous Europe, devoid of conflict-promoting nationalisms and capable of participating in a common front against the Soviets.[4] However, during the 1950s anxieties began to emerge in Washington as to the benefits of the European integration process for US interests, and by the early 1960s it had become clear that Europe might become a major economic competitor. The economic success of the evolving common market contrasted with chronic US balance-of-payments problems, prompting US concerns over access to foreign markets.[5] As successive US Administrations sought to redefine the concept of Atlantic Partnership and Community, the linkage between economic and defence 'interdependence' served to point up the contradictions in US-European relations.

As the two 'big ideas' for European security were developed, in collective defence terms within the Atlantic Alliance, and in integrative terms within the Europe of the Six, the WEU was effectively bound by its treaty obligations to restrict its own development and function to whatever provided support to these primary organizations. However, as a compromise solution to convergent national concerns, the WEU was inevitably an untidy and ill-defined institution, lacking any clear blueprint for its functional or legal mandate. Importantly, once the Federal Republic had been successfully incorporated into NATO in 1955, a lack of consensus emerged amongst members on the direction that the 'hybrid' WEU should take. Given the lack of member agreement as to the preferred nature of transatlantic and European community development, it is unsurprising that the extent to which the WEU could and should seek to pursue its dual aims of promoting European integration and Atlantic Alliance was as contentious as the means by which this might be achieved. Hence, national players sought to utilize the WEU to forward their own visions of what would constitute an acceptable institutional order.

Against this backdrop, this chapter explores the nature of the WEU's dual support role by examining the development of the institution during the period from its formation in 1955 to its decline into 'somnolence' in 1973 in the context of the broader institutional environment. During these years the potential functions of the WEU were the subject of much debate. An examination of those functions that the WEU developed as well as those which were limited or stillborn demonstrates the perceived utility of the WEU in meeting the interests of participant states. In so doing, it highlights the tensions that existed within Europe as the centre for integration, within the NATO alliance as the constituency for collective defence, and between these two processes as central elements of the European security environment.

THE EARLY DEBATE: WHAT ROLE FOR THE WEU?

That the role of the WEU at its creation was at best ambiguous was reflected in the debate between Council and Assembly regarding the WEU's mandate and commitments. This debate was illustrative of wider concerns about the nature of the Atlantic relationship and the desirability of an integrated and truly united Europe. At the Assembly's opening session in Strasbourg, on 5 July 1955, Paul Henri Spaak, the Belgian Foreign Minister and Chairman of the WEU Council, announced the Council's intention to pursue a policy of peace, to reinforce security, to strive for unity and to encourage the gradual integration of Europe with closer co-operation internally and with the other European organizations.[6] However, despite this grand rhetoric, the Council position was to be essentially minimalist, with the Council proclaiming by 1956 that 'at present WEU should be regarded only as the repository of the solemn undertaking to afford mutual assistance embodied in Article V of the revised Brussels Treaty, and the guardian of procedure laid down in Article VIII'.[7] Hence, the de facto position determined by the Council was that the WEU should essentially be restricted to supervising the Agency for the Control of Armaments and the Standing Armaments Committee, with defence obligations being fulfilled through NATO.[8]

The WEU Assembly, established under Article IX of the MBT as the recipient of Council reports, had undertaken as its first task the writing of its own Charter, Article 1 of which defines its powers as discussing any matters arising from the MBT, including those raised by the Council reports. Purely consultative in nature, the Assembly was able to establish its own institutional structure and rules of procedure under the Charter, with business being conducted on the lines of 'general debate' followed by referral to committees, on the basis of whose reports Assembly recommendations could be made to the Council.[9] The Assembly position with regard to WEU competence was essentially maximalist, seeking a far broader role for the WEU than that perceived by the Council, including both the active promotion of European integration and the supervision of defence responsibilities encharged to NATO. In the 1956 report of the Assembly's Defence Questions and Armaments Committee (DQAC) it was requested of the Council 'not to take too restrictive a view about its relative competence with regard to NATO', and following Council rejection of an Assembly invitation to debate the matter in October 1956, the Assembly was to make repeated requests that the Council 'urgently review their present interpretation of the amended Treaty of Brussels with regards to functions of Western European Union in the defence field'.[10] The Assembly was also keen to establish its own role in this regard. Although it was recognized that, for the Council, it was 'right and practical that their general responsibility for security should be discharged through NATO', this should not preclude the communication of relevant information to the Assembly, where, 'if we discuss the issues in common, in a European Assembly, this forms a valuable corrective to the tendency in all national parliaments to look at plans involving considerable sacrifice solely from the point of view of immediate national advantage, rather than in the perspective of European security as a whole'.[11]

This liberal interpretation of the Assembly's role was agreed by the Council, after initial reticence, in its second Annual Report in February 1957, in which it was stated, 'The Council appreciate the Assembly's desire to consider broader aspects of defence than those to which the Council must limit themselves and to debate these activities against the background of a general policy'. This was a significant decision of the Council, recognizing the WEU Assembly as the only European assembly mandated to discuss defence. The Council went on to recognize the legitimacy of the Assembly's demands for adequate documentation on those defence matters that it was entitled by its Charter to discuss, conceding the obligation to furnish such information in Annual Reports and accepting that joint meetings between Council and Assembly representatives might be useful.[12] However, although the Assembly would meet to discuss a range of reports produced by its General Affairs Committee (GAC) and DQAC, 'the Council would frequently respond to subsequent Assembly Recommendations by bald assertions that the issue had been noted or that the matter was one reserved for NATO'.[13] Despite numerous Assembly attempts to get some political accountability from the Council, the Assembly lacked the teeth to do much more than disagree with the specific content of Council reports.[14] Although formally sensitive to the Assembly's concerns, the Council's position remained essentially a minimalist one. The consequence of Council intransigence was a disheartened Assembly. Thus it was noted as early as 1956 that 'the members of the Assembly only attend the meetings of the committees and the plenary sessions of the Assembly out of politeness or a sense of duty and not because they are convinced of the prime importance of the Assembly and of the problems which it discusses'.[15]

The interests of the major continental powers in the early development of the WEU were reflected in the maximalist position of the Assembly. Defence through NATO may have been recognized as a necessity of European dependence, but the six continental members of the WEU had continued to develop their interest in an integrated Europe in the area of low politics. At the conclusion of their Messina Conference, 1–3 June 1955, the six resolved that the moment had come 'to go a step further' towards the construction of 'united Europe', beginning in the economic sphere through the process of constructing a European common market and developing an organization for the peaceful development of atomic energy.[16]

The WEU had been devised as a result of the failure of integration in the defence field, but it had also been conceived with the broader aim to 'promote the unity and encourage the progressive integration of Europe'. During the ratification debate on the Paris Agreements in the French National Assembly on 23 December 1954, Prime Minister Pierre Mendès France identified the WEU's broad area of competence and noted that 'the contribution to the construction of Europe is infinitely more important to the future of our civilisation than the military clauses of the agreements which are now before you'.[17] Equally the West German Chancellor, Konrad Adenauer, stated that the WEU had 'primarily political significance and aims' and would be 'the starting point and nucleus of future European policy'.[18] Consequently, for the continental members of the WEU pursuing economic integration through ongoing negotiations on an EEC, the WEU represented something more than a largely symbolic support for an Atlantic defence commitment. As the US NAC delegation was to report to Washington after a meeting in Paris in May 1955, for Adenauer and for Spaak (who chaired the preparatory committee on 'relaunching' Europe initiated at Messina), the WEU 'must have a life of its own' and be free to discuss whatever problems it saw fit. The WEU had distinct functions from those of NATO, including the significant function of arms control, and 'some of those who had helped establish WEU believed it would grow and lead towards greater cohesiveness [of] its members in certain fields'.[19]

An explanation of the Council's minimalist position may be found in the attitudes of the British towards their own creation. Clearly for the UK Government, the WEU was something of an 'unwanted child', an entity which had served its purpose by ensuring a German contribution to NATO and thus an American commitment to the Continent. The British essentially perceived the WEU as a European element of the Atlantic Alliance. Some may have hoped that the WEU had succeeded in convincing the UK of its inextricable security links with Europe, but British attitudes towards its WEU commitments over the following years were soon to dispel any early optimism.[20] Despite the UK Government's 1954 association agreement with the ECSC, it did not share the continental enthusiasm for the European integration process and had chosen to withdraw, in November 1955, from the Spaak Committee's preparatory discussions on economic integration, which was being pursued by the ECSC Six. As a 'great power' with significant transatlantic and Commonwealth interests, British disengagement was largely based on false assumptions regarding the ability of the Europeans to come to agreement without UK involvement.[21] The British Government sought a broader approach to European economic co-operation, as reflected in its Free Trade Area (FTA) plans, which sought to include all OEEC states in a customs union within which internal tariff barriers on manufactured goods (notably excluding agriculture) would be abolished. These plans did not, however, include a common external tariff as envisaged for the EEC. Political integration, as promoted by the EEC proposals, was clearly to be excluded from this purely economic arrangement, and the FTA proposals were motivated at least in part by the desire of the British Government to undermine the negotiations taking place between the Six.[22]

Indeed, political integration, as envisaged through the enhancement of political dialogue within the WEU was, from London's view, more likely to undermine than to enhance the Atlantic relationship. Consequently, the British Government had been keen to promote the broader Council of Europe over the more 'concentrated' WEU as an appropriate political forum for discussion of European affairs. In an effort to rationalize the institutional framework it was agreed, in June 1956, that the WEU would limit its activity to discussion of the military aspects of defence so as to avoid duplication with the Council of Europe, although it reserved the right to extend discussion to the political where there was a direct link to military issues.[23]

In January 1957, the UK Foreign Secretary, Selwyn Lloyd, put forward his 'Grand Design' proposals. These foresaw the Atlantic Alliance providing the high military and political direction to Europe, a single Atlantic Assembly overseeing semi-autonomous commissions, and membership varying dependent on the issue, covering all aspects of Western co-operation.[24] Sold as a means to rationalize the increasing number of European institutions, the 'Design' was essentially an Atlantic option, intended to prevent the establishment of a 'little Europe' by grouping the Messina Six within a broader Atlantic framework.

The British Government was, however, on the horns of a defence dilemma. Whilst it had become clear that the UK could not sustain its defence burdens at the prevailing rate, 'our [sic] international standing would suffer if we sought relief by a unilateral reduction in defence expenditure'.[25] US action over Suez had convinced the British that, although the Anglo-American relationship remained vital, the UK's 'special relationship' was in question[26] and the UK might be better able to influence its American ally if it 'were part of an association of Powers which had greater political, economic and military strength'.[27] In Lloyd's Grand Design proposals he argued that only through the possession of thermo-nuclear weapons could a country play the role of a great power but that Britain alone could not 'go the whole distance . . . If we try to do so we will bankrupt ourselves'. Pooling resources with the European powers through the WEU might enable Britain to reduce its defence burden and develop a significant presence within NATO, with Britain becoming a thermo-nuclear power in association with the WEU. Although Lloyd refers to a nuclear-competent WEU as 'the third great power', he goes on to state, 'Such an association would not be a "Third Force" between America and Russia. Its object would rather be to develop into one powerful group within the North Atlantic Treaty Organisation (NATO), almost as powerful as America and perhaps in friendly rivalry with her'. Lloyd did envisage a 'closer political association' but stated that 'there need be no supranational machinery not responsible to Governments. Nor need we ever come to a complete merging of forces. The machinery of W.E.U. could serve, developed in due course as was necessary for closer co-operation both in the nuclear and conventional field'.[28]

Without support in the British Cabinet, the nuclear proposals for the WEU were rejected in favour of seeking closer US-UK nuclear collaboration, although it was recognized that the potential for the WEU to develop as a more cohesive European element within NATO might find favour with a US supportive of European unity. Indeed, Lloyd's nuclear proposals would have required a complete reorientation in British foreign policy, an abandonment of the Commonwealth and a sharing of nuclear secrets with Europe that was hardly likely to gain the support of the US.[29]

US reaction to the concepts behind the Grand Design, in terms of both the Assembly rationalization proposals and the defence implications of a more cohesive WEU, were predictable. Noting that British proposals would 'require careful study', the US Administration was clearly resistant to any British initiative for institutional change that might dilute the integrative development of the European institutions.[30] Equally, whilst the US retained interest in the WEU, both as an arena for European political discussion of defence interests and in terms of its 'activities in fields clearly assigned to it, in particular arms control', the Administration questioned the 'desirability [sic] conceiving WEU as "inner circle" in NATO . . . NATO primacy in political and military field must be clearly recognised'.[31] With little further to commend it to the British, the WEU would be effectively undermined as an expression of European identity, being limited to a 'defence support role' to NATO.

Having rejected the British Grand Design as an attempt to undermine European integration by enlargement,[32] the Assembly sought clarification of the role of the WEU. Recommendations in the Assembly's GAC report of April 1957 included more regular Council meetings to discuss major issues concerning European interests and the co-ordination of instructions given to the permanent delegates of member states to NATO and the UN. It also recommended that the Council re-examine the relationship between the UK and the Six after ratification of Euratom and the Common Market so as to co-ordinate efforts to achieve European unity. In noting that the 'moral and political imbalance' in NATO resulting from US leadership was 'harmful to the efficiency of the Organisation', the report had gone on to state that 'the necessary balance can only be established if the principal powers of Western Europe transcend their differences . . . and unite, finally, to achieve European integration'. Hence it had been determined that the WEU, as one of the bases of European unity, could contribute to both defence and integration through the provision of the 'political framework' for European unity.[33] However, British opposition to any attempt to make the WEU an organization for political co-operation was evidenced by the narrow Assembly majority for the report's recommendations. Paul Borcier, who was to become press attaché for the WEU, suggests that this 'reflected the difficult circumstances in which WEU found itself and revealed the Assembly as a cross-roads of conflicting designs'.[34] British resistance to European integration denied the WEU a significant political role in the construction of the new European order, 'the measure of the unfulfilled promise of the WEU' being assessed in terms of the 'measure of the political will of the British Government to use it'.[35] It was the UK's refusal to play a constructive part in the WEU in its early years that was to contribute to the institution's political decline.[36] By 1957, the activities of the WEU were to be limited further by the successful completion of one mandated task and the rationalization of European responses in another.

SHEDDING RESPONSIBILITIES

Under the provisions of the October 1954 Franco-German Saar Agreement, the WEU had been explicitly tasked with the resolution of the status of the Saar region, a matter of continuing friction in the Franco-German relationship. As part of the Paris 'package', the Saar Agreement had provided for a referendum of the Saarlanders on a proposed 'European Statute' for the area. Provision was made, should the Statute be approved, for the WEU Council to appoint a European Commissioner for the Saar. This Commissioner would be responsible for overseeing observance of the Statute and representing the foreign and defence interests of the Saarlanders in advising the WEU Council, to whom he would be responsible, and the Saarlanders would have direct representation within the Council of Europe and the WEU Assembly.[37]

Whilst a convergence of views on the desirability of a European Statute for the Saar had finally been reached between the French and West Germans in the months following the Paris Agreements, the three-month period between the promulgation of the forthcoming referendum and its realization on 23 October 1955 saw the emergence of a vociferous body of political 'objectors' in the newly restored sovereign Federal Republic. Despite requests from the WEU Plebiscite Commission that German politicians refrain from interference in the referendum campaign, as expressly required by the Franco-German agreement, the propaganda of the pro-nationalist German parties became increasingly urgent. The subsequent overwhelming rejection of the Statute came as something of a surprise, and, in light of the ongoing Messina process, it was reported that many were 'shaken by this disavowal of integration'.[38] Following the referendum, the WEU

Commission in the Saar functioned as a caretaker government, establishing an International Tribunal to ensure fair and unprejudicial voting in the forthcoming election to determine the national status of the Saarlanders. After further negotiations between the French, German and Saar Governments, during which economic concessions were provided for France, the Saar was incorporated into the Federal Republic on 1 January 1957, spelling the end of the WEU's unique supervision role.[39] Paving the way for Franco-German reconciliation, the Saar resolution was seen as an early coup for the WEU,[40] and the satisfaction of one of its few specifically mandated tasks.

As responsibility for resolving the Saar situation came to a successful end, the WEU was busy 'shrinking' its commitments in other areas of its remit. The cultural and social activities of the WEU, the responsibility for which it had inherited from the WU, had become focused on specialized areas of, for example, public administration (providing annual courses for government officials), education (conferences, youth activities, sponsorship of exchanges) and the arts. Nevertheless, the WEU Assembly and the Consultative Assembly of the Council of Europe found themselves duplicating efforts in these areas, and whilst they had some success in avoiding this through consultation, by 1957 the Consultative Assembly was calling for the removal of WEU competence in these areas as the level of duplication 'would gradually lead to a state of confusion and thus not merely impede progress, but bar the way to European unification'.[41] Given its wider membership it was agreed that the Council of Europe would be the preferred institution for cultural and social affairs, and following agreement in 1960, the WEU's Expert Committees and their competencies in these areas were transferred to the Council of Europe as part of the rationalization of European institutions.[42]

BRITAIN MOVES CLOSER TO EUROPE

By 1957, having successfully provided a resolution to the Saar dispute and begun the transfer of its social and cultural competencies to the Council of Europe, the WEU's future direction seemed uncertain given the lack of consensus amongst the member states.

The Treaties of Rome, establishing the EEC and Euratom, had been signed by the ECSC Six in March 1957. In providing for the removal of internal tariffs, the freedom of labour, capital and enterprise movement and a community budget, the Six had taken clear steps towards community-building in Europe.[43] However, before the ink was dry on the Rome agreements, the return to office of French President Charles de Gaulle in June 1958[44] quickly spelt the end of any consensus on the future of the European project. Adamantly opposed to European integration during the 1940s and 1950s, de Gaulle identified the potential benefits to France of the EEC as a loose confederal system of European states. Such an entity could enhance French leadership in Western Europe and contribute to weakening the influence of the external powers of the 'Anglo-Saxons'. Many Europeanists feared that the UK might act as a buttress against supranational institutions, but de Gaulle's concern was rather that the UK might prevent the development of the EEC as a 'vehicle of French grandeur',[45] whilst integration based on a model preferred by the US could only provide for enhanced US influence. As Hoffmann notes, for de Gaulle, 'the alternative to a Gaullist policy *for* Europe would be an American policy *in* Europe, either promoted by America's "clients" or filling the vacuum left by conflicting European policies that would cancel each other out'.[46] De Gaulle recollected the basis of his post-war strategy in his memoirs, stating that 'I intended to assure French primacy in Western Europe by preventing the rise of a new [German] Reich that might again threaten its safety; to co-operate with East and West, and, if need be, contract the necessary alliances, on the one side or the other, without ever accepting any kind of dependency; to persuade the states along the Rhine, the Alps and the Pyrenees to form a political, economic and strategic bloc and to press forward this organization as one of the three world powers, and, should it become necessary, as the arbiter between the Soviet and Anglo-American camps'.[47]

The French vision was clearly at odds with that of its federalist-minded allies. Fearful of Franco-German domination of the EEC, the smaller states, most notably the Belgians and Dutch, sought an integrated political union which might constrain the French, whilst the presence of the UK could provide a balance to Franco-German influence. Consequently, they promoted the gradual enhancement of integration within the context of progressively enlarging European Communities, rejecting any moves to undermine NATO, whilst de Gaulle looked towards developing an intergovernmental arrangement for co-operation amongst the Six across a broad range of issues, including defence and foreign affairs.[48]

The WEU Assembly's winter Session of 1958 marked a shift in British policy that was to lead to the promotion of the WEU as a vehicle for enhanced European political co-operation. In November 1958, the UK's alternative FTA plan, intended to associate the EEC with the wider Europe, had been rejected by the Six.[49] This, combined with a decline in the 'special relationship' with the US after Suez and a muting of Commonwealth relations,[50] had led to a change in British attitudes to Europe. Whilst the British Government continued to harbour fears about economic integration, increased co-operation within the WEU might provide a means of drawing Europe closer to the UK, preventing the emergence of a widening gap as integration took off amongst the Six.[51] Consequently, during the winter Session of the WEU Assembly in 1958, the UK began to promote political competence for the Assembly.[52]

Despite Britain's resistance to direct participation in the 'European project', the majority within the Assembly of the WEU was keen to keep the European Communities door open for the UK. Consequently, at its June

1959 Session, the Assembly established a political secretariat to ensure regular consultation between Britain and the Six, and the new Secretary General, Mr Badini Confalonieri, dedicated himself 'wholeheartedly to the task of making Western European Union a bridge over the Channel'. The Assembly went on to 'affirm the importance of the political functions of Western European Union' and to encourage the Council to 'develop and increase political consultation'.[53] Meeting in Paris at the Assembly's subsequent November–December Session, Confalonieri suggested that the WEU Council of Ministers could become a 'clearing house' for relations between the Six and the UK.[54] In order to further promote the political role of the Assembly, the Michaud Report of December 1959 facilitated a reorganization of the structure of the Secretariat-General and established joint meetings between the WEU Council and the Assembly at the level of the GAC.[55]

Throughout 1959, efforts to patch up the apparent divide between Britain and the Six continued apace. The US had consistently given support to Community-building in Europe, accepting the short-run economic disadvantages for the US on the basis that full integration would tie Germany and Italy into Europe, whilst 'in the long run Europe would be economically and politically stronger and that was important in meeting the Communist threat'.[56] Given US encouragement of the EEC the British sought to persuade both the US and its European neighbours of its European credentials. The UK Government had continued to promote the idea of a wider European Free Trade Area after its rejection by the EEC Six in November 1958, leading to the formation of EFTA, a loose trading association of what became known as the 'outer Seven', the UK being joined by the non-EEC states of Austria, Denmark, Norway, Portugal, Sweden and Switzerland. Established in May 1960 under the Stockholm Convention signed in November 1959 (to be enlarged later by the inclusion of Iceland and Finland), the EFTA was essentially a negative contrivance, brought about by the absence, in the face of the actions of the Six, of any 'realistic alternative course of action'.[57]

Nevertheless, the British Chancellor of the Exchequer, Derick Heathcoat-Amory, 1st Viscount Amory, was keen to 'sell' his Government's EFTA initiative as a major UK concession, stating that 'whilst the degree of political association may not satisfy the US it should be recognized that no U.K. Government has ever come so far before'. Association through the EFTA could provide the European link, he argued, that was crucial to the continuing political and economic unity of Europe, without which NATO would be likely to run into 'rough water'.[58] Any hope that the EFTA initiative might offer leverage for Britain to have some form of close association with the EEC was soon to prove unfounded.[59] At the same time, the US continued to encourage UK membership in the Communities on the grounds that it might put an end to the EFTA, 'with its "unhealthy" tinge of neutrality', and 'counteract any European pretensions to "third force" status and help to weld Europe more firmly into the Atlantic partnership'.[60]

By the December 1959 WEU Assembly debates, the British Minister of State for Foreign Affairs, John Profumo, was able to announce officially a revision of British policy, stating that 'whereas when WEU came into being we in Britain were determined to draw Europe closer together, we are now determined to draw closer to Europe'. In response to the agreement of the Six in November 1959 to intensify their political consultation and have regular quarterly (foreign) Ministerial consultative meetings on political questions, Profumo suggested that 'political consultations among the Six . . . might immediately be followed by a meeting of the Western European Union Council at Ministerial level'.[61] By establishing the WEU as the 'keystone of British policy in Europe', the British hoped to prevent a gap from developing between themselves and the Six.[62] As the first of these Council meetings took place in February 1960, the British continued to promote alternatives to the EEC, seeking to use the WEU as a bridge between the Six and the seven remaining OEEC states that were negotiating the looser EFTA agreement.[63] However, it soon became evident that, because only one of the EFTA Seven was actually a member of the WEU, there were clear limitations to the WEU's utility in this regard. A British observer was to note at the time that in order for the WEU to be useful as an instrument of greater co-operation with mainland Europe, the British would have to move beyond 'using the Union as a useful tool to get round the embarrassment caused by the creation of the Six; at the moment the omens are mixed'.[64]

Having considered the potential for the UK's partial membership of the Communities throughout 1960,[65] the Assembly of the WEU adopted Recommendation 53 in November, proposing that negotiations begin for the UK to join the three Communities.[66] This document has not occupied the 'place of honour' in the archives of Europe-building proposed by Borcier, although it does demonstrate that WEU states had agreed to 'an authentic programme of European Community action providing for British participation, subject to London's readiness to play its part'.[67] Transmitted to the Council and Heads of Government, the Assembly initiative received wholehearted support, and it was agreed that the Council would go forward with the recommendation to promote discussion between representatives of the WEU 'Seven' and the Commission of the EEC to prepare agreement for accession of the UK.

Having taken 'soundings' throughout the autumn of 1960 through unofficial contacts in the WEU, the British Prime Minister, Harold Macmillan, had come to the view that any arrangement with the Common Market would have to be founded on the basis of the Treaty of Rome and, therefore, that Britain should apply to join the Six.[68] This revolutionary shift in the UK policy orientation from the Commonwealth and EFTA to the EEC may be explained largely in commercial terms as a reaction to the decline in British trade with the Commonwealth, at a time when the EEC's significance to British industry as a buyer and a competitor had increased.[69] However, it is clear that Macmillan was also motivated by his recognition of the limitations of UK influence over US policy, although whether his change of heart was driven by the desire to 'hedge against the unreliability of British influence' by seeking a European alternative or by 'a continuation of the pursuit of the Anglo-American special relationship by other means', given US hostility towards the UK's EFTA option, is contestable.[70] On 31 July 1961 Macmillan announced to the House of Commons his intention to apply for full British membership in the EEC under Article 237 of the Treaty of Rome, and on the first day of August 1961, the British chose the WEU Council meeting as the forum for their official notification to the Six of their accession intentions.[71] Having established the WEU as the bridge across the Channel, Britain now sought to use it as a vehicle for facilitating its approach and accession to the Europe of the Six. As the Deputy Secretary General of the WEU was to note, 'that this was the forum chosen illustrates the role played by the WEU as the prefiguration of the enlarged European Community, and the intimate connection of the WEU with the whole process leading up to the British decision'.[72]

Following the official notification of British intentions, the Council of the WEU was to provide one forum for dialogue on UK accession to the EEC. Subsequent reports submitted to the WEU Assembly found delegates from its seven member states unanimous in their optimism regarding the negotiations and keen to promote all efforts to reach a successful conclusion, providing that any future agreement 'in no respect allow a weakening of European integration on a Community basis, as laid down in the letter and enshrined in the spirit of the Treaties of Paris and Rome'.[73] In addition to contributing technical assistance to the negotiators,[74] transmitting reports via the Council to negotiators in Brussels, the Assembly was to act as a forum and testing ground for a range of new European ideas, as a liaison and contact institution between politicians of the Continent and UK, and as a public relations agency and psychological promoter for the concept of a Seven Power Europe.[75] As the only institution that contained only and all of the Seven, it was ideal for this role.

FRANCE AND FOUCHET

The Fouchet Committee, mandated by the Six to study the problems of European co-operation, accepted a draft treaty submitted by the French Government on 19 October 1961 as the basis for subsequent discussions on political union. The first set of draft proposals of the Fouchet Committee foresaw the establishment of a 'Union of States', the aims of which were to include the adoption of common foreign and defence policies, although it was noted that this would contribute to a strengthening of the Atlantic Alliance.[76] The EU was to be based on unanimous decision-making within a Council of Government Heads, supported by a Permanent Political Committee and a Consultative Parliament. However, on 18 January 1962, de Gaulle presented a revised draft treaty to the Committee,[77] in which any reference to NATO or provisions for new memberships were excluded, and

economic policy would come under the auspices of this new intergovernmental body, effectively watering down the extant supranational provisions.
For de Gaulle, the French position on European integration was clear; whilst
co-operation was a necessary condition for European influence in the international environment, intergovernmentalism was to be the key. This was
equally true of economics as it was of politics, for, as all economic issues
were essentially political, they should not be left to supranational bureau-
crats but must be the remit of states.[78]

Meeting in Luxembourg on 20 March and Paris on 17 April, the Foreign
Ministers of the Six could reach no agreement. It is paradoxical that Britain,
excluded from the Fouchet discussions, would have been more in favour of
de Gaulle's 'Europe des Patries' than his fellow EEC cohorts were. Certainly,
the original Fouchet draft had the support of the British Government, which
favoured a loose form of international association for Europe, whilst stating
its acceptance that European Political Union would require a defence interest and that 'a European point of view on defence would emerge'.[79] Even
for the European federalists, the first draft was an acceptable step towards a
truly united Europe given the provision for revision after three years and the
priority of first involving Britain in any future union.[80] The second Fouchet
draft not only moved away from the incremental federalism implied by the
Treaty of Rome but carried significant implications for the developing relationship with the UK and the future of the transatlantic relationship.[81]

The WEU Council had been effectively sidelined by the Community discussion on political union and UK accession, and it failed to meet whilst
negotiations for British entry into the EEC were taking place in Brussels
in 1962.[82] Nevertheless, the Assembly continued to provide a forum for
dialogue on the provisions and implications of UK accession to the Communities, not least in its examination of the potential for its own absorption
into the European Parliament (EP) if the enlargement negotiations should
succeed.[83] The address by the British Lord Privy Seal, Edward Heath, to the
WEU Assembly a week before the Paris meeting polarized debate on these
issues.[84] In his 'préamble anglais' Heath argued the case for British inclusion in discussion on the future structure of Europe, a position that resulted
in Belgian and Dutch refusal to sign any proposals for political union that
excluded the UK.[85] At the same time, the French refused to accept recognition of the primacy of the Atlantic Alliance framework, as demanded by the
other five EEC states, within the draft provisions of the Fouchet proposals.
Thus, the rejection of both 'Fouchet Plans' was largely a consequence of
persistent disagreement amongst the Six over the nature of political union,
the place of the UK within that union, and the place of defence both within
the union and within the broader Atlantic Alliance. That the negotiations
on political union took place concomitantly with the British entry negotiations was not coincidental. For de Gaulle, it was imperative that the political
character of the EEC should be determined before British entry.

THE WEU AND ARMS CONTROL

Since the WEU's inception in 1955, member states had sought to utilize the institution in the pursuit of their varying national preferences for the development of the European integration process. Equally, the WEU had been mandated with specific 'defence' tasks, with the MBT containing within it a significant Article V commitment to collective defence. The agreement in Article IV to 'rely on the appropriate military authorities of NATO for information and advice on military matters' suggested that the WEU had been emasculated as a serious defence-management institution, and the WEU Council maintained a consistently minimalist position with regard to defence issues.[86] However, the scope of the WEU's defence interests was clearly potentially as wide as that desired by its members. The WEU had indeed been mandated with two other significant 'military' functions, one related to arms co-operation and the other to arms control, the latter being particularly significant in that it had enabled the acceptance of the Paris Agreements of 1954.

The asymmetrical arms specifications contained within the MBT had limited member states' possession, manufacture and deployment of a range of armaments, both conventional and non-conventional. The most restricted member of the WEU, West Germany, had, in effect, bought its place in Europe at the expense of a heavily controlled military rearmament programme.[87] Britain, whilst excluded from these restrictions, had enabled continental acceptance of the modified treaty largely on the basis of its inscribed commitments to troop deployments on mainland Europe.[88] Consequently, the maxima and minima prescribed by the WEU Treaty, which were to be managed through the Council's ACA, were a central element of the post-war structures for the management of defence in Europe.

By the mid 1950s, the prospects for the development of an effective arms control regime through the auspices of the WEU did not, however, appear promising given growing concerns over the nature of the US defence commitment to Europe. Acceptance of European defence dependency on US military capability and commitment had been severely shaken by events in 1956: the 'relative inaction' of the US during the Hungarian crisis and its outright opposition to its allies' interests in Suez had convinced many in Europe 'that the United States treats its friends worse than its enemies'.[89] Assembly reports urging the maintenance of substantial conventional forces reflected European concerns that 'it was unquestionably impossible from a psychological viewpoint for the representatives of European peoples physically in contact with the potential enemy to entrust their electors' safety wholly to the deterrent effect of the American nuclear force'.[90] The question of appropriate and efficient force structures for transatlantic defence had been the subject of much heated debate within the WEU Assembly since its inception. The declining credibility of the US's 'Massive Retaliation' strategy for extended deterrence, particularly following the Soviet Sputnik launch of

1957, led to Assembly promotion of the emerging 'flexible response' posture, officially proposed by US Defence Secretary Robert McNamara only in 1962.[91] Concurrent concerns over the potential for war-fighting in the European theatre, including the use of tactical nuclear weapons, increased European desires for greater control over the use of nuclear weapons and the development of NATO strategy.

The British position throughout the 1950s remained consistently Atlanticist, recognizing the requirement for US leadership in Western Europe. Clinging to its great-power status, the British Government sought to maintain its 'special relationship' with the American administration and to promote the centrality of NATO while simultaneously announcing a defence policy based on developing its own 'independent' nuclear deterrent capability even in the face of American opposition. In the parliamentary debates on the 1955 Defence White Paper, which announced British intentions to develop its own hydrogen bombs, Britain's Defence Secretary, Harold Macmillan, argued strongly against reliance on the American deterrent, seeing it as a 'dangerous doctrine' that would 'surrender our [British] power to influence American policy, and deprive us of any influence over the selection of targets'.[92] However, despite the rhetoric of independence, in the face of budgetary and technological constraints, as incoming Prime Minister in 1957 Macmillan had accepted that 'forging relations with the United States' would inevitably be a requirement of British nuclear development. In an agreement reached in Bermuda in March 1957, Macmillan secured American nuclear-armed Thor missiles to support the limited British nuclear force of V bombers until such time as the British independent deterrent capability could be developed.[93] Fears raised by the launching of the Soviet Sputnik satellite in October 1957 provided a more conducive environment for greater Anglo-US nuclear co-operation. With the signing of the joint UK-US Declaration of Common Purpose in the same month, a special 'inter-dependence' was grudgingly accepted by the US in return for the UK's foreign and strategic support against the Soviet threat.[94] For Macmillan, the 'great prize' of the October agreement was the promised repeal of the McMahon Act, which had limited UK-US nuclear collaboration, the lifting of which in July 1958 was to pave the way for an enhanced 'special relationship' between the two powers.[95]

Britain had been excluded from the nuclear arms restrictions of the WEU Treaty, but it was clear that a significant reduction in British conventional forces would be required in order to facilitate a nuclear programme that would be inevitably exhaust the defence budget. At the same time, the British Foreign Secretary was to note the 'paradoxical' situation in which the UK, as a former occupying power and now ally in Germany, was facing a severe balance-of-payments problem, whereas the West Germans, without the UK's defence budget burdens, had become the UK's largest commercial competitor. Some reduction of British forces in West Germany was increasingly inevitable.[96]

Given the UK's WEU commitments to continental force deployments, the WEU Council asserted its right to 'rule' on any proposed cuts.[97] The formal announcement of British conventional force reductions came to the WEU Council on 14 February 1957, and the Council then requested SACEUR's opinion on the likely impact on European defence. In an effort to avoid the souring of UK-Six relations that these proposals were likely to promote, Macmillan sought to 'sweeten the pill' of a decreasing UK conventional presence by the offer of greater co-operation on non-nuclear arms research and development within the WEU.[98] At the Special Session of the WEU Council in London on 18 March 1957, the British Foreign Minister insisted that conversion and reduction were the only means by which Britain could maintain a viable commitment to Europe within its means. Despite general concern amongst the other six WEU members, a compromise solution was found by which the WEU Council agreed to wait on SACEUR's report, in effect acquiescing to UK proposals for a two-year phased conventional force reduction under SACEUR consultation. In May the NAC unanimously accepted the British proposals for conventional/nuclear force balance,[99] as articulated in the British White Paper of April 1957, and only subsequently did the British Foreign Minister address the WEU Assembly regarding the British policy.[100] Presenting the second Annual Report of the Council to the Assembly, the Council Chairman, Spaak, marked a notable change of emphasis in WEU Council's thinking when he defended the UK's nuclear position and Council acceptance of a withdrawal of 13,500 British troops from the Continent. Although only half of that 'requested' by the British, the evidence suggests that this acceptance was only grudgingly given, after British threats of a unilateral withdrawal.[101] These withdrawals contributed to a decline in British prestige amongst the Six and resulted in the carrying of an Assembly motion of no confidence in the Council in May 1957, although it lacked a sufficient majority to become effective. In January 1958, the Council accepted a further 8,500 withdrawals.[102] The British continued to remain short by several thousand on their reluctantly agreed figure of 55,000 continentally deployed forces after 1959.[103]

As for the French, engagement in the Algerian Civil War, which had begun in November 1954, only months after the fall of Dien Bien Phu, had become another 'thorn in the side' of French interests, leaving France unable to fulfil its WEU or NATO commitments. The tensions that had developed between the French and American Governments earlier in the decade as a result of US pressure for the EDC had been exacerbated by American action over Indo-China. The French were to learn that 'to invite direct American intervention in an overseas conflict was to risk being undermined and finally supplanted by the superpower ally'.[104] Whilst the British consistently reduced their conventional minima, ostensibly so as to facilitate their nuclear weapons programme, the French, still seething from the humiliation of Suez, sought to develop their own nuclear capability for cases in which US interests might conflict with their own.[105]

By November 1956, the French Prime Minister Guy Mollet had set in motion a programme for the production of weapons-grade plutonium, at the same time establishing the foundations for an operational military nuclear programme, despite the clear restrictions of the MBT. Denouncing the WEU controls on French nuclear development as discriminatory, the Mollet Government refused to submit the level of stocks of its nuclear weapons to a majority decision of the WEU, hence breaking its obligations under the MBT. At the same time, the French sought to encourage Franco-German co-operation, claiming that nuclear capabilities were being developed for experimental rather than 'production' purposes.[106] The 'Protocole de Colomb Bechar', signed in January 1957, established a Franco-German Committee to oversee research and development (R&D) in advanced weapons and materials, with a French-Italian-German Arms Pool (FIG) being established by the end of the year, to include the military application of nuclear energy in the prospective co-operation list.[107]

Whilst Adenauer had identified the European integration route as the most effective passage to German reconstruction, at the same time the West German position during the early 1950s had been largely accepting of its place in the American alliance system from which the West German state had effectively emerged. It may be argued that West Germany had indeed gained the most from the Paris Agreements, the discriminatory arms control provisions of the WEU having provided for its rehabilitation, but consensus on Germany's place in the new architecture of European security was never assured.[108] On the very day that the FRG had joined NATO, the Social Democrats had proposed the waiving of West Germany's military obligations under the Paris Agreements, suggesting that a united Germany become an equal partner in a new WEU-based European security system, within the framework of the UN.[109] A range of possible options for the management of a united Germany had been aired, and the subsequent 'disengagement' debate included Eden's proposals at the July 1955 Geneva Summit for 'a demilitarised area between East and West' and the Rapacki Plan of 1957, which envisaged a 'denuclearised zone' covering Poland, Czechoslovakia and the two Germanys.[110]

Adenauer had consistently sought a relationship of constructive engagement with the US, but even this seemingly impervious alliance began to show signs of strain by the late 1950s. The US rollback strategy, formulated under Dulles in 1953 as an active strategy of liberation, found little practical application during the Soviet repression of the Hungarian Uprising in 1956, and it became clear to the West Europeans that fears of general war would compel superpower acceptance of each other's unofficially recognized spheres of influence. For the US, NATO's strategic objective was essentially preservation of the status quo in Europe through the deterrence of Soviet attack. Any further interference would be inevitably unprofitable. The belief that only through the strength of an allied West could the Soviets be brought to the negotiating table over the status of East Germany was severely shaken by the realities of the superpower stand-off.

Awakened to the realities of allied strategy by the tactical exercise code-named 'Carte Blanche' (20–28 June 1955), in which German territory was subject to a high level of nuclear 'bombing', the problem for Germany, as for much of Europe, was the feasibility of European rearmament plans in the light of American nuclear strategy for Europe.[111] If West Germany needed convincing of its place in US strategy, two events in the late 1950s served to demonstrate this clearly. During the Iraqi conflict in July 1958, American aircraft deployed from West German territory without host consultation or prior warning, and with the evident possibilities of retaliation or at least significant diplomatic damage to Bonn's relations with the Arabs. The evolving Berlin crisis later that year sharpened German concerns as Dulles made clear that 'vital interests of the United States—notably peace—were not to be compromised by rigid adherence to the principle of non-recognition of the G.D.R.'[112] As, by the end of the decade, the NATO alliance had failed to deliver on Adenauer's promised 'reunification through allied negotiating strength', the debate within the FRG on its military future grew increasingly heated as Germany's second-class status began to grate.

In terms of their WEU commitments, the West Germans became remiss in meeting force goals, sought greater armaments procurement and carried out their integrative interests in less contentious areas. Between 1958 and 1964 there were six amendments to the arms limitation provisions of the MBT, allowing the FRG to produce warships, small submarines and guided missiles in line with NATO requirements. However, the West Germans failed to build the conventional forces demanded by their NATO commitments.[113] As La Feber notes, by the autumn of 1956, having 'bargained its military rearmament to regain its sovereignty . . . [t]he Adenauer government cut service time for draftees, refused to spend its full authorization for arms, and reduced force goals from 500,000 to 325,000. Adenauer instead ominously began to request missiles, artillery capable of firing nuclear shells, and fighter bombers which could hail thermo-nuclear bombs'.[114] This shift in policy was explained by Adenauer largely on the basis that 'Western Europe's conventional capabilities were now so depleted that NATO had no choice but to use tactical nuclear weapons to respond to a Soviet attack'.[115] If intended to reinforce deterrence rather than to provide for defence, tactical nuclear weapons could ensure an early tripwire to US nuclear retaliation, enhancing deterrence credibility and moving NATO strategy away from reliance on conventional war-fighting options.

Seeking some level of nuclear control, Adenauer had expressed some interest in nuclear arms-sharing through the WEU as early as October 1956. Within the next 18 months, his Defence Minister, Franz Josef Strauss, was to dismiss the openly reported support of some within the French Administration for an independent German nuclear programme,[116] acknowledging that the Federal Republic would fulfil its obligations under the Paris Agreements. However, Strauss did not see these obligations as ruling out participation in collaborative nuclear research, with the FRG representative to the WEU noting that 'co-operation in the production of nuclear weapons was likely to be limited to studying the application of nuclear propulsion to submarines and other ships'.[117] Insisting that WEU members should be invited to join FIG in order to 'collaborate', Strauss even went so far as to suggest that West Germany might contribute to the construction of a WEU-controlled European nuclear force. The inclusion of Britain would be central to make such a force credible, although the British Defence Minister, Duncan Sandys, rejected Strauss's overtures during the Bonn talks in March 1958.[118] Strauss further advocated weapons and equipment standardization, collaborative weapons research and development and the integration of European air defence and air raid warning systems. As Haas notes, 'Germany became the spokesman in the WEU Council for the vigorous integration of important aspects of defence policy, countering the British insistence on maintaining national autonomy'.[119] For the FRG, the WEU could once again provide the vehicle for German military development in a manner that would also enhance European integration whilst contributing to broader Atlantic defence.

Grosser suggests that as early as 1957 the failure of the WEU to control the armaments of its members had led to its decline as a relevant organization. Although his prediction of its imminent death was clearly premature,[120] it did become increasingly clear as the decade progressed that the WEU was not up to its original arms control tasks. The French continued to develop their nuclear programme despite the conditions of the MBT, the West Germans called for qualitative enhancement of their weapons systems, whilst the British failed to meet the conventional force minima agreed under the treaty. The WEU's ACA had some success in terms of establishing force level controls but proved unable to secure the necessary legal right to on-site inspection without prior warning.[121] As for obtaining reliable information from member governments and private firms and establishing effective inspection procedures, the ACA remained hampered until the institutionalization of procedures late in 1957. In the same year, physical inspections of military establishments began to take place, national budgets were reviewed, and defence-related factories were identified and inspected. However, as the Assembly complained, without the relevant assignment of police and military forces subject to the ACA's jurisdiction, the task of managing arms maxima remained problematic. The Council's refusal to allocate the necessary funds for the required expert personnel to inspect atomic weapons production did little to enhance the ACA's credibility.

Throughout the 1960s the Assembly continued to report on the problems of verification and control of force levels in Europe, urging respect for the letter of the MBT.[122] However, it seems evident that, whilst the WEU had offered a degree of confidence and visibility in its early years, which in turn would contribute to stability during a period of post-war transition, the original arms control task had become increasingly irrelevant given both external developments and national demands. In fact, the ACA had lost its original raison d'être, the issue having become not one of keeping force levels down but of keeping them up. US concerns regarding the lack of burden-sharing and the assumption that the US would 'carry the NATO can' were to become consistent features of the Alliance relationship. By the end of 1958, speaking with considerable warmth, US President Dwight D. Eisenhower was demanding to know when the US contribution to the Alliance, intended as a temporary fix for European shortcomings, was to be met by an equivalent European response. 'We should ask' he demanded, 'when the hell these other people are going to do their duty . . . These other NATO powers cannot go on forever riding on our coattails . . . All of these nations seem to be trying to figure out how little they themselves can do and how best to leave us to do the rest of the job'.[123] As the Americans continued to press for increases in conventional force levels and, by 1958, for the acceptance of intermediate- and short-range nuclear missiles in Europe under US or 'dual key' control, the WEU Assembly was to provide both informed reports and an important forum for open European debate. Agreement reached within the Assembly was to enable significant endorsement of NATO decisions, including early support for the contentious 'flexible response' doctrine that was to become the mainstay of NATO strategy in Europe. However, national priorities determined that relative capabilities would remain a perennial issue of contention within the broader Alliance.

ARMS CO-OPERATION AND THE NUCLEAR DEBATE

Where the WEU had some limited 'success' in the management of defence capabilities was through its effective 'absorption' of alternative multinational arms co-operation efforts that were potentially at variance with NATO interests. During the Paris negotiations of 1954, the French Premier Mendès France had gone so far as to propose a supranational arms pool plan to maintain tight controls on German equipment and to get a good share of the WEU-wide contracts for French industry. On the basis of the French initiative, the 'watered-down' WEU Standing Armaments Committee (SAC) had been established following a decision of the first WEU Council meeting in May 1955. With an advisory function for the standardization of equipment, the SAC was intended to promote efficiencies in the use of common resources through the exchange of information on current equipment as well as technological and scientific research and development, bi- and trilateral armaments co-operation, and the adoption and common manufacture of certain weapons, co-ordinated with the efforts of NATO's Standardization Agency. Under its auspices, the *ad hoc* group of the six continental members' Chiefs of Staff and War Office representatives had facilitated agreements on the specification requirements of a range of military equipment. The SAC maintained a close relationship with the FINABEL organization, which had been initiated in 1953 to harmonize European strategic thinking on joint armaments production.[124] However, US discouragement of closer European co-operation in defence production outside of the NATO framework had enhanced national and industrial disinclination, and these attempts to rationalize weapons production had produced only limited substantive results.[125]

By 1958, fearing 'uncontrolled' European nuclear advances within the FIG programme, the US Administration had put forward a set of proposals for nuclear sharing, including the deployment of first-generation Intermediate Range Ballistic Missiles (IRBMs; Thors and Jupiters) in NATO countries and the initiation of a 'co-ordinated programme of research, development and production of a selected group of modern weapons systems, including IRBMs'.[126] Deployed IRBMs were to be under a dual-key arrangement whereby the host state built and manned the bases, whilst the US maintained custody of the warheads and a veto over launch decisions. However, the French were not prepared simply to be a landing stage for American-controlled nuclear weapons and sought to use the FIG alternative as a means of levering the Americans into some real nuclear sharing. Given the limitations of the NATO and FIG options, and fearing isolation from an increasingly collaborative Franco-German axis, the British promoted the WEU as an acceptable framework for arms co-operation. For Britain, this WEU-based participation could best be achieved 'by first concluding bilateral agreements with the principal countries concerned' and then bringing these under the WEU umbrella.[127] The British had initially excluded discussion of co-operation on nuclear weapons; the research, design and development of ballistic missiles; strategic bombers and their equipment; and biological and chemical warfare from the remit of the emerging WEU Steering Committee architecture.[128] However, given more favourable US attitudes to some level of co-operation with the Europeans on weapons systems, the UK sought possibilities to co-operatively develop a European delivery system on the basis that engagement with Europe might also enhance British EFTA proposals. As long as the UK refused to discuss IRBMs within the Steering Committee structure, the French were likely to seek aid from the US for a FIG IRBM over which the UK would have no influence and from which it might well be excluded. Indeed, a further FIG agreement, signed by the three countries' Defence Ministers on 7 April 1958 as 'the basis for the future joint development of nuclear weapons', was clearly intended as leverage to get some technical assistance from the Americans.[129] However, by offering to co-operate on a liquid-fuelled IRBM with both FIG and the WEU, Sandys was able to persuade Jacques Chaban-Delmas, the French Defence Minister, at the April 1958 NATO Ministerial Conference that arms co-operation projects of bilateral and trilateral groups could be pursued within the WEU framework.[130]

The subsequent agreement, whilst encouraging 'collective plans for co-operation in defence research, development and production', determined that 'such plans should be presented to NATO through the Secretariat General' and that 'proper provision should be made to give any interested

NATO country which can make a positive contribution, the opportunity to associate itself with any such plans'.[131] Once again, the British had found a use for a WEU option. British-sponsored arms production through multilateral co-operation within the framework of the WEU would weaken exclusive tripartite developments within FIG whilst countering the continentals' feeling that Britain stood apart from Europe.[132] In connecting FIG to NATO through the WEU, Britain had also ensured that European arms development contributed to her wider Atlantic interests.[133]

The question of the control and ownership of nuclear weapons was to be a recurring source of irritation within the Alliance. De Gaulle's return to office in June 1958 had further worsened Franco-American relations, already undermined by the Americans' refusal to 'bail the French out' over Algeria, a decision which had been seen as a significant factor in the fall of the Fourth Republic.[134] Condemning 'graduated deterrence' as a 'euphemism for a United States withdrawal of her nuclear umbrella',[135] de Gaulle increased French efforts to build up a nuclear 'force de frappe' intended to provide a lever not only against the Soviets but also against the Anglo-American leadership of the Atlantic Alliance. However, the concept of Franco-German collaboration in the nuclear field as a means to 'build a Continental Front against Anglo-American domination of NATO' was discarded.[136] De Gaulle's desire to see France as a major actor led him to propose, in September 1958, a 'directoire a trois' between the US, the UK and France that would better meet the global interests of a nuclear-capable France than the largely outmoded NATO alliance. De Gaulle proposed that tripartite discussion and co-operation on world affairs would be conducted by the 'three great powers', each of which would exercise 'hegemony' in the area in which it had most concerns, where nuclear development would be promoted between the three, and where joint nuclear decision-making would provide each with a veto over any use of the nuclear weapons of the other two unless under direct attack.[137]

Although there was some acceptance of the need to 'modernize' NATO, and a desire by the US and British to maintain French commitment to the Alliance, it was clear that de Gaulle's proposals for nuclear sharing and tripartite decision-making were 'impossible'.[138] For the British and Americans, these proposals were yet another example of Gaullist extremism, underlining their belief that 'de Gaulle feels that the present NATO might as well be scrapped and a fresh start be made under triumvirate auspices'.[139] His proposal having been rejected, de Gaulle's distaste for the Anglo-Saxons led the French to increasingly distance themselves from the Alliance. By March 1959 France had informed NATO states of its intention to withdraw the French Mediterranean fleet from NATO command.[140]

The potential for a WEU 'solution' to the problem of nuclear sharing had first been raised by the UK's Grand Design in 1956. In December 1959 the idea of a WEU-based European deterrent was raised again with WEU Assembly approval as Recommendation 40.[141] The report on which this recommendation was based proposed 'the creation of a joint European strategic nuclear force . . . as a complement to the US Strategic Air Command'. The transfer of national nuclear forces to WEU control and direction, whilst eliminating the danger of competition between European countries, would make the WEU the 'fourth nuclear power, with joint power of decision on the use of strategic weapons', until such time as the American and European forces might become part of a 'common NATO pool'.[142]

Although the Assembly's proposals met with all-party disapproval in London,[143] the WEU option continued to be debated throughout the early 1960s as a potential answer to the nuclear-sharing conundrum.[144] As a concept, the WEU option had some virtues: it could provide a framework in which the FRG could contribute to the maintenance and construction of a European nuclear capability and participate in the strategic planning process but remain under the arms control arrangements of the WEU Treaty. France would not need to develop an expensive independent (and proliferating) capability,[145] being able to share Britain's nuclear assets and know-how. A WEU nuclear arrangement might also spell the end of the UK's nuclear 'special relationship' with the US, whilst offering France 'an additional counter to Germany, as when Britain's association with WEU eased France's acceptance of German rearmament in NATO'.[146]

As the British continued to seek US support for their 'independent' deterrent, the possibility of a WEU-based collaborative approach was mooted, if only as a means of levering some further 'privileged' concessions from the Americans. The British had benefited from the modification of the McMahon Act in 1958, enabling some level of 'special relationship' to develop with the US in the area of nuclear collaboration. By 1957 the UK independent nuclear programme had produced both atomic and hydrogen bomb capability, but the development of missile technology had undermined the utility of the vulnerable V bombers as an effective delivery system. After Britain abandoned its increasingly obsolete Blue Streak ballistic missile project in February 1960, Prime Minister Macmillan was able to secure in the following month a preferential agreement for the supply of the US Skybolt missile, to which it could fit British warheads.[147] But by November 1962 Presidential approval had been given for the unilateral abandonment of the costly and over-running Skybolt project, and the ensuing crisis in UK-US relations reflected the British view that they had once again been let down by their American ally.[148] Nevertheless, an affordable and credible alternative had to be found if Britain was to remain a nuclear power. Addressing the WEU Assembly in December 1962, British Defence Minister Peter Thorneycroft's proposals for Anglo-French co-operation in the establishment of a European deterrent may be seen as a cynical attempt to pressure the Americans, particularly in light of the forthcoming bilateral Nassau Summit.

Certainly the British proposals were not entirely without credence. Through collaboration the British could obtain financial support for maintaining a strategic nuclear deterrent. The WEU option could achieve the political objective of ending the US nuclear monopoly in the Alliance without undermining the Alliance itself, given the accepted subordination of the WEU to NATO. Through the WEU Council's 'out-of-area' remit a WEU-based deterrent might also provide for greater influence over extra-European concerns, an area of interest that it was felt had been consistently disregarded by the Europeans' American ally. As Mulley asserts, the WEU option 'could have been the beginning of a truly European approach to both foreign and defence policies . . . it would have assisted the solution of the problem of a divided Europe and produced the political and economic unity which is so essential if Europe is to play its proper role in the world'.[149] Dougherty was to write in 1962, 'If the United States wishes to encourage the further integration of Europe, with the British fully participating, there is no more appropriate instrument at hand for the purpose than the WEU'.[150] Nevertheless, although in the past the WEU had provided the compromise position to the failure of Europe to meet US expectations, its Assembly-proposed solution to the nuclear-sharing problem proved not to be integrative enough for the Americans, Atlanticist enough for the British or French enough for the French.

US plans for a nuclear-capable Multilateral Force (MLF) within NATO, pursued between 1960 and 1964, sought to satisfy European concerns regarding nuclear sharing by diffusing some of its nuclear force geographically within a mixed-manned fleet. However, the US remained intent on the maintenance of exclusive control over nuclear warheads.[151] Although the Federal Republic was encouraged by the possibility of some closer co-operation on nuclear issues, for the French and British there was little to be gained by assigning nuclear weapons directly to NATO if the control system remained American. As one commentator was to remark, given the US insistence on veto power, the MLF represented little more than a 'façade' or, as a European Ambassador described it to him, a 'gimmick'; the Gaullists referred to the whole 'charade' as the 'multilateral farce'.[152] Nuclear 'colonisation' was rejected by both the French and the British in favour of increased nuclear independence.[153]

However, US preferences with regard to Europe's development did not augur well for the European deterrent option. The Democrats had taken office in the US in 1961. The following year the new US President, John F. Kennedy, had put forward his Grand Design as a means of addressing the realities of Europe's increasing economic competitiveness, whilst at the same time discouraging the nuclear proliferation which seemed to be a potential response to the strategic incoherence of NATO's deterrence policy in the light of Soviet military developments. The Americans' support for the Marshall Plan, NATO, the ECSC and the EEC had been based on the assumption, explicit in the Grand Design concept, of the building of a 'larger edifice', an Atlantic Partnership between the US and an integrated Europe. The US did 'not regard a strong and united Europe as a rival but as a partner', although the Europeans clearly had some way to go in terms of 'forming the more perfect union which will some day make this partnership possible'.[154] Until such time as this 'perfect union' could emerge, the US would continue to support the economic and political development of Europe in the expectation that European policies would accord with American interests.[155]

At the economic level, increasing trade liberalization, facilitated through the passing of the US Trade Expansion Bill in January 1962, was to lead to a balanced transatlantic partnership, forthcoming British entry into the EEC being seen as a central plank in the achievement of that policy objective.[156] At the military level, Europe should be prepared to increase its share of the conventional force burden,[157] forsake national nuclear deterrents and accept US control of nuclear weaponry until such time as a unified Europe could become a potential military partner and could then have a share in the control of the Alliance nuclear forces.[158] Just as the Marshall Plan had been preceded by the OEEC as a means of stimulating European co-operation, Kennedy concluded that the Europeans must decide on the means by which they could develop a deterrent capability or a formula for joint political control, and a plan for development, deployment and military strategy, before the US could think of assisting them. However, that the US Administration was not in favour of a European deterrent, officially on the basis that this would be a contribution to proliferation and to the complexity of strategic calculation, suggests a level of ambiguity in Kennedy's Grand Design concept.[159]

The interchangeability of 'partnership' and 'community', as the stated objective of Kennedy's Grand Design concept, was reflective of the lack of clarity within the US on the desired nature or 'precise form' of this new transatlantic relationship.[160] Certainly 'partnership', understood as a relationship between two autonomous powers, differed from the concept of 'community', at least in terms familiar to the European experience of integrating institutions and procedures for common purpose and values.[161] It seemed clear that Kennedy's Grand Design represented at best a 'minimalist' view of community based on enhanced co-operation, communication and representation, rather than a 'maximalist' or Atlantic federalist approach.[162] At the same time, the language of partnership diverted US attention from the real problem of adapting American leadership of the Alliance. The focus on 'partnership' ignored the fact that economic and strategic trends were travelling in different directions as the onset of missile technology increased the strategic distance or inequality between the US and Europe. A resurgent Europe would inevitably seek to have a more 'responsible' role in the Alliance, although, in Buchan's view, this was in terms of influence over the formulating of strategy, what he termed '*controle*', rather than necessarily through direct operational '*control*'.[163] Since the modification of the McMahon Act in 1958 to enable the 'special treatment' of the UK, the ambiguity in US nuclear proliferation policy had seemed evident to observers, with Wohlstetter noting the US tendency to unintentionally incentivize allies 'to demonstrate a nuclear capability of their own, and so become eligible for help'.[164] If US policy was truly the avoidance of proliferation of nuclear capability across the Alliance, sensitive management of the internal process of alliance consultation might seem a more effective method than rhetorical support for some hypothesized future integrated European deterrence capability. Equally, it was argued, the 'Europeans would be well advised to concentrate their attention less on putting their fingers on the trigger of American strategic weapons and more on tying the United States so closely to a true Atlantic Union that even in the American perspective the fate of Germany or France would not appear different from that of Alaska or Florida'.[165]

The ambiguity of successive US positions encouraged a general political malaise amongst European players, accustomed as they were to dependence, resistant to defence integration and fearful of a weakening US commitment. However, it did little to offset the growing frustrations of an increasingly economically powerful Europe. Once again the US seemed to be attempting to push Europe further than it wanted to go down the integrative path, whilst appearing more than ambiguous about the potential 'partnership' outcome in terms of defence.

The deal struck at Nassau on 18 December 1962 spelt the end of any truly European project in the nuclear field. Accepting the US offer of Polaris missiles, for which the UK could provide submarines and warheads, Britain also agreed to assign its strategic V bomber and Polaris submarine forces to NATO, although under the 'supreme national interest' clause these forces could be withdrawn for national use at times of national emergency.[166] Within the WEU Assembly the difficulties inherent in simultaneously developing nuclear capability and ensuring conventional forces to avoid escalation to nuclear war had been recognized, and the Nassau decision was subsequently seen as at least a step towards a common NATO deterrent and away from national nuclear forces.[167] Whilst Richardson has argued that the Nassau Agreement was intended to 'restrain forces making for nuclear proliferation by taking the first step toward a supra-national nuclear force in Europe', this would seem to be stretching the point, short-term provision to the UK having undermined potential medium-term co-operation in Europe. However, it is true that the Nassau Agreement ended the US nuclear monopoly in the Alliance and so may be represented as 'a victory of America's Atlanticists over "hegemonialists"'.[168]

The question of the impact of the Polaris agreement on Britain's European policy is a contentious one. Bowie has argued that the Nassau deal undermined Britain's European interests by encouraging a British illusion regarding the UK's specialness, which 'cut directly across the more basic objective of fostering a united Europe, so necessary for an effective partnership'.[169] Nevertheless, as Freedman and Gearson suggest, 'the goal that was apparently lost at Nassau was hardly realisable in any case', given de Gaulle's resistance to British EEC membership.[170] What is clear is that the Nassau Agreement did little to satisfy the French, who portrayed this 'betrayal' as another illustration of the lack of British 'European-ness'[171] and an attempt by the Anglo-Saxons to create a permanent division of labour within the Alliance.[172] Despite de Gaulle's vigorous promotion of the French nuclear weapons programme, initiated under the Fourth Republic, the French lagged far behind the British, who had benefited from their favoured status with the US. At Nassau, Kennedy had 'brought Britain back under his own aegis, not without giving himself the luxury of a little humiliation of his French partner by offering him Polaris rockets that the French strike force could not use', as the French lacked both the necessary warheads and submarines.[173] The US-UK deal may not have determined French policy with regard to the UK's EEC accession, or, indeed, the continuance of its own nuclear programme, but it certainly provided further 'grist for the mill' of French Anglo-cynicism.

THE FRENCH CHALLENGE

In his press conference of 14 January 1963, de Gaulle denounced British nuclear policy, rejected the MLF concept, reaffirmed his determination to go ahead with an independent nuclear force and announced the French veto of British entry into the Common Market.[174] De Gaulle had already determined, before the Nassau Agreement, that British membership in the EEC should be rejected on the basis that it would serve only to dilute the Community and undermine French leadership of it.[175] Nevertheless, the Nassau deal confirmed de Gaulle's perception of British over-dependence on the US and their potential to act as Atlanticist spoilers for his vision of European community. With the failure of the Fouchet Proposals, and at the insistence of the French, negotiations on British accession to the Communities were discontinued on 29 January 1963. In this final decisive act, de Gaulle spelt not only the rejection of British plans in Europe, but also the end of Kennedy's partnership concept. As one commentator was to note, de Gaulle's 'exclusion of Britain from membership in his "Europe" prevents an Atlantic Partnership from being bilateral . . . he has made it impossible for his "Europe" to approach even partial equality with the United States'.[176]

Following the French rejection of UK accession to the EEC, it was recorded that 'it was generally believed that such a crisis would shake WEU to its foundations by putting it in a position from which it was difficult to see how it would extract itself. Contrary to expectations the effect was quite the opposite'.[177] Rather than undermining the WEU, problems in the Communities context actually served to stimulate it into action. Given the French veto on further accession talks, the WEU could provide the vehicle for the promotion of further links between the UK and the Six, preventing exclusion and isolation, and demonstrating the British interest in deepening European co-operation, whilst awaiting the political demise of de Gaulle.[178]

As early as 5 June 1963, Heath was asking the WEU Assembly for a 'Western European Union review of interests which member states have in common outside the NATO area, and the means which they deploy in support of these interests'.[179] By 10 July, the Council of Ministers of the EEC agreed, on the basis of a West German initiative, to hold quarterly meetings in the framework of the WEU, attended by members of the EEC Commission, to exchange views on the European economic situation and extra-European issues. The French had rejected regular meetings of the Permanent Representatives of the Six with the British mission in Brussels, whilst the French preference for the Council of Europe had no support amongst the other five. Consequently, the French 'fell back' on the intergovernmental WEU, which, with no Brussels seat, was as far removed as possible from the 'organic relationship with the institutions of the Communities'.[180] Thus, the 'political necessity' of the WEU was once again evident as the Council sought to build bridges between the UK and the Six, meeting for the first time in 18 months at The Hague on 25–26 October 1963.[181] At this meeting, the Council discussions included the forthcoming GATT (General Agreement on Tariffs and Trade) negotiations, agricultural issues, EFTA activity and relations between Britain and the EEC. Significantly, this link between the UK and the Six ensured that Britain was adequately represented at the European conference tables and helped to overcome the perceived possibility of an 'economic fragmentation' of Europe.[182] As de Gaulle's vision of Europe dominated the EEC throughout the decade, his resistance to the enhancement of supranational integration within the Community, his continuing rejection of UK advances and his increasing disengagement from the Atlantic Alliance served to demonstrate that the French Government was at odds with its European partners on every issue concerning the future direction of Europe.[183] The WEU provided the important institutional arena in which this 'thorn in the side' of the progress of the other European players could be illuminated, and the Europe of the Seven could be symbolically represented.

The French policy decisions with regard to British EEC membership and NATO co-operation in 1963 contributed to an already evident Atlantic 'drift', where transatlantic allied co-operation was to be severely tested by the lack of any shared 'vision' of European futures. Despite some national dissatisfaction with the benefits of Alliance membership,[184] there remained a general consensus on the part of the European allies that US commitment to NATO was a requirement of European defence.[185] However, with Kennedy's Grand Design in tatters, US policy in Europe was clearly in need of revision.

By the mid 1960s the US policy-determining assumption that European integration was inherently in the American interest was beginning to be seriously questioned. The implementation of the EEC's Common Agricultural Policy and the resultant 'chicken war' of 1963–4 had contributed to a growing sense within the US political elite that it was time to 'end the handouts' to an increasingly competitive and ungrateful Europe.[186] Although US support for European integration had ensured the interests of the post-war US—contributing to the prevention of intra-European war and the resurgence of German militarism, and promoting the necessary economic development to ensure a stable 'partner' against the emerging Soviet menace—these objectives had largely been satisfied.[187] European claims for equality with the US, 'to which Europe is historically entitled', were increasingly met by 'unofficial' grumblings within the US political community about the 'arrogance' of European demands, 'as if something that does not exist, and has never existed, can be entitled to anything'.[188] If, at least for the Americans, European unity was not the aim in itself but a means of strengthening the Atlantic Alliance, then European integration efforts should be judged accordingly. A united and inevitably more assertive Europe, even post de Gaulle, might not necessarily be in US interests.[189] The further promotion of political integration, and particularly the encouragement of a European nuclear force implied within Kennedy's Grand Design, clearly would be a worrying development if in the hands of a Europe beyond Washington's control.[190] Given that 'partnership' no longer seemed possible or, increasingly, desirable, the orientation of US policy began to shift from the conceptual 'dumbbell' to a 'concentric circles' model of transatlantic relations,[191] in which a closely knit Europe would be contained within a broader Atlantic Community, overseen by the US hegemon.

With US 'patronage' of Europe tested by the new realities of the decade, satisfaction with US leadership amongst the Europeans was equally 'qualified'. The Cuban Missile Crisis of October 1962 had brought the world to the brink of nuclear war. And whilst this 'cathartic' experience had led to a more co-operative superpower relationship,[192] both the credibility of Alliance nuclear strategy and the developing superpower condominium (suggested not least by the bilateral negotiations resulting in the 1963 Test Ban Treaty) raised fears of impotence and exclusion amongst the European allies.[193] The perception in the US of a 'growing consensus in the new Europe, even among those who completely disagree with de Gaulle's charted course, that the time has come to bring an end to American hegemony'[194] had some credence. This 'consensus' was in part a reflection of a 'new European loyalty' that had grown during the decade through the habits of European co-operation, a loyalty which was 'not necessarily hostile to America, though there is [sic] a danger of that excess'.[195] Whilst US engagement with Europe remained an accepted requirement of the European order, it was an 'inescapable fact' that enhanced European unity would result in the decline of American hegemony, but that this in turn should result in a more responsible Europe capable of contributing to Western security and development:[196] in turning the American perception on its head, there were those in Europe who had begun to argue that what was needed for the new era was less Atlantic Community, more Europe.

Kissinger succinctly represented the condition of Atlantic relations by the mid 1960s when he asserted, 'What makes current disputes so complex is that they really involve basic assumptions about the nature of Atlantic relationships, the future of Europe and the relative influence of the various partners. For the first time since the war there exists an open challenge not just to the technical implementation of American plans but to the validity of American conceptions. Our strategic conceptions no longer go unquestioned; our preferences concerning the organisation of Europe and the most efficient Atlantic relationship are being contested'.[197] The US was having to deal with a Europe different from the ravaged, impotent one of the early post-war period and was finding it 'most difficult to adjust to conditions in which American leadership is no longer unquestioned'.[198]

It was French attitudes that were to create the real challenge to the US-prescribed order. The Franco-German Elysée Treaty of 22 January 1963 'appeared from the outset as an attempt by Paris to snatch Germany from American influence, just as the Nassau accords had turned Great Britain away from the offers of association with France'.[199] De Gaulle's efforts to enhance bilateral co-operation as a foil to American (and British) influence had minimal success given German concerns, particularly following the election of the pro-Atlanticist Government of Ludwig Erhard in late 1963, to avoid any implied anti-Americanism, a commitment that dissuaded the French from pursuing the defence clauses of the Elysée Treaty.[200] Nevertheless, the treaty did become a symbol for the French, not only of Franco-German rapprochement, but of the 'affirmation of French will'.[201]

French national strategy under de Gaulle had increasingly drawn the French away from NATO, despite his recognition of the continuing necessity for allied military solidarity in the face of mutual threats. Bozo notes that by 1963 the French conception of the national role in the defence of Europe was 'manifestly at odds' with the NATO concept: 'to increased integration it opposed the principle of national command; to a linear and static defence it opposed mobility starting from a rear position; and to a capability for prolonged conventional resistance it opposed the prospect of early use of tactical and strategic nuclear firepower'.[202] The conditionality of French engagement with NATO over its air defence plans in 1960 had been but a foretaste of increasing resistance to NATO military integration efforts. In 1963 de Gaulle removed the French Atlantic Fleet from the Supreme Allied Command, Atlantic (SACLANT) as he sought to assert the principle of national control over French forces.[203] By 1965 the Secretary General of NATO was moved to declare 'France under de Gaulle as not any longer a full working member but rather as an associate member of NATO . . . the French will to co-operate in NATO has practically disappeared'.[204] In a handwritten note to the US Government on 8 March 1966, de Gaulle announced the severance of French ties with the military organization of NATO, requesting that within one year all NATO commands be withdrawn from French territory. However, by virtue of the WEU accords, French forces would remain in Germany and France would remain a signatory of the Washington Treaty.[205] Severely shaken by the French departure, the Alliance experienced a crisis of confidence, with the Americans' 'empty chair' policy for France in NATO reflecting their belief that the French remained essential to the maintenance of an effective security order for the West.[206]

PAPERING OVER THE CRACKS?

Once the initial shock of the French departure from NATO had subsided, the Europeans sought a means by which to demonstrate continuing European cohesion in defence in order to prevent the potential damaging effects for both the Community and the Alliance of French 'exclusion'. The WEU might have seemed the ready-made vehicle for continuing European defence interaction, but the French quickly rejected close co-operation within the WEU on the grounds that it was too 'Atlanticist' in its leanings. This resistance also reflected French displeasure at the manner in which the WEU was being utilized as a means of smoothing UK entry into the EEC. As the WEU Council became a focus of Ministerial efforts to promote the UK's EEC accession, the Assembly took up the task of engaging the French in dialogue and debate in an environment inclusive of the other Six and exclusive, but not undermining, of the US.

Efforts within the WEU to resolve the nuclear-sharing debate and to limit further nuclear proliferation within the Alliance continued throughout the 1960s.[207] The Duynstee Reports, developed in the two years following the Nassau agreement and proffered by the DQAC of the WEU Assembly, proposed the development of a 'single NATO nuclear force . . . based on a European and an American component', under a single command, into which allied nuclear forces should be integrated. In addressing directly the issue of political control, Duynstee envisaged a single NATO Political Executive, with decisions determined by a qualified majority voting within a weighted system.[208] In this way, the proposed new force might satisfy both US concerns regarding the uncontrolled use of allies' national capabilities and European fears of US unilateralism. Despite general approval within the WEU Assembly, the NATO nuclear force proposals were poorly received in national capitals. Given French and British rejection of the MLF, the allied nuclear force proposals were increasingly seen by Washington as both divisive and inadequate as an exercise in non-proliferation or acceptable nuclear sharing.[209] In light of the negotiated US-Soviet nuclear test-ban treaty, the MLF project was officially abandoned in 1964.[210]

In the same year, the new British Prime Minister, Harold Wilson, put forward his Atlantic Nuclear Force proposals for a UK-US nuclear force that might retain the UK's status, which was threatened by the Assembly proposals.[211] In fact, it was not until 1967, following the departure of France from NATO's integrated command and with the establishment of NATO's Nuclear Planning Group, that the nuclear-sharing problem was 'resolved'. This select group would report to the larger Nuclear Defence Affairs Committee (including all but France and Iceland), share information regarding both US and Soviet nuclear force levels and discuss the development of doctrine for the use of tactical nuclear weapons in Europe in the event of Soviet aggression. The notion of a European deterrent was raised again by Heath as UK Leader of the Opposition in 1967 and by Lord Carrington, Heath's

Defence Minister following the Conservative Party's election victory in 1970, but neither idea was developed, and both may be seen as little more than Europhile rhetoric in the light of ongoing EEC accession negotiations.[212]

In the spring of 1967, the British decision to withdraw forces east of Suez[213] was a reflection of a more Euro-focused policy determined by largely economic considerations. Commitments were clearly outstripping resources as the British economy faltered, leading to the eventual devaluation of the pound in November 1967. The consistently low growth rate of the British economy throughout the 1960s contrasted with the much higher performance of the EEC Six, the development of the custom union having established a privileged combined European market of 250 million people.[214] British fears of supranationalism within the Community had been dampened by the Gaullist insistence on national caveats exemplified in the Luxembourg Compromise of 1966, whilst Commonwealth concerns regarding the impact of British membership in the EEC had declined as a consequence of precedent-suggesting agreements reached between the Six on preferential trade terms for ex-dependent African states.[215] At the WEU Ministerial Meeting of 10 May 1967 the British Foreign Secretary, George Brown, made the UK's second application for membership in the EEC on behalf of the Wilson Government, only to be rejected by de Gaulle less than a week later. Wilson was 'fully aware' of the certainty of the French veto, the second application being primarily tactical, serving to isolate de Gaulle within both France and the EEC and to deny Heath, the pro-Europeanist Leader of the Conservative opposition, a 'platform on which to attack the government', given rising popular support for entry into the EEC.[216]

Largely in response to this second French veto, at the Rome meeting of the WEU Council on 21 October 1968, Belgian Foreign Minister Pierre Harmel put forward a plan for closer co-operation between the UK and the Six within the WEU. The scope of this co-operation was to include a range of issues not covered by the Rome Treaty, including defence, foreign policy, technology and monetary affairs.[217] Despite French resistance, at the WEU Council meeting in Luxembourg in February 1969, it was agreed to consult on some foreign policy matters within the WEU before national decision-making. In the light of a decision to hold a meeting of the Permanent Council to discuss the situation in the Middle East, de Gaulle instituted a French boycott of the Council.[218] It was clear to the French that, by another act of 'diplomatic terrorism', the actions of the other six WEU members were intended to force the hand of the French Government, with the proposed meeting being 'one more step in the escalation, in which the British and their supporters have been indulging, to get around the French refusal to discuss among the seven British membership of the Common Market'.[219]

Within the WEU, the debate on the institution's political role continued. The unanimity rule within the Council had resulted in decision-making at the level of the lowest common denominator. Given de Gaulle's resistance to UK efforts to 'exploit' the WEU in its EEC accession agenda, it was noted that 'the six Ministers who want to act are forced to appear before the Assembly and in the eyes of public opinion as if they agreed with the only one who systematically boycotts their organisation'.[220] The high point of tension between the Council and Assembly came with the Assembly's rejection of the Council's Annual Report in June 1967, in which the Council ruled out anything that might constitute a political assessment of its activities.[221] The Assembly was to be relegated to the position of a talking shop, with the Council rejecting any supervisory or guidance role for the one European Assembly able to discuss the full range of political issues. In his speech to the WEU Assembly in October 1968, the Assembly President, Vittorio Confalonieri, expressed his concern that the Council did not share the 'ambitious' Assembly view that the role of the politicians represented within the WEU was to speed up 'the transformation of the utopian to the possible, the possible into the necessary, the necessary into a reality that the untamable way of history will continually oblige us to revise and develop'.[222] This 'frustrating asymmetry' did result in a level of disillusionment with the institution. Nevertheless, the Assembly persevered in its tradition of informative and unique political reporting[223] and proved itself an effective body in articulating debate and sounding out the views of all seven members.[224] Indeed, the Dutch Foreign Minister was to note the profound significance of the WEU to the West European powers as 'the only political and military forum to which they have recourse when the harmony of their relations is threatened'. In the context of the late 1960s, he went on to state that the 'WEU provides the only acceptable means of progressing toward European unification . . . It is fortunate that this organisation exists . . . it shows them the road to take . . . thanks to WEU it is often solidarity which triumphs rather than narrow nationalism'.[225]

MANAGING ADJUSTMENT

By the time of Richard Nixon's inauguration as US President in January 1969, relations between the US and Western Europe were at best uncertain; perennial concerns regarding burden-sharing and leadership combined with economic and strategic developments to raise questions about the continuing relevance of the post-war Atlantic order. During the Presidency of Lyndon B. Johnson (Kennedy's successor following the President's assassination in 1963), the Vietnam War had become a major preoccupation of both the US Administration and the American people, whereas the Gaullist defection from NATO had served to undermine the centrality of the transatlantic relationship. At the economic level, there was considerable unease on both sides of the Atlantic regarding the Americans' place in the world economy. The Kennedy Round of trade negotiations had concluded relatively successfully in 1967, but subsequent US efforts to manage a burgeoning balance-of-payments deficit by 'printing the dollar' had severely undermined the

Bretton Woods system of fixed exchange on which the West's economic stability had been based.[226] The costs of alliance at a time of economic instability were further highlighted as the progressive de-Stalinization of Eastern Europe resulted in a perceived reduction of threat, as more 'liberal' forms of communism appeared to offer new opportunities for positive engagement. The policy approach of Ostpolitik, which first emerged under the West German Foreign Minister Willy Brandt in 1966, was based on engagement and co-operation with the East, which, though in large part officially supported by the US, suggested a loss of US leadership and control of the management of Western relations with the East.[227] In an effort to multilateralize the processes of détente and simultaneously ensure some level of US influence, the Harmel Report of 1967 sought to redefine NATO's role by setting détente alongside the collective defence function of the Alliance. The Mutual and Balanced Force Reductions (MBFR) initiative announced by the NAC in June 1968 was an expression of this 'transformation'.[228] However, the Soviet invasion of Czechoslovakia in 1968, combined with the strengthening of the Soviet fleet in the Mediterranean and the speed of the Soviet's nuclear build-up, suggested the limits of détente and led to renewed European optimism regarding the benefits of alliance and the Atlantic order.[229] Significantly, for the French, hopes of rapprochement with the Soviets (and the consequent assumption that they had room to manoeuvre in the Alliance) had been dashed by the Soviet treatment of dissenters; clearly the 'Russians were not prepared to allow the Czechoslovaks to do to them what de Gaulle was doing to the United States'.[230]

With Nixon in the White House a new style of transatlantic relations was quickly to emerge whereby old assumptions regarding the benefits of an integrated Europe were challenged by the pragmatic requirements of American power. Just as the President's New Economic Policy marked a new era of international economic relations in which the US would pursue a trade and monetary policy that put its own economic interests first,[231] Nixon's 'structure of peace' was to depend on a fully burden-sharing and strategically compliant Europe doing its part in support of the bipolar stability determined by the superpower balance. In what Duke suggests was reminiscent of the 'Dullesian' approach of the 1950s, the President was to warn the US allies in his address to the NAC in December 1970 that 'NATO's conventional forces must not only be maintained, but in certain key areas strengthened. Given a similar approach by our allies, the United States will maintain and improve its own forces in Europe and will not reduce them unless there is reciprocal action from our adversaries'.[232]

One means of managing the requirement for a more effective European contribution was through co-operation on armaments, as some level of integration of European arms production seemed to offer the only means of providing for the weapons standardization and high unit production which would create the necessary cost efficiencies to meet US demands. However, there was an apparent contradiction in the US position of requiring a greater European capability whilst resisting European-based armaments co-operation on the grounds of industrial competition.[233] The WEU had provided a vehicle in the past for some level of co-operation, but despite some ambitious schemes for joint programmes of research, development and arms production, little was achieved in the way of co-operative European armaments production during the 1960s. Although the potential broad benefits of enhanced European armaments co-operation may have seemed evident to many, national interests and economic differences combined with industrial pressures to limit co-operation. As one commentator was to note, in the area of armaments co-operation 'common sense comes up against 2,000 years of national defence, 2,000 years of national armament industries which have their own vested interests and are reluctant to commit hara-kiri forthwith on the altar of Europe and integrated defence'.[234]

Although some bi- and multilateral negotiations resulted in degrees of standardization, fears of upsetting the Americans by giving the impression of caucus-forming within NATO led to any project of importance being referred to the NATO Armaments Committee.[235] Given that, as Mulley was to note at the beginning of the decade, 'it is widely held in the arms industry that the transfer of projects from WEU to NATO often leads merely to their being taken over by American industry', it is unsurprising that WEU efforts at arms co-operation remained limited.[236] Nevertheless, the WEU Assembly, as part of its general interest in defence dialogue, maintained an active role in promoting European technological and industrial co-operation. Acting as a 'pressure group' it was to submit numerous programme recommendations to the Council, organize conferences on European technology and promote the concept of Europe-wide co-operation in scientific and technical fields.[237]

In fact, the WEU was to be sidelined as a forum for European armaments co-operation by the establishment in 1968 of the Eurogroup on an initiative of the British Defence Minister, Denis Healey. By providing a 'ginger group within NATO', the Eurogroup could enable the Europeans to demonstrate their commitment to Alliance burden-sharing and efficiencies in the absence of French resistance and in the light of increasing US demands.[238] The Eurogroup provided for consultation and co-operation on European defence matters; one significant role was to communicate more effectively the realities of European contributions in defence to the Americans. However, it was in the area of deliverables that the Eurogroup was to respond to mounting US pressures in 1971[239] by announcing a $1b 'package' of provisions through its European Defence Improvement Programme, although it was to prove less effective in areas such as joint production of armaments, which, it was felt, might 'interfere with United States exports'.[240]

The Eurogroup was essentially an 'Atlantic creature', motivated by the requirements of alliance management and lacking the European constituency to articulate a strong European voice in defence matters. In response to the ascendancy of Eurogroup, the French increasingly promoted the WEU as an autonomous organization with broader European potential.[241] By the inclusion of all three major European states and the exclusion of the US, the WEU provided a means of keeping the French involved in some level of defence dialogue, enabling the Europeans to 'let off steam' without fundamentally damaging the Alliance, promoting collective thinking about European issues and dissipating the divisive nationalism of the Gaullist vision. As the Deputy Secretary General of the WEU was to note in 1970, the role of the WEU Assembly in providing a continuous exchange of information with member governments with regard to defence matters at this 'stage' of European development was 'indispensable'.[242]

PREPARING THE WAY: THE WEU POST DE GAULLE

Following the departure of de Gaulle from office and his replacement by Georges Pompidou in June 1969, agreement was reached at the December Hague Summit on the reopening of EEC accession negotiations, to begin the following June. In response, Harmel made clear to the WEU Assembly in the Session held one week after the Hague Summit that 'henceforth priority would go to the European Community . . . the European Communities remain the original core from which a European idea is developing and will continue to develop'.[243] Once again, as enlargement discussions began within the EEC, the Six renewed their consideration of a political community in Europe. The resulting Davignon Report of October 1970 led to a series of regular meetings between Foreign Ministers and senior Foreign Ministry officials, collectively referred to as European Political Co-operation (EPC), a process outside of the Treaty of Rome and intended as a vehicle for the harmonization of members' foreign policies.[244] Although committing the Six to nothing less intergovernmental than the WEU arrangement, the significance of the Davignon Report was that it demonstrated the political choice of the Six, 'opting away from WEU towards the Economic Community, yet nevertheless independent of it'.[245] As Gordon was to note, with the establishment of EPC as an element of the EEC and the reopening of negotiations on accession, 'the turn of the decade seemed to some observers to mark the end of the line for WEU'.[246]

In June 1971 the Amrehn Report of the Assembly's GAC sought to establish what the 'tasks and competences' of the WEU should be 'in view of the extension and strengthening of the European Common Market'.[247] This report identifies the debate in Europe on the precise competencies of the extended Community, a debate that opposed two camps: those who sought an exclusively economic inter-relationship, and the integrationalists who advocated decisive co-operation in the additional areas of defence, foreign policy and technology. Although the WEU Assembly was sensitive to the inter-relationship between these areas, it noted that few states would be prepared to accept the same level of integration allowed in economics to operate elsewhere, most particularly in defence. For this reason the report suggests that two separate organizations might be better than having to 'bring the more advanced communal structures down to the level of the more backward'. Proposals were aired for the eventual fusion of the EP and WEU Assembly and the inclusion of the WEU's executive organs in the EC as the basis of its political and defence wing,[248] but the Assembly argued that the Parliament would be unable to provide initiative and control for so many areas of public life, whilst the many years of experience in defence matters accrued by the WEU Assembly made it a specialist in these areas. A merger of the WEU and the EC would also raise the question of the automatic assistance clause of the Brussels Treaty, a stronger clause than NATO's Article 5, given that not all members of the EC were WEU members or sought Article 5 cover. The dissolution of the WEU would also compel a reconsideration of the supervision and control of armed forces clauses and, if they were to continue, the management of these clauses and their extension to the rest of the Community. For these reasons the French Deputy of the GAC advocated 'evolution of the Political Union from the WEU'.[249] The Davignon proposals had suggested a declining role for the WEU, although the debates within the Assembly suggested its enhancement as the basis of a political and defence community until such time as Europe had matured sufficiently to enable the 'ultimate merger'.[250] The Assembly further recommended to the Council that steps should be taken within the WEU to 'work out a European defence policy within the framework of the North Atlantic Pact'.[251]

In fact, as EEC enlargement became an imminent reality, the WEU began to look increasingly unhealthy at the Ministerial level. British interest in WEU development had been largely satisfied by its coming accession to the EEC. Equally, for many in Europe, British EEC membership was seen as the means of 'lifting the most obvious constraint on its [the EEC's] progress from an economic to "political" stage of existence', because the schism between the three major powers had been removed.[252] French cynicism regarding the WEU as a vehicle of UK interests had been replaced by a cautious opportunism in which the WEU was identified as a possible vehicle for promoting further European co-operation in those foreign- and defence-related areas still outside of the Community's remit. However, given French resistance to Atlanticism, the WEU was not the means of achieving serious co-operation in defence terms for Europeans, representative as it was of the Europeanist/Atlanticist split.[253] Increasingly, the EC seemed to represent the only means of developing any kind of effective foreign policy dialogue.[254] With the accession of the UK to the EC in 1973, the WEU Council ceased to meet, its political activities having effectively come to a halt in 1972 as it gradually sank into Ministerial hibernation.[255] However, the Assembly and its Committees continued to provide a forum for dialogue on political issues and to promote closer European identity in defence in the absence of an Executive. Indeed, the WEU provided the only forum in which this European defence debate could be heard.

REFLECTIONS

The WEU was established in 1955, following the modification of the 1948 Brussels Treaty in October 1954, as a response to immediate and pressing needs. As part of a broader framework of security relationships established under the Paris Agreements, it played a central role in accommodating the requirements of European security concerns. In its subordination to NATO for defence, the WEU had become firmly part of the Atlantic defence vision and thus the Cold War international structure, and it reflected European acceptance of defence dependency. The structural overlay had resulted in a decline in high politics in Europe, the EDC having demonstrated that European defence integration was not viable. As economic integration took shape between the ECSC Six within the emerging EEC context, and with the Council of Europe taking on the social and cultural aspects of European co-operation, the role of the WEU in this new security order seemed uncertain. As the WEU had been established with the dual support role of promoting both collective defence and European integration, the lack of any vision for this 'hybrid' institution led to its reactive development. When tensions between state interests created difficulties in either of the primary organizational structures, states sought to utilize the WEU as a means of satisfying their particular concerns. The preceding contextual discussion serves to highlight the areas of major tension that existed between states seeking to pursue their interests within the WEU's broad functional pillars of furthering European integration and managing alliance.

One major area of tension that persisted throughout the period examined in this chapter was the lack of consensus on the preferred breadth and depth of European integration. Significantly, the British free trade area approach was at odds with the deeper economic integration taking place between the Six within the emerging EEC. Despite general support amongst six of the seven WEU members for British entry into the new community, following de Gaulle's election in 1958, the French staunchly opposed it, believing the UK to be a 'Trojan horse' bent on establishing an Atlanticist order. Whilst accession desires led the UK to encourage increased political co-operation between European states, de Gaulle's nationalism was to constitute a significant hurdle to closer European integration during the period, restricting both the deepening of the community and its enlargement.

Within the Alliance context, the major issues of contention resulted from concerns over the nature of the US commitment to Europe and were highlighted by de Gaulle's rejection of NATO's integrated military structure in 1966. European concerns that their defence dependency was resulting in a lack of control over NATO strategy led to efforts to readjust their position within the Alliance. However, efforts to enhance their independent and collective capabilities were met by 'contradictory' US behaviour. On the one hand, the US encouraged increased burden-sharing by its European allies, but, on the other, it resisted any greater European competency that would undermine US leadership within the Atlantic relationship. These tensions were evidenced most clearly in the area of arms control, arms co-operation and the nuclear-sharing debate.

The tensions resulting from the crossover between alliance and integrative interests also became more evident during this period. Washington's insistence on the primacy of the Atlantic structure linked the development of an integrated Europe to the satisfaction of US interests. However, the assumption of the benefits of European integration for Atlantic interests was increasingly called into question by the emerging 'iceberg' of an economically competitive Europe. For Europeans, defence required a US presence, with the defence Alliance providing the stability for European developments in the 'low-politics' arena where European economic integration was to be the first step towards an even closer union. As Europeans benefited from the successes of economic integration, US dominance within NATO was seen to have a negative influence on Europe's ability to co-operate within it. Enhanced European integration might provide a means of balancing the unhealthy asymmetry in transatlantic relations, but US fears of a more assertive Europe threatened to undermine the cohesion of NATO. The search for a balance within the transatlantic relationship that would satisfy all players provided the context for developments within the Alliance and Community frameworks. The WEU's dual imperatives placed it at the crossroads of these two, potentially competing, designs.

The WEU proved itself able to act as an 'enabler' for European construction throughout the period examined in this chapter, and this in turn provides an explanation of the development of WEU activity. In the 'low-politics' areas, alternative economic frameworks for European co-operation were debated within the WEU arena, with Britain promoting the WEU's political role as it sought to get closer to its European 'partners'. On British application for EEC membership, the WEU Assembly was to become a significant element in the process of Europe-building by providing reasoned reports and debate on the details of the enlargement proposals and by offering a forum for discussion and negotiation.[256] Following French rejection of UK accession, the harmony of European relations was challenged by de Gaulle's stranglehold on the EEC as the primary vehicle of European integration. The WEU, as the one institution that included at least and no more than the Seven, was able to step into the breach and prevent a schism from developing between the UK and Continental Europe.

In contrast to Hoscheit and Tsakaloyannis's suggestion that the WEU was 'drawn into the dispute' between Britain and the Six, resulting in its 'further relegation',[257] the evidence suggests that the WEU provided a useful lever, not only for the British, but for the five EEC supporters of UK accession, in efforts to pave the way for eventual British entry. As a 'balancing factor in the oscillations of the process of European unification',[258] the WEU proved itself to be a convenient tool in managing this crisis in the European integrative process by providing an arena for keeping alive discussions on

British entry. Once the British achieved accession, the WEU had served its purpose. The pursuit of its political development appeared to have been only a 'cosmetic initiative to pave the way for Britain's entry into the EC';[259] once that was accomplished, political development was transferred to the evolving EPC of the primary organization for European integration, the EEC. Nevertheless, the manipulation of this new function was useful in providing leverage against French resistance and had led to British acceptance of the EPC within the emerging Community structures. Just as the WEU's social and cultural activities had contributed to increased European co-operation in these areas until their transfer to the Council of Europe in 1960, it has been argued that the development of the WEU's political competence was to provide a small step in the incremental process of European integration, contributing to the 'steady trickle' of co-operation that was wearing away the 'solid rock of national exclusiveness'.[260] Equally, in isolating defence from the evolving EPC structure, the WEU had ensured that the problematic area of defence integration did not contaminate the young Communities, who were not yet sufficiently developed to manage this assault on the core of national existence.

Within the Atlantic Alliance context, concerns regarding the lack of European influence led to a debate on acceptable levels of dependence that was reflected in efforts to enhance national capabilities and promote European co-operation. Given the WEU's subordinate position to NATO, it was identified as a means of rebalancing the Alliance, reflecting European desires for a greater say and contributing to the overall efficiency of the broader alliance system. However, the WEU was of limited utility in the development of a more balanced transatlantic alliance relationship. US dominance had hamstrung the institution, the minimalist position taken by the WEU Council being a reflection of divergent alliance visions, with the British insistent on NATO precedence and the French resistant to European co-operation in the 'Anglo-Saxon' framework.

The arms control provisions of the WEU were designed to provide the internal security required by the Europeans to enable a managed rearmament of Germany in support of the Atlantic Alliance. However, the WEU failed to secure the necessary conventional forces for European defence, requiring a nuclear solution to NATO's defence needs. As the UK 'nuclearization' policy resulted in a decline in its conventional force commitment to the continent, the WEU failed to prevent French nuclear development—a reflection of independent defence thinking. That said, the WEU did continue to provide the context for a (reducing) British continental presence and for a scrutinized German contribution to European defence. These elements were equally relevant to the European dimension; the WEU's arms control provisions provided the means of securing a balance in Europe and the confidence for the promotion of further European co-operation in low-politics areas.

Arms co-operation had been recognized as an area in which European co-operation might enhance the contribution of Europe to burden-sharing within the Alliance by providing for efficiencies and helping to overcome the technological dependency on the US. Committed to this task, the WEU's SAC proved largely ineffective as the US insistence on Alliance preference, and national resistance to the subordination of their own defence industries, meant that Europeans saw little benefit from the SAC procedures. The WEU did succeed, however, in tying the multilateral arms co-operation emerging in FIG into the WEU framework and thus prevented a potentially 'competing' system from developing within Europe. The NATO body Eurogroup was eventually to supplant the WEU as the vehicle for co-operative arms arrangements in the light of US demands, as the French 'departure' from NATO led to increased restrictions on the WEU as a body for effective alliance management. In terms of nuclear sharing, the WEU was to prove unacceptable as a vehicle for developing a European nuclear deterrent; the UK and France resisted the loss of prestige and control evident in the European alternatives. Nevertheless, it provided a vehicle for articulation of European concerns regarding lack of influence over NATO strategy and had encouraged a reluctant US to consider the alternatives, resulting in the Nuclear Planning Group within NATO. In effect, the WEU obliged NATO to take the problem seriously and adopt a working solution to what had proven a divisive source of persistent irritation within the Alliance.

The WEU did provide a forum for European dialogue on defence: a significant if constrained role following the French departure from NATO. In terms of alliance cohesion, the WEU Assembly's recommendations may not have resulted in concrete action, but they did enable the establishment of legitimizing joint positions in support of Alliance policy. Its annual reports on defence preparedness and critiques of NATO strategy, as well as its debates on general defence matters, provided 'a certain degree of parliamentary supervision over the work of NATO and Western European defence policy in general'.[261] As a 'watchdog' of European defence, the WEU enabled areas of concern to be considered and discussed, whilst new ideas could be aired before being expressed in the 'hallowed halls' of NATO's Supreme Allied Command and hence amongst the national governments.[262] Notably, in enabling the development of a European perspective and representation, the WEU was to contribute to a sense of 'Europeanness', which was a central element of the integrative process. Despite being occasionally at odds with NATO, this 'Europeanness' was not, in substance, a threat to Atlantic cohesion, being essentially supportive of the overall interests in the stability of the Alliance. By 1973 French resistance to NATO had crippled any effective Ministerial consensus within the Council of the WEU on defence issues, European integration having taken the low-politics path of the EEC after UK accession. However, the Assembly continued with its work even after the WEU Council had ceased to function.

Examination of WEU development and activity during the period from its inception to its Ministerial hibernation in 1973 illuminates three key themes. Firstly, the lack of agreement on the WEU's role resulted in institutional development in response to the immediate interests of individual states, rather than as part of any long-term plan. Consequently, the specific functions of the WEU were to be inconsistently developed, evolving and devolving throughout the period according to 'subjective' criteria. The WEU retained its central supporting role to the primary organizations of collective defence and European integration, and states sought to utilize it in pursuit of their particular interests in these arenas, blocking WEU activity when further developments were not in their immediate interests.

Secondly, as Duke suggests, the WEU's ambiguity as both an 'Atlanticist' and 'Europeanist' institution served to undermine its effectiveness,[263] as evidenced by British resistance to its development as a vehicle of integration in its early years[264] and French resistance to it as a promoter of political and defence dialogue in an Atlantic framework. Nevertheless, this ambiguity also proved to be a strength as the WEU was utilized to support the interests of both alliance and integration. That these functions were at times complementary, or even mutually dependent (as for example in the case of British EEC accession), and at other times at cross-purposes demonstrates the importance of the WEU's apparent ambiguity. The flexibility of its broad mandate and institutional competence enabled it to change focus to satisfy particular interests, whilst serving an articulating role in the management of the 'sticky' parts of the broader co-operative process.

Finally, these factors are illustrative of the supporting nature of the institution, with the WEU's development reflecting the primacy of NATO and the EEC as vehicles of collective defence and integration. The WEU was utilised only when the primary organizations proved insufficient to meet national interests. Consequently, when the WEU looked self-consciously at development it did so in the light of how it might contribute to the wider order, giving up responsibilities where they might better be achieved elsewhere. The devolution of functional areas by the WEU may be seen as only a partial failure of the institution to be effective in its support role. Institutional rationalization and the development of other organizations at the WEU's expense may be identified as a success of the institution as it sought to contribute to the 'greater good' of the security structure for Europe. The release of much of its social and cultural activity to the Council of Europe in 1960, and of its political function to the EPC on enlargement are examples of this process. However, when the primary organizations required 'the duty doctor on call',[265] or when the 'European ship' required re-floating,[266] the WEU was, at least on occasion, able to provide the 'first aid' or 'motor' required. By 1973, with integration remitted to the EC and the WEU's ability to function in the defence support role severely hampered by the Europeanist-Atlanticist divide within the Council, the WEU was to recede into its 'traditional role of a fallback position in case all else fails',[267] whilst the 'quiet' work of the Assembly kept alive the promise of a future European identity in defence.

NOTES

1. A. Grosser, 'Suez, Hungary and European integration', *International Organization*, vol. 11, no. 4, May 1957, p. 471.
2. K. Kyle, *Suez,* New York: St Martin's Press, 1991, pp. 456–60 and 559.
3. The Suez debacle had done much to accelerate the European project. The West German Chancellor Konrad Adenauer suggested to the French Prime Minister Guy Mollet that 'Europe will be your revenge' for the humiliation of US abandonment. See M. Vaisse, 'Post-Suez France', in W. M. R. Louis and R. Owen (eds) *Suez 1956: The Crisis and its Consequences,* Oxford: Oxford University Press, 1989, p. 336.
4. Wolfers notes that American support of European unity had been 'one of the few persistent and bipartisan features of post-war United States policy'. A. Wolfers, 'Integration in the West: the conflict of perspectives', *International Organization*, vol. 17, no. 3, May 1963, p. 755.
5. See H. C. Wallich, 'The United States and the European Economic Community: a problem of adjustment', *International Organization,* vol. 22, no. 4, September 1968, pp. 841–54.
6. WEU Assembly, *Proceedings,* (Session 1, Part 1), 'Official report of debates', July 1955, pp. 23–5. Initially holding its sessions at the Parliamentary Assembly building of the Council of Europe in Strasbourg, the Assembly moved to its permanent home in Paris in 1959, where it was later joined (1990) by the WEU Institute for Security Studies.
7. WEU Assembly, *Reply of the Council to the Supplementary Questions in the Report of the Committee on Defence Questions and Armaments,* doc. 17, 10 July 1956.
8. In 1957, the Council reiterated its position to the Assembly that 'sole responsibility for planning defence policy and organizing common defence' had been transferred to NATO as of April 1951, and whilst there was a certain devolution of military tasks to the WEU under the Paris Agreements, 'no steps were taken to re-establish military planning or command machinery'. WEU Assembly, *Second Report of the Council to the Assembly of WEU,* doc. 37, 25 February 1957.
9. See M. M. Ball, *NATO and the European Union Movement,* London: Stevens and Sons, 1959, p. 364; M. Palmer and J. Lambert, *European Unity: A Survey of the European Organisations,* London: Allen and Unwin, 1968, p. 330, for details of institutional arrangements.
10. DQAC, Recommendation 6 in WEU Assembly, *Proceedings* (Session 2, Part 2), vol. 4, 1956, p. 117.
11. WEU Assembly, rapporteur Mr Fens, *Activities of Western European Union in the Sphere of Security and the Production and Control of Armaments,* doc. 12, 17 April 1956, p. 71.
12. WEU Assembly, *Second Report of the Council,* doc. 37.
13. C. Gordon, 'The WEU and European defence cooperation', *Orbis,* vol. 17, no. 1, spring 1973, p. 251.
14. The Assembly's Charter provides for a 'motion of disapproval' of the Council report. For full discussion of the issue see M. Curtis, *West European Integration,* New York: Harper Rowe, 1965, chap. 5.
15. WEU Assembly, rapporteur Mr Senghor, *Activities of WEU in the Cultural Field,* doc. 21, 19 September 1956.
16. 'Resolution adopted by the Foreign Ministers of the ECSC Member States', Messina, 1–3 June 1955. The UK, 'as a State belonging to W.E.U and associated with the E.C.S.C.', was invited to participate in the deliberations on future European integration initiated at Messina.

17. Cited in P. Borcier, *The Political Role of the Assembly of WEU*, Paris: WEU Assembly, 1963, p. 6.

18. Cited in P. Borcier, *The Assembly of Western European Union: Its Contribution to the Defence and Building of Europe since 1955*, Paris: WEU Assembly, 1975, p. 42.

19. 'Telegram from US Delegation at the NAC Ministerial Meeting to Department of State, Paris, 11 May 1955', *FRUS 1955–1957, Western European Security and Integration*, vol. 4, doc. 7, pp. 19–21.

20. C. Schmid, *Ten Years of Seven Power Europe*, Paris: WEU Assembly, 1964, p. 12.

21. See W. Kaiser, *Using Europe, Abusing the Europeans: Britain and European Integration, 1945–63*, London: Macmillan, 1999, p. 60. Moravcsik notes that this was not an entirely unreasonable assumption, given that 'leading Continental participants felt that the French political and economic weakness would probably lead to a looser free trade arrangement, the economic equivalent of the WEU'. A. Moravcsik, *The Choice for Europe: Social Purpose and State Power from Messina to Maastricht*, London: UCL Press, 1998, p. 129.

22. D. Gowland and A. Turner, *Reluctant Europeans: Britain and European Integration, 1945–1998*, Harlow: Longman, 2000, p. 112.

23. Palmer and Lambert, *European Unity*, 1968, p. 336, noted that 'in practice this has not restricted the WEU Assembly from the discussion of the politics as well as the military aspects of defence'.

24. TNA: CAB 129/84: CP (57) 6, 'The Grand Design' (Co-operation with Western Europe), Memorandum by the Secretary of State for Foreign Affairs, 5 January 1957.

25. TNA: CAB 128/30: CM 3 (57), 'Co-operation with Western Europe: Minutes of a Cabinet Meeting', 9 January 1957.

26. The emerging close relationship between the Federal Republic and the US, and particularly between Adenauer and Eisenhower, suggested that the FRG was to be a 'senior partner' in the Alliance and fears of potential US-German economic dominance of a new Europe had motivated the Benelux states and Italy to look towards the formation of a European economic bloc as the means of curtailing this. See RIIA, *Survey of International Affairs 1954–1955*, London: Oxford University Press, 1960, p. 104.

27. TNA: CAB 128/30: CM 3 (57), 'Co-operation with Western Europe'.

28. TNA: CAB 129/84: CP (57) 6, 'The Grand Design', p. 2.

29. TNA: CAB 128/30: CM 3 (57), 'Co-operation with Western Europe'.

30. 'We would in any case hope there is no intention on British part to propose inclusion of CSC, Common Market and Euratom Assembly in parliamentary scheme. Former would have some real powers of decision, might eventually be directly elected, and have special role to play in development six country integration movement'. Circular Telegram from the [US] Secretary of State to Certain Diplomatic Missions', Washington, 6 March 1957, *FRUS 1955–1957. Western European Security and Integration* (1955-1957), vol. 4, doc. 227, pp. 534–6.

31. 'Circular Telegram from the [US] Secretary of State to Certain Diplomatic Missions, Washington, 6 March 1957', p. 535.

32. The British plan would create a 'vague amorphous body, whose internal working would be of unprecedented complexity, and within which the real powers already won by some Assemblies might gradually sweep away'. WEU Assembly, rapporteur Mr van Naters, *European Assemblies—the 'Grand Design'*, doc. 45, 5 April 1957.

33. See WEU Assembly, rapporteur M. Senghor, *The Future Role of the WEU in Political, Economic, Cultural and Legal Matters*, doc. 41, 5 April 1957, pp. 73 and 404–5.

34. Borcier, *The Political Role of the Assembly of WEU*, p. 15.
35. N. Salter, 'Western European Union: the role of the Assembly 1954–1963', *International Affairs*, vol. 40, no. 1, January 1964, p. 35.
36. Confalonieri notes, 'Until December 1958 the contradictory positions of the Six and of the UK condemned WEU to be no more than a forum, but an important forum for defence questions, carrying out but little weight in the political field'. V. Confalonieri, *Ten Years*, Paris: WEU Assembly, 1964, p. 77.
37. This vote was to include acceptance by the French and Germans and the assent of the Saarlanders themselves. See Palmer and Lambert, *European Unity*, p. 341.
38. Nearly 68% voted against the Statute, with a turn-out of 96.59%. RIIA, *Survey of International Affairs 1955–1956*, p. 103.
39. See E. J. Patterson, 'The Saar Referendum', *European Yearbook*, vol. 4, 1956, pp. 226–39.
40. A. Cahen, *The Western European Union and NATO: Building a European Defence Identity within the Context of Atlantic Solidarity*, London: Brasseys, 1989, p. 5.
41. Council of Europe, Resolution 128, May 1957.
42. See WEU Assembly, rapporteur Mr Struye, *Creation of a Fourth Assembly*, doc. 34, 15 December 1956.
43. Entering into force on 1 January 1958, the institutions of the EEC and Euratom were modelled on those of the ECSC, sharing a parliamentary Assembly and Court of Justice. However, these new Communities had a Commission instead of a High Authority for an executive, demonstrating a weakened federalism and a strengthening of member governments in the Council, a position accentuated by Charles de Gaulle's election in 1958 and the merging of the executive Commission in 1965.
44. Returning as the 'saviour of France', De Gaulle's Presidential powers were to be significantly enhanced by the new Constitution of the Fifth Republic, introduced on 5 October 1958.
45. J. Dougherty, 'European deterrence and Atlantic unity', *Orbis*, vol. 6, no. 3, fall 1962, p. 396.
46. S. Hoffmann, 'The European process at Atlantic cross-purposes', *Journal of Common Market Studies*, vol. 3, no. 2, June 1964, p. 98. Also see H. Lange, 'European integration and Atlantic partnership', *Atlantic Community Quarterly*, vol. 1, no. 4, winter 1963–4, p. 514.
47. C. de Gaulle, *War Memoirs: Salvation, 1944–46*, New York: Simon and Schuster, 1960, pp. 204–5.
48. 'The path to be followed must be that of organized co-operation between States, while waiting to achieve, perhaps, an imposing confederation'. De Gaulle, speech cited in Political and Economic Planning (PEP), *France and the European Community, Occasional Paper 11*, London: PEP, 1961, p. 18.
49. See A. S. Milward, *The Rise and Fall of a National Strategy 1945–1963*, London: Frank Cass, 2002, pp. 265–309, for a discussion of the failure of the FTA proposals. Ellison notes Harold Macmillan's 'hysterical' reaction to the ensuing failure of the FTA plan, 'suggesting that Britain withdraw its troops from the Continent, leave the WEU and the North Atlantic Treaty Organisation (NATO)' and construct a 'Fortress Britain', although the more conciliatory and pragmatic Whitehall perspective was to prevail. J. Ellison, 'Britain and the Treaties of Rome, 1955–1959', in R. Broad and V. Preston (eds) *Moored to the Continent? Britain and European Integration*, London: Institute of Historical Research, 2001, p. 46.
50. See C. R. Schenk, 'Decolonization and European economic integration: the Free Trade Area negotiations, 1956–58', *Journal of Imperial and Commonwealth*

History, vol. 24, no. 3, September 1996, pp. 444–63, for discussion of the changing economic relationship between the Commonwealth, Europe and the UK.

51. See R. L. Pfaltzgraff Jr, *Britain Faces Europe,* Philadelphia: University of Pennsylvania Press, 1969, pp. 61–8.

52. The UK delegate Peter Kirk, speaking to the Assembly on 18 December 1958, stated, 'Of course, this is a political Assembly. Its main task may be to discuss defence, but the fact remains that it is also an Assembly of politicians representing seven nations. We are politicians and that is why we are here and we must be able to discuss politics'. WEU Assembly, *Proceedings,* vol. 4, (Session 4, Part 2), 'Minutes and official report of debates', December 1958, p. 142.

53. See summary of 1st Part of the 5th Session in *International Organization,* vol. 13, no. 4, autumn 1959, pp. 663–4, and the report on which the discussion was based, WEU Assembly, rapporteur Mr Michaud, *Activities of Western European Union in Political Questions,* doc. 36, 20 May 1959 (Resolution 36).

54. Summary of 2nd Part of the 5th Session, *International Organization,* vol. 14, no. 2, spring 1960, p. 363.

55. WEU Assembly, rapporteur Mr Michaud, *Policy of Member States of Western European Union,* doc. 148, 13 November 1959 (Resolution 38).

56. 'Memorandum of Conversation', London, 8 December 1959, *1958–1960. Western European Integration and Security, Canada (1958–1960),* vol. 7, part 1, doc. 81, pp. 175–85, here p. 179. It was assumed that, once the EEC was 'permanently on the road', the US could 'apply more pressure' to get them to adopt 'outward looking policies' and could 'press for a more liberal trade policy without jeopardising the Community and our political objective' (p. 179).

57. Kaiser, *Using Europe, Abusing the Europeans,* p. 101. Also see Gowland and Turner, *Reluctant Europeans,* pp. 113–16.

58. 'Memo of Conversation', London, 8 December 1959, p. 177.

59. Gowland and Turner, *Reluctant Europeans,* pp. 114–15.

60. J. Major, 'President Kennedy's "Grand Design": the United States and a united Europe', *The World Today,* vol. 18, no. 9, September 1962, p. 387.

61. See a condensed version of Profumo's address to the WEU Assembly in 'Determined to draw closer to Europe', *European-Atlantic Review,* winter 1959–60, p. 5, and see WEU Assembly, *Proceedings,* vol. 4, (Session 5, Part 2), 'Minutes and official report of debates', December 1959, pp. 60–1.

62. See P. Kirk, 'Keystone of European unity', *European-Atlantic Review,* winter 1959–60, p. 4.

63. The OEEC was to become the Organization for Economic Cooperation and Development (OECD) with the inclusion of the US and Canada in 1960.

64. Kirk, 'Keystone of European unity', p. 5.

65. The Conte Report of the GAC had recommended UK membership in Euratom, although this was rejected by the Six who sought a more cohesive Europe. See WEU Assembly, rapporteur Mr Conte, *Policy of Western Europe—The Varying Fortunes of the Building of Europe,* doc. 168, 30 May 1960 (Recommendation 48).

66. WEU Assembly, rapporteur Mr Molter, *The Policy of Member States of Western European Union,* doc. 184, 17 November 1960.

67. Borcier, *The Political Role of the Assembly of WEU,* p. 35.

68. For Macmillan's rationale see A. Sampson, *Macmillan: A Study in Ambiguity,* London: Penguin, 1967, p. 207.

69. See J. Tratt, *The Macmillan Government and Europe: A Study in the Process of Policy Development,* Basingstoke: Macmillan, 1996, pp. 107–8, for export figures and for broader discussion of the factors informing the UK policy-making process regarding the accession issue.

70. Ashton argues that Macmillan's failure to persuade US President Dwight D. Eisenhower to take a more conciliatory line with the Soviet leader Nikita Khrushchev over the U2 spy plane incident at the Paris Summit of May 1960 exposed British impotence and the limitations of the Anglo-American relationship in facilitating British interests. See discussion in N. J. Ashton, *Kennedy, Macmillan and the Cold War: The Irony of Interdependence*, Basingstoke: Palgrave Macmillan, 2002, pp. 131–3.
71. The UK Government's formal application to the EEC for membership was made on 9 August 1961.
72. Salter, 'Western European Union', p. 39.
73. WEU Assembly, rapporteur Mr Leynen, *Progress in Negotiations for the Entry of the United Kingdom in to the European Economic Community*, doc. 219, 11 December 1961 (Recommendation 71). See also docs. 235, 3 May 1962, and 252, 2 December 1963, on *Progress in Negotiations...*
74. See for example the WEU Assembly, rapporteur Mr Mathew, *The Policy of Member States of Western European Union—Implementation of Recommendation 53: Examination of Arrangements Necessary for the Accession of the United Kingdom to the European Economic Community*, doc. 200, 29 April 1961; the Mathew Report of November 1962 (doc. 249) considered the legal implications for the British Constitution of EEC accession, and in the same month, M. Albert Sorel (France) reported on the consequences of British accession for Community institutions (doc. 248).
75. See WEU Assembly, rapporteur Mr Confalonieri, *The Future Pattern of Europe*, doc. 228, 4 April 1962. Borcier suggests that the 'psychological contribution' of the WEU Assembly in preparing the way for British application for accession to the Communities during this period 'is impossible to overemphasise'. Borcier, *The Political Role of the Assembly of WEU*, p. 32.
76. This Article (2) had been added to the original draft on the insistence of Adenauer amongst others. See S. Duke, *The Elusive Quest for European Security*, London: Macmillan, 2000, p. 47.
77. See *The Financial Times*, 15 March 1962, which has the two drafts side by side.
78. See reference to de Gaulle's 15 May press conference in C. Johnson, 'De Gaulle's Europe', *Journal of Common Market Studies*, vol. 1, no. 2, 1962, p. 162.
79. *European Political Union. Text of a Statement by the Lord Privy Seal, the Right Honourable Edward Heath, MBE, MP, to the Ministerial Council of Western European Union in London on April 10, 1962*, Cmd. 1720, London: HMSO, May 1962.
80. The Dutch, most resistant to de Gaulle's plans for an intergovernmental political union, recognized that their 'tactical' insistence on UK membership would ensure French abandonment of the project rather than the dilution that British membership might ensure. See discussion in J. Vanke, 'An impossible union: Dutch objections to the Fouchet Plan, 1959–62', *Cold War History*, vol. 2, no. 1, October 2001, pp. 95–112.
81. The Luxembourg compromise of 1966 was to disabuse federalists of any potential for enhanced integration under de Gaulle. See note 180.
82. Curtis notes the relative ineffectuality of the WEU Council as a contributor to the solution of the accession issue. *West European Integration,* p. 105.
83. See for example WEU Assembly, rapporteurs F. J. Goedhart and R. Cardona, *The Future Organisation of Western Defence*, doc. 231, 3 May 1962.
84. *European Political Union.* Cmd. 1720, May 1962.
85. Duke, *The Elusive Quest for European Security*, pp. 48–9.
86. From 1958, the WEU Council regularly discussed classified information with the Assembly's committees and provided special briefings for interested

members at the behest of the Assembly (and notably against a NATO ruling). However, it was noted in 1972 that the WEU Council 'has retained a general consultative function at quarterly ministerial meetings but these meetings have practically never been used for consultation about defence'. B. Burrows and C. Irwin, *The Security of Western Europe*, London: Charles Knight, 1972, p. 122.

87. See Protocols II and III of the MBT, especially Protocol III, Annex 1, 'Declaration by the Federal Chancellor'.

88. See Protocol II, Article VI of the MBT.

89. See 'Western European Chiefs of Mission Conference, Paris, 6–8 May 1957: Summary of Conclusions and Recommendations', *FRUS 1955–1957, Western European Security and Integration*, vol. 4, doc. 251, pp. 600–7 (here p. 602). Also see G. Crowther, 'Reconstruction of an alliance', *Foreign Affairs*, vol. 35, no. 2, January 1957, pp. 180–1.

90. P. Borcier, *Eight Years Work for European Defence: A Political Survey*, Paris: WEU Assembly, p. 16. See WEU Assembly, rapporteur J. J. Fens, *Explanatory Memo to Recommendation 5*, doc. 28, 3 October 1956 and *Explanatory Memo to Recommendation 8*, doc. 38, 27 March 1957.

91. The Assembly position was restated many times; See Recommendation 21, 12 October 1957; Recommendation 23, 4 July 1958; and Recommendation 35, 17 June 1959.

92. *Hansard* reference cited in A. Grosser, *The Western Alliance: European-American Relations since 1945*, London: Macmillan, 1980, p. 170. Also see Sampson, *Macmillan*, p. 104.

93. J. Turner, *Macmillan*, London: Longman, 1994, p. 133.

94. See I. Clark, *Nuclear Diplomacy and the Special Relationship: Britain's Deterrent and America 1957–66*, Oxford: Clarendon Press, 1994, pp. 8–17.

95. J. Ellison, *Threatening Europe: Britain and the Creation of the European Community, 1955–58*, London: Macmillan, 2000, p. 167.

96. 'Memorandum of Conversation', Paris, 11 December 1956, *FRUS 1955–1957.Western European Security and Integration*, vol. 4, doc. 44, p. 123.

97. See *The New York Times*, 27 July 1956; *Le Monde*, 22 July 1956, for comment.

98. TNA: CAB 128/31: CC(57), 13th Cabinet Conclusions, 22 February 1957.

99. See comment on the NAC survey of the technical and strategic implications of this conversion in WEU Assembly, *Report of the Debates* (Session 3, Part 1), May 1957, doc. 51, pp. 114–16.

100. *Defence: Outline of Future Policy*, Cmd. 124, London: HMSO, April 1957. The White Paper also abolished conscription without notifying the Council.

101. WEU Assembly, *Second Report of the Council to the Assembly of WEU*, doc. 37 and, for discussion see WEU Assembly, *Proceedings*, vol. I, (Session 3, Part 1), 6 May 1957, pp. 84 and 90–7.

102. See WEU Assembly, *Third Report of the Council to the WEU Assembly*, doc. 79, February 1958, p. 15.

103. See Palmer and Lambert, *European Unity*, p. 326; Grosser, *The Western Alliance*, p. 447.

104. M. Harrison, *The Reluctant Ally: France and the Atlantic Alliance*, London: John Hopkins University Press, 1981, pp. 39–40; R. Challener, 'Dulles and De Gaulle', in R. O. Paxton and N. Wahl (eds) *De Gaulle and the United States*, Oxford: Berg, 1994, pp. 148–51.

105. Vaisse, 'Post-Suez France', p. 338.

106. As Stikker points out, 'it should not be overlooked that it is this same treaty which controls German armament, and under which Germany renounced the production of atomic, biological and chemical weapons in Germany'. 'France and its diminishing will to co-operate', *Atlantic Community Quarterly*, vol. 3, no. 2, summer 1965, p. 198.

107. See *Documents Diplomatiques Français 1957,* Paris: Imprimerie Nationale, 1991, pp. 717–18 and 762–3, for FIG agreements, signed 20 and 27 November 1957.
108. See G. A. Craig, 'Germany and NATO: the rearmament debates, 1950–1958', in K. Knorr (ed.) *NATO and American Security,* Princeton: Princeton University Press, 1959, pp. 236–59, for discussion.
109. 'Programme for the Four-Power negotiations on German reunification', *Europa Archiv,* June 1955, pp. 7932–6.
110. See E. Hinterhoff, E. *Disengagement,* London: Stevens and Sons, 1959, for complete texts of the Eden and Rapacki plans. For discussion of the disengagement debate in the late 1950s, see G. F. Kennan, *Russia, the Atom, and the West,* New York: Harper, 1957, and 'Disengagement revisited', *Foreign Affairs,* vol. 37, no. 2, January 1959, pp. 187–210; G. Williams, *The Permanent Alliance: The European American Partnership, 1945–1984,* Leyden: A.W. Sijthoff, 1977, p. 39.
111. Craig, 'Germany and NATO', p. 240.
112. R. Morgan, *The United States and Western Germany: 1945–1975,* Oxford: Oxford University Press, 1975, p. 90. The construction of the Berlin Wall in 1961, substantiating the division of Germany, was to further demonstrate Western impotence.
113. See Curtis, *West European Integration,* p. 107, for discussion.
114. W. La Feber, *America, Russia and the Cold War,* New York: John Wiley and Sons, 1976, p. 206; L. S. Kaplan, 'Adenauer's Germany: uneasy partnership', *International Organization,* vol. 15, no. 4, autumn 1961, pp. 618–29.
115. W. F. Hanreider, *West German Foreign Policy 1949–1963: International Pressure and Domestic Response,* Stanford: Stanford University Press, 1967, p. 153.
116. See statement by the French General Chassin, reported in *The Times,* 24 September 1957.
117. TNA: FO 371/135577, Foreign Office to Bonn, Tel. no. 106 saving, 12 February 1958, p. 1.
118. B. Heuser, *NATO, Britain, France and the FRG: Nuclear Strategies and Forces for Europe, 1949–2000,* Basingstoke: Macmillan, 1997, p. 150.
119. E. B. Haas and P. H. Merkl, 'Parliamentarians against ministers: the case of the Western European Union', *International Organization,* vol. 14, no. 1, winter 1960, p. 47.
120. Grosser, 'Suez, Hungary and European integration', p. 477.
121. For workings of the ACA see WEU Assembly, *Third Report of the Council to the WEU Assembly,* doc. 79, pp. 18–22. For a full report of the activities and structure of the ACA during this period see G. Cantu, *The Agency for the Control of Armaments of the Western European Union,* Paris: WEU, 1973.
122. Its Defence Committee report by Mr Georges Housiaux led to intensive discussions in 1962, 1963 and 1964 in the WEU Assembly.
123. 'Memorandum of Discussion at the 390th Meeting of the NSC, 11 December 1958', *FRUS 1958–1960, Western European Integration and Security, Canada,* vol. 7, part 1, doc. 163, pp. 366–9.
124. Originally called FINBEL, reflecting the membership of France, Italy and the Benelux states, this loose organization, led by the Army Chiefs of Staff Committee, expanded to include West Germany in 1956, the UK in 1973 and later Spain (1990) and Greece and Portugal (1996), adopting the name FINABEL as it grew. Its original objective of achieving co-ordination in armaments was gradually expanded to include conceptual study on issues such as the harmonization of doctrine, interoperability and co-operation between land forces.
125. See Third Report of the Council to the Assembly, Assembly doc. 79, February 1958, p. 23.

126. See text of Communiqué from NATO Heads of Government meeting, Paris, *Department of State Bulletin*, 6 January 1958.
127. TNA: DEFE 13/339, 21 March 1958.
128. TNA: DEFE 10/378: ADSC(58), Meeting 1, 13 February 1958, p. 5.
129. Heuser, *NATO, Britain, France and the FRG*, p. 157.
130. See 'Editorial note', *FRUS 1958–1960. Western European Integration and Security, Canada*, vol. 7, part 1, doc. 131, pp. 314–15, and doc. 133, 'Memorandum from the Assistant Secretary of State for European Affairs (Elbrick) to Secretary of State Dulles, 24 April 1958', pp. 317–19.
131. TNA: DEFE 13/339: Annex A, European Arms Cooperation: Proposals approved by the NAC, 17 April 1958.
132. For discussion of British attitudes to FIG and WEU co-operation see S. N. M. O'Driscoll, *British Policy towards the French Military Nuclear Programme, 1954–60*, unpublished PhD thesis, Wolfson College, Cambridge, 1996, pp. 167–222.
133. TNA: PREM 11/3721, Sandys to Macmillan, 24 March 1958.
134. US official policy with regards to what were seen as fundamental French interests in Algeria was perceived by the French as 'distinctly unsupportive and even downright hostile'. M. S. Alexander and J. F. V. Keiger, 'France and the Algerian War: strategy, operations and diplomacy', in M. S. Alexander and J. F. V. Keiger (eds) *France and the Algerian War 1954–62*, London: Frank Cass, 2002, p. 20.
135. G. L. and A. L. Williams, *Crisis in European Defence: The Next Ten Years*, London: C. Knight, 1974, p. 11. NATO did not formally adopt flexible response until 1967, after French withdrawal from the integrated command.
136. Morgan, *The United States and Western Germany*, p. 67.
137. See W. L. Kohl, *French Nuclear Policy*, Princeton: Princeton University Press, 1971, p. 72.
138. I. M. Wall, 'De Gaulle and the Anglo-Saxons', in Alexander and Keiger, *France and the Algerian War*, p. 129.
139. 'Telegram from Secretary of State Dulles to the Department of State, Paris, 17 December 1958', *FRUS 1958–1960. Western European Integration and Security, Canada*, vol. 7, part 1, doc. 177, p. 399. Also see *FRUS 1958–1960. Western European Integration and Security, Canada*, vol. 7, part 2, docs. 81 and 83, for de Gaulle's calls for change in NATO.
140. 'Telegram from the Mission at the NATO and European Regional Organisations to the Department of State, Paris, 6 March 1959', *FRUS, 1958–1960. Western European Integration and Security, Canada*, vol. 7, part 1, doc. 196, pp. 420–1.
141. F. W. Mulley, 'A European nuclear deterrent?' from the Report on the State of European Security to the Fifth Session of the Assembly of the WEU, November 1959, in *Survival*, vol. 2, no. 1, January–February 1960, pp. 34–6.
142. Mulley, 'A European nuclear deterrent?', p. 36. The report did not envisage joint nuclear production or the sharing of atomic secrets.
143. The proposals envisaged that the UK would put at least some of her nuclear warheads and V bombers under the joint decision-making power of the seven WEU member states, thus ending any special UK relationship with the US and her pretence at being a 'superpower'. F. W. Mulley, *The Politics of Western Defence*, New York: Praeger, 1962, p. 88.
144. The WEU Assembly continued to articulate European anxieties about nuclear proliferation and the desire within Europe for a nuclear capacity to satisfy legitimate concerns. See Assembly Recommendation 57, adopted 2 December 1960, and Recommendation 69, adopted 13 December 1961. See B. T. Moore, *NATO and the Future of Europe*, New York: Harper, 1958, pp. 207–9.

145. There had been some enthusiasm expressed in the French Government for a European nuclear option in 1962, if a European political authority could be established. The failure of the first Fouchet plan was to undermine this idea, which in any case had no support from de Gaulle. Heuser, *NATO, Britain, France and the FRG*, p. 152.

146. R. E. Osgood, *NATO: The Entangling Alliance*, Chicago: University of Chicago Press, 1962, p. 289.

147. Baylis notes that London and Washington had very differing interpretations of the nature of the commitments within the Skybolt agreements reached at Camp David, Macmillan arguing that the supply of Polaris had been implied in the event of Skybolt cancellation. This ambiguity was to lead to considerable 'souring of relations' following Skybolt cancellation. J. Baylis, *Ambiguity and Deterrence: British Nuclear Strategy, 1945–1964*, Oxford: Clarendon Press, 1995, pp. 290–1.

148. The sale of US Hawk missiles to Israel in August 1962, despite earlier agreement with the British that neither should contribute to a Middle East arms race by the offer of their indigenous systems, had left Macmillan with an 'enduring taste of bitterness' and provided the context for the Skybolt crisis of confidence in US reliability. Ashton, *Kennedy, Macmillan and the Cold War*, pp. 161–4.

149. Mulley, *The Politics of Western Defence*, p. 89.

150. Dougherty, 'European deterrence and Atlantic unity', p. 412.

151. For discussion of the MLF see A. L. Burns, 'NATO and nuclear sharing', in Knorr (ed.) *NATO and American Security*, pp. 151–75; H. A. Kissinger, 'The unsolved problems of European defense', *Foreign Affairs*, vol. 40, no. 4, July 1962, pp. 531–9.

152. E. Goodman, *The Fate of the Atlantic Community*, New York: Praeger, 1975, p. 417.

153. For discussion see E. V. Rostow, 'Fission or fusion', *Survival*, vol. 5, no. 4, July–August 1963, pp. 166–71.

154. For Kennedy's Grand Design ideas see his 4 July 1962 'Declaration of Interdependence', *Department of State Bulletin*, vol. 55, no. 1426, 23 July 1962, p. 132.

155. For a useful contemporaneous discussion see J. Kraft, *The Grand Design*, New York: Harper, 1962.

156. See H. A. Kissinger, *The Troubled Partnership*, New York: McGraw-Hill, 1965, p. 4; S. Vanhoonacker, *The Bush Administration (1989–1993) and the Development of a European Security Identity*, Aldershot: Ashgate, 2001, p. 71.

157. Agreement had been reached in 1961 with the West German Government to offset the costs of US military deployments in the FRG through that Government's purchase of US military equipment, an agreement that persisted until 1975.

158. See J. L. Heldring, 'Atlantic partnership: European unity', *Survival*, vol. 7, no. 1, January–February 1965, p. 36.

159. J. Richardson, 'The concept of Atlantic Community', *Journal of Common Market Studies*, vol. 3, no. 1, 1964–5, p. 1.

160. Pfaltzgraff, *Britain Faces Europe*, p. 331. Mahan argues that the lack of a coherent policy approach by the Kennedy Administration was due in large part to the 'president's blurred ideas about security, European integration, tendency towards economic simplicity, and his overriding Cold War fears'. See E. R. Mahan, *Kennedy, De Gaulle and Western Europe*, Basingstoke: Palgrave Macmillan, 2002, p. 168.

161. The language of Atlantic community and partnership emerging from the US in the 1960s attracted some powerful critique from those who highlighted

the distinction between the European and US community concept. See, for example, S. Hoffmann, 'Discord in community: the North Atlantic Area as a partial integration system', in F. O. Wilcox and H. Field Haviland (eds) *The Atlantic Community, Progress, and Prospects,* New York: Praeger, 1963; J. Richardson, 'The concept of Atlantic Community', *Journal of Common Market Studies,* vol. 3, no. 1, March 1964, pp. 1–22.

162. The Paris Declaration of the Atlantic Convention of NATO Nations, 19 January 1962, had proposed 'the creation of a true Atlantic Community' which 'must extend to the political, military, economic, moral and cultural fields', including suggestions for the development of NATO's Parliamentary Conference into a Consultative Assembly to 'review the work of all Atlantic Institutions'. See C. A. Herter, *Toward an Atlantic Community,* New York: Harper and Row, 1963. The North Atlantic Assembly, a less ambitious body replacing NATO's Parliamentary Conference, was formed in 1966 as a non-treaty-based organization, unlike the WEU Assembly.

163. See A. Buchan, 'A British view', *Survival,* vol. 4, no. 1, January–February 1962, p. 12; A. Buchan, 'The reform of NATO', *Foreign Affairs,* vol. 40, no. 2, January 1962, p. 180; K. Birrenbach, 'The reorganization of NATO', *Orbis,* vol. 6, no. 2, summer 1992, p. 246.

164. A. Wohlstetter, 'Nuclear sharing: NATO and the N+1 country', *Foreign Affairs,* vol. 39, no. 3, April 1961, p. 356.

165. Birrenbach, 'The reorganization of NATO', p. 251.

166. See *Polaris Sales Agreement,* Cmd. 1995, London: HMSO, 1963.

167. Indeed, the pre-Nassau Assembly's Recommendation 83, 4 December 1962, calls for a NATO, rather than European, deterrence force. See Salter, 'Western European Union', p. 43.

168. Richardson, 'The concept of Atlantic Community', p. 9. Also see A. Buchan and P. Windsor, *Arms and Stability in Europe,* London: Chatto & Windus for the Institute for Strategic Studies, 1963, for a discussion of the implications of a joint European deterrent.

169. R. R. Bowie, 'Tensions within the Alliance', *Survival,* vol. 6, no. 1, January–February 1964, p. 29.

170. L. Freedman and J. Gearson, 'Interdependence and independence: Nassau and the British nuclear deterrent', in K. Burk and M. Stokes (eds) *The United States and the European Alliance since 1945,* Oxford: Berg, 1999, p. 197.

171. De Gaulle had proposed during discussions in Rambouillet on 14–16 December, in advance of Prime Minister Macmillan's Nassau meeting with Kennedy, that the British might cooperate with France in developing a Skybolt replacement. F. Costigliola, 'Kennedy, De Gaulle, and the challenge of consultation', in Paxton and Wahl (eds) *De Gaulle and the United States,* p. 185.

172. See Hoffmann, 'Discord in community', p. 541.

173. J. Lacouture, *De Gaulle: The Ruler 1945–1970,* London: Harper Collins, 1992, p. 376.

174. President de Gaulle, press conference, 14 January 1963, reported in 'President de Gaulle's views', *Survival,* vol. 5, no. 2, March–April 1963, pp. 58–62. See E. U. Fromm, 'President de Gaulle's vision of Europe', *Atlantic Communities Quarterly,* vol. 4, no. 2, summer 1966, pp. 224–8.

175. See discussion in G. Warner, 'Why the general said no', *International Affairs,* vol. 78, no. 4, October 2002, pp. 869–82.

176. L. Hartley, 'Atlantic partnership—how?', *Orbis,* vol. 8, no. 1, March 1964, p. 145.

177. Ministry of Foreign Affairs and External Trade, 'Western European Union: history and opinions', *Memo from Belgium,* no. 109–10, February–March 1969, p. 12.

178. See N. P. Ludlow, *Dealing with Britain: The Six and the First UK Application to the EEC,* Cambridge: Cambridge University Press, 1997, p. 227.
179. Heath cited in Salter, 'Western European Union', p. 44.
180. Salter, 'Western European Union', p. 44.
181. Ministry of Foreign Affairs and External Trade, 'Western European Union', p. 15.
182. F. K. von Plehwe, 'WEU's part in European cooperation', *Aussenpolitik,* vol. 21, no. 2, 1970, p. 152.
183. De Gaulle's withdrawal of the French Permanent Representative to the EEC over proposals to enhance Commission and parliamentary controls resulted in the EEC 'empty chair' crisis in March 1965, and the resultant Luxembourg Compromise of 29 January 1966, which was to acknowledge member states' right to veto legislative proposals when 'important' national interest' were at stake. See D. Dinan, *Europe Recast: A History of European Union,* Basingstoke: Palgrave Macmillan, 2004, pp. 104–8; Moravcsik, *The Choice for Europe,* pp. 193–6.
184. For a discussion of national concerns see J. D. Lodge, 'Can NATO be restored?', *Orbis,* vol. 10, no. 3, fall 1966, pp. 729–30.
185. Fromm, 'President de Gaulle's vision of Europe', p. 226. That De Gaulle agreed to the renewal of the Washington Treaty in 1969 suggests that his interest was in reform rather than dissolution. F. O. Miksche, 'Western Europe: security through integration, *Orbis,* vol. 13, no. 1, March 1969, pp. 162–3.
186. See Senator Frank Church (Democrat), speech to the National War College, Washington, 'Reappraising American policy', *Survival,* vol. 5, no. 5, September–October 1963, pp. 234–5. Agricultural issues were the topic of the 1963/7 Kennedy Round of GATT negotiations. See H. Smith, *European Union Foreign Policy: What it is and What it Does,* London: Pluto Press, 2002, pp. 59–60.
187. L. Norstad, 'European unification and Atlantic unity', *Atlantic Community Quarterly,* vol. 2, no. 2, summer 1964, pp. 186–9.
188. Heldring, 'Atlantic partnership: European unity', p. 33.
189. Given that 'The price of a spanner in the machinery of Atlantic cooperation is, most definitely, too high a price to pay' for European unity, van der Beugel was to suggest that at 'the present moment the cause of Western cooperation is probably best served by stagnation in the process of political unification of Europe, at least the Europe of the Six'. E. H. van der Beugel, 'The clash in Europe', *Atlantic Community Quarterly,* vol. 3, no. 1, pp. 30 and 32.
190. Heldring, 'Atlantic partnership: European unity', p. 36.
191. Hartley, 'Atlantic partnership—how?', p. 151.
192. Williams and Williams, *Crisis in European Defence,* p. 3.
193. For de Gaulle, the Test Ban Treaty was a superpower attempt to establish a nuclear monopoly and 'squeeze' out French developments. S. Sloan, *NATO, the European Union, and the Atlantic Community: The Transatlantic Bargain Challenged,* Oxford: Rowman and Littlefield, 2005, p. 44. The WEU Assembly welcomed any moves towards non-proliferation but regretted the lack of consultation in NATO or with the WEU, 'the absence of which represented a serious threat to the cohesion of the Alliance'. Recommendation 96, adopted 4 December 1963.
194. Church, 'Reappraising American policy', p. 234.
195. V. Calvocoressi, 'The evolution of Europe', *Survival,* vol. 5, no. 5, September–October 1963, p. 199.
196. See A. Spinelli, 'Atlantic pact or European unity', *Foreign Affairs,* vol. 40, no. 4, April 1962, p. 545, who argues that *pax Americana,* whilst a necessary condition of the early post-war order, was serving to obstruct European unity, which 'failed to prosper wherever the ground was covered with Atlantic vegetation'.

197. Kissinger, *The Troubled Partnership*, pp. 4–5. Henry Kissinger, at this time a Harvard academic and political consultant to a range of government agencies in the US, was to be highly influential in US foreign policy, becoming President Nixon's National Security Advisor in 1969 and Secretary of State in 1973, appointments he was to retain under Nixon's successor, President Gerald Ford.

198. Kissinger, *The Troubled Partnership*, p. 6.

199. Although the Franco-German Treaty had been a long-planned arrangement. Lacouture, *De Gaulle: The Ruler 1945–1970*, p. 376.

200. The treaty provided for, amongst other things, regular meetings of Heads of Government and Foreign Ministers, the harmonization of military doctrine, combined operational research and joint arms projects. See Franco-German Treaty, *Documents on Germany 1944–85*, US Department of State Publications, 9446, Office of the Historian, Bureau of Public Affairs, p. 834.

201. Aron notes that, whilst the EDC had been seen by the French as 'The European Army (that) destroys the French Army and rebuilds the German Army' and 'an expression of American will', de Gaulle's signature of the Elysée Treaty had the support of 61% of the French, with only 10% against. R. Aron, 'Old nations, new Europe', *Dædalus*, vol. 93, no. 4, winter 1964, p. 47.

202. F. Bozo, *Two Strategies for Europe: De Gaulle, the United States, and the Atlantic Alliance*, trans. S. Emanuel, Lanham, MD: Rowman and Littlefield, 2001, p. 133.

203. Bozo, *Two Strategies for Europe*, pp. 46–7 and 129–35.

204. Stikker, 'France and its diminishing will to co-operate', p. 197. See C. De Gaulle, press conference at the Elysee Palace, 29 July 1963, *Survival*, vol. 5, no. 5, September–October 1963, p. 238.

205. 'Reflections on the quarter', *Orbis*, vol. 10, no. 1, spring 1966, pp. 3–6. See DQAC Report to the WEU Assembly, rapporteur D. Sandys, *State of European Security: France and NATO*, doc. 375, 11 June 1966.

206. D. Acheson, 'One of our firemen is resigning', *Atlantic Community Quarterly*, vol. 4, no. 2, summer 1966, p. 163; L. Norstad, 'Defending Europe without France', *Atlantic Communities Quarterly*, vol. 4, no. 2, summer 1966, p. 179.

207. 'A cynic might point out that the British deterrent exists but is not independent, while the French deterrent is independent, but does not exist'. C. Johnson, 'France's deterrent', *Survival*, vol. 5, no. 2, March–April 1963, p. 60.

208. EU Assembly, *State of European Security: A NATO Nuclear Force*, doc. 251, 16 October 1962; see also WEU Assembly, *State of European Security* reports: *The NATO Nuclear Force after the Nassau Agreement*, doc. 268, 26 April 1963; *The NATO Nuclear Force*, doc. 290, 30 October 1963 (Recommendation 98); *Aspects of Western Strategy*, doc. 320, 20 October 1964 (Recommendation 110).

209. Mahan, *Kennedy, De Gaulle and Western Europe*, pp. 148–58.

210. See L. Lauris, 'Defending Europe without France', interview in *Atlantic Community Quarterly*, vol. 4, no. 2, summer 1966, p. 184; Lodge, 'Can NATO be restored?', p. 724.

211. Heuser, *NATO, Britain, France and the FRG*, p. 158.

212. G. Aybet, *The Dynamics of European Security Co-operation 1945–1991*, London: Macmillan, 1997, pp. 118–19.

213. See *Statement on the Defence Estimates 1967*, Cmd. 3203, London: HMSO, February 1967; this refocusing of military commitments was to continue over the two successive White Papers of 1968 and 1969.

214. The average annual growth in real gross domestic product of EEC members between 1961 and 1967 significantly outstripped that of the UK, with France and West German growth at 5.6% and 4.4% respectively, whilst the UK average

stood at 2.9% in the same period. P. J. N. Sinclair and I. M. Zarzosa, 'Transfers, trade, food and growth: Britain and the European Union over 40 years', in R. Broad and V. Preston (eds) *Moored to the Continent? Britain and European Integration*, London: Institute of Historical Research, 2001, p. 151.

215. For a broader discussion of the motivations behind the Wilson Government's application for EEC membership see A. May, *Britain and Europe since 1945*, London: Longman, 1999, pp. 42–5.

216. See W. Kaiser, 'Party games: The British EEC applications of 1961 and 1967', in Broad and Preston (eds) *Moored to the Continent?*, pp. 68–71; P. Catterall, 'Conclusion: the ironies of successful failure', in O. J. Daddow (ed.) *Harold Wilson and European Integration: Britain's Second Application to Join the EEC*, London: Frank Cass, 2003, pp. 243–52.

217. See WEU Assembly, rapporteur Mr van der Stoel, *Political Organisations of European Defence*, doc. 481, 16 June 1969.

218. The French boycott was at both the Ministerial and Permanent levels, although they did continue to meet and co-operate with the agencies in Paris, that is, the ACA, Secretariat of the SAC, and the Assembly. Von Plehwe, 'WEU's part in European cooperation', p. 150.

219. 'Press Commentary' by French Foreign Ministry, 14 February 1969, cited in E. Barker, *Britain in a Divided Europe: 1945–1970*, London: Weidenfeld and Nicolson, 1971, p. 233.

220. Etienne de la Vallee Pussin, 'England kept waiting on the doorstep of the European Communities', in Ministry of Foreign Affairs and External Trade, 'Western European Union', p. 44.

221. WEU Assembly, *Motion to Disagree with the Content of the Annual Report of the Council*, doc. 413, 14 June 1967.

222. V. Confalonieri, 'The building of Europe must take priority', 14th Session of the WEU Assembly, October 1968, in *Memo from Belgium*, 1969, pp. 21–3.

223. Burrows and Irwin, *The Security of Western Europe*, p. 43. Borcier noted that despite some damning newspaper comment about the worthiness of the Assembly, nowhere else could reports be found providing 'such a wealth of data, of comparative figures, conveying with equal clarity the present extent of Western European defence efforts'. Borcier, *Eight Years Work for European Defence*, p. 11.

224. Palmer and Lambert, *European Unity*, p. 340, note the importance of the Assembly in promoting discussion on political union after the failure of Fouchet, and Gordon notes that the Assembly 'could not avoid becoming an educator of national parliamentary opinion'. Gordon, 'The WEU and European defence cooperation', p. 252.

225. Foreign Minister Joseph Luns cited in *Memo from Belgium*, p. 16.

226. See H. Wallich, 'The United States and the European Economic Community: a problem of adjustment', *International Organization*, vol. 22, no. 4, autumn 1968, pp. 841–54.

227. Brandt vigorously pursued this policy, initiated in 1966, after becoming Chancellor in 1969; in recognizing the status of East European states as a precondition of engagement, this represented a significant shift from the Hallstein Doctrine of non-recognition rigidly adhered to by Adenauer. See E. J. Kirchner and J. Sperling (eds) *The Federal Republic of Germany and NATO: Forty Years After*, Basingstoke: Macmillan, 1992, pp. 7–8.

228. MBFR talks were not to begin until 1973 due to Soviet resistance. Sloan, *NATO, the European Union, and the Atlantic Community*, p. 49.

229. See L. Hartley, 'The Atlantic Alliance: institutional developments for the 1970s', *Orbis*, vol. 13, no. 1, March 1969, pp. 299–311.

230. Williams and Williams, *Crisis in European Defence*, p. 26.

231. Nixon's New Economic Policy, announced on 15 August 1971, included the suspension of gold-to-dollar convertibility, spelling the effective end of the Bretton Woods system, and the imposition of a surcharge on imports not already restricted by quota. See B. J. Cohen, 'The revolution in Atlantic economic relations: a bargain comes unstuck', in W. Hanreider (ed.) *The United States and Western Europe,* Maas: Winthrop, 1974, pp. 106–33.

232. Cited in Duke, *The Elusive Quest for European Security,* p. 56.

233. F. O. Miksche, 'Western Europe: security through integration, *Orbis,* vol. 13, no. 1, March 1969, p. 166.

234. Borcier, *Eight Years Work for European Defence,* p. 27.

235. The NATO Armaments Committee was replaced in 1966 by the Council of National Armaments Directors (CNAD) to provide alliance-wide information on national projects.

236. Mulley, *The Politics of Western Defence,* p. 195.

237. Borcier, *The Assembly of Western European Union,* p. 49. In April 1967, for example, the Assembly established a Committee on Scientific, Technological and Aerospace Questions to promote a European policy for space and technological cooperation.

238. The Eurogroup excluded France, Portugal and Iceland. For a discussion of Eurogroup's formation and early development see C. Damm and P. Goodhart (rapporteurs), 'The Eurogroup: an experiment in European defence co-operation', Military Committee, North Atlantic Assembly, October 1972, P.147, MC(72)8.

239. The 1971 Mansfield resolution was to call for a 50% in-year withdrawal of US troops stationed in Europe if the allies proved unable to meet expected contributions, although this and subsequent resolutions were defeated on the grounds that unilateral withdrawal would threaten the ongoing MBFR process under 'negotiation' with the Soviets. See Williams and Williams, *Crisis in European Defence,* p. 273; M. Quinlan, *European Defence Cooperation: Asset or Threat to NATO?,* Washington, DC: Woodrow Wilson Center Press, 2001, pp. 6–7.

240. Burrows and Irwin, *The Security of Western Europe,* p. 53.

241. Goodman, *The Fate of the Atlantic Community,* p. 571.

242. Von Plehwe, 'WEU's part in European cooperation', p. 151.

243. The institutions of the three European Communities (EEC, Euratom and ECSC) had merged in 1967, although each community maintained an independent legal identity under its separate originating treaty.

244. For a pessimistic contemporaneous view of the possibilities of the Davignon proposals see C. Gordon, 'European defence: a return to Brussels?', *Foreign Service Journal,* vol. 48, no. 22, 1971, pp. 19–21 and 36–7.

245. Burrows and Irwin, *The Security of Western Europe,* p. 121.

246. Gordon, 'The WEU and European defence cooperation', p. 253.

247. WEU Assembly, rapporteur Mr Amhren, *Evolution of the European Institutions,* doc. 543, 14 June 1971 (Recommendation 204).

248. The WEU Assembly had also resisted calls for its absorption into the Atlantic Assembly as proposed, for example, by the 1966 de Freitas Charter, on the basis that the NATO Conference of Parliamentarians, which became the North Atlantic Assembly in 1967, did not have the official status of the WEU Assembly, even though frequently the same delegates dealt with the same issues in both. For discussion see C. Brumter, *The North Atlantic Assembly,* Dordretch: Martinus Nijhoff, 1986, pp. 28–9.

249. M. Destremau cited in F. K. von Plehwe, 'WEU and the European institutions', *Aussenpolitik,* vol. 22, no. 4, 1971, pp. 421–2.

250. See for example WEU Assembly, rapporteur Lord Gladwyn, *The Brussels Treaty and the European institutions: prospects for Western European Union,* doc. 554, 4 November 1971.

251. See the Amhren Report: WEU Assembly, *Evolution of the European Institutions*, doc. 543.
252. F. Duchene, 'The strategic consequences of the enlarged European Community', *Survival*, vol. 15, no. 1, January–February 1973, p. 2.
253. Williams and Williams, *Crisis in European Defence*, p. 253.
254. One commentator was to note, 'Observers in Paris believe that an EEC back-cloth would stand the best chance of strengthening defence contacts with France'. H. Stanhope, 'Spreading the butter over 27 years of peace in Europe', *The Times*, 23 August 1972.
255. Following a decision by the Council on 24 May 1972, meetings of WEU member state representatives in advance of meetings of the UN and other organizations had ceased, and the discussion within the Council had diminished. WEU Assembly, *Western European Union: Information Report*, 38th Ordinary Session (part 2), February 1993, p. 10.
256. Noel Salter, Deputy Secretary General of the WEU Assembly from July 1955 to March 1963, refers to the Assembly as a 'motor force', helping to 'push governments in the direction toward which their thoughts were already turning'. 'Western European Union', p. 38.
257. J. M. Hoscheit and P. Tsakaloyannis, 'Relaunching the Western European Union: an overview', in P. Tsakaloyannis (ed.) *The Reactivation of the WEU: The Effects on the European Community and its Institutions*, Maastricht: EIPA, 1985, p. 1.
258. Von Plehwe, 'WEU's part in European cooperation', p. 152.
259. Aybet, *The Dynamics of European Security Co-operation*, p. 120.
260. Haas and Merkl, 'Parliamentarians against ministers', p. 42.
261. Palmer and Lambert, *European Unity*, p. 346, describe this as the WEU's 'most useful function'.
262. Kirk provides an example of WEU's 'watchdog' role, citing the DQAC Fens Report of 1957, which analysed the details of the gaps in the integrated defence of Western Europe—evidence that SACEUR was glad to have aired. With regard to its 'testing' function he notes that proposals for raising the capacity limit of shipping permitted to Germany in order to secure the Baltic flank were first launched in the Assembly to identify the response, before being put forward to Ministers by the SACEUR. 'Keystone of European unity', p. 4.
263. Duke states that 'almost from the outset the WEU was viewed with suspicion. It was not the supranational foundation for European unity that the EDC could have been nor did it entirely escape federalist leanings'. Duke, *The Elusive Quest for European Security*, p. 39.
264. Salter suggested that had the UK 'come forward with bold political leadership, had she even honoured the political intention of the amended Brussels Treaty, Western European Union could have become the vehicle of future unity, which would then have included Great Britain'. 'Western European Union', p. 35.
265. Borcier concluded his 1963 study of the WEU Assembly by describing the WEU 'at ministerial level' in this way, whilst he considered its Assembly as 'equal to its ill-defined but noble mission in the service of Europe'. Borcier, *The Political Role of the Assembly of WEU*, conclusions.
266. 'The WEU conference hall has sometimes provided a point of departure for the resumption of negotiations that have reached deadlock elsewhere'. Von Plehwe, 'WEU's part in European cooperation', p. 152.
267. Burrows and Irwin, *The Security of Western Europe*, p. 126.

3 The Path to Revitalization
1973–89

Throughout the 1970s the WEU lay dormant at the Council level, but its Assembly stoically maintained an active role in the promotion of European discussion on defence issues. The evident lack of Ministerial interest in the institution during this period of 'somnolence' can largely be explained by the relative effectiveness of other organizations, notably NATO and the EC, in satisfying the interests of national players. These broad interests had been articulated within the dual aims of the Brussels Treaty, with collective defence and the promotion of European unity providing for both external and internal security. The satisfaction of collective defence interests had been ensured through the coupling of US capability to Europe within NATO, whilst European integration had taken place within the EC, providing for the low politics of internal security, most notably within the economic arena.

However, as satisfaction of national interests through the primary institutions declined during the 1970s, tensions mounted, at both the Atlantic and European levels, which threatened to undermine the basic security structure of Europe. The revitalization of the WEU—a 'first aid' institution designed to support the development of a broad range of security interests through the promotion of other, primary organizations—may be interpreted as a response to this perceived 'sickness' within the preferred organs. Indeed, the WEU's revitalization, which was to begin formally in 1984 following over 10 years of dormancy, must be understood in terms of this support function within the 'dual context of the process of European integration and developments in the Atlantic Alliance'.[1] This chapter analyses the transatlantic and European tensions that were to lead to this revitalization. The WEU's subsequent contribution to the satisficing of undermining concerns within the context of the ongoing development of the primary organizations is then examined through an exploration of its development and activity throughout the period of its revitalization, leading up to the final years of the Cold War.

TRANSATLANTIC TRAVAILS

Although many of the transatlantic tensions of the 1960s appeared to have been resolved by the early 1970s, significant pressures developed during the decade that called into question the nature of the relationship between the US and Western Europe. The 'shock' of French 'separation' from NATO in 1966 had contributed to the consolidation of US leadership as the allies sought stability through consensus.[2] Nevertheless, throughout the 1970s, general acceptance of dependence on the US by its European partners was at best fragile.[3] The first Nixon Administration had instituted a more 'confrontational' approach to the European NATO allies, insisting on increased burden-sharing and continuing the military manpower reductions in Europe that had begun under the Johnson Administration.[4] Fears of decoupling were exacerbated by US unilateral actions in the economic sphere, including the end of the Bretton Woods system following Nixon's suspension of dollar convertibility in August 1971 and the imposition of increased import taxes on European goods.[5]

US National Security Advisor Henry Kissinger's 'Year of Europe' speech of 23 April 1973 had called for an Atlantic Charter which was to reflect the linkage between defence and economics and was intended to reinforce US leadership at a time when a developing Europe was becoming a powerful economic, and potentially political, competitor.[6] In defining the European states as 'regional' powers, Kissinger's 'insensitive' unilateral proposals led to a worsening of transatlantic relations. Even the traditionally Atlanticist British, under the Conservative Government of the Europhile Edward Heath (1970–4), were 'not amused by this intervention', which the UK Prime Minister likened to his 'standing between the lions in Trafalgar Square and announcing that we were embarking on a year to save America!'[7] Compelled to assert their determination to establish themselves 'as a distinct and original entity', expressed in the EC's 'Declaration of Identity' in Copenhagen later that year, the EC member states sought to define Europe's distinctive place in the international system and reassert their commitment (at a time of enlargement) to the construction of a United Europe.[8] NATO's Ottawa Declaration of 19 June 1974 was intended to smooth relations, not least by recognizing the significance of French and British nuclear capabilities to the Alliance's deterrence posture. However, the OPEC (Organization of the Petroleum Exporting Countries) oil crisis, Arab-Israeli War and US-Soviet détente contributed to rising tensions within the Alliance throughout the early 1970s.[9] The French Foreign Minister Michel Jobert was the most articulate of those speaking 'for Europe'. Nevertheless, his proposals for the renewal of the WEU in 1973 had been rejected offhand by the other Europeans as the 'usual' French Anti-Americanism, and continued French efforts to arouse a unified European response met with general indifference from European states all too aware of their continuing defence dependency and unused to collective political action.[10]

Concerns regarding the competence and reliability of American leadership, both in the global environment dominated by rapidly changing superpower relations and, more directly, in US policies towards its European allies, continued to grow throughout the 1970s.[11] Washington's foreign policy failure in Vietnam, the Watergate scandal and setbacks in Angola, Ethiopia and Iran had led to a loss of self-confidence in Washington. During the Ford Administration (1974–7), agreement was reached on the Soviet-initiated Conference on Security and Co-operation in Europe (CSCE), a mechanism of the détente favoured by the Europeans. The Democratic US Administration that was to follow (1977–81) initially inspired very favourable transatlantic relations as President Jimmy Carter sought to adopt a human rights agenda in US foreign policy.[12] However, by the end of the 1970s the Cold War was once again dominating Washington's international agenda: the 1979 Soviet invasion of Afghanistan and the apparent failure of détente witnessed the beginnings of a US military build-up and a return to a more realist perspective on US international engagement.

FOREIGN POLICY DIVERGENCE

By the beginning of the 1980s, European concerns regarding the strategic, political and economic implications of US policy and rhetoric had begun to cast serious doubt on the continuing efficacy of the Atlantic Alliance structure.[13] It had become evident that, given the degree of European resurgence, particularly in the economic field, the Alliance was in serious need of an overhaul to reflect Europe's rising power.[14] Central to the developing crisis in Alliance relations was an evolving divergence in the American and European perceptions of threat. This became increasingly evident following the inauguration of President Ronald Reagan in January 1981, with his extreme Cold War rhetoric, rejection of détente and revitalization of containment.[15] A 'conscious reaction to the idealist internationalism' of the Carter approach, Reagan's 'realist internationalism' rejected the obstructive liberalism that, it was argued, had prevented a more effective realpolitik engagement with the Soviet bloc.[16] For Reagan, détente had failed to prevent Soviet aggression, as demonstrated by the invasion of Afghanistan in 1979 and the imposition of martial law in Poland in 1981. However, for the states of Western Europe détente had proven largely successful, reducing regional tensions and providing opportunities for increased trade. Reagan's tough-talking anti-communism may have won the hearts and minds of his people, but for many in Europe Reagan was 'a bellicose ideologue leading the country into a dangerous global confrontation with international communism'[17] with potentially serious implications for the security of the Alliance. In appealing to the forces of democracy to resist 'totalitarian evil' in his 'crusade for freedom', Reagan was to challenge the states of Europe to join him in the 'struggle between right and wrong, good and evil',[18] to face up to the 'evil empire' of the Soviet Union: not just a test of military strength but a struggle of 'moral will and faith'.[19] Although fearful of a decline in American support for the Alliance, concerns that Washington might drag Europe into a destructive conflagration led Europeans to seek more effective means of influencing the European security environment.

Despite the traditional foreign policy diversity of European states, from the beginning of the 1970s there had been an evident broadening of the European perspective from a Eurocentric introspection to an 'out-of-area' focus that reflected Europe's rising status. Europeans' limited ability to influence the external environment had been illuminated by emerging 'out-of-area' crises, notably the Arab-Israeli War and OPEC oil crisis, in which transatlantic foreign policy divergence highlighted European impotence.[20] What was particularly significant about the Reagan Doctrine of global interventionism was that in interpreting international events through a Cold War lens, Washington had come to expect its NATO allies to co-operate outside of the immediate Atlantic area in the pursuit of 'communist containment'.[21] As the US sought to re-establish its leadership following the years of self-doubt in American politics, pressure for allied support was an expression of a more assertive US posture; if American interests were threatened globally, European allies must be judged on their readiness to come to the aid of the US. For Europeans, despite the rhetoric of 'Atlantic Community' and efforts to expand the scope of the Alliance both geographically and sectorally, NATO had been specifically constructed as a limited and clearly defined military alliance. Any broader remit was viewed as unwelcome political leverage rather than a treaty obligation.[22] The concerns of European states regarding what many saw as Washington's 'dangerous and counter productive bias toward ideological oversimplification, public posturing, and premature force'[23] in regional situations, principally in the Middle East, led them to seek means by which to distance themselves from too close a connection with US policy.[24]

The implications of Reaganite policy, during what Halliday has referred to as 'the second Cold War'[25] period of Reagan's first term, clearly extended beyond the military sphere. With many Europeans already unhappy with apparent US mismanagement of the global economy, Reagan's massive increases in defence spending were to turn the US from the 'world's largest creditor to world's largest debtor [state] in four years', increasing European anxieties about international economic recession.[26] For European states, the economic benefits of East-West trade were matched by the strategically significant advantages of the reduction in reliance on Middle East sources of oil.[27] US efforts during 1980–1 to enforce the cancellation of a massive European gas pipeline deal with the Soviets, with the imposition of 'extra-territorial' trade bans on foreign subsidiaries of US companies that were manufacturing equipment under license for the pipeline, were justified by the Administration on the basis of a Cold War rationale, but met with a 'cool' reaction in Europe. Reagan's subsequent lifting of the grain embargo initiated by Carter, raising US grain sales to Moscow by 50% in 1983 under domestic pressure from farmers, further called into question the sensitivity and consistency of US foreign policy actions.[28]

ARMS POLICY AND STRATEGIC INCOHERENCE

By the late 1970s the military and strategic balance had begun to favour the Soviets. Their deployment of SS-20s (mobile, intermediate-range ballistic missiles equipped with three independently targetable nuclear warheads and capable of reaching all of Western Europe), which had begun in 1977, called into question the credibility of NATO's military posture. The West's flexible response strategy, reliant on levels of allied superiority for its rationale, had become 'inflexible response in practice'.[29] Soviet strategic parity and theatre nuclear superiority undermined the credibility of US nuclear guarantees and shifted the onus for deterrence onto NATO's limited conventional forces in Europe. In 1979 Kissinger was to note that 'the European allies should not keep asking us to multiply strategic assurances that we cannot mean, or if we do mean, we should not want to execute because if we execute, we risk the destruction of civilisation'.[30]

The deployment of Intermediate-range Nuclear Forces (INF) in Western Europe in December 1983 was intended to reassure the Europeans about American commitment and to fill the apparent 'window of vulnerability' in NATO's flexible response strategy.[31] In 1979 the decision was taken to deploy Cruise and Pershing II in Western Europe, at the same time as arms control agreements were negotiated with the Soviet Union as part of the détente process. Drawing on President Carter's original dual-track strategy, the INF deployments were to become another element of Reagan's position of negotiating from strength. Although welcomed by participating European governments as a means of ensuring continued US 'coupling', lack of influence over bilateral superpower arms talks had lessened enthusiasm for the deployment amongst some government elites.[32] Equally, the siting had been accompanied by a growing and vociferous peace movement and increased concerns amongst European publics regarding Reagan's apparent belief in war-fighting strategies limited to a European theatre.[33] Equally, the irony of the two-track policy was not lost on European publics; as Lellouche notes, where arms control had become an important stabilizing element of the superpower relationship, it also provided 'bizarre justification, in the domestic politics of most European countries, for continued defence efforts'.[34]

Reagan's announcement, in March 1983, of plans for the Strategic Defense Initiative (SDI), or 'Star Wars', programme occurred only shortly after the controversial INF deployment. A fundamental break from traditional post-war US policy, SDI represented a dramatic shift in strategic doctrine away from the established NATO strategy of deterrence. Widely unpopular amongst European strategists,[35] SDI appeared to be a scientifically improbable and futuristic defence system, but one that, in Reagan's words, would have the effect of making nuclear weapons both 'impotent and obsolete'.[36] Despite Reagan's assurances of American commitment to European defence,[37] SDI heightened alarm in the Western European states about potential decoupling of American and European strategy and a return to something resembling a 'fortress America' emphasis in US strategic doc-trine.[38] Inevitable Soviet counter-research and deployment would leave even the limited British and French deterrents valueless and force them into a con-ventional arms build-up, and any breach of the Anti-Ballistic Missile Treaty would predictably lead to a further stimulation of the superpower arms race and increase instability on a global scale. Clearly the Star Wars issue offered little to increase European confidence in the strategic guarantee of the US or the future efficacy of NATO doctrine.

The SDI project exacerbated concerns in Europe over the extent of Euro-pean dependence on American technology. Europe was increasingly aware of its growing technological backwardness and economic vulnerability to both US and Japanese capital—tensions which were to build up by the mid 1980s with, for example, the Westland helicopter affair of 1985, which led to Defence Minister Michael Heseltine's resignation from the British Gov-ernment over US 'commercial imperialism'.[39] At the same time the concept of joint arms projects seemed attractive in terms of 'the need to avoid dupli-cation of systems, to rationalise the use of resources, to promote standardisa-tion, and to face the growing costs of weapons'.[40] As Reagan's arms projects threatened European producers, it became clear that a high level of Euro-pean co-operation would be necessary in order to rationalize production. However, this would require not only common manufacture and export but also a political commitment in terms of force postures and defence strate-gies. By the mid 1980s it was generally acknowledged in Europe that arms co-operation might provide the only acceptable alternative if Europe was to be able to produce the next generations of sophisticated weaponry.

BURDEN-SHARING

The burden-sharing debates of the 1970s, which were to be a constant of Alliance relations, had led to suggestions that greater European co-operation in defence research, development and production might enable the Euro-peans to contribute to defence requirements in a more efficient manner. Consequently, the Independent European Programme Group (IEPG) was established in 1976 with the aim of harmonizing national defence equip-ment schedules, so as to avoid duplication of the defence effort. Independent of NATO, the IEPG consisted of all of NATO's European members, except Iceland, and included the French. For this reason it was seen as a potentially more useful mechanism for co-ordinating European defence production than the Eurogroup,[41] although national and commercial interests ensured that progress in co-operation remained limited.

By the 1980s, the perennial problem of defence provision had reached a new peak. Inflationary tendencies had added to rising equipment costs and affected the real value of defence budgets at a time when new-generation technology was adding to defence expenses. As the inefficiency of national procurement systems amongst NATO allies became increasingly evident, NATO sought new initiatives to capitalize on technological advantages in conventional capability.[42] The Europeans argued that they had been modernizing their forces and increasing their share of the defence burden while the US had been distracted by their Vietnam commitments. Europe's share of NATO expenditures had risen from 23% in 1969 to 39% in 1981, and low draftee numbers and high land costs amounted to significant hidden costs.[43] At the same time, US defence spending, amounting to 7.6% of the gross domestic product, was largely directed outside of Europe, and the US benefited from seven times the arms sales of Europe.[44] Nevertheless, the marginally defeated Nunn-Roth Amendment of 1984 reflected growing US opinion regarding what was seen as the ungrateful and costly failure of Europeans to meet their share of the defence burden, and it served as an impetus to European defence co-operation in the knowledge that declining US commitment was inevitable in the future.[45] Defence analysts on both sides of the Atlantic were beginning to see the need for the development of a greater European 'independence' in security identity,[46] but what the burden-sharing debate chiefly illustrated was the need for the Europeans to actively do something to keep the US in Europe.

DEVELOPMENTS IN THE EC

The link between integration and security co-operation had been largely absent within the Communities context following the failure of the EDC in 1954. However, events during the 1970s began the process of 'reconnection' by renewing interest in security and defence in Western Europe. The EPC mechanism denoted the separation of security from political-economic relations and was a backward step when compared with the EDC or the Fouchet Proposals. Given the lack of consensus on the future direction of the integration project, the particular idiosyncratic positions of EC member states and the NATO membership of most, foreign policy continued to be pursued under national auspices. The consequent ineffectiveness of the EPC in dealing with the growing number of external issues that increasingly suggested a requirement for some form of common European position began to have a negative effect on European confidence. By the mid 1970s it was widely believed that 'the disintegration of Western Europe as a political entity could well occur if by the end of the decade no common institutions or common goal have been forged in the field of defence and foreign policies'.[47]

The significance of foreign and security policy for a developing EU had been evidenced in the Copenhagen Report following the 1 January 1973 enlargement of the three European Communities (EEC, ECSC and Euratom).[48] However, the EPC vision was essentially that of Europe as a 'civilian power', seeking to adopt a 'soft security' approach to which it was best fitted.[49] Indeed, the EPC did have some success in converging views through diplomatic concentration on issues such as the CSCE and UN representation[50] and through the use of sanctions, aid and trade.[51] The Tindeman Report of December 1975 had been rejected as too radical in suggesting that Europe would be incomplete without a common defence policy. However, by the early 1980s pervasive unilateralism in both the style and the substance of American policy had begun a profound change in sections of the European public as many began to feel that their security was, in some way, out of their hands.[52] For an increasing number of West Europeans, a greater degree of self-sufficiency would help to redress the 'loss of dignity' that had accompanied years of dependence on the US. Although Europe's national political elites proved generally supportive of the maintenance of alliance links, rising popular discontent with Washington's policy approach and NATO strategy combined with a growing sense of political independence amongst regenerated polities.[53] Economic reconstruction had taken priority in the post-war period, but by the early 1980s a rejuvenated Western Europe became more assertive in its relations with the US, and a number of issues began to surface that had previously been overlain by the structural imperatives of the time.

As perceptions of transatlantic divergence increased, European concerns were reflected in a 1981 report by the four leading Western international relations institutes that argued for a new transatlantic bargain in which 'Europe would assume greater responsibility in dealing with the Soviet threat and in securing Western interests in the Third World; in so doing it would acquire new influence over US policy and gain more sensitive attention to its perspectives'.[54] The report's 'principal nations' approach, which proposed a European security core of 'capable' states, was largely rejected by those who feared a 'directoire' from whose decision-making they would be excluded. Nevertheless, the report had spelt out some serious concerns that prompted a European response. In the EC's London Report of 13 October 1981, promoted by the British Foreign Minister Douglas Hurd and made possible by François Mitterrand's accession as French President, the EPC had been given competence in the political aspects of security, although the nature and intent of the commitment were left vague.[55] The Genscher-Colombo Initiative[56] led to the adoption of the 'Solemn Declaration of Stuttgart' in June 1983, which envisaged 'joint action on the basis of intensified consultation, in the area of foreign policy, including the co-ordination of the positions of Member States on the *political and economic* aspects of security, so as to promote and facilitate the progressive development of such positions and actions in a growing number of foreign policy fields'. Although an important declaratory step towards the development of a European Union, the scope of security co-ordination remained limited, and the declaration clearly refrained from suggesting a common foreign policy.[57]

The lack of practical co-operation within the EPC, demonstrated by limited responses to the crises in the Middle East, Afghanistan, South Africa and the Falklands, further served to undermine confidence in the EC's ability to provide an answer to what was seen by many as a significant European problem. The EC did impose economic sanctions against Iran (1980), the Soviet Union (1982) and Argentina (1983), but the lack of a single institutional arrangement for external policy, with the separation between political guidance (EPC) and economic response (EC), was problematic. Indeed, as Hoscheit and Tsakaloyannis were to note, 'the more ambitious the Ten's political initiatives had been, the starker their political limitations (and the credibility gap between words and actions) has been'.[58]

By the time the international relations institutes released their second report, in 1983, the worsening transatlantic crisis led them to call for the EC to 'make a deliberate effort to become the European pillar of a Western security policy' in order to counter Reaganist unilateralism, and respond to worsening East-West relations and the rise of the peace movement across Europe.[59] Continued opposition by the Atlanticist Danes, anti-Atlanticist Greeks and neutral Irish to further development of security co-operation within the EC led to frustration amongst the other members.[60] Alfred Cahen, the WEU's first post-revitalization Secretary General (1985–9), stated that it was 'the accumulation of these failures, or near failures, each time efforts are made to give the European Community genuine opportunities for working together in the security field—as well as a growing interest, at both the public and at the governmental level, in problems concerning the defence of Europe—which are the basis for the initiatives aimed at re-launching WEU'.[61]

MOTIVATIONS FOR WEU REVIVAL

The previous discussion serves to illustrate the major political challenges that now faced the members of the WEU and required adaptation of the institutional framework of European defence and security. Having neglected the WEU since 1973, individual states discovered particular motivations for supporting its revitalization. At issue was how the WEU might fulfil the requirements for European defence as perceived by the 'Big Three' of Europe: the French, West Germans and British.

The French were the prime movers in the reactivation of the WEU. The significant shift in French attitudes towards NATO in the 1980s had a considerable effect on attempts at European defence co-operation on a number of levels. Given developments in Soviet conventional and nuclear capability, the credibility of the French 'independent' strategic nuclear deterrent rested upon the larger interdependence of the security environment. French autonomy required a strong NATO and a committed West Germany within it. However, NATO appeared to be becoming increasingly incoherent at the same time as French concerns were growing about Soviet actions in Afghanistan and Africa.

Although President Mitterrand was evidently less anti-American than his Fifth Republic predecessors, his basic strategic philosophy was not fundamentally different: believing Moscow to be in the ascendant, France would seek to alter the superpower balance in favour of the US so as to maintain an equilibrium that would ensure Europe's independence.[62] If NATO was losing its way, the Europeans must seek a means of re-establishing it. Whilst the French were not prepared to return to NATO's integrated military command, the need for a 'healthy' alliance would require a degree of European co-operation to ensure the necessary rebalancing of interests and influence. In fact, France and the US had common currency in seeking the strengthening of Western alliance, although the traditional burden-sharing approach of the US did not match French aspirations for a rebalancing of transatlantic influence through the development of an inherently European element within the Alliance structure. As one commentator notes, that France was to become the new 'special partner' of the Alliance suggests how bad the crisis in NATO had truly become.[63]

The possibility of West Germany moving towards some kind of neutralism,[64] particularly given the unprecedented popularity of the peace movement in Europe, heightened French fears, which had already been increased by the weak response of the Federal Republic to the imposition of martial law in Poland in December 1981.[65] By upgrading Franco-German security co-operation, France hoped to strengthen West Germany's stability and tie the Federal Republic more firmly into the Western system.[66] Thus in October 1982 France instigated the revision of the 1963 Franco-German Treaty, establishing twice yearly Foreign and Defence Minister meetings and three joint commissions on strategy, military co-operation and arms procurement. In 1983, as part of a restructuring of the French armed forces, the Force d'Action Rapide (FAR) was established, consisting of a five-division air-mobile and armoured force for use both as a power-projection capability in support of French overseas interests and as a rapid-deployment mobile reserve for Central Europe.[67] Significantly, the FAR reflected a recognition that the French deterrent was becoming little more than a 'nuclear Maginot Line' in the face of Soviet military superiority[68] and that French security required extended 'sanctuarization', entailing a greater commitment to protect its Eastern neighbour.[69] The FAR was to become both a physical and a symbolic representation of a new French readiness to participate in forward conventional defence in support of its West German ally, and as such it supported French interests in promoting closer Franco-German partnership as the core of a new Europe. But this new commitment was equally symbolic of a realignment of French policy, a rejection of what had become an increasingly disingenuous and unsustainable 'splendid isolation' and a major step towards an active engagement with allied strategy in Europe.[70]

From the start of his Presidency in May 1981, Mitterrand made the reactivation of the WEU a central theme of his European policy.[71] The Franco-German relationship was to be the linchpin of any future Europeanized defence arrangement, with the WEU providing the 'two-plus-five' nursery for developing the European defence identity central to its realization.

And, of course, being intergovernmental in nature, the WEU could serve as a convenient international forum for consultation and debate, without incorporating the supranational elements that might be damaging to French autonomy. The organization had the significant attribute of already being in existence, if not evidently awake, and so might be put into operation fairly rapidly and without adding to the institutional weight of the defence regime.[72] The WEU had within it a body for armaments co-operation, the SAC, and a framework that could provide for the symbolically and politically important removal of the conventional arms limitations still imposed on the Federal Republic. By bringing France 'back into the reckoning', the WEU would satisfy its European partners, who were also keen to seek a rapprochement with France at a time of strategic uncertainty.[73] As Poos states, 'Since such a consultation process could not take place either within the alliance framework or under the aegis of the European Communities, the only viable alternative, for the time being, was WEU'.[74]

In fact, the WEU was to serve two apparently contradictory elements of French defence policy. On the one hand, it would bring France nearer to its allies, complementing NATO solidarity; on the other hand, it would maintain French distance from NATO's integrated command and enhance an independent view of European security in line with France's broader European interests. In this sense it is true to say that the French were 'playing both a European and Atlanticist role'.[75]

The Federal Republic had resisted French initiatives to help rejuvenate the WEU in 1973, but a growing unease had been developing since the 1970s based on an underlying 'perception of a conflict between national and foreign interests'.[76] Whilst the maintenance of the NATO 'umbrella' and the development of détente were central, although often incompatible, elements of the West German security position, the policies and style of the American leadership during the early 1980s had significant effects.[77] For some, the American guarantee had become a dangerous condition, the Alliance a means of German containment and the Soviet threat an unrealistic myth.[78] West European integration had traditionally been seen as a legitimate area in which Germany might pursue its foreign policy, but unlike France, the Federal Republic had avoided taking any position of leadership in the integrative process. However, given its rising economic power, the Federal Republic began to seek a greater political role within a more assertive Western Europe. At the same time, alliance stability would require that West Germany take on the larger costs and responsibilities that would go with that role.

The decline of overt French anti-Americanism cleared the way for the Federal Republic to act without having to make a political choice between the US and Europe. For the Germans, the WEU held certain promises in terms of both short- and long-term interests. It could provide for the removal of the last of the restrictions on West German conventional weapon production,[79] bring France nearer to NATO and strengthen the

Alliance through the enhancement of the European pillar. At the same time, support of WEU revitalization could demonstrate to the German public that the Federal Republic was not dominated by the US and could provide a step towards closer European co-operation. In the longer term a regenerated WEU would provide a framework for co-ordinating European security policy and would therefore give greater weight to German concerns in its dealings with the US.[80]

Britain proved to be the most unenthusiastic of the 'Big Three' in its approach to WEU revitalization. Certainly, throughout the 1970s the UK did have concerns regarding American leadership, not least in terms of the 'unilateralism' of American policy towards its NATO and global interests. The British defence posture had been in gradual decline since the mid 1960s, although the UK had consistently failed to rationalize its strategic position and military commitments in the light of economic realities.[81] Whilst keen to find more effective means of utilizing declining defence resources, Britain was concerned that any moves in the direction of European defence co-operation should not undermine nor overlap the work of NATO. Shying away from co-operation that might overtly promote any grand project for an EU, UK Governments had consistently promoted alternative multilateral fora in their search for defence efficiencies, most notably the Eurogroup (1970) and the IEPG (1976). By 1981, following the election of the Thatcher Government in 1979, defence spending was to reach a new post-war high, although the Government was keen to promote more effective use of defence resources at a time of low economic growth.[82] Sharing the cost burden at a time of declining public spending created a dilemma for a government determined to maintain its position as 'second amongst equals' within the Alliance,[83] and by 1981 the British had begun to encourage the extension of dialogue on the economic aspects of security within the EPC.

The new British Prime Minister, Margaret Thatcher, was less at odds with US policy towards the East than her European counterparts, the promotion of the transatlantic 'special relationship' being a central plank of the UK Government's international policy. With Reagan in the White House, a close friendship and mutual respect was to develop between the two leaders as a consequence of an empathy that was both ideological and more personal, resulting in an extraordinarily intense and largely unprecedented relationship between modern Heads of State.[84] This relationship was to be enhanced by the eventual US support of UK interests during the Falklands Crisis of 1982. However, tensions persisted between London and Washington over US foreign adventurism, starkly illustrated by the US invasion of the British Commonwealth state of Grenada in 1983,[85] which was to solicit angry condemnation from Thatcher as an unacceptable assault on sovereign rights and a humiliation for the British Government, the Foreign Secretary having assured the House of Commons on the day before the invasion that he had 'no knowledge' of any such US intention. 'Dismayed' by the US action, Thatcher notes that 'at best, the British Government had been made to look impotent; at worst we looked deceitful', and this as she was coming under increasing pressure to renegotiate the terms of the forthcoming US cruise missile deployment to Britain so as to ensure 'dual control' in the face of unpredictable US actions.[86] The dilemma for the British Government was to find a means of enhancing its influence on US policy without undermining the US engagement seen as central to the UK's broader international interests.

As Franco-German defence co-operation developed during the early 1980s, the British were largely dragged along in their lukewarm acceptance of WEU revitalization by concerns that 'France and West Germany might just get their collective act together and jointly ensure their own leadership of a new development', as they had in the economic sphere.[87] This in turn would inevitably impact on the UK's relationship with the US. Having treated the WEU with what a senior British official referred to as 'benign neglect', the UK now faced a situation in which the costs of ignoring this 'irrelevant' institution might prove too high.[88] For the British, the value of the WEU was to lie in its 'practical action, not in its symbolism'.[89] For London, as for Bonn, the WEU offered a means of drawing France closer to NATO while restraining excesses of 'Euro-fancy' and providing what Forster has described as 'multinational cover'[90] for a directoire between France, West Germany and the UK that would be acceptable to the smaller European states.[91] Most important, the WEU was not to be a rival or substitute for NATO, but rather a means of enhancing the Europeans' defence contribution to the broader transatlantic alliance.

For the Americans, efforts towards greater European competence in defence created another dilemma, reflecting what was to become the central paradox of transatlantic relations. The concept of a European pillar in an equal transatlantic partnership had gained official support in the US as the Atlantic Alliance had begun to lose credibility in the late 1970s.[92] However, the assumption that a stronger Europe would necessarily be unambiguously in US interests had been irrevocably called into question by Kissinger's 1973 'Year of Europe' speech. A degree of what UK Foreign Secretary Geoffrey Howe referred to as 'Europessimism' had developed in the US, the dilemma for the Americans being that a more competent European pillar would also be a more assertive one.[93] Consequently, Europeans found themselves in an unenviable position of having to meet what were essentially contradictory requirements if they were to satisfy American concerns. If the pillar remained essentially a symbolic one, the Europeans would be chastised for failing to take on their share of the defence burden; if it became effective, it would threaten to undermine domestic American support for the Alliance, certainly in the transitional stages. Many commentators on both sides of the Atlantic questioned the utility of the pillar concept, arguing that the Alliance had never been either a symmetrical or a bilateral relationship.[94] Indeed, even as late as 1989, the then WEU Secretary General Willem Van Eekelen was to note that, given the incongruence of the membership and scope of the EC and NATO, 'the image of a dumbbell or two pillars upholding the same frieze is too neat and tidy to fit international realities', although it came 'closest to European aspirations'.[95]

Although the requirement for some rebalancing of the Alliance was widely recognized, there seemed little agreement on just what that 'balance' should entail.[96] What the Americans sought, in one view, was a means to 'alter the Alliance without changing it', that is, for the Europeans to pay more of the cost of defence while following policies determined in Washington.[97] However, as Kissinger was to note in his 1984 'Plan to Reshape NATO', structural changes to the Alliance, with a 'more rational balance of responsibilities', would be needed, rather than 'traditional burden-sharing', if Europeans were to contribute effectively to a vibrant alliance.[98]

As for the French plans for WEU revitalization, the US was at first suspicious, as it was of any independent European initiative.[99] The revitalization of the WEU was likely only to add another competing procedure for defence dialogue and co-operation, resulting in unnecessary duplication of efforts and greater strain on already limited budgets.[100] Whilst the WEU had clearly been seen as a means of supporting NATO in the 1950s, the changing structural environment raised American fears about the effects that a vehicle with competency in a distinctly European defence dimension might have for their position within the Atlantic Alliance. Most significantly, the WEU might prove itself another ineffectual expression of European angst, simply adding institutional complexity and increased demands for European influence while offering little in the way of meaningful support to the Alliance. Consequently, the official government position was that the US could see no need to revitalize the WEU, as the Eurogroup provided a suitable forum for the arms co-operation required for effective burden-sharing.[101]

REVITALIZATION

The French Minister of Foreign Affairs, Claude Cheysson, made tentative proposals for the re-launching of the WEU in the French National Assembly as early as 2 December 1981. However, it was not until 2 February 1984, having gained the support of the West German and Belgian Governments, that French revitalization plans were circulated.[102] Following a meeting of Foreign Ministers in Paris on 12 June 1984, the Rome meeting of the Foreign and Defence Ministers of the Seven (26–27 October) led to the adoption of the Rome Declaration,[103] which initiated the process of WEU revitalization. In this 'certificate of rebirth',[104] the Seven agreed to establish the WEU as 'the European centre for the Member States' common reflection and concerted action on security matters'. The declaration identified those areas which had become of serious concern in transatlantic relations—defence questions, disarmament and arms control, European arms co-operation, European contributions to the Atlantic Alliance, and the development of East-West relations—as those in which to hold 'comprehensive discussions'. That NATO remained 'the foundation of Western Security' was made clear; 'better utilisation of the WEU' would be a contribution to this security by creating 'greater solidarity' amongst all the allies. In restating the treaty goals, the long-standing aim to 'promote the unity and encourage the progressive integration of Europe' was highlighted, as was the objective of closer member-state co-operation internally 'and with other European organisations'.

In order to carry out the stated aims of enhanced co-operation, the WEU was to be redesigned: the Rome Declaration provided for a new diplomatic framework that was intended to make for a more vibrant and effective organization. Formally approved at the Luxembourg Foreign and Defence Ministers' meeting of 28 April 1987,[105] a number of new intergovernmental organs were established so as to improve consultation procedures. Provision was made for at least twice-yearly meetings of Foreign and Defence Ministers, establishing the WEU as the one institution where both ministries were represented together at the highest level. Within the year, one commentator was able to note, 'Ministers have become accustomed to discuss very frankly and in a relaxed atmosphere key issues affecting European security, whether strategic questions, East-West relations, arms control, direct or indirect threats or regional security'.[106]

Other institutional changes included the introduction of a Presidency of the Council, with a one-year term, and regular meetings by Political Directors from the Foreign Ministries and representatives from the Ministries of Defence, with this group in turn contributing to regular 'enlarged' meetings of the Permanent Council of Ambassadors in London. The Rome Declaration also paved the way for the creation of Special Working Groups (SWGs) with experts from the foreign and defence ministries meeting to deal with specific matters entrusted to them, the first SWG being established in 1985 to discuss the implications of SDI for European security. That SWG was to be subsumed within a high-level SWG in April 1987, this new group being tasked to look at a broader range of issues relating to European security interests, and to be joined by two sub-groups dealing with security in the Mediterranean and organizational issues respectively. With the high-level SWG focusing on the political aspects of security, a new Defence Representatives Group was formed to concentrate discussion on military matters.

The smooth conduct of meetings for all of these intergovernmental groups was to be ensured by the administrative expertise of the Secretariat General. Daily contact between civil servants in the capitals was to be enhanced in the spring of 1988 through the establishment of WEUCOM, the WEU's communications network, designed for the fast exchange of WEU-related information and facilitating much closer links between key personnel and departments.

The intergovernmental elements of the WEU were the ones that would be most significantly improved, although the Assembly had remained the most active part of the WEU during the period of Council somnolence, producing a range of reports for national parliamentary consumption and consistently seeking to establish itself as the 'instrument for European consultation on security policy'.[107] Indeed, the Assembly had proven itself a useful arena for European 'joint reflection' on a range of foreign and security policy issues, alongside that taking place within the EPC framework.[108] The Rome Declaration (and the 'Platform' to follow) identified a more prominent role for the Assembly, with paragraph 9 emphasizing the Assembly's increasing importance as the only European parliamentary body treaty-mandated to discuss defence. Following revitalization, the Assembly sought not only to enhance its relationship with the Council and its various working groups but also to establish consultation and co-ordination procedures with the Council of Europe, the European Parliament (EP) and the North Atlantic Assembly (NAA).[109] Having committed itself to 'the improvement of East-West relations through the promotion of contact and dialogue' in the Venice Communiqué of April 1986, the WEU established official relations between its Assembly and the Supreme Soviet in April 1987.

For all the symbolic importance of reactivation,[110] the process of 'breathing new life' into the organization was to prove disappointingly slow. Indeed, one year after the Rome Declaration, the President of the WEU Assembly was moved to complain, 'There we have the WEU Treaty charging us to define a policy on security and defence; we have a Council in London which is organized in such a way as to be able to operate continuously—but instead of using this forum the members engage in bilateral talks and the foreign ministers travel around as if the WEU were non-existent'.[111] Cahen suggests an institutional dimension to the problem, recalling how difficult it had been to 'concretise' the organizational structures of the WEU, with defence officials finding the working practices of Foreign Affairs officials over-deliberative and indecisive.[112] The initial 'sluggishness' may also be explained by the British reservations (closely supported by the Dutch) regarding the potential impact of enhanced European co-operation on NATO.[113] In February 1985, in light of the forthcoming US-Soviet Nuclear and Space Talks to begin in Geneva in March, the WEU states were given clear direction by US Assistant Secretary of State Richard Burt that the US 'did not wish a European position to be expressed' on SDI development or arms control which might serve to undermine the US' negotiating position. Consequently, the British Government vetoed any joint statements on these issues by the WEU, a compliant Council dutifully suspending consideration of such matters.[114] This compliance did, however, raise an important issue. Given the commitment to enhanced consultation, if the WEU was neither to duplicate NATO activity nor potentially undermine it through the establishment of an effective caucus, it remained unclear what its role was to be. Although Cahen's quiet diplomacy was to prove effective in terms of promoting long-term change, the decision not to appoint a high-profile political figure to the post of Secretary General of the WEU reflected the lack of certainty as to the organization's future direction.

In the light of the EPC's limitations in overcoming national preferences in its low-politics deliberations, high expectations of a newly revived and institutionally reformed WEU may have contributed to an unreasonable sense of disappointment in the institution's early performance. Efforts to further European co-operation on defence issues had continued both within the EC context and in bilateral agreements. With the French holding the rotating Presidency of the EEC in the first half of 1984, Mitterrand had called for the 'relaunch' of the EPC and established an Intergovernmental Committee to consider how co-operation within the EEC might be improved. The subsequent Doodge Report of March 1985 identified the significant reservations of the Irish, Dutch and Greeks regarding the extension of EPC competence.[115] France and West Germany were unsuccessful in their attempt at the following Milan Summit of June 1985 to 'introduce binding political consultation on security matters within the framework of "Political Union"'[116] but did gain support for an Intergovernmental Conference (IGC), beginning in September, during which a Political Committee would consider the issue of formulating a Common Foreign and Security Policy for the EC.

Given the ongoing efforts to develop a security profile within the EC, there were those who suggested that WEU reactivation was 'a traditionally nation-state oriented policy' intended to constrain integrative behaviour within the EC context by creating a 'competitive multinational institution'.[117] Tensions had arisen between the WEU Assembly and the EP, which had, since its Klepsch Report dealing with armaments procurement in 1978, sought to establish a security role for itself and had challenged the WEU's authority, particularly following the introduction of direct elections to the EP in 1979.[118]

It is certainly true that the WEU and EC/EPC would find themselves with overlapping competencies,[119] and that success within the WEU could potentially marginalize the EPC. However, the WEU's contribution to integration must be identified in terms of the impact that its revitalization had on the 'defence-shy', non-WEU states of Denmark, Ireland and Greece within the EC. In what may be described as a 'vortex effect', WEU reactivation 'impelled' states to concentrate their thoughts and adopt a more positive attitude to the political aspects of the EC, if they did not want to be relegated to the 'second league'.[120] This was particularly true for Greece, the most recent state to accede to the EC. Both Turkey and Norway, as non-EC states, had shown interest in the WEU as a means of compensating for their absence from the EPC, and the possible accession of Turkey to the WEU might seriously impinge on Greek influence over the security environment. The inclusion of a commitment to closer co-ordination of policy on political and economic security aspects under Title III of the 1987 Single European Act (SEA), the first major amendments to the 1957 Treaty of Rome establishing the EEC,[121] and may be seen as an attempt by non-WEU EC members to avoid the risk of exclusion from this important area of European debate.[122] Although the SEA did little more than codify established

EPC practice, it represented an important shift in providing a legal basis for political co-operation on security matters; Article 30(1) established the longer-term objective 'to endeavour jointly to formulate and implement a European foreign policy'.[123] Significantly, the provisions of the SEA stipulate that it must not impede closer co-operation 'within the framework of the Western European Union or the Atlantic Alliance'.[124]

Thus precedence was given to the WEU as a vehicle for developing the elusive European defence identity in the absence of EC consensus. Indeed, the failure of EC members to agree on a defence dimension for Europe contributed to the ongoing pursuit of revitalization of the WEU as a representation of a defence identity of the willing. The '10–3' forum provided by the WEU could promote co-operation amongst Europe's defence-responsible states, unblocked by the EC's 'free-riders'. That the WEU was nothing other than a 'second-best' option, intended 'as a device to keep this important area of European co-operation (defence) active which the Community and the Ten are at present unable to exploit', had been made clear by the participating Foreign Ministers at its reactivation.[125] As Cahen was emphatic in pointing out, 'should circumstances change, the WEU would bow to the primacy of European Political Cooperation'.[126]

THE WEU FINDS A VOICE: REYKJAVIK

The emergence of Mikhail Gorbachev as leader of the Soviet Union in March 1985 spelt the beginnings of the end of the Cold War structure.[127] Facing economic stagnation and internal political instability, Gorbachev began a process of 'openness' (glasnost) and 'restructuring' (perestroika), encouraging debate on the future direction of the Soviet system and its international engagement in the spirit of 'new thinking' (novye myshlenye). As a new détente emerged between the superpowers, the Soviets sought to establish an 'interdependent' relationship with the West, de-emphasizing the role of military power and searching instead for economic and political mechanisms for meeting Soviet security objectives.[128]

The European powers had generally welcomed the new era of arms control made possible by Gorbachev's accession, although superpower summit-level negotiations raised concerns in Europe regarding their exclusion from the Soviet-US dialogue. Washington's earlier insistence that Europeans refrain from discussing ongoing arms control issues within the WEU, fearing that signs of allied dissent might undermine or complicate negotiations, did little to reassure its European allies that their defence interests would necessarily be met in a rapidly changing global arena.[129] Although the Europeans were broadly supportive of Reagan's zero option on INF, it was felt that the implications of the proposed INF Treaty, without subsequent significant expenditure on conventional arms build-up, would result in incoherence in the flexible response doctrine as applied to Europe, and cast doubt on the US commitment to remaining a 'European power'.[130] Consequently, the WEU's Council of Ministers, in their Venice Communiqué of 30 April 1986, stressed 'the particular interest to Europe' of the INF negotiations, underlining the need for balanced conventional forces throughout Europe and emphasizing the WEU members' efforts in the context of multilateral fora such as the Comprehensive Ban on Chemical Weapons talks in Geneva and those on MBFR in Vienna.

The crunch was to come at Reykjavik. In summit-level superpower talks in the Icelandic capital, the US President turned what was intended as a 'preparatory prise de contact' into a serious negotiating summit.[131] With both Reagan and Gorbachev keen for a political success, only Reagan's insistence on maintaining SDI saved him from embarrassing Soviet acceptance of proposals that would have unilaterally undermined his European allies' vital security interests and decoupled West European and American strategies only three years after INF deployment.[132] Reagan's stated commitment to the 'elimination of all ballistic missiles from the face of the earth' not only was generally of concern to the members of the WEU, in terms of the effects on NATO strategy and the nuclear guarantee, but was particularly worrying to the British Government, given its dependence on US supplies and satellite targeting back-up for its planned Trident replacement.[133] In the realization that European interests would only be heard if Europeans managed to find a way of articulating and acting upon a common position in a coherent manner, the WEU met in Ministerial meetings on 13–14 November 1986. These meetings resulted in joint conclusions, enabling UK Prime Minister Thatcher to gain agreement at her Camp David meeting with President Reagan later that month that allied priorities in arms control would be recognized.[134] Cahen was to note the importance of the concerted WEU response to the Reykjavik talks, stating that, as Thatcher acted on the brief wired to her from the WEU, 'then, for the first time, we were in business'.[135] Certainly, concerns regarding Reagan's apparent willingness to phase out the US commitment to Europe, with its impact on UK Trident procurement, had contributed to British acquiescence in the development of WEU competence.[136] In her speech to the Conservative Party Conference on 12 October 1984, Thatcher seemed to have warmed to the idea of some level of defence co-operation in Europe, although in tending to 'see the European Community as an arm of NATO' she was certainly at odds with her European counterparts.[137] In accepting the WEU as a tool of convenience, Thatcher remained highly suspicious of the European pretensions for the WEU and sceptical of its Atlantic utility. By the time of her infamous Bruges speech of 20 September 1988, Thatcher's tone had hardened; rejecting the notion of a European 'superstate', the British Prime Minister promoted 'that Europe on both sides of the Atlantic—which is our noblest inheritance and our greatest strength'.[138] NATO remained the primary organization for the security of Europe, and whilst Thatcher reluctantly recognized the need to develop the WEU, this was 'not as an alternative to NATO, but as a means of strengthening Europe's contribution to the common defence of the West'. In fact, her Foreign Secretary noted in his memoirs that 'Margaret could never be trusted not to snort impatiently whenever the three letters WEU crossed her path'.[139]

THE PLATFORM

By the mid 1980s the sense of growing separation from US decision-making on matters fundamental to European interests was widespread across the European capitals. In December 1986, Jacques Chirac, the first French Prime Minister in 24 years to address the WEU Assembly, called for a European Security Charter setting out the principles by which European security efforts should be guided.[140] The Council's high-level SWG, which was to supplant the SDI-specific SWG in April 1987, prepared the report which was to form the basis of the subsequent 'Platform' Declaration, promulgated at The Hague on 27 October 1987, that effectively completed the process of WEU revitalization.[141] A 'watered-down' version of the charter called for by the French, the Platform can nevertheless be seen as something of a diplomatic watershed for the WEU, representing an expression of European intentions for the organization and defining an embryonic European security identity. The Platform is clear in its commitment to the Atlantic Alliance, stating that the security of Western Europe could 'only be ensured in close connection with our North American allies'. However, the language of the Platform suggests a more assertive European position, underlining the interdependent nature of the transatlantic relationship, where 'Just as the commitment of the North American democracies is vital to Europe's security, a free, independent and increasingly more united Western Europe is vital to the security of North America'. Significantly, the Platform identified the WEU as an important contributor to the broader process of European Unification, a process that would 'remain incomplete as long as it does not include security and defence'. Thus, the new intention to 'develop a more cohesive European defence identity' through WEU auspices was placed firmly within the dual context of European construction and Atlantic Community.

In establishing the criteria on which European security should be based, the Platform, like the Rome Declaration before it, was reflective of areas of tension within the Alliance context. In an environment of ongoing arms control negotiations, it served to reaffirm the centrality of nuclear deterrence, with explicit mention of the role of French and British national capabilities, whilst a commitment to détente and arms control as complements to defence, taking 'into account the specific European security interests', was also highlighted.[142] The Platform proceeded to outline the member states' intentions to 'assume fully their responsibilities' in the fields of Western defence, arms control and disarmament, and East-West dialogue and co-operation, establishing key areas for development. Outlined under

Section IIIa 4 of the Platform, Western defence was to be ensured through a commitment to six key areas, it being agreed subsequently that each area would be examined further by a 'responsible' member state for review in the forthcoming April and November WEU Ministerials. West Germany was to consider the implications of the commitment dear to its national interest 'to defend any member country at its borders', whilst the French took responsibility for deliberating on the 'best possible use of the existing institutional mechanisms' so as to ensure the highest level of Defence Ministry involvement in the WEU's work. The British were to report on member-state contributions to the common defence, with Belgium and Luxembourg tasked to examine opportunities for the improvement of consultation and the extension of co-ordination between member states in security and defence matters. The Italians and Dutch shared responsibility for consideration of the fifth and sixth commitments outlined in part IIIa of the Platform, to make more effective use of existing resources and to concert member states' policies on crises outside of Europe in so far as they affected security interests.[143]

The Platform seemed to offer something to everyone. However, there was some resentment in Italy over the Franco-British prominence in the document, and concerns were expressed about the apparent nuclear fixation of the document at a time of flux in East-West relations and about the possibility of encouraging US isolationism, concerns largely shared by the Dutch.[144] Britain had been resistant to the notion of a 'security charter' for fear that it might sound like a replacement for Kissinger's Atlantic Charter, and even the name was a matter of contention amongst the Seven. One commentator was to note 'a certain air of unreality . . . while the text of the platform declares the intention to build the security dimension of an "integrated Europe" the title dares not even suggest that NATO might be affected'.[145] In fact, it was only after reassurances from the French, during the Luxembourg Ministerial in the preceding April, regarding the guaranteeing of national positions and the pre-eminence that nuclear deterrence would have in the declaration, that the British reversed their rejection of the Platform, drawing other wavering states along with them. The Platform was generally well received in Washington; President Reagan's reaction was largely positive, defining it as a means of strengthening a more equal Atlantic partnership.[146] Nevertheless, conscious of potential US sensitivities, the WEU's Secretary General was keen to point up the contribution of the revitalized organization to Atlantic solidarity, noting the coincidence of 'spirit and substance' between the Platform and the following Communiqué of the Atlantic Summit of 2–3 March 1988.[147] Indeed, it has been noted that the WEU's revitalization 'did not appear to provoke much reaction among U.S. political leaders, the media, defense consultants, or even teachers of regional integration', and this may be explained by the incremental manner of the WEU's awakening, as much as by any assumed institutional irrelevance.[148]

THE WEU AND ARMS: CONTROL AND CO-OPERATION

In terms of 'internal' arms control, the role of the ACA had diminished throughout the 1970s. Controls on conventional armaments had been gradually relaxed in order that the FRG might contribute more effectively to NATO. In the Rome Declaration a commitment was made that the 'remaining quantitative controls on conventional weapons' were to be entirely lifted by January 1986, although controls on ABC weapons remained in place.[149] Given that the ACA had never shown itself successful in establishing ABC controls,[150] its residual activity was to follow up the work of the multilateral disarmament talks that had become a key feature of the 1970s and 1980s. Consequently, the ACA was to be reorganized and downsized, and, following discussions within the Permanent Council, it was agreed at the Bonn Ministerial of 23 April 1985 to establish three small 'Agencies for Security Questions' to consider the areas of arms control negotiations, security and arms co-operation respectively, with the ACA coming under the first of the new agencies until their merger under the Secretariat General following the Platform in October 1987, and eventual demise in 1989.

Although the WEU's internal arms control role had become largely obsolete, the implications of superpower discussions on arms control agreements for the national force plans and arms production, not to mention basic strategy and commitment, of European states were increasingly apparent. This realization had served to highlight the significance of Europe knowing its own collective mind in order to have some influence on the developing arms control regime. The WEU was to provide the forum in which this consensus could be achieved and articulated, the 1984 Rome Declaration having committed the WEU members to 'seek to harmonise their views' in this area central to European interests. The Reykjavik experience in the winter of 1986 had a significant positive impact on Europeans' confidence in their collective voice, and by the time of the 1987 Hague Platform the tone of the WEU statements on European arms control interests had become markedly more assertive.

Consequently, although Reagan's zero option on INF had been largely accepted due to the extent of Soviet concessions,[151] NATO's March 1988 discussions on the removal of longer-range INFs (the double zero option) resulted in an 'ambiguous compromise' reflecting a lack of allied consensus.[152] Further negotiations on shorter-range INFs (around the Soviets' triple zero proposal), whilst welcomed in some quarters of the Federal Republic, where concerns about the singularity of these 'German killers' proved politically influential, were largely resisted by British, French and West German officials, who feared the progressive de-nuclearization of Western Europe and its conceptual separation from US strategic interests.[153]

The implications of Reykjavik and the INF issue had effectively permeated the European psyche and attitudes towards the further dismantling of existing NATO strategy.[154] The Hague Platform had asserted that 'Arms control policy should, like our defence policy, take into account the specific European security interests in an evolving situation. It must be consistent with the maintenance of the strategic unity of the Alliance and should not preclude closer European defence co-operation'.[155] The WEU in itself had little direct role in the arms control process, but it was able to provide the security forum for high-level, well-informed discussion of arms control issues, which was to feed back into national decision-making. Indeed, the WEU member states proved themselves invaluable during the Conventional Forces Europe (CFE) negotiations in March 1989, particularly in the supervision of force reductions, in the management of recalled personnel and in the verification procedures. In terms of negotiation and decision-making, although much of this may have been unilaterally American, NATO's High Level Task Force played a considerable role, the WEU member states' representatives within the Task Force being identical to those within the WEU's SWG. Given this 'coincidence', and 'depending on procedures, timing and objectives', one commentator was able to conclude that by the end of the decade it seemed likely that 'the WEU indirectly [would play] a considerable role in conventional arms control policy-making'.[156] This conclusion would seem to be supported by the statements of Ministers at the time. At their meeting on the 18–19 April 1988, Mr Van den Broek, the Dutch Foreign Minister, was able to assure the WEU's Ministerial Council that 'Ministers had addressed the current major issues relating to arms control and defence requirements from a European perspective and [that] they had instructed the special working group to study these questions with the aim of harmonizing European views. In this way, a more effective European input into Alliance thinking on such issues as the comprehensive concept of arms control and disarmament could be achieved, thereby contributing to a further strengthening of the Alliance as a whole'.[157] Equally, Howe was moved to comment, following the British Presidency of the WEU in 1988, that 'we have had valuable exchanges of views on all the main arms control issues over the past year'.[158]

Just as arms control had become a significant area of common concern for WEU states during the 1980s, the scepticism of the 1970s with regard to European arms collaboration began to be replaced in the early 1980s by an acceptance that a way had to be found to make European arms collaboration work. In its Rome Declaration (para.7) the WEU had committed itself to 'provide a political impetus to institutions of co-operation in the field of armaments', but despite the WEU's mandate for arms collaboration, the performance of its SAC had proven 'disappointing'.[159] Rather, the WEU had tended to 'defer' to the Eurogroup, the IEPG or NATO's arms co-operation body, the Council of National Armaments Directors (CNAD), identifying its own role in terms of 'providing the necessary political impetus for, and practical contribution to, the various efforts undertaken in this field'.[160] The Rome Declaration had identified the IEPG as an institution to be particularly encouraged given that its 'main objective is to promote European cooperation and also to contribute to the development of balanced cooperation within the Atlantic Alliance'.[161] Promoted by the British and Dutch, IEPG reinvigoration coincided with that of the WEU, meeting at the Foreign and Defence Minister level for the first time in 1984. Following their landmark report 'Towards a Stronger Europe' of 1986, an action plan for a European Defence Market was developed in 1988, and the IEPG established a permanent Secretariat in Lisbon.[162]

Despite a developing awareness of the need for increased European arms co-operation, national interests continued to predominate. Concern over the emerging technical dependence of Western Europe on the US, implicit in the Star Wars programme, had led President Mitterrand to urge Europeans to take a common stand against SDI co-operation on the grounds that participation would involve further subordination to the American military-industrial complex with damaging implications for Europe's technology trade. Equally, if the Europeans were to devise any European defence identity it would seem to depend on some level of joint arms production and standardization and a move away from dependence on American technologies, and this would have to take place within the context of a broader political commitment. European initiatives in the area of technology co-operation were to include the EC's Commission-run European Strategic Programme of Research in Information Technology (ESPRIT, 1983)[163] and the European Research Co-ordination Agency (EUREKA, 1985), a non-EC framework for co-operation between European businesses and research institutes focusing on the practical application of technologies.[164] Agreeing at their Bonn Ministerial in April 1985 to 'continue their collective consideration in order to achieve as far as possible a co-ordinated reaction of their governments to the invitation of the United States to participate in the [SDI] research programme',[165] the Ministers of the WEU member states expressed their governments' continuing desire and intent to seek a European response to the issue of technology dependency. However, no common position could be found between the member states,[166] and US sweeteners, in the form of lucrative contracts, were quickly snapped up by the national military-industrial groups.[167] Competition and national interest once again took precedence, as each state negotiated separate terms for its participation in the industrial research funding.

American support for European arms co-operation was consistently at best ambivalent. Whilst collaborative arms projects might in theory be efficient and cost-effective, and lead to useful standardization, in practice they frequently led to greater costs and less efficiency in production.[168] Even if European collaboration might create defence resource efficiencies, contributing to burden-sharing and consequently to US security interests, as Ledogar was to note, it 'may not be in the interest of certain United States defence industries or their friends in Congress, or of those desiring the surest, safest control of technology flow to the East, nor, perhaps, of United States commercial competitiveness in general'.[169]

It is evident that, although greater efficiency might serve to placate some of the American concerns regarding European burden-sharing, arms co-operation served longer-term interests in a more specifically European perspective.[170] In the same way as WEU revitalization had promoted development and co-operation in the EPC framework, Garnham notes that 'as the WEU revived, states such as Denmark, Norway, and Spain, which were excluded from the WEU, sought to energize the IEPG as well'.[171] Additionally, Aybet has suggested that the WEU, by providing for a dialogue on the 'higher politics' of European security, enabled a kind of reverse spill-over to take place where practical co-operation within the IEPG was, at least in part, a response to the revival of high politics within the WEU.[172] Subsequently, as European governments moved increasingly in favour of enhanced European arms co-operation,[173] the WEU's role became that of a 'talking shop'. Functional co-operation was to take place within alternative fora.

That the WEU was to be utilized as a support organization rather than a primary centre for arms co-operation is made clear by the documents relating to revitalization. Indeed, efforts to rationalize the WEU in order that it might more effectively perform the duties for which it was reactivated led to the transferral of the SAC Secretariat to one of the newly formed 'Agencies for Security Questions' in January 1986, with the SAC itself not meeting after 1985. In November 1989, as arms co-operation developed in the broader framework of the IEPG and in EC industrial policies,[174] the SAC was finally disbanded, along with the other Security Agencies.[175]

The WEU's role extended into making better use of existing resources, which might give Washington signals that Europe was taking its commitments seriously, but this proved a difficult area given that force planning carried the inevitable implications of treading on the toes of NATO. Bilateral co-operation had continued to take place between European states, most notably between the French and the Germans, who had reached agreement, in the summer of 1987, on a Franco-German Brigade, to consist initially of 4,000 soldiers, to be deployable by 1988. This joint force was to be supported by the new Franco-German Defence Council, established in January 1988, consisting of Foreign and Defence Ministers, Heads of Government and Chiefs of Staff, with a small Secretariat in Paris.[176] Seen as a potential core of European co-operation in defence, Britain's reservations regarding this new piece of Franco-German collaboration were based on the perennial fears of undermining NATO (and the UK's own influence within it) by the establishment of a competing structure.[177] Without the promise of at least long-term British participation, the Brigade's future opportunities seemed limited. For the British at least, the WEU might provide the vehicle that could contain any such pretensions in an environment conducive to Alliance support and one in which British influence was secured.[178]

OPERATIONAL ACTIVITY

Free from the constraints of NATO's Article 6 provisions, the Brussels Treaty had empowered WEU member states to confer when confronted by threats outside of the immediate European or allied defence area that might threaten European security interests.[179] This commitment had been specifically recognized within the Rome and Platform documents as constituting an area where progress could be made within the WEU framework. The US had sought, since the Carter Presidency, to enhance 'out of area' co-operation through the NATO framework, Carter having proposed the establishment of a Rapid Deployment Joint Task Force drawn from US forces and assigned to NATO for 'out-of-area' deployment, with a subsequent requirement for increased European presence to cover the shortfall in the NATO area. This idea was taken further by the Reagan Administration, which proposed the formalization of allied contributions to 'out-of-area' activity, including direct military participation, peacetime military presence and provision for US access to airspace and bases.[180] These efforts had been largely resisted by the Europeans, who shared neither Washington's globalized vision of the East-West conflict nor necessarily the Americans' manner of managing it. The traditional European diversity of 'out-of-area' interest prescribed a more *ad hoc* informalism in the management of external crises. For the UK, the Falklands experience in 1982 had served to illustrate the benefits of being able to act quickly, unconstrained by the requirements of broad coalition-building. France continued to resist any US-prescribed constraints on its freedom of manoeuvre, and the West Germans shied away from the potential for entanglement in external conflicts, which could be an explosive problem domestically, given its constitutional constraints.[181] In order to resist US pressure for formalized NATO-based co-operation 'out-of-area', without undermining the Alliance, the Europeans needed to demonstrate their effectiveness in informal co-operation outside of NATO.[182]

As the Iran-Iraq War escalated in 1986–7, the danger to maritime navigation in the Arabian Gulf provoked the first step in the development of the WEU's operational role. In response to the presence of Soviet warships in the Gulf from early 1987, acting as invited escorts for Kuwaiti oil tankers threatened by the ongoing conflict, the US deployed a large naval force to protect re-flagged Kuwaiti vessels and counter Soviet influence in the region.[183] The Americans had made a formal proposal at the NATO Defence Planning Group meeting on 26 May 1987 that the NATO framework might be used to co-ordinate shipping protection. This proposal was rejected by the Europeans who were keen to divorce the crisis from any East-West connotation through promoting UN rather than NATO involvement. The loss of the US-escorted Kuwaiti tanker *Bridgeton* to a mine in July was the first of a growing number of merchant vessel losses whilst under US protection. Despite the immense resources of the US Navy, these incidents served to point up its woeful lack of Mine Counter Measures (MCM), which amounted to only three ancient minesweepers in service. The Europeans, on the other hand, were much better resourced in this area at least; the relatively insignificant Belgian Navy, for example, counted 27 modern MCM vessels amongst its fleet.[184] If the US Navy was not to be further embarrassed by its inability to protect, it had become apparent that it required the Europeans alongside.

The UK had been operating the Armilla patrol to protect British-flagged shipping in the Gulf since 1980, and in the summer of 1987 it announced its intention, along with the French, to send 'independent' minesweepers to the area as the threat to shipping increased. With keen resource interests in the region, other European members of the WEU felt constrained by both public opinion and limited capability from pursuing nationally independent or US-led activity. However, unfettered by the geographic limits imposed by the Washington Treaty, the WEU had reinforced, in the Rome Declaration of 1984, its members' commitment to 'consider the implications for Europe of crises in other regions of the world' (para.8). George Younger, UK Defence Minister since Heseltine's resignation in January 1986, had drawn together plans earlier in the year, along with his Dutch and French counterparts, for a possible WEU operation in the area, and on 20 August 1987 the Dutch Presidency of the WEU convened a special meeting for political consultation on the Gulf crisis. Although it quickly became apparent that a joint WEU action was out of the question, these discussions laid the ground for the deployment of MCM vessels by the Belgians and Dutch under a joint operation, to be code-named 'Octopus'. Following an attack on an Italian freighter in September, the Italian Government determined to deploy a considerable maritime force, securing the deployment of naval vessels from five of the seven WEU member states. Not all of the WEU's members were as keen as the Belgians and Dutch to promote the organization as the most acceptable multinational vehicle for action.[185] The French saw the WEU as too closely tied to NATO, whilst British Prime Minister Thatcher rejected the proposals of her own Defence Ministry for a WEU fleet with rotational command, her Foreign Secretary at the time remarking that 'For her the notion that any Royal Navy ship should be under command of any "foreigner"—unless he was an Anglo-Saxon—was quite unthinkable'.[186] Nevertheless, given their joint interest in the maintenance of freedom of navigation in the Gulf, the WEU member states agreed, at their meeting of 15 September, that the process of 'concertation' of WEU states' activity in the Gulf should be gradually enhanced.[187]

Working side by side with the US in the Gulf,[188] the WEU structure co-ordinated national operations on three levels: high-level consultation took place at the Presidency capital, the Hague, between political and military experts from the Foreign and Defence Ministries of the seven; Points of Contact within the national naval staffs met in the capitals on a rotating basis; and regular contact was established between naval commanders in the Gulf. Command and control, rules of engagement (ROE) and the activity of naval deployments remained essentially national,[189] reflecting the political sensitivities of the situation, but these three levels of co-operation facilitated through the WEU provided for a more efficient use of resources and enhanced operational effectiveness. Designated 'zones' were quickly established for search-and-clear activity, and efforts were made by navy staffs to harmonize national programmes so as to ensure a sufficiently high readiness capability in the areas of concern.[190]

Particularly noteworthy was the effect of this arrangement on the articulation of common European aims in the Gulf region.[191] And this was to include all seven WEU members: the Federal Republic, given its constitutional constraints, replaced units sent to the Gulf within the Alliance area, and Luxembourg provided financial contributions to its Benelux partners.[192] Following the August 1988 cease-fire, this concerted effort in support of common aims was continued as WEU states co-operated in Operation Clean Sweep, involving the co-ordination of the 'Calendar' forces along with the French and Italian national detachments to undertake mine clearance operations along key shipping routes in the southern Gulf, a task completed by December.

There were clear limitations on WEU activity in the Gulf, not least the lack of operational co-operation by the French. Neither should the level of efficiencies achieved be overstated. The Dutch Point of Contact noted that only 7 MCM vessels with 1 or 2 support ships might have done the job, rather than the 15 and 5 respectively deployed, and 1 or 2 frigates, rather than the 3 or more assigned, this overprovision reflecting a lack of co-operation resulting from national prerogatives.[193] Nevertheless, the then Dutch Defence Minister, Willem van Eekelen, was moved to state that 'our practical arrangements within the WEU framework have been justified, are workable and have been put into practice'.[194] In their first effort at common action, the WEU states had established an *ad hoc* and flexible arrangement that had contributed to the satisfaction of common aims. Largely an incremental development that had emerged from immediate military, as well as political, requirements, the WEU's experience in the Gulf was to provide for the elucidation of a set of common politico-military principles for future concerted military action in operations out of the NATO 'area'.[195]

But the success of the Gulf operation needs to be recognized not simply in terms of the political and operational co-operation that was achieved under the WEU. This 'successful piece of improvisation' had raised the visibility of the WEU and, by demonstrating that it could play a supportive role in relation to NATO, had a significant effect on both US and European attitudes to the Union.[196] The success in the Gulf had demonstrated that the WEU could perform useful roles that lay effectively outside of NATO's remit; it could enable Europeans to disassociate themselves from too close a connection to US policy while participating in areas of European interest, and it could provide for an emerging European identity in very substantive and visible terms without undermining Atlantic cohesion or being seen as anti-American. Cahen has gone so far as to identify the Iraqi President Saddam Hussein and the Soviet leader Mikhail Gorbachev as unknowing 'sponsors' of the WEU, given the specific dynamics of the period, where 'glasnost' had undermined the potential for Soviet opposition to European activity in the Gulf.[197] In the development of its 'out-of-area' competency, the WEU had proved an asset both to Europe and to the Alliance in general.

ENLARGEMENT AND THE CO-LOCATION DEBATE

Two other issues occupied the WEU in the final years of the decade. The first was enlargement: reactivation of the WEU in 1984 had awakened interest in a number of states in membership in the organization, although the Council of the WEU had decided to delay membership expansion until such time as the revitalization process was complete. The process of enlargement was subsequently initiated at The Hague on 26 May 1988, when invitations were offered to Spain and Portugal to begin accession negotiations, to be continued in London under the UK Presidency of the WEU from July. Provided for under Article IX of the original Brussels Treaty, accession criteria included the acceptance of the sentiment, conditions and commitments of the MBT, the Rome Declaration and the Hague Platform. The Accession Protocol was signed on 14 November 1988, and Spain and Portugal became full members on 27 March 1990.

For Spain, membership in the WEU was to continue its course of integration into the West European economic and political system following the Franco years of ostracism, during which it had been largely regarded as the 'last Nazi-Facist state' in post-war Europe.[198] Given its geo-strategic position, bilateral agreements with the US had provided for a politically palatable 'de facto' membership of the NATO alliance[199] until Franco's death in November 1975, and the subsequent establishment of a democratic system opened the door for Spain's eventual accession to NATO in May 1982. NATO membership had been sold to the Spanish people against the vigorous opposition of the political left, not only as a means of modernizing the Spanish armed forces and securing Spanish defence interests, but significantly as a means of expediting Spanish entry into the EC, with all of the political and economic benefits that might accrue. Rejection of the referendum on NATO withdrawal held by the socialist Gonzalez Government in March 1986, only months after the Spanish accession to the EC in January, was a reflection of this desire to further integrate into the European system, despite the Spanish Government's insistence on exclusion from NATO's integrated command and the non-deployment of nuclear weapons on its soil during peacetime.[200] The Spanish bid for WEU accession in early 1987 reflected that desire to emphasize its European credentials, whilst ensuring its place in the multilateral structure of European organizations. The WEU would provide a forum for military co-operation, inclusive of states 'serious' about defence and replete with a parliamentary assembly in which Spanish defence concerns might receive a more sympathetic hearing than in the Atlantic context.[201] At the same time, Spanish accession to the WEU would undermine the potential for the development of an inner 'informal directorate' from which Spain might otherwise be excluded.[202] Under leftist opposition, Gonzalez negotiated for special status for Spain, including the maintenance of the Spanish non-nuclear stance whereby Spain would not accept nuclear forces on its territory during peacetime, although it accepted a political commitment, as expressed in the Platform document, to the principle of a forward defence and nuclear deterrence strategy relying on a combination of nuclear and conventional forces. As a 'concession' for entry into the WEU, the Spanish Government agreed to the creation of a rapid action force capable of operating with both the French FAR and the Franco-German Brigade for operations in the Mediterranean.[203] The issue of the contested status of Gibraltar was dodged by interpreting the arbitration requirements of the Brussels Treaty to be relevant only to post-accession disputes.[204]

Despite its less than democratic political system, Portugal's wartime activities ensured that it did not suffer from the post-war exclusion from the emerging Western system that Franco's Spain did, and as a founding member of NATO, Portugal was fully integrated into the NATO command structure. The young Portuguese democracy sought to secure stability and influence through its international engagements and, given Spanish enthusiasm for WEU membership, considered that it would be against Portuguese interests to risk exclusion from an organization which the Spanish clearly perceived to be of such potential value to their own international position. Like their British supporters for accession, the Portuguese viewed the WEU as a means of providing a practical contribution to NATO, rather than an expression of an inherently desirable Europeanization of defence.

For the newly reinvigorated WEU, accession was to provide greater balance to the previously northern-dominated Union without diluting the organization, in which there was a consistently affirmed 'determination to develop a more cohesive European defence identity which will translate more effectively into practice the obligation of solidarity contained in the (modified Brussels) Treaty and in the North Atlantic Treaty'.[205] Enlargement to include Spain and Portugal would ensure the membership of the nine major defence contributors in Western Europe, geo-strategically spread and significantly equipped with military assets. Yet the question of membership was, once again, to reflect the uncertainty of the ongoing role of the WEU, with the conditions for accession raising political questions regarding the relationship of the WEU to both the NATO alliance and European integration. Membership of NATO, if not its integrated command, was a requirement of the Platform and, given the WEU's reliance on NATO for the substance of its Article V, would seem a necessary, if not sufficient, condition of membership. The Platform also refers to the commitment of the WEU members to 'build a European Union in accordance with the Single European Act, which we all signed as members of the European Union', suggesting that membership of the EC would be another precondition, excluding Turkey and Norway, for example, from WEU membership. Greece and Turkey, both of whom had shown interest in membership since revitalization, agreed on a joint consultation mechanism with the WEU at the Ministerial level in 1989, but the slow process of enlargement in the 1980s may be explained, at least in part, by the lack of clarity as to the WEU's place in the institutional arrangements of European security. As an article in *The Times* was to suggest on the day after Spanish and Portuguese entry, the 'determination' with which accession was sought reflected 'the WEU's success in re-establishing itself as a major institution'. However, the article continues, as an enlarged 'club' capable of establishing European caucused positions to present to a disaffected US, the WEU pillar of the Alliance might 'topple the structure it supports . . . The bigger the WEU grows, the more delicate the balancing act it will have to perform in Nato'.[206]

The other major area of discussion at the end of the decade was that of organizational location. In 1987 the then Dutch Defence Minister, van Eekelen, noted the 'risk that WEU is too absorbed in inward-looking, organizational deliberations', adding that the 'revitalization in 1984 of WEU was a *political* one; the organizational aspects are subsidiary to that aim'.[207] Nevertheless, it was largely 'politics' that led to the disagreements over organizational change that 'all but paralysed' the organization during 1988–9 and reflected deep divisions over the desired nature and intent of West European security co-operation.[208] The British canvassed support for a permanent relocation of the scattered elements of the WEU to Brussels, but the French resisted on the basis that such a move would subordinate the WEU by too close a proximity to NATO. Compromise proposals resulted in a London seat for the intergovernmental organs, including the Secretariat, whereas Paris was to keep the Assembly and become home to a new WEU Institute for Security Studies, which had the tasks of carrying out research, encouraging awareness through seminars and meetings and establishing a database of issues relating to European security.[209] As part of the general rationalization of the WEU to meet its changing role, Cahen was to recall that the effective transformation of its Agencies into the Institute for Security Studies was not a 'suppressive' act, but rather an example of the dynamism of the organization.[210]

Indeed, the WEU Secretary General was to note as early as 1987 that 'Major structural and organizational surgery has been undertaken in order to transform an organization once set up to control rearmament into a political forum for security debate. Like an old house, the façade has been kept, but behind the edifice has been rebuilt from the foundations upwards'.[211] The new intergovernmental machinery had been most significant in establishing the WEU as a forum in which regular institutionalized discussion at the level of senior officials could be undertaken in an atmosphere of 'plain speaking'.[212] The improved dialogue and institutional performance within the WEU at all levels enabled converging positions to emerge in a number of issue areas, which in turn produced a greater European confidence of expression.

Despite the successes of co-ordinated action in the Gulf, in areas in which the Europeans did not share the foreign policy perspective of the Americans, the role of the WEU in developing and articulating concerted positions was generally to be weak.[213] Kissinger had warned against any independent European foreign policy, commenting in response to criticisms of the US bombing of Tripoli in April 1986 that 'if this kept going on, if the United States felt obliged to intervene in many places and if the Europeans . . . participated in the opposition against us, then the Alliance . . . would lose support in the United States'.[214] However, the lack of a substantive European position was only in part the result of American pressure on European governments to comply with Washington's strategic demands. European states continued to act essentially on their individual interests. The British, most closely concerned with their 'special relationship' with the US, acquiesced to US activity, although with increasing reservations,[215] and the French sought an independent line, distancing themselves from American policy. None proved ready to accept the costs of joint action, and even in those areas where a common European position was established, the combination of collective inadequacies, national orientations and US pressures ensured a European inability to translate common interests into substantive policy.[216]

Consequently, the WEU was to provide for continuous dialogue amongst member states on issues of European significance, but the lack of ready convergence ensured its role, as Forster suggests, as a 'ginger group rather than a caucus, concerned with consultation rather than policy-making'.[217] The WEU's key role may have been as a platform for joint deliberation, essentially developing ideas that might be implemented elsewhere. However, this important task had resulted in a degree of 'mission creep' into areas of co-operation and operational activity excluded from any early interpretation of its role.

REFLECTIONS

Following British EEC entry in 1973, the WEU had retired into a period of Ministerial slumber. In consort with the French rejection of the 'Atlanticist' Union as a vehicle for defence co-operation, British disinclination to undermine the primary NATO structure for the provision of European defence ensured that the WEU fell into disuse: only the Assembly maintained its role of keeping alive a defence dialogue between European states. By the early 1980s, however, a number of changes had occurred in the international environment that called into question the continuing efficacy of the primary institutions of alliance and integration, with tensions emerging within and between both of these 'communities of interest'. Integrative tensions arose from disparate perceptions of how European development should take place within the Communities context, whereas, in terms of the Alliance, acceptance of increasingly 'unilateral' US leadership was questioned as foreign policy divergence and strategic incoherence created a schism between US and European interests. The 'tense' relationship between the more assertive and externally focused EC, seeking to define its role in the global order, and the US-led Alliance was a predictable feature of changing power relations. The revitalization of the WEU in 1984, and its subsequent development throughout the decade, may be understood in terms of its utility in satisficing these tensions and providing the vehicle for the necessary adaptation, both perceptually and substantively, of the institutional order.

The revitalization of the WEU had been largely a response to the emerging concerns amongst European states about their position within the Atlantic Alliance. During the 1950s the WEU had served the interests of the US-dominated Alliance, and the lack of political will to move beyond its NATO support role was indicative of the decline of 'high politics' in Europe and its degree of structural subordination. That the WEU again played a support role in the 1980s demonstrated the persistence of the bipolar structure in which European security still depended on the might of its American allies. However, with Europe confused and intimidated by apparent inconsistencies in American policy, particularly in the strategic field where perceptions (trust, commitment, credibility) are as powerful as intent, and increasingly at odds with the US over trade and financial matters, the development of a European identity might seem a logical consequence, particularly given the rising expectations of an economically powerful Europe. The increased unilateralism and perceived dogmatic, anti-communist bellicosity of US foreign and defence policy activity during the first Reagan Administration raised tangible concerns amongst many Europeans. Fears of possible entanglement in an unnecessary Reaganite conflict were intensified by Washington's desires to draw Europe into 'out-of-area' co-operation within NATO to meet its global agenda. Furthermore, the proposed SDI had rocked the relative contentment with the strategic relationship in terms of deterrence doctrine and nuclear guarantees that had persisted during the 1970s, whilst bilateral superpower arms control activity further undermined European satisfaction with the Alliance as the 1980s progressed. Fearful of both abandonment and entrapment in their relationship with NATO, the Europeans' commitment to the alliance was consistently tried by events.[218] As perennial burden-sharing issues re-emerged, so did a recurrent alliance dilemma: whilst the US required greater European efforts in support of alliance interests, the greater European assertiveness which was likely to accompany any declining dependency threatened to undermine Atlantic cohesion. This familiar tension was intensified by the growing interest of many within an increasingly powerful Europe in pursuing the development of a security dimension for the integration of the European space.

The reactivated WEU clearly acknowledged the continuing relevance of the Atlantic relationship,[219] but, significantly, it identified the range of Alliance contentions as those areas in which closer European co-operation would serve to enhance the security of all allies. This was illustrative of a new European confidence and a rising disaffection with an alliance structure that did not reflect the realities of the decade. The WEU's revitalization took place 'not outside, but in the very context of the Alliance',[220] but the WEU of the 1980s represented the interests of a less timid Europe, and in seeking to address the requirements of structural change it enabled NATO to evolve to meet the new circumstances of the era. In so doing, it raised issues previously unaddressed as a result of European dependence and articulated, in a conservative and generally un-presupposing manner, the requirements of an emergent European pillar within the confines of a recognizable, if perhaps less rigid, Atlantic Alliance.

The WEU was to have practical effects in providing the diplomatic infrastructure for defence dialogue and co-operation in keeping with Atlantic requirements for a more effective European contribution. As it provided the only institutionalized European ministerial and parliamentary mechanism for discussion of security and defence issues, the significant improvements of the consultation network of the revitalized WEU enabled the Europeans to establish concerted positions on areas of Alliance interest. Alliance coherence required a level of 'rebalancing', as highlighted by the events at Reykjavik,[221] and the positioning of the WEU in relation to the Alliance enabled common European interests and potentially alliance-damaging concerns to be aired effectively. This was particularly significant in terms of edging France closer to NATO, a function enhanced by the exclusion from the WEU of those EC members not 'serious' about defence.

The WEU's symbolic role, representing for many a desire and commitment to a European defence identity, had relevance not simply in terms of integrationist intent, but also in mollifying European publics for whom defence had become a distantly manipulated concern. For the WEU, the act of 'being' was potentially as significant as the act of 'doing', providing the perceptive lens that enabled state acceptance of alliance in light of domestic discontent. The destabilizing effects of Europe 'speaking with one voice' within the alliance, not least in terms of US perceptions of a decline in its own authority, were to be mitigated by a ready acquiescence, particularly on the part of the British, to limit WEU co-operation where US leadership essentially satisfied national concerns.

Perhaps most significantly, as a result of its counter-mine operations in the Gulf, the WEU demonstrated to the US that it was not attempting to undermine or replace NATO, and that it might have a significant role in specific defence areas not covered by the Washington provisions. It was not the Atlantic answer, but it proved an acceptable solution. Once the WEU member states accepted the IEPG mechanism as the most effective forum for arms co-operation activity, satisfying US concerns over burden-sharing and European worries about over-dependency, the arms control elements of the WEU were dropped in order to provide for an effective German contribution to defence. Nevertheless, in its commitment to the discussion of arms control activity, the WEU provided for a European contribution to the arms control debate: acting as a vehicle for the articulation of European concerns over the impact of the superpower agreement on the strategic viability of the emerging European order.

In the three decades following the creation of the WEU, developments within the EC framework had led to the establishment of Europe as a vibrant and dynamic global region. Once the European partners had established both an economic and (limited) political dimension to European construction, the scope of further integration had become an issue of contention amongst them. For many, the logical 'next step' in the integrative process was the development of a European defence competence, and despite the resistance of those who sought to retain the Community as a 'civilian power', the number of co-operative ventures and declarations of intent suggested a growing commitment within the enlarging Community to the eventual development of a European security dimension. Efforts to develop the EPC as its 'natural home' met with only limited successes, not least as new members brought their own national constraints to play. Nevertheless, events within the broader security environment emphasized, particularly for the French and Germans, the requirement for a strengthened European 'voice' as frustration at the lack of progress on foreign, security and defence co-operation within the Community threatened to undermine the fragile consensus on which the developing EU was to be built.

The new competencies of the WEU, formulated under the Rome Declaration and reinforced in the Platform document, established it as the European centre for co-operation and consensus-building on security matters with a commitment to the development of European unity. However, the resurrected WEU was to satisfy a number of contrasting interests in relation to the integration of Europe. In one sense, the WEU must be seen as 'an EPC on security',[222] providing both example and momentum for future developments in this area, and it was a response, at least in part, to the limitations of the Community in developing its own 'high-politics' competencies. Representing an alternative constituency in which such interests could be met, the WEU provided 'an example of what can be achieved through cooperation on the European plane and as [sic] a device to keep this important area of European cooperation active'[223] until such time as the EC states could resolve their differences.

However, not all were convinced of the contribution of WEU revitalization to the European construction process. The shifting of 'sexy' European issues such as arms control and nuclear affairs to the WEU might detract from the appeal of the EPC as an arena for dialogue, whilst the 'natural' spillover between foreign policy and defence interests would be disconnected by the separation of institutional competencies.[224] Certainly, it has been argued that WEU revitalization was in part a 'negative' response to efforts by the EP to develop its own security role. Given the rejection by some member states of the development of enhanced integration in the security sphere, the revival of the WEU in the mid 1980s can be explained in terms of traditional nation-state-oriented policy, intended to limit European integration within the EC by the creation of a competing multinational arena, with the added benefit, particularly in the British view, of preventing the emergence of any alternative Franco-German directoire. As an autonomous vehicle for dialogue and co-operation in those security areas of concern to many in Europe, the WEU did not directly compromise the civilian nature of the EC. Consequently, an important role of the WEU, particularly for the neutral Irish, was that of a 'lightning conductor to keep the dangerous currents of bloc militarism away from the general fabric of the European Community'.[225]

From any of these perspectives, the WEU provided 'political relief' in the Europeanization process.[226] However, the political implications of revitalization served to push the 'reluctant' EC members to accept a greater level of political competence for the emerging Union at the risk of becoming second-division players in the emerging order. The acceptance of the WEU's precedence in the SEA was but a short-term expedient in preparation of further political developments within the Union. Through the provision of institutional knowledge and functional mechanisms for core state dialogue and co-operation, the WEU was to provide for a timely and pragmatic development of European defence co-operation which did not undermine the internal consensus of the Community, but which did provide for increased European confidence in their collective interests and abilities in the security field.

Secretary General Cahen placed the revitalized WEU firmly within the context of European construction when he concluded, 'If everyone among the "Twelve" were able to accept, truly and without afterthoughts, a full European dimension of security, then the WEU should put its future and even its very existence in question, and be ready to melt into the mainstream of the European construction. But as long as that is not the case, the WEU is the only place where a European dimension of security can be developed, and it has to fulfil that role completely'.[227] That there remained a significant gap between European rhetoric and substantive WEU security activity is evident: national goals still predominated in the calculations of European governments, leading to inevitable diversity and individuality of interest despite frequently compelling reasons for co-operation, evidenced, for example, by the lack of a concerted WEU response to SDI.[228] Nevertheless, by providing the framework of co-operation and consensus-building, the WEU enabled the progressive interaction that was to lead to a growing Euro-consciousness amongst participating states and a tendency to associate European with national interests in a pervasive relationship, which may be somewhat overstated as 'European identity' but which was more than co-operative pragmatism. It is Dezcallor who points most cogently to the significance of the WEU in this broader context of the construction of a European security dimension when he states that:

> To start moving in a certain direction, however, is in itself important because it reveals the birth of a political will which in the future may set more ambitious goals. It is imperative to combine the modesty of today's goals with a compelling vision of what might be possible tomorrow, thus motivating the Europeans out of their complacency about their dependent position . . . By starting a process of political co-operation

in security matters, it might be feasible to build incrementally a body of doctrine about the nature of West European political interests, points of view, and attitudes towards the world.[229]

Although the WEU was not to realize the full extent of a European security identity during the 1980s, it did take important steps in maintaining the momentum towards its eventual development.

The WEU was also identified during the 1980s as an increasingly necessary bridge between Alliance and Community interests. Given the potential that a European security dimension could compete with Alliance interests, the WEU provided for a transition in the transatlantic relationship, in which a resurgent Europe could assume an increasing defence role without undermining the fundamental cohesion of the Alliance. In facing the new challenge of bridging the divide between the traditionally Atlantic-oriented defence organization and the West European economic structures, the WEU was able to provide a co-ordinated institutional response to the blurring of this previously clear distinction. For the pragmatic British, who remained sceptical of European rhetoric, the WEU's bridging role was important in that it provided for 'a healthy relationship with our North American allies, which remains the key to European security'.[230] Britain perceived the WEU as an adjunct to the existing European security arrangements, and its success was seen only in terms of the supporting and strengthening effect that it had as 'a servant of NATO, not an understudy'.[231] The alternative European approach to the WEU was characterized by the French, who identified the institution as an embryonic defence arrangement for Europe that occupied a position incorporating both a 'security policy' and a 'European policy'.[232] In fact, the WEU was able to accommodate the disparate perspectives of all European players, enabling some level of resolution of problems incumbent in their security relationships and facilitating the emergence of an embryonic European security identity. As Clarke was to state, 'The WEU presently stands as a half-way house between NATO and the EC; supplementing the existing defence work of one and encouraging more defence work within the other'.[233] The WEU had both the framework and the remit to serve this function, and it provided the Europeans with the wherewithal to acquire the experience necessary for the development of a substantive and effective pillar within the Alliance. As Howe acknowledged at the time, 'All the members of WEU agree that the North Atlantic Alliance needs to have a strong European pillar. At the same time, we have felt the need to develop a common defence identity as Europeans. The work on which we are embarked responds to both needs'.[234]

In sum, the WEU was reactivated and developed on the basis of convergent rather than shared motives, and the lack of a clear vision of the WEU's role was reflected in the protracted nature of its revitalization. Indeed, it could be argued that the WEU's actions during this period were largely symbolic and achieved little of absolute significance, its achievements being meagre in the grand strategic context of the period. However, the WEU was promoted as a contribution to both Atlantic solidarity and European integration,[235] proving itself useful to both sides of the Atlanticist/Europeanist debate in an environment in which it was recognized that 'something must be done' if the primary organizations were unable to host the 'institutional competency' debate. The WEU's role was, by necessity, a dynamic and transitional one, which remained responsive to the full gamut of Western security interests and reflective of the environment to which they related. Consequently, the WEU's inherent ambiguity and capacity to be 'different things to different people' allowed, against a background of faltering institutional mechanisms elsewhere, for adaptation of both the Alliance and Community to meet particular interests. Thus the WEU had become a recognized and significant vehicle for the pursuit of structural change in a transforming Europe, serving as a mechanism for gradual institutional adaptation, concurrently providing support to both the Atlantic Alliance and an embryonic European security identity.

NOTES

1. A. Cahen, *The Western European Union and NATO: Building a European Defence Identity within the Context of Atlantic Solidarity,* London: Brasseys, 1989, p. 391. See P. Schmidt, 'The WEU—a union without perspective', *Aussenpolitik,* vol. 37, no. 4, 1986, pp. 389–90.
2. See F. Bozo, *De Gaulle, the United States and the Atlantic Alliance: Two Strategies for Europe,* Lanham: Rowman and Littlefield, 2001, p. xvi–xvii.
3. For discussion see J. R. Schaetzel, *The Unhinged Alliance: America and the European Community,* New York: Harper Row, 1975; H. Mendershausen, *Outlook on Western Solidarity: Political Relations in the Atlantic Alliance,* Santa Monica: Rand, 1976.
4. See D. Stuart, 'NATO in the 1980s: between European pillar and European home', *Armed Forces and Society,* vol. 16, no. 3, spring 1990, p. 423.
5. For discussion of the Nixon-Kissinger policy of 'hegemony on the cheap', see D. P. Calleo, 'NATO's middle course', *Foreign Policy,* no. 69, winter 1987–9, pp. 138–42.
6. See 'The year of Europe', Address to the Associated Press Annual Luncheon, New York, 23 April 1973, in H. Kissinger, *American Foreign Policy,* 3rd edn, 1979, pp. 100–3; W. Wallace, 'Atlantic relations: policy co-ordination and conflict. Issue linkage among Atlantic governments', *International Affairs,* vol. 52, no. 2, April 1976, pp. 163–79.
7. Edward Heath, *The Course of my Life: My Autobiography,* London: Hodder and Stoughton, 1998, pp. 492–3.
8. The 'Declaration of Identity' of 14 December 1973 has been described as an 'act of desperation', given EC impotence in the face of US policy and international events. C. Hill and K. Smith (eds) *European Foreign Policy: Key Documents,* London: Routledge, 2000, p. 92.
9. Dependence on Middle East oil led Europe to adopt a more pro-Arab stance than the US, with the EU launching Euro-Arab dialogue in 1974, to the frustration of the Americans. Détente was generally favoured by the Europeans, but there were fears, particularly in France, of a developing superpower

condominium. See R. McGeehan, 'European defence cooperation: a political perspective', *The World Today,* vol. 41, no. 6, June 1985, pp. 116–19; G. F. Kennan, 'Europe's problems, Europe's choices', *Foreign Policy,* no. 14, spring 1974, pp. 3–16.

10. K. E. Jørgensen, 'The Western European Union and the imbroglio of European security', *Co-operation and Conflict,* vol. 25, no. 3, 1990, p. 137.

11. When asked in 1979, 'How much confidence do you have in the ability of the United States to deal wisely with present world problems?', 53% of those in a British poll had little or no confidence, with 14% undecided. *Public Opinion,* vol. 2, no. 2, March–May 1979, p. 14.

12. See J. Dumbrell, *A Special Relationship: Anglo-American Relations from the Cold War to Iraq,* 2nd edn, Hampshire: Palgrave Macmillan, 2006, pp. 94–104.

13. See J. G. H. Halstead, 'The security aspects of European integration: a Canadian view', *Journal of European Integration,* vol. 9, nos. 2–3, winter/spring 1986, pp. 177–92.

14. For the crisis in confidence in the Atlantic Alliance by the early 1980s see R. R. Bowie, 'The Atlantic Alliance', *Daedalus,* vol. 110, no. 1, winter 1981, pp. 53–70; A. von Geusau (ed.) *Allies in a Turbulent World: Challenges to US and Western European Co-operation,* Lexington: Heath, 1983.

15. D. Allen and M. Smith, 'Western Europe in the Atlantic system of the 1980s: towards a new identity', in S. Gill (ed.) *Atlantic Relations beyond the Reagan Era,* New York: St Martin's Press, 1989, p. 92. For a useful discussion of the first Reagan Administration's 'containment' policy see C. Wolf Jr, 'Beyond containment: redesigning American policies', *Washington Quarterly,* vol. 5, no. 1, winter 1982, pp. 107–17.

16. S. P. Ramet, 'The United States and Europe: toward greater cooperation or a historic parting?—an idealist perspective', in S. P. Ramet and C. Ingebritsen (eds) *Coming In from the Cold War. Changes in US-European Interactions since 1980,* Lanham: Rowman and Littlefield, 2002, p. 4.

17. Reagan said, of his use of ideology, that 'to grasp and hold a vision, to fix it in your senses—that is the very essence, I believe, of successful leadership—not only on the movie set, where I learned it, but everywhere'. Cited in T. L. Deibel, 'Reagan's mixed legacy', *Foreign Policy,* no. 75, summer 1989, p. 51. For a more generous revisionist study of Reagan's foreign policy approach see J. Arquilla, *The Reagan Imprint: Ideas in American Foreign Policy from the Collapse of Communism to the War on Terror,* Chicago: Ivan R. Dee, 2006.

18. 'The Evil Empire', President Reagan's speech to the British House of Commons, June 8, 1982, online at http://www.mtholyoke.edu/acad/intrel/evilemp. htm.

19. President Reagan's address to a meeting of the National Association of Evangelicals in Orlando, Florida, on March 8, 1983, online at http://www.nationalcenter.org/ReaganEvilEmpire1983.html.

20. In 1973 Jobert, the French Minister of Foreign Affairs, was to complain that European dependency was resulting in her being 'treated like a non-person, humiliated in its non-existence'. Cited in McGeehan, 'European defence cooperation', p. 118.

21. C. Layne, 'Atlanticism without NATO', *Foreign Policy,* no. 67, summer 1987, pp. 26–7.

22. See T. Draper, 'The Western misalliance', *Washington Quarterly,* vol. 4, no. 1, winter 1981, pp. 13–69.

23. D. P. Calleo, *Beyond American Hegemony: The Future of the Western Alliance,* Oxford: Wheatsheaf Books, 1987, p. 80.

24. The US' perceived pro-Israeli bias in its policy for the Middle East led the EEC member states to adopt the ineffective, but politically significant, Venice

Declaration of July 1980, which announced a co-ordinated policy position for the region based on the desire for a long-term Middle East settlement including consideration of the Palestinian problem and the stabilization of pro-Western Arab regimes. See E. A. Kolodziej, 'Europe: the partial partner', *International Security,* vol. 5, no. 3, 1980–1, pp. 104–31. Also see R. E. Hunter, 'What crisis?', *Washington Quarterly,* vol. 5, no. 3, summer 1982, pp. 53–8.

25. F. Halliday, *The Making of the Second Cold War,* London: Verso, 1983.
26. Stuart, 'NATO in the 1980s', p. 425.
27. See J. W. Holmes, 'The dumbbell won't do', *Foreign Policy,* no. 50, 1983, p. 15.
28. E. A. Kolodziej and R. A. Pollard, 'The uneasy alliance: Western Europe and the United States', *Wilson Quarterly,* winter 1983, p. 119.
29. S. Nunn, 'NATO: saving the alliance', *Washington Quarterly,* vol. 5, no. 3, summer 1982, p. 21.
30. H. A. Kissinger, 'NATO: the next thirty years', *Survival,* vol. 21, no. 6, November–December 1979, pp. 265–6. Also see P. Lellouche, 'Does NATO have a future? A European view', *Washington Quarterly,* vol. 5, no. 3, summer 1982, pp. 40–52; M. H. Harrison, 'Our Atlantic quagmire', *Washington Quarterly,* vol. 5, no. 3, summer 1982, pp. 67–73.
31. For a useful overview of NATO nuclear strategy during the period see M. O. Wheeler, 'NATO nuclear strategy, 1949–90', in G. Schmidt (ed.) *A History of NATO: The First Fifty Years. Volume 3,* Basingstoke: Palgrave, 2001, pp. 121–39.
32. See W. Krieger, 'NATO and nuclear weapons', in Schmidt, *A History of NATO,* p. 113.
33. M. J. Hillenbrand, 'American foreign policy and the Atlantic Alliance', in W. Goldstein (ed.) *Reagan's Leadership in the Atlantic Alliance,* New York: New York University Press, 1986, p. 46.
34. P. Lellouche, 'Europe and her defence', *Foreign Affairs,* vol. 59, no. 4, March 1981, p. 815.
35. For discussion see C. Bertram, 'Strategic defence and the Western Alliance', *Daedalus,* vol. 114, no. 3, summer 1985, pp. 279–96.
36. Reagan cited in R. E. Osgood, 'Reagan's foreign policy in a post-war perspective', in Goldstein (ed.) *Reagan's Leadership in the Atlantic Alliance,* p. 31. Also see S. Smith, 'The Strategic Defence Initiative: is it technically and strategically defensible?' in Goldstein, *Reagan's Leadership in the Atlantic Alliance,* p. 176.
37. R. Reagan, Address to the Nation by the President Ronald Reagan, 23 March 1983, 'Peace and national security', *Daedalus,* vol. 114, no. 3, summer 1985, pp. 369–71.
38. A. Cyr, *US Foreign Policy and European Security,* London: Macmillan, 1989, p. 133.
39. See J. Palmer, *Europe without America: The Crisis in Atlantic Relations,* Oxford: Oxford University Press, 1988, pp. 8 and 21. Also see M. Uttley, 'Defence procurement and industrial policy', in S. Croft, A. M. Dorman, W. Rees and M. Uttley (eds) *Britain and Defence 1945–2000,* London: Pearson Education, 2001, pp. 122–3.
40. R. Dezcallor, 'On Western European defence', *Washington Quarterly,* vol. 10, no. 1, 1987, p. 166.
41. Willem van Eekelen, future Chairman of the Eurogroup and Secretary General of the WEU, was to note the work done by the organization 'to put the message across to the American politicians, officials and the public that we are contributing a fair share to NATO'. W. van Eekelen, 'The Eurogroup and the US-European dialogue', *NATO Review,* vol. 36, no. 4, August 1988, p. 9.

42. The 'Airland Battle 2000' initiative, for example, was intended to exploit Soviet doctrinal weakness, dislocating the Soviet second echelon with technologically enhanced front-line forces. See Nunn, 'NATO: saving the alliance', p. 23.

43. Kolodziej and Pollard, 'The uneasy alliance', p. 118.

44. P. Corterier, 'Two views from West Germany: what do we need changed in NATO?', in Goldstein (ed.) *Reagan's Leadership in the Atlantic Alliance*, p. 86.

45. The 1984 Amendment threatened a withdrawal of 30,000 US troops from Europe if the Europeans failed to meet specific performance expectations in line with the annual 3% of GDP defence-spending increases agreed by member states at the NATO Washington Summit in May 1978. Failing by three votes in the Senate, it was followed in 1985 by a successful amendment to provide extra funding for particular transatlantic co-operative NATO projects as a reward and inducement for good allied performance in burden-sharing. I. Gambles, 'Prospects for West European security cooperation', *Adelphi Paper*, no. 244, autumn 1989, p. 11.

46. See H. Bull, 'European self-reliance and the reform of NATO', *Atlantic Quarterly*, vol. 1, no. 1, spring 1983, pp. 25–43.

47. G. L. and A. L. Williams, *Crisis in European Defence: The Next Ten Years*, London: C. Knight, 1974, p. 255.

48. The UK, Denmark and Ireland became EEC members in 1973, and Greece acceded in 1981.

49. See F. Duchêne, 'Europe's role in world peace', in R. Mayne (ed.) *Europe Tomorrow*, London: Fontana/Collins, 1972, pp. 32–47, here p. 43. For a critique of the concept see H. Bull, 'Civilian power Europe: a contradiction in terms?', *Journal of Common Market Studies*, vol. 21, no. 4, September–December 1982, pp. 149–70.

50. See Halstead, 'The security aspects of European integration', p. 184; R. Rummel, 'European-American crisis management cooperation' in W. J. Feld, *Western Europe's Global Reach, Regional Cooperation and Worldwide Aspirations*, New York: Pergamon, 1979, p. 220.

51. For discussion of the EPC in the 1970s see W. Wallace, 'A common European foreign policy: mirage or reality', in B. Burrows, G. Denton and G. Edwards (eds) *Federal Solutions to European Issues*, London, Macmillan, 1978, pp. 174–86. Also see S. Nuttall, 'Two decades of EPC performance', in E. Regelsberger, P. de Schoutheete de Tervarent and W. Wessels (eds) *Foreign Policy of the European Union: From EPC to CFSP and Beyond*, Boulder: Lynne Rienner, 1997, pp. 19–39.

52. Alfred Cahen refers to a 'marked coolness of a growing sector of European opinion with regard to Atlantic security and, in the Atlantic context, to European security'. A. Cahen, 'Relaunching WEU: implications for the Atlantic Alliance', *NATO Review*, vol. 34, no. 4, August 1986, p. 11. Also see S. Hoffmann, 'Cries and whimpers: thoughts on West European-American relations in the 1980s', *Dædalus*, vol. 113, no. 3, summer 1984, p. 231.

53. See D. Möisi, 'Domestic priorities and the demands of alliance: a European perspective' in 'Special issue: Defence and consensus: the domestic aspects of Western security, part III: papers from the IISS 24th annual Conference' *Adelphi Paper*, no. 184, summer 1983, pp. 12–16. For a study of trends in public support for NATO and attitudes to a European security and defence competence between 1976 and 1992 see P. Manigart and E. Marlier, 'European public opinion on the future of security', *Armed Forces and Society*, vol. 19, no. 3, spring 1993, pp. 335–52.

54. K. Kaiser, T. de Montbrial and D. Watt, *Western Security: What Has Changed? What Should be Done?*, New York: Council on Foreign Relations, 1981, p. 48.

55. For the London Report see 'Report on European political cooperation', *Bulletin of the European Communities*, vol. 14, no. 3, 1981, p. 14–17.

56. See 'Draft European Act', *Europe Documents*, no. 1178, 19 November 1981. The West German and Italian Foreign Ministers had sought the inclusion of defence issues within the EPC remit, with European Parliament and Commission input enhancing linkage to the EC. For discussion see D. W. Urwin, *The Community of Europe: A History of European Integration since 1945*, 2nd edn, London: Longman, 1995, pp. 221–2.

57. 'Solemn Declaration on European Union, European Council, Stuttgart 19 June 1983', *Bulletin of the European Communities*, vol. 16, no. 6, 1983, p. 25 (author's italics). The European Council was to provide general guidelines for the EPC, whilst the Council Presidency would report to the European Parliament.

58. J. M. Hoscheit and P. Tsakaloyannis, 'Relaunching the Western European Union: an overview', in P. Tsakaloyannis (ed.) *The Reactivation of the Western European Union: The Effects on the European Community and its Institutions*, Maastricht: EIPA, 1985, p. 13.

59. K. Kaiser, T. de Montbrial, W. Wallace and E. Wellenstein, *The European Community: Progress or Decline?*, London: RIIA, 1983, p. 11.

60. Keatinge notes the 'logical incompatibility' within Irish doctrine with regard to European integration, which 'insists on the parallel evolution of political and economic integration with the transfer of decision-making competences matching economic convergence', and their position of permanent neutrality. P. Keatinge, 'Ireland and the Western European Union', in Tsakaloyannis (ed.) *The Reactivation of the Western European Union*, p. 106.

61. Cahen, 'Relaunching WEU', p. 9.

62. D. Garnham, *The Politics of European Defense Cooperation*, Cambridge: Ballinger, 1988, p. 35.

63. S. Serfaty, 'Atlantic fantasies', *Washington Quarterly*, vol. 5, no. 3, summer 1982, p. 75.

64. This is what Schmidt refers to as 'neutrality pacifism' and Grant as 'the three West German isms—nationalism, neutralism, and pacifism'. See Schmidt, 'The WEU—a union without perspective', p. 391; R. Grant, 'French defence policy and European security', *Political Science Quarterly*, vol. 100, no. 3, fall 1985, p. 417.

65. Many in France took this 'as an index of their neighbour's anxiety about its own security before the Soviet threat'. S. F. Wells, 'The United States and European defence co-operation', *Survival*, vol. 27, no. 4, July–August 1985, p. 161.

66. D. S. Yost, 'France, West Germany and European security co-operation', *International Affairs*, vol. 64, no. 1, winter 1987–88, pp. 97–100.

67. For details of the make-up of the FAR, which was largely formed from pre-existing French Army units, see G. Turbe, 'France's rapid deployment forces', *International Defence Review*, vol. 20, no. 8, August 1987, pp. 1023–6.

68. See R. S. Rudney, 'Mitterand's New Atlanticism: evolving French attitudes towards NATO', *Orbis*, vol. 28, no. 1, spring 1984, p. 83–101.

69. See B. Brigouleix, 'The Franco-German cement of the EC edifice', *European Affairs*, no. 3, autumn 1987, pp. 62–7. Also see H. G. Poettering, 'Germany's and France's interest in a European security policy', *Aussenpolitik*, vol. 32, no. 2, 1986, pp. 176–86.

70. See discussion in D. A. Ruiz Palmer, 'Between the Rhine and the Elbe: France and the conventional defence of Central Europe', *Comparative Strategy,* vol. 6, no. 4, fall 1987, pp. 471–512.

71. See J.-C. de Swann, 'Mitterrand and the Gaullist dilemma over European integration', *International Relations,* vol. 12, no. 2, August 1994, p. 22. WEU Assembly Reports from 1982 demonstrate that the WEU increasingly came to act as a platform for the views of the French Defence Minister M. Charles Hernu.

72. Taylor argued for the 'tidying up' of institutional structures given 'the current reluctance of governments to set up any new bodies'. T. Taylor, 'Alternative structures for European Defence cooperation', in K. Kaiser and J. Roper (eds) *British-German Defence Co-operation—Partners within the Alliance,* London: RIIA, 1988, p. 180.

73. See M. Clarke, 'The Europeanisation of NATO and the problem of Anglo-American relations', in M. Clarke and R. Hague (eds) *European Defence Co-operation: America, Britain and NATO,* Manchester: Manchester University Press, 1990, p. 40.

74. J. F. Poos, 'Prospects for the WEU', *NATO Review,* vol. 35, no. 4, August 1987, p. 16.

75. K. R. Holmes, 'Europeanising NATO', *Washington Quarterly,* vol. 7, no. 2, spring 1984, p. 60. Also see F. Heisbourg, 'The British and French nuclear forces: current roles and challenges', *Survival,* vol. 31, no. 4, July–August 1989, pp. 301–20.

76. Dezcallor, 'On Western European defence', p. 160. For a discussion of the principal security dilemmas for the FRG see R. Seidelmann, 'German defence policy', in E. H. Fedder (ed.) *Defence Politics of the Atlantic Alliance,* New York: Praeger, 1980, pp. 67–82.

77. For a discussion of divergent German-US perceptions of the Soviet invasion of Afghanistan and the Iranian hostage issue see W. R. Smyser, 'Turmoil in German-American relations', *Washington Quarterly,* vol. 3, no. 3, 1980, pp. 106–17. Also see L. D. Edinger, 'The German-American connection in the 1980s', *Political Science Quarterly,* vol. 95, no. 4, winter 1980–1, pp. 589–606.

78. See E. Pond, 'The security debate in West Germany', *Survival,* vol. 28, no. 4, July–August 1986, pp. 322–36. These views persisted amongst the German public throughout the decade: opinion polls conducted in 1989 found that only 9% felt that nuclear deterrence was an acceptable basis for NATO strategy, and less than one-quarter saw the Soviet Union as a military threat. See E. Schmahling, 'German security policy beyond American hegemony', *World Policy Journal,* vol. 6, no. 2, 1989, pp. 379–81.

79. This had finally covered only some types of strategic bombers, mines and long-range missiles, but removal of these constraints would be a significant symbolic change. See Hoscheit and Tsakaloyannis, 'Relaunching the Western European Union', p. 15.

80. See Hans-Dietrich Genscher, Foreign Minister of the FRG, 'Aspekte der Partnerschaft zwischen Europa und den USA', speech to US Chamber of Commerce, Stuttgart, 25 October 1984, in *Bulletin,* no. 128, 30 October 1984, p. 1133. Also see S. Keukeleire, 'Franco-German security cooperation', in E. J. Kirchner and J. Sperling (eds) *The Federal Republic of Germany and NATO: Forty Years After,* Basingstoke: Macmillan, 1992, p. 138.

81. The 'orthodox' view of UK defence adaptation from 1945 perceived the British defence decline as essentially economically driven, reactive and *ad hoc* in nature, although others argue that British defence policy has been more rationally determined by the requirements of the changing security situation.

See M. Dockrill, *British Defence Policy since 1945*, Oxford, Blackwell, 1988, pp. 125–31.

82. L. Freedman, 'British defence policy', in Fedder (ed.) *Defence Politics of the Atlantic Alliance*, p. 52; K. Hartley and E. Lynk, 'The political economy of UK defence expenditure', *RUSI Journal*, vol. 125, no. 1, March 1980, p. 30.

83. See *Statement of the Defence Estimates, Defence in the 1980s*, London: HMSO, 1980, p. 41, for the British defence posture.

84. Dumbrell, *A Special Relationship*, pp. 106–7.

85. Ostensibly undertaken in order to 'rescue' US citizens on the island following a coup, the invasion was likely motivated by the loss of US international credibility following the high casualties sustained in Lebanon, and by the perceived need to send a message of resolve to local adversaries in Cuba and Nicaragua. See D. Ryan, *The United States and Europe in the Twentieth Century*, London: Pearson Education, 2003, p. 100.

86. M. Thatcher, *The Downing Street Years*, London: HarperCollins, 1993, pp. 331–2.

87. D. Allen, 'Britain and Western Europe', in M. Smith, S. Smith and B. White (eds) *British Foreign Policy: Tradition, Change and Transformation*, London: Allen and Unwin, 1988, p. 179. Also see comments by Admiral Sir James Eberle in Wells, 'The United States and European defence co-operation', p. 166.

88. Interview at UK Ministry of Defence, 19 July 1991.

89. Clarke, 'The Europeanisation of NATO', p. 39. This concern for the 'practical' was to become a consistent theme of the UK's approach to the WEU.

90. A. Forster, 'The ratchet of European defence: Britain and the reactivation of Western European Union, 1984–1991', in A. Deighton (ed.) *Western European Union 1954–1997: Defence, Security, Integration*, Oxford: European Interdependence Research Unit, 1997, p. 32.

91. Italy and the Benelux countries had resisted the exclusive Principal Nations approach and sought to exercise influence over the Big Three through the auspices of the WEU. See P. Tsakaloyannis, 'Constructing a European security pillar: domestic constraints', in P. Tsakaloyannis (ed.) *Western European Security in a Changing World: From the Reactivation of the WEU to the Single European Act*, Maastricht: EIPA, 1988, p. 4.

92. For discussion see M. Clarke and R. Hague, 'Britain, America and the future of NATO', in Clarke and Hague (eds) *European Defence Co-operation*, p. 154. Also see *NATO in the 1990s*, Special Report of the North Atlantic Assembly, Belgium, May 1988; D. Greenwood, 'Constructing the European pillar: issues and institutions', *NATO Review*, vol. 36, no. 3, June 1988, pp. 13–17.

93. G. Howe, 'The European pillar', *Foreign Affairs*, vol. 63, no. 2, winter 1984–5, p. 338. Also see E. Ravenal, 'Europe without America: the erosion of NATO', *Foreign Affairs*, vol. 63, no. 5, summer 1985, p. 1030.

94. See C. Bertram, 'Western Europe's strategic role: towards a European pillar' in 'The changing strategic landscape', *Adelphi Paper*, no. 235, spring 1989, pp. 109–11; Holmes, 'The dumbbell won't do', pp. 3–32.

95. W. van Eekelen, 'Future European defence co-operation: the role of the WEU', *European Strategy Group Occasional Paper*, September 1989, p. 32.

96. See W. Wallace, 'With Europe—for better or worse', *New Statesman*, vol. 113, 17 April 1987, pp. 12–13.

97. Mattox refers to the American attitude as 'supportive in principle, but somewhat schizophrenic, or at least ambivalent, in practice'. G. A. Mattox, 'The United States' perspective on the growth of a European pillar', in Clarke and Hague (eds) *European Defence Co-operation*, p. 123.

98. H. A. Kissinger, 'A plan to reshape NATO', *Atlantic Community Quarterly*, vol. 22, no. 1, spring 1984, pp. 41–51. For a useful discussion of US elite

images of Europe and transatlantic relations in the early to mid 1980s see C. M. Kelleher, 'America looks at Europe: change and continuity in the 1980s', *Washington Quarterly*, vol. 7, no. 1, winter 1984, pp. 33–49.

99. This was to remain true throughout the revitalization process, particularly given the Gaullist tendencies of the French Prime Minister Jacques Chirac. However, as Zakheim was to note, 'though a Gaullist, Chirac is not De Gaulle, nor is his defense minister, André Giraud, anti-American. Defense relations between France and the US are better than they have been for years'. D. S. Zakheim, '"New" Western European Union: uniting Europe or dividing NATO?', *Armed Forces Journal International*, vol. 125, December 1987, pp. 86–7.

100. W. Wallace, 'Relaunching the Western European Union: variable geometry, institutional duplication or policy drift', in Tsakaloyannis (ed.) *The Reactivation of the Western European Union*, p. 39.

101. Wells, 'The United States and European defence co-operation', p. 166.

102. See the Belgian Foreign Minister's favourable anticipation of French proposals in his report published in *Le Monde* on 23 December 1983.

103. WEU Council of Ministers, *Rome Declaration*, 26–7 October 1984, implemented in Bonn, 22–23 April 1985. For the text of relevant documents see WEU, *The Reactivation of WEU, Statements and Communiqués 1984–1987*, Batley: WEU, 1988.

104. A. Cahen, 'Western European Union: birth, development and reactivation', *Army Quarterly and Defence Journal*, vol. 17, no. 4, October 1987, p. 394.

105. For discussion see A. Cahen, 'The emergence and role of the WEU', in Clarke and Hague, *European Defence Co-operation*, pp. 60–1. Also see WEU Assembly, Extraordinary Session, *The European Pillar of the Atlantic Alliance: Part 1. The Reactivation of the WEU*, doc. 1089, 16 March 1987.

106. Luxembourg's Foreign Minister Poos, 'Prospects for the WEU', p. 17.

107. Schmidt, 'The WEU—a union without perspective', p. 390.

108. See for example WEU Assembly, rapporteur Mr Muller, *Africa's Role in a European Security Policy—Chad*, doc. 957, 31 October 1983; rapporteur Lord Reay, *Situation in the Middle East and European Security*, doc. 978, 24 May 1984; rapporteur Mr Martine, *Europe and the Aftermath of the War between Iran and Iraq*, doc. 1162, 10 November 1988.

109. Cahen, *The Western European Union and NATO*, p. 34.

110. WEU Council of Ministers, *Venice Communiqué*, 29–30 April 1986. Jørgensen suggests that during the revitalization process 'the WEU's most "substantial" qualities seem to be located at the rhetorical and symbolic levels'. 'The Western European Union and the imbroglio of European security', p. 150.

111. Cited in a report by P. Ruge, 'Terrorismus bedroht Europa', *Die Welt*, 25 April 1986, p. 6. See B. Bloom, 'Enthusiasm wanes in Europe for reviving the WEU', *Financial Times*, 29 April 1986. For an unsurprisingly more optimistic account see Secretary General Cahen's speech to the Plenary Session of the WEU Assembly, 2 December 1985, 'The future of Western European Union', text published in *Europe Documents*, no. 59, 31 December 1985.

112. Cahen, interview with author, 25 January 1997.

113. The British Secretary General of NATO, Lord Carrington, was particularly concerned about the effects that the WEU might have on transatlantic relations, stating that 'to build a European defence identity by weakening the security link between Western Europe and North America would put at risk the security we seek to strengthen'. Carrington cited in *Agence Europe*, no. 4164, 18 September 1985.

114. See WEU Assembly, *The European Pillar of the Atlantic Alliance*, doc. 1089, p. 6. The three issues on the agenda of the Nuclear and Space Talks were to be INF, strategic offensive arms, and defence and space weapons.

115. *Report of the Ad Hoc Committee for Institutional Affairs to the European Council, Brussels,* 29–30 March 1985. This report did, however, become the basis for much of the future work on institutional reform that was to lead to the Single European Act and Maastricht Treaty.

116. Schmidt, 'The WEU—a union without perspective', p. 395.

117. R. Seidelmann, 'WEU and EC—competition or cooperation for Western Europe's security', in Tsakaloyannis (ed.) *The Reactivation of the Western European Union,* pp. 62–5.

118. Note the Haagerup Report adopted by the EP in November 1982 dealing with the security dimensions of foreign policy, and the Fergusson Report of October 1983 calling for pragmatic co-ordination of arms production and arms exports.

119. Areas of overlap included East-West relations, the CSCE, the Middle East and the Mediterranean, whilst issues such as SDI clearly had economic as well as security and defence implications. Interestingly, no formal consultations between the EPC and WEU were provided for in the Rome Declaration or Single European Act.

120. See P. Tsakaloyannis, 'Greece and the reactivation of the WEU', in Tsakaloyannis (ed.) *The Reactivation of the Western European Union,* p. 100. Also see C. Thune, 'Denmark and the Western European Union', in Tsakaloyannis (ed.) *The Reactivation of the Western European Union,* p. 93.

121. *The Single European Act,* Luxembourg, 17 February 1986. The SEA included amendments to all three Communities, most significantly creating the conditions for an internal market within the EEC and replacing many areas of unanimity in decision-making with provisions for Qualified Majority Voting. The SEA was intended chiefly to create a single market by 1992. Under Title III, Article 30, the SEA provided for 'the formalisation of what already existed in EPC practice, plus an EPC Secretariat', retaining the emphasis on intergovernmentalism but strengthening co-ordination between the EPC and the EC Commission and improving consultation between the EPC and EP. For structure, rules and security competence of the EPC see P. Jannuzzi, 'European political co-operation: moving towards closer integration', *NATO Review,* vol. 36, no. 4, August 1988, pp. 11–16; S. Duke, *The Elusive Quest for European Security: From EDC to CFSP,* London: Macmillan, 2000, pp. 69–72.

122. See P. Tsakaloyannis, 'The EC from civilian power to military intervention', in J. Lodge (ed.) *The European Community and the Challenge of the Future,* London: Pinter, 1989, p. 471.

123. See E. J. Kirchner, 'Has the Single European Act opened the door for a European security policy', *Journal of European Integration,* vol. 13, no. 1, autumn 1989, pp. 1–14, for discussion.

124. *The Single European Act,* Article 30(6a).

125. Report by Foreign Ministers of WEU, 12 June 1984, cited in WEU Assembly, *Thirtieth Annual Report of the Council to the Assembly,* doc. 1006, 1 March 1985, p. 25.

126. Cahen, 'Western European Union: birth, development and reactivation', pp. 394–5.

127. Executive power in the Soviet Union sat with the General Secretary of the Communist Party. Gorbachev replaced Konstantin Chernenko in this role (and as Chair of the Presidium of the Supreme Soviet, the de jure head of state), becoming President of the Union of Soviet Socialist Republics, the highest political office once this new role was established in March 1990.

128. Ryan, *The United States and Europe in the Twentieth Century,* pp. 106–7.

129. See 'Washington s'inquiete des initiatives de l'Union de Europe occidentale', *Le Monde,* 3 April 1985; B. Bloom, 'US objects to European moves on defence policies', *The Financial Times,* 2 April 1985.

130. R. E. Hunter, 'Will the United States remain a European power', *Survival,* vol. 30, no. 3, May–June 1988, p. 215. Reagan's zero option may have been 'a clever ploy rather than a bona fide strategy', intended to make modernization of nuclear forces acceptable to Europeans, on the assumption that the Soviets would not consider scrapping their SS-20 capability; Gorbachev called Reagan's bluff with his January 1986 proposals for the elimination of all nuclear weapons by 2000. C. Bertram, 'Europe's security dilemmas', *Foreign Affairs,* vol. 65, no. 5, summer 1987, p. 949.

131. M. Howard, 'A European perspective on the Reagan years' in 'Special issue: America and the World 1987', *Foreign Affairs,* vol. 66, no. 3, 1987–8, p. 479. Also see J. Schlesinger, 'Reykjavik and revelations: a turn of the tide' in 'Special issue: America and the World 1986', *Foreign Affairs,* vol. 65, no. 3, 1986, p. 430.

132. The summit offered Reagan the opportunity to enhance his profile as a peace-builder, whilst improving Republican chances in the November Congressional elections. Gorbachev was eager to avoid the domestic political backlash of another failed arms negotiation following the Geneva Summit of 1985. Both men later referred to the Reykjavik Summit as a 'turning point' despite its failure, demonstrating how close the two superpowers were and laying the ground for more fertile talks to come. See M. Duric, *The Strategic Defence Initiative,* Aldershot: Ashgate, 2003, pp. 66–98. Also see M. Gorbachev, *Memoirs,* London: Bantam, 1997, pp. 536–42.

133. Reagan cited in Howard, 'A European perspective on the Reagan years', p. 479. The then UK Foreign Secretary notes in his memoirs that Reykjavik led to a 'curious shift' in the previously 'critical' attitude of European states to the British and French nuclear deterrents in the face of a potentially destabilizing unilateral US arms control deal. G. Howe, *Conflict of Loyalty,* Basingstoke: Macmillan, 1994, p. 523.

134. In securing the Anglo-US Trident deal, Thatcher also gained agreement with Reagan on his negotiating objectives on INF elimination, although the 'deal' omitted only the aspiration to a total phase-out of strategic nuclear weapons within 10 years, accepting a 50% reduction in superpower strategic weapons within 5 years and a ban on chemical weapons. See L. Barber and P. Riddel, 'Thatcher wins Reagan promise on modernizing UK deterrent', *The Financial Times,* 17 November 1986. This won her some respect from Europeans despite her Euroscepticism. See S. Erlanger, 'Mrs Thatcher under European eyes', *New Statesman,* 26 June 1987.

135. Cahen, interview with author, Paris, 25 January 1997.

136. Thatcher's Bruges speech to the College of Europe, 20 September 1998, cited in M. Thatcher, *The Downing Street Years,* London: Harper Collins, 1993, p. 745.

137. J. Campbell, *Margaret Thatcher. Volume Two: The Iron Lady,* London: Jonathan Cape, 2003, p. 307.

138. For the text of Thatcher's speech to the College of Europe (the 'Bruges Speech') see http://www.margaretthatcher.org/speeches/displaydocument. asp?docid=107332.

139. Howe, *Conflict of Loyalty,* p. 544.

140. Duke, *The Elusive Quest for European Security,* p. 76.

141. WEU Council of Ministers, *Platform of European Security Interests,* The Hague, 27 October 1987.

142. See UK Foreign and Commonwealth Office commentary on the Platform in their memorandum, 'The political impact of disarmament and arms control', *Third Report of the Foreign Affairs Committee,* 1987–8, HC 280, London: HMSO, 1988, pp. 22–4.

143. M. Clarke, 'Evaluating the new Western European Union: the implications for Spain', in K. Maxwell (ed.) *Spanish Foreign and Defence Policy*, Boulder: Westview Press, 1991, p. 171.

144. Garnham, *The Politics of European Defense Cooperation*, p. 120.

145. H. Sonnenfeldt, 'The European pillar: the American view' in 'The changing strategic landscape', *Adelphi Paper*, no. 235, spring 1989, p. 98.

146. 'Remarks by the President to World Net', Washington, DC: Office of the White House Press Secretary, 3 November 1987, p. 5. Also see van Eekelen, 'Future European Defence Co-operation', pp. 17–18.

147. Cahen, *The Western European Union and NATO*, pp. 18–22.

148. R. Rummel, 'Modernising transatlantic relations: West European security cooperation and the reaction in the United States', *Washington Quarterly*, vol. 12, no. 4, autumn 1989, p. 88.

149. *Rome Declaration*, 'Institutional Reform of WEU', 1984, section III3a.

150. WEU Assembly, rapporteurs Mr Henares and Mr Tummers, *Western European Union: Information Report*, February 1993, pp. 18–19.

151. The INF Treaty, signed in December 1987, agreed to the destruction of intermediate- and shorter-range deployed US and Soviet ground-based ballistic and cruise missiles with a range of 500–5,500 km within three years. See L. E. Davis, 'Lessons of the INF Treaty', *Foreign Affairs*, vol. 66, no. 4, spring 1988, pp. 720–34, for discussion.

152. L. A. Dunn, 'Considerations after the INF Treaty: NATO after the global double zero', *Survival*, vol. 3, no. 3, May–June 1988, p. 22; J. Joffe, 'Europe's American pacifier', *Foreign Policy*, no. 54, spring 1984, p. 80.

153. In fact, WEU members could not come to an agreed position over the 'triple zero option' at their April 1987 Ministerial in Luxembourg, agreeing only to the need for a measured and 'unhasty' response. See F. Bonnart, 'West Europeans agreed they had nothing to say', *International Herald Tribune*, 28 May 1987.

154. Given the implications of arms control measures, the UK's Foreign Minister, Geoffrey Howe, supported the WEU as a forum to prepare for potential reduction of the US defence commitment to Europe. See Report on Brussels Speech, 'Howe hints NATO must be ready for US cuts in Europe', *The Guardian*, 17 March 1987.

155. WEU Council of Ministers, *Platform of European Security Interests*.

156. Jørgensen, 'The Western European Union and the imbroglio of European security', pp. 146–7.

157. Cited in Cahen, *The Western European Union and NATO*, p. 46.

158. G. Howe, 'The WEU: the way ahead', *NATO Review*, vol. 37, no. 3, June 1989, p. 13.

159. E. J. Mesaros, 'NATO-Europe and the United States: the "two way street" concept', in Feld (ed.) *Western Europe's Global Reach*, p. 240.

160. See the WEU Council of Ministers, *Bonn Communiqué*, 23 April 1985.

161. *Rome Declaration*, 'Institutional Reform of WEU', 1984, section III3d. 'The IEPG is Janus-faced. Transatlantic cooperation is one face; the second face is improved European competitiveness *against* American defense contractors, a US armaments market two and a half times larger than Western Europe's, and research and development spending approximately five times greater than Europe's'. Garnham, *The Politics of European Defense Cooperation*, p. 126.

162. See R. Nibblett, 'Defence implications of EC 92: a primer', *National Defence*, no. 74, December 1989, p. 22.

163. See Communication from the Commission to the Council, COM (83) 258 final, 2 June 1983, in *Bulletin of the European Communities*, Supplement 5/83, pp. 25–34. For discussion of European initiatives in this area see M. Lucas, 'The

Strategic Defence Initiative and the European response in high technology research and development', in Gill, *Atlantic Relations beyond the Reagan Era*, pp. 179–95.

164. F. Fenske, 'France and the Strategic Defence Initiative: speeding up or putting on the brakes?', *International Affairs*, vol. 62, no. 2, spring 1986, p. 235; C. Arnaud, 'What is Eureka?', *NATO Review*, vol. 34, no. 3, June 1986, pp. 12–15. For the British perspective on these initiatives see S. George, *An Awkward Partner: Britain in the European Community*, Oxford: Oxford University Press, 1998, pp. 200–1.

165. WEU Council of Ministers, *Bonn Communiqué*, 23 April 1985.

166. The long and drawn-out process to report stage opened the WEU up to considerable criticism at the time. See WEU Assembly, *The European Pillar of the Atlantic Alliance*, doc. 1089, p. 7.

167. For discussion see Howard, 'A European perspective on the Reagan years', p. 480; and G. de Carmoy, 'Changing French perspectives: the Atlantic Alliance and the United States', in Goldstein, *Reagan's Leadership in the Atlantic Alliance*, p. 96.

168. The European Fighter Aircraft, for example, cost an estimated $60m each, compared to around half this for F-16 Agile Falcon or F-18 Hornet 2000. See Sonnenfeldt, 'The European pillar: the American view', pp. 96–7.

169. S. Ledogar cited in Sonnenfeldt, 'The European pillar: the American view', p. 97.

170. D. Garnham, 'US disengagement and European defense cooperation', in T. G. Carpenter (ed.) *NATO at 40: Confronting a Changing World*, Lexington: Lexington Books, 1990, pp. 75–91.

171. Garnham, *The Politics of European Defense Cooperation*, p. 123. The UK's Defence Minister, Heseltine, was particularly encouraging of IEPG utilization, in line with ongoing efforts by the British Government to encourage defence collaboration as part of its New Management Initiatives.

172. G. Aybet, *The Dynamics of European Security Co-operation 1945–1991*, London: Macmillan, 1997, p. 160.

173. For the British position see *Statement on the Defence Estimates*, vol. 1, London: HMSO, 1987, p. 46. Also see discussion in T. Taylor and K. Hayward, *The UK Defence and Industrial Base: Issues and Future Policy Options*, London: RUSI/Brassey's, 1989; E. Schmaling, 'German security policy beyond American hegemony', *World Policy Journal*, vol. 6, no. 2, spring 1989, p. 384.

174. See F. Heisbourg, 'A European defence industry: dream or reality', *NATO's Sixteen Nations*, vol. 33, no. 8, January 1989, pp. 24–7. In fact, by 1989, national and collaborative weapons projects had lost much of their political impetus as a consequence of the 'arms control blight'. See T. Taylor, 'Conventional arms control—a threat to arms procurement', *The World Today*, vol. 45, no. 3, July 1989, pp. 121–4.

175. WEU Assembly, *WEU: Information Report*, February 1993, pp. 18–20.

176. See W. J. Feld, 'Franco-German military cooperation and European unification', *Journal of European Integration*, vol. 12, nos. 2–3, 1989, pp. 151–64; W. Weidenfeld, '25 years after 22 January 1963: the Franco-German Friendship Treaty', *Aussenpolitik*, vol. 39, no. 1, 1988, pp. 3–12.

177. M. Evans, 'Paris ignores Thatcher over joint brigade', *The Times*, 30 March 1988, p. 11.

178. See W. Wallace, 'European security: bilateral steps to multilateral cooperation', in Y. Boyar et al. (eds) *Franco-British Defence Cooperation*, London: Routledge/RIIA, 1989, pp. 171–80.

179. At member-state request, 'the Council shall be immediately convened in order to permit them to consult with regard to any situation which may constitute

a threat to peace, in whatever area this threat should arise, or a danger to economic stability'. MBT, 1954, Article VIII, para. 3.

180. For discussion of the development of the 'out-of-area' issue see Aybet, *The Dynamics of European Security Co-operation 1945–1991*, pp. 153–6.

181. Hoscheit and Tsakaloyannis, 'Relaunching the Western European Union', p. 17.

182. As Schmidt states, for the sake of Alliance cohesion the Europeans needed to find a means of countering the growing American perception that the Europeans 'are interested everywhere but engaged nowhere'. Schmidt, 'The WEU—a union without perspective', p. 398.

183. A. de Guttry and N. Ronzitti (eds) *The Iran-Iraq War (1980–1988) and the Law of Naval Warfare*, Cambridge: Grotius, 1993, pp. 159–60.

184. M. R. DeVore, 'A convenient framework: the Western European Union in the Persian Gulf, 1987–1988 and 1990–1991', *European Security*, vol. 18, no. 2, June 2009, p. 232.

185. Belgium and the Netherlands went on to explicitly define their force as a European one in 'close collaboration' with the WEU; the Belgium Council of Ministers noted in a press conference on 25 March 1988 that 'thanks to the intense dialogue within the context of the WEU . . . well co-ordinated operations have been conducted'. Reproduced in de Guttry and Ronzitti (eds) *The Iran-Iraq War (1980–1988) and the Law of Naval Warfare*, p. 476. The Italians, with a perceived 'special interest' in the area, retained a national orientation throughout.

186. He went on to note that 'at the cost of much goodwill the arrangements already accepted had to be unstitched'. Howe, *Conflict of Loyalty*, p. 546.

187. E. Grove, *Maritime Strategy and European Security*, London: Brasseys, 1990, p. 61, suggests a definition of the noun 'concertation' from the adjective 'concerted', meaning 'mutually planned' and 'arranged in parts'.

188. Grove, *Maritime Strategy and European Security*, p. 64, notes the established meetings of MCM squadron commanders in the Gulf as 'an excellent example of subtle, low key integration of the various "European" and American activities'.

189. Their lack of anti-aircraft and anti-shipping capability led the Belgian and Dutch forces to seek British protection, leading to bilateral agreements with the British Armilla, resulting in the integration of Belgian and Dutch forces under the British command structure as the combined Operation Calendar in June 1988.

190. W. van Eekelen, *Debating European Security*, The Hague: SDU Publishers, 1998, pp. 50–1.

191. See W. van Eekelen, 'WEU and the Gulf Crisis', *Survival*, vol. 32, no. 6, November–December 1990, pp. 519–32.

192. See M. Chichester, 'Allied navies and the Gulf War: strategic implications', *Navy International*, no. 93, June 1988, pp. 318–21, for details of the deployments.

193. W. Mabesoone, 'European cooperation—naval lessons from the Gulf War', *NATO's Sixteen Nations*, vol. 34, no. 1, 1989, p. 74.

194. Van Eekelen speaking at a press conference concluding the WEU Ministerial Council on 19 April 1988, cited in Cahen, *The Western European Union and NATO*, p. 48.

195. For the seven principles, see van Eekelen, 'WEU and the Gulf crisis', p. 524.

196. UK Ministry of Defence official, interview with author, London, 19 July 1991.

197. Cahen, interview with author, Paris, 25 January 1997.

198. M. Smith, *NATO Enlargement during the Cold War: Strategy and System in the Western Alliance*, Basingstoke: Palgrave, 2000, p. 129.

199. Spanish co-operation with NATO had been secured on the basis of the Madrid Pacts of 1953, with Spain receiving economic aid from the Americans in exchange for airbases on Spanish territory, and by the 1970s Spanish air and naval facilities had become an 'integral part of NATO strategy and war planning', despite the absence of any Article 5 guarantee. Smith, *NATO Enlargement during the Cold War*, p. 135.
200. These two conditions of Spain's continuing NATO membership were provisos in the referendum, which asked whether it was advisable for Spain to remain in the Atlantic Alliance, alongside the provision that the US presence on Spanish territory would be reduced. The result of the referendum was a yes vote of 52.5% and a no vote of 39.8%, with 40% abstention.
201. B. George and M. Stenhouse, 'Western perspectives of Spain', in Maxwell, *Spanish Foreign and Defence Policy*, p. 95.
202. See Garnham, *The Politics of European Defense Cooperation*, p. 121.
203. In her analysis of the Soviet reaction to the Spanish entry bid, Clark notes that 'the WEU is perceived to play a key role' in the expansion of European defence co-operation, with Spain, according to a report in *Izvestiya* on 3 March 1988, 'taking a step towards the idea long nurtured by pan-Europeanists to establish a new military bloc on the continent, that would not only not oppose NATO but would, on the contrary, supplement it'. See S. Clark, 'Soviet perspectives on Spanish security policy', in Maxwell, *Spanish Foreign and Defence Policy*, p. 148.
204. Clarke, 'Evaluating the new Western European Union', pp. 173–4.
205. Protocol for the Accession of the Portuguese Republic and the Kingdom of Spain to the Treaty of Economic, Social and Cultural Collaboration and Collective Self-Defence, signed at Brussels on 17th March 1948, as amended by the Protocol modifying and completing the Brussels Treaty, signed at Paris on 23 October 1954.
206. 'Closer Western Union', *The Times*, 15 November 1988, p. 15.
207. W. van Eekelen, 'The management of the WEU: political/organizational aspects', in Tsakaloyannis (ed.) *Western European Security in a Changing World*, p. 47.
208. Gambles, 'Prospects for West European security cooperation', p. 32; 'WEU stagnation tied to London-Paris quarrels on defense', *International Herald Tribune*, 4 March 1988.
209. 'Ministerial decision concerning the setting-up of a WEU Institute for Security Studies, Brussels, 13 November 1989', online at www.weu.int/key%20 texts.htm. Also see WEU Assembly, rapporteur Mr Roman, *The WEU Institute for Security Studies*, doc. 1430, 31 October 1994, for a discussion of the institute's origins and early debates over its role. Roman identifies the remarks by French Prime Minister Michel Rocard, in his speech to the Institut des hautes études de defense nationale on 15 November 1988, as the 'point of departure' for these debates, where Rocard called for the creation of an ISS tasked to 'propagate a defence spirit', helping to develop a 'shared grammar' to underpin a common European voice in defence and to 'enable WEU, still uncertain of its course, better to choose its direction'.
210. Cahen, interview with author, Paris, 25 January 1997.
211. Cahen, 'Western European Union: birth, development and reactivation', p. 395.
212. C. Krupnik, 'European security and defense cooperation during the Cold War', in A. Moens and C. Antstis (eds) *Disconcerted Europe: The Search for a New Security Architecture*, Boulder: Westview Press, 1994, p. 18.
213. Areas of contention included the US bombing of Libya, the mining of Nicaraguan harbours and American actions in Grenada, aggravated by the Irangate debacle that had thrown 'not only the substance of American policies but also

the credentials of the foreign policy machine into the melting pot'. M. Smith, *Western Europe and the United States: The Uncertain Alliance*, London: Allen and Unwin, 1984, p. 24.

214. Channel 4 interview, 24 September 1986, cited in Palmer, *Europe without America*, p. 169.

215. A Market and Opinion Research International poll in the *Sunday Times*, 23 February 1986, found that half of all those polled thought the US as big a threat as the Soviets, 59% considered Reagan to be untrustworthy with British interests and 54% thought that Reagan did not have sound judgement.

216. Areas in which the EC took a position in direct opposition to Washington's policy and interests included support for the Contadora Group's peace initiative of 1984 and the Arias plan of 1987, both of which were attempts to deal with the troubles in Central America. See Allen and Smith, 'Western Europe in the Atlantic system of the 1980s', p. 105.

217. Forster, 'The ratchet of European defence', p. 34. Reference to the WEU as a 'ginger group' is made by Howe, the then UK Foreign Minister, in 'The WEU: the way ahead', p. 13.

218. For discussion of this security dilemma see J. M. O. Sharp, 'After Reykjavik: arms control and the allies', *International Affairs*, vol. 63, no. 2, spring 1987, pp. 239–57; and G. Snyder, 'The security dilemma in Alliance politics', *World Politics*, vol. 36, no. 4, July 1984, pp. 461–96.

219. The Rome Declaration makes clear this commitment (see paras. 4, 5 and 6), as does the Platform document (see Section III, paras. 3 and 4, and Sections 1 to 4, which define European security within the terms of Atlantic Alliance). In this they have remained faithful to the original perception that 'there is no credible defence of the West (that is also Western Europe) without the Alliance, that European security cannot be guaranteed by the Europeans alone and that the logic behind the Washington Treaty remains as strong today as it was in 1949'. Cahen, 'The emergence and role of the WEU', p. 56.

220. Cahen, *The Western European Union and NATO*, p. 18.

221. Van Eekelen noted the suggestion of the Dutch Atlantic Foundation President, Pieter Dankert, that European historians would divide the second half of the 20th century into a pre-Reykjavik and post-Reykjavik period, the Reykjavik Summit marking the 'rise of Euro-politics', although he also remarks that this is a reflection of national and 'traditional' trends rather than 'the success of alternative European movements'. Van Eekelen, 'The management of the WEU', p. 41.

222. Cahen, 'The emergence and role of the WEU', p. 59.

223. See the Foreign Ministers' report of 12 June 1984, cited in A. Pijpers, 'Western European Union and European political cooperation: competition or complementarity?', in Tsakaloyannis (ed.) *The Reactivation of the Western European Union*, pp. 82–3.

224. Pijpers, 'Western European Union and European political cooperation', p. 83.

225. P. Keatrige, 'Ireland and the Western European Union', in Tsakaloyannis (ed.) *The Reactivation of the Western European Union*, p. 107.

226. R. Seidelmann, 'WEU and EC—competition or cooperation for Western Europe's security', pp. 72–3.

227. Cahen, 'The emergence and role of the WEU', p. 59.

228. Calleo, *Beyond American Hegemony*, p. 181.

229. Dezcallor, 'On Western European defence', p. 168.

230. Howe, 'The WEU: the way ahead', p. 15.

231. Clarke and Hague, 'Britain, America and the future of NATO', p. 154.

232. Poos, 'Prospects for the WEU', p. 18.

233. Clarke, 'The Europeanisation of NATO', pp. 37–8.

234. Howe cited in Cahen, 'Relaunching WEU', p. 9.
235. Bull adopts the term 'Europeanist' in 1983 to describe the alternative to Atlanticism or neutralism, stating that 'it does not imply the break-up of NATO, but it does require its reform: the transfer from North American to European hands of a greater share of the burden of European defence, and along with it of a greater share of responsibility for decisions'. Bull, 'European self-reliance and the reform of NATO', p. 25.

4 Post-Cold War Challenges and Opportunities
1989–97

The fundamental changes to the global strategic environment brought about by the end of the Cold War called into question the role of those bodies designed, developed and institutionalized according to Cold War determinants. In November 1988, Soviet Leader Mikhail Gorbachev had announced to the UN General Assembly the adoption of a 'defensive' Soviet military doctrine and the unilateral and major withdrawal of Soviet forces from Europe, in the spirit of the ongoing and largely successful superpower arms control negotiations.[1] This coincided with the processes of Soviet 'restructuring' (perestroika) and 'opening' (glasnost), which foreshadowed the major international changes to come, as the Soviet satellites loosened their communist ties.[2] The fall of the Berlin Wall in November 1989 symbolized a process of radical transformation emerging from the Soviet 'retreat' and created new challenges for the Western Alliance, led by the US Administration of George H. W. Bush. Predicated on a transatlantic defence arrangement, articulated through the NATO military alliance, the Cold War had laid the conditions for a transatlantic system that had tied together the interests of the US and Western Europe for 40 years. With the collapse of the Soviet Union, the primary external and common threat, the institutional 'glue' that had held the Alliance together was severely weakened. The potential for new co-operative and productive international relationships, combined with the uncertainty of continued allied commitment on both sides of the Atlantic, resulted in the requirement for a fundamental reappraisal of the structures of security. In attempting to meet the new challenges and opportunities that the post-Cold War environment might offer, states looked critically at the institutions that had provided for their post-war security and considered how these institutions might adapt in order to satisfy the requirements of a new order. NATO's rationale had been based on the enormity of the perceived Soviet threat and an ineffectual Europe's requirement for strong American leadership. With the apparent decline in the Soviet menace and, consequently, the common rationale for collective defence, the imperative for member acceptance of the national costs of alliance seemed less compelling for states seeking to determine their place in the emerging post-Cold War system. The opportunities for a 'peace dividend', resulting from a decline in threat, and therefore in the requirement for alliance commitment, were evident on both sides of the Atlantic, as states sought to secure the potential economic benefits of a new co-operative European order. Shaken by the changed external environment and by internal dissent, the Alliance's continuing relevance was inevitably questioned. NATO's London Declaration on a Transformed Alliance of 6 July 1990 emphasized the continuing rationale for a strong defensive alliance in an age of continuing uncertainty. However, it also identified the broadening of the security environment, and the need to overcome the Cold War heritage of suspicion and mistrust. Driven, at least in part, by the desire to 'prepare the ground for German unification and continued German membership of the Alliance',[3] the London Summit did establish the requirement for a significant reassessment of NATO's mechanisms for the management of this new security environment. A new strategic concept was clearly required to bring NATO into the post-Cold War era, as was a strategy that recognized a diverse and less predictable range of 'challenges' for NATO. Cold War force structures intended to meet the massed Soviet forces would also require reform, giving way to rapidly deployable, highly flexible and mobile capabilities to meet the more diffuse threat base. Indeed, if NATO was to remain relevant it would have to change: the inter- and intra-alliance simplicity of the bipolar age had been replaced by a complex environment of uncertain commitments, multifarious risks and strategic uncertainties.

The decline in threat from the East, foreshadowing the imminent unification of an economically and politically strong Germany, and the increased likelihood of a declining American commitment to Europe coincided with the impetus created by Gulf War I for greater European defence independence. The EC had become 'the foremost proponent of "soft security" because of its huge internal market and economic strength',[4] a feat made possible by its reliance on the US for much of its 'hard' security requirements. However, the West Europeans had been increasingly struck by the inability of the Community to match its international influence with its economic capabilities. The challenges of a changing world prompted many to question the Community's place and the extent to which this 'new order' might require a more dynamic and assertive Europe, equipped with common policies and capabilities beyond the traditionally 'soft' options of economic and social integration. Under the auspices of the EPC, the EC had increasingly come to recognize and represent its members' joint interests in its broader policy orientation towards the international environment.[5] For many, defence was the inevitable next step in the integrative process towards a full-fledged EU.[6] An IGC was to take place in December 1990, to take the necessary steps for the final stages of Economic and Monetary Union (EMU), ground prepared by the provisions of the SEA. On an initiative of the Belgian Government, and following a Franco-German request of the Irish EC Presidency in April 1990, agreement had been reached at the following Dublin European Council in June to also hold an IGC on European Political Union (EPU) to run in parallel with that on EMU.[7] Europe's political development required reconsideration given the potential challenges and opportunities offered by the major changes in the international environment accompanying the ending of the Cold War. Whilst much of the agreed agenda of the IGC on EPU was to be 'internally' focused on the Community's institutional efficiency and democratic accountability, the most contentious of issues was to be the proposal for a Common Foreign and Security Policy (CFSP) whereby the Community might fully exercise its international influence by seeking to fill the security 'gap' left by the receding powers both within Europe and beyond.

The WEU had been re-awakened in 1984 in response to the level of national dissatisfaction with the organizational structures for security as they reflected the political realities of the 1980s. By the turn of the decade, the WEU was to find itself at the heart of debates regarding the future institutional management of the emerging Europe. As the institutions of European security, NATO and the EC, embarked on their own processes of reflection and revision in light of massive international change, the possible contribution of the WEU to the management of this new environment, and specifically in support of the transitioning of the primary organizational structures for its management, was to become a significant area of debate. Through an examination of national perspectives and environmental and organizational change, this chapter considers the role of the WEU in accommodating this essential transformation of the post-Cold War institutional order, highlighting the central areas of tension as states sought to satisfy their ongoing interests during this period of global uncertainty and international flux.

NATIONAL PERSPECTIVES ON INSTITUTIONAL CHANGE

Having played a significant role in the development of the existing security framework in Europe, Britain, whilst choosing not to be isolated by abstention, had pursued an essentially negative line towards European integration, seeking to dampen the integrative process where possible. Desirous of maintaining its 'special relationship' with the US and of strengthening the Atlantic Alliance, the British Government had acted with great scepticism when confronted with suggestions that Europe might develop a common, independent (of the US) and effective defence entity. For the British, as the Foreign Secretary was to state, 'European security without the United States simply does not make sense'.[8] As the provider of capabilities and leadership, the US had an indispensable role in the Alliance, and talk of a European defence identity not only was unrealistic and impractical but was likely to damage the fundamental relationship on which European defence rested.[9] Clearly, NATO would require adaptation to meet the challenges of the new world 'disorder', but any developments towards an enhanced European defence dimension must be tempered, indeed directed, by the requirement to keep the Americans 'in' and committed to Europe. At the same time, the

UK would need to retain a measure of influence over European initiatives, as a lack of involvement could result in British marginalization both in the Community and in the transatlantic relationship. Prime Minister Margaret Thatcher was strongly opposed to German unification without the 'breathing space in which a new architecture of Europe could be devised where a united Germany would not be a destabilizing influence/over-mighty subject/bull in a china shop'. If premature, it would encourage speedier and deeper integration (in order to tie Germany 'in' to Europe), whilst offering US decoupling predicated on German-led federal stability.[10] A unified Germany, with its economic potential and its particular relationship with the interests of the broader Europe, might also be seen by the US as the stronger partner for European security management. Given this US predisposition, Thatcher argued that attempts would need to be made to sustain a policy orientation that allowed for sufficient European defence development to satisfy American demands, whilst outwardly protecting the Alliance against European 'excesses'.[11]

Although the French Government was to take some tentative steps towards greater deliberative co-operation with NATO, its independent position with regard to nuclear forces, multinational corps and the integrated alliance structure remained largely unchanged in the early post-Cold War years.[12] For the French, keen to restrict US influence in Europe, the ending of the Cold War and the subsequent likelihood of a declining US presence in Europe opened up real possibilities for an enhanced European defence profile. It had remained a basic principle of French policy that West European unity could be complete only once it included defence and security matters, despite a distinct lack of definitional clarity in official positions as to just what this might entail.[13] However, the prospect of a unified Germany served to clarify French thought, with European integration providing the means of ensuring a German contribution to French interests. Although the impetus for closer economic union was seen by many as largely a response to the dominance of the German mark within the Community,[14] political union would help to corral a united and powerful Germany within the institutions of a politically cohesive and competent Europe. The opportunity presented itself for Europe to assert its interest in developing an effective security and defence identity to complement its economic strength, even if this might require some decline in French independence. Steinberg clearly articulated the predominant French view of the early post-Cold War years when he stated that 'The US security relationship has prevented the emergence of a political structure capable of addressing Europe's security requirements, both in Europe and globally, as well as the military structures to support it . . . Europe can only achieve its rightful international stature if it becomes more independent from the United States'.[15] Hence, the French sought to confine NATO—and thus the US—by limiting it to the provision of an insurance function against any emergent military threat and to the provision of those resources for peacekeeping and enforcement efforts that were beyond

European capabilities, as Europe developed its security and defence identity outside of the Alliance.[16]

For West Germany, the end of the Cold War seemed likely to resolve its primary post-war policy concern of achieving international acceptance of reunification. Chancellor Helmut Kohl had announced his 10-point plan for reunification to the Bundestag on 28 November 1989, with the speed and 'unilateralism' of his action taking his uninformed counterparts in France and Britain by surprise. When Kohl succeeded in gaining support for German self-determination at the Strasbourg European Summit of 8–9 December, reunification was closely linked to a German commitment to ever closer European integration. Entrenchment within the institutional framework of European integration had enabled the Federal Republic to establish for itself a pivotal European role. The further Europeanization of German policy, within an ever closer political and economic union of Europe, was seen to be politically expedient if a united Germany was to find an influential role for itself in Europe that met with European approval.[17]

As the key 'beneficiary' of the Soviet demise, Western Europe's largest and most competitive economy would, on unification, also support the largest conventional force in Europe.[18] NATO had served the post-war interests of West Germany, enabling a military rehabilitation acceptable to its neighbours, whilst preventing Soviet aggression. The new environment raised questions about the continuing utility of an alliance originally intended to 'keep Germans down' and traditionally directed against Germany's eastern neighbours, the stability and reconstruction of which had become a paramount national concern. Germany continued to accept the relevance of NATO as an insurance against a renewed Eastern threat, but it favoured the CSCE as the institutional framework for pan-European security co-operation, incorporating the wider co-operative mechanisms required for Eastern European reconstruction.

During the 'two-plus-four' negotiations on German unification, which took place between East and West Germany and the four major powers with residual rights (UK, US, France and the Soviet Union), beginning in January 1990, the US had been keen to promote acceptance of a unified Germany as a full member of NATO. Driven by concerns regarding potential German neutrality, re-nationalization of defence and the loss of a potential Soviet balancer, the Bush Administration's concerns were reminiscent of those informing the debates of the early 1950s that preceded the Federal Republic's NATO accession.[19] Mindful of a conventionally armed Germany's continuing reliance on the transatlantic link for its military security, Kohl was persuaded by President Bush of the desirability of a united Germany's membership in NATO at their summit of February 1990. The Chancellor was to win Soviet agreement on the basis of renewed renunciation of ABC weapons as established in the MBT,[20] a commitment to the inviolability of its external borders and a US-provisioned financial package to support the repatriation of Soviet forces from East Germany in advance of the implementation of

NATO structures.[21] Following the signing of the Treaty of Final Settlement with Respect to Germany on 12 September, which provided for full sovereignty, Germany was officially united on 3 October 1990 and welcomed as a full member of NATO on the same day.

As domestic unrest following German unification resulted in electoral successes for the extreme right-wing Republican Party, it was widely recognized that embracing the EC and clinging to NATO could only reassure neighbours nervous of Germany's future intentions.[22] France, with whom the FRG had established a close, if sometimes fraught, post-war working relationship, remained the European partner of choice: Bonn sought to resist the French 'decoupling' suggested by President François Mitterrand's announcement, at the end of the London NATO Summit in July 1990, of his intentions to withdraw all French troops from German soil by 1994.[23] The German Foreign Ministry was keen to develop a joint security policy within the EPC framework, as a natural progression of the integration process and as a means of providing an enhanced German security role that did not intimidate its neighbours. Equally, maintaining close relations with Washington was seen as essential to German economic and security interests.[24] Consequently, the best medium-term option would require the enhancement of European defence integration, whilst not undermining the European consensus on the building of a closer Union and, at the same time, reassuring the Americans of Germany's 'good ally' status.

The US had similarly re-evaluated its security interests in the light of the Soviet decline. The likelihood that the future security problems of Europe would be regionally confined, and that the integrative process itself would prevent the development of a hegemonic threat within the Community area, raised questions regarding the continued necessity of a US presence in Europe. Emerging non-European interests, not least in the economic sphere, required the fostering of new relationships that might themselves be undermined by too close ties with Europe, the costs of alliance suggesting to many the desirability of decoupling US and European security.[25] As the requirements of the domestic agenda drew attention 'back home', Europe was seen by some as 'an increasingly unreliable partner' and a potential competitor as fears of a powerful economic 'fortress Europe' grew.[26] Nevertheless, the official US position remained that the allies shared common interests and goals and that, in a time of transition, the Alliance was a basis for stability. If the East did not provide the traditional concerns of the Cold War period, those concerns were only muted or transformed into fears of weapons proliferation, technology transfer and the potentially destabilizing consequences of the re-nationalization of defence, all of which might affect US interests fundamentally. The extent of US efforts to secure full NATO membership for a united Germany was an expression of the American belief that 'the Alliance would continue to be the major lynchpin of US policy towards Europe'.[27]

Increasingly, Washington had recognized the need for European support for its international action, illustrated not least by the recent Gulf operations:

clearly the new challenges of the post-Cold War world would require the development of a reformed and more balanced partnership. This process of partnership redefinition had been signalled by Secretary of State James Baker's 'New Atlanticism' speech, delivered in Berlin on 12 December 1989, in which he outlined the changes in relationship, both between East and West and among Western states, in which the EC would increasingly perform as an international actor through its common institutions.[28] Although some in Europe feared a US troop withdrawal and a decline in US commitment to the Alliance, the message from Washington was that NATO remained the institution of choice for the satisfaction of US interests on the continent. However, a new relationship would need to be developed between the US and Europe: co-operative EC relations with the US would be facilitated by closer and possibly treaty-based agreement, whilst NATO would need to adapt to the new security environment by developing its political functions, most significantly its consultation and co-operation processes, both between allies and with the Eastern European states.

The subsequent Transatlantic Declaration of 20 November 1990 set out the conditions for a renewed transatlantic partnership, acknowledging the need to balance responsibilities and burdens more equitably in the light of an emerging European security identity.[29] By December, agreement had been reached within the NAC that 'A European security and defence role, reflected in the construction of a European pillar within the Alliance, will not only serve the interests of the European states but also help to strengthen Atlantic solidarity'.[30] However, US interest in redefining the transatlantic relationship was largely confined to the pursuit of burden-sharing: Washington was clearly opposed to any European military role that might permit European action without NATO consent or undermine NATO or the US leadership role within it. Thus, US policy suffered from inherent inconsistencies. Despite the language of partnership, the limits of economic co-operation were quickly highlighted by the break-down of the Uruguay Round of trade talks in December, whilst the transatlantic security relationship was dogged by the apparent contradiction of the US' repeated support for a stronger West European defence role at the same time as it warned Europeans against taking any substantive moves in that direction.[31]

And what of the WEU's role in relation to these internal and external requirements of European security organization? Since its revitalization in 1984 the WEU had institutionalized a defence forum for the discussion of those issues of concern to Europeans. The co-ordination of military activity during the Tanker War in the Gulf in 1987–8 had demonstrated an embryonic capability to serve the operational interests of both European and transatlantic defence. The WEU's potential political and military competencies seemed to offer an obvious ready-made vehicle for enhancing European security and defence collaboration. In political terms, the WEU might prove less problematic as a means of developing a European defence dimension than the EC, given its exclusion of the neutral states, its intergovernmental nature and its long experience of defence dialogue. The WEU could also prove sufficient to meet US requirements for greater burden-sharing in defence, whilst contributing to a rebalancing of European input and influence within the transatlantic relationship. And, in the worst-case scenario of a future US disengagement, the WEU might provide a valuable 'safety net' for a Europe alone.[32] Although there was agreement amongst both the Europeans and the US that some level of Europeanization was necessary to reflect the new realities of the post-Cold War environment, and that the WEU might provide a 'first step' in this process, the extent of that Europeanization was a matter of often bitter disagreement. Consequently, the position and role of the WEU in any new security architecture became an issue of considerable contention.

THE WEU AND THE GULF 'OPPORTUNITY' (MARK II)

On 2 August 1990, Iraq invaded Kuwait, in response to what Saddam Hussein perceived as Kuwait's illegal exploitation of oil reserves, in contradiction to agreed quotas and as encouraged by a US Administration keen to undermine the Iraqi regime.[33] Adopted on the very day of the invasion, UN Security Council (UNSC) Resolution 660 condemned the invasion as a direct contravention of international law and called for the immediate and unconditional withdrawal of Iraqi forces from Kuwait. Four days later, Resolution 661 went further in ordering an economic and military boycott of Iraq, the enforcement of which would require an international military presence. Hence, with a new spirit of solidarity amongst the UN's Permanent Members (P5), the Gulf crisis was the first post-Cold War conflict to test out the effectiveness of international institutional security arrangements in meeting the emerging challenges of the new order.

The EC, under its EPC provisions, proved itself quick to act, formally condemning the invasion at its extraordinary Ministerial meeting of 10 August and instituting a number of measures, including the imposing of an oil embargo on Iraq and Kuwait, the freezing of Iraqi assets and the suspending of scientific and technical co-operation.[34] Ongoing disputes regarding the future of any security identity for Europe precluded consensus within the EC on the desirability of any military action,[35] but it was recognized that the WEU might again take on the role of a 'pivotal' organization, providing an alternative collective vehicle for European co-operation in this 'out-of-Europe' crisis, one which, by working closely with the US, would not undermine NATO.[36]

Following the WEU's activities in the Gulf during the Tanker War, the WEU Council had roundly rejected the establishment of permanent procedures and structures for consultation and co-ordination to deal with future crises as recommended by the Assembly.[37] Although the Council acknowledged that 'coordination of the action of armed forces of WEU countries can certainly be envisaged under the auspices of WEU', it insisted that it was 'not WEU's responsibility to announce in advance that member states are prepared to coordinate such action': in fact, it appeared to be advocating the primacy of the EC's mechanisms for determining the political context in which national decisions for collective action might be taken.[38] Nevertheless, it was accepted that the mechanisms for concertation developed during the WEU's first Gulf experience might be reconstituted effectively.

The Administration in Washington, also drawing on the experience of the 1987–8 operations, promoted WEU co-ordination of the European naval effort in support of US action in the area. On 7 August, the Ministerial Counsellor from the US Embassy informed the Deputy Secretary General of the WEU of US interests, and the Secretary General received a letter from Secretary of State Baker, dated 16 August, welcoming WEU co-operation and identifying areas of operations that might be best suited for WEU action. These were further elaborated on in US Secretary of Defense Dick Cheney's letter of 20 August, including logistics, chemical weapons protection and financial support to Turkey in addition to minesweeping, air and sea lift and ground deployments as areas where WEU member contributions could be most useful.[39]

At the prompting of the Assembly, the French Presidency of the WEU called a meeting of the WEU Foreign and Defence Ministers, held in Paris on 21 August under Article VIII (para. 3) of the MBT. In a reversal of the French position in the 1987–8 Tanker War, President Mitterrand had come to see the WEU as a means of promoting European integration as well as enhancing the French profile in global affairs. As a demonstration of the linkage and coherence of the EC and WEU approaches, invitations to attend this meeting were extended to the three non-WEU EC members, Denmark, Greece and Ireland (the latter chose not to attend), whilst, at German and British insistence, Turkey was also included. The outcome of the meeting was a decision to 'closely coordinate their operations in the area' in support of UNSC measures, whilst also facilitating 'cooperation with other countries deploying forces in the region, including those of the United States'.[40] Determining to adopt the three-tier mechanism for naval co-ordination established in 1987, the Ministerial Council instructed that an *ad hoc* group of Foreign and Defence Ministry Representatives was to ensure the effective co-ordination of member-state contributions. Heading up Points of Contact in national capitals, the *ad hoc* group was to provide for high-level consultation and establish the politico-military guidelines that were to frame the co-ordination between the commands of national naval units throughout the crisis. Naval points of contact were, as in 1987, established within national ministries, but with the additional mechanism of a permanent unit at the Naval Staff Headquarters in Paris tasked with identifying areas for co-ordination, monitoring WEU vessels in the Gulf area and acting as an information exchange for member states' defence staffs. Regular contacts between task commanders in theatre were also provided for, the three-tier structure enabling the co-ordination of activities from national capitals to naval forces in the area.[41]

Following the Ministerial, and under its authority, the WEU's first meeting of national Chiefs of Defence Staff was held in Paris on 27 August 1990 to establish military guidelines for the co-ordination of the embargo operation in support of the politico-military deliberations of the *ad hoc* group. Whilst no agreement had been reached on a WEU operation per se, specific joint guidelines for naval coordination in the Gulf in support of the embargo enforcement were established, including 'mission definition, scale and type of deployments, exchange of information, logistic and operational support, and mutual protection of deployed units'.[42] WEU member states were to retain complete sovereignty in terms of deployment of forces and missions assigned, but through the mechanisms for 'concertation', their contributions could be co-ordinated effectively.

Efforts to co-ordinate the international implementation of UN sanctions were made during the Bahrain Naval Conference of 8–9 September 1990, initiated by Washington and co-chaired by the WEU along with the US and Arab contributors. Discussion with US Naval Commanders in the region resulted in an agreed WEU sea area, which, following a meeting of senior officers of the four major European naval contributors (the UK, France, Italy and the Netherlands) onboard the deployed French destroyer *Dupleix* (10–14 September), was divided into zones; arrangements were made for national units to share and rotate through the zonal patrols.[43] This co-ordination was to be facilitated through the formalized 'conferences of in-zone commanders of WEU naval forces' which were to be held in advance of the broader meetings of states engaged in the embargo.[44]

As attempts to secure a peaceful resolution reached a low point, following an Iraqi assault on six Embassies in Kuwait on 14 September, the WEU called a second Ministerial meeting (on 18 September) to plan for the additional co-ordination requirements of any future land and air deployments. Further agreement was reached on the harmonization of member states' forces and the pooling of logistic support capabilities. Within this framework, co-operation began on air and sea transport arrangements and the escort of shipping in the Mediterranean and Red Seas. At the height of the embargo operation, there was a significant WEU presence with up to 45 warships and auxiliaries in the area from WEU member states, carrying out three-quarters of all control measures.[45] Alongside the UK, which was the largest European contributor to the maritime presence, six other WEU states had vessels in the area,[46] with Luxembourg offering 'substantial' financial aid. In the final stages of unification, Germany maintained that its constitutional constraints prevented deployment other than for 'defence purposes', confining its contribution to the deployment of minehunters and support ships to the Eastern Mediterranean to replace warships from the NATO Mediterranean command that had been sent to the Gulf.[47] Throughout the deployment, however, the extent of the WEU's 'concertation' procedures was to prove divisive, with the British leading the resistance to the French WEU Presidency's call for greater WEU command, including a proposal for rotational 'tactical control' of all WEU ships in the area.[48] The French promotion of WEU co-ordination could resolve the political problem of how to 'contribute to any military operations in the Gulf without openly giving the appearance of following US leadership'.[49] The British preferred to co-ordinate their activities with the 'English speaking forces' of the wider coalition, most significantly the Americans, and opposed the WEU command option on the basis that the institution lacked the structures to provide the politico-military oversight required.[50]

On 29 November, the UNSC, under Resolution 678, authorized the use of 'all necessary means' to implement the immediate and unconditional withdrawal of Iraqi forces from Kuwait, as demanded by Resolution 660, if agreement had not been reached by 15 January 1991. As last-ditch efforts by the Americans and the EC failed to secure Iraqi compliance,[51] the US-led Operation Desert Storm was initiated on 17 January 1991. Alongside American forces, the British and French had been quick to respond with the deployment of air and land assets to the area; the Italians provided forces for the air campaign, and the Dutch made frigates available to the coalition. Such a limited number of member-state contributors made the WEU's offer of co-ordination unnecessary, particularly given the national preference of the majority for direct co-ordination with US forces within the UN-sanctioned coalition.[52] The British determined to place their troops directly under American operational control, whilst the French maintained their national command.[53] The WEU was to take no active part in the land or air war, although it continued to co-ordinate the naval embargo operations and acted as a joint co-ordinating body to ensure the supply of necessary equipment and munitions to the British and French forces in Saudi Arabia.[54]

Following the cessation of hostilities on 28 February 1991, the WEU machinery was used to co-ordinate the minesweeping operations of the five contributing WEU states, along with the US and Saudi vessels.[55] German ships took part in this post-conflict activity, escorting the British, French, Italian, Belgian and Dutch ships under WEU auspices.[56] Responding to the formal request of the European Council to study the military aspects of humanitarian relief, given the growing Kurdish refugee crisis, the WEU considered the possibility of a further WEU presence in the area.[57] In the event, a lack of European consensus led to these operations being conducted by national contingents under American leadership. Operation Provide Comfort, authorized under UN Resolution 688, which sought to end civil repression and ensure access to humanitarian aid through the provision of 'safe' areas in Northern Iraq, was to be supported by 30,000 troops from NATO countries.[58] Nevertheless, the WEU discussions had served to raise European awareness of the needs of the suffering Kurdish population. Operation Safe Haven, the deployment for which began on 20 April 1991, was conducted by British and Dutch amphibious forces, with Royal Air Force and land support, to provide assistance both to the Kurds and to the Turkmen Arabs in the region. This operation was actively assisted by WEU-organized 'co-ordination and cooperation' of logistical and material support from other European states, offering some limited experience of humanitarian operations under broad WEU auspices.[59]

Looking back over the conflict had led to some frustration amongst European states, the 'feeble mechanisms' available for co-ordinating separate national policies throughout the crisis having deprived them of an effective forum for action, resulting in the Community as a whole 'having to respond to an agenda set by others, notably the United States'.[60] Early co-operation within the EC through the EPC mechanism had proven relatively successful in terms of providing for the use of measures short of war, with the WEU facilitating a level of military co-operation in support of the UN-endorsed and EC-supported embargo.[61] However, once the conflict escalated to war, the frenetic diplomatic activity of European state Ministers served only to demonstrate both the failure of European consensus and the lack of effective institutional machinery for European co-operation in areas seen as vital to common European interests.[62] That is not to say that the EC was entirely ineffectual. As Sir Leon Brittan, Vice-President of the Commission, was to argue, 'The EC acted effectively where it had a role: enforcing the UN sanctions; helping with refugee problems; arranging budgetary support for the countries neighbouring Iraq which were hardest hit by the crisis, and so on. But it could not do more . . . the Community should not be attacked for not being what its Member States have not wanted it to become'.[63] Nevertheless, when a crisis took on a military dimension, the exclusion of such matters from the remit of the EPC dictated that national rather than European responses predominated.[64]

The Gulf crisis had revealed the limitations of Europe, in terms of both capabilities and collective will. The absence of an effective mechanism for common European security and defence deliberation and decision-making, and the military means to execute those decisions, had led Roland Dumas, the French Foreign Minister, to note that 'we were beginning to live on incantations, illusions and lots of second thoughts'.[65] Whilst the EC's limitations during the Gulf conflict acted only to confirm the impossibility of a true European defence identity to the Atlanticists, the Europeanists were to argue that only through greater co-operation and integration at the political as well as military level could Europe ever have the international influence that its economic position suggested.[66]

What is clear is that the failure of the Europeans to find any means for providing collective action in the Gulf would have inevitably damaged Euro-American relations, and it was largely in this sense that the WEU was able to play its pivotal role. The WEU demonstrated its potential as a vehicle for mobilizing and articulating collective responsibility, acting as the co-ordinator of European actions, but equally as a convenient *ad hoc* vehicle for European-American co-operation in an 'out-of-Europe' crisis.

The largely accepted interpretation of the Washington Treaty created geographic constraints for NATO-mandated action, political sensitivities also suggesting that NATO would not necessarily be the preferred institutional arrangement for 'out-of-area' military activity. As Buchan argues in his examination of the Gulf engagements, 'Any force bearing a NATO imprint would have been unacceptable, not only to the French but also to Arab participants in the anti-Iraq coalition to whom WEU (if they actually know what these initials stand for) smacks far less of Western neo-imperialism than NATO would'.[67] Equally, given the limits of European support for any Alliance-based action, the WEU was to enable the commitment of forces outside of Europe by states for whom such a commitment would have been politically problematic without the 'European' credentials of the WEU.[68] As a 'source of legitimation for European responses', the WEU 'umbrella' provided the domestic political palliative for Dutch and Belgian military contributions to the Gulf action, and was an absolute requirement for Spanish and Italian involvement.[69]

British and French standing with the US had risen significantly as a consequence of their engagement in the Gulf. Germany's posture during the conflict, however, had served to undermine the US' previously held misconception that the newly unified state might prove to be their 'special' partner in the new security order.[70] What the WEU had demonstrated, in providing the necessary institutional machinery for at least some level of European military co-operation, was its potential to contribute to the protection of what were perceived as shared transatlantic interests in a NATO 'out-of-area' situation. Roland Dumas, as Chair of the WEU Council, seemed rather more optimistic about the WEU's performance than he had appeared regarding the EC's. He stated, 'A great step forward has been taken in the quest for common security and common defence . . . this crisis has shown that the WEU countries are capable of coming together, taking joint decisions, giving political guidance and, what is more, translating into action their stated political will'.[71] The speed with which the crisis presented itself and was then resolved militated against its utility as a testing ground for future institutional multinational co-operation,[72] although the limitations of *ad hoc* structures for co-ordination and planning were to provide lessons for an unpredictable future where the requirement for a rapid co-ordinated response might become the norm.[73] Unfolding in the course of the IGC on EPU and during deliberations on the future strategic direction of NATO, the experiences of the Gulf conflict would inevitably impact on the conclusions of these institutional debates.

THE IGC, 1990–1

Of the areas of discussion on the agenda of the Community's IGC on EPU, launched in Rome on 14 December 1990, the development of a CFSP was to generate much of the debate; the relationship of the WEU to this policy area quickly became a central consideration.[74] In a letter circulated a week before the opening of the IGC, President Mitterrand and Chancellor Kohl added substance to their earlier proposals, suggesting that the IGC 'review how the WEU and Political Union might establish a clear organic relationship and how, therefore, the WEU, with increased operational capacities, might in time become part of Political Union and elaborate, on the latter's behalf, a common security policy'.[75]

In preparation for the IGC, discussions had taken place within the WEU on its future role. As the IGC was likely to have profound implications for the WEU, this was clearly an opportune time at which to consider the possible revision of the (Modified) Brussels Treaty, which was to reach its 50th year in 1998, after which provision was made for member states' withdrawal with one year's notice on application. Equally, such a discourse would ensure that the views of WEU states on the future of the organization might feature, at least to some extent, in the ongoing discussions on an EU. The subsequent 'Personal Reflections of the Secretary General on the Future of European Security and Defence Cooperation' of 22 November 1990 recognized the complementary nature of the European (WEU/EC), Atlantic (NATO) and pan-European (CSCE) security arrangements.[76] As an autonomous organization bridging the Atlantic Alliance and an integrating Europe, the WEU had the benefit of excluding the neutrals (who limited the potential of the EPC), its members being committed to the construction of a security- and defence-competent EU. The WEU was unique amongst European organizations in bringing together both Foreign and Defence Ministers, and its Article V and unrestricted geographic mandate offered significant opportunities for the organizational management of European security and defence, whilst working in close co-operation with NATO. For the new Secretary General (the former Dutch Defence Minister Willem van Eekelen replaced the Belgian diplomat Alfred Cahen in 1989), the challenge facing the WEU from the EC's IGC and the NATO review process was 'to continue the "cross-roads" function and ensure the twin essentials of transatlantic and European co-operation'.[77] The WEU's objective in relation to the EC, he argued, 'should be to demonstrate more clearly, by developing its contacts and actions, that it represents the defence dimension of the European integration process'. At the same time, by demonstrating a 'coherent European approach' the WEU might 'influence the Alliance's evolution, strengthen the European component and define the respective roles of the US and Europe in a new "transatlantic security contract"'.[78] Operational responsibilities successfully taken on by the WEU would also help to raise the organization's credibility and enhance the effectiveness of its bridging function.[79] Through its Platform and post-revitalization accession Protocols, the WEU was committed to 'the construction of an integrated Europe [which] will remain incomplete as long as it does not include security and defence',[80] and the Reflections noted the requirement for a 'gradual approach', sensitive to the limits of European consensus and capability, for which the WEU had distinct 'institutional advantages'.[81]

Not all commentators were quite so struck by the unique utility of the WEU for adapting the institutional architecture of the new Europe, however, with one peevishly suggesting that 'the management of the targeted WEU is reacting as all managements do when under threat of takeover. It is stressing that no other organization can serve the defence interests of European shareholders better than the WEU, and that they should leave well enough alone'.[82] Nevertheless, it was evident that as an autonomous defence organization, bridging the Atlantic divide, providing for the enhancement of intergovernmental European defence co-operation and linked to the emerging aspirations of the evolving EU, the WEU might offer a working vehicle for development in the absence of consensus on more 'radical' transformation elsewhere.

Deliberations within the IGC on EPU were illustrative of the debates taking place between European states over the future direction of the integrative process in Europe, the continuing relevance of both NATO and the transatlantic security link, and the role that the WEU might play in this uncertain and evolving environment. Of the two broad-based coalitions that developed during the conference, the UK and the Dutch, with some support from the Portuguese and Danes, took an essentially Atlanticist position whereby a CFSP for the emerging Union was to be resisted on the grounds that it might weaken NATO and the transatlantic link, which remained at the core of European defence. Any development of European competence in foreign and security matters should be essentially in 'soft security' activity, with the WEU remaining as NATO's European pillar for limited 'hard' security and defence co-operation.[83] The Europeanists, led by the French and including Belgium, Luxembourg and Spain, sought an explicit defence role for the new EU, as part of an integral CFSP, although the French largely concurred with the UK view that any CFSP should be on an intergovernmental basis.[84] Germany had chosen to walk a difficult 'tightrope' between these two positions: supporting the maintenance of a strong Atlantic Alliance, Bonn identified defence integration as a desirable stage in the gradual process of uniting Europe, where a closer WEU-EU relationship might provide the means of legitimizing, and not least to its own population, more active German participation in post-Cold War 'out-of-area' military operations.[85]

As negotiations on the development of the CFSP got underway in early 1991 under the Luxembourg Presidency, Foreign Ministers Roland Dumas and Hans-Dietrich Genscher sought to establish the French and German positions in a joint statement of 4 February, when they suggested that 'the WEU will constitute the channel of co-operation between the European Political Union and NATO', and that integration of the WEU into the EPU should be considered for decision by 1996–7.[86] In fact, this initiative represented something of a compromise given the lack of consensus on a future CFSP for the Union. The statement recognized the importance of NATO and the unanimity requirement for CFSP activity, whist proposing an 'organic relationship' between the WEU and the EU, with the WEU serving as 'the nucleus of a European defence entity but at the same time . . . the European pillar of the Alliance'. It appeared that France might be prepared to move away from its standard 'independent' position on the development of a European defence dimension, and it would certainly need to establish closer co-ordination with its WEU partners to fulfil the stated objectives.

That there were divergent views on the optimal relationship between the WEU, NATO and the developing EU was evidenced in the language as much as the substance of the debate. Conceptually, Luomna-aho has suggested that the static architectural metaphors of the WEU as both a European 'pillar' of the Atlantic Alliance and a 'bridge' between the US and Europe, favoured by the Atlanticists, may be seen to distinguish this approach from the Europeanists' more 'organic' and integral concept of the WEU as the 'arm' of an evolving EU.[87] Forster also notes the Atlanticist perspective of a WEU 'bridge' that permanently links NATO and the EU, whereas the Europeanists preferred the concept of a WEU 'ferry' 'gradually transporting its defence function to the European Union'.[88] Whilst a compromise might be found in the substance of the relationship to be determined in the IGC, the distinct conceptual underpinnings of the two approaches suggested a necessary ambiguity in the prescribed nature of the WEU that might satisfice in the short term, but which suggested longer-term limits to its utility.

The Atlanticists' concerns over US perceptions of the Europeans' deliberations on defence had been given substance in the infamous Bartholomew Telegram[89] sent by the Bush Administration to its European allies and presented to the WEU Foreign and Defence Ministers meeting in Paris on 22 February 1991.[90] Reacting to the Franco-German proposals for WEU subordination to the EU Council, as outlined in their February 'letter', the Memorandum cautioned the Europeans on the dangers of developing too close a link between the WEU and the EC, stating that 'developing a European security component—solely within the EC— . . . could lead to NATO's marginalization'. The US recognized the logic behind the gradual development of a security dimension within political union, but the 'primary yardstick against which proposals and institutional innovations' should be measured should be 'whether they actually enhance Alliance defensive capabilities and make Europe more secure'. Warning of the 'danger that positions which seem to emphasize European over transatlantic solidarity or institutional changes which diminish the centrality of the Alliance could pose for American opinion on and support for the transatlantic partnership', the stated US view was that the 'defence and security dimensions of European union should not extend beyond those states that have undertaken mutual defence commitments within the Atlantic Alliance'. The US did accept that, as the representation of a 'European security identity', there could be a 'distinct and obvious role for the WEU and a different basis for transatlantic collaboration based on NATO-WEU linkage' outside of Europe, as demonstrated in the Gulf. But the WEU should not compete with NATO's missions nor, through its subordination to the EU, 'accentuate the separation and independence of the European pillar from the Alliance' and thus weaken the 'integrity of our common transatlantic security and defense'. The Europeans had shared concerns that increasing European competency might lead the US to reconsider its commitment to Europe, but this heavy-handed message did much to harden European attitudes and served to shift opinion further towards the French position on the necessity of a European defence component.[91] By March 1991 it was reported that 8 of the 12 EC governments were ready to back the Franco-German plans, with the WEU, under the supervision of the European Council, acting as a 'bridge' between the EC and NATO until such time as it could be 'absorbed into the Community's foreign policy'.[92]

The British, in the meantime, had come to identify the WEU as a means of resolving their particular dilemma, by providing for an enhanced intergovernmental European profile and capability without undermining the Atlantic Alliance. Thus, on 19 February 1991 at the Churchill Memorial Lecture in Luxembourg, the British Foreign Secretary, Douglas Hurd, was to go further than ever before in foreseeing closer links between the EC and the WEU. Identifying the WEU as a bridge connecting 'the Twelve, concentrating on foreign policy, security policy; and NATO concentrating on defence', Hurd recognized the potential advantage of providing for a (limited) responsibility for the EC and WEU in areas of security policy, including the management of arms proliferation, counter-terrorism and actions outside of Europe under UN mandate or under the CSCE.[93] European Council co-ordination and guidance on security policy might also be acceptable to the British, but any proposals for the merger of the WEU or its defence functions into the new EU were solidly rejected.[94] This included proposals by the President of the EC Commission, Jacques Delors, that, 'all provisions relating to external aspects—foreign policy, security, economic relations and development co-operation'—having been taken on under one title, with the European Council being responsible for identifying common 'essential interests' including defence, the solidarity of interests should be expressed 'by taking over Article V of the WEU Treaty'.[95] For the British, any such proposals were unrealistic, undesirable and undermining of both European solidarity and Alliance interests. The Alliance was the institution of defence, and the WEU's commitment to nuclear deterrence would be unacceptable both to the current EC membership (neutral Ireland) and to potential incoming neutral states (Austria, Sweden and Finland), whilst the EU's envisaged relationship with the transforming Soviet Union and the question of extended memberships would inevitably become more difficult if EU deterrence frontiers were to be established.

Having rejected French, German and Italian proposals for the absorption of the WEU into the future EU, the British Government sought to demonstrate its new-found commitment to greater European unity by backing, in

March 1991, the concept of an independent European Reaction Force under the control of the WEU, for use outside the NATO area in consultation with the Alliance.[96] Such a force, with its differentiated 'out-of-area' role, would be 'compatible' with NATO's territorial defence role, whilst WEU forces and staffs would be drawn from the same 'pot' as those assigned to NATO roles, coming under 'either NATO or WEU commands, depending on the contingency with which they were dealing'.[97] The WEU option thus represented a compromise between the UK and its EC partners keen to begin the construction of a European defence identity, the British position remaining essentially minimalist and pragmatic. In seeking a 'non-NATO-competitive' operational role for an upgraded autonomous and intergovernmental WEU, loosely connected to a 'soft' security-limited EU, both Atlantic and European interests could be addressed, at least in part and for the medium term.

NATO: SEARCHING FOR A ROLE

Just as the deliberations of European states on the future of the EC were to have implications for WEU development, so efforts to define NATO's post-Cold War role influenced national perspectives on the utility of the WEU. As discussions continued within NATO on the new Strategic Concept for the organization, the cart was put somewhat before the horse with the agreement, following the meeting of NATO's Defence Planning Committee and Nuclear Planning Group in May 1991, on the Alliance's new force structure, in advance of any clear articulation of NATO's concept for its use. Consisting of Main, Defence, Reaction and Augmentation Forces, the new force structure included a multinational Allied Rapid Reaction Corps (ARRC) of 50,000–70,000 troops for Allied Command Europe under UK leadership.[98] Excluded from the ARRC as non-contributors to NATO's Defence Planning Committee, where much of the planning for this new force structure had taken shape, the French regarded the 'Anglo-Saxon'-heavy corps as a means of undermining European efforts to develop their own defence identity: offers of potential WEU command of the ARRC under certain NATO-determined conditions were summarily rejected by the French.[99] Whilst the WEU Secretary General reacted to the ARRC announcement with calls for a WEU force capable of intervention in and out of Europe so as to insure against any future instability, the Assembly President reacted more critically, denouncing the NATO decision as a reinforcement of an outdated bipolar system, based on an Alliance dominance likely to squeeze out any European efforts in the security arena.[100]

Toning down the heavy-handed views expressed in the February Bartholomew Telegram, Secretary of State Baker laid out US policy towards the development of a European Security and Defence Identity (ESDI) in his letter to the European capitals of 16 April 1991. Under the Baker Plan, the measurement for the acceptability to Washington of any future development of an ESDI was to be calculated in relation to five key principles. These principles were to form the basis of discussion for the following NATO Summit in Copenhagen.[101] Although the US supported their European allies' arrangements for expressing a common foreign and security policy (Principle 1), those developments must 'strengthen the integrity and effectiveness of the Atlantic Alliance', with NATO remaining the primary institution for discussion of policy related to the security of its members, wherever the origin of debate (Principle 2). NATO's collective defence role must be retained through the 'effective integrated military structure' of the Alliance (Principle 3), and the US would support European allies in their efforts to 'protect vital interests and uphold the rule of law beyond Europe itself' (Principle 4). Also, European allies should be encouraged to 'open their common defence policy deliberations to all European members of NATO' in order to prevent divisiveness and encourage transparency between institutions (Principle 5).[102]

The June 1991 meeting of the NAC in Copenhagen saw the beginnings of a convergence of views, as the French felt able to agree to the final communiqué, which established that NATO was the 'essential forum' for consultation among its members, that NATO's integrated military structure must be maintained[103] and that transparency and complementarity were required between the EC, WEU and NATO, with appropriate institutional linkage developed so as to ensure that NATO members not engaged in EC/WEU developments would be 'adequately involved' in decisions that might affect their security.[104] In exchange for restated European support for NATO, the US was prepared to offer explicit encouragement for greater European co-operation in defence. In further identifying NATO's new military and political tasks, Washington held that there was no possible substitute for NATO. Significantly, however, a statement was included in the communiqué welcoming 'efforts further to strengthen the security dimension in the process of European integration' and 'the progress made by the countries of the European Community toward the goal of political union, including the development of a common foreign and security policy'. The development of a European 'security identity and defence role', defined in terms of a 'European pillar within the Alliance', was welcomed as a means to 'reinforce the integrity and effectiveness of the Atlantic Alliance'. How far this support would stretch was not clear, and it may be seen as something of a 'non-decision' in the light of the apparent operational incapacity of alternative institutions.[105]

Where there did seem to be a level of consistent encouragement, as clearly expressed by Baker's Principle 4, was in the development of an 'out-of-Europe' role for the Europeans. As William H. Taft IV, former US Permanent Representative on the NAC, noted, 'If NATO is not to be used outside Europe, Europeans should develop the political and military capability to defend their out-of-area interests in some other way', given that future European security interests were likely to be dominated by 'out-of-area' concerns.[106] The development of an 'out-of-area' option, where the WEU had already proven its worth, certainly began to appear the least contentious path for the further development of any European capability. The strategic significance of any such developments, however, would inevitably create areas for potential future transatlantic tension, where 'external' competence would surely promote increasing calls for a matching 'internal' dimension to European capabilities. As the British Commander of NATO's Second Allied Tactical Air Force, Air Marshall Sir Roger Palin, suggested in light of the Gulf experience, it 'would indeed be ironic if events outside Europe helped to forge the WEU as an institution that could have a long-term potential within Europe, for which it was of course originally established'.[107] Indeed, resistant to the WEU's incorporation into the EC, the WEU's Secretary General had suggested back in February 1991 that the organization should have 'autonomy of action' that would permit 'a minimum of military structures' in order to allow it to be involved in regional crises both in and outside of Europe. There would be strategic benefits from such a development, he argued, highlighting the role that the WEU might play 'in tackling security crises in eastern Europe without immediately involving NATO since to bring in NATO might be to risk the involvement of the Soviet Union which we wish to avoid'.[108] As events continued to unfold in Yugoslavia, the focus of discussion on an appropriate geographic operational role for the WEU began to shift very much towards the organization's European vocation, as van Eekelen was to highlight in a presentation at the NATO Staff College the following October: 'The crux of the problem we all face as Allies', he stated, 'is the extent to which a European defence identity can be developed which has not only a role outside Europe but also within our continent'.[109]

YUGOSLAVIA: CALLING EUROPE'S BLUFF

The disintegration crisis in Yugoslavia began in earnest with the February 1991 Slovenian and Croatian calls for independence from the faltering Yugoslav Federation. This provided the transitioning and somewhat introspective institutions of Europe with an opportunity to test their emerging competencies in the first post-Cold War crisis in Europe. Coinciding with the IGC on Political Union, the outcome of which would be determined in the concluding negotiations to be held in Maastricht in December, observers' perceptions of any realistic prospects for a future CFSP might well be formed on the basis of the Twelve's ability to respond to this 'European' problem.

In support of the preservation of Yugoslavian unity, consensus was reached within the EPC framework that unilateral expressions of independence would not be recognized by the EC member states.[110] This decision was in line with the US' position expressed by Secretary of State Baker during his visit to Belgrade on 21 June 1991, when he had also reassured the

Europeans that the US did not intend to adopt an interventionist policy for what was not, after all, considered a matter of vital US interest.[111] Indeed, it has been suggested that, given the imminence of US Presidential elections, the Bush Administration was 'all too happy' if the EC was 'ready to burn its fingers', the Yugoslav crisis providing the Community with a good testing ground for its (overblown) aspirations in what was seen as a potential political 'quagmire'.[112] Consequently, when, on 25 June, Slovenia and Croatia formally declared their independence, the EC felt free to take the role of lead organization for multinational action in the region: here was an opportunity for Europe to prove its mettle.

As the Yugoslav People's Army intervened in the breakaway areas at the behest of the Federal Parliament in Belgrade, a hurriedly constructed EC Troika successfully brokered an agreement providing for financial aid to the region on the implementation of a cease-fire, secured on the basis of the army's return to barracks and a 90-day halt on the implementation of Slovenian and Croatian independence. The Brioni Accords of 3 July 1991 were to provide for the EC's first 'peacekeeping' operation, the deployment of a team of observers to monitor the Troika-brokered cease-fire. As Serb/Croat fighting intensified throughout July, the EC deferred aid and instituted an arms embargo on all of Yugoslavia, acting within the framework of the CSCE for political legitimacy.

Throughout the second half of 1991, an EC Troika of Foreign Ministers shuffled between Belgrade and Ljubljana in an attempt to broker peace, the activity of the Community contrasting with the apparent inactivity of both NATO and the WEU. Initiating the Hague Peace Conference on 7 September, the EC sought to establish a common line and 'broke new ground' in its relationship with the WEU when it effectively issued it with 'political orders'; the WEU Council agreed to examine the feasibility of adopting a more active role in support of EC efforts.[113] French-initiated discussions within the WEU Council in August had rejected the possibility of a WEU cease-fire supervision role, the consensus being against any entangling force involvement in the messy business that was Yugoslavia.

At the WEU Council Extraordinary Meeting at The Hague on 19 September, agreement on a WEU contribution remained elusive. Although there was strong popular support amongst WEU/EC states for intervention in the region to prevent Serbian aggression, political disputes over the recognition of Croatian and Slovenian independence, the maintenance of the integrity of the Federation and perhaps more fundamentally the role and nature of the CFSP led to incoherence and an inability to act.[114] The UK Government, supportive of Yugoslav unity, argued that states must retain their rights to pursue national interests in the region (through the UN and CSCE) and, highlighting the risks of conflict escalation, rejected any significant WEU engagement, without the presence of the Americans. Indeed, the then Foreign Secretary Douglas Hurd recalls the proposals for a WEU peacekeeping force with disdain, referring to French-inspired efforts as 'gesture politics, on a par with the empty proclamation by our Luxembourger President at the time that the crisis in Yugoslavia was the hour of Europe'.[115]

The French, also keen to promote the retention of the Federation, supported intervention once a cease-fire had been established. Despite the clear capability limitations of the WEU for carrying out such action, the French favoured its use for broader political reasons, the promotion of a WEU force providing 'the seed for the creation and elaboration of a "European" defence force and hence a European defence policy'.[116] The Germans, constitutionally forbidden from deploying forces outside of the NATO area, had cultural and historical links to the region that led them to persuade the Italians and Benelux states that independence for Croatia and Slovenia in the light of Serb aggression was the only road to peace. However, given that the only two EC/WEU states capable of military intervention both favoured maintenance of the Federation, military engagement in support of the German objective was unlikely. Indeed, the 'urgent pleadings' of the German Foreign Minister, Hans Genscher, for European intervention in the region 'intensely irritated' the British, who felt that Germany was 'pushing the EC towards a military intervention in which Germany itself would be neither able nor willing to contribute';[117] one senior official was reported as commenting, 'If the Germans' do not intend to participate (in the proposed WEU force), they would be better to shut up'.[118]

Tasked by the WEU Council, which was acting on the request of the EPC following their Ministerial of 19 September,[119] the WEU Ad Hoc Group on Yugoslavia came up with four possible options for intervention on the basis of a permissive environment facilitated by a clear UN mandate: these ranged from logistical support for EC monitors to the deployment of a sizeable peacekeeping force (up to 50,000 personnel).[120] Meetings of military representatives from WEU states took place between 15 and 25 October to discuss the potential planning requirements of the four options, and following their meeting of 18 November, the WEU Council expressed the preparedness of WEU states to contribute to the establishment of humanitarian corridors and take part in peacekeeping operations if accepted by 'all parties' in the conflict and on the basis of an effective cease-fire. Whilst it still remained outside the EC's gift to direct WEU activity, this WEU response initiated by the initial 'mild' EPC request was to become, as Palmer notes, the 'nearest the EC came to putting WEU troops into Bosnia'.[121] In reaction to WEU Assembly Recommendations 511 and 512 in November for an immediate and co-ordinated response,[122] the Council stipulated that 'the provision of contingents for humanitarian or peace-keeping operations is a matter to be decided nationally and that any national decisions to commit forces should be taken with due regard for the overall political context, to be judged in the framework of a common foreign and security policy'.[123] Given the lack of any consensus on what that policy should be, the member states failed to task the WEU with even the least difficult of the options discussed. This lack of European agreement, reflective of national positions towards a common security and defence dimension that were being debated within the ongoing IGC, was to make a nonsense of European pretensions at a coherent security capability, consensus having fallen roundly at the first fence!

THE IGC NEGOTIATIONS

By the winter of 1991, on the tail of the Gulf War, with Yugoslavia descending into ever deeper crisis, and with the disintegrating Soviet Union offering the potential for a range of new security challenges within a Europe of uncertain borders, the future institutional management of this new security environment had become an increasing concern.

Within the context of the IGC on EPU the debate on the future foreign, security and defence identity of Europe raged on.[124] The draft treaty, circulated by the Luxembourg Presidency in April 1991 as a 'non-paper', had proposed a single institutional arrangement but with separate intergovernmental pillars for foreign and security policy and for justice and home affairs, removed from the standard decision-making machinery of the EC and reporting to the European Council.[125] With the treaty accepted in its second draft form as the basis for negotiations,[126] the pillar concept gained support following the Dutch Presidency's attempts at the September Ministerial meeting to introduce an alternative draft.[127]

An unlikely partnership emerged in October with an Anglo-Italian joint proposal on security and defence within the Union.[128] The Italians, who had been the most overtly supportive of the development of a European foreign, security and defence competency, including proposing the merger of the EU and the WEU, had come to recognize the need for a compromise if any development in these areas was to be possible.[129] Building on the WEU's discussions of 27 June in Vianden the proposals envisaged that the future EU would work towards the formulation of a common defence policy, but not yet a common defence, and that the WEU would operate on a twin track, serving as both the defence component of the EU and the European pillar of the Alliance. NATO would 'remain the essential forum' for defining the security and defence commitments of the European members of the NATO alliance, with the WEU acting as the bridge between the Alliance and the Union. The proposal also envisaged the creation of a European action force, already mooted by the British, although it was to be limited to action outside the NATO area, and was to be subordinate to NATO.[130]

In response to these proposals, France, Germany and Spain, in a joint statement, argued that 'foreign and security policy is a necessary component of a Political Union. Such a union should include all questions related to security and defence and should lead to a common defence; the execution of the foreign and security policy should be decided by qualified majority voting'.[131] However, drawing on British preparedness to consider the possibility of a new European defence force, only days after the trilateral joint statement, Mitterrand and Kohl presented a 'draft treaty' attached to their joint letter to the Dutch President of the European Council on 11 October 1991. This heralded acceptance of a much stronger role for the WEU as an agent of Community security than had previously been advocated by the French or Germans. The 'draft treaty' proposed that CFSP decisions and actions might be 'developed and implemented entirely or in part by the WEU', which would be an 'integral part of the process of European Union' based on an 'organic link' between the EU and WEU, although the details of this link remained vague.[132]

Announced in a footnote to this statement was the intention to broaden the existing Franco-German Brigade as the basis of a 70,000–100,000-strong European corps (Eurocorps), initially available to the WEU, but with the possibility of later adoption by the EU.[133] The Franco-German concept extended the scope of this European force beyond the Anglo-Italian proposals for a European capability, neither limiting its potential action to out-of-NATO area, nor subordinating it to NATO. For the French, the new force was to represent 'a symbol . . . of common defence in the making, of European military integration outside the structure of NATO'.[134] For Germany, Eurocorps was to provide an enhanced European capability consistent with its promotion of an eventual supranational European defence framework, whilst arresting the French 'drift towards re-nationalisation' suggested by Mitterrand's force withdrawal threat of the previous September.[135] At the same time, this initiative would represent to the Atlantic Alliance a means of binding France more closely 'by the back door' into NATO's military structures.[136] The Franco-German plans were welcomed enthusiastically by Belgium and received a positive response from Spain and Luxembourg, with Italy's Foreign Minister, Gianni de Michelis, stating that he did not see 'any contradiction between the Anglo-Italian statement and the Franco-German initiative' despite the very clear differences in the proposed scope and institutional 'fit'.[137] Given the 'in-area' as well as 'out-of-area' mandate of the new corps, the British condemned the Franco-German proposals as a means of seeking to establish rival military structures that might undermine NATO and Britain's position within it, particularly given that the developing UK-led ARRC was constrained to 'in-area' activity.[138] These concerns were heightened by the suggestion that the CFSP might utilize the WEU 'entirely or in part', raising the possibility of an alternative hub for an emerging European defence identity.[139] Whilst resisting the Franco-German Eurocorps initiative, the British were equally unprepared to accept any decision on the proposed 'organic link' between the WEU and EU without a 'clear understanding' that this did not imply WEU subordination nor undermine NATO primacy.[140]

Efforts to break the apparent deadlock over the future of any Community defence policy through a Five Power 'round table' between the UK, France, Germany, Italy and the Netherlands (holder of the EC Presidency) led to accusations that the 'big four' EC states were seeking to 'take control of a future common foreign policy and to disregard the positions of the smaller states', with the Dutch European Affairs Minister suggesting that the EC's 'changed position in the world has made the larger EC member states hungry for power'.[141] It was these differences that led, during the WEU Ministerial meeting of 29 October 1991, to intense disagreements over the nature of any future European defence policy.[142] However, the British Government was to signal a move towards compromise in its statement of 31 October 1991, in which it was prepared to envisage 'a neutral review' at a 'certain time' to consider the need for revision 'in the longer term perspective of a common defence policy compatible with the common defence we already have with our allies in NATO'.[143]

Despite the general cross-political party consensus within the UK against the development of an EU competency in defence, disputes within the Conservative Government between the Euro-sceptics and those more sympathetic to the European cause followed the replacement of Prime Minister Thatcher by John Major in November 1990. This resulted in a level of ambiguity in perceptions of the UK's desired outcome in negotiations on the CFSP, with one commentator suggesting that 'Britain is the only country which has no clear objective in the negotiations other than to minimize the outcome, and that, inevitably, has been an invidious negotiating position'.[144] Nevertheless, it could be argued that it was British intransigence on the CFSP issue that preserved the WEU as the intergovernmental institutional vehicle for enhanced European security co-operation.[145] Throughout the negotiations, the UK continued to insist that the WEU should 'remain autonomous, subservient to neither NATO nor the European Community',[146] a position criticized by the WEU/EU-merger proponents as at best 'conservative . . . using ambiguity over the role of the WEU to obstruct clear radical change in European security'.[147]

As the British continued to push for the 'equidistance' of the WEU between the EU and NATO, the French sought a closer WEU/EU link that could be reflected in membership and control, with forces available to NATO only after consultation.[148] On the eve of the NATO Summit in Rome, Chancellor Kohl sought to put a rather more NATO-friendly 'spin' on his Government's calls for a closer WEU/EU link. In a speech warmly received in the Bundestag, he recognized the Alliance's 'existential importance' but argued that this did not 'relieve Europeans of the task of reflecting on what specific, particularly political, contribution we can make to confront the new challenges and risks facing us . . . A united Europe without a common defence is, in the long run, not feasible. That is not an expression of doubt in the durability of the Atlantic alliance, nor an effort to set up a competing body'; rather, he identified it as a move towards responding to long-standing US demands for greater European responsibility.[149]

The NATO Summit in Rome, on 7–8 November 1991, represented an important step in the development of future options both for the Alliance and for Europe. In the resulting declaration the requirement for a new security architecture for Europe was acknowledged, where challenges 'cannot be addressed by one institution alone, but only in a framework of interlocking institutions', a framework in which 'NATO, the CSCE, the European Community, the WEU and the Council of Europe complement each other'.[150] As part of the Alliance's new Strategic Concept, announced at the Rome meeting and designed to better fit the organization for the new strategic environment, NATO was to develop a new 'political' function, offering 'the hand of friendship' to former adversaries in the East and reaffirming its Article 4 provisions for allied consultation and response co-ordination across the broadened risk spectrum, scaling down force capabilities whilst maintaining an insurance defence capability in case of a resurgent threat.[151] Explicit within the new Concept was the recognition that the 'creation of a European identity in security and defence will underline the preparedness of the Europeans to take a greater share of responsibility for their security and will help to reinforce transatlantic solidarity'.[152] Although NATO appeared to be signalling US acceptance of a European defence identity, this was clearly defined in terms of a pillar of the Alliance. NATO was to remain 'the essential forum for consultation' and the 'venue for agreement in policies bearing on the security and defence commitments' of its members, the enhanced European role primarily being in contributing to Alliance 'integrity and effectiveness'.[153] The sensitivities of the US position were to be evidenced by President Bush's comments at the conclusion of the summit, when he was reported as telling his European counterparts, 'If you want to go your own way, if you don't need us any longer, say so', the implications of such a statement not being lost amongst allies fearful of a potential transatlantic decoupling.[154]

Given that the position of the WEU in relation to the EC and NATO was central to differing visions of the desired security architecture, the summit declaration did little to clarify what the role of the WEU was to be, although it went so far as to welcome 'reinforcement' of the WEU 'both as the defence component of the process of unification and as a means of strengthening the European pillar of the Alliance, bearing in mind the different nature of its relations with the Alliance and with the European Political Union'.[155] Nevertheless, in acknowledging that NATO was essential, whilst giving approval to the development of European multinational forces such as the new Eurocorps, the Rome 'deal' enabled the convergence of British and French positions and cleared the way for a decision at Maastricht.

THE MAASTRICHT TREATY

The Treaty on European Union (TEU), agreed at Maastricht in December 1991 on conclusion of the IGC deliberations, was completed and signed on 7 February 1992, to enter into force on 1 November 1993.[156] The new treaty was to transform the Communities' structure into a three-pillar EU. The integrated Communities of the EEC (renamed the European Community or EC under the Maastricht Treaty[157]), the ECSC and Euratom, formed the first pillar, the new EC being enhanced by provision for Economic and Monetary Union. Alongside this pillar would sit two additional intergovernmental pillars, extending the remit of the Union into the two new areas of Common Foreign and Security Policy (CFSP) and Home and Justice Affairs.

Under Title V of the new treaty, provision was made for the establishment of the CFSP, replacing the EPC and forming the second pillar of the Union. This policy was to include all questions related to the security of the Union, 'including the eventual framing of a common defence policy, which might in time lead to a common defence'.[158] The aspirational nature of these commitments was a reflection of the state of agreement reached during the IGC, where a common foreign and security policy was to be established, a common defence policy assured (but in the longer term) and a common defence placed at 'arm's length', with no certainty of its development. The CFSP was to be implemented in accordance with the co-operation mechanism set out in Article J.2 of the TEU, in which, subject to the guidelines set by the European Council, 'common positions' could be defined on the basis of unanimity within the Council of Ministers. Article J.3 of the treaty provided, where the Council so decided, for decisions on implementation measures through 'joint action' by weighted majorities, although this was to apply only to a limited range of issues that did not have defence implications, and was subject to the caveat of national measures in the case of vaguely defined 'imperative need'.[159] The Commission was to be 'fully associated' with the work carried out under the CFSP and, along with member states, was to have the right to refer questions and submit proposals on CFSP matters to the Council (Article J.8). The Presidency, which was to represent the Union on CFSP matters, was (along with the Commission) to keep the EP informed of CFSP developments and to consult with the EP, ensuring that its views were considered; the EP would have the right to ask questions and make recommendations to the Council (Article J.7).[160]

In terms of the treaty's defence provisions, responsibility was to fall to the WEU, the relationship between the WEU and the EU being laid down under Article J.4.2, where it was stated that 'the Union requests Western European Union (WEU), which is an integral part of the development of the Union, to elaborate and implement decisions and actions of the Union which have defence implications'. The lack of clear definition, determined by the failure to reach a definitive position on the nature of a common defence for the Union, required the additional provision of a renegotiation commitment on the basis of a report by the European Council in 1996.[161] Until such time, the WEU was to play the role of the defence arm of the Union, effectively separating 'hard' security from the remit of the EU itself.

Both the Europeanists and the Atlanticists 'sold' Maastricht as a success. The Europeanists had succeeded in breaking the taboo on defence and establishing a commitment to future development, whilst the Atlanticists had succeeded in keeping defence outside of the integrated institutions by placing responsibility with an institutionally distinct WEU, diluting the

CFSP by the vague commitment to the 'eventual' framing of a Common Defence Policy. The treaty was a clear break from the past in that it placed no limit on the scope of the security debate to be considered collectively by the Europeans in their newly constructed Union, but the allocation of the defence role to the autonomous WEU was acceptable only in the short term to integrationists, who saw this 'division of labour' as an unnatural block in the integrative process. Nevertheless, this 'compromise' position, opening up the potential for further defence developments whilst avoiding any clear path for action, may be seen as one of the treaty's virtues given that the principle of a political union with a common defence policy was established. The post-Maastricht potential for the development of an effective European CFSP would inevitably be dictated by the Union's capacity to identify and define common interest.[162]

For many, overloading the EC system with the over-ambitious introduction of 'hard-core' security policies, given the diversity of national security concerns and the lack of a common European identity in defence, could create a potentially negative spill-over into other policy areas. Thus, it was argued, the 'complexity of traditional interest lines and the task of aggregating national positions would become so enormous that the present system would stagnate or even collapse'.[163] In placing defence with the WEU, and assuming only a gradual development of EU competencies in these areas, the Maastricht Treaty recognized the failures of the premature defence-first strategy attempted in the early years of the European integrative process. Jacques Delors, President of the European Commission, was to note the importance of 'transitional arrangements' in this incremental process, 'notably in the area of defence where the West European Union can play a very useful role', providing that the end vision of a single EU remained clear.[164] Thus, the Maastricht agreement had provided 'a door leading towards the possible long-term goal: full commitment by all European Union member countries to a common foreign and security policy, including defence',[165] and in so doing it intrinsically connected the WEU to this European process.

The debates that resulted in the Rome and Maastricht decisions could be regarded as something of a funnelling exercise in which institutional competition was compromised and national interests satisfied in at least the short to medium term. The WEU was central to the development of this compromise. As a ready-formed and institutionalized arrangement, the WEU had been identified by both sides of the Atlanticist/Europeanist divide as a useful tool for transition purposes. Whether an impermanent body awaiting subsumption into an emergent security- and defence-competent EU, or a substantive expression of a European defence identity (and competency) within a reformed and rebalanced Atlantic partnership, the WEU was to facilitate two divergent approaches to European defence co-operation during the early post-Cold War years. Through the development of a greater operational capability, matched by an institutional will, the WEU was to take on the challenge of both an adapting Alliance and a transforming 'community' Europe.

THE WEU DECLARES ITSELF 'WILLING'

The Alliance's Rome Declaration and the Treaty on European Union had left open a range of options for European defence management and institutional development in the early 1990s, and reflected the developmental uncertainty of the declaratory compromise. The disintegration of the Soviet Union in December 1991, preceded by the dissolution of the Warsaw Pact in July, had finally spelt the end of the old order. However, continuing instability in Russia and its near abroad, Central and East European overtures for institutional inclusion and a developing Yugoslav crisis provided the broader environmental context for a European security quandary influenced by changes in national governments. The debate on the desirable pace, breadth and depth of European integration and the continuing management and value of the transatlantic relationship remained essentially unresolved.

The Declarations on Western European Union of 10 December 1991, appended to the Maastricht TEU, defined the WEU's dual role and its relationship with the EU and NATO.[166] In the first of the two declarations, entitled 'The Role of the Western European Union and its Relations with the European Union and with the Atlantic Alliance', the WEU member states agreed 'on the need to develop a genuine European security and defence identity and a greater European responsibility on defence matters' and that this identity should be 'pursued through a gradual process involving successive stages'. Acknowledging that the WEU was to form an 'integral part of the process of the development of the European Union and will [sic] enhance its contribution to solidarity within the Atlantic Alliance', the member states established the objective to 'build up WEU in stages as the defence component of the European Union'. To this end, the WEU was tasked 'at the request of the European Union, to elaborate and implement decisions and actions of the Union which have defence implications, it will formulate common European defence policy and carry forward its concrete implementation through the further development of its own operational role'. At the same time, the Declaration established the WEU as 'a means to strengthen the European pillar of the Atlantic Alliance': with these dual functions in mind, the WEU determined to establish closer working relationships with both the EU and NATO.

For the two European institutions (EU and WEU) this was to be facilitated through co-operation and the harmonization of working methods, the synchronization of meetings and the eventual harmonization of the sequence and duration of their respective Presidencies.[167] To enhance this process, the WEU Secretariat and Permanent Council seats were to be moved to Brussels, to become effective in January 1993, although Paris resisted the total co-location plans of the British, retaining the Assembly and Institute in the French Capital, ostensibly to avoid too close a connection between the organizational workings of the WEU and NATO. Nevertheless, closer co-operation was also to be sought between the WEU and the Alliance, in order to ensure the 'necessary transparency and complementarity between the emerging European security and defence identity and the Alliance'. In the development of its capabilities, responsibilities and role, the WEU was to act 'in conformity with the positions adopted in the Atlantic Alliance', which was to 'remain the essential forum for consultation among its members and the venue for agreements on policies bearing on the security and defence commitments of Allies under the North Atlantic Treaty', although the Declaration foresaw the introduction of 'joint positions agreed in WEU' into the Alliance consultation process.[168]

As the WEU was thus placed at the confluence of Alliance and Union, its role as interlocutor between NATO and the EU was clearly to become a significant one. Nonetheless, the utility of the institution would be fully realized only if it was to provide for some level of substantive defence contribution in the light of demands from within both primary 'constituencies' for a more active European defence posture. Hence, the first Declaration had envisaged the strengthening of the WEU's operational role by 'examining and defining appropriate missions, structures and means', including the establishment of a military Planning Cell; closer military co-operation, particularly in the field of logistics, transport, training and strategic surveillance; regular meetings of WEU Chiefs of Defence Staffs; and the development and identification of military units answerable to the WEU. The WEU's Satellite Centre, to be functional by April 1993, would contribute to the WEU's capability, training European experts in the interpretation of satellite data and imagery, and facilitating the verification of arms control agreements and the monitoring of environmental and out-of-Europe crises (proliferation and ballistic missile protection being emergent European concerns).[169] Other proposals included enhanced co-operation on armaments with the aim of establishing a European armaments agency, and the development of the WEU's Institute into a European Security and Defence Academy.

In the WEU's second Declaration attached to the Maastricht Treaty, the issue of memberships was addressed in order to 'put the relationship between the WEU and the European States on a new basis for the sake of stability and security in Europe'. If the WEU was to act as the defence arm of the EU, the benefits of membership congruence between the two institutions were evident. Indeed, as the WEU's Secretary General was to note, without it 'the potential for convergence would not be exploited and ambiguities would arise between the CFSP of the EU and the operational activities of the WEU'.[170] Following the Danish 'no' campaign on ratification of the Maastricht agreement in June 1992, it was established that whereas the TEU did make reference to the eventual goal of a 'European defence' it imposed no obligation on any member to join the WEU or any future European Army.[171] Greece had insisted on full WEU membership if it was to sign on to the TEU, whilst Ireland had considered its 'neutral' status to be protected by Article J.4.4 of the TEU, which commits the Union to take into account the 'specific character of the security and defence policy of certain member states'. In fact, the WEU sought to overcome the 'incongruence' problem by offering either full membership or 'observer' status to EU states, ensuring that if neutrality (Ireland) or Atlanticism (Denmark) prevented acceptance of the conditions of full membership under Article XI of the MBT, a level of institutional convergence might still be facilitated by the offer of less 'onerous' levels of membership within the WEU.

At the same time as the WEU sought to facilitate a closer relationship with the EU by means of expanded and differentiated membership, its commitment to enhanced linkage with NATO led to the offer of associate membership to those European member states of NATO who were not members of the EU. Representing another form of differentiation short of full membership within the WEU, this provided associate members with the 'possibility of participating fully in the activities of WEU'. Through this process of enlargement, it was envisaged that the WEU would be able to provide a link between NATO and the EU, preventing the isolation of non-EU European NATO members from the evolving European process by providing for transparency in the working method of this 'integral' part of the Union. However, the extent to which the associate members should be accommodated under the WEU provisions was contentious, as the less Atlanticist-minded states sought to ensure a clear distinction between full and associate memberships so as to emphasize the European credentials of the organization.

At the WEU Ministerial Council meeting in Petersberg near Bonn in June 1992, agreement on the conditions of the various statuses was reached.[172] Observer status would enable attendance at Council meetings (unless restricted by a majority vote of full members, or half plus the Presidency) and working groups, and observers would be invited to speak on request; as for all but full members, this status carried no collective defence guarantee nor any voting powers within WEU bodies. The conditions of associate membership included the same right of attendance at Council meetings as for observers but also provided for permanent liaison with the Planning Cell, association with member decisions and participation in the implementation of those decisions (unless subject to majority disapproval), including military operations, on the same basis as full members. They would also be connected to the WEUCOM system of communication and would be expected to make a financial contribution to the organization. Following discussions within the framework of the WEU's SWG, a protocol of accession for Greece[173] and the admittance of Denmark and Ireland as observers, and of Iceland, Norway and Turkey as associate members, was agreed at the Rome meeting of 20 November 1992.[174]

PLANNING FOR ACTION

The WEU Council's Petersberg Declaration of 19 June 1992 sought to move forward the positions taken in the declarations attached to the Maastricht

Treaty, by outlining and developing substantive areas for progress. In fact, the key issue to be addressed by the Council was what the WEU was actually to do, given its stated commitments as the defence component of the EU and the means of strengthening the European pillar of the Alliance. After due Council consideration, and alongside its long-standing Article V commitment to collective self-defence, the WEU was to establish the scope of its missions, a task set which was collectively to take on the Petersberg name. Given the intention that the WEU become more 'assertive in international peacekeeping and even peacemaking efforts', the role of WEU forces would extend beyond the Article V commitment of collective self-defence (effectively provided by NATO) to include the 'Petersberg Tasks' of humanitarian and rescue missions, peacekeeping, peacemaking and crisis management. Significantly, the Petersberg Declaration provided that 'As the WEU develops its operational capabilities in accordance with the Maastricht Declaration, we [the member states] are prepared to support, on a case-by-case basis and in accordance with our procedures, the effective implementation of conflict prevention and crisis-management measures, including peacekeeping activities of the CSCE or the United Nations Security Council'.[175] This commitment contrasts with the position taken at NATO's Ministerial meeting in Oslo two weeks earlier, where NATO had declared in very similar language its intent to support, on a case-by-case basis, CSCE peacekeeping activities but had excluded any specific commitment to the UN.[176]

Central amongst the Petersberg provisions were those relating to the strengthening of the WEU's operational role. By identifying forces and mission types, and by establishing the concomitant planning mechanisms, the WEU would be able to fulfil its functions as the defence component of the EU and the means of strengthening the European pillar of NATO. The Petersberg Declaration developed the concept of Forces Answerable to the WEU (FAWEU) whereby member states designated those military units and headquarters they would be willing to make available for use under the authority of the WEU, to act on decisions taken by the WEU Council, although the participation of national forces in specific operations would remain a sovereign decision. Drawn from across the whole spectrum of their conventional forces, FAWEU were to include forces with NATO missions and multinational units such as the Eurocorps.[177] Significantly, in pre-Petersberg meetings the French and German Defence Ministers had agreed to establish the WEU as the 'political roof' over the Eurocorps, which would not in itself constitute a European Army but only one of a range of forces potentially available for WEU operations.[178]

The development of the Planning Cell, envisaged under the Maastricht Declaration, was an important first step in providing the WEU with the planning capability that it would require if it was to truly develop operational competence. Major General Marcello Caltabiano of the Italian Air Force was to be the first Director of the Cell, established on 1 October 1992 and becoming operational the following April, located along with the

Secretariat in Brussels. Supported by a small permanent military staff and a Military Delegates Committee,[179] the Planning Cell was to be responsible for keeping updated lists of FAWEU, developing generic plans for the employment of forces under WEU auspices and making recommendations for the necessary command, control and communication arrangements, including standing operating procedures, for headquarters that might be selected for WEU operations.[180]

The Petersberg decisions recognized that the majority of the military forces available to the WEU would be 'double-earmarked' and thus also assigned to NATO's integrated structure. Subsequently, NATO should be consulted before FAWEU with NATO missions were used in WEU operations. NATO had welcomed the development of the WEU's operational capability 'in ways that complement and are fully compatible with the common defence we enjoy in the Alliance'. In order to ensure the continuing 'operational coherence' of NATO, agreement had been reached amongst Alliance Ministers in Oslo that the 'primary responsibility' of FAWEU would remain NATO collective defence under the Washington Treaty.

Post-Petersberg, in an effort to clarify inter-institutional relationships, an Annex was approved by the EU (29 October 1993) and WEU (22 November 1993) Councils to be attached to the Document on the Implementation of the TEU outlining further the situations in which the WEU might be militarily or otherwise engaged. These were to include situations where Union security interests were directly concerned; where the Union acknowledged the need for WEU military observers, cease-fire, peacekeeping, sanction-monitoring and peace-enforcement support where it was politically and economically involved in a specific crisis; in response to a CSCE or UN request where the Union identifies the WEU could make a contribution; and where humanitarian efforts required logistic support. Were the EU to request WEU support as part of a broader Union action, 'mutual information and consultation procedures' were to be put into place to promote coherence, although WEU autonomy in 'operational decisions, including military planning, rules of engagement [ROE], command structures, deployment and withdrawal' was to be ensured.[181] Continuing efforts to establish a clear working relationship between the WEU, the EU and NATO reflected the level of disagreement on the desired nature of the Union's security role,[182] but with the decisions at Maastricht, Petersberg and Rome the path had been established for a wide range of possible WEU missions.

YUGOSLAVIA: THE WEU FINDS A ROLE

As the crisis in Yugoslavia had continued to deepen during early 1992, the EC had sought to exercise leadership and had pursued a range of 'soft' options for its diplomatic resolution. By March 1992, only three months after the Maastricht agreement, one commentator had been moved to report that European responses to the crisis could 'lead one to conclude that a joint security and foreign policy is already being translated into reality. Given due consideration to first visits of the three European foreign ministers, the dispatch of civilian observers, continuous efforts to effect a ceasefire, the convention of the peace conference at the Hague with prospects of a long term political agreement—all this goes to show that in its foreign policy the Community is far more united internally than would have been considered possible at the beginning of last year'.[183] However, this upbeat commentary did not reflect the general absence of European consensus evidenced in national foreign policy approaches and highlighted in the security area where the role and application of force were a matter of acute divergence between member states.

The EC member states in their EPC Extraordinary Meeting, only days after the Maastricht Council Declaration on a CFSP in December 1990, had agreed on the conditions for the recognition of Slovenia and Croatia by 15 January 1992.[184] German recognition of the breakaway republics in advance of the agreed date had served only to further undermine the credibility of the EC Peace Conference under the Chairmanship of Lord Carrington, already undermined by Serbian intransigence.[185] Whilst diplomatic efforts stumbled on in the face of limited political consensus, the targeting of the EC's ineffective and unarmed civilian cease-fire monitors demonstrated the 'limitations of an exclusively civilian approach to the conflict'.[186] Indeed, initial optimism was beginning to give way to a realization of institutional limits. Just as the Community's 'ineffectuality' during the Gulf War had led to a 'loss of heart' amongst some Europeans with regard to their plans for a security dimension for the Union, the crisis unfolding in Yugoslavia was to further undermine faith in the potential for any effective European response to common security interests. Certainly, the failure of European diplomacy in the face of escalating violence made the enthusiastic declaration in July 1991 by Troika member Jacques Poos that this was the 'hour of Europe' seem sadly optimistic and wildly premature in the face of interest divergence amongst the major European states.[187] The failure of European peace efforts resulted in the gradual emergence of the UN as the primary security organization in the area. The UN Protection Force (UNPROFOR) had been established in February 1992 to support the diplomatic peace initiatives being played out by the EC. As the violence spread, the UN began to take a leading role in negotiations as the legal and political requirements of a more coercive posture, and the absence of any apparent effective alternative, demanded that it take an increasingly active part if the crisis was to be resolved.

The lack of European consensus regarding the use of military power during the Yugoslav crisis had denied the WEU, the EU's designated defence 'contractor' under the provisions of Maastricht, any significant role. Nevertheless, in the Petersberg Declaration of June 1992 the WEU member states had identified operations outside of the NATO area, and in support of peacekeeping under a CSCE or UN mandate, as a differentiated path for the

WEU, along which European interests could be met, co-ordination encouraged and broader Alliance interests supported without treading on NATO areas of activity. The WEU's contribution to 'out-of-Europe' interests had been demonstrated in the Gulf, firstly during the Tanker War of 1987–8 and subsequently in support of UNSC Resolutions 660 to 662, participating in the naval embargo imposed in response to the Iraqi invasion of Kuwait in 1990. However, the WEU's utility in Europe, but out of the NATO area, was both contentious as a concept and unproven in substance. The German Defence Minister was to describe the Petersberg Declaration as an organizational 'milestone', but it was evident that demonstrable failure to meet the expectations of Petersberg might make of it a 'millstone' around the neck of an over-ambitious Europe, unable to live up to its own over-inflated rhetoric.[188]

Somewhat ironically, disagreement on the precise nature of the WEU's 'new' military role was reflected in the Council debate on Yugoslavia on the very day of the promulgation of its Petersberg Declaration. Nevertheless, the resultant 'Declaration on the Yugoslav Crisis' demonstrated a level of consensus, stating that 'WEU is prepared, within the bounds of its possibilities, to contribute towards effective implementation of United Nations Security Council resolutions in connection with the conflict in the former Yugoslavia'.[189] The Council once again tasked an Ad Hoc Group of Foreign and Defence Ministry representatives to consider the WEU's possible role, this time in terms of the specifics of implementing these resolutions. In recognition of the fact that this offered 'scope . . . for WEU widening its role', the WEU's Secretary General perceived the WEU's peacekeeping role to include the 'preventative deployment of forces; the enforcement of economic sanctions with the support of military resources; the provision of humanitarian assistance and protection of safe areas with the aid of armed forces, and the implementation of an approved peace plan, with recourse to force against any parties failing to comply with its provisions'.[190] The Declaration made clear the WEU member states' commitment to utilize the organization in support of the UNSC resolutions. However, it also demonstrated a 'striking' organizational awareness of the WEU's operational limitations, where the encouragement of member-state engagement might be its primary task.[191]

The EC, having failed to secure an agreement with the Serbs following the overwhelming vote for independence in Bosnia-Herzegovina (1 March 1992), had opted for recognition of the republic on 6 April, determining to support this decision through coercive sanctions on Serbia and Montenegro in line with UNSC Resolution 757. On the basis of the deliberations of the Ad Hoc Group, the WEU Council, meeting in Helsinki on 10 July in the margins of the CSCE Summit, agreed to a limited operational role in support of Resolutions 713 and 757 in monitoring the Adriatic coast for sanction-busting,[192] with surveillance to be carried out in international waters in the Otranto channel and at other points off the Yugoslav coast. The Italians, who were holding the Presidency of the WEU at the time, offered to co-ordinate the monitoring mission of the WEU's Maritime Contingency Force (WEUMARCONFOR) through their Fleet Commander in Chief Admiral Angelo Mariani, with the WEU flotilla to be placed under the operational control of the Italian Naval Staff Headquarters and to consist initially of Belgian, French, Italian, Portuguese, Spanish and British warships supported by four patrol aircraft and land-based helicopters. The adoption of the Ad Hoc Group's joint planning directive, common ROE and working guidelines for participating vessels was to provide further substance to the mission,[193] and the forces of the WEU's Operation Sharp Vigilance were deployed to the northern Adriatic from 16 July 1992.

The WEU's decision came at a time of increasing US interest in some form of engagement in the Yugoslav crisis. There was certainly no appetite in Washington for a major US military commitment to what was perceived as essentially a 'European problem'. However, there was rising domestic disquiet at the Bush Administration's inactivity, particularly problematic for the White House in the run-up to a Presidential election, whilst broader concerns began to emerge in Washington regarding the potential impact of unchecked Serbian aggression on the Islamic world. Equally, as one commentator was to note, 'If NATO continued to shrug its strategic shoulders at the problem then the case for a fundamental revision of its military role in Europe and for the replacement of its command structure by a European organisation would be greatly strengthened'.[194] Utilizing NATO in a limited role in the region might satisfy public concerns, ensure continued US influence and establish an Alliance 'footprint' to counter any 'secessionist' pretensions amongst European allies.

The NATO Council, not to be overshadowed, convened on the same day that the WEU Council determined their Maritime mission, to agree on a NATO monitoring mission to match that of the WEU. Operation Maritime Monitor, which was to draw on NATO's Standing Naval Forces Mediterranean (STANAVFORMED), was to patrol along the coast of Montenegro. Working in co-operation with the WEU mission, the serendipitous holding of NATO's Commander, Allied Naval Forces, Southern Europe (COMNAVSOUTH) post by an Italian Admiral ensured a relatively smooth co-ordination between the two missions as they utilized NATO's Allied Naval Forces Southern Europe Headquarters in Naples, eventually rotating areas of operation in the Otranto channel and off the Montenegrin coast. With support from maritime-patrol aircraft and Airborne Warning and Control System (AWACs) radar surveillance aircraft, and using standard NATO procedures and communications, the warships of the two operations were data-linked, enabling them to share sea and air traffic information gathered in their respective sectors.[195] Initial concerns regarding the co-ordination of these two missions were quickly dispelled by the 'largely seamless'[196] manner of their operation, the Italian on-scene commander suggesting one week into the operations that 'it seems that we have already achieved maximum co-operation'.[197]

The NATO engagement in monitoring in the Adriatic is particularly significant in that it marked the beginnings of a redefinition of NATO's role. Despite the political agreement on a new UN support role having to await official recognition at the NATO Ministerial Session in December,[198] with Maritime Monitor the Alliance had effectively assumed an 'out-of-area' role under the auspices of a UN mandate, redefining itself beyond traditional 'collective defence' and subsequently bringing the US into the conflict. The political motivation for the conducting of two distinct operations was evident, as each represented potentially diverse interests in the future organization of European security.[199] And the monitoring operations certainly offered the opportunity for organizational visibility at potentially little risk: as Fairhall was to note, 'Both organisations have flotillas of warships patrolling the Adriatic, even though there is virtually nothing for them to do—because the main sanction-busting is taking place along the Danube'.[200]

With the failure of the Carrington Plan, authority shifted in August 1992 to the Vance-Owen-led EC-UN London International Conference on the Former Yugoslavia.[201] The UNSC issued increasingly strong sanctions against Serbia and Montenegro as Bosnian Serb aggression frustrated the delivery of humanitarian assistance, calling on its members either nationally or through regional arrangements to take the necessary steps in support. However, transatlantic disagreement over the preferred option for a peaceful settlement had done little to enhance the peace process. Throughout the summer of 1992, the Bush Administration had come under increasing public pressure to 'do something' about Yugoslavia, amidst fears that the conflict could spread throughout the Balkans region. The calls of US Presidential candidate William Jefferson 'Bill' Clinton for US-supported air strikes against those disrupting the humanitarian effort (although ground troops remained out of the question) were roundly rejected by the 'impartial' Europeans, resistant to any 'selective' ethnic targeting on the grounds that this could only extend the conflict, and with an eye to the safety of their own troops in theatre. By the end of 1992, Washington was considering the lifting of the arms embargo against Bosnia and began to put pressure on the EC and UN to do more to isolate the Serbian protagonists.[202]

Following the inauguration of Clinton as US President in 1993, the White House's frustration with the failure of international efforts became increasingly evident: this was despite continuing resistance, not least from within the Pentagon, to US military engagement in what was seen as an intractable 'ethnic tangle with roots reaching back a thousand years', the resolution of which provided for no clear military mission.[203] Initially, the US continued to look to Europe to manage the ongoing crisis despite its clear lack of success in the region. However, the lack of US support for the Vance-Owen Peace Plan of January 1993, on the basis that the '10-province' solution would reward Serb aggression, undermined European mediation efforts by encouraging the Bosnian Muslims to believe that a better deal might be achieved by holding out. As the EC/UN-mediated plan stumbled towards its rejection in May 1993, efforts by the US, UK, France, Russia and Spain to find an *ad hoc* resolution through their Joint Action Plan, in bypassing both the UN and the Europe of the Twelve, further undermined the Vance-Owen efforts and any pretensions at a common European response.[204]

As the international efforts at crisis resolution staggered on, efforts at collectivizing military support for the diplomatic process through the WEU had continued apace. On the basis of the principles agreed at the August 1992 London Conference, the WEU Council affirmed, at their Extraordinary Ministerial meeting of 28 August, their support for UN military escort of humanitarian convoys. Whilst these escorts should be organized by the UN, the WEU communiqué emphasized the member states' 'collective will to contribute military, logistic, financial and other means' to the UN's humanitarian operations in Bosnia-Herzegovina, with the WEU Presidency submitting to the UN Secretary General in September a list of possible contributions by member states. The WEU went so far as to pass on to the UN plans for a significant land operation drawn up by its Planning Cell and envisaging a WEU deployment of 5,000 troops, including three infantry battalions, to reinforce UNPROFOR. However, a lack of consensus on the means by which this contribution should be made led to the operation being 'handed over' to an expanded UNPROFOR later that month.[205]

Whilst agreement on a co-ordinated WEU land contribution had proven elusive, the less risk-intense maritime mission continued to offer a visible sign of European co-operation in support of the international effort. On 16 November 1992, in line with the provisions of UNSC Resolution 787, both WEU and NATO switched operations from 'monitoring' to 'enforcement' of the UN-mandated trade embargo of Serbia and Montenegro. In Operation Sharp Fence and Maritime Guard respectively, the two forces sought to institute what amounted to a full-scale naval blockade in the Adriatic by 'stop-and-search' operations if necessary. The desire to co-ordinate NATO-WEU-EU activity in the area was clearly articulated by the invitation to joint discussions on the ongoing crisis extended by the WEU Council, with the President of the EC and the Secretary General of NATO joining the WEU Council for their meeting in Rome on 20 November. Nevertheless, the presence of two distinct maritime operations, performed by separate defence organizations, within a limited operating area did not escape comment and provided evidence of the 'contesting plans and rival ambitions' that hounded efforts to develop coherent security and defence for the European space. As the NAA was to report in May 1993, the performance of the institutions of security in managing the crisis in Yugoslavia suggested that the NATO concept of 'interlocking institutions' was either 'sheer nonsense or fundamentally premature'.[206]

Eventually, common sense prevailed. With NATO's superior and extant command and control arrangements, unity of command could best be achieved by adapting NATO's structures to accommodate the political requirements of joint control.[207] At a Joint Session of the NAC and the

Council of the WEU, held on 8 June 1993, a combined NATO/WEU single command and control arrangement was agreed under the joint authority of the Councils of both organizations for the combined Operation Sharp Guard.[208] Overall operational control was delegated to the Italian Admiral Vandini, double-hatted as the NATO COMNAVSOUTH and Commander of the 'pooled' Combined Task Force 440, a joint headquarters being established by the attachment of a WEU contingent to the COMNAVSOUTH headquarters in Naples.[209] As MILCOM ADRIATIC, the joint Military Committee of NATO and WEU military representatives was to control, under the political authority of the WEU and NATO Councils, a fully integrated task force and was to represent the 'birth' of a 'genuine partnership'.[210]

Having replaced Sharp Fence and Maritime Guard on 15 June 1993, Sharp Guard was to provide for a level of co-ordination that could meet French demands for a visible European operation under European political control, at the same time demonstrating the potential for a European capability to act 'alongside' NATO in accordance with broader Alliance interests. The full integration of French ships in the joint framework was an expression of the level of pragmatic rapprochement achieved with NATO. French participation in NATO's political and military structures reached new levels as military requirements dictated enhanced co-operation with capable allies.

With diplomatic efforts continuing apace, member states had sought to utilize the WEU further to enhance the European contribution to the international effort. Within the WEU, consideration had been given since the end of 1992 to UNSC proposals for 'safe areas' and the WEU's potential contribution to their protection. By March 1993, the WEU Council was able to endorse contingency plans for a projected WEU-protected area in Sarajevo. However, in the face of mounting violence and continuing diplomatic failure, with US domestic pressure rising and with no realistic multinational alternative in sight, NATO had become increasingly involved in support of UNSC resolutions.[211] Operation Deny Flight (April 1993), in support of UNSC Resolution 816, was to result in the firing of NATO's first combat shots on 28 February 1994, bringing down four Serbian Galeb aircraft that were in violation of the UN-mandated no-fly zone over Bosnia-Herzegovina.[212] The incumbent WEU Secretary General was to note that the result of this engagement 'on the ground' was limited, 'but there was no more talk of a WEU role in Sarajevo', as NATO firmly took the reins.[213]

By June, the UNSC had authorized (Resolution 836) the use of air power to defend the safe areas. NATO provided close air support to UNPROFOR and threatened retaliatory air strikes if the safe areas were shelled.[214] With escalating violence, continuing targeting of civilians by the Bosnian Serbs and the increasing likelihood of a UN withdrawal, Operation Deliberate Force was initiated in August 1995, the intensity of the NATO air strikes serving to drive the Serbs to the negotiating table. On 14 December 1995, the US-brokered Dayton Peace Accords were signed in Paris, providing for the division of Bosnia-Herzegovina into a loose federation of two parts; the peaceful implementation of the plan was to be supported by a 60,000-member NATO implementation force (IFOR). The EU would support the civil aspects of the peace agreement through a package of measures including financial and technical aid for the rebuilding of essential infrastructure.

WEU participation in the efforts that led to the eventual peace agreement in the Balkans, whilst limited in nature, represented perhaps the best the Europeans could achieve in this relatively untried area of defence co-operation outside of NATO. The combined NATO-WEU Operation Sharp Guard had adjusted its activity as the UNSC gradually suspended its embargo on commercial goods and small arms; by November 1995 the embargo mission had been limited to heavy weapons and ammunitions alone. Indeed, the Americans had already 'partially' reduced their commitment to embargo enforcement when, in November 1994, Washington took the unilateral decision to instruct US ships not to pursue the enforcement of the arms embargo against Bosnian or Croatian vessels in the joint embargo operation: this was to draw unusually harsh criticism from the WEU states, who continued their operations despite the US' selective participation.[215] As van Eekelen tactfully notes, 'it proved possible in the following weeks to limit the impact of the US decision on Sharp Guard'[216] as practical co-operation overcame political constraints, but the unilateral nature of the US decision did little to reassure Europeans of the surety of their ally's commitment to future 'grey-area' operations.[217] Nevertheless, when officially terminated by UNSC Resolution 1074 in October 1996 (having been suspended in July), the Sharp Guard operation accounted for 74,000 ship challenges and represented a major international effort to restrict the movement of arms and goods into the region.[218] As a development of the WEU's ability to contribute to such operations in the future, and on the basis of experiences in the Adriatic, the Planning Cell, tasked by the WEU Council, developed 'Combined Endeavour', a maritime operation plan for the use of maritime forces answerable to the WEU, which was to provide 'a mechanism for generating and exercising WEU maritime forces', under the Council's authority, for future participation in a range of Petersberg missions.[219]

The other WEU contributions to the resolution of the Yugoslav conflict were to be small scale, but they were nonetheless of some significance. In May 1993, following decisions taken at the Luxembourg Extraordinary Council meeting of 5 April 1993 and the subsequent Memoranda of Understanding, agreement was reached between the WEU and the three riparian states of Romania, Hungary and Bulgaria on a co-ordinated police and customs action on the Danube in support of the UN embargo.[220] The Danube had been recognized as the main 'loophole' in the sanctions-enforcement regime, with the embargo operations being carried out in the Adriatic when much of the suspect traffic utilized the internal waterway. The concept put together by the WEU's Ad Hoc Group at the request of the Council was of a non-military operation, acceptable to the three 'river-side' states fearful of Serbian reprisal and potentially open to German participation. The

WEU went on to support a police and customs operation along the Danube, helping to establish, and provide personnel for, a co-ordination and support centre and three control areas, one in Mohacs in Hungary, one in Ruse in Bulgaria and the main base in Calafat in Romania.[221] The operation was conducted under the national authorities, but with WEU command of the fast patrol boats and vehicles provided to support the national efforts. The Danube operation proved successful in carrying out a total of 6,748 inspection checks with the discovery of 422 embargo infringements.[222] However, it was also significant in that it facilitated the close co-operation of civil police and customs services, a new departure for the WEU operations and an area to become increasingly significant in security terms within the new Europe. And for the three participating NATO and EU 'waiting-room' states, an opportunity had been provided to demonstrate their commitment and utility in the satisfaction of European security interests with the possible enhancement of their membership prospects.

The other major contribution of the WEU in the former Yugoslavia was the result of a request for WEU assistance on 5 October 1993, weeks before the TEU actually came into force. The EC's General Affairs Council had requested of the WEU that it consider how it might support the EU Administration planned for the divided town of Mostar as part of its contribution to the General Framework Agreement for Peace. Following the appointment of the EU Administrator, Hans Koschnick, the following April, the WEU Council agreed to a WEU presence 'to supervise and control the police, including their training' and, by early July, had deployed a police contingent to assist in the establishment of a unified Bosnian/Croat police force for Mostar under the Administrator's authority.[223] With participation in the contingent initially restricted to the WEU member states, the acceptance of Austrian, Swedish and Finnish assistance led to the WEU police group reaching 182 personnel by the following summer.[224] As part of the EU presence, and funded by the EU, the police action in Mostar offered a limited and conscribed role for the WEU which did not step on either NATO or UN 'toes', although it was to prove a difficult task given the lack of Bosnian readiness to co-operate across the ethnic divide. The WEU's involvement came to an end with the transfer of the EU Administrator's responsibilities to the local authorities in October 1996, after which the UN's International Police Task Force absorbed the WEU's role.[225]

The failure of the European institutional mechanisms to secure a speedy and effective political settlement in the former Yugoslavia was, at least in part, the consequence of national resistance to meeting the costs of a coherent and broadly based policy that might in turn provide for military action. Without common foreign policies and defence resources much of the EU's efforts were directed at managing internal divergence rather than actively establishing and implementing policy, leading to the adoption amongst frustrated members of *ad hoc* rather than CFSP-based action.[226] But the EU, and indeed the WEU, should not be judged too harshly on this apparent missed opportunity to demonstrate a new commitment to external action. Given the level of internal cohesion, the relative newness of the CFSP concept and the significant lack of experience in the management of external crisis situations, the EU had demonstrated, at least in its early diplomatic activity and in the absence of other 'interested' parties, the desire to find a capacity for action so evidently lacking in the Gulf debacle.[227] Equally, the WEU had demonstrated the political will to act and the capability to do so rapidly and effectively, in low-level embargo support tasks under UN mandates, but also in response to EU requests for policing support in Mostar. Whilst a consensus had not yet emerged amongst members of the EU or WEU regarding the extent and nature of external engagements, the events in Yugoslavia did demonstrate that in terms of the institutional management of a European defence policy, concerns had moved from questions of principle to questions of technicality. As Gnesotto suggests, the relationship between the EC/EU and WEU in this sense had become a 'normal' one, 'the latter becoming a technical instrument at the disposal of the former'.[228]

In fact, the limitations of the EU/WEU response to the Yugoslav crisis also provided an opportunity for NATO, severely creaking at the joints in the absence of any apparent raison d'être, to find itself a new role. NATO had been caught 'off guard' by the speed with which the WEU had launched its initial Sharp Vigilance operation in the Adriatic, and the 'quiet competition' which initially ensued between the WEU and NATO was largely inspired by Washington's desire to demonstrate the continuing relevance of the US-led Alliance.[229] By 1993 NATO had taken on the role of peace-enforcer in Yugoslavia and, in moving 'out of area', had found a means of remaining 'in business'. At the same time, the clear limitations of the Europeans led even the most 'Europeanist' of states to recognize that a working security system would require an Atlanticist dimension. In the SACEUR Agreement, signed by the Chiefs of Defence Staff of the participating nations in January 1993, the French agreed to NATO operational command of Eurocorps in case of crisis[230] and, despite some concerns that the WEU should not become a 'poor cousin' picking up the Alliance's 'left-overs',[231] accepted the principle that these forces would only be deployed under WEU auspices to serve the goals of the EU in the event of NATO failure to act. This decision was a reflection of a new 'pragmatism' brought about by the experiences in Yugoslavia, removing a long-standing point of strain in the France-NATO relationship.[232]

The WEU's ability to demonstrate the institutional flexibility to adapt to the operational requirements of the Alliance's transforming security agenda was significant in overcoming the potential negative 'fall out' of competitive institutional interests. Acting on the one hand as an expression of common European concerns, but on the other hand engaging with the US through *ad hoc* collaboration with NATO in the Adriatic, the WEU was able to satisfy both constituencies, overcoming initial 'gridlock' and enabling successful 'interlock' between participating organizations. Arguably more significant at the political rather than the operational level, WEU activity in the Yugoslav crisis provided a 'real' example of the potential complementarity between the emerging CFSP and broader Alliance interests. However, the limitations of the WEU were also evident. An Assembly report on the WEU's Adriatic operations highlighted the specific requirement for a developed military infrastructure and for clear political guidance and a mandate for those in command and control of WEU operations. With an eye to the forthcoming NATO Summit, the report did note the contribution of the WEU operations to 'the achievement of the political aim, namely the bringing together of the Atlantic Alliance (NATO) and its European pillar (WEU)', a relationship that might be further developed by a formal agreement with NATO providing for WEU access to Alliance assets and infrastructure.[233] Just as the working 'political' relationship between the WEU and NATO had been enhanced following the move to Brussels, (with the establishment of Secretariat co-operative mechanisms, the holding of Joint Council meetings and the attendance of the respective Secretary Generals at Ministerial meetings), the WEU Council was to break new ground in November 1993 by suggesting that the WEU might utilize NATO's communication systems, command facilities and headquarters for WEU operations. Representing what Jopp has referred to as 'the first important joint input from WEU members to the Allied decision-making process', this proposal was to set the stage for a new relationship between the WEU and the Alliance.[234]

THE WEU AND THE BROADER EUROPE

As member states sought to determine the nature and role of the institutions of European security in meeting the challenges of the post-Cold War environment, the question of the relationship of these institutions to the broader Europe presented its own dilemmas. Unable to isolate themselves from the security risks raised by the fragmentation of the Eastern Bloc, the primary institutions of European security had begun to consider the potential for enlargement as one element of their broader outreach to the East. The states of Central and Eastern Europe (CEE) sought a framework that might offer them military and economic security in the new post-Cold War order, as both East and West recognized the potential benefits that might accrue from 'belonging' to a broad European 'security community' based on a commitment to democracy and human rights and facilitated by a range of interlocking institutions.[235]

Consequently, the EC had embarked on a programme of inclusion in December 1991, establishing a practical plan for the association of CEE states through the provision of 'Europe Agreements', individually tailored to the interests and situations of the 10 most 'progressive' states, and intended to provide for the gradual establishment of a close relationship based on free trade, political dialogue, economic and financial co-operation and cultural discourse.[236] Decisions reached by the European Council in Copenhagen, on 21–22 June 1993, explicitly linked the co-operation provided for under the Europe Agreements to the 'objective of membership', establishing a 'structured relationship' of enhanced consultation with the CEE states on matters of common interest across all three pillars of the EU, including the CFSP, to be followed by membership of the Union in the long term once certain criteria had been met.[237]

NATO resisted the notion of any immediate enlargement, but had begun the process of 'outreach' to its former Cold War antagonists by the establishment, in the same month as the EC's 'Europe Agreements' plans were unveiled, of the North Atlantic Co-operation Council (NACC). As a forum for dialogue between NATO and the former Warsaw Pact states, it was to provide for discussions on issues to include civil-military relations, arms control measures, defence conversion and political consultation on regional disputes such as that between Russia and Ukraine over the Crimea and the Black Sea Fleet.[238] Without offers of membership, which were problematic not least to the extent that NATO had still to determine its own place as a defence provider in an environment lacking a common and dominant threat, the NACC was to provide for dialogue, co-operation and confidence-building transparency as a contribution to regional stability.

Just as the primary institutions sought to extend security through outreach and expansion,[239] the WEU had also begun to carve itself out a role in the 'eastern engagement' process. In an effort to establish a climate of co-operation and understanding with the CEE states, the WEU Assembly had initiated a dialogue at its Extraordinary Session in Luxembourg in March 1990, inviting representatives from the national parliaments of the Warsaw Pact states to attend the Assembly as observers and discuss issues of concern. Reinforced by the Secretary General's diplomatic visits in the following months,[240] it was thought that the Assembly initiative, by 'pooling ideas' and 'drawing together the new strands of thinking being developed in both east and west', could potentially play a significant role in overcoming the continental Cold War divide.[241] The recently established WEU Institute for Security Studies, opened in Paris on 1 June 1990, had been entrusted with the task of 'collaboration with existing institutes, to organize meetings with institutes in countries not belonging to Western Europe, particularly those in the Warsaw Pact countries',[242] as part of its broader mission to develop the common 'grammar' of a European strategic culture of defence cooperation. This was to include the development of a seminar programme for Foreign and Defence Ministry representatives of WEU and Visegrad states, with an intensified dialogue emerging following the decisions of the WEU's Vianden Ministerial in June 1991, including the award of scholarship opportunities to CEE researchers.

In line with emerging EU policy, the WEU sought to develop a strategy of differentiation in its relationships with its eastern neighbours, whereby states that had reached particular political standards could benefit from a closer level of co-operation with the WEU.[243] This co-operation was formalized at the Extraordinary Meeting of 19 June 1992: those states with, or in the process of negotiating, Europe Agreements with the EC were invited by the WEU Council to 'strengthen existing relations by structuring the dialogue, consultation and cooperation' with the WEU. This new structured arrangement would enable the CEE states to 'acquaint themselves with the future security and defence policy of the European Union and find new opportunities to co-operate with the defence component of the Union and with the European pillar of the Atlantic Alliance as these develop'.[244]

The resultant Forum for Consultation established between the WEU Permanent Council and the Ambassadors of Bulgaria, Czechoslovakia, Estonia, Hungary, Latvia, Lithuania, Poland and Romania met for the first time, in London, on 14 October 1992. Providing for annual meetings between Foreign and Defence Ministers, and at least twice yearly Ambassadorial meetings, the Forum was to be supported by an *ad hoc* Troika at the senior official level pursuing consultations on specific security issues. Based on a commitment to promote dialogue, consultation and co-operation, the emphasis was to be on 'formulating mechanisms for consultation on crisis situations, with a view to developing co-operation on conflict prevention and crisis management'.[245]

Meeting some resistance from NATO on the grounds that it might detract from the work taking place within the NACC, the WEU's Forum emphasized the complementary and non-duplicative nature of its work, concentrating on 'specifically European subjects'[246] supportive of the broader co-operation taking place within the NATO body, constituting as it did a smaller group of CEE states, selected on the basis of their proximity to the criteria for EU membership.[247] Indeed, the Forum was to prove its effectiveness in developing consultation partner co-operation when, following the Forum's Rome Ministerial of 20 May 1993, the WEU provided the practical civil aid which was to form the basis for the first Danube operation of June 1993, enforcing the embargo against Serbia. This development of co-operative practice had long-term implications, helping to establish a 'community of interests' between the WEU and those states seeking accession to the EU.

Although a degree of consensus had facilitated a level of co-ordinated institutional outreach to the CEE states, the issue of institutional enlargement was to prove highly contentious as distinct national agendas resulted in member-state disagreement on the desired constituencies of the major organizations. Discussions taking place following the signing of the Maastricht Treaty in 1992 demonstrated fundamental differences in the institutional 'visions' of the major players.[248] The British generally favoured EU widening, largely as a means to block further deepening of the integrated space, arguing that as a 'civilian power', able to include neutral states and extend 'soft' links with the East, the EU might be better able to establish a stable and prosperous European space than if it were to seek to become a more traditionally 'power-based' super-state. However, there was no UK support for either WEU or NATO enlargement on the basis that this might undermine the cohesion and efficiency of both organizations, whilst unilateral WEU enlargement might set the organization up as a European competitor to NATO.

The French, for their part, were resistant to any early enlargement of the institutions, but for very different reasons to the British. Recognizing the potential benefits of enlargement in terms of the EU's geo-strategic position and economic clout, the French were clearly concerned that the introduction of neutral states, culturally predisposed to the utilization of soft leverage through economics and diplomacy, might undermine the development of a defence dimension for the Union.[249] Consequently, the French argued that the initiatives undertaken by the Twelve existing members in the areas of Economic, Monetary and Political Union should be consolidated before the EU considered any further enlargement.[250] Equally, it was argued that the presence of new states in the WEU, as the embryo of a concerted European defence for Europe, might serve only to dilute the process, whilst NATO enlargement was resisted on the grounds that it could only enhance American influence in Europe: the French preferred the CSCE as a vehicle for pan-European security co-operation.

The Germans remained consistently pro-enlargement for both the EU and NATO, and subsequently for the WEU as the defence arm of the EU and the European pillar of the Alliance. Just as the economic and political stability of Europe post-Second World War was dependent on German recovery, enhanced by its participation in Alliance and Community, the situation of the CEE states post-Cold War required an institutional response. Drawing these states in to a political, economic and security framework that in turn could draw them up a 'developmental' ladder of economic growth and political 'maturity' could assure European stability and development. At the same time, extending institutional borders would ensure that Germany would cease to be a front line in a divided Europe. However, a level of caution towards the favoured widening and deepening of the European institutions was evident in the German approach, the experience of its own reunification having illuminated some of the potential challenges of integrating the East.[251]

As compromise was reached on proposals for a limited enlargement of the EU, negotiations with the four EFTA states, Sweden, Austria, Finland and Norway, being sanctioned at the European Council meeting in Edinburgh in December 1992, it became increasingly evident that any enlargement of the primary institutions would create complexities given the linkage between NATO, the EU and the WEU. The enlargement of the EU, with its inferred access to WEU membership, raised the difficulty of new members' access to WEU collective defence guarantees, effectively provided by the Alliance, for those states not members of NATO. The Dutch Foreign Minister was to argue that this 'Royal Road' was conceived of in order to provide a path from the EU, through the WEU, to NATO in such a way that 'no one could take offence, because that would mean objecting to the E.C.'[252]

The 'Royal Road' may have been popular with many of the aspirant states in CEE, but the potential ramifications of a strategy that offered 'implied' NATO membership without concomitant NATO controls ensured general agreement that this back door to NATO guarantees had to be closed. In fact, the first post-Cold War wave of EU enlargement, with the accession of the neutral states of Austria, Finland and Sweden in 1995, skirted the problem of 'extended' guarantees as these states sought only 'non Article V carrying' observer status in the WEU. WEU observer status enabled a level of participation for neutral states, ill-disposed to and constitutionally prohibited from direct defence collaboration, in the EU's security and defence aspirations, although it did suggest that the WEU might be 'hamstrung' in terms of any future merger option with a membership-divergent EU.[253] In what became known as the Cahen Doctrine, the WEU states accepted the principle that any new full, and therefore guarantee-carrying, members of the WEU must also be full members of NATO, whilst the prerequisite of EU membership was established in order to maintain the coherence of the WEU's role as the instrument of the EU's emergent defence policy.[254]

STRENGTHENING THE ALLIANCE: NATO, ESDI AND THE ROLE OF THE WEU

The NATO Summit in Brussels on 10–11 January 1994 was to mark a watershed in US acceptance of the benefits of an ESDI for the broader transatlantic Alliance. Efforts at co-operation through the WEU had served to demonstrate that a more co-ordinated Europe was not necessarily a threat, and indeed might be an asset, to NATO and American interests if it was managed within an Atlantic context. Ambassador Robert Hunter was later to spell out the thinking behind the Clinton Administration's more 'relaxed' approach to the construction of an ESDI through the development of the WEU. The US offered support of the WEU as a means of 'preventing the renationalisation of defence', 'focusing minds on security' and providing 'a home for the Germans', whilst 'the more the European allies help themselves, the more Congress is likely to pay for transatlantic defence'.[255] Welcoming the entry into force of the Maastricht Treaty and the establishment of the EU, the Declaration of Heads of State following the Brussels Summit gave 'full support' to the development of an ESDI 'in the longer-term perspective of a common defence policy within the European Union [which] might in time lead to a common defence compatible with that of the Atlantic Alliance'. Recognizing that the 'Alliance and the European Union share common strategic interests', the declaration went on to 'support strengthening the European pillar of the Alliance through the Western European Union, which is being developed as the defence component of the European Union'.

In order to facilitate this, the Alliance's organization and resources were to be adjusted, and closer co-operation and transparency to be encouraged

through consultation, including joint Council meetings of the two organizations. Most significantly, it was agreed to 'make the collective assets of the
alliance available, on the basis of consultations in the North Atlantic Council, for WEU operations undertaken by the European allies in pursuit of their
common foreign and security policy'.[256] This declaration of intent was to
refocus military-level relationships, with the WEU, specifically acting as the
defence arm of the EU, having resort not only to the collective capabilities of
the European allies but also to those of the Atlantic Alliance itself.

In further support of a more effective European pillar, the Brussels Declaration endorsed the development of the Combined Joint Task Force (CJTF)
concept by which multinational, tri-service headquarters, deployed as self-
contained elements of the NATO command structure, could also provide
for the participation of states not within the integrated military structure
of NATO itself. Drawing on the experiences of Operations Desert Storm,
Deny Flight and Sharp Guard, the CJTF was to enable action by 'coalitions
of the willing', in circumstances in which mobility and flexibility would be
key determinants of success.[257] Providing for coalitions of interest that could
'by-pass' the consensual necessities of traditional NATO decision-making,
an increasing requirement given the loss of 'cold war' threat consensus,[258]
the CJTF inside NATO's regional commands would be able to launch a
military operation on behalf of the WEU, using joint NATO assets and
non-European personnel, 'under the orders of the operational commander
appointed by the WEU under the political authority of the WEU Council'.[259]

In offering the WEU the possibility of an operational capability that
national constraints were likely to preclude for the foreseeable future, the
CJTF could prevent unnecessary duplication and enable Europeans to act
in support of their CFSP.[260] However, the provision of 'loaned' facilities
was not to be automatic, requiring NAC approval on a case-by-case basis,
raising the question of an American veto over potential missions decided
by Europeans. Equally, the CJTF proposals were regarded with suspicion
by some, most notably the French, who regarded the US-initiated 'offer'
as a means of pre-empting the development of separate European military
structures, such as the Eurocorps, which would be directly answerable to
the WEU.[261] For the British, the CJTF concept offered a suitable means
of facilitating potential European action within an Alliance framework, if
notionally under the direction of the WEU. British officials argued that the
offer of availability of collective NATO assets and the evolution of the CJTF
would increase the range of national and multinational forces available to
the WEU, offering, at least 'in principle . . .a wide range of options from
which we [sic] can select to get the right combination of military capability
and the right political "label" for each case'.[262]

Although it was generally accepted that the WEU could benefit from 'separable but not separate assets' provided through NATO, the French were
not alone in raising concerns that the WEU must not forgo the development
of an autonomous planning and operational capability if it was to be able

to act either independently or for the EU.[263] This concern for a level of European autonomy was considered a 'moot point' by those who foresaw no possibility, at least within the following 10 years, that Europe could reach agreement on any issue that was important enough to require operational potential without the agreement of the US. As a senior NATO official in Brussels commented, the 'WEU has no military significance—it is a symbolic forum to express European unity', being neither 'sexy' nor relevant, particularly in light of NATO's new confidence and given the redefinition of the Alliance's scope ('out-of-area') and role (peacekeeping).[264]

RWANDA: THE FAILED TEST

Notwithstanding the limitations of European capabilities, the evidence of the WEU's operational activity over the coming years was to suggest that the lack of political will, rather than operational capabilities, was to be the significant limiting factor. Deep-seated national differences in the perception of problem and solution had resulted in the failure to reach political consensus on the committal of WEU forces to Bosnia.[265] This problem was to re-emerge as another 'opportunity' arose for WEU action, this time in Rwanda, an 'out-of-Europe' crisis, and in the face of a dire requirement for international intervention to prevent a humanitarian disaster. Events in Somalia in 1993 had soured the initial post-Cold War international taste for UN-sanctioned military intervention in areas well beyond national territories and without clear national interests at stake. Public disgust at the hacking to death of 24 Pakistani peacekeepers in July, followed by the September images of the bodies of US helicopter pilots being dragged through the streets of Mogadishu, reinforced international resistance to future military engagement in peacekeeping tasks.[266]

As violence erupted in Rwanda in April 1994, the French put forward proposals for WEU member states' contribution to an interim force, whilst the force for the UN Assistance Mission for Rwanda (UNAMIR) was readied. These proposals came up against considerable opposition in the WEU Permanent Council meetings held on 17 and 21 June. At its second meeting, the WEU Council did agree to task the Planning Cell with the monitoring and co-ordination of the contributions of member states in support of UN-mandated action in the region, although no agreement on a WEU operation could be reached.[267]

Despite the UN's prior mandate for an operation in Rwanda, the French continued to seek European legitimation, raising the issue of its proposed intervention at the Corfu European Council in the same month, marking what Vasconcelos referred to as 'a growing trend towards the Europeanization of France's African policy'.[268] The French announced the start of the Rwanda Operation Turquoise in support of UN Resolution 929 at the Council's following meeting of 24 June.[269] The WEU's Planning Cell continued to monitor and report on WEU member contributions to the region, including the provision of financial, medical and transportation aid. However, the WEU's Secretary General noted his organization's lack-lustre performance when he suggested that 'the best we could say of our involvement was that to a certain extent WEU had acted as a catalyst by continuously listing the most urgent needs in the area'.[270]

Even given the WEU's rather dismal performance, the missed opportunity of Rwanda did spur debate on the possible future role for the organization in African crisis management in support of UN mandates. If capable of mobilizing European support and helping in the co-ordination of European contributions, the WEU might offer a vehicle for action at every stage, from prevention to peacekeeping, in line with its Petersberg 'commitments'. Indeed, the WEU might find Africa 'the most plausible environment for operational solidarity': potentially it could offer the most 'appropriate test cases and seedbeds for cohesion and co-ordination', standing as it did largely outside Alliance (or Russian) interest.[271] Jointly launching an African peacekeeping initiative in November 1994, the French and British identified the role that the WEU might play in support of the improvement of African capabilities and in assisting the Organization of African Union in its peacekeeping role. This initiative was supported by the European Council, meeting in Madrid in December 1995, when it requested of the WEU that it 'plan and implement special actions in order to strengthen the participation of African countries in UN forces'.[272] Although the WEU was to become increasingly interested in developing options for humanitarian and emergency response missions,[273] the option of enhancing the Africans' ability to take a leading role in security provision within the continent had significant appeal to a Europe politically ill-disposed to the costs of direct engagement and aware of African sensitivities to 'benign' interventions by Western powers in African crises.[274]

EXPANDING MEMBERSHIPS: ASSOCIATE PARTNERSHIP AND THE WIDER EUROPE

Given continuing resistance, not least from the Russians, to any NATO enlargement[275] and the inevitably slow pace of the economic developments required for EU expansion, the WEU had sought to enhance further its own role in the process of integrating the East. Having agreed at their meeting of 22 November 1993 that WEU relations with the CEE states 'should be broadened and deepened in parallel to the closer co-operation of these states with the European Union',[276] the WEU Council of Ministers, meeting in Luxembourg on 9 May 1994, had issued the Kirchberg Declaration, establishing the status of associate partner of the WEU. As associate partners, the former members of the now defunct Forum would have periodic access to Council meetings and could take part in discussions, although without the power to block decisions of the Council. They could be invited on a case-by-case basis to take part in the WEU's SWGs, have permanent observer status in the Assembly, have a liaison arrangement with the Planning Cell and associate themselves with decisions taken with regard to humanitarian, peacekeeping and peacemaking tasks and take part in their implementation. This WEU 'family' of differentiated members, which was to number 28 states by 1996, offered a 'unique' opportunity for CEE participation in discussion at the highest decision-making level.[277] Presented as 'a concrete contribution by WEU towards preparing these states for their eventual accession to the European Union',[278] this initiative was seen as complementary to the broader 'good neighbours' consultation and negotiation process to be established by the EU's 'Stability Pact' launched in the same month.[279]

The Kirchberg initiative was also presented as being 'fully complimentary to co-operation within the Alliance framework' and, in particular, to that occurring through NATO's Partnership for Peace (PfP) programme, initiated in January 1994 as a vehicle for enhanced military co-operation without guarantees.[280] As NATO membership moved tantalizingly closer following NATO's acceptance of the principle of enlargement at their January 1994 Brussels Summit, and the subsequent publication of the 'Study on NATO Enlargement' in September 1995,[281] the new status of WEU associate partner was to provide for the enhancement of the CEE states' consultation and co-operation with NATO's European members.[282]

At the same time, given the evident requirement to pacify the Russians in the light of any future NATO enlargement, WEU efforts in promoting dialogue and co-operation with the Russian establishment would seem to have been propitious.[283] The President of the Russian Federation, Boris Yeltsin, had warned of the emergence of a 'Cold Peace' as a consequence of NATO's enlargement aspirations, with an increasingly isolated Russia potentially turning towards anti-Western attitudes, whilst the prospects for the continuing development of a co-operative European system, not least in the area of arms limitation, might be an early casualty.[284] The Russian response to the WEU's granting of associate partner status to the CEE states was, however, one of only mild annoyance. Traditional Soviet hostility to the WEU either as a vehicle of German rearmament or as a largely insignificant element of a wider US-dominated Atlantic system had been replaced in the post-Cold War period by a more positive approach, identifying the WEU as a contributor, if essentially a fairly low-priority one,[285] to a broader European Partnership concept. In this Russian vision, as elaborated by Defence Minister Pavel Grachev during negotiations on participation in NATO's PfP, a bloc-free European security system would emerge, under the auspices of the CSCE, which would 'oversee the efforts of the WEU, the EU and the CIS', with the NACC developed as its military wing.[286]

Despite its early rejection of the PfP, in the hope of effecting some constraint on further NATO enlargement, Russia was eventually to sign the joining protocol in Brussels on 22 June 1994, its alternative vision for

Europe having been roundly rejected. In the same month, Russia and the EU signed their Partnership and Cooperation Agreement (PCA) in Corfu, the beginnings of an institutionalization of this 'strategic' relationship based on acknowledged common interests in not only trade and energy but the elaboration of a workable 'Security Model' for the new Europe.[287] With its connections to the EU as determined under Maastricht, and to the Atlantic Alliance as its European pillar, developing relations with an 'expanded' WEU offered potential influence over two more significant agendas. An essentially 'toothless' defence organization, the WEU could provide a non-threatening forum linked to the integrating process in Europe and generally acceptable to the Kremlin.[288]

The WEU Council, whilst keen to promote stability and increase transparency and co-operation between Russia and the West, recognized that there was little need to duplicate activity being developed within the NATO and EU spheres, particularly with regard to issues outside of the organization's competence. Politely rejecting Foreign Minister Andrey Kozyrev's suggestion in October 1995 for a Russian-WEU Consultative Council, the WEU preferred to continue its development of a largely *ad hoc* and flexible framework of co-operation, which was to put the 'emphasis on substance rather than form'.[289] Initiated by the WEU Council the previous March, political consultation at both ambassadorial and parliamentary levels was to result in practical co-operation with both Russia and Ukraine.[290] By November 1995, a commercial deal had been struck between the Russian state armaments company, Rosvoorouzhenie, and the WEU Satellite Centre for the supply of Russian satellite imagery, whilst discussions were eventually to lead to agreements on a framework for negotiation of bilateral deals to facilitate the provision of Russian and Ukrainian long-haul transport assets for WEU Petersberg operations.[291] Co-operation on arms control discussion, such as the Open Skies Treaty negotiations, proved constructive,[292] and proposals were made for potential arms production co-operation between the Western European Armaments Group (WEAG) and the Russian arms export company. At the same time as enabling this low-profile and practical mechanism for enhanced transparency and co-operation between the West and Russia, the WEU was also to provide an important forum for dialogue, conducted as it was largely within the context of the broader WEU family, intended to promote understanding between Russia, its neighbours and the West.

The member states' interest in expanding the WEU's area of engagement as a contribution to wider security and stability did not end at the borders of Europe. Their desire to utilize the organization to enhance relations in the Southern Mediterranean had been evident since the WEU's revitalization. A sub-group on Mediterranean matters had been established in 1986, becoming a Council advisory Working Group in 1993, with subsequent documentation supporting a growing engagement with the region. The WEU's Mediterranean Dialogue, launched in 1992 to provide for an exchange of views on Mediterranean security and defence issues, eventually included seven states: Algeria, Egypt, Israel, Mauritania, Morocco and Tunisia, with Jordan the last to join, in March 1998. With dialogue conducted largely on a bilateral basis between WEU officials and Mediterranean partner Ambassadors in Brussels, the WEU framework offered a level of confidence-building in Mediterranean states, which were nervous about the implications of increased Western interest in their region. However, without the opportunity for important South-to-South discussion, and tending towards 'dissemination of information on the development of WEU itself, rather than on the possibilities for actual cooperation or even exchange of expertise', the achievements remained 'very modest', as the Mediterranean partners largely prioritized the NATO Mediterranean Dialogue, or the EU's Barcelona Process (initiated in 1995), over the WEU option.[293]

THE WEU REFLECTS: SOME 'PRELIMINARY CONCLUSIONS'

Following the 1994 NATO Brussels Summit, and in light of the forthcoming 1996 IGC review of the EU's security and defence provisions,[294] the WEU sought to develop a common view on what the defence role of the institutions of the new Europe should be. At the Noordwijk meeting of the WEU Council on 14 November 1994, the Permanent Council offered up their 'Preliminary Conclusions on the Formulation of a Common European Defence Policy', a task set for them in the Kirchberg Declaration of May.[295] Recognizing that 'institutionally and substantively, the development of a common European defence policy in WEU must be seen in the context of broader European and transatlantic relationships, which are closely intertwined', the study offered an initial contribution to the discussion of what the objectives, scope and required means of that policy might be. Acknowledging that the development of such a policy would depend upon an as yet undetermined 'judgement of the role the European Union wishes to play in the world and the contribution it wishes to make to security in its immediate neighbourhood and in the wider world', the report sought to lay out some essential areas for common reflection.

Defining a common European defence policy as 'an element of security policy in a wider sense', the report directed it 'towards the reduction of risks and uncertainties that might threaten the common values, fundamental interests and independence of the Union and its member states', enhancing security and stability by 'ensuring a commensurate European participation in collective defence, and by an active engagement in conflict prevention and crisis management in Europe and elsewhere, in accordance with Europe's importance'. The significance of collective defence alliances as established by the Brussels and Washington Treaties was highlighted by the report, a 'basic assumption' of a European defence policy being the 'collective cooperative approach to defence'. Four levels of European responsibility and interest in defence for WEU states were identified: the security and defence of their own peoples, the projection of security and stability throughout Europe, the fostering of stability in the Southern Mediterranean; and the promotion of security, stability and democratic values in the wider world, 'including through the execution of peacekeeping and other crisis-management measures under the authority of the UN Security Council or the CSCE, acting either independently or through WEU or NATO'. Intended to complement the work being undertaken by the EU's CFSP Working Group on security, the 'Preliminary Conclusions' envisaged further WEU 'military analysis' to provide insight into the potential role of defence instruments alongside the EU's diplomatic and economic levers in meeting the EU's security and defence needs.

Outlining the requirements for the development of WEU decision-making, planning, command and control, and capabilities to enhance its operational role, the Noordwijk report also identified the ability of the institution, as demonstrated by its actions in Mostar and on the Danube, to perform combined civilian/military activities in support of the Petersberg Tasks. Welcoming NATO's recently declared support for an ESDI, the report also identified the requirement to 'take into account' NATO processes and 'developments in the transatlantic partnership', requirements highlighted by the introduction of the CJTF concept and NATO's adoption of 'new tasks' in the crisis-management field.

As the first Council meeting at which all associate partners participated, Noordwijk is also memorable for two other events, the first of these being the appointment of a new Secretary General, José Cutileiro of Portugal, the last of the WEU Secretary Generals to be 'single-hatted' in that role. Secondly, Noordwijk is notable for the clear note of censure in the Council of Ministers' Declaration, issued on the same day as the Permanent Council's 'Conclusions', of the US' unilateral decision to withdraw from the naval arms embargo of the Bosnian Serbs.[296] The extent to which the apparent enthusiasm for the determination of a common European position on security and defence, and significantly for the elaboration of the WEU's operational role, evidenced in both the Noordwijk Declaration and the 'Conclusions', was prompted by the US action is, however, difficult to determine.[297]

Following the Noordwijk meeting, efforts at defining the WEU's contribution to a common European defence continued apace. With the aim of establishing a 'comprehensive Common European Defence Policy Statement in the perspective of the Intergovernmental Conference of 1996', the WEU Ministers had tasked the Permanent Council in Noordwijk with initiating a common reflection amongst all 27 differentiated members and partners of the WEU. In this 'reflection' the Council had envisaged a two-part process; firstly, the development of shared analysis of the security issues facing Europe and, secondly, a common position on 'appropriate responses', building on the 'preliminary conclusions' and including the financing, consultation and politico-military support mechanisms 'to enable the organisation to react promptly to crises'.[298]

By the time of the Lisbon Ministerial of 15 May 1995, the first stage of the 'reflection' had been completed, with the 'common reflection' of the 27 outlining for the first time the common interests of this wider European constituency as well as the potential risks to European security.[299] At Lisbon the WEU Council also reached agreement on a number of practical enhancements of WEU capabilities. These were to include the establishment of a Politico-Military Group to advise the Council on crises and crisis management, supported by a Situation Centre offering 24-hour monitoring of potential crises and an Intelligence Section (comprising initially five intelligence analysts) within the Planning Cell to enhance the operational viability of the WEU.[300] Experiences in the Balkans had helped to expose the limits of the WEU's intelligence-gathering capability, the US having withdrawn its intelligence support along with its forces from the naval arms embargo, prompting the President of the WEU Assembly to state that this proved 'just how much Europe needs to be autonomous where intelligence gathering, satellite reconnaissance and logistic support are concerned'.[301] The WEU's limitations in both the collection and processing of intelligence, relying on national assets, had led the WEU states to seek enhanced intelligence-sharing of NATO assets[302] alongside efforts to promote a specifically European capability attuned to the more 'subtle' intelligence needs of the Petersberg Tasks agenda and not dependent on American resources.[303] Accepting the Satellite Centre as a permanent body of the WEU, having successfully completed its experimental stage, the Council at Lisbon tasked its Space Group to continue consideration of three possibilities for enhancing the WEU's capability to use satellite imagery for security purposes: the establishment of a WEU satellite system, participation in developing multinational programmes[304] and the procurement of imagery for WEU use.[305] Although the Assembly continued to promote the first and second options, because of cost and the uncertainty of multinational developments, the emphasis was to remain on enhanced satellite data access for the Centre's interpretation, in itself a unique collective European facility for civil and military security support.

At Lisbon, the decision by France, Italy and Spain (to be joined later by Portugal) to establish multinational land and maritime forces (EUROFOR and EUROMARFOR) for operations at the behest of the WEU was welcomed by the Ministers;[306] with the announcement of the Anglo-French European Air Group at the binational Chartres Summit the previous November, this brought the number of multinational FAWEU up to eight.[307] However, earlier Assembly efforts to encourage Council consideration of a European Rapid Action Force 'to which the member countries of WEU should make commitments including greater integration of training and equipment' had been met with irritated disinterest by the Council, who had informed the Assembly that such consideration was simply 'not on the agenda'.[308] For the Council, the possibility of drawing on NATO assets and the development of the CJTF concept took precedence in their efforts to further 'operationalize' the WEU. Nevertheless, the implementation of decisions made at Kirchberg, Noordwijk and Lisbon provided for new mechanisms and capabilities for the WEU, which was to hold its first CRISEX exercise in order to test its operational response system at the end of the year, these developments all contributing to a sense of 'onward movement' in a Europe stultified by its failures in Yugoslavia.[309]

CO-OPERATION IN ARMS: THE WEAG AND WESTERN UNION ARMAMENTS ORGANISATION (WEAO)

It would be generous to state that the WEU's efforts during the Cold War to enhance European defence equipment co-operation had met with anything other than limited success. In the post-Cold War environment of the early 1990s, domestic expectations of a peace dividend dictated greater efficiencies from declining budgets, whilst the defence industrial sector recognized the need to rationalize if it was to be competitive in a defence market dominated by the 'high-tech' Americans. As defence industries began to seek European collaboration and merger as a rational response to the profit requirements of shareholders,[310] there were clearly potential integrative benefits that might accrue through extending the scope of the European single market and enhancing an area of European defence co-operation.[311]

Article 223 of the TEU had preserved state protection of domestic defence industries, despite the EC Commission's support for the adoption of single market rules in this sector on the basis that, without collaborative research and production of military equipment, the EU would become increasingly dependent on the US market.[312] However, with the WEU identified as the core of an emerging European defence identity, the French and Germans had promoted arms co-operation as an area for development by the WEU in support of a developing CFSP, a position accepted in the WEU's Declaration annexed to the Maastricht Treaty, in which the objective of 'enhanced cooperation in the field of armaments with the aim of creating a European armaments agency' was included.[313] In recognition of the desirability of developing a single focus for armaments co-operation within Europe, it was agreed at the meeting of Defence Ministers of the Independent European Programme Group (IEPG) states in Bonn, on 4 December 1992, that the 13-nation institution would transfer its functions to the WEU. On the same day the WEU Council announced the creation of a new organization, the WEAG, as the IEPG's successor.[314] The National Armaments Directors (NADs) of the participating states, under the guidance of their Defence Ministers, were to ensure efficient use of resources by harmonizing operational requirements, facilitating reciprocal opening up of national defence markets, strengthening the European defence technical and industrial base and improving co-operation in research and development.[315] In November 1993, the WEAG Defence Ministers, in a meeting with the WEU Council, agreed to the establishment of an Armaments Secretariat within the WEU's Brussels framework as the 'institutional' element for armaments co-operation working to the NADs.[316]

Nonetheless, Europe remained dogged by the perennial issue of national protection as the strategic interests of governments in defence production had as much a domestic economic basis as a 'defence efficiency' one.[317] Recognizing that the conditions for the establishment of a functioning European Armaments Agency (EAA) responsible for procurement activity for WEU states did not exist, the WEU Council had welcomed, at their Noordwijk meeting in November 1994, the Franco-German initiative to establish a Joint Armaments Cooperation Structure for bilateral co-operation on the development of a common industrial strategy until such time as an EAA could be realized. To be developed within the Brussels Treaty framework, the Organisation Conjointe de Cooperation en matière d'Armaments (OCCAR) was to emerge from this initiative in November 1996, with the UK and Italy as members. Seen largely as a transitional organization and lacking the legal identity required for the granting of contracts, it was intended to provide a more *ad hoc* vehicle for the management of shared arms projects amongst a group of willing states in the absence of a broader consensus.[318]

At their November 1996 meeting in Ostend, the WEU Council gave their approval to the establishment of the WEAO as an 'executive' arm of the WEAG, and as a subsidiary body of the WEU, in an effort to promote further co-operation.[319] The WEAO's executive Research Cell was established in 1997, with the legal personality necessary to enable it to make contracts for research and technology activities and with the intention that it would become the executive body of a future EAA once the time was right. Agreement on any level of common acquisition strategy, on the procurement of collective WEU strategic assets or even on the centralization of hiring contracts proved elusive.[320] Nevertheless, as Quinlan notes, initiatives within the WEU framework did contribute to the collective machinery that 'fostered regular contact among procurement chiefs, and thereby strengthened a habit of dialogue that must have helped in the various deals reached'.[321] The WEU was also to contribute to the rationalization of the institutional mechanisms underpinning European efforts at developing operational capability and armaments co-operation: becoming effective in January 1994, the Eurogroup sub-groups EUROLONGTERM, EUROCOM and EUROLOG (to become the Western European Logistics Group [WELG]) were transferred to the WEU,[322] whilst a Council Working Group on the Transatlantic Forum preserved the Eurogroup's important public information role across the Atlantic.[323]

A COMMON CONCEPT AND THE MADRID OPTIONS

In November 1995, the 27 participating states presented their 'Common Concept' at the WEU Council Meeting in Madrid, beginning with the 'first stage' reflections on the challenges and risks of the new European security conditions, and developing this further by identifying the competencies and limitations of the WEU in the field of crisis management and prevention.[324] Not quite the White Paper called for by the French at Noordwijk,[325] the 'Common Concept' did seek to establish a common set of values and interests across the range of full, observer and associate members and partners of the WEU (constituting, as they did, the EU-plus and NATO memberships). These were identified in three categories: democracy, human rights and the rule of law; Europe's worldwide economic interests (including technology and access to energy and resources); and the security of European citizens worldwide. New risks were outlined: the potential for armed conflict; the proliferation of weapons of mass destruction; international terrorism, crime, drug trafficking and unmanaged or illegal immigration; and environmental challenges. Following a 'canter' through Europe's significant relationships with other regions of the world, the 'Concept' took a 'first cut' at identifying the contributions that WEU member states might make to European security, either nationally or through collective action. The 'Concept' identified the institution's role in co-ordinating non-military activity, as it had done in Mostar and on the Danube, and stated that the WEU should also be capable of 'mounting military operations in support of crisis-management tasks'. It went on to identify the gaps in European capabilities, alongside the political and operational lessons gained from experiences in Yugoslavia, with the most pressing areas for attention including force generation, command and control mechanisms, reconnaissance and intelligence, strategic lift, levels of standardization and interoperability, and defence industrial capability.

This critical assessment of the WEU's contribution to the security of Europe was further developed in the 'WEU Contribution to the European Union Intergovernmental Conference', adopted at the Madrid Ministerial and formed on the basis of the WEU's own review of the provisions of its Declaration attached to the Maastricht Treaty of 1991.[326] In assessing the organization's post-Maastricht development, and specifically its relations with the EU and NATO and its operational role, the paper identified three possible options for future WEU-EU relations. The 'reinforcement' option, favoured by Britain, provided for a closer partnership between the EU and an autonomous intergovernmental WEU largely on the same basis as that established under Maastricht. The 'merger' option foresaw the complete integration of the WEU into the EU and was favoured by the Germans and, as a long-term objective, by all but the British. The 'subordination' option, by which legal and institutional links would establish areas where decisions of the EU would require a political commitment of the WEU to act, offered a middle ground acceptable to France in the light of its 'intergovernmentalist' leanings. Given the varying interests of the central players, the WEU's Madrid Contribution was, in line with the Westendorp Report of the EU, to represent a range of possibilities rather than any agreed future for the development of the European Union's defence competency.[327]

Perhaps the most striking of the reflections presented in the WEU's own review was its pessimism regarding the organization's operational development. In fact, by the spring of 1995 the WEU Council had been forced to recognize that the strengthening of the WEU's operational role depended on 'NATO's elaboration of the combined joint task force (CJTF) concept', and the Madrid 'Contribution' reinforced this requirement for the use of Alliance assets and 'in particular the successful implementation of the CJTF concept'. Despite the WEU's efforts in developing its operational capability in line with its Maastricht commitments, the Council was down-beat about the WEU's progress, noting even that 'the FAWEU concept has still not been put into practice in a way that would confirm the existence of a WEU capability effectively to generate force packages'.[328] With post-Cold War defence budgets amongst European NATO states 10% below their 1989 figures, a significant drop in military personnel and equipment had resulted in a massive decline in the number of operational units available, suggesting that the WEU would find it difficult to raise sufficient national forces to carry out any significant military tasks.[329] All in all, this analysis could only bolster the concept of the WEU as a European pillar of NATO and undermine the more optimistic view of those Europeanists keen to see the development of an effective CFSP.

NATIONAL POSITIONS AND THE IGC

The March 1996 date set for the opening of the IGC in Turin, as provided for under Article J.4.6 of the Maastricht Treaty, was inevitably premature given the TEU's protracted ratification. Nevertheless, the conference, informally referred to as 'Maastricht II', proceeded with a raft of issues on the agenda intended to enhance the EU's cohesion and effectiveness, not least in the process towards Monetary Union and in the rationalization of decision-making and inter-pillar activities in preparation for future enlargement. The future direction of the Union's foreign and security policy aspirations was also to have been a central part of these discussions. However, the enthusiasm that had marked the Maastricht IGC was clearly lacking in the lead-up to the concluding meetings in Amsterdam, expectations of the potential for an effective CFSP having been muted by the slow pace of development and the exposure of European pretensions in Yugoslavia.[330] With the decisions taken in Maastricht in 1991, the European states had demonstrated their desire to develop their collective ability within the EU context as an active external security player through the establishment of a CFSP. However, events in the early 1990s in Europe had demonstrated the apparent lack of political will to engage militarily without the Americans. Matched by the economic necessity to avoid duplication of capability, experience had highlighted the requirement for intra- and inter-institutional rationalization to ensure coherence and effectiveness in meeting security challenges.

A New Transatlantic Agenda and Joint Action Plan had been signed at the US-EU Summit in Madrid on 3 December 1995, consisting of a non-binding executive agreement to work together across a broad agenda of common interests including global and regional trade issues and the management of global challenges, notably international crime and terrorism, humanitarian issues, environmental degradation and disease.[331] These agreements reflected an improvement in US-EU relations, resulting in enhanced bilateral co-operation, although this was to be complicated by the partial developments within the EU's CFSP. Establishing the EU's intentions and capabilities in this policy area, and the relationship between it and the Atlantic Alliance, would be an important task for the states meeting together in the EU's IGC. The future role of the WEU in these developments, as an expression of both the extent of European commitment and the transatlantic condition in defence relations, was again to be central to the discussions. As the IGC approached, national positions on the future of the CFSP and its relationship to the WEU began to coalesce.

Despite British resistance to an EU-WEU merger, there was evidence of a significant shift in the Government's assessment of the benefits of enhanced European defence co-operation in the period leading up to the second IGC. By 1995 the British Government had instituted two rounds of significant post-Cold War defence cuts. The first, 'Options for Change' in 1990, enforced deep cuts in UK defence expenditure and significant reductions in manpower.[332] In 1994 the UK Ministry of Defence, finding itself a focus of the Treasury's efforts to reduce Government expenditure at a time of economic downturn, took further cuts in 'Front Line First: The Defence Costs Study', which aimed to achieve the required savings in support areas and through greater efficiencies without adversely affecting front-line forces.[333] Neither of these policy approaches appeared to have been accompanied by any serious review of the UK's strategic position.[334] Senior officials continued to reject any suggestion of the rationalization of capabilities through European co-operation as being contrary to the requirements of national self-defence.[335]

The underlying reality, however, was that Britain could neither act independently nor depend absolutely on Cold War allies in post-Cold War crises.[336] Although remaining predictably Atlanticist in outlook, and critical of gestures towards 'unrealisable' European capability, by the autumn of 1994 a serious thaw in British attitudes towards European defence co-operation was detectable. US acceptance of an ESDI at the January 1994 NATO Summit had paved the way for a gradual broadening of British support for a European Common Defence Policy, although this was still clearly linked to the enhancement of the Atlantic Alliance. Experiences in Yugoslavia had suggested to the British that the US might not always be prepared to engage in European conflicts.[337] At the same time, Anglo-French relations had greatly improved as a consequence of shared experience as defence-competent states, largely taking the lead in command of UNPROFOR. One commentator suggested that by April 1995 Anglo-French military relations were 'at their best since Suez'.[338] In a memorandum sent out to all EU member states in March 1995, the British Government had 'set out its stall' in advance of the forthcoming IGC.[339] Although NATO remained the primary institution for Article 5 defence, burden-sharing might require a task delineation whereby the Europeans must be 'ready and able to take the lead, or to act on their own'. Given its diplomatic and military strengths, the British Government had identified that a CFSP and 'future European defence arrangements' would be areas where Britain would take a key role, with the WEU providing the basis for military activity 'consistent with our [sic] NATO obligations' and within the scope of the Petersberg Tasks. To this end, the WEU should be strengthened in its ability to plan, conduct and control operations, avoiding duplication with NATO and supported by NATO assets. The suggestion in the memorandum that co-ordination could be enhanced through the creation of a WEU Summit (the reinforcement option) consisting of the Heads of State of the 18 full, associate (European non-EU NATO members) and observer member states, to which the European Council could make proposals, was perceived as a means of ensuring a permanent division between military activity and the institutions of the EU and received little support from the UK's continental partners.[340]

In their March 1996 White Paper laying out the UK Government's aims for the intergovernmental review of the TEU, the British had rejected any WEU-EU merger on the grounds that the institutional autonomy of the WEU ensured continued intergovernmentalism in defence, which was a 'non-negotiable' of British policy and a position that they were to defend continually over the following months.[341] Franco-German proposals of February 1996 for the enhancement of the CFSP decision-making process through the extension of Qualified Majority Voting (QMV) to joint positions and the introduction of effective opt-outs through 'constructive abstention' were equally resisted by the British as an unacceptable deepening of integration.[342] However, increasingly isolated in its attitudes to the CFSP, and keen to prevent a further drift towards federalism in light of the Maastricht II talks, the British Government launched a 'charm offensive', presenting their insistence on intergovernmentalism as a 'pro-European' rather than pro-nation-state position, with 'institutional separation' ensuring that understandable resistance to supranationalism in defence did not have the effect of 'diluting in any way the single institutional mechanism of the Treaty of Rome'.[343]

Keen to move away from the highly political 'institutional' debates regarding the future role and direction of the WEU and the developing CFSP, the British Conservative Government of John Major used its Presidency of the WEU in the first half of 1996 to establish a programme of pragmatic development of Europe's defence capabilities.[344] Addressing the WEU Assembly on 23 February, Prime Minister Major spelt out the UK Presidency's objectives, central to which was the aim of ensuring that the WEU become fully operational as speedily as practicable.[345] With this in mind, a number of operational initiatives were successfully undertaken such as the implementation of a coherent WEU exercise programme, the establishment of the agreed Situation Centre within the Planning Cell, the development of the 'Eurolift' strategic airlift concept for WEU operations and the opening of the UK's Operational Sea Training facilities to other WEU members (in the expectation of the extension of similar national offers) to enhance WEU maritime training opportunities.

With a stated priority of promoting closer working links with NATO, another success of the British Presidency was the conclusion of a Security Agreement between the WEU and NATO that provided for the flow of classified information between the two organizations, whilst joint meetings of the NATO and WEU Councils continued to promote greater inter-institutional complementarity and transparency.[346] The British Government also began to work closely with the French on the operation of CJTFs, the success of which was seen as a prerequisite if the WEU was truly to become operationally effective. For the British, these 'practical' developments were intended largely to fill a capability gap at a time of transition and preserve the organizational status quo, and their apparent Euro-focus during their WEU Presidency was intended to enhance the NATO-ization of Europe, rather than the Europeanization of NATO, which was the aim of the French. Nevertheless, the practical operational development of the WEU over which the British presided coincided with the requirements of a much broader vision for Europe than that held by successive British Governments: once again British pragmatism was providing for the small incremental steps from which European leaps would emerge.

The Germans, meanwhile, had remained keen to promote an integrated and inclusive Europe, based on supranational structures and open to the East. Enthusiasm for closer integration in defence had, however, been tempered by transatlantic sensitivities. At the same time, there was continuing domestic resistance to any reinterpretation of (West) German constitutional constraints on military activity, the restrictive view of 'legal' use of German forces being historically determined. Under Article 87a of the Basic Law, the deployment of German forces had been limited to cases of direct territorial attack and the support of collective defence within the Alliance. The post-Cold War shift to 'out-of-area' activity suggested the requirement for either a redefinition or a rewriting of the Constitution if Germany was to retain any influence in this important area of policy.

Through engagement in multinational operations under UN mandates, firstly under the auspices of the WEU with German escorts of minesweepers after the first Gulf War, and later through contributions to the WEU and NATO embargo in the Adriatic, Germany had begun a process of 'changing by doing'.[347] By July 1994 the German Constitutional Court had ruled that German forces could contribute to peacekeeping missions in support of NATO, the UN and the WEU, by its reinterpretation of Articles 24 (1) and (2). This enabled participation in a collective security system and opened up the possibility of a broad mission range, both in and 'out-of-area', for potential German participation under the authorization of a decision by the Bundestag.[348] With this 'legal' block to German military activity removed (although political resistance proved more intractable), Berlin could approach the forthcoming IGC as a 'player' in terms of its readiness to contribute to an evolving security and defence competence for the Union.[349] With the Germans choosing to adopt a joint approach with the French to the IGC negotiations, differences over the level of acceptable integration were offset to a degree by the softening of French attitudes to the Alliance.[350] Keen to see the extension into the realm of defence of the integration that had served German interests well in other sectors of European co-operation, the Germans led the way in promoting WEU integration into the EU.[351]

Changes in the French Government during the mid 1990s had instituted an apparent shift in French defence thinking. The 1994 French Defence White Paper, commissioned by the new Balladur Government, had suggested a major softening of French policy towards NATO, promoting adaptation but significantly identifying the Alliance as the 'main arena' for transatlantic security consultation and for the establishment of the ESDI.[352] This reassessment of French principles may be explained in part by the decreasing relevance of nuclear deterrence, the independence of which had been a constant constraint on French relations with the Alliance, and by the post-Cold War requirement for non-Article 5 'intervention' missions, identified at Brussels as an area of Alliance interest and recognized as an area of European failure.[353]

In the spring of 1995, Mitterrand had been replaced by Jacques Chirac as the French President, opening up a new stage of French rapprochement with the Alliance. A keen Europeanist in defence terms, Chirac acknowledged that efforts to develop an independent European defence competence were doomed to failure in the prevailing climate, whilst maintaining a distance from NATO was likely only to undermine French ability to influence the Alliance agenda. Chirac's Gaullist credentials gave him the domestic credibility that enabled him to 'narrow the gap' between France and the Alliance, signalling his acceptance of closer Alliance ties in exchange for NATO reforms. For Chirac, this 'temporary accommodation' with NATO was intended as a means of promoting French interests in the development of an ESDI, 'being more Atlanticist today in order to be more European tomorrow'.[354] Re-entering NATO's Military Committee in December 1995, the French deployed forces in IFOR under NATO command in the same month and agreed to attend Ministerial meetings of the NAC and to send staff to the NATO training colleges in Naples and Oberammergau as well as the NATO Situation Centre, all under the Military Committee's jurisdiction. French military reforms, outlined the following February, foresaw a modernized military, downsized and professionalized in line with British forces, and better fitted to the new international security environment, with the possibility of full French re-engagement with a properly reformed Atlantic Alliance.[355]

Given NATO's continuing commitment to develop the procedures for WEU-led operations using CJTFs outside of NATO structures, the French grudgingly came to accept the potential benefits of this new provision, whilst pressing for further concessions at the three-plus-one talks between the UK, France, Germany and the US that preceded the NATO Berlin Summit.[356] At the same time as a level of rapprochement had been taking place with the Alliance, the cooling of Franco-German relations that had occurred following the election of Chirac, who had been seen as something of a nationalist 'bogey man' by German politicians, had begun to reverse by late 1995. This had culminated in agreement on a Franco-German 'common strategic concept' at the bilateral meeting in Nuremberg on 9 December, providing for closer co-operation on security and defence policies, on approaches to strategy and missions of armed forces, and for common guidelines on armaments policy.[357] French concern to enhance the ability of the feeble CFSP, hamstrung by the unanimity requirement, to represent European interests had led France to co-operate with the Germans in their proposals for 'constructive abstention' and more 'integrated' decision-making within the CFSP, despite deeply held concerns regarding the transfer of power away from sovereign states.[358]

BERLIN AND THE 'GRAND BARGAIN'

By the time of the Berlin NATO Council Meeting of Foreign and Defence Ministers in June 1996 the 'Grand Bargain' had been struck, establishing the relationship between NATO and the evolving European defence identity. The Berlin Communiqué of the NAC had effectively set the level for future institutional developments, in which NATO was established as the primary and 'first choice' defence organization, itself 'an integral part of the emerging, broadly based, cooperative European security structure'.[359] Recognizing the requirement for adaptation in order to improve the Alliance's capability to carry out a full range of missions, the Berlin Communiqué established the nature of that adaptation, including the 'important qualitative step forward' of building the ESDI 'within NATO', and thus enabling the Europeans to make a 'more coherent and effective contribution to the missions and activities of the Alliance as an expression of our shared responsibilities; to act themselves as required; and to reinforce the transatlantic partnership'.[360]

A first objective for Alliance adaptation was ensuring Alliance military effectiveness both in its traditional collective defence role and also in a range of 'new roles in changing circumstances'. Based on the concept of 'one system capable of performing multiple functions', the Alliance would adopt flexible arrangements for carrying out a variety of missions, taking into account national decisions on participation and adopting differing aspects of command and control on a case-by-case basis, through the further development of the CJTF concept. The second Alliance objective of preserving the transatlantic link was to be promoted by 'full transparency between NATO and WEU in crisis-management', whilst the third objective of developing the ESDI within the Alliance would be advanced by preparing the ground that would 'permit the creation of militarily coherent and effective forces capable of operating under the political control and strategic direction of the WEU'. This was to be based on the identification of 'separable but not separate' Alliance assets for WEU-led operations, and the 'elaboration of appropriate multinational European command arrangements within NATO, consistent with and taking full advantage of the CJTF concept, able to prepare, support, command and conduct the WEU-led operations'.

Made possible by French rapprochement with the Alliance and acquiescence on the CJTF, the agreements reached at Berlin spelt out NATO's control over the WEU, the latter being largely dependent on borrowed assets: this would be the case even in terms of its planning for the exercise of command and force elements for possible WEU operations, which would require submission, through NATO's Military Committee, for NAC approval. Although the essential elements of the CJTF 'bargain' were to be agreed in Berlin, much remained to be determined in terms of the operational practicalities of the relationship, including the specific means by which NATO assets for WEU operations would be identified, released, monitored and returned. At the same time, the sphere for any possible WEU-led missions was left uncertain, given NATO's reinforced commitment to engaging in non-Article 5 operations and to developing its ability to carry out new roles and missions relating to crisis management and conflict prevention with a wide and varying range of potential partners.[361]

Hence, the ESDI was to be constructed within the Alliance, with the WEU representing that identity and operationally enhanced through the CJTF concept, which would enable access to NATO capabilities and assets outside of NATO's integrated military structure. France would reintegrate into the Alliance, in exchange for a degree of NATO restructuring, including the provision of 'separable' assets for European actions under WEU auspices. In fact, as Hill and Smith suggest, the CJTF concept became the means of 'satisfying honour' on both sides of the Atlanticist/Europeanist divide, although the degree of NATO control over assets, and therefore over 'European' operations, suggested the high price paid by those seeking autonomous European capability in security and defence terms.[362]

Throughout 1996, the French led efforts to gain US agreement on the transfer of NATO's Southern Command in Naples, Allied Forces Southern Europe (AFSOUTH), to a European Command. This not only was intended to demonstrate US 'good faith' in rebalancing the Alliance to better represent European interests but was also an attempt to secure a highly visible European achievement to offset French domestic critics of Alliance rapprochement.[363] The US had proven staunchly unwilling to limit their freedom of action in the increasingly strategically important Eastern Mediterranean, where the US Sixth Fleet provided a major presence. The failure to gain US acceptance of this 'demand' led to protracted disagreements between Paris and Washington, stalling further French re-engagement with the Alliance.[364] Clearly there were limits to US political flexibility over transatlantic leadership.

As talks on the future direction of the CFSP within the EU continued within the context of the ongoing IGC, US intractability over AFSOUTH and the level of NAC control over assets to be provided for WEU operations continued to concern those seeking a greater European role in security and defence activity. The contradictions inherent in the ambition to both enhance NATO primacy and promote an ESDI had begun to dispel the myth of any substantive Europeanization of NATO.[365] In preparation for the NATO Madrid Summit of July 1997, work had begun on military planning for a range of military missions identified by the WEU,[366] on NATO-WEU information-sharing and consultation mechanisms and on the modalities for release and return of Alliance assets and capabilities made available for WEU-led operations.[367] Consideration had also been given to the terms of reference and appointing principles for the double-hatting of personnel within the NATO command structure for WEU-led operations, as envisaged in Berlin, including the enhancement of the traditionally European Deputy Supreme Allied Commander Europe (DSACEUR) post, as a Command option in a European operation under the CJTF concept.[368]

As the Amsterdam Summit of the EU neared, not all were so optimistic about the CJTF's development at both the conceptual and practical levels. One commentator noted the 'sad fact' that the CJTF concept had 'been given little concrete meaning since January 1994', and that this had led the WEU to adopt a 'wait and see approach . . . limiting itself to reacting to NATO proposals for the practical interpretation of the concept'.[369] More fundamentally, questions had begun to be raised regarding the requirement for the CJTF concept, given the nature of WEU missions to date. Van Eekelen, the former Secretary General of the WEU, reflected in 1997 that 'we have all made the mistake of exaggerating the need for NATO assets . . . for our operations in the Adriatic, in the Iraq crisis of 1990, on the Danube and in Mostar, the size of each WEU operation was such that these assets were not needed', whilst the likelihood of larger operations without US participation seemed increasingly slim.[370] With little need for the headquarters arrangements required for NATO-type operations and being worked up within the CJTF concept, the WEU did lack command arrangements appropriate to the types of missions in which it was most likely to be engaged. The resistance to 'duplication' between organizations could arguably be denying the WEU the capability required to be the effective operational organization in support of both the EU and NATO that it had set out to make of itself under its Maastricht objectives.

THE GREAT LAKES AND ALBANIA: THE WEU
'AVOIDING THE NETTLE'

The WEU's failure to intervene in Rwanda in 1994 had set an unfortunate precedent as the crisis emerged in the African Great Lakes region in the autumn of 1996. Largely in response to the Rwanda debacle, an initiative had been launched within the WEU to examine possible support actions in African crises. A fact-finding mission on peacekeeping had taken place during August 1996, with WEU representatives from the Planning Cell visiting Ethiopia, Kenya, Malawi and Tanzania to look at how this initiative might be progressed.[371] Nevertheless, consensus on action remained elusive. The plight of the 1.5 million displaced people, fleeing the refugee camps established by the international community on the Rwanda-Zaire border as they came under attack from Laurent Kabila's rebel army, appeared only to add to Western inertia. UNSC Resolution 1080 of 14 November 1996 had mandated a Multinational Force under Chapter VII of the UN Charter to support the provision of humanitarian aid and the repatriation of Rwandan refugees from eastern Zaire. The WEU Council of Ministers, having discussed a potential WEU response to the crisis at its Ostend meeting of 19 November, declared its intent to study possible contributions to the delivery of aid and logistic support to the region and the potential for training of African contingents. In its Joint Action three days later, the EU requested of the WEU that it 'examine as a matter of urgency how it can, for its part, contribute to the optimum use of the operational resources available' to support the humanitarian aid effort in the region, but it received no response.[372] A lack of agreement between key WEU states as to the best focus for support in the region precluded any agreement on further action: with France, Belgium, Spain and Italy favouring an intervention, the British, Dutch and Portuguese rather subscribed to the US position,[373] with the complexity of the situation preventing any ready solutions in an environment in which international engagement might be interpreted as 'colonial' opportunism. By December, as the refugees returned to Rwanda without the requirement for intervention, further deliberation on any potential WEU engagement proved redundant, events having essentially resolved themselves.

The civil crisis that began to emerge in Albania in the same year offered yet another opportunity for the WEU to demonstrate its utility in the management of security interests, this time inside Europe, as political irregularities and the failure of the domestically popular pyramid investment schemes precipitated major civil unrest and disorder. As the situation deteriorated with the collapse of civil authority, spreading violence and a stream of refugees heading towards Italy and Greece, these two states led the call for an EU intervention. Following an EU fact-finding mission in March 1996, accompanied by representatives from the Organisation for Security and Co-operation in Europe (OSCE), the WEU and the Council of Europe, it was recommended that the EU act as the lead agency for the provision of emergency humanitarian assistance and the re-establishment of an effective police force. Italy sought to use the WEU, on the basis of these recommendations, as the institution for planning and running the military contribution to a Multinational Protection Force in what would have been a Petersberg-type mission, but efforts by the Southern Europeans to call a Special Session of the WEU to discuss these proposals were rejected by the British and Germans.[374] Forced to go 'ad hoc', the Italians initiated Operation Alba as a 'coalition of the willing' under UN authority[375] to support the delivery of humanitarian supplies in Albania and re-establish an effective police capability. Deploying on 15 April, the force consisted of around 6,000; the Italians were the major contributors, supported by the French, Greeks, Spanish, Turks, Romanians, Austrians and Danes—a truly European adventure but bypassing the organizational structures intended to provide, through the EU, WEU and NATO, for just this sort of eventuality. Extended beyond its original three-month mandate, Operation Alba remained active to ensure security for the OSCE-monitored parliamentary elections in July.[376]

The lack of consensus between the 10 WEU member states and their subsequent inability to act effectively in joint operations, as demonstrated by these crises, threatened to undermine the credibility of the organization, as states chose to act in *ad hoc* coalitions of the interested and able. If the WEU was to be either a useful European pillar of the Alliance or an embryonic European capability for autonomous action in support of the EU's CFSP, it would require both the will and capability to carry out operations, potentially utilizing the CJTF concept when the US was disinclined to act. These failures to find any coherence between the national policies of WEU member states did not bode well. When asked 'how a consensus on military operations could ever be achieved by WEU's 10 members, which rarely see eye to eye on defense and security issues', Cutileiro attempted to downplay the significance of Albania as the most recent example of institutional inertia, suggesting that 'at this point, it would probably take a much larger crisis on our doorstep for Europeans to agree'.[377] However, the failure to agree to take on the Albanian crisis-response operation was later defined by one senior EU observer as a 'decisive moment', dealing a 'death blow' to the WEU and its future aspirations as the defence organization of choice for European crisis-management operations.[378]

It was not until 2 May 1997 that the WEU Council finally found the institution a role in Albania. Agreed at '18' (the full, observer and associate member states) and later including the associate partners in discussion, the Council approved the establishment of a small Multinational Advisory Police Element (MAPE) to advise on issues of police organization, border control and public order as a contribution to the wider international effort to stabilize Albania. The advance party having 'smoothed the way' for the main element's deployment, with the successful negotiation of the Memorandum of Understanding between the WEU and the

Albanian Government on 24 June, 24 police personnel from 14 states from within the broad WEU 'family' deployed in time to provide policing advice in advance of the 29 June election. Drawing on its experience gained in Mostar, the WEU's MAPE was to expand in personnel and duration, providing advice on the restructuring and democratization of the police service to the Albanian Ministry of Public Order, including the development of a new State Police Law and the training of around 3,000 police officers in training centres in Tirana and Durres.[379] Clearly, WEU aspirations were not confined to police operations, and experiences in Mostar and MAPE might not 'hold good' for potentially more challenging Petersberg-style operations; nevertheless, it was evident that these experiences were not without 'developmental value'.[380] The first operation to be run from the WEU headquarters, with the Director of the Planning Cell as the point of contact for the operation, MAPE was also to become the first operation conducted at the full WEU complement of 28 states, offering a valuable opportunity for operational participation on an equal footing for all of the extended 'membership' and in close co-operation with a range of international organizations and bilateral initiatives.[381]

Although this low-level action was to prove a success for the WEU, experience had demonstrated that developing consensus on crisis-management operations required a level of common interest between member states that was at best unlikely. In recognition of the limitations of crisis-management mechanisms that required complete consensus, or collective assets, the possibilities of less restrictive decision-making processes and operational facilities that might enhance the ability of interested parties to take the lead in collective actions were explored in the context of the evolving institutions. Europe's failures to prevent and react effectively to crises were not so much the fault of the institutions but of the member states, unable to respond in a 'common and coherent' manner as crises unravelled.[382] The experiences of the French-led Operation Turquoise in Rwanda and the Italian-led Operation Alba in Albania had provided operational lessons with regard to 'lead nation' provisions for consensus-light activity. Approved by the WEU Council in their 13 May 1997 Paris Declaration, the French proposal for a WEU 'framework nation' approach was first identified as a means of managing difficulties of political consensus, operational coherence and rapid reaction for 'autonomous' WEU operations.[383] Under this approach a 'lead nation' could provide the infrastructure and key components of a European operational headquarters, including command arrangements and support activities such as logistics, drawing on existing national or multinational assets and under the political direction of the WEU Council. This concept was to be adopted subsequently by the EU for operations without recourse to NATO assets, with Africa providing the venue for the first 'framework nation' operation as the French led the first autonomous EU operation, Artemis, in the Democratic Republic of the Congo in July–September 2003.[384]

THE AMSTERDAM OUTCOME

With the agreements articulated in its Berlin Communiqué, NATO had stolen a march on the EU. Welcoming the development of an ESDI, NATO had diluted its possible development within the Union by declaring its rightful place to be within the Alliance. Moreover, member-state approval of NATO's CJTF provisions marked recognition of the reality of European weakness and continued dependence. The CFSP had not lived up to the expectations of its supporters, and this particularly in the area of security and defence. The relationship between the WEU and the EU's CFSP had not developed as many had hoped, given the Maastricht intention of placing the WEU as an 'integral part' of Union development. In the period following the signing of the Maastricht Treaty, only one Article J.4.2 WEU/CFSP activity had occurred: the EU's request of 27 June 1996 that the WEU prepare generic contingency plans for a possible evacuation operation.[385] There had been little WEU attendance at EU General Affairs Council meetings, and the linkage between WEU- and CFSP-related staffs within the Council Secretariat and Commission had been largely 'disappointing'.[386] Whilst liaison had been poor between the EU and WEU in practice, the NATO-WEU relationship had strengthened significantly, reflecting, as Bretherton and Volger have suggested, a 'greater affinity between the organizational cultures, and indeed the personnel, of the two organizations', supported by a security agreement that enabled NATO-WEU information-sharing not entrusted to their 'civilian' institutional partner.[387] If the WEU was to continue as the intended 'defence component' of the EU, both the nature of that relationship and the processes to facilitate it would require clarification.

In the run-up to the Amsterdam Summit, the issue of the WEU's place in the CFSP arrangement remained particularly contentious. The majority of EU member states sought the full integration of the WEU into the EU, proposals for a staged merger of the WEU with the EU being submitted to the Dutch Presidency of the EU by six of the WEU's full members.[388] Beginning with a White Paper agreement on common defence policy, and followed by the merger of the Secretariats and provision for the WEU to be bound by European Council decisions, these proposals foresaw WEU absorption completed with the final stage of Council and Assembly responsibilities being transferred to the EU institutions. Common defence could be provided through incorporation into the CFSP, but with opt-out, or through an opt-in protocol attached to the treaty, whilst the committal of forces would remain a national decision.

The British continued to insist on the WEU's autonomy for essentially 'Atlanticist' reasons. The change of government following the UK general election of May 1997 had resulted in little alteration to this position; Tony Blair's Labour Administration was defence 'sensitive' given the 'wilderness years' his Party had experienced under the leadership of the 'unilateralists', Michael Foot and Neil Kinnock.[389] Seeking time to 'bed in' and in light of a promised Strategic Defence Review, the new British Government questioned the ability of the Europeans to reach the consensus on defence interests that had been so evidently lacking in foreign policy to date. The autonomy of the WEU continued to facilitate defence-minded European states working in close co-operation with the EU without being constrained by an ever increasing 'neutralist' membership. This was significant not least in ensuring the continuance of a credible mutual defence agreement, as the merger of the WEU into the EU would call into question the continuing NATO commitment to underwrite the WEU's Article V guarantee.[390]

Favouring the weakest of the Madrid options, the British found 'merger' unacceptable, whilst WEU 'subordination', suggested by French proposals that the European Council might 'instruct' the WEU to act for it, were equally rejected. At the WEU's meeting of Foreign and Defence Ministers in Paris on 13 May 1997, the new Foreign Secretary, Robin Cook, signalled what was described as 'a small but atmospherically significant move . . . towards accepting a limited role for the European Union in defence matters'.[391] The UK Government, Cook announced, would be prepared, whilst retaining WEU autonomy, to consider ways of 'reinforcing' WEU-EU links and would acquiesce to the inclusion of the Petersberg Tasks into the provisions of the new post-Amsterdam EU Treaty. This was a level of reinforcement potentially acceptable to the 'neutrals' as well, who were keen to retain the 'civilian' status of the EU but, having been active supporters of Petersberg-type activity in Mostar and Albania as WEU observers, recognized humanitarian and peacekeeping tasks as compatible with neutrality.[392] The merger of an increasingly operational WEU, along with its 'defence' commitments, into the EU would, however, suggest a potential 'militarization' of EU policy and require a significant and highly problematic reconsideration of 'neutrality', which was at best premature.[393]

As a further contribution to the discussions taking place within the IGC, and in light of the up-coming NATO Summit on adaptation and enlargement to take place in Madrid in July, the WEU's Council of Ministers met in Paris the month before the Amsterdam Summit, to set down the WEU's 'pivotal role . . . in accordance with the agreements reached at Maastricht which are [sic] being reviewed in the IGC and the decisions taken in Berlin'. The resulting declaration identified how the WEU had sought to carry out this connecting role of enabling 'Europeans to shoulder their responsibilities in the field of security and defence in Europe and beyond whilst reinforcing the transatlantic link' by its contributions, not least in the area of operational development, acknowledging how the WEU had become increasingly operationally capable in the field of crisis management, able to draw on national, multinational and NATO assets and capabilities. Constituting a 'genuine framework for dialogue and cooperation among Europeans on wider European security and defence issues', the WEU had, through its practical contribution to the promotion of the ESDI concept within the Alliance, sought to enable Europeans to make a 'more coherent and effective contribution to missions and activities of the Alliance', whilst remaining committed to 'build up WEU in stages as the defence component of the Union'. The Council stated clearly its members' willingness to contribute fully to the 'finalisation of the security and defence aspects of the IGC'. However, its articulation of the areas of progress being made in the practical development of inter-institutional co-ordination and operational competency through WEU auspices suggested that WEU 'dissolution through merger' would be at best premature and potentially counter-productive from both Atlanticist and Europeanist perspectives.[394]

The agreements reached at the Amsterdam Summit of 16–17 June 1997 were presented in the Treaty of Amsterdam (TOA), amending the TEU and the treaties establishing the European Communities, the key defence provisions of which were to be incorporated into the new consolidated version of the Treaty on European Union.[395] At Amsterdam, a level of enhanced integration in the highly contentious area of CFSP development was enabled, by reaching a form of words generally acceptable to all, although the CFSP provisions reflected once again an uneasy compromise between European states on the future of a common defence policy for the EU.[396] The CFSP provisions were laid down within Title V of the consolidated TEU. In Article 17.1 (TOA J.7.1) the scope of the EU's CFSP remained largely unchanged, including 'all questions relating to the security of the Union', although Article 17.2 (TOA J.7.2) explicitly included the WEU-defined Petersberg Tasks as part of the remit of the EU, constituting a significant integration of an element of the WEU 'acquis' into the EU framework.[397] Two further opportunities for significant development in security and defence were opened up under Article 17.1. Firstly, the EU committed to the 'progressive', rather than 'eventual', framing of a common defence policy, which 'might lead to a common defence', suggesting a practical ongoing development of common policy towards defence, if not a common defence or necessarily the capability to support it. The WEU's commitment, expressed in its Declaration attached to the Maastricht Treaty, that it would 'formulate a common European defence policy and carry forward its concrete implementation' had raised concerns that this might lead to the framing of potentially distinct WEU and EU policies for defence; this ambiguity was removed with the Amsterdam statement that the WEU 'supports the Union in framing the defence aspects of the Common Foreign and Security Policy as set out in this Article', the concluding reference suggesting that the substance of this policy was to be confined to the Petersberg Tasks identified therein.[398]

The Amsterdam Treaty retained the institutional separation of the EU and WEU, just as it recognized that the Union would 'respect the obligations of certain Member States, which see their common defence realized in NATO . . . and be compatible with the common security and defence policy established within that framework'. However, a second significant opportunity for development was offered by the commitment to foster 'closer institutional relations with the WEU with a view to the possibility of the integration of the WEU into the Union'; both the development of a common defence and the merger of the WEU with the EU would require only that 'the European Council so decide', and that their recommendation be adopted by member states, 'in accordance with their respective constitutional requirements'.[399] The WEU was to remain an 'integral part of the development of the Union, providing the Union with access to an operational capability' to carry out the Petersberg Tasks, now incorporated into the Union and at the core of the developing CFSP. The new wording of Article 17.3 (TOA J.7.3) allowed that the EU might 'avail itself' of the WEU, rather than make 'requests' (as in the original TEU J.4.2) that it 'elaborate and implement policy', a subtle enhancement of EU authority over the WEU; in such cases relating to the Petersberg Tasks, all EU members should be able to 'participate fully on an equal footing in planning and decision-taking in the WEU', to be facilitated by EU and WEU Council agreement on the necessary practical arrangements.

The decisions taken at Amsterdam also reflected recognition of the limitations of the CFSP decision-making processes, evidenced by the EU's lack of effective response to the crises in Rwanda and Albania. Rejecting the British concept of a separate Heads of State forum for CFSP matters, a new strategic role for the EU Council was established in the determination of Common Strategies, which were to set out the objectives, durations and means to be made available for CFSP actions, adding direction to EU planning.[400] These strategies would then be implemented by the Council. To enhance Council decision-making on CFSP matters, QMV was to be introduced 'when adopting joint actions, common positions or taking any other decision on the basis of a common strategy [or] when adopting any decision implementing a joint action or a common position'. However, the general principle of unanimity in the Council's CFSP decision-making remained, with provision for national vetos of the application of a qualified vote and with the clear exemption of decisions having military or defence implications.[401] In a further effort to overcome the problems of limited consensus, and specifically in these military- and defence-related areas where the EU had been hamstrung in even approaching the WEU as its 'operational arm', a system of qualified (constructive) abstention was introduced to allow for a degree of flexibility, whereby EU joint actions with military or defence implications could not be impeded by abstentions unless they represented more than one-third of the weighted vote; this enabled the adoption of decisions on Petersberg operations even where, for example, the five non-WEU states chose to abstain.[402] Although intended to remove an impediment to decision-making by the EU in 'tasking' the WEU under its joint actions, the Amsterdam provisions did not imply any diminution of the WEU Council's right of determination, in regard to either self-initiated actions or those passed to it by the European Council.[403]

In seeking to enhance the profile and coherency of the EU's CFSP, the rotational six-month EU Presidency, which held responsibility for the implementation of CFSP common measures under the authority of the Council, was to be assisted by a High Representative for CFSP, a post allocated to the Secretary General of the Council, responsible for the 'formulation, preparation and implementation of policy decisions, and, when appropriate acting on behalf of the Council at the request of the Presidency, through conducting political dialogue with third parties'.[404] A Policy Planning and Early Warning Unit (PPEWU) was also envisaged in the Council's General Secretariat to work alongside the small CFSP unit in monitoring international developments and determining areas of the world of foreign and security policy relevance for CFSP focus, including analysis, recommendations and strategies for the CFSP to contribute to the Council's policy formulation. In an effort to overcome the poor liaison between the WEU and EU, personnel would be drawn from the General Secretariat, member states, the Commission and the WEU.[405]

The response of the WEU to the Amsterdam Treaty was articulated in its 'Declaration on the Role of Western European Union and its Relations with the European Union and with the Atlantic Alliance', adopted by the WEU Council on 22 July. To be appended to the TOA, the Declaration incorporated the relevant Amsterdam provisions, acknowledging the WEU's agreement on the treaty's prescribed development of the EU-WEU relationship.[406] Recognizing the desire to enhance its role as an 'integral part of the development of the Union providing the Union with access to an operational capability', notably in the context of Petersberg Tasks, the WEU set out the range of measures 'already in hand in WEU'. These included the harmonization of Presidencies and the close co-ordination of the work of the staff of the Secretariat General of the WEU and General Secretariat of the Council of the EU, whilst the WEU Council also noted arrangements to allow relevant EU bodies, to include the PPEWU, to draw on the resources of the WEU Planning Cell, Situation Centre and Satellite Centre. All of these efforts were intended to enhance co-operation between the two organizations, and particularly the co-ordination of consultation and decision-making processes in crisis situations.[407]

Just as the WEU Declaration reproduced the tone and prescription of the relevant TOA provisions for the enhancement of its relations with the EU and its CFSP, it also reflected that of NATO's Madrid Declaration of 8 July. The NATO Declaration had re-affirmed the positions adopted at Berlin, giving NATO's 'full support for the development of the European Security and Defence Identity by making available NATO assets and capabilities for WEU operations'.[408] It went on to prescribe reinforcement of the NATO-WEU relationship as the articulation of the evolving ESDI within the Alliance; given the rejection at Amsterdam of a merger between the EU and WEU, 'or even [of] an integration process over the medium term', this was largely welcomed by Atlanticists and Europeanists alike. The provision of NATO assets and capabilities in support of WEU operations would resolve the WEU's immediate 'dilemma' of how to provide a concrete expression of that European identity in defence.[409] The CJTF concept would enable Europeans to contribute to the range of Petersberg Tasks on the basis of 'sound military principles and supported by appropriate military planning' and with 'militarily coherent and effective forces capable of operating under the political control and strategic direction of the WEU'.[410] The WEU Declaration re-emphasized the institution's role as an 'essential element of the development of the ESDI within the Atlantic Alliance', which remained the 'basis of collective defence . . . and the essential forum for consultation among Allies and the framework in which they agree on policies bearing on their security and defence commitments under the Washington Treaty'. To this end, the WEU identified the need, and prescribed the appropriate actions, to 'strengthen institutional and practical cooperation with NATO' in parallel with its developing relationship with the EU.[411]

In the concluding section of the Declaration, a new identity was articulated for the WEU, with the organization being described as the 'European politico-military body for crisis-management'.[412] To that end, the WEU would be operationally progressed through the development of its crisis-management capability, 'updated as WEU gains [sic] experience through exercises and operations'. This, in turn, would contribute to the formulation of objectives, scope and means for a Common European Defence Policy by facilitating the definition of principles for the use of the WEU states' armed forces for Petersberg Tasks, the organization of operational means and the enhancement of capability (particularly in the areas of strategic mobility and intelligence provision) for WEU operations.[413] In line with its commitment to closer co-ordination with the EU and NATO, the WEU aimed to open up maximum participation in all of its operations to associate members and observer states, including increasing access to the activities of its Planning Cell, Situation Centre, Satellite Centre and its newly provisioned Military Committee.[414] Through the development of its operational role, and the fostering of closer relations with both NATO and the EU, the WEU would facilitate an evolution of Europe's security and defence architecture, where 'political ideal' was to be inevitably tempered by the practicalities of both capability limitation and the immaturity of the European collective impulse.

REFLECTIONS

In the post-Cold War era the role of the primary institutions and their influence on the European security agenda had been fundamentally questioned. The combination of external and internal challenges resulted in a significant shift in the nature of both Alliance and Community in the European context. The dissolution of the Soviet bloc had removed much of NATO's original raison d'être, whilst concerns regarding the rising power of a unified Germany were to enhance European states' interest in seeking closer integration, not least as a means of ensuring that German power might be harnessed for the European good. As NATO sought to establish a more political role based on a broader concept of security interests, the EC moved towards a closer economic union, with a defence competency to support its 'soft' security role. The part the WEU was to play in the process was increasingly identified as a significant one by the constituents of both of the primary organizations. Throughout the period under examination in this chapter, from the end of the Cold War in 1989 to the institutional consolidation signified by the Amsterdam and Madrid Summits of 1997, the WEU sought to fulfil its 'support' role for both the evolving EU and the Atlantic Alliance.

The duality of the WEU had been evident since its foundation but had become increasingly identified following the Maastricht Treaty, which had established the WEU as the 'defence component' of the Union alongside its commitment to contribute to the 'solidarity' of the Alliance. Duke had suggested that this might lead to 'acute institutional schizophrenia in the WEU, or worse, the collapse of the WEU as it is [sic] torn between conflicting loyalties'.[415] In fact, once again, this duality was to be the WEU's key institutional attribute. As a conduit between the EU and NATO, the WEU facilitated an acceptable juxtaposition between the two organizations, whilst providing for adaptation in both. Through the development of its operational and institutional capability and the extension of its membership, the WEU was to contribute to a process of institutional transition by accommodating a range of diverse interests with regard to the nature and scope of development of each of the primary organizations and the relationship of one to the other. Significantly, the WEU was able to demonstrate throughout this period that European security and defence co-operation in the EU context was 'perfectly compatible' with commitments to transatlantic defence.[416] The interplay between alliance and integrative interests had led to national resistance to developments in one arena that might impact negatively on the other. However, the incremental development of the WEU as an external organization, supportive of both processes, served to dissipate these tensions by providing a testing ground for developments, far enough removed from the primary organizations to mitigate the negative effects of potential failure.

The major areas of tension within the primary organizations of security and defence during the period were a consequence of differing national perspectives on the preferred scope of integration, on the US leadership role in an adapting Atlantic Alliance and on the relationship between the emerging EU and NATO. As Europe began to address the issues of developing a defence identity, the integration debate moved into the realms of high politics and became increasingly and inextricably connected to the debate regarding the future of NATO and the transatlantic link. Consequently, the tensions that emerged throughout the post-Cold War period were a complex response to these interconnecting interests.

Within the EC, the requirement for some greater level of foreign policy coordination in order to effectively navigate a European path in an uncertain post-Cold War environment was recognized by all members. However, for many, defence was an integrative step too far. The decisions taken at Maastricht reflected the uneasy compromise between those who sought a defence competence for the evolving Union and those who wished to keep Europe a civilian power. The French sought an intergovernmental defence competency for the Union as a means of harnessing German strength in support of Europe, enhancing European power not least in relation to the remaining superpower. A reunited Germany sought security integration in Europe in line with its policy of promoting German development within the 'reassuring' context of European integration, whilst contributing to the rebalancing of the Atlantic Alliance through which West German defence interests had been traditionally secured. For the British, persistent Atlanticism led to resistance against any European pretensions that might lead to an undermining of NATO, seen as the mainstay of European defence, whilst any defence arrangement within the Community context would compromise Irish neutrality and restrict the potential for enlargement of the 'soft security' zone provided by the Union.

The Maastricht agreement, in establishing the WEU as an autonomous defence arm of the EU, was to provide a means of overcoming the seemingly intractable problem of meeting these divergent interests. In separating the defence element from the Union, the difficult issue of the neutrals was overcome and consequently the door left open for the enlargement of the EU to include Austria, Sweden and Finland. The interests of the French in promoting closer defence ties with Germany were provided for in an intergovernmental organization that was to be an 'integral' part of the Union. Germany was able to demonstrate its interest in promoting closer European integration without undermining its relationship with NATO, and the UK had ensured that European defence co-operation, whilst contributing to the broader Alliance, would be developed pragmatically amongst the key European players.

At Maastricht, the EU had committed itself to the 'eventual framing of a common defence policy, which might in time lead to a common defence',[417] although the failure of the EU member states to agree on an effective programme of development for a common defence policy was in part a consequence of the lack of clarity about its meaning. In its Declaration attached to the Maastricht Treaty, the WEU had committed itself to formulate this policy and to 'carry forward its concrete implementation through the further development of its own operational role'. Consequently, efforts to define the nature of this policy took place within the WEU: its 'Preliminary Conclusions', presented at Noordwijk in November 1994, and later its 'Common Reflection' of all 27 European states within the broad WEU 'family' of May 1995, offered input into the discussion about the objective, scope and means of any future European defence policy.[418] That the WEU's 'Contribution' to the 1996 IGC constituted a range of options, rather than the comprehensive European defence policy statement envisaged in Noordwijk, reflected the lack of consensus on the next step for the development of this policy area.[419] However, as a forum for and expression of the developing debate, not least through the work of its Assembly and Institute, the WEU offered insight into areas of emerging consensus. The identification of the Petersberg Tasks as areas 'short of defence' in which to promote effective European co-operation, and the WEU's operational experiences in carrying them out, suggested a working model for scoping EU defence policy.[420] Proving an acceptable division of labour for the neutral states, the scope of the EU's common defence policy was effectively bounded by explicit reference to the Petersberg Tasks in the TOA provisions, areas for co-operation tested in the WEU and subsequently adopted into the acquis of the Union.

The EU's commitments to a CFSP, including provisions for the development of a common defence policy and potentially a common defence, brought it into close proximity with the Alliance as the key provider of that defence for the majority of the EU's member states. The WEU was to enable the linkage between these two constituencies, through the opening up of associate memberships and observer status, facilitating dialogue and co-operation on defence issues in an environment inclusive of the interests of European members of both the EU and NATO. At the same time, as the interests of post-Soviet Europe opened up the possibilities for a new 'inclusive' European security order, the role of institutions in the engagement of emerging 'independent' states had presented new challenges of 'outreach' and enlargement. The WEU supported the management of these processes within the primary organizations, through the extension of its differentiated membership structure, with associate partner status facilitating CEE engagement with European security and defence outreach in line with that taking place within the EU and Alliance. In this way, the WEU helped to prepare the emerging democracies for membership in the primary organizations, offering practical co-operation in the form of participation in exercises and low-level operations as well as the political dialogue that was to connect them to the 'cultural zone' of democratic Europe.[421] Whilst divergent national interests had led to competing views on the pace and scope of institutional enlargements, the WEU provided a proving ground for the gradual integration of CEE states in a manner acceptable to Russia and complementary to both alliance and integrative interests. This may indeed have been, as one commentator suggests, one of the WEU's most important achievements.[422]

In operational terms, WEU activity in the Gulf and Yugoslavia had demonstrated both the potential for and the limitations of European defence co-operation. In 1991 the WEU-co-ordinated action in the Gulf had enabled a European deployment in line with international community objectives as articulated through the UN. More pointedly, the WEU had facilitated a visible European action in support of US interests and activity in the region and, in doing so, had evidenced the practical benefits of a European dimension for collective military action outside the NATO operating area. The early action of the WEU in the Adriatic, in July 1992, had, however, caught

NATO somewhat on the back foot. Subsequent NATO action may be seen partially as a response to US concerns regarding European assertiveness, although it was to lead to practical NATO-WEU co-ordination in an area of common interest in the joint Operation Sharp Guard. The failure of the EU's embryonic CFSP to meet its promise during the Yugoslav crisis eventually led an uneasy Washington to sanction NATO action in an unprecedented 'out-of-area' intervention role, sanctioned by the UN, which offered an institutional 'lifebuoy' to an increasingly directionless Atlantic Alliance. In this context, Washington came to recognize the benefits that a more effective European defence identity might offer, both as a direct contribution to a more operationally active Alliance, and as a potentially independent crisis-management 'actor', although preferably under some level of US influence. As an 'integral' part of the developing EU, the WEU had proven its practical utility in a range of small-scale operations, falling within the delineated area of the Petersberg Tasks, providing the political 'cover' for enhanced European engagement that was potentially problematic within NATO. If an emerging ESDI could be promoted through the WEU and 'captured' within the broader Alliance context, an operationally capable WEU could satisfy US requirements for commitment-rebalancing within the Alliance, enabling Europeans to take on crisis-management roles with the option of US abstention from operations outside of pressing national interests.[423] US acceptance, in principle, of the development of an ESDI within the Alliance at the 1994 Brussels Summit encouraged the British to seek further practical European defence co-operation as a means of enhancing NATO. At the same time, as the political and capability limitations on defence activity were demonstrated by the lack of EU 'tasking' of WEU operations and the scale of WEU engagements, the French, as the most ardent supporters of a 'European' defence, came to accept the requirements of US leadership, at least in the medium term; these factors contributed to a greater pragmatism in French attitudes both to the future development of a Common European Security and Defence Policy and to the French relationship to NATO. Consequently, the French and British positions began to converge on the WEU.

The CJTF concept, although 'condemning' Europe to a level of continued dependency, was a practical solution to the problem of limited European capabilities. The WEU's part in developing this concept in co-operation with the Alliance was to enhance the potential for a European crisis-management capability without undermining the coherence of the Alliance based on continuing US leadership. As Gordon argues, to an extent the Europeanization of NATO, suggested by the ESDI and accompanying CJTF concepts, was little more than a comfortable 'illusion', resulting from the vested and various interests of the key players in making it appear so: Paris required a cover for Alliance rapprochement given Europe's lack of ambition; Berlin a European 'success' to support domestic approval of Monetary Union; the British a 'cap' to any further European pretensions.[424] Nevertheless, in support of its position as the acceptable face of an ESDI within the Alliance, and a potential beneficiary of the provision of NATO capabilities under the CJTF concept, the WEU would be able to 'tap in' to NATO planning, command, intelligence and military assets in support of European operations in the absence of European alternatives, whilst its NATO-friendly profile enabled it to facilitate the development of the mechanisms and habits of European defence co-operation, a required precursor to further European initiatives.[425] At the same time, the promotion of co-operative mechanisms between the WEU and NATO had contributed to a 'culture of co-operation' between the two organizations and their national representatives at both military and civilian levels that was to prepare the ground for the future relationship between the EU and NATO.

The development of WEU allocated forces, as national and multinational FAWEU, had also served the dual functions of enhancing the Alliance and promoting European co-operation. Firstly, it provided demonstrable European commitment to take on more of the cost of defence, easing Alliance tensions over burden-sharing and bringing France closer to the NATO structure. These forces also served to demonstrate a substantive European identity and capability in security matters, enabling the WEU to act, if only in a limited sense, independently of NATO. And the WEU had proven itself capable of conducting non-military operations, including those potentially more relevant to the security challenges facing the new Europe. WEU activity in Mostar and Albania provided a proving ground for new European structures for the complex activity of crisis management. The development of the WEU's Planning Cell, Situation Centre, Intelligence Section and Satellite Centre, with the provision for a Military Committee in support of Council deliberations, all contributed to an enhanced capability for the WEU to plan, conduct, monitor and support European missions. These practical arrangements met with US interests, despite the WEU's limited actions. As the US Ambassador to NATO, Robert Hunter, was to note, 'we do not, as Americans, see the test of the WEU's effectiveness as being whether or to what extent it actually engages in military operations. The test is rather the activity of creating the ESDI, the willingness to use it, and the preparations to undertake those matters which could come before it—preparations which, in themselves, could prove to be the WEU's most important contribution to European security'.[426]

By the mid 1990s, any expectation of a temporary WEU dependence on NATO infrastructure and capabilities in its role as the defence arm of the Union and European pillar of NATO had been replaced by a sense of permanence. Realism required that the ESDI be built within the Alliance. European limitations were evident not only in capability terms, where pressure on defence budgets and the requirements for post-Cold War military restructuring contributed to capability shortfalls.[427] The failure of political will to engage in any significant military action without the Americans was evident not only in the former Yugoslavia but also in the 'failed opportunities' in Rwanda and Albania, operations potentially within the capability of European states and model Petersberg Tasks. As satisfaction with the EU's foreign and security performance declined and ambitions became muted at a European level, careful development of any European competence in defence would be required, to avoid the risk of undermining US commitment to NATO when no alternative was in sight. However, if Europe did not yet have the answers, the WEU might provide a vehicle for adaptation whilst it searched for them.

In fact, the WEU was to fill a gap not only in European but also in NATO development. Fears that a distinct military organization might accelerate the dissolution of NATO proved unrealistic, as the WEU remained closely enough linked, slowly enough developed and non-competitive enough in function to contribute rather than detract from Allied interests. Once again, the WEU could help to satisfy two apparently contradictory requirements of US policy: on the one hand, it offered a more coherent and militarily competent contribution to common security and defence interests, necessary not least in terms of continued Congressional support for US defence engagement with Europe. On the other hand, the WEU ensured American primacy within the transatlantic defence relationship through facilitation of the development of the ESDI within a US-led NATO. As the 'main institutional embodiment' of a European 'hedging strategy',[428] WEU operational development would also provide a degree of insurance against any loss of US commitment, possible even if NATO were to persist. Paradoxically, efforts to enhance EU security and defence co-operation might well undermine US commitment to Europe, even if intended as a means of complementing the Alliance, by disincentivizing the Atlantic option. The WEU, historically embedded within the Atlantic structures, mitigated some of this 'moral hazard' that might accrue from too apparent a divide with the US,[429] enabling European capability and role enhancement without further contributing to transatlantic drift.

If the 'tug of war' over the WEU's proximity to NATO and the EU, as suggested by debates within the pre-Maastricht IGC and revisited throughout the 1990s, was evidence of a 'fight for dominance' between those two organizations,[430] the WEU's positioning by 1997 suggested that NATO had far greater 'pull' than the inexperienced, disorganized and undetermined EU 'team'. That both organizations identified the WEU as a useful instrument, however, was increasingly evident throughout the post-Cold War transition years;[431] it was not the preferred option for defence co-operation but a 'satiating' mechanism able to move forward the process of change in the security and defence structures of Europe at a pace acceptable to all, if not optimal. As a hybrid organization promoting both alliance and integration activity, the WEU could be identified as Atlanticist or Europeanist in nature, and this ambiguity had again enabled compromise as national interests converged at the level of functional change. The incremental, pragmatic developments that took place within the WEU on the basis of this convergence of interests had enabled the acceptance of piecemeal transition for both the Alliance and the EU, preventing their stagnation or regression as each sought to adapt to meet new international realities. As a 'necessary aspiration, a linchpin of the

CFSP', the WEU represented the furthest point of European consensus on a common defence policy for the Union:[432] for NATO it provided for the not entirely comfortable but accepted necessity of Alliance reform in the light of changing power relations in a new Europe. Without the 'sentimental' attachment of the primary organizations, the WEU nevertheless fulfilled its traditional task as a 'support' or 'intermediary',[433] its hybrid nature, its bridging constituency and its malleability as a symbol of potentially conflicting aspirations placing it at the heart of the European security transformation process.

NOTES

1. The Washington INF Treaty, eliminating all land-based intermediate-range nuclear missiles, had been signed by Reagan and Gorbachev on 8 December 1987, talks on CFE and Confidence and Security Building Measures (CSBMs) were opened in March 1989, and the Strategic Arms Reduction talks reopened in Geneva the following June.

2. Poland attained its first non-communist-led government for 40 years in August 1989, and on 23 October the newly democratic Republic of Hungary was formed. As a steady stream of East German refugees sought to leave the Democratic Republic for the West via Budapest and Prague, political protests demanding reform led to the resignation of the East German Cabinet in November and the opening of East German borders with the West as Berliners exploited the uncertain political environment to tear down the Berlin Wall. Political protest against communist rule spread across Central and Eastern Europe, resulting in the fall of communist regimes and the institution of democratic governments in Czechoslovakia, Bulgaria and Romania over the following months.

3. Vanhoonacker suggests that this was the 'main purpose' of the declaration. S. Vanhoonacker, *The Bush Administration (1989–1993) and the Development of a European Security Identity*, Aldershot: Ashgate, 2001, p. 118.

4. J. Delors, 'European unification and European security' in 'European security after the Cold War: part II papers from the IISS annual conference', *Adelphi Paper*, no. 284, January 1994, p. 11.

5. See R. Zandra, 'Towards a European identity', in N. Gantz and J. Roper, *Towards a New Partnership: US—European Relations in the Post-Cold War Era*, Paris: WEU Institute for Security Studies (WEU ISS), 1993, pp. 70–1.

6. J. Delors, 'European integration and security', *Survival*, vol. 33, no. 2, March–April 1991, p. 107.

7. 'Kohl-Mitterrand letter to the Irish Presidency, 19 April 1990', *Agence Europe*, 20 April 1990.

8. For the text of his Berlin speech see D. Hurd, 'Europe's defence and security in the 1990s', *Arms Control and Disarmament Quarterly Review*, no. 19, January 1991, pp. 18–26.

9. D. Keohane, 'The approach of British political parties to a defence role for the European Community', *Government and Opposition*, vol. 27, no. 3, July 1992, p. 301. This view was generally shared across the spectrum of the British political system, with Labour Opposition Leader Neil Kinnock commenting, 'I do not accept a defence identity for the European Community. The best assurances for European security lie in our existing relations with the countries of North America'. J. Palmer, 'Kinnock blocks EC socialists' plan',

The Guardian, 5 December 1991, p. 8. Also see N. Kinnock, 'International security in a changing world: the Labour Party perspective', *RUSI Journal,* vol. 136, no. 2, summer 1991, pp. 1–5.

10. M. Thatcher, *The Downing Street Years,* London: HarperCollins, 1993, p. 814.
11. See D. Keohane, 'Britain's security policy and NATO in the 1990s', *Arms Control,* vol. 12, no. 1, May 1991, p. 75.
12. Foreign Minister Roland Dumas, commenting on the French decision to join the Alliance's Strategic Review Group in March 1991, stated that this 'changes nothing in France's relationship' to NATO and that there was 'no question of returning either surreptitiously or more openly' to the integrated military command structure. Cited in D. S. Yost, 'France and West European defence identity', *Survival,* vol. 33, no. 4, July 1991, p. 331.
13. Yost, 'France and West European defence identity', p. 335; A. Menon, A. Forster and W. Wallace, 'A common European defence', *Survival,* vol. 34, no. 3, autumn 1992, p. 104.
14. Economic integration had 'virtually turned Western Europe into a Deutsch-mark zone, prompting the French and Italian governments to demand an economic and monetary union (EMU), which would give them some say in German monetary policy'. E. Mortimer, 'European security after the Cold War', *Adelphi Paper,* no. 271, summer 1992, p. 53.
15. J. B. Steinberg, 'The case for a new partnership', in Gantz and Roper, *Towards a New Partnership,* pp. 111–12. Also see P. Lellouche, 'France in search of security', *Foreign Affairs,* vol. 72, no. 2, spring 1993, p. 128.
16. S. Gregory, *French Defence Policy into the Twenty-First Century,* Basingstoke: Macmillan, 2000, p. 105.
17. This is reflected in Bluth's assessment in 1992 that 'the kind of leadership that Germany now needs to exercise in Europe is politically acceptable only in the context of European integration'. C. Bluth, 'Germany: towards a new security format', *The World Today,* vol. 48, no. 11, November 1992, p. 198. The former West German Chancellor Helmut Schmidt was to comment that it was 'good that our political leaders—aware of the rising discomfort of our neighbours—work for a transformation of the European Community into a political union and a currency union and thus firmly unite Germany with the other nations of Europe', cited in K. Caitlin, 'The new Europe', *World Press Review,* vol. 39, no. 2, February 1992, p. 32.
18. Mortimer, 'European security after the Cold War', p. 9.
19. Risse highlights the negotiating 'process of communication, argumentation, and persuasion rather than traditional power-based bargaining', whereby Soviet interests were also to be accommodated in US efforts to construct the post-Cold War security order. J. Risse, 'The Cold War's endgame and German unification', *International Security,* vol. 21, no. 4, spring 1997, p. 159. Also see his reviewed texts, F. Elbe and R. Kiessler, *A Round Table with Sharp Corners: The Diplomatic Path to German Unity,* Baden-Baden: Nomos, 1996; P. Zelikow and C. Rice, *Germany Unified and Europe Transformed: A Study in Statecraft,* Cambridge, MA: Harvard University Press, 1995.
20. Germany's renewal of its renunciation of nuclear weapons in the WEU and of non-proliferation treaties within the context of the 'two-plus-four' agreement meant it would continue to require the nuclear guarantee the US offered in this area. See R. Rummel, 'Integration, disintegration, and security in Europe: preparing the Community for a multi-institutional response', *International Journal,* vol. 47, no. 1, winter 1991–2, pp. 69–70.
21. For US influence on the unification process see R. D. Blackwill, 'German uni-fication and American diplomacy', *Aussenpolitik,* vol. 45, no. 3, 1994, pp. 211–25.

22. Brenner suggests that this represented a German statement to the effect of 'temptation, get thee behind me'. M. J. Brenner, 'EC: confidence lost', *Foreign Policy,* no. 91, summer 1993, p. 35.

23. For discussion of German policy, see L. Gutjahr, 'Stability, integration and global responsibility: Germany's changing perspectives on national interests', *Review of International Studies,* vol. 21, no. 3, July 1995, pp. 301–17. For discussion of Franco-German bilateral co-operation see P. Schmidt, 'The Franco-German Defence and Security Council', *Aussenpolitik,* vol. 40, no. 4, 1989, pp. 360–71.

24. See Menon et al., 'A common European defence', p. 105.

25. By 1996 US trade with the growing Asia-Pacific economies was to account for 40% of US trade, being 50% greater than that with Western Europe. See P. H. B. Godwin, 'A new Pacific community: adjusting to the post-Cold War era', in H. J. Wiarda (ed.) *U.S. Foreign and Security Policy in the Post-Cold War Era: A Geopolitical Perspective,* Westport: Greenwood Press, 1996, p. 21.

26. Steinberg, 'The case for a new partnership', p. 7.

27. Vanhoonacker, *The Bush Administration,* p. 115.

28. J. Baker, 'A new Europe, a new Atlanticism, architecture for a new era', *US Policy Information and Texts,* no. 175, 12 December 1989.

29. 'Declaration on US-EC Relations', *Europe Documents,* no. 1622, 23 November 1990. The Transatlantic Dialogue initiated by the declaration included biannual meetings of the Presidents of the US, EC and European Council, although these were to prove fairly ineffective given long-standing disagreements, most notably over trade issues. See W. C. Thompson, 'European-American co-operation through NATO and the European Union', in D. Mahncke, W. Rees and W. C. Thompson (eds) *Redefining Transatlantic Security Relations: The Challenge of Change,* Manchester: Manchester University Press, 2004, p. 116; H. G. Krenzler and W. Kaiser, 'The Transatlantic Declaration: a new basis for relations between the EC and the USA', *Aussenpolitik,* vol. 42, no. 4, 1991, pp. 363–72.

30. Communiqué of the NAC, Brussels, 18 December 1990, para. 5

31. Rummel, 'Integration, disintegration, and security in Europe', p. 84.

32. M. Jopp, R. Rummel and P. Schmidt, 'Integration and security in a new Europe: inside and beyond a West European pillar', in M. Jopp, R. Rummel and P. Schmidt (eds) *Integration and Security in Western Europe—Inside the European Pillar,* Boulder: Westview Press, 1991, p. 289.

33. The causes of the 1990–1 Gulf War are widely debated in the literature; those identified include Saddam's paranoid psychology, Iraq's territorial claims, the military 'distraction' of Saddam's post-Iran-Iraq army and the failure of US diplomacy and deterrence (contrived or otherwise). For discussion see L. Mylorie, 'Why Saddam invaded Kuwait', *Orbis,* vol. 37, no. 1, winter 1993, pp. 123–34; M. Khadduri and E. Ghareeb, *War in the Gulf, 1990–1991: The Iraq-Kuwait Conflict and its Implications,* Oxford: Oxford University Press, 1997; L. Freedman and E. Karsh, *The Gulf Conflict 1990–1991: Diplomacy and War in the New World Order,* London: Faber and Faber, 1994, pp. 19–63; A. Danchev and D. Keohane (eds) *International Perspectives on the Gulf Conflict, 1990–1991,* Basingstoke: Palgrave Macmillan, 1994.

34. For discussion see N. Gnesotto and J. Roper (eds) *Western Europe and the Gulf: A Study of West European Reactions to the Gulf War,* Paris: WEU ISS, 1992.

35. Zandra, 'Towards a European identity', p. 65. Also see Delors, 'European unification and European security', p. 102.

36. S. Duke, *The New European Security Disorder,* Basingstoke: Macmillan, 1994, p. 232.

37. Recommendation 475 in WEU Assembly, rapporteur Mr Pieralli, *European Security and Events in the Near and Middle East,* doc. 1202, 26 October 1989.

38. 'Any national decisions to commit forces should be taken with due regards for the overall political context which is in fact a matter for EPC'. Permanent Council's reply, April 1990, to Assembly Recommendation 475.

39. See A. Jacomet, 'The role of WEU in the Gulf crisis', in Gnesotto and Roper (eds) *Western Europe and the Gulf,* p. 163. M. R. DeVore, 'A convenient framework: the Western European Union in the Persian Gulf, 1987–1988 and 1990–1991', *European Security,* vol. 18, no. 2, June 2009, p. 236, noted that the military was not so enthusiastic about being burdened with 'an independent non-hierarchical military command' coexisting in the same theatre as the US-Saudi-led coalition.

40. Communiqué issued at the completion of the WEU Ministerial Meeting, Paris, 21 August 1990. This agreement reflected the lack of consensus on the desired status of the WEU in the conflict, in relation to both UN authority and the US coalition. See DeVore, 'A convenient framework', p. 237.

41. See W. van Eekelen, 'WEU and the Gulf crisis', *Survival,* vol. 32, no. 6, November–December 1990, p. 526.

42. M. Chichester, 'The Gulf: the Western European Union naval deployment to the Middle East', *Navy International,* vol. 96, no. 2, February 1991, p. 40.

43. These zones were situated in the North and South of the Straits of Hormuz, the Gulf of Oman, the Straits of Bab el Mandeb and the Gulf of Tirana in the Red Sea.

44. E. Grove, 'A European navy: new horizon or false dawn', *Jane's Navy International,* vol. 101, no. 9, November 1996, p. 14.

45. W. van Eekelen, *Debating European Security 1945–1998,* The Hague: SDU Publishers, 1998, p. 53.

46. Belgium, France, Spain, Italy and the Netherlands, with Portugal loaning a logistic support vessel.

47. Chichester, 'The Gulf', p. 41.

48. Van Eekelen, *Debating European Security,* p. 52.

49. Duke, *The New European Security Disorder,* p. 232.

50. S. Duke, *The Elusive Quest for European Security: From EDC to ESDP,* London: Macmillan, 2000, p. 85. See WEU Assembly, rapporteur J. de Hoop Scheffer, *Consequences of the Invasion of Kuwait: Continuing Operations in the Gulf Region,* doc. 1248, 7 November 1990. Also see E. Grove, *Maritime Strategy and European Security,* London: Brasseys, 1990, p. 63.

51. See J. K. Cooley, 'Pre-war Gulf diplomacy', *Survival,* vol. 33, no. 2, March–April 1991, pp. 125–39, for discussion of these diplomatic efforts to avert war.

52. Van Eekelen, *Debating European Security,* p. 53.

53. In fact, NATO facilities were utilized to some extent, particularly in the co-ordination of air and sea lift and the provision of NATO bases for troop and supply transit. See T. D. Young, *Preparing the Western Alliance for the Next Out-of-Area Campaign: Linking NATO and the WEU,* Carlisle, PA: US Army War College, 15 April 1991, for discussion.

54. Freedman notes that the WEU 'distinguished itself in co-ordinating naval forces, but not in a particularly demanding situation', and offered nothing in the way of ground force co-operation. Nevertheless, he suggests that 'it seems to have done enough for it to be seen as the basis of a new European Defence Community (at least in its 'out-of-area' role)'. L. Freedman, 'The Gulf War and the new world order', *Survival,* vol. 33, no. 3, May–June 1991, p. 199.

55. The UK took over the co-ordination of the MCM operation, and the Italians and the French co-ordinated the continuing blockade of the Straits. See Grove, 'A European navy', p. 14.

56. See WEU Assembly, rapporteur J. de Hoop Scheffer, *The Gulf Crisis—Lessons for Western European Union,* doc. 1268, 13 May 1991, p. 16.

57. The WEU Foreign Ministers meeting coinciding with the European Council meeting of 8 April 1991, cited in WEU Assembly, rapporteurs Mr Henares and Mr Tummers, *Western European Union: Information Report*, February 1993, p. 22.

58. For an interesting discussion of the implications of Operation Provide Comfort for future enforcement action see J. Cockayne and D. Malone, 'Creeping unilateralism: how Operation Provide Comfort and the no-fly zones in 1991 and 1992 paved the way for the Iraq crisis of 2003', *Security Dialogue*, vol. 37, no. 1, March 2006, pp. 123–41.

59. See G. Wilson, 'WEU's operational capability—delusion or reality', in G. Lenzi (ed.) *WEU at Fifty*, Paris: WEU ISS, 1998, p. 55; and WEU Assembly, rapporteur Mr Palis, *Participation of European Forces in Crisis Management: Reply to the Annual Report of the Council*, doc. A/1803, 3 December 2002.

60. J. Palmer, 'Defending the indefensible', *The Guardian*, 29 January 1991, p. 19.

61. EPC and WEU Ministerial meetings were held on the same day, providing a level of coherence between the two bodies.

62. The lack of cohesion of the European stance was typified by the British Prime Minister Edward Heath and former German Chancellor Willy Brandt's efforts to secure the release of hostages in direct contravention of the EC Twelve's agreement not to negotiate with Baghdad.

63. L. Brittan, 'International security in a time of change: Europe within NATO', *RUSI Journal*, vol. 136, no. 2, summer 1991, p. 36. Brittan argues for the absorption of the WEU over time into an EDC, 'based on the European Community, but separate from it', allowing for variable memberships but adopting where possible Community practice.

64. See C. Closa, 'The Gulf crisis: a case study of national constraints on Community action', *Journal of European Integration*, vol. 15, no. 1, autumn 1991, pp. 47–67.

65. Cited in P. Webster, D. Gow and J. Wolfe, 'Europe tries to reaffirm leading role diluted in crisis. France calls for EC Emergency Summit', *The Guardian*, 12 March 1991.

66. See P. V. Jakobsen, 'The Twelve and the Gulf crisis', in K. N. Jørgensen (ed.) *European Approaches to Crisis Management*, The Hague: Kluwer Law International, 1997, pp. 31–2.

67. D. Buchan, 'Whither WEU?', *European Affairs*, 1991, p. 70.

68. P. M. Haslach, 'The Western European Union: a defence organisation in search of a new role', *Europe*, January–February 1991, p. 19.

69. T. C. Salmon, 'Testing times for European Political Cooperation: the Gulf and Yugoslavia, 1990–1992', *International Affairs*, vol. 68, no. 2, April 1992, p. 244.

70. See Vanhoonacker, *The Bush Administration*, p. 126.

71. Cited in W. van Eekelen, Presentation by the Secretary General to Third General/Flag Officers' Course, NATO Defense College, Rome, 31 October 1991 (SG: 31.10.91).

72. This was a five-month crisis and a 43-day war. See W. van Eekelen, 'Naval Co-operation in WEU', *Marine Policy*, vol. 18, no. 6, November 1994, p. 535.

73. See Assembly Recommendation 493, WEU Assembly, rapporteur J. de Hoop Scheffer, *The Consequences of the Invasion of Kuwait: The Pursuit of Operations in the Gulf Region*, doc. 1248, 7 November 1990, which calls for the establishment of a European observation satellite centre and verification centre given the significance of intelligence for the prevention and management of crises. The Assembly also called for examination of the possibility of creating a naval on-call force for out-of-Europe co-ordination of naval operations, possibly to include airmobile assets to establish a European rapid reaction force.

74. See 'Conclusions of the Presidency', *Bulletin of the European Communities,* vol. 23, no. 12, December 1990, pp. 7–18.
75. For discussion and selected text of the Mitterand/Kohl letter see S. Nuttall, *European Foreign Policy,* Oxford: Oxford University Press, 2000, pp. 125–6. This document also recommended that joint security policy decisions could be taken within the European Council (the periodic summit meetings of the EC Heads of Government), and whilst decisions should 'in principle' be taken unanimously, provision could be made for the adoption of certain decisions by majority, particularly in terms of Council implementation arrangements.
76. See van Eekelen, *Debating European Security,* pp. 64–7.
77. W. van Eekelen, 'The WEU: Europe's best defence', *European Affairs,* no. 4, winter 1990, p. 10.
78. Van Eekelen, *Debating European Security,* pp. 65–6.
79. Van Eekelen, *Debating European Security,* p. 61.
80. WEU Council of Ministers, *Platform on European Security Interests,* The Hague, 27 October 1987, para. 2.
81. Van Eekelen, *Debating European Security,* p. 65.
82. Buchan, 'Whither WEU?', p. 69.
83. See A. Moens, 'The formative years of the new NATO: diplomacy from London to Rome', in A. Moens and C. Antis (eds) *Disconcerted Europe: The Search for a New Security Architecture,* Boulder: Westview Press, 1994, p. 37.
84. Menon refers to the 'increasing tensions' between two strands of French policy: support for greater European defence co-operation and a 'declaratory emphasis placed on national independence and self-reliance'. A. Menon, 'Explaining defence policy: the Mitterand years', *Review of International Studies,* vol. 21, no. 3, July 1995, p. 286.
85. M. Jopp, 'The strategic implications of European integration', *Adelphi Paper,* no. 290, July 1994, p. 9. Also see E. Pond, 'Germany in the new Europe', *Foreign Affairs,* vol. 71, no. 2, September 1992, pp. 114–30.
86. 'Joint initiative on establishing a Common European Foreign and Security Policy', 4 February 1991. See French Foreign Ministry, *Bulletin d' information,* 5 February 1991.
87. M. Luomna-aho, '"Arms" versus "pillar": the politics of the Western European Union at the 1990–91 Intergovernmental Conference on Political Union', *Journal of European Public Policy,* vol. 11, no. 1, February 2004, pp. 106–27.
88. A. Forster, 'The European Community and Western European Union', in Moens and Antis (eds) *Disconcerted Europe,* p. 103.
89. For the full text of the Under Secretary of State's telegram, selectively cited throughout this paragraph, see van Eekelen, *Debating European Security* (Annex 2), pp. 340–4. Staffed by the Assistant Secretary of State for European Affairs, James Dobbin, the telegram is also referred to as the 'Dobbins demarche'. See J. Dumbrell, *A Special Relationship: Anglo-American Relations from the Cold War to Iraq,* 2nd edn, Hampshire: Palgrave Macmillan, 2006, p. 234.
90. At the same meeting, the French WEU Presidency unveiled its document 'WEU's Role and Place in the New European Security Architecture' (Presidency's Conclusions), developed from the Secretary General's earlier 'personal reflections'. This became the working document for the WEU's SWG, Ministers, delegates and Secretariat in establishing a draft declaration for annexing to the Maastricht agreement.
91. See A. Moens, 'Behind complementarity and transparency: the politics of the European security and defence policy', *Journal of European Integration,* vol. 16, no. 1, fall 1992, pp. 41–2.

92. J. Palmer, 'Britain faltering in effort to tie EC defence to NATO', *The Guardian*, 28 March 1991, p. 9. Van Eekelen had proposed in February that the WEU might be brought under the European Council, although he accepted that there might be problems in terms of the binding nature of decisions on the WEU, given the presence of three non-WEU members in the Council. For concerns raised see J. Palmer, 'WEU warned against closer ties with EC', *The Guardian*, 23 February 1991, p. 10.

93. See *Agence Europe*, 20 and 23 February 1991.

94. See D. Buchan, 'Hurd seeks to keep defence out of Rome Treaty', *Financial Times*, 20 February 1991.

95. These proposals were articulated during Delors' Alastair Buchan Memorial Lecture to the International Institute for Security Studies in London, 7 March 1991. The Poettering Report of the EP, adopted after some dissent on 10 June 1991, also advocated the development of a common security policy, including the incorporation of the WEU Treaty commitments into the CFSP (Resolution A3–0107/91).

96. J. Palmer, 'Hurd supports independent European force', *The Guardian*, 27 March 1991. See John Major's foreword to the British White Paper *Developments in the European Community*, Cmd. 1457, London: HMSO, 1991.

97. D. Hurd, 'No European defence identity without NATO', *Financial Times*, 15 April 1991. This 'out-of-area' role was consistently promoted by the British Government over the following months. See for example Defence Secretary Tom King's statement: 'I see the WEU as being ready to play a role in areas where NATO could not operate or would choose not to operate', cited in 'Waking up the sleeping beauty: EEC-community in agreement over joint defence policy', *Jane's Defence Weekly*, 4 January 1992, p. 21.

98. This corps was to comprise four divisions residing in Germany: two would be British, one based on an Italian division with Greek and Turkish support, and one made up of Dutch, German, Belgian and British forces. Supported by US air and sea lift, an initial rapid deployment (within 72 hours) of 5,000 mobile forces was envisaged. See L. S. Kaplan, *NATO Divided, NATO United: The Evolution of an Alliance*, Westport: Praeger, 2004, p. 112.

99. A. Menon, 'From independence to cooperation: France, NATO and European security', *International Affairs*, vol. 71, no. 1, January 1995, p. 24.

100. W. Feld, *The Future of the European Security and Defence Policy*, Boulder: Lynne Rienner, 1993, pp. 81–2. Lansford suggests that the ARRC was designed to counter the WEU, operations in the Gulf and Yugoslavia having encouraged NATO's out-of-area aspirations. T. Lansford, *Evolution and Devolution: The Dynamics of Sovereignty and Security in Post-Cold War Europe*, Aldershot: Ashgate, 2000, p. 162.

101. C. Krupnik, 'Not what they wanted: American policy and the European Security and Defence Identity', in Moens and Antis (eds) *Disconcerted Europe*, p. 126.

102. Cited in van Eekelen, *Debating European Security*, p. 83.

103. The second point disappeared in the NAC's Rome Declaration of November, probably as a means of assuring French signature.

104. For the Copenhagen Communiqué see *NATO Review*, vol. 39, no. 3, June 1991, pp. 30–3.

105. As NATO's Secretary General noted in his Washington speech on 9 October 1991, 'We must be realistic and realize that neither the emerging European Political Union nor the WEU will have for the foreseeable future an operational defence capability able to be deployed without US/NATO assistance in domains like air support, strategic lift, logistics and communications requirements'. Cited in A. Hartley, 'Maastricht's problematical future', *The World Today*, vol. 48, no. 10, October 1992, p. 181.

106. W. H. Taft, 'European security: lessons learned from the Gulf War', *NATO Review,* vol. 39, no. 3, June 1991, p. 11.

107. Cited in D. A. R. Palmer, 'The future of West European security and defence cooperation—a United States perspective', in P. Schmidt (ed.) *In the Midst of Change: On the Development of West European Security and Defence Cooperation,* Baden-Baden: Nomos, 1992, p. 165.

108. W. van Eekelen in J. Palmer, 'NATO may reject overture', *The Guardian,* 16 February 1991, p. 9.

109. W. van Eekelen, Presentation by the Secretary General to Third General/Flag Officers' Course, NATO Defense College, Rome, 31 October 1991.

110. 'Declaration by the informal European Political Cooperation Ministerial Meeting on Yugoslavia', Château de Senningen, 26 March 1991, in C. Hill and K. E. Smith (eds) *European Foreign Policy: Key Documents,* London: Routledge, 2000, p. 362, doc. 4b/61.

111. Secretary Baker, 'US concerns about the future of Yugoslavia. Excerpts from Remarks at the Federation Palace, Belgrade, Yugoslavia, June 21 1991', *US Department of State Dispatch,* 1 July 1991.

112. Vanhoonacker, *The Bush Administration,* p. 175.

113. Salmon suggests that, over the following few weeks, the WEU, 'on this matter at least, [was] becoming the military arm of the EC'. 'Testing times', p. 250. Also see J. Palmer, 'Debate brings union closer', *The Guardian,* 21 September 1991, p. 6.

114. Lucarelli suggests that, whilst the national interests of member states with regards to Yugoslavia were not entirely clear, the UK, France and Germany had 'interest in *using* Yugoslavia as an instrument' of broader policy towards NATO and the CFSP. S. Lucarelli, 'Europe's response to the Yugoslav imbroglio', in Jørgensen (ed.), *European Approaches,* p. 39.

115. With these WEU peacekeeping proposals dependent on the cease-fire holding and consent of all parties, Hurd noted that 'no-one proposed for a moment that European troops should fight their way into Croatia or impose a settlement'. D. Hurd, *Memoirs,* London: Little Brown, 2003, p. 448.

116. J. Gow, *Triumph of the Lack of Will: International Diplomacy and the Yugoslav War,* London: Hurst, 1997, pp. 161–2. Also see R. Tiersky, 'France in the new Europe', *Foreign Affairs,* vol. 71, no. 2, spring 1992, pp. 131–46, for discussion of French policy on Yugoslavia.

117. Q. Peel, L. Silber and E. Mortimer, 'Divisions over Yugoslav crisis: Dutch call for intervention force will draw WEU disagreement', *Financial Times,* 17 September 1991.

118. R. Mauthner and Q. Peel, 'The crisis in Yugoslavia: Europe split over role in Yugoslavia—peacekeeping plan for WEU underlines differences among member states', *Financial Times,* 18 September 1991.

119. In fact, the EPC request had been a modest one in which it was stated that EC member states 'welcome that the WEU explore ways in which activities of the [EC] monitors could be supported . . . It is their understanding that no military intervention is contemplated'. 'Declaration on Yugoslavia', EPC Extraordinary Ministerial, The Hague, 19 September 1991, reproduced in Hill and Smith (eds) *European Foreign Policy,* p. 364, doc. 4b/65.

120. The report of the Ad Hoc Group was presented to an Extraordinary Ministerial Session of the WEU Council in Brussels on 30 September 1991. See van Eekelen, *Debating European Security,* p. 147.

121. J. Palmer, 'Kohl faces crisis over air crews', *The Guardian,* 22 June 1993, p. 18.

122. See WEU Assembly, rapporteur Mr Goerens, *European Union and Developments in Central and Eastern Europe,* doc. 1293, 27 November 1991; and rapporteur Mr De Hoop Scheffer, *Operational Arrangements for WEU—the Yugoslav Crisis,* doc. 1294, 27 November 1991.

123. See WEU Assembly, rapporteurs Mr Henares and Mr Tummers, *Western European Union: Information Report*, February 1993, pp. 29–30.

124. For discussion of national stances during the IGC see F. Laursen and S. Vanhoonacker (eds) *The Intergovernmental Conference on Political Union: Institutional Reforms, New Policies and International Identity of the European Community*, Maastricht and Dordrecht: EIPA and Martinus Nijhoff, 1992.

125. 'Draft Treaty Articles with a View to Achieving Political Union', Brussels, 17 April 1991, *Europe Documents*, no. 1709/1710, 3 May 1991.

126. 'Conclusions of the Presidency', *Bulletin of the European Communities*, vol. 24, no. 6, June 1991, pp. 8–19.

127. 'The Dutch Draft Treaty towards European Union', *European Documents*, no. 1734, 3 October 1991.

128. 'An Anglo-Italian Declaration on European Security and Defence, 5 October 1991', *European Documents*, no. 1735, 5 October 1991. Blair notes the significance for the British of demonstrating that they were not alone in their vision of a NATO-attached ESDI; Foreign Secretary Hurd played a 'crucial' role in securing Italian support for the declaration as 'a direct attempt [by the British] to challenge both the Franco-German alliance within the negotiations and a means of countering any future federalist aspirations in this policy area'. A. Blair, 'UK policy coordination during the 1990–91 Intergovernmental Conference', *Diplomacy and Statecraft*, vol. 9, no. 2, July 1998, p. 169.

129. Whether the declaration was seen as an Italian success in persuading the UK to move closer to a 'more European position' (largely by the Italians) or as an Italian move towards Atlanticism (largely by the French), the British and Italian Governments certainly chose to interpret the document with an Atlanticist or Europeanist emphasis respectively. See M. Cremasco, 'The future of West European security and defence cooperation—the case of Italy', in Schmidt (ed.) *In the Midst of Change*, pp. 98–9.

130. H. Pick, 'Britain softens on EC defence policy', *The Guardian*, 5 October 1991, p. 8.

131. French, German and Italian joint statement cited in R. van Beveren, 'Military aspects', in Gantz and Roper, *Towards a New Partnership*, p. 133.

132. Franco-German 'Draft Treaty on Political Union: Common Foreign and Security Policy', see *Atlantic Document*, no. 74, 18 October 1991.

133. The Corps, comprising 4,200 men in October 1991, was to have a permanent Headquarters in Strasbourg with an initial command of 35,000 men.

134. Menon et al., 'A common European defence', p. 110.

135. D. von Wolff Metternich, 'The Franco-German Brigade: a German perspective', *RUSI Journal*, vol. 136, no. 3, autumn 1991, p. 48. Also see K. P. Stratmann, 'The future of West German security and defence co-operation—German perspectives', in Schmidt (ed.), *In the Midst of Change*, pp. 48–9.

136. Brenner suggests that German concerns about the possibility of American disengagement, and the potential for being placed in strategic limbo, led Bonn to accept French 'pushing' over the Franco-German corps and that this 'placed Germany in the position of being whipsawed between the Americans and the French, between NATO and the sovereign, independent Europe envisaged for the future'. Brenner, 'EC: confidence lost', p. 37.

137. See J. Palmer, 'EC backs proposals for European army', *The Guardian*, 17 October 1991. Following the final Franco-German agreement on Eurocorps at La Rochelle on 21 May 1992, Belgium (1993), Spain (1995) and Luxembourg (1996) joined.

138. H. Pick, 'Britain signals doubts on Bonn-Paris joint force plan', *The Guardian*, 14 February 1992; 'Franco-German corps strains NATO's post Cold War strategic relations', *Aviation Week and Space Technology*, vol. 136, no. 22, 1992, p. 23.

139. Franco-German 'Draft Treaty on Political Union'. Foster describes the Eurocorps as a 'third force' between NATO and the WEU, connected to both and yet independent of each, and potentially a future hub of European decision-making in defence. E. Foster, 'The Franco-German Corps: a 'theological' debate?', *RUSI Journal*, vol. 137, no. 4, August 1992, p. 64.

140. See J. Eisenhammer, 'Britain and France fail to narrow the gap on defence', *The Independent*, 30 October 1991.

141. Cited in S. Helm and D. Usborne, 'EC "security council" mooted', *The Independent*, 30 October 1991.

142. D. Gow, 'WEU leaders divided over future role', *The Guardian*, 30 October 1991.

143. H. Pick, 'Britain sets out its summit stall', *The Guardian*, 1 November 1991, p. 14.

144. B. Johnson, *Daily Telegraph*, 1 November 1991. Also see A. Forster, 'The ratchet of European defence: Britain and the reactivation of Western European Union, 1984–1991', in A. Deighton (ed.) *Western European Union 1954–1997: Defence, Security, Integration*, Oxford: European Interdependence Research Unit, 1997, pp. 36–7.

145. See for example D. Chuter, 'The United Kingdom', in J. Howorth and A. Menon (eds) *The European Union and National Defence Policy*, London: Routledge, 1997, p. 116.

146. Major cited in H. Pick, 'Major draws line on defence links', *The Guardian*, 8 November 1991, p. 11.

147. Oxford Research Group, *Defence and Security in the New Europe: Who Will Decide?*, Current Decisions Report, no. 7, November 1991, p. 17.

148. Van Beveren, 'Military aspects', p. 134.

149. He identified that only in agreement with NATO would troops be assigned to the WEU, and that Germany would not reassign any of its NATO troops. Cited in D. Gow, 'Kohl affirms Germany's support for the alliance', *The Guardian*, 7 November 1991.

150. NATO, 'Rome Declaration on Peace and Cooperation', *Europe Documents*, no. 1744, 13 November 1991, para. 3

151. *The Alliance's New Strategic Concept*, NATO, November 1991, para. 40.

152. *The Alliance's New Strategic Concept*, para. 22.

153. 'Rome Declaration on Peace and Cooperation', para. 6.

154. Bush cited in 'Bush warning to Europe', *The Independent*, 8 November 1991. A leaked Pentagon draft paper of February 1992 stated that the US should 'prevent any collection of friendly or unfriendly nations from competing with the United States for superpower status', although this was toned down in the final version of the paper, *National Military Security 1992*, which simply stated that 'the preservation and expansion of alliances was given the highest priority'. Cited in Van Beveren, 'Military aspects', p. 138.

155. 'Rome Declaration on Peace and Cooperation', para. 7.

156. *Treaty on European Union including the Protocols and Final Act with Declarations, Maastricht, 7 February 1992*, Treaty Series no. 12, Cm 2485, London: HMSO, March 1994.

157. The Treaty Establishing the European Economic Community (the Treaty of Rome) was renamed the Treaty Establishing the European Community (TEC).

158. TEU, Title V, 'Provisions on a Common Foreign and Security Policy', Article J.4.1.

159. The range of issues where a qualified majority may determine 'joint actions' was defined by the European Council in their Lisbon Report of June 1992, including arms control considerations, CSCE questions, nuclear non-proliferation, and arms technology transfer to the Third World. See *Atlantic News*, no. 2438, 30 June 1992.

160. See Smith for discussion of CFSP mechanisms and procedures as established at Maastricht, their comparison to former EPC structures and their development post-Maastricht. M. Smith, 'What's wrong with the CFSP? The politics of institutional reform', in P.-L. Laurent and M. Maresceau (eds) *The State of the European Union. Volume 4, Deepening and Widening*, Boulder: Lynne Rienner, 1998, pp. 152–60.

161. The WEU also committed itself to a parallel review, the timing being significant as the Brussels Treaty provided for the possibility of membership withdrawal in 1998, 50 years after the signing of the original treaty.

162. N. Gnesotto, 'European Union after Minsk and Maastricht', *International Affairs*, vol. 68, no. 2, April 1992, pp. 224–5.

163. M. Jopp and W. Wessels, 'Institutional frameworks for security co-operation in Western Europe: developments and options', in Jopp et al. (eds) *Integration and Security in Western Europe*, p. 59.

164. Delors, 'European unification and European security', p. 105.

165. Zandra, 'Towards a European identity', p. 59.

166. For the Declarations on Western European Union annexed to the Treaty on European Union, 7 February 1992, and issued on the occasion of the European Council at Maastricht, 10 December 1991, see Cm 2485, London: HMSO, 1994, pp. 131–3.

167. This was to include the 'establishment of close co-operation between the Council and Secretariat-General of WEU on the one hand, and the Council of the Union and General Secretariat of the Council on the other', arrangements for closer co-operation and consultation with the Commission as appropriate, and the 'encouragement of closer co-operation between the Parliamentary Assembly of the WEU and the European Parliament'. Declaration 1, Section A, para. 3.

168. Declaration 1, Section B. 'Where necessary, dates and venues of meetings will be synchronised and working methods harmonised. Close co-operation will be established between the Secretariats-General of WEU and NATO'. The first formal meeting of the Councils of NATO and the WEU took place in Brussels on 21 May 1992. The first introduction of a 'joint position' agreed in the WEU into the Alliance consultation process concerned the operational rules for multinational teams engaged in the CFE arms control process, a position adopted by the Alliance.

169. Following studies on the possible uses of space technology by the *ad hoc* Space Group, established as a subsidiary body of the WEU Council in 1989, the WEU Council agreed at their meeting in Vianden in June 1991 to the development of a satellite data interpretation centre for an experimental period of three years, to be constructed in Torrejon, Spain (1 January 1992), by a consortium of more than 30 European companies. For discussion see A. McLean, 'Integrating European security through space', *Space Policy*, vol. 11, no. 4, November 1995, p. 244.

170. W. van Eekelen, 'WEU prepares the way for new missions', *NATO Review*, vol. 41, no. 5, October 1993, p. 11.

171. Provisions made under the Edinburgh European Council agreements of 12 December 1992 enabled a Danish 'opt out' of the defence provisions of the TEU, necessary to ensure public acceptance of the treaty in the second Danish referendum.

172. WEU Council of Ministers, *Petersberg Declaration*, Bonn, 19 June 1992.

173. Greece was given the status of 'active observer' until ratification of its accession in 1995, a process slowed by Dutch resistance. See Nuttall *European Foreign Policy*, p. 242.

174. The Turkish, supported by Washington, were keen to have full participation in, and indeed membership of, the WEU, but this was rejected by those

members which sought to develop the WEU as a future arm of the Union. See WEU Assembly, rapporteur Mr Moyer, *Turkey,* doc. 1341, 6 November 1992. For discussion of the impact of accession issues on the pre-declaration debate see H. Pick, 'After the summit: NATO declares points win to Britain', *The Guardian,* 12 December 1991, p. 2; J. Palmer and M. White, 'Maastricht Summit / votes, vetoes and compromises: issues which have caused divisions', *The Guardian,* 11 December 1991, p. 3.

175. In establishing out-of-territory peace support operations as a key objective of the WEU, Petersberg moved the institution away from its former collective defence role, the Article VIII.3 provisions for 'consultation' of the MBT being insufficient to provide the legal basis for this change. Equally, its status as a regional organization under Article 52 provisions of the UN Charter, and therefore available to act under UN mandate, has been a matter of contention since its inception. For discussion see M. Ortega, 'Some questions on legal aspects', in Lenzi, *WEU at Fifty,* p. 2; W. Eric Beckett, *The North Atlantic Treaty, the Brussels Treaty, and the Charter of the United Nations,* London: Stevens and Sons, 1950; J. Roper, 'The contribution of regional organisations in Europe', in A. Otunnu and M. Doyle (eds) *Peacemaking and Peacekeeping for the New Century,* Lanham: Rowman and Littlefield, 1998, pp. 255–71.

176. NAC Ministerial Meeting, *Final Communiqué,* Oslo, 4 June 1992.

177. Officially declared FAWEU at the WEU's Council of Ministers meeting in Rome in May 1993, the Eurocorps was to stand alongside other multinational FAWEU including the Multinational Division (Central) (Belgium, the UK, the Netherlands, Germany), the UK-Netherlands Corps, the Spanish-Italian Amphibious Force (agreed September 1997) and the 1st German/Dutch corps headquarters, all of these also being declared to NATO.

178. See van Eekelen, *Debating European Security,* p. 126.

179. Responsible for providing advice to both the Planning Cell and their Permanent Representatives, the delegates were distinguished from their NATO equivalent (MilReps) by the nomenclature MilDel, although only the French and Belgians did not 'double-hat' this role.

180. For details of Planning Cell operational procedures see S. de Spiegeleire, 'From mutually assured debilitation to flexible response: a new menu of options for European crisis management', in Lenzi (ed.) *WEU at Fifty,* pp. 27–31. For an early assessment of Planning Cell development see WEU Assembly, rapporteur Mrs Baarveld-Schlaman, *The WEU Planning Cell,* doc. 1421, 19 May 1994. Also see Lt Gen M. Caltabiano (then Director of the WEU Planning Cell), 'The military dimension of the WEU', *RUSI Journal,* vol. 138, no. 3, 1 June 1993, pp. 7–9.

181. For further detailed discussion of the Annex provisions see van Eekelen, *Debating European Security,* pp. 212–14.

182. EU-WEU relations were to be improved through the mutual exchange of relevant information via the respective Presidencies, and between the Secretary General and Council, with cross-participation of staff at relevant meetings determined on a case-by-case basis by the Presidencies. Synchronization of meetings would be encouraged, and Commission attendance would be permitted at WEU meetings as part of the Presidency delegation. Restrictions on the transmission to the EU of secure information that NATO supplied to the WEU limited this exchange and caused some inter-institutional angst, the NATO-WEU relationship proving more co-operative. Nuttall describes the evolved 'network of contacts' as 'dense, although not necessarily rich'. *European Foreign Policy,* pp. 244–5.

183. Roper, 'Yugoslavia and European security', p. 2.

184. The EC's Badinter Commission, a judicial body established to adjudicate on the recognition of new post-Soviet states, determined the legal basis for the break-up of federal Yugoslavia into independent states.

185. German recognition came on 23 December, the Serbs having formally rejected the EC Peace Plan for an association of sovereign republics in November 1991 on the grounds that this constituted dissolution of the Federation.

186. Five EC monitors were shot down in a marked helicopter in January 1992. C. Bretherton and J. Vogler, *The European Union as a Global Actor*, London: Routledge, 1999, p. 209.

187. Poos cited in the *Financial Times*, 1 July 1991. See G. F. Treverton, 'The year of European disunification', *Current History*, vol. 91, no. 568, November 1992, pp. 353–8.

188. Volker Ruhe cited in D. Gow, 'Blockade of Yugoslav army urged', *The Guardian*, 20 June 1992.

189. WEU Council of Ministers, *Declaration on the Yugoslav Crisis*, Bonn, 19 June 1992.

190. Van Eekelen, 'WEU prepares the way for new missions', p. 22.

191. L. Vierucci, 'WEU: a regional partner of the United Nations', *Chaillot Paper*, no. 12, Paris: WEU ISS, December 1993, pp. 25–6.

192. Resolution 713 (25 September 1991) provided for a general and complete embargo on all deliveries of weapons and military equipment to Yugoslavia, and Resolution 757 (30 May 1992) extended sanctions against Serbia and Montenegro to include a trade embargo, the freezing of assets abroad and the prohibition of air traffic and services related to aircraft and weapons.

193. Wilson notes that the WEU's common maritime ROE were produced two months ahead of NATO's, although they had been developed by SACEUR's staff. 'WEU's operational capability—delusion or reality', p. 56.

194. M. Chichester, 'Maastricht, the Adriatic and the future of European defence', *Navy International*, vol. 97, no. 11/12, November–December 1992, p. 361.

195. P. Beaver, 'WEU/NATO tighten naval blockade', *Jane's Defence Weekly*, 25 July 1992, p. 6.

196. T. Ripley, 'Isolating Yugoslavia', *International Defense Review*, vol. 27, 1994, p. 75.

197. Rear Admiral Carlo Alberto Vandini cited in Beaver, 'WEU/NATO tighten naval blockade', p. 6.

198. 'Communiqué issued by the Ministerial Meeting of the North Atlantic Council, Brussels, 17 December 1992', in *NATO Review*, vol. 40, no. 5, December 1992, pp. 28–31.

199. Autolycus, 'Adriatic ops—NATO and/or the WEU?', *Naval Review*, vol. 81, no. 1, January 1993, pp. 23–4.

200. D. Fairhall, 'Yugoslav civil war', *The Guardian*, 11 August 1992.

201. Lord Owen replaced Carrington as the EC's Special Representative, and Cyrus Vance co-chaired the London talks as UN Special Envoy; the conference opened on 26–27 August, the UK having taken the EC Presidency.

202. Vanhoonacker, *The Bush Administration*, p. 181.

203. C. L. Powell, *A Soldier's Way: An Autobiography*, London: Hutchinson, 1995, p. 559. Influential texts in this regard include J. J. Mearsheimer's 'Back to the future: instability in Europe after the Cold War', *International Security*, vol. 15, no. 1, summer 1990, pp. 5–56; and S. P. Huntington's 'The clash of civilisations?', *Foreign Affairs*, vol. 72, no. 3, summer 1993, pp. 22–49.

204. A. G. Kintis, 'The EU's foreign policy and the war in former Yugoslavia', in M. Holland (ed.) *Common Foreign and Security Policy: The Record and Reforms*, London: Pinter, 1997, p. 157. Another ad hoc grouping, the Contact Group (Germany, France, the US, Russia and the UK), which was formed in London on 26 April 1994 to try to develop some coherent and co-ordinated response in the light of the failure of the international effort, further undermined the credibility of those organizations involved.

205. Van Beveren, 'Military aspects', p. 141.
206. The report goes on to note the 'policy paralysis' consequent on the inertia and buck-passing of institutional rivalry and immaturity. Report of the NAC, cited in *Atlantic News*, no. 2527, 27 May 1993, p. 4.
207. See R. H. Palin, 'Multinational military forces: problems and prospects', *Adelphi Paper*, no. 294, April 1995, p. 26.
208. For discussion of Operation Sharp Guard see WEU Assembly, rapporteurs M. Martin and K. Speed, *An Operational Organisation for WEU: Naval Co-operation—Part One: Adriatic Operations*, doc. 1396, 9 November 1993.
209. As Task Force 440, a pool of ships from WEUMARCONFOR and NATO's STANAVFORMED and Standing Naval Forces Atlantic (STANAVFORLANT) provided three operational Combined Task Groups (CTG), each commanded by a Rear Admiral or Commodore and consisting of around six ships per group. CTG 440.01 patrolled the Montenegrin coast, CTG 440.02 covered the Straits of Otranto, and CTG 440.03 consisted of ships in training or resting in port. Command of the CTGs was rotated around the three force commanders. The operation was supported by maritime patrol aircraft run by Combined Task Force 431 in Naples and a Forward Logistic Site at the Italian Naval Air Station, Grottaglie, responsible for co-ordinated logistic support to all Sharp Guard ships. For discussion see E. Grove, 'Navies in peacekeeping and enforcement: the British experience in the Adriatic Sea', *International Peacekeeping*, vol. 1, no. 4, winter 1994, p. 467.
210. Van Eekelen, 'WEU prepares the way for new missions', p. 22. The double-hatting of most NATO and WEU representatives further facilitated this co-operation.
211. It has been argued that it was 'above all the debilitating effect that the crisis was having on NATO, that galvanized Clinton into action and provided the impetus for the US diplomatic intervention that led to the Dayton Accord'. F. S. Larrabee, 'US policy in the Balkans: from containment to strategic reengagement', in C. P. Danopoulos and K. G. Messas (eds) *Crisis in the Balkans: Views from the Participants*, Oxford: Westview, 1997, p. 285.
212. This was in response to the siege of Sarajevo, following the market shelling of 5 February, the UN Secretary General having called for a NATO-backed ultimatum of air strikes if the heavy weapons exclusion zone was not respected.
213. Van Eekelen, *Debating European Security*, p. 164.
214. UNSC Resolution 836, 4 June 1993. The safe areas included Sarajevo, Srebrenicia, Bihac, Zepa, Goradze and Tuzla.
215. This criticism was evident in the WEU's Noordwijk Declaration of 14 November 1994. See N. Gnesotto, 'Lessons of Yugoslavia', *Chaillot Paper*, no. 14, Paris: WEU ISS, March 1994, for discussion of the Yugoslav conflict.
216. Van Eekelen, *Debating European Security*, p. 177.
217. Significantly, this unilateralism had worrying implications for the development of the 'separable but not separate' concept of capabilities underpinning the Combined Joint Task Forces proposals.
218. NATO, Regional Headquarters Allied Forces Southern Europe, 'Operation Sharp Guard', *AFSOUTH Fact Sheets*, 18 August 2003. Ripley argues that the actual impact of the arms embargo was negligible given Serbian stockpiles and Croatian/Slovenian land and air routes and that economic sanctions had a greater effect against Serbia, whose economy was being 'wrecked by its isolation'. Ripley, 'Isolating Yugoslavia', p. 79.
219. The final draft of the WEU Operation Plan (OPLAN) 001 was produced in March 1994. See WEU Assembly, rapporteur Sir K. Speed, *An Operational Organisation for WEU: Naval and Maritime Co-operation*, doc. 1415,

10 May 1994. Also see W. van Eekelen, 'Naval cooperation in WEU', *Marine Policy*, vol. 18, no. 6, November 1994, p. 536.

220. WEU Council of Ministers, *Declaration on Implementation of UN Sanctions in the Former Yugoslavia*, Luxembourg, 5 April 1993.

221. The Assembly was to report that 10 patrol boats and 270 specialists had been seconded from WEU member states to monitor river traffic, working in close co-operation with the EC and CSCE. See WEU Assembly, rapporteur Mr De Decker, *The Situation in the Former Yugoslavia*, doc. 1468, 12 June 1995.

222. WEU Press Release, 'Termination of the WEU Danube Embargo Enforcement Operation', Brussels, 2 October 1996.

223. In fact, the WEU activity in support of the EU Administration in Mostar was not on the basis of a formal request under the J.4.2 provisions of the TEU as no 'defence' issue was involved. See M. E. Smith, *Europe's Foreign and Security Policy: The Institutionalization of Cooperation*, Cambridge: Cambridge University Press, 2004, p. 204.

224. These three states acceded to the EU in 1995, becoming observer states in the WEU in the same year.

225. The UN International Police Task Force in the rest of Bosnia and Herzegovina had numbered 1,700 during the WEU's Mostar operation.

226. See C. J. Smith, 'Conflict in the Balkans and the possibility of a European Union common foreign and security policy', *International Relations*, vol. 13, no. 2, August 1996, pp. 1–22. The French were particularly active in encouraging European multinational deployment, including the small 'rapid reaction force' of French, British and Dutch forces deployed to support the UN presence in June 1995. Gregory, *French Defence Policy*, p. 139. Also see C. Hill, 'The capabilities-expectation gap, or conceptualising Europe's international role', *Journal of Common Market Studies*, vol. 31, no. 3, September 1993, pp. 305–28.

227. Rummel, 'Integration, disintegration, and security in Europe', p. 78.

228. Gnesotto, 'European Union after Minsk and Maastricht', p. 227.

229. G. W. Rees, *The Western European Union at the Crossroads: Between Trans-Atlantic Solidarity and European Integration*, Oxford: Westview, 1998, p. 85.

230. See Lt Gen H. Willman (then Commander Eurocorps), 'The European Corps—political dimension and military aims', *RUSI Journal*, vol. 139, no. 4, August 1994, p. 29.

231. Vice-President of the French National Assembly's Defence Commission cited in R. Grant, *The Changing Franco-American Security Relationship: New Direction for NATO and European Defense Cooperation*, Arlington: US-CREST, 1993, p. 33.

232. See R. P. Grant, 'France's new relationship with NATO', *Survival*, vol. 38, no. 1, spring 1996, p. 61.

233. See WEU Assembly, *An Operational Organisation for the WEU*, doc 1396.

234. M. Jopp, 'The defence dimension of the European Union: the role and performance of the WEU', in E. Regelsberger, P. de Schoutheete de Tervarent and W. Wessels (eds) *Foreign Policy of the European Union: From EPC to CFSP and Beyond*, Boulder: Lynne Rienner, 1997, p. 159.

235. See discussion in S. Rohan, 'Constructing a European security community: the role of institutions', in V. Popa (ed.), *International Public Law: Between Desires and Reality*, Timisoara: Helicon, 1999, pp. 59–76. For the seminal work on security communities see K. W. Deutsch et al., *Political Community and the North Atlantic Area*, Princeton: Princeton University Press, 1957.

236. The 10 to ratify the Europe Agreements were Hungary, Poland, the Czech and Slovak Republics, Bulgaria, Romania, Latvia, Lithuania, Estonia and Slovenia. See M. J. Baun, *A Wider Europe: The Process and Politics of European Union Enlargement*, Oxford: Rowman and Littlefield, 2000, pp. 30–7. Earlier

EC initiatives included the PHARE programme, established in 1989 to provide direct grants to promote market, and later democratic, reform, and the European Bank for Reconstruction and Development, which began lending to the CEE private sector in 1991.

237. See P.-C. Müller-Graff, 'Legal framework for relations between the European Union and Central and Eastern Europe: general aspects', in M. Maresceau (ed.) *Enlarging the European Union: Relations between the EU and Central and Eastern Europe,* London: Longman, 1997, pp. 27–40.

238. See NACC, 'Work plan for dialogue, participation and cooperation', NATO HQ, Brussels, 10 March 1992, in *NATO Review,* vol. 40, no. 2, April 1992, pp. 34–5.

239. 'Expansion' refers here to the institutional provisions for engagement short of enlargement.

240. See W. van Eekelen, 'WEU's post-Maastricht agenda', *NATO Review,* vol. 40, no. 2, April 1992, pp. 13–17, for discussion.

241. W. van Eekelen, 'Building a new European security: WEU's contribution', *NATO Review,* vol. 38, no. 4, August 1990, p. 20. Also see the WEU Council of Ministers, *Brussels Communiqué,* 23 April 1990.

242. 'Ministerial decision concerning the setting-up of a WEU Institute for Security Studies, Brussels, 13 November 1989', online at www.weu.int/key%20texts.htm.

243. See the WEU Council of Ministers, *Paris Communiqué,* Paris, 10 December 1990, and *Vianden Communiqué,* Luxembourg, 27 June 1991. In fact, the Visegrad states of Hungary, Poland and Czechoslovakia were disappointed by the Council's failure to further differentiate between themselves, as the most 'progressive' states in terms of democratic and market reforms, and the other 'Europe Agreement' states, as proposed by the Assembly. See P. Dunay, T. Kende and T. Szűcs, 'The integration of Central and Eastern Europe into the Common Foreign and Security Policy of the European Fifteen', in Maresceau (ed.) *Enlarging the European Union,* pp. 339–40.

244. WEU Council of Ministers, Extraordinary Meeting of the WEU Council with States of Central and Eastern Europe, *Bonn Declaration,* 19 June 1992.

245. Van Eekelen, 'WEU prepares the way for new missions', p. 21.

246. A. Podraza, *The Western European Union and Central Europe: A New Relationship,* RIIA Discussion Papers, no. 41, London: RIIA, 1993, p. 29.

247. That the 'forum' offer was made only to Europe Agreement states was intended to ensure that WEU's outreach was not 'placed in competition with the North Atlantic Co-operation Council'. See WEU Assembly, rapporteur Mr Goerings, *European Security Policy—Reply to the Thirty-seventh Annual Report of the Council,* doc. 1342, pt. 1, 6 November 1992.

248. See Commission report, 'The Challenge of Enlargement', *Europe Documents,* no. 1790, 3 July 1992.

249. For a contemporaneous discussion of the motivations behind French support for the development of a European identity in security and defence see P. H. Gordon, *A Certain Idea of France: French Security Policy and the Gaullist Legacy,* Princeton: Princeton University Press, 1993, pp. 172–8.

250. Jopp et al., 'Integration and security in a new Europe', pp. 73–4.

251. Jopp, 'Strategic implications', pp. 56–7.

252. 'Kooijmans on NATO, US relations, Europe', *De Volksrant,* 19 October 1993, cited in M. Mihalka, 'Squaring the circle', *RFE/RL Research Report,* vol. 3, no. 12, 25 March 1994, p. 9.

253. Concerns regarding the negative influence on CFSP development of the EU accession of the three neutrals included their potential rejection of future efforts to develop a common defence policy, their proximity to Russia (Finland) and their lack of interoperability, although it was also recognized that they could

add to the overall political weight of the EU in international affairs, contribute to the European defence industrial base and provide a positive contribution through their experiences of peacekeeping activity. See M. Jopp, 'Developing a European security and defence identity: the specific input of present and future new members', in F. Algieri, J. Janning and D. Rumberg (eds) *Managing European Security*, Gütersloh: Bertelsmann Foundation, 1996, pp. 71–4.

254. Never formally adopted, the Cahen Doctrine is outlined by the former Secretary General in WEU Assembly, *Enlarged Security: The Security Problems Posed by the Enlargement of NATO and the European Institutions*, Colloquy, Athens, 11–12 March 1997, pp. 61–2. For a discussion of the complexities of the question of memberships see T. Flockhart, 'The dynamics of expansion: NATO, WEU and EU', *European Security*, vol. 5, no. 2, summer 1996, pp. 96–218.

255. US Ambassador to NATO Robert E. Hunter cited in *The Economist*, 25 February 1995, p. 21.

256. *Declaration of the Heads of State and Government*, NATO Headquarters, Brussels, 10–11 January 1994.

257. The provision of a NATO operational headquarters with 100 staff, equipment and supplies to support the UNPROFOR in Bosnia in November 1992 may have been the 'source' of the CJTF concept, enabling NATO support for ground action without the Congressionally unacceptable deployment of forces. Bretherton and Volger, *The European Union as a Global Actor*, p. 210.

258. C. W. Mayn, 'A working Clinton Doctrine', *Foreign Policy*, no. 93, winter 1993–4, p. 5.

259. A. Cragg, 'The Combined Joint Task Force concept: a key component of the Alliance's adaptation', *NATO Review*, vol. 44, no. 4, July 1996, pp. 3–6. Also see WEU Assembly, rapporteur Mr Baumel, *Draft Recommendation on the Evolution of NATO and its Consequences for WEU*, doc. 1410, 23 March 1994, adopted by Standing Committee of WEU Assembly in Paris, 3 May 1994; C. Barry, 'NATO's Combined Joint Task Forces in theory and practice', *Survival*, vol. 38, no. 1, spring 1996, pp. 81–97.

260. B. George, *After the NATO Summit* (UK), General Rapporteur. Draft General Report, International Secretariat, NATO Centralized Media Service, May 1994.

261. D. Fairhall and J. Palmer, 'NATO keeps its options open to help Yeltsin', *The Guardian*, 9 December 1993.

262. D. Heathcoat-Amory, 'The next step for Western European Union: a British view', *The World Today*, vol. 50, no. 7, July 1994, p. 135.

263. See T. Taylor, 'Challenges for Western European Union operations', in Deighton (ed.) *Western European Union 1954–1997*, pp. 145–55. For a discussion of French attitudes to CJTF see Menon, 'From independence to cooperation', pp. 19–34.

264. Briefing by Policy Planning Section, NATO HQ, 12 July 1994.

265. 'East gets a lukewarm answer', *The Guardian*, 22 June 1993, p. 8.

266. See G. Evans, 'Responding to crises in the African Great Lakes', *Adelphi Paper*, no. 311, August 1997, p. 55.

267. W. Kühne, 'Lessons from peacekeeping operations in Angola, Mozambique, Somalia, Rwanda and Liberia', in W. Kühne, G. Lenzi and A. Vasconcelos (eds) 'WEU's role in crisis management and conflict resolution in sub-Saharan Africa', *Chaillot Paper*, no. 22, Paris: WEU ISS, December 1995, p. 35.

268. A. Vasconcelos, 'Should Europe have a policy on Africa', in Kühne et al. (eds) 'WEU's role in crisis management', p. 14.

269. Resolution 929 authorized a two-month interim operation to protect safe zones for refugees fleeing the Hutu militias, which remained in place until handed over to UNAMIR II at the end of August.

270. Van Eekelen, *Debating European Security*, p. 224.
271. Recommended by a joint UK-French paper in November 1994, an African peacekeeping initiative was launched within the WEU. G. Lenzi, 'WEU's role in sub-Saharan Africa', in Kühne et al. (eds) 'WEU's role in crisis management', pp. 48, 59 and 64.
272. *Presidency Conclusions*, European Summit, Madrid, 15–16 December 1995.
273. At their meetings in Noordwijk (November 1994) and Lisbon (November 1995) the WEU Council encouraged further consideration of this area of potential WEU activity, including endorsement of a document at Lisbon, based on an Italian-UK proposal, proposing a WEU Humanitarian Task Force capable of offering specialized logistic support to the WEU or other multinational operations.
274. C. Echeverria, 'Cooperation in peacekeeping among the Euro-Mediterranean armed forces', *Chaillot Paper*, no. 35, Paris: WEU ISS, February 1999, pp. 6–7.
275. For an analysis of the early post-Cold War articulation of Russian policy towards any future NATO enlargement see S. Crow, 'Russia asserts its strategic agenda', *RFE/RL Research Reports*, vol. 2, no. 50, December 1993, pp. 1–8.
276. Cited in R. Zandra, 'Widening and deepening', *WEU ISS Newsletter*, no. 11, April 1994, p. 1.
277. The 'family' was to comprise 10 full members, 3 associate members, 5 observers and 10 associate partners, with Slovenia becoming the 10th associate partner in 1996. Associate partners were excluded from Council discussions on issues related to Article V, relations with the EU and NATO, and institutional affairs. See M. Wohlfeld, 'Closing the gap: WEU and Central European countries', in Lenzi (ed.) *WEU at Fifty*, p. 81.
278. WEU Council of Ministers, *Kirchberg Declaration*, Luxembourg, 9 May 1994.
279. A response to the conflict in Yugoslavia, where issues of territorial integrity and national minorities had become security issues, the 'Stability Pact in Europe: The documents adopted by the Paris Conference', *Europe*, doc. 1887, 31 May 1994, committed CEE states through bilateral agreements to principles of 'good neighbourly relations', areas indicated for consideration including trans-border co-operation, minority issues and issues of cultural, legal, economic and environmental co-operation. See T. Ueta, 'The Stability Pact: from the Balladur Initiative to the EU Joint Action', in M. Holland (ed.) *Common Foreign and Security Policy*, pp. 92–104.
280. *Kirchberg Declaration*, Part II. Extending co-operation to all CSCE members, PfP was to establish bilateral accords between NATO and individual CSCE states, acting effectively as a staging post for longer-term enlargement on the basis of states' demonstration of their intent and acceptability for membership. Co-operation was to develop in the areas of peacekeeping, crisis management and disaster relief and was facilitated through joint training and planning.
281. See *NATO Handbook*, Brussels: NATO Office of information and Press, 2001, pp. 61–2.
282. See M. Wohlfeld, 'The WEU as a complement—not a substitute—for NATO', *Transition*, vol. 1, no. 25, 15 December 1995, pp. 34–6 and 64.
283. See WEU Assembly, rapporteur M. Cazan, *The Consequences of the Madrid NATO Summit and the Development of WEU's Relations with Central and Eastern European Countries and Russia*, doc. 1585, 5 November 1997.
284. Comment during Yeltsin's speech at the Budapest CSCE Summit, December 1994, cited in J. Dean, 'Losing Russia or keeping NATO: must we choose?', *Arms Control Today*, vol. 25, no. 5, June 1995, p. 6. Repercussions were to be evidenced in the slow progress towards ratification of START II and negotiations on the Open Skies Treaty, along with ongoing question marks over continuing Russian engagement with the CFE process.

285. In an early collaborative work between the WEU's Institute for Security Studies and the Russian Academy of Science, it was noted that the 'WEU remains a barely detectable "blip" on the political radar screen', with Russians viewing the WEU 'with a mixture of sympathy and interest, but also with some scepticism about its independent role and actual operational and political possibilities', although it was to prove a practical arrangement for the development of co-operative practice. D. Danilov and S. de Spiegeleire, 'From decoupling to recoupling: a new security relationship for Russia and Western Europe', *Chaillot Paper*, no. 31, Paris: WEU ISS, April 1998, pp. 7–8.

286. See M. Mihalka, 'European-Russian security and NATO's Partnership for Peace', *RFE/RL Research Report*, vol. 3, no. 33, 26 August 1994, p. 44. Wohlfeld, 'Closing the gap', p. 88.

287. The PCA came into effect on 1 December 1997, providing for Ministerial, parliamentary and senior official forums addressing a wide scope of economic issues. The EU's Action Plan for Russia of May 1996 was to extend the scope of this co-operation, including the establishment of an SWG tasked with supporting the elaboration by the Organisation for Security and Co-operation in Europe (OSCE) of a Common and Comprehensive Security Model. Danilov and De Spiegeleire, 'From decoupling to recoupling', pp. 9–15.

288. See A. Sergounin, 'Russian domestic debate on NATO enlargement: from phobia to damage limitation', *European Security*, vol. 6, no. 4, winter 1997, p. 57. Wohlfeld, 'Closing the gap', p. 88.

289. See R. Tibbels, 'WEU's dialogue with Russia and the Ukraine', *NATO's Sixteen Nations*, Special Supplement, 1998, p. 44.

290. The mechanisms for co-operation with the WEU 'family' included regular meetings between the Secretary General and Permanent Representative of the Presidency-holding state and the Russian and Ukrainian Ambassadors, high-level official visits, points of contact for information exchange between the WEU Secretariat and Presidency and the Russian and Ukrainian Embassies, and gradual development of parliamentary contacts and co-operation between the WEU's Institute for Security Studies and Russian/Ukrainian academic communities.

291. Ukraine was concerned that too hasty a NATO enlargement might position it between an enraged Russia and an expanded Alliance, at a time when it was seeking to stress its European vocation through close association with the EU. Hence, the WEU was identified as a useful vehicle for cosying up to its preferred, but less accessible, organizational partners. For a discussion of the Ukrainian and Russian positions see P. van Ham, 'Ukraine, Russia and European security: implications for Western policy', *Chaillot Paper*, no. 13, Paris: WEU ISS, February 1994.

292. Since revitalization the WEU had discussed practical member-state co-operation for implementing arms control agreements including the Conventional Forces Europe treaty verification regime, with an Expert Group working on the possibility of constructing multinational inspection teams including CEE states, of training inspectors and of finding the means to establish an effective and economic means of implementing the 'Open Skies' agreement. See W. van Eekelen, 'WEU after two Brussels Summits', *Studia Diplomatica*, vol. 47, no. 2, 1994, p. 44.

293. See I. Lesser, *The Future of NATO's Mediterranean Initiative: Evolution and Next Steps*, Santa Monica: Rand, 2000, p. 40; and S. Biscop, *Euro-Mediterranean Security: A Search for Partnership*, Aldershot: Ashgate, 2003, pp. 51–2.

294. In the WEU's Declaration 1 attached to the Maastricht Treaty a review of the WEU's own provisions had been promised, to take place in 1996.

295. See WEU Council of Ministers, *Preliminary Conclusions on the Formulation of a Common European Defence Policy*, Noordwijk, 14 November 1994, cited extensively below.

296. WEU Council of Ministers, *Noordwijk Declaration,* Noordwijk, Netherlands, 14 November 1994.
297. T. Dodd, *Towards the IGC: Developing a Common Defence Policy,* RP 95/45, International Affairs and Defence Section, House of Commons Library, 6 April 1995, p. 20.
298. J. Cutileiro, 'WEU's operational development and its relationship to NATO', *NATO Review,* vol. 43, no. 5, September 1995, p. 9.
299. WEU Council of Ministers, *Common Reflection on the New European Security Conditions,* Lisbon, Portugal, 15 May 1995.
300. Post-Noordwijk the role of the Planning Cell had been enlarged to include compiling ROE for WEU missions, preparing standard operating procedures for selected headquarters, and planning and evaluating exercises. For the WEU's 'operational doctrine' and details of the Planning Cell see B. Rosengarten, 'The role of the Western European Union Planning Cell', in Deighton (ed.) *Western European Union 1954–1997,* pp. 157–65; Brig. G. Messervy-Whiting, 'The refinement of the WEU's operational capability', *NATO's Sixteen Nations,* Special Supplement, 'The 50th Anniversary of the Brussels Treaty', 1998, pp. 9–14.
301. Sir Dudley Smith cited in S. Kay, *NATO and the Future of European Security,* Lanham: Rowman and Littlefield, 1998, p. 130. The Satellite Centre had proven useful in its monitoring of the embargo against Serbia on the Danube, indicating truck movement in shallow waters in contravention of the embargo. See van Eekelen, *Debating European Security,* p. 100.
302. See WEU Assembly, rapporteur Mr Baumel, *A European Intelligence Policy,* doc. 1517, 13 May 1996. The NATO-WEU agreement signed in June 1996 provided for intelligence exchange between the two organizations, although caveated.
303. For discussion see WEU Assembly, *Proceedings of a Colloquy on a European Space Based Observation System, March 24–5, 1995,* Paris, 1995. The Assembly were active supporters of a European satellite observation capability and, through the work of their Technology and Aerospace Committee, had also promoted discussion of a European ballistic missile defence as a further area for collaborative development of space-based technology. See WEU Assembly, rapporteur M. Lenzer, *An Anti-missile Defence for Europe,* doc. 1363, 17 May 1993; C. Covault, 'WEU seeks European missile defence plan', *Aviation Week and Space Technology,* 18 January 1993, pp. 25–6. Also see WEU Assembly, rapporteur Mr Atkinson, *Transatlantic Co-operation on European Anti-missile Defence,* pt. 1, doc. 1435, 9 November 1994, and pt. 2, doc. 1588, 4 November 1997.
304. The Council sought to encourage European consortium in the development of systems such as the Helios 2 and ill-fated Horus projects.
305. WEU Council of Ministers, *Lisbon Declaration,* Lisbon, Portugal, 15 May 1995. The Satellite Centre sought to obtain its imagery from a wide source base of commercial suppliers, including the US Landsat, French Spot, Canadian Radarsat, Indian IRS and, once operational in 1996, the Franco-Italian-Spanish Helios defence observation satellite.
306. The Southern Mediterranean states were not so enthusiastic, as these multinational forces stood outside the authority of the organizational structures in which they had established a dialogue and had an evidently Mediterranean, and potentially interventionary, vocation. Offers of co-operation with EUROFOR and EUROMARFOR for those states engaged in the WEU Mediterranean Dialogue in May 1997 contributed to a lowering of concerns amongst the Mediterranean partners. See Biscop, *Euro-Mediterranean Security,* pp. 53–4. Also see WEU Assembly, rapporteur M. Lipkowski, *Security in the Mediterranean Region,* doc. 1543, 4 November 1996.

307. Whilst EUROMARFOR was to consist of pre-structured force packages, EUROFOR had no forces pre-assigned to it, and the UK-France Airgroup based in High Wycombe had no standing operational structures. See 'EUROFOR and EUROMARFOR:WEU's new Latin twins', *RUSI Newsbrief*, vol. 15, no. 7, July 1995, pp. 49–51; and Dodd, *Towards the IGC*, p. 17.

308. WEU Assembly (Session 40, Part 1), *Replies of the Council to Recommendations 547 to 556*, doc. 1423, 8 June 1994, Recommendation 552, pp. 20–2.

309. Initiated as a Eurocorps exercise within the framework of the Petersberg Declaration, WEU CRISEX 95–96 became a full WEU exercise, conducted in three phases, beginning in Brussels in December 1995 with the setting up of consultation procedures at the strategic level. Phase two, conducted in June 1996, validated the decision-making and force generation processes as well as the command and control procedures between the strategic decision-makers in Brussels and the operational commander. Phase three, in December 1996, tested the force commander and the deployment of force concept within a peacekeeping scenario. See Rosengarten, 'The role of the Western European Union Planning Cell', pp. 166–7.

310. A. Politi, 'Western European Union and Europe's defence industry', in Deighton (ed.) *Western European Union 1954–1997*, p. 139.

311. Rees, *The Western European Union at the Crossroads*, p. 71.

312. Smith, 'What's wrong with the CFSP?', pp. 165–6.

313. Declarations on Western European Union.

314. The IEPG and subsequent WEAG consisted of the 10 full WEU members plus Turkey, Denmark and Norway. Van Eekelen noted the difficult task of persuading the non-WEU states of the benefits of the IEPG transfer, fearing as they did a less equal status in the organization. Van Eekelen, *Debating European Security*, pp. 283–5.

315. See WEU Assembly, rapporteur Mr Colvin, *European Armaments Restructuring and the Role of the WEU*, doc. 1623, 9 November 1998. for a useful overview.

316. For a discussion of the WEAG structure, including the work of its four panels on equipment, R&D, procedures and study on a European Armaments Agency, see A. Schlieper (then Chairman of the WEAG-NADs and Deputy Chairman of the WEAO Board of Directors), 'Armaments cooperation in the WEU', *NATO's Sixteen Nations*, Special Supplement, 'The 50th Anniversary of the Brussels Treaty', 1998, pp. 62–6.

317. P. van Ham, 'The prospects of a European security and defence identity', *European Security*, vol. 4, no. 4, winter 1995, p. 539. Also see I. Anthony, 'Arms procurement after the Cold War: how much is enough to do what (and how will we know)?', *International Affairs*, vol. 74, no. 4, October 1998, pp. 871–83. Whilst the French were to remain highly protectionist, the British had continued the process of gradually opening up its defence market, through collaboration and competition, which had begun in the 1980s. See G. de Fraja and K. Hartley, 'Defence procurement: theory and UK policy', *Oxford Review of Economic Policy*, vol. 12, no. 4, winter 1996, pp. 70–88.

318. And this without the 'burden of a large institutional bureaucracy and the tradition of work sharing which had been regarded as the fatal flaw of many previous endeavours'. M. Rogers, 'Identity crisis: European defence', *Jane's Defence Weekly*, 3 June 1998, p. 51. In 1998 the OCCAR Convention was signed by the four Defence Ministers, coming into effect in January 2001, giving the organization a legal identity. S. Fraser, 'OCCAR—five years on', *Military Technology*, Special Issue, vol. 28, 2004, p. 20.

319. Ministers at the Ostend meeting also signed a Memorandum of Understanding on THALES, Technology Arrangements for Laboratories for

Defence European Science, intended to implement government-supported joint research and information exchange, provided to industry and defence agencies in order to enhance technology development and interoperability between defence forces.

320. See Duke, *The Elusive Quest for European Security,* p. 270; and discussion in WEU Assembly, Symposium, *European Co-operation on the Procurement of Defence Equipment* (Munich, 1–2 October 1997), Paris: WEU Assembly, 1997.

321. M. Quinlan, *European Defence Cooperation: Asset or Threat to NATO?,* Washington, DC: Woodrow Wilson Center Press, 2001, p. 11. Given the historically central strategic standing of the national defence industry during the Cold War, Politi notes the constituent advantage of the WEU, in linking together NATO and EU members alongside the CEE states, along with special dialogue with Russia and Ukraine, in enabling a level of informal dialogue on post-Cold War defence industrial development 'in full view of the sister organisations'. A. Politi, 'The future of the European defence industry', in Lenzi (ed.) *WEU at Fifty,* pp. 69 and 78.

322. Transfer was agreed in principle by Eurogroup Defence Ministers on 25 May 1992 and welcomed by the WEU Petersberg Declaration the following June. EUROCOM's objective was to promote tactical land communication system interoperability. The WELG aimed at increased WEU member co-operation in logistics support for WEU missions and greater efficiency and harmonization of acquisition and logistics policy and doctrine applicable to WEU operations. EUROLONGTERM's role was the development of the conceptual basis for long-term military planning between WEU states, on which military capabilities and equipment requirements beyond a 10-year time frame might be determined. See Council of Europe (ed.) *European Yearbook Volume 42 (1994),* The Hague: Martinus Nijhoff, 1996, p. 8.

323. See E. Derycke, 'The Transatlantic Forum', *NATO's Sixteen Nations,* Special Supplement, 'The 50th Anniversary of the Brussels Treaty', 1998, pp. 55–6.

324. WEU Council of Ministers, *European Security: A Common Concept of the 27 WEU Countries,* Madrid, Spain, 14 November 1995.

325. The French had originally sought a summary of national White Papers. See van Eekelen, *Debating European Security,* p. 250.

326. WEU Council of Ministers, *WEU Contribution to the European Union Intergovernmental Conference of 1996,* Madrid, Spain, 14 November 1995.

327. Reflection Group Report, chaired by Carlos Westendorp, Brussels, 5 December 1995.

328. WEU Assembly, rapporteur Mrs Aguiar, *The Future of European Security and Preparations for Maastricht II,* doc. 1458, 16 May 1995.

329. Coffey reports that UK operational units were down by 30% in Germany and over 40% in the UK. See J. I. Coffey, 'WEU after the second Maastricht', in Laurent and Maresceau (eds) *The State of the European Union,* p. 123.

330. See P. van Ham, 'The EU and WEU: from cooperation to common defence?', in G. Edwards and A. Pijpers (eds) *The Politics of European Treaty Reform: The 1996 Intergovernmental Conference and Beyond,* London: Pinter, 1997, pp. 306–25, for discussion of the IGC negotiations.

331. For critical assessment of the New Transatlantic Agenda see R. Ginsberg, 'US-EU relations: the commercial, political and security dimensions', in Laurent and Maresceau (eds) *The State of the European Union,* pp. 297–316.

332. Dorman notes that 'Options' was carried out in a 'strategic vacuum', resulting in the British Defence Forces retaining 'essentially the same basic force composition as they had during the Cold War but on a smaller scale'. A. Dorman, 'Crises and reviews in British defence policy', in A. Dorman, S. Croft, W. Rees

and M. Uttley (eds) *Britain and Defence, 1945–2000: A Policy Re-evaluation,* London: Longman, 2001, pp. 20–1.

333. De Fraja and Hartley, 'Defence procurement', pp. 70–1. Between 1990 and 1996, UK defence spending dropped from 4% to 3.2% of the gross domestic product.

334. In response to the Defence Minister's announcement of his 'Front Line First' plans, Labour MP Donald Anderson complained to the House of Commons that there was 'still no defence review, no attempt to strike an overall balance between commitments and resources . . . The Government has no coherent strategy'. House of Commons, *Hansard,* vol. 246, 14 July 1994, col. 1177.

335. Defence Minister Malcolm Rifkind, interview with *Newsnight,* BBC, 14 July 1994.

336. One senior British official had been drawn to comment, 'In Britain there has been no attempt to construct an honest intellectual rationale for the force structure. We have no foreign and defence policy'. Cited in J. Adams, 'British defence cuts dismay Pentagon', *The Sunday Times,* 17 July 1994.

337. Alliance cohesion had been weakened by the disputes over the arms embargo in Yugoslavia, whilst a Republican landslide in the November 1994 Congressional elections, on the back of the US 'route' in Somalia, suggested a more neo-isolationist US foreign policy stance, with declining provision for US military assistance both in Europe and further afield.

338. Dodd, *Towards the IGC,* p. 17. This co-operation was evidenced in the formation of the European Air Group; in collaborative defence procurement, such as the Common New Generation Frigate Programme, 'Project Horizon'; and perhaps most symbolically in the celebrations of the 90th anniversary of the Entente Cordial!

339. *Memorandum of the United Kingdom Government Approach to the Treatment of European Defence Issues at the 1996 Inter-governmental Conference,* distributed to EU members in March 1995 and cited throughout this paragraph.

340. See C. Bellamy, 'Defence memo outlines UK's Euro-strategy', *The Independent,* 2 March 1995; *Atlantic News,* no. 2699, 4 March 1995; B. Clark, 'UK more sceptical on European defence', *Financial Times,* 16 March 1995; M. Sheridan, 'UK urges bigger role for WEU', *The Independent,* 1 March 1995.

341. *A Partnership of Nations: The British Approach to the European Union Intergovernmental Conference 1996,* Cmd. 3181, London: FCO, March 1996. (The *Memorandum* of March 1995 was published as an annex to this paper.) The British also argued that the presence of the EU neutrals would constrain the ability of Europe to act if a merger was to take place.

342. Constructive abstention would allow a state to determine not to participate itself, but without preventing other states from acting on behalf of the Union. See *Agence Europe,* no. 6677, 29 February 1996, pp. 3–5.

343. Heathcoat-Amory, 'The next step for Western European Union', p. 135.

344. See House of Commons Defence Committee, *Western European Union,* Session 1995–96, 4th Report, London: HMSO, 8 May 1996, especially para. 46 on the British WEU Presidency agenda.

345. C. Bellamy, 'Major opposes EU role in defence', *The Independent,* 24 February 1996.

346. For the British 'pragmatic' development of WEU capability see WEU Council of Ministers, *Birmingham Declaration,* 7 May 1996. Interviews held at the FCO, 1996.

347. P. Schmidt, 'German strategic options', in C. Bluth, E. Kirchner and J. Sperling (eds) *The Future of European Security,* Aldershot: Dartmouth, 1995, pp. 32–3.

348. For a detailed discussion of the Constitutional Court's rulings see W. Von Heinegg, 'Decision of the German Federal Constitutional Court of 12 July 1994', *Netherlands International Law Review*, vol. 41, no. 3, December 1994, pp. 285–311. Also see K. Kinkel (then German Minister of Foreign Affairs), 'Peacekeeping missions: Germany can now play its part', *NATO Review*, vol. 42, no. 5, October 1994, pp. 3–7.

349. Fears of an increasingly assertive Fourth Reich were, however, overplayed in the light of popular resistance to an increased military role and budgetary constraints on defence expenditure. See M. Walker, 'Overstretching Teutonia: making the best of the Fourth Reich', *World Policy Journal*, vol. 12, no. 1, spring 1995, pp. 10–12.

350. See R. Niblett, 'The European disunion: competing visions of integration', *Washington Quarterly*, vol. 20, no. 1, winter 1997, pp. 105–7.

351. D. White, 'Britain isolated over EU defence merger', *Financial Times*, 15 November 1995; I. Mather, 'Still at odds on the shaky road to a common defence policy', *The European*, 12 April 1996.

352. Livre Blanc sur la Defénce, La Documentation Française, March 1994.

353. See C. G. Cogan, *Forced to Choose: France, the Atlantic Alliance and NATO— Then and Now*, Westport: Praeger, 1997, p. 131.

354. Jean-Claude Casanova cited in Gregory, *French Defence Policy*, p. 125.

355. See R. Tiersky, 'France, the CFSP, and NATO', in Laurent and Maresceau (eds) *The State of the European Union*, pp. 177–88.

356. C. Millon, 'France and the renewal of the Atlantic Alliance', *NATO Review*, vol. 44, no. 3, May 1996, pp. 13–16. Ambassador Robert Hunter, the US Permanent Representative to NATO, commented that Chirac's 'courageous decision' to accept the 'proposition that the ESDI should be built within NATO, not outside it and in competition with it; that it should be supportive of the transatlantic link rather than a rival to it' made for 'quite startling' progress towards the opening of CJTFs to the WEU, a work that proceeded 'as a more or less technical exercise ever since'. R. Hunter, 'The US and Europe— a parting of the ways or new commitments?', in E. Foster and G. Wilson (eds) *CJTF—a Lifeline for a European Defence Policy*, London: RUSI, 1997, pp. 73–4.

357. Early German concerns regarding Chirac had been confirmed by the lack of European consultation preceding the resumption of French nuclear tests in the summer of 1995 and his announcement the following February of his intention to abolish conscription. G. Hendriks and A. Morgan, *The Franco-German Axis in European Integration*, Cheltenham: Elgar, 2001, pp. 119–22.

358. Rees, *The Western European Union at the Crossroads*, p. 117.

359. NAC Ministerial Meeting, *Final Communiqué*, Berlin, 3 June 1996, here para. 3, commonly referred to as the Berlin Communiqué and referenced throughout this section.

360. M. Bentinck (then Head of Defence Policy in NATO's Defence Planning Operations Division), 'NATO's structural reform and the ESDI', in Foster and Wilson (eds) *CJTF—a Lifeline*, p. 79.

361. The Berlin Communiqué notes NATO's ambition to increase the participation of partner countries and to integrate new members into the Alliance's military structure, whilst adopting flexible arrangements to enable 'selective' participation.

362. Hill and Smith (eds), *European Foreign Policy*, p. 232.

363. Gregory, *French Defence Policy*, p. 113.

364. On 12 June 1997, Washington declared that the matter was formally closed. Hendriks and Morgan, *The Franco-German Axis in European Integration*, p. 121.

365. Howorth suggests that by 1997 'hegemony was unacceptable, balance unattainable' in the transatlantic relationship. J. Howorth, 'Foreign and defence policy cooperation', in J. Peterson and M. Pollack (eds) *Europe, America, Bush: Transatlantic Relations in the Twenty-first Century*', London: Routledge, 2003, p. 15.

366. The WEU Planning Cell provided NATO's Combined Joint Planning Staff with six illustrative mission profiles for WEU operations that might require NATO assets for consideration: separation of parties by force, conflict prevention, assistance to civilians, imposition of sanctions, containment, and the guarantee and denial of movement. WEU input into the NATO Defence Planning Process following the NAC decision at Berlin and agreement at the WEU's Ostend Ministerial on 19 November 1996, resulted in a WEU contribution to NATO's 1997 Ministerial Guidance which set the parameters for the following planning cycle and ensured consideration of the WEU's requirements related to the Petersberg Tasks. See A. J. K. Bailes, 'WEU and NATO', *NATO's Sixteen Nations*, Special Supplement, 'The 50th Anniversary of the Brussels Treaty', 1998, pp. 49–50.

367. Bentinck, 'NATO's structural reform and the ESDI', p. 83.

368. For discussion of the developing DSACEUR role see General Sir J. MacKenzie (then DSACEUR), 'ESDI in NATO', *NATO's Sixteen Nations*, Special Supplement, 'The 50th Anniversary of the Brussels Treaty', 1998, pp. 51–4. By the time of the Madrid Summit, the core of three CJTF HQs had been established within NATO HQs in Naples, Brunsuum and Norfolk, Virginia, and greater detail was given to the CJTF concept, including the arrangements for release, monitoring and return of NATO assets. See A. Cragg, 'Internal adaptation: reshaping NATO for the challenges of tomorrow', *NATO Review*, vol. 45, no. 4, July–August 1997, p. 34.

369. G. de Nooy, 'NATO's structural reform and the ESDI: a good idea wasted', in Foster and Wilson (eds) *CJTF—a Lifeline*, p. 86.

370. W. van Eekelen, 'Europe's role and the CJTF', in Foster and Wilson (eds) *CJTF—a Lifeline*, pp. 63–5.

371. Echeverria, 'Cooperation in peacekeeping', p. 27. The Planning Cell proceeded to construct a database to identify suitable available training facilities and opportunities across Europe in support of African peacekeeping development.

372. Document 96/670/CFSP: Council Decision of 22 November 1996 adopted on the basis of Article J.4.2 of the TEU on the elaboration and implementation of a Joint Action by the Union in the Great Lakes region.

373. G. Olsen, 'Western Europe's relations with Africa since the end of the Cold War', *Journal of Modern African Studies*, vol. 35, no. 2, June 1997, p. 316.

374. Silvestri suggests that UK opposition was largely 'prompted by unwillingness to reinforce the prospect of a strong EU-WEU common military action a few months before the Amsterdam Conference' given the pressure for merger, whilst German resistance resulted from pessimism about possible success, limited domestic support and an 'unwillingness to increase German exposure in the Balkans'. S. Silvestri, 'The Albanian test case', *International Spectator*, vol. 32, nos. 3–4, July 1997, pp. 92–3.

375. UNSC Resolution 1101, 28 March 1997.

376. For a discussion of responses to the Albanian crisis see E. Foster, 'Ad hoc in Albania: did Europe fail?', *Security Dialogue*, vol. 29, no. 2, June 1998, pp. 213–17; and F. Tanner, 'Conflict management and European security: the problem of collective solidarity', paper prepared for the first Geneva Centre for Security Policy Seminar, Leukerbad, Switzerland, 21–22 August 1998, online at http://www.isn.ethz.ch/3isf/Online_Publications/WS4/Tanner.htm.

377. Cited in G. de Briganti, 'WEU spurns Albania but promises future humanitarian tasks', *Defence News*, 7–13 April 1997.

378. Views expressed during discussions on 'The Demise of the Western European Union: Lessons for European Defence', Chatham House, London, 10 May 2011.

379. Given the poor level of police training and the positive response to the WEU's activities, the original three-month deployment was extended, first to October and then to April 1998, with the option of further extensions.

380. Admiral R. de Morales (then Director of the Planning Cell), 'The WEU's Multinational Advisory Police Element in Albania', *NATO's Sixteen Nations,* Special Supplement, 1998, p. 6.

381. This was to include information exchange at the politico-military level in Brussels and co-operation with the European Commission's PHARE programme on public administration reform, drawn up largely on the basis of MAPE advice; with OSCE and Council of Europe activities through the co-ordination of the 'Vranitzky Group'; and with a range of national assistance initiatives. De Morales, 'The WEU's Multinational Advisory Police Element in Albania', p. 60.

382. Tanner, 'Conflict management and European security', p. 8.

383. See WEU Council of Ministers, *Paris Declaration,* Paris, 13 May 1997, paras. 21–2. Also see A. Missiroli, 'Flexibility and enhanced cooperation after Amsterdam—prospects for CFSP and the WEU', *International Spectator,* vol. 33, no. 3, August–September 1998, p. 115.

384. M. Reichard, *The EU-NATO Relationship: A Legal and Political Perspective,* Aldershot: Ashgate, 2006, p. 96.

385. Smith, 'What's wrong with the CFSP?', p. 164.

386. Van Eekelen, replaced as WEU Secretary General by Cutileiro in 1994, noted that 'if the relationship between the WEU and NATO is not perfect, it is nonetheless heaven compared to that between the WEU and the EU. I was invited only once to a meeting of the General Affairs Council when they discussed Yugoslavia, and I do not believe that my successor has yet been present there'. Van Eekelen, 'Europe's role and the CJTF', p. 60.

387. Bretherton and Vogler, *The European Union as a Global Actor,* pp. 205–6. See also J. Paganon, 'Western European Union's pivotal position between the Atlantic Alliance and the European Union', in Deighton (ed.) *Western European Union 1954–1997,* pp. 93–102.

388. France, Germany, Belgium, Italy, Luxembourg and Spain, with the support of the Dutch Presidency. See *Agence Europe,* no. 6941, 24–25 March 1997, pp. 4–5. In fact, this was a gradualist approach to the development of a truly European defence competence, referred to in the Spanish case as 'realist Europeanism', 'Europeanist in objectives, intergovernmentalist in methods and gradualist in terms of processes adopted'. E. Barbé, 'Spain and CFSP: the emergence of a "major player"?', in R. Gillespie and R. Youngs (eds) *Spain: The European and International Challenges,* London: Frank Cass, 2001, pp. 48–50.

389. See R. Whitman, 'Amsterdam's unfinished business? The Blair government's initiative and the future of the Western European Union', *Occasional Paper,* no. 7, Paris: WEU ISS, 1999, p. 5.

390. J. Goulden, 'The WEU's role in the new strategic environment', *NATO Review,* vol. 44, no. 3, May 1996, pp. 21–4.

391. J. Lichfield, 'Cook says EU may have a defence role', *The Independent,* 14 May 1997.

392. See for example 'Security co-operation', *The Irish Times,* 15 May 1995, which refers to the first high-profile Irish delegation attendance at the WEU Council meeting in Lisbon as an 'important symbolic step in Ireland's deepening security co-operation with our [sic] EU partners', reflecting a recognition on the

part of all of the attending neutrals of the need to be fully informed of WEU developments in the run-up to the IGC debate.

393. I. Mather, 'Neutral states dither', *The European*, 19 May 1995.
394. WEU Council of Ministers, *Paris Declaration*, Paris, 13 May 1997.
395. Consolidated Version of the Treaty on European Union (incorporating changes made by the Treaty of Amsterdam), *Official Journal*, C 340, 10 November 1997. The provisions on CFSP come largely within Title V, Articles 11–28.
396. Treaty of Amsterdam Amending the Treaty on European Union, the Treaties Establishing the European Communities and Certain Related Acts, signed 2 October 1997, ratified 1 May 1999.
397. F. Pagani, 'A new gear in the CFSP machinery: integration of the Petersberg Tasks in the Treaty on European Union', *European Journal of International Law*, vol. 9, no. 4, 1998, p. 742. See WEU Assembly, rapporteur Mr Vrettos, *WEU after Amsterdam: The European Security and Defence Identity and the Application of Article V of the Modified Brussels Treaty*, doc. 1584, 19 November 1997, for a critical assessment of the impact of this integration.
398. See van Eekelen, *Debating European Security*, p. 271.
399. Consolidated TEU Article 17.1 (TOA J.7.1). The 'constitutional' reference does suggest an opt-out even following European Council agreement, and, of course, unanimity principles ensured an effective national veto on such a recommendation.
400. Consolidated TEU Article 13 (TOA J.3). Bretherton and Volger, *The European Union as a Global Actor*, p. 189.
401. Consolidated TEU Article 23.2 (TOA J.13.2). More clearly defined, joint actions address 'specific situations where operational action by the Union is required'; common positions 'define the approach of the Union to a particular matter of a geographic or thematic nature'. Consolidated TEU Articles 14 and 15 (TOA J.4 and J.5).
402. French and German proposals for 'enhanced cooperation' in defence, enabling a level of 'variable geometry' already provided for in the Maastricht 'opt-outs' over monetary union and social policy and in the Schengen border agreement, had found little support and were dropped from the final draft. See *Agence Europe*, no. 20009, 29 October 1996. For discussion of 'multi-speed', 'variable geometry' and 'á la carte' approaches to overcoming the lack of consensus see Missiroli, 'Flexibility and enhanced cooperation after Amsterdam', pp. 103–4.
403. Article VIII of the MBT had provision for WEU Council decision-making at less than consensus, it being required only to 'decide by unanimous vote questions for which no other voting procedure has been or may be agreed', although this possibility had not been actively pursued.
404. Consolidated TEU Article 18.3 and 26 (TOA J.8.3 and J.16).
405. For a discussion of the role of the PPEWU see J. Lodge and V. Flynn, 'The CFSP after Amsterdam: the Policy Planning and Early Warning Unit', *International Relations*, vol. 14, no. 1, April 1998, pp. 7–21.
406. WEU Council of Ministers, *Declaration of Western European Union on the role of Western European Union and its Relations with the European Union and with the Atlantic Alliance*, Brussels, 22 July 1997 (Brussels Declaration).
407. See Section A of the declaration on 'WEU's relations with the European Union: Accompanying the implementation of the Treaty of Amsterdam'. Other areas included co-operation in armaments, within the framework of the WEAG, the EU and the WEU in the context of the rationalization of the European armaments market and the establishment of an EAA; co-operation with the Commission; and improved security arrangements with the EU.
408. NAC, *Madrid Declaration on Euro-Atlantic Security and Cooperation Issued by the Heads of State and Government*, Madrid, 8 July 1997.

409. 'WEU stands today as the only reference point in terms of European defence, and can now draw on NATO assets for certain operations. Its prospects are better now than they have ever been'. President of the WEU Assembly Lluis Maria de Puig cited in A. Kintis, 'NATO-WEU: an enduring relationship', *European Foreign Affairs Review,* vol. 3, no. 4, December 1998, p. 555.

410. Para. 11 of the WEU declaration of July 1997 mimics here the NATO Berlin Communiqué of 1996, para. 7, and as restated in the July 1997 Madrid Declaration, para. 18.

411. See Section B of the declaration, entitled 'Relations between WEU and NATO in the framework of an ESDI within the Atlantic Alliance'. Areas for developing co-operation included crisis-consultation mechanisms; involvement in NATO's defence planning process; operational links for the planning, preparation and conduct of WEU operations using NATO assets; the framing of an agreement on the transfer, monitoring and return of NATO assets and capabilities; and liaison on command arrangements.

412. See Section C of the declaration, entitled 'WEU's operational role in the development of the ESDI'.

413. This was to include 'generic and contingency planning and exercising, preparation and interoperability of forces, including participation in the NATO defence planning process'. *Declaration of Western European Union*, 22 July 1997, section C, para. 14.

414. At their Paris meeting in May 1977, the Council determined to establish a WEU Military Committee, intended to support the Council in military matters and facilitate improved co-operation with NATO. An implementation plan was approved at the Erfurt Ministerial meeting in November.

415. Duke, *The New European Security Disorder,* p. 235.

416. See Address by Dr Javier Solana, Secretary General of the WEU, Council of Ministers Session at 21, Marseille, 13 November 2000.

417. TEU, Title V, 'Provisions on a Common Foreign and Security Policy' Article J.4.1.

418. It is interesting to compare the 'Common Concept' with the European Security Strategy of December 2003, where a similar threat base is identified by the High Representative for CFSP, Javier Solana, in his efforts to provide a common 'vision' from which to develop a coherent security strategy for the EU. See *A Secure Europe in a Better World—The European Security Strategy,* approved by the European Council, Brussels, 12 December 2003.

419. K. E. Jørgensen, 'The WEU: sleeping beauty is awake', in T. Flockhart (ed.) *From Vision to Reality: Implementing Europe's New Security Order,* Boulder: Westview Press, 1998, pp. 86–7.

420. W. van Eekelen, interview with author, The Hague, January 1997.

421. J. Baylis, 'European security between the "logic of anarchy" and the "logic of community"', in C. C. Hodge (ed.) *Redefining European Security,* New York: Garland, 1999, p. 21, suggests the WEU took a 'combination' approach, offering inclusion through direct involvement akin to the OSCE, whilst preparing the ground for gradual integration more in line with the 'exclusive' EU/NATO method.

422. Wohlfeld, 'Closing the gap', p. 79.

423. Cutileiro described the 'main purpose' of the WEU by 1996 as developing the operational means to deal with security crises 'in which North Americans will not want to become directly involved'. The WEU Secretary General excluded 'major threats' from the WEU purview, these being the remit of NATO, which was 'the cornerstone of European defence'. Address by José Cutileiro, 'WEU's pivotal position between the Atlantic Alliance and the European Union', Association for Western Cooperation, Reykjavik, 12 September 1996.

424. P. Gordon, 'Does Western European Union have a role?', in Deighton (ed.) *Western European Union 1954–1997*, p. 109.
425. Till notes the organization's impact on maritime co-operation, for example, as it proved able to 'reflect, and determine, a slow growth in the habits of cooperation in practical, empirical, day to day issues'. G. Till, 'Europe's maritime strategy: present context and future directions', in G. de Nooy (ed.) *The Role of European Naval Forces after the Cold War*, The Hague: Kluwer Law, 1996, p. 35.
426. Hunter, 'The US and Europe', p. 76.
427. See WEU Assembly, rapporteur Mr Blaauw, *Europe's Role in the Prevention and Management of Crises in the Balkans*, doc 1589, 5 Nov 1997, p. 2; and P. H. Gordon, 'Europe's uncommon foreign policy', *International Security*, vol. 22, no. 3, winter 1997–8, pp. 92–3.
428. De Spiegeleire, 'From mutually assured debilitation to flexible response', p. 19.
429. De Spiegeleire, 'From mutually assured debilitation to flexible response', p. 19.
430. Moens, 'Behind complementarity and transparency', p. 39.
431. 'The number of critics still calling the WEU ineffectual is dwindling . . . More and more analysts have begun to take the fully awakened Rip van Winkle of Europe as a serious security player for the future'. C. Barry, 'Forging a new trans-Atlanticism', in C. Barry (ed.) *Reforging the Trans-Atlantic Relationship*, Washington, DC: National Defence University Press, 1996, p. 14.
432. J. B. Collester, 'How defence 'spilled over' into the CFSP: Western European Union (WEU) and the European Security and Defence Identity', in M. Green Cowles and M. Smith (eds) *The State of the European Union. Volume 5: Risks, Reform, Resistance, and Revival*, Oxford: Oxford University Press, 2000, p. 377.
433. Quinlan, *European Defence Cooperation*, p. 25.

5 The Final Compromise
1997–2011

During the mid 1990s, the largely unexpected re-emergence of NATO suggested something of a 'missed opportunity' for any truly European defence co-operation.[1] The demise of the Cold War bipolar overlay in Europe had cast a new light on a complexity of multifarious security challenges. This had suggested a fertile ground for the developing European Union, keen to exercise its new-found confidence in the pursuit of common external interests. However, as Europe's aspirations came up against the political realities of Bosnia, the immediate state reflex had not been to strengthen collective military competence through co-operation within the EU context, but rather to put individual national efforts towards a reinvigorated NATO. Given the EU's untested and limited institutional provisions in the sphere of crisis management, events in the Balkans had failed to provide the external impetus for positive change, rather 'scaring the horses' into the more familiar harness of alliance with their North American ally. Having entered the fray in response to the EU's impotence in conflicts in its own backyard, NATO had begun a gradual transformation, reasserting its relevance as the primary European security organization. Member states had embraced the Petersberg Tasks as an area of 'competence' for the EU in the 1997 Amsterdam Treaty, but the absence of any further significant provision for CFSP development suggested a lack of common will to move beyond the muddy compromise of 'outsourced' defence through the contracted arrangement with the WEU. As the decade progressed, NATO looked towards redefinition with the development of its new Strategic Concept, to fit it for the security challenges of a new century, whilst the 'false dawn' of EU defence was largely sidelined by the bright hope of the developing project of Economic and Monetary Union.

Left largely 'on hold' by the distractions of these primary institutions, the WEU had continued in its familiar role as institutional nanny throughout the 1990s, patiently seeking opportunities to develop and demonstrate closer European defence co-operation, whilst enhancing the relationship with NATO on which it continued to rely. By 1997 NATO's Berlin and Madrid Ministerials and the EU's Amsterdam Summit had firmly established the WEU as an organization that might support their ongoing interests, whilst the WEU retained its treaty-based ability to act independently should the member states so decide.[2] Having become the 'embodiment of ESDI' within the Alliance, to which it had been increasingly drawn throughout the decade, the WEU seemed secured for the foreseeable future as keeper of the European defence flame until such time as the EU could fulfil what many assumed to be its destiny as a full-fledged political and military actor. It certainly appeared that the time had not yet proved ripe for any major steps in the development of EU security and defence capability: economic integration might provide the necessary foundations, but experience suggested that it was not in itself sufficient to overcome pervasive sovereign assertion against integration in defence. This, combined with a UK-led resistant Atlanticism that largely defined transatlantic and European constituencies as at odds, if not in opposition, suggested a slow pace of change towards an uncertain future for the EU and a long haul for the WEU, the chosen articulation of the EU's unfulfilled promise. The conclusion reached at the WEU's Erfurt Ministerial of November 1997 was upbeat: despite the dramatically altered political environment of the decade, the WEU remained 'a valuable part of the European security architecture'. In the post-Amsterdam climate of continuing defence dependency, a full-spectrum EU crisis-management capability, as suggested by the incorporation of the Petersberg Tasks, required a reinforced relationship with the politico-military WEU with its recourse to the assets and capabilities of NATO. Hence, 'the enhancement of WEU's pivotal role between the European Union and NATO' remained a 'high priority on WEU's agenda'.[3]

The half-century anniversary of the Brussels Treaty in 1998 focused reflection on the past and future of the institution,[4] not least as the treaty provided for optional member-state withdrawal at the 50-year point.[5] Guido Lenzi, the Director of the WEU Institute for Security Studies, took this opportunity to question the effect that having both NATO and the EU as 'suitors' might have on the WEU's future development. 'Logically', he concluded, 'WEU ought now to constitute the bridge and possibly the conveyor belt between [NATO and the EU], providing the EU with a more solid operational underpinning and NATO with a more coherent European political commitment, for whenever specific needs arise that can motivate them to interact'.[6] However, as NATO increasingly asserted its 'operational priorities' and the EU sought to determine the 'political mandate' for any European missions, the WEU had been discouraged from taking the initiative and, Lenzi feared, might find its ability to act either independently or in support of the other organizations 'smothered' by its position 'tucked in the embrace of EU and NATO'.[7] The WEU's former Secretary General, Willem van Eekelen, appeared equally uncertain about the prognosis for this erstwhile 'reserve' organization, which he saw as increasingly 'swamped by NATO' and thwarted by the dual challenge of being considered either as a useless institution, unable to offer any real possibility of European military competency, or as an unwanted competitor and duplicator of the Alliance.[8]

DÉJÀ VU IN THE BALKANS

As the Kosovo crisis intensified through 1998 and into 1999 it provided the backdrop for a developing debate regarding the future of any European defence ambitions. The peace established by the Dayton Accords in Bosnia in 1995 had left unresolved tensions that bubbled on in Slobodan Milošević's new Federal Republic of Yugoslavia (FRY), which incorporated the former republics of Serbia and Montenegro.[9] The largely autonomous Serbian province of Kosovo, an Albanian-dominated region to the south, and the historical cradle of Serb nationalism, had been denied the prospect of secession. By early 1998, the increasingly active and violent forces of Kosovan independence, represented by the Kosovan Liberation Army (KLA), were being met by heavy Serbian resistance, resulting in an escalating cycle of violence throughout the summer.[10] KLA attacks on Serbian paramilitary targets and suspected 'collaborators' were met by brutal and indiscriminate reprisals against the ethnic Albanian Kosovan population. International pressure for an end to the violence and for negotiation on Kosovo's status was 'cold shouldered' by Belgrade as the Serb Government remained determined to maintain the integrity of the republic.[11]

With the EU supporting the reconvened Contact Group's diplomatic efforts to seek a negotiated settlement in the region,[12] the WEU Ministers, at their Rhodes Council of 11–12 May 1998, considered how the WEU might also contribute to the international effort. The decision was taken to task the Permanent Council to consider extension of the WEU's ongoing police advisory role in Albania (MAPE), given the spill-over of displaced Albanian Kosovans, to include advice on border and crowd control and further training and equipping of the Albanian police. A study by the WEU's Military Staff in July considered options to extend the organization's role beyond this uninspired 'training' commitment to include an international police mission in Albania, concluding that an estimated 600 police officers would be required, as well as a further 20,000 troops for the military protection force needed to establish a 'secure environment'. These figures provided the unenthusiastic Council with 'a good excuse to abandon the idea of an international police operation in Albania' and to 'sit on its hands' awaiting further developments. This lack-lustre response did not go unnoticed. Expressing his disappointment at the limitation of the WEU proposals, the European Commissioner, Hans van den Broek, was dismissive of the WEU's utility as a vehicle for enhancing European security co-operation, stating that the 'absence of result-oriented activities makes any discussion of WEU's role in the European security architecture a highly theoretical one'.[13]

With the US reticent to engage in another European conflict, the ensuing humanitarian crisis clearly necessitated some demonstration of international resolve if the warring parties were to be drawn to negotiate. In June, the NATO air exercise over Albania and the former Yugoslav Republic of Macedonia, Operation Determined Falcon, was intended to demonstrate the Alliance's capability to 'project power rapidly into the region'.[14] As this had little evident effect on the rising level of violence, 'endless discussions' on who should do what, where and how illustrated the failure of Europe and the US to match words with deeds. By the autumn it was estimated that 250,000 Albanian Kosovans had been driven from their homes and 50,000 found themselves without shelter as the winter approached.[15] In the face of a humanitarian disaster, and amidst charges of ethnic cleansing against the government in Belgrade, UNSC Resolution 1199 provided a trigger for unspecified 'further action and additional measures' in light of continuing non-compliance with the Security Council's demands.[16] With a growing international consensus on military action given mounting evidence of Serbian atrocities, and with the threat of NATO air strikes on the table, a deal was finally struck. On 3 October 1998, Milošević agreed to a plan, approved by the Contact Group and negotiated by US Special Envoy Richard Holbrooke, requiring a draw-down of Serbian forces and the deployment of an OSCE verification team, supported by airborne surveillance. But as Europe reflected on this, the second major crisis of the decade in the Balkans, the sense of *déjà vu* must have been palpable. In the much-reported view of the then US Ambassador to NATO, negotiating success had been clearly based on US power, and the 'harsh reality' was that only the US could effectively 'marry military power and diplomacy as a means of managing—and resolving—crises'. The simple lesson for the EU was that 'without more military muscle to back it up, the EU's Common Foreign and Security Policy could never duplicate the "Holbrooke effect"'.[17]

THE EUROPEAN INITIATIVE

During 1998 a significant shift became evident in British Government attitudes towards Europe, a shift that was to signal the 'beginning of the end' for the WEU. Prime Minister Tony Blair's 'New Labour' had entered office in May 1997 with a 'new broom', intent on reappraising Britain's relations with Europe and reassessing the UK's broader security interests. For the most Europhile UK Government since British entry into the EEC in the 1970s, Britain should place itself as a leader in Europe, capable of influencing both the US and her European partners through active engagement.[18] Pro-Europe rhetoric was nevertheless tempered by the realities of domestic Euro-scepticism, internal political divisions (not least over the economy)[19] and pervasive Atlanticist leanings that militated against any immediate and radical change in policy.

Indeed, when it came to defence, there was little early indication of a change from the behaviours and attitudes of the previous Conservative Government. Prime Minister Blair had been quick to reassure the House of Commons following the 1997 Amsterdam European Council that, whilst he had been keen to bring 'a fresh and constructive approach to Europe and to the negotiations', he had resisted any efforts towards 'developing an unrealistic Common Defence Policy' in the EU. 'We said that we would preserve NATO, not the European Union, as the cornerstone of the defence of Europe', he strutted, 'and we did', winning inclusion for the first time of an explicit treaty recognition of the position of NATO as 'the foundation of our and other allies' common defence'. Blair had been equally unambiguous about the future of the EU-WEU relationship—for him it was clear that 'getting Europe's voice heard more clearly in the world will not be achieved through merging the European Union and the Western European Union', as the latter's autonomy facilitated the most productive link between the Alliance and Europe's premature security and defence aspirations.[20]

The foreign policy-led *Strategic Defence Review* (*SDR*), published in July 1998, reflected the new Government's desire to reinstate the UK as a world player, whilst acknowledging the limitations imposed by necessarily declining defence budgets.[21] The *SDR*, intended to modernize and rationalize the overstretched UK armed forces and fit them for the future expeditionary, rapid-response requirements of the new security environment, emphasized power projection and strategic mobility over more traditional concerns of territorial defence.[22] In recognising that future operations would 'almost always be multinational', with the UK 'working as part of a NATO, UN or Western European Union force, or ad hoc "coalition of the willing"', the *SDR* made clear that NATO was to remain the primary European security organization, with the WEU providing the European pillar within the Alliance.[23]

However, only months after the publication of the *SDR*, the Blair Government had undergone an apparent change of heart over European defence. Speaking at the informal EU Summit held at Pörtschach in Austria on 24–25 October, the British Prime Minister enthusiastically argued 'for Europe to take a stronger foreign and security role' following its 'unacceptable' performance in Bosnia and Kosovo. This would require that the EU develop 'its own effective military capability able to take on Petersberg tasks', including effective decision-making structures, along with flexible and deployable forces for a credible underpinning of the CFSP. Significantly, Blair signalled that the WEU was 'less than ideal' as the instrument for ensuring this development and offered for the first time the 'possible integration' of the WEU into the EU as an option, a position favoured by the majority of the other EU member states but up to this point consistently rejected by the British.[24] Representing something of a 'Pandora's box', the British proposals were intended to open up debate rather than provide a definitive plan. In essence, the British sought a more effective EU intergovernmental decision-making system for defence matters, where Europe could carry out 'independent' military action through access to capabilities complementary to those of NATO. Beyond these basic interests nothing had been decided.[25]

So what explains this apparent seismic shift in the orientation of British policy, and specifically this 'new thinking' on the role of the WEU? It is apparent that a number of factors were at play as the new Labour Government 'bedded in'. With the British holding the rotating Presidency of the EU (January to the end of June 1998), it is perhaps not entirely surprising that the issue of European defence co-operation was to catch the attention of a largely Europhile and ambitious Prime Minister keen to make his mark in a Europe which was sliding once again into conflict and to enhance British influence as the US partner of choice.

The policy area of greatest significance for the EU in 1998 was the Single Currency to be instituted for 11 of the EU member states on 1 January 1999.[26] British domestic and political disquiet with the EU, and Treasury concerns about the cost of convergence, had led to the adoption of a slow pace of engagement in this fundamental area of European integration: UK entry into the EMU would be progressed only once certain criteria had been met and following a subsequent referendum of the British people. Given that this was unlikely to take place before the next General Election, the UK's aspiration to place itself at the heart of Europe was rather undermined by its 'distance' from this mainstream integrative project. The degree of correlation between Britain's self-exclusion from the EMU and the decision to adopt a more positive defence policy towards Europe is debatable. It is apparent, however, that the Blair Government was keen that the UK's influence in the EU should not be diminished by this exclusion, and this immediate concern would have provided a permissive environment for such a proposal to be seen with merit. With its defence shift, the British Government appeared to have been offering a compensation strategy in an area in which it had credible capability, a kind of perverse spill-over taking place where limitations in one area of policy drove forward actions in another.[27] With the Pörtschach meeting only two months before the launch of the Single Currency this may also help to explain how it was seen as policy 'on the hoof'.[28] And as this could potentially make the UK Government a 'leader rather than a spoiler' in this area of European affairs in which Britain had a comparative advantage, it opened up the possibility of establishing a close relationship with the French (as the other prime military-competent nation within the EU) and thus countering the dominance of the Franco-German 'axis' which had, over time, provided the engine of EU development.[29] Although defence was currently on the back burner of EU business, it was not likely to remain so as the EU 'project' intensified. Blair was later to argue, in defence of his Government's 'new' position, that 'it would be a tragic mistake—repeating mistakes of British European policy over the past few decades—if Britain opted out of the debate on European Defence Policy and left the field to others. This is a debate that we must shape and influence from the start, because our vital strategic interests are affected by it'.[30]

After the experience of the inadequacies of the EU's CFSP in Bosnia, the heightening of the Kosovo crisis during the UK's EU Presidency had served to highlight the impotence of the Europeans in managing security challenges in their own neighbourhood. By the summer of 1998 the EU had been forced to accept that it was unable to prevent further escalation of the conflict as diplomatic pressure on Belgrade to seek a peaceful settlement, including the imposition of military and economic sanctions, had little effect.[31] The British Prime Minister had been 'appalled' when briefed on the limited capability that the Europeans could offer to any potential NATO campaign in Kosovo[32] and was equally concerned by the impenetrable complexity of untried mechanisms for any EU-led action (incorporating the WEU and drawing on NATO assets).[33] If this lack of European capability continued, the credibility of Europe as a significant partner for the US would be in jeopardy, potentially undermining the very foundations of the Alliance. Without some rebalancing, the health of the Alliance was at risk, and only through greater co-operation in the European context could this be achieved. The British political investment in the WEU as the security institution of choice for collective European efforts, as the bridge between the EU and NATO and the focus of a European defence identity, had reached the limits of its likely pay-off, suggesting that the WEU had outlived its usefulness. Indeed, continuing attachment to the institution might even become an obstructive symbol of British resistance to greater co-operation with her European allies.[34] The lack of collective political will to pursue the ESDI route had resulted in a serious credibility gap in the institutionalization of collective European defence efforts. At the same time, Amsterdam had at least opened up the possibility of a more coherent crisis-management role for the EU, whilst European potential was indicated by the enthusiasm of the 'neutrals' for an active EU humanitarian presence, by national preparedness to engage in localized crises (as demonstrated by the Italians in Albania) and by the welcome removal of constitutional barriers to German participation in 'out-of-area' multinational peacekeeping.

And when it came to influence over the UK's key ally, the environment also seemed conducive to a change of direction. The Clinton Administration in Washington appeared to be increasingly exclusive of its allies in its dealings with matters of significant strategic interest for Europe, such as the Middle East. But this disinterest also manifested itself in an apparent decline in US resistance to European collective defence efforts.[35] In promoting a more effective 'defence Europe', the British Government could not only encourage the development of Europe as a more capable defence partner for the US but also ensure a special place for Britain at the heart of that relationship. Outlining the direction of his thinking in his November 1997 Guildhall speech, Blair called for a UK 'strong in Europe and strong with the US', stating that there was 'no choice between the two. Stronger with one means stronger with the other'. However, he went on to emphasize the purpose of this dual policy: 'Our aim should be to deepen our relationship with the US at all levels. We are the bridge between the US and Europe. Let us use it. When Britain and America work together on the international scene, there is little we can't achieve'.[36]

During the final months of the British EU Presidency, Blair had commissioned an FCO 'sweeping review' of the UK's approach to the EU, to be led by the diplomat Robert Cooper. The Government's new thinking presented at Pörtschach reflected the review's conclusion that it was crucial for the UK to demonstrate that it favoured closer integration in a number of areas, including foreign and defence policy; its confidential memorandum of May 1998 included recommendations for controversial new initiatives in these areas. The FCO proposals, elucidated in the 'think piece' by Charles Grant of the Centre for European Reform,[37] included the creation of a fourth EU pillar for defence policy which would subsume the Modified Brussels Treaty Article V provision and from which states could elect to opt out. The EU's second pillar would remain responsible for the softer end of crisis management, including conflict prevention and more traditional peacekeeping, whilst a new fourth pillar would deal with the harder aspects, including peace enforcement, for which NATO would provide the military capability. A new EU Council of Defence Ministers would be responsible for authorizing military action by requesting the use of NATO forces, and the WEU would be dismembered with transferral of its functions to the other two organizations.[38] This new structure would enhance CFSP credibility by enabling the EU to call on NATO military capabilities and would satisfy long-held continental desires for a WEU-EU merger, whilst allowing for EU enlargement to include those who did not seek a defence element. It would also contribute to the enhancement of NATO (and the US commitment to it) by confirming the Alliance's primary status and role. The WEU, which was in Grant's view 'going nowhere', would enhance the EU and NATO by this dying act of self-sacrifice, finally being 'put out of its misery'.[39]

It seems unlikely that, at the time of the Pörtschach statement, the Prime Minister had determined that the disposal of the WEU was necessarily the optimum option. Rather, he added some 'meat' to the initiative by suggesting four non-exclusive 'options' for institutional change: strengthening the ESDI in NATO, scrapping the WEU, creating a fourth pillar and establishing a European Defence Council.[40] By the time of the first informal meeting of the EU Defence Ministers in Vienna on 4 November 1998, the fourth-pillar approach had been sidelined, with the British Defence Minister, George Robertson, arguing for the simplification of the institutional structure, rather than further complication with new pillars.[41] Referring to the experiences of Bosnia and Kosovo, the big question of European defence, he argued, was surely whether 'when we press the button for action, is it connected to a system and a capability that can deliver'.[42] Prioritizing NATO, having not ruled out the possibility of enhancing the WEU, and insisting on the centrality of intergovernmentalism within any future arrangement, he argued that the 'cumbersome' nature of the EU-WEU-NATO relationship militated against the development of effective deliverable capability.[43] For the UK this was not to be about institutional semantics or some political ideal. What Europe needed, Blair had asserted at the Edinburgh meeting of the NAA (to be renamed the NATO Parliamentary Assembly), was 'genuine military operational capability' and 'genuine political will' to act, without which

European defence was no more than an 'empty shell'.[44] And whilst Blair asserted that he had 'no preconceptions' as to the optimum institutional architecture of any future European defence, in presenting the possibility of an EU-WEU merger, he had launched a process of European reflection in which the UK had successfully redefined itself from 'brakeman' to 'engine' of European development.[45]

Conservative opposition to what was seen as Blair's radical departure from a traditional and largely cross-party consensus on defence co-operation was raised in the House. Seemingly content with reported Government acceptance of a new Head for CFSP (something that had been proposed in the previous Conservative Government's 1996 White Paper), many in the Conservative Party were concerned by the surprise *volte face* on the WEU that, they believed, threatened to 'stand the whole of the Government's approach on its head'. Having only months before 'singled out' the WEU for 'special consideration' in the TOA, suggesting a 'strengthening of the WEU's position in the family of European organisations', the Prime Minister was now casting doubt on Britain's future co-operation with the organization. 'What conclusion', the Under Secretary of State for Defence John Spellar was asked, 'are people supposed to draw about the future of the WEU', which had hardly been given a 'ringing endorsement' by Blair's recent comments, and what did this policy shift imply with regards to the agreements set out in the TOA?[46]

Unsettled not least by the lack of parliamentary notification or discussion of the new proposals, the domestic Opposition 'forces' had just cause to query the potential changes that the Blair Initiative implied. But the extent to which this was a truly 'revolutionary' change in British politics, or in the approach of the incumbent Labour Government to the positioning of the UK in the world, is questionable.[47] The UK's persistent core principles—the maintenance of the state's relative status, its ability to actively engage in and influence global affairs, and its preference for international co-operation, both military and otherwise, in support of national interests—remained evident in subsequent British policy. The shift was rather one of detail, with Blair identifying the European option as a means of achieving UK objectives within these 'core preferences' at a time of changing power relations.[48] With Europe in the ascendant, and a Pacific-leaning US more inclined to unilateralism, leadership in Europe offered a repositioning of the UK as a 'pivotal' power between these two major actors. UK influence could derive from this unique interlocutor position, not in itself 'new' for the UK, but the maintenance of which would require a rebalancing of its crucial relationships. If the UK was to retain its influence with the US (which remained a priority objective of British policy under Blair), it would need to enhance its relationship with the Europeans, for one derived at least in part from the other. At the same time, European co-operation offered the opportunity of global influence in its own right, and the UK's interest could be best met through leadership rather than the follower-ship that had largely defined its earlier relations. The 'diplomatic revolution' came in the choice of Europe as the means of achieving international influence,[49] but although the inclination towards greater European co-operation clearly had some normative resonance within the new Government,[50] it was also a logical response in line with a traditional UK policy orientation towards core national interests.

THE FRENCH VIEW

The shifting of the British position coincided with a developing 'new mood' in Paris. Collective European action through the institutions of the EU had long been identified by Paris as a means by which US power could be counterbalanced, whilst enhancing the French 'presence' and interests where its own influence was weak or the cost of independent action prohibitive. The breadth of the security challenges facing the European region, combined with the limitations on any national response, ensured continuing French promotion of the EU's CFSP and a form of integrated defence within the EU that did not challenge national primacy.[51] Threatened with marginalization by the surprising reassertion of NATO through the mid 1990s, France had also begun to seek a closer relationship with the Alliance. The new interventionism of the post-Cold War environment required a French voice within the decision-making environs of the one serious military organization able and prepared to engage in support of French defence interests. And so, whilst Paris retained the Gaullist conviction of French exceptionalism largely in opposition to US power, the relationship with NATO had warmed significantly. By the autumn of 1998 the French had become the commanding framework nation for the all-European NATO Extraction Force in Macedonia, with the role to assist in any evacuation of the OSCE verification teams in Kosovo. As a demonstration of French willingness to participate 'flexibly' within NATO's integrated command structure as good and active allies,[52] this engagement had also offered the opportunity to 'spotlight' the potential utility of a European-only mission in support of Alliance interests, a point not lost on the Americans[53] and in line with French policy on the promotion of European initiatives in the area of security and defence.

In this context, and with the launch of the euro and the WEU anniversary approaching, President Jacques Chirac had first mooted new proposals for the future of the WEU in his August address to French Ambassadors in Paris, prior to the British Initiative. The French President had changed his mind about the WEU: having been significant in elaborating the Hague Platform to promote the development of the WEU in the 1980s, his enthusiasm had waned as the organization had failed to attract the political support required to make effective his European defence ambitions.[54] At the WEU's Rome Ministerial in November 1998, where it was agreed to launch a process of informal reflection on Europe's security and defence, the French outlined a series of proposals for the WEU, calling for a decision on its future by the April Ministerial.[55] Paris suggested that the WEU become, at least in the short term, a Defence Agency within the second pillar of the EU, representing a form of 'enhanced co-operation', as seen in the first and third pillars, and allowing for its gradual integration. With close defence co-operation between a 'core' of full members, and mechanisms for wider participation (as already promoted through the WEU's differentiated memberships), this Agency would enable other interested states to 'plug in' to European defence activity without the complications of treaty change or the requirement for neutrals' disengagement or approval.[56] Composed of the Foreign and Defence Ministers of interested member states the Agency would provide the political and strategic authority and direction for EU military operations, and would include within it structures for 'analysis, planning and military means'. These means would include enhanced multinational European forces, capable of mounting joint European operations, whilst it was proposed that the Agency might also draw on NATO assets, with collective defence remaining the primary remit of NATO.[57]

Rather overtaken by events, Chirac's Defence Agency proposals suggested a closer relationship between the political and military aspects of the CFSP than the fourth-pillar approach initially favoured by the British, whilst enabling the maintenance of the WEU's Article V commitment through the provision for neutral 'distance'. With both approaches suggesting that the WEU's demise was clearly on the table, the flexibility at the heart of each option was suggestive of divergent European futures. The British vision was a decentralized one of a core Europe of common activities and procedures around which different associations of like-minded states followed sectoral interests within distinct institutional arrangements, whilst the French vision was essentially a centralized one in which enhanced co-operation would provide a 'half-way house' to a more competent and coherent EU.[58]

And so, by the autumn of 1998, both the British and the French had come to the conclusion that their interests might be best met by greater co-operation with their 'former bête noir', the EU and NATO respectively.[59] This coincidence of assessment provided for a 'meeting of minds' over the future direction of European defence co-operation. Primarily motivated by distinct objectives—the British by the maintenance of the Alliance and the French by the prospects of enhanced European integration—interest began to converge on the benefits of pragmatic development of greater European co-operation within the EU framework.[60] Largely a practical consideration for the British, co-operation on European defence with a more NATO-amenable Paris would offer London immediate benefits in its influence in Europe and more essentially with the US, whilst the French could take the opportunity to steer the UK towards an inextricable engagement with Europe that could have lasting and profound effects on the future of the Union.

ST MALO: THE BEGINNING OF THE
END FOR THE WEU

On 3–4 December 1998 a 'historic agreement' was reached between the French and British at the conclusion of their summit meeting in St Malo, with the formal removal of the long-standing British resistance to the development of a substantive defence competence within the EU itself.[61] In acknowledging that 'the Union must have the capacity for autonomous action, backed up by credible military forces, the means to decide to use them, and a readiness to do so in order to respond to international crises', the St Malo Declaration provided the impetus for rapid development of a common European security and defence policy backed by credible operational capabilities.[62] A 'masterpiece of diplomatic language',[63] the meeting-point of the two national positions is evident throughout the Declaration and is nowhere clearer than in its stated common purpose: in 'strengthening the solidarity between the Member States of the European Union, in order that Europe can make its voice heard in world affairs, whilst acting in conformity with our respective obligations in NATO, we are contributing to the vitality of a modernised Atlantic Alliance'. Referring to common defence policy rather than a common defence, the Declaration made explicit the intergovernmental (non-federal) nature of European defence decision-making; Europe's ability to act would be drawn from a range of national and multinational assets, offering no suggestion of a European Armed Force. Europe was to develop capabilities for meeting 'international crises' in line with the Petersberg Tasks outlined in the provisions of the TOA, whilst NATO would remain 'the foundation of the collective defence of its members'. Significantly, the Declaration offered the prospect of 'autonomy' for European actions, although the level of this was not defined, and the aspiration to 'take decisions and approve military actions where the Alliance as a whole is not engaged' muted any challenge to the primacy of NATO and the transatlantic arrangement.[64]

Although the preferred future of the WEU was not clearly articulated in the Declaration, agreement on the common purpose of developing an 'autonomous' and tangible defence role for the EU did seem to suggest a shared Anglo-French belief that the WEU, as a 'subcontractor' for European defence, had reached the limits of its utility. Retention of the WEU's Article V was envisaged in the declaration, but otherwise the prospects for the organization looked bleak. The Franco-German Summit that had preceded the St Malo meeting had affirmed WEU integration into the EU as a common position, and the absence of collective defence from the St Malo proposals for the EU's common defence policy seemed likely to make them palatable to 'neutral' states already accepting of Petersberg Tasks within CFSP under the TOA. The WEU's historic role in filling the gap between Atlanticist and Europeanist desires appeared to have been truly supplanted by an emerging complementarity of interests. The declaration implied that the EU's scavenging of WEU functions might be extensive, and not only in the area of decision-making and military capability management; it was argued that the EU 'must be given appropriate structures and a capability for analysis of situations, sources of intelligence and a capability for relevant strategic planning, without necessary duplication taking account of the existing assets of the WEU and the evolution of its relations with the EU'.[65] And alongside the declaration, Anglo-French bilateral co-operation was to be intensified, aimed at 'improving the ability to plan and execute a combined response to crises in areas of mutual interest' and seeking to strengthen co-operation in 'operations, logistics, intelligence, civil-military affairs, media handling, and personnel and liaison'. This could provide the basis for broader and more inclusive co-operation aimed at operations 'outside NATO territory where NATO does not take the lead'.[66]

The timing of the St Malo Declaration appeared to be fortuitous given forthcoming events. Broadcast weeks before the launch of the EU's single currency, it preceded by only a few months the coming into force of the EU's TOA and the Washington celebrations of NATO's 50th anniversary, at which a new Strategic Concept for the Alliance was to be unveiled. Having crossed the 'European Rubicon' in acknowledging the requirement for an autonomous military capability for the EU, Blair had enabled a new era to begin in European integration, in which a more balanced and direct partnership in defence might be established between the US and Europe.[67]

A week after the St Malo meeting, at the European Council in Vienna, Germany, which was to take up the first synchronized Presidencies of both the WEU and EU Councils in January, was invited to consider further the issues raised by the Anglo-French Declaration in light of the forthcoming meeting in Cologne (3–4 June), where it would be discussed. This represented something of an opportunity for the recently elected Government of Gerhard Schröder and his Social Democrat/Green coalition to influence the international agenda. Once Schröder's Administration replaced the conservative Kohl Government in September 1998, a new enthusiasm for Germany to find its 'proper' post-unification place at the centre of Europe emerged in German politics.[68] Traditional partner reassurance through demonstrated Europeanism was to be accompanied by a post-'post-national' orientation to seek out a self-defined national interest, embedded in an active multilateralism with key European partners and, most particularly, through triangulation of the Anglo-French 'club'.[69] Berlin had little attachment to the WEU, one of whose original functions had been to keep strict control on German rearmament, and had consistently perceived the institution in purely instrumentalist terms. Recognizing the WEU's role as an interlocutor between the EU and NATO, and as a promoter and facilitator of European security and defence dialogue, Germany had long considered the WEU as a temporary, but necessary, institution if the EU was eventually to become the Alliance's second pillar.[70] But the WEU had proven itself largely ineffectual when it came to military co-operation, and the time had come for a streamlining of organizations. A security- and defence-competent EU, within which Germany had a much more significant presence than in the WEU or NATO relationships, would provide greater German influence over core areas of interest, contribute to the enhancement of the European 'project' and ensure a more balanced partnership in the Alliance.[71] The German vision was of NATO retained for collective defence and the EU developing a crisis-management role, which would require not only full integration of the WEU into the EU but the abandonment of intergovernmentalism in the CSFP domain if the EU was not to be paralysed by the lack of internal consensus.[72]

Identifying the St Malo Declaration as a 'good starting point for further steps', Chirac and Schröder's joint declaration of 11 January 1999 sought further consideration of a gradual absorption of the WEU into the EU.[73] In its February think piece entitled the 'Internal Reflection of WEU on European Security and Defence', the German Presidency offered a range of questions about the means by which Europe might develop a crisis-management capability as described at St Malo, forming the basis of debate within the EU and WEU.[74] The subsequent Reinhartshausen paper, tabled at the informal meeting of the EU Foreign Ministers on 13–14 March 1999, and later revised to reflect the language of the NATO Washington Communiqué, became the 'blueprint' for the forthcoming Cologne Report to be delivered at the end of the German EU Presidency.[75] Alongside discussion in the EU forum, tripartite talks between the French, British and Germans had resulted in an emerging consensus on some common lines of development, including the absence of EU Commission or Parliament involvement in the intergovernmental arrangements for defence, the role of NATO as the provider of collective defence and the EU as crisis manager and the requirement for political and military bodies in the EU able to draw on national, multinational and NATO assets to fulfil those crisis-management tasks.[76]

In the absence of the British 'alibi' for the maintenance of the WEU, however, a not altogether expected support for the organization began to emerge. Sceptical about British motivations behind its intentions for the WEU, the French began to consider whether the benefits of an Article V-carrying, defence-oriented and solely European institution might be lost in any 'merger' of the institutions. Given the continuing lack of consensus on the range of security issues facing Europe, WEU subordination to the EU might make any European security action more difficult, whereas retaining its autonomy could avoid EU-induced paralysis and leave open a range of options for influence by NATO/WEU member states.[77] Hence, throughout the first quarter of 1999, having been a driving force behind the WEU-EU merger proposals, the French began to speak of the 'useful role' played by the WEU as a bridge between the EU and NATO, and to argue that there should be no hasty absorption of the WEU into the EU until such time as the EU was developed sufficiently in capability and will to play the world role to which it was ultimately suited.[78]

The initial reaction in Washington to the St Malo Declaration had been, perhaps surprisingly, largely supportive. In an article in the *Financial Times* on 7 December, US Secretary of State Madeleine Albright welcomed the Blair Initiative, stating that 'our interests are clear: we want a Europe that can act. We want a Europe with modern, flexible military forces that are capable of putting out fires in Europe's backyard and working with us through the alliance to defend our common interests'. Albright argued that 'European efforts to do more for Europe's own defence make it easier, not harder, for us to remain engaged', although this was caveated by an emphasis on the importance of avoiding her 'three Ds', 'the triple dangers of decoupling (of European and NATO decision-making), duplication (of defence resources) and discrimination (against non-EU/NATO members)', in the developing architecture.[79] Washington sought to initiate early bilateral NATO-EU discussions on the implications of the St Malo proposals, but fears of US attempts to determine the development and outcome of the EU's new project led to persistent rebuttals from the new German EU/WEU Presidency.[80]

With the situation deteriorating in Kosovo, the British Prime Minister concentrated his efforts on placating Atlanticist concerns at home and abroad, developing a highly practiced narrative around the theme of the necessity for practical European capability development, rather than institutional 'fixes', in order to free the US from the necessity of engagement in 'every disorder in our own backyard'.[81] Nevertheless, the perennial dilemma of too much or too little Europe began to reassert itself in the months following the Anglo-French agreement. Just as Blair argued that a greater European defence co-operation was a requirement for a strong alliance, US Deputy Secretary of State Strobe Talbott reminded his London audience in March that 'if ESDI is misconceived, misunderstood or mishandled, it could create the impression—which could eventually lead to a reality—that a new European-only alliance is being born out of the old, trans-Atlantic one', and that this could 'weaken, perhaps even break those ties' between the US and Europe on which both NATO and the wider Atlantic Community were built.[82]

As the German EU/WEU Presidency prepared its forthcoming report for the Cologne Council, events in the Balkans could not help but colour the debate. With pressure mounting for a speedy resolution of the Kosovan crisis, the Chair of the WEU Assembly reflected an emerging European consensus that, if Europe was to 'break the monopoly of the US', which was 'trying to resolve the Kosovo problem in its own way', the European organizations needed to find the collective strength to engage.[83] But EU requests of the WEU, its 'defence' agent under the CFSP provisions, to act for it in matters of security and defence amounted to a not entirely irrelevant, but hardly convincing, peripheral engagement in support of the wider peace. Three missions of note were conducted in the region by the WEU on the basis of the TEU Article J.4.2 provisions for the implementation of actions with defence implications. The first EU request of 9 November 1998 led to the WEU De-mining Assistance Mission to Croatia (WEUDAM), launched on 10 May 1999 to provide 'advice, technical expertise and training support' to the Croatians in clearing their waters of the munitions left behind from the earlier Balkan conflict.[84] Also at the EU's request, the WEU Satellite Centre had initiated a 'general security surveillance' mission in November 1998, gathering information on the security situation in the Kosovo region, including refugee movements and compliance with the October agreements, and producing reports for NATO, the OSCE and the EU, supported by the WEU's Military Staff.[85] And on 2 February 1999, on the basis of a further Article J.4.2 EU request, the WEU Council approved plans to enhance MAPE's geographic scope and mobility, and to expand its advisory and training mission to include other government ministries and directorates. From April, the WEU mission was also to support the Albanian police in 'receiving, registering, supervising and escorting' Kosovan refugees, including the establishment of the Albanian police joint crisis centre, with MAPE teams in support of police directorates near the Kosovan border.[86] However, any EU pretensions at exercising strategic influence through the 'operational capability' of the WEU seemed to have been discounted at an early stage.

Ongoing negotiations between the parties to the Kosovan conflict, led by the Contact Group, had culminated in the Rambouillet Accords of February 1999, providing for a cease-fire, a peace settlement (to prepare the ground for a decision three years hence on Kosovo's status) and the deployment of an international peacekeeping force within Kosovo to uphold that settlement.[87] With NATO member-state agreement on the requirement for military action to avert a humanitarian disaster, and with NATO's credibility on the line given the preceding months of posturing, Milošević's rejection of the interim settlement opened the door for the NATO air assault, Operation Allied Force, beginning on 24 March 1999. Intended to lead to speedy capitulation, and with minimal casualty risk for the US forces engaged, Washington determined a strategy for NATO forces that, on the face of it, demonstrated the continuing 'vitality' of the Alliance as it approached its 50th birthday. However, deep concerns about the nature of the operation, about the ability to influence its conduct and about capability to act provided for a growing undercurrent of unease on both sides of the transatlantic partnership.[88]

THE WEU FIGHTS BACK

As the vultures began to circle around the condemned, but not yet sentenced, body of his organization, José Cutileiro, the WEU's Secretary General, sought to present an altogether optimistic picture of its capabilities and merits, in the hope that it might be spared. 'One of the many disobliging things that has been said about WEU', he noted in his RUSI address only weeks before the Washington Summit, 'is that it has a great future behind it'.[89] But the WEU's role, he stated, was to 'straddle the gap' between those motivated by the desire to see a defence dimension in the EU and those keen to ensure that any separate European defence activity did not damage NATO:

until that gap could be closed the WEU would need to continue in its 'historical mission'. Although supportive of the development of a 'credible' EU defence capability, he advised a cautious approach to its development that did not 'call everything into question prematurely', ignoring hard-earned achievements in a rush for institutional tidiness. 'How can we', he had asked his Assembly colleagues at their November 1998 session, 'without openly repudiating all the decisions taken at Maastricht, Amsterdam, Berlin and Madrid, decide that the mechanisms and procedures put in place on the basis of those decisions are inadequate at the very time when they are just being finalised and have not yet been put to the test?'[90] Extolling the WEU's virtues, Cutileiro argued, despite the flimsy response to the ongoing Kosovo situation, that the 'WEU today not only could handle a military operation where the US chose not to take part, but could handle a three-way operational partnership with the EU providing political leadership and NATO lending us the necessary assets and capabilities'.[91]

And the WEU had, indeed, been active in promoting its relations with both NATO and the EU, as well as developing its institutional arrangements so as to enhance its own ability to act. The WEU's military structures had undergone a significant reorganization in 1998, as the WEU Council sought to develop more effective practical arrangements for the planning and conduct of European operations. A Military Committee of Chiefs of Defence Staffs of all WEU full, associate member and observer states (to be joined by associate partners and others on a case-by-case basis) had been established, represented in permanent session by the Military Delegates Group with a permanent Chairman and responsible to the WEU Council. The Military Committee was to be supported by an enhanced Military Staff under a three-star general/flag officer, which would include the Planning Cell, Situation Centre and Intelligence Centre. This new structure was intended to improve the coherence of the WEU's military operational capability through the provision of guidance and advice to the WEU Council on military matters, including the implementation of the Petersberg Tasks and all matters related to FAWEU and NATO transferred assets for WEU missions. The Military Committee would also oversee the work of the Military Staff in its evaluation of contingency and operational plans, assist in the provision of military intelligence, contribute to the WEU input into the NATO defence planning process and encourage consultation between the WEU and NATO.[92]

The completion of a 'framework document' on the modalities for NATO asset transfer, monitoring and return for WEU missions had proven elusive.[93] But the principle of NATO inclusion of WEU requirements into its own defence planning process had been fully accepted, with WEU-led operational support requirements being factored into NATO's 1998 biannual Ministerial Guidance and Force Goals assessments.[94] WEU military staff had even been permitted to observe NATO planning for the Kosovo operation, a degree of 'NATO-ization' that might have been politically unwelcome to some in Europe, if it had not been for the extent of co-operation that had developed in the WEU-EU relationship.[95] Communication and information exchange between Councils and Secretariats (including the EU Commission) had been expanded and improved, and the Amsterdam CFSP provisions had been exemplified in the WEU's acceptance and implementation of the EU's first Article J.4.2 requests. And as the WEU had improved its relations with each, it had also acted as a 'transformer' or 'decompression chamber' between NATO and the EU, 'absorbing and dampening the different currents or pressures on both sides'.[96] Alongside the practical co-operation that the WEU had achieved over recent years, its major contribution to security and defence might be seen to reside in the creation of the benign political conditions under which that co-operation could develop and blossom. The dismal performance of Europe in response to events in Kosovo could not be denied, with a report from the WEU Assembly's Political Committee clearly expressing the organization's frustration at the 'size of the European mouse that has [sic] come out of all of these mountains', that 'Europe's political voice is still so slow to speak and so confused when it does, and why Europe's mailed fist is not stronger to strike after all the resources we have put into it'. Nevertheless, it argued, 'we cannot afford to throw away all the careful effort spent on setting up the technical and political conditions' under which this mouse might learn to roar.[97] A lot of political capital had been invested in developing the links that enabled a level of co-operation between the WEU, NATO and the EU's developing policy area, and these were far too hard won to be done away with lightly and without first establishing the necessary political and organizational mechanisms and behaviours to replace them.

THE WASHINGTON SUMMIT: CHANGING PARTNERS

As NATO celebrated the Alliance's 50th anniversary at the Washington Summit on 24–25 April 1999, at the height of the Kosovo engagement, the stage was set for a new era of Euro-Atlantic security co-operation. A revised Security Concept was launched for the Alliance, updated to meet a 21st-century security climate of complex new risks, including 'oppression, ethnic conflict, economic distress, the collapse of political order, and the proliferation of weapons of mass destruction'.[98] The summit reaffirmed member states' commitment to collective defence and the transatlantic link, whilst calling for a new resolve to transform to meet the challenges of the new environment, including crisis prevention and crisis-management activity.[99] Highlighting an enhanced role for 'partnership and dialogue', the summit welcomed three new members (Poland, the Czech Republic and Hungary) to the Alliance, introduced the Membership Action Plan as a 'practical manifestation' of the Alliance's 'Open Door' policy and welcomed Spain's full integration into NATO's military structure as an important 'milestone' for the organization. Introducing a Defence Capabilities Initiative to promote

European capability development so as to meet the spectrum of Alliance missions, the summit also gave full support to the progress made towards the development of an ESDI 'within the Alliance'.[100]

In the Washington Communiqué following the summit the Alliance members acknowledged 'the resolve of the European Union to have the capacity for autonomous action so that it can take decisions and approve military action where the Alliance as a whole is not engaged', and welcomed the 'new impetus' in strengthening European policy in security and defence. In so doing, it confirmed the views expressed in the St Malo Declaration (and to be the repeated 'mantra' in the forthcoming EU agreements at Cologne and Nice) that 'a stronger European role will help contribute to the vitality of our Alliance for the 21st Century, which is the foundation of the collective defence of its members'. The communiqué noted 'with satisfaction' the progress achieved in implementing the Berlin decisions for NATO support to WEU-led operations, including the developed CJTF and command arrangements. But the emphasis appeared to shift from the WEU as a representation of an ESDI within the Alliance to support for a common European policy in security and defence (acknowledging the EU's resolve to prepare for 'autonomous' actions), even in advance of any deliberations to take place within the Cologne European Council meeting in June. The Alliance declared its readiness to 'adopt the necessary arrangements for ready access by the European Union to the collective assets and capabilities of the Alliance, for operations in which the Alliance as a whole is not engaged militarily as an Alliance'. This was to include 'assured EU access to NATO planning capabilities'; 'the presumption of availability' to the EU of pre-identified NATO capabilities and common assets; the identification of a range of command options for EU operations, including the further development of the DSACEUR role; and the adaptation of the NATO defence planning system to 'incorporate more comprehensively the availability of forces for EU-led operations'.[101] In building on the mechanisms for 'consultation, co-operation and transparency' existing between the WEU and NATO, a new direct relationship between NATO and the EU was thus envisaged, which implied acceptance that the end of the line had come for the 'go-between' WEU in the light of the new European initiative. None of this, of course, implied a 'blank cheque' in support of proposed developments within the EU. The communiqué still described an ESDI as 'within NATO', requiring close co-operation between NATO, the WEU and, 'if and when appropriate, the European Union' to ensure an effective European contribution to Alliance interests. This suggested 'an ongoing blindspot' when it came to the significance of the St Malo proposals,[102] although both the Washington Communiqué and accompanying Strategic Concept did seem to suggest that the Americans had come to recognize the likelihood that the EU would supplant the WEU as the focus for any European defence identity and hence would be a necessary partner in the new security architecture.

The Washington Summit proved too early for any real consensus to have emerged amongst the Europeans on the future of the ESDI/Common European Security and Defence Policy (CESDP) post St Malo. At the WEU's Ministerial meeting in Bremen on 10–11 May, members welcomed agreement on a framework document for the release of Alliance assets and capabilities for WEU-led operations and, in stating their commitment to the development of an effective European defence and security policy, agreed to begin preparations for enabling EU access to WEU resources.[103] But the nature of the NATO-EU defence relationship was still undecided. France and Germany, supported by the majority of other WEU members, appeared to favour a merger of the WEU and EU, giving the EU operational capacity with direct control, supplemented by NATO assets through the CJTF concept.[104] The British favoured a construct whereby the EU had political authority to initiate crisis-management operations, but the means to carry them out would be provided through pre-designated European assets *within* NATO, facilitated by the CJTF arrangements.[105] The 'neutral' observers rejected any move towards an EU Article V, whilst the associate partners and members feared exclusion from defence discussions taking place within the organization to which they did not belong.[106] As one commentator had concluded, it was going to be 'easier to consign the WEU to history's dustbin than to parcel out its functions between the EU and NATO'.[107]

In the lead-up to Cologne, the question of the place of 'collective defence', the Article V issue, had become a major sticking point in deliberations about the nature of any future EU-based security and defence capability. At the Bremen meeting, the 'neutral' or 'non-allied' states had made clear their concerns about the German Presidency's draft proposals for a WEU-EU merger.[108] Having been prepared to adopt the Petersberg Tasks of peace-keeping and crisis management, requiring national policy shifts that had yet to 'bed in', these 'post-neutral' states had serious reservations about any future defence assumptions for the EU. For the Austrian Government, which had refused over-flight rights to NATO during the spring air strikes on Serbia, sustaining 'residual neutrality' had become a major political concern.[109] Likewise, the Irish and Finns, whilst encouraging the development of an EU peacekeeping capability in support of UN/OSCE mandates, rejected any prospect of a WEU-EU merger that might result in an effective EU Article V.[110] But it was the Swedish who were the most hard set against the draft report. The Swedish Defence Minister, Björn von Sydow, made clear at Bremen that, whilst his government were supportive of the St Malo initiative, it was keen that the EU adopt what Merlingen and Ostrauskaitė refer to as a 'holistic view of peace support operations that brought together military and civil dimensions', for which it should be equipped.[111] Driven by the national demands of domestic support, von Sydow emphasised the 'soft' aspects of crisis-management as a means of sweetening the pill of an EU security and defence capability, the Swedish Government making clear that it would not accept a militarization of the EU, implied by the merger of the WEU or the adoption in any form of its mutual defence guarantee.[112] Neither were the post-neutral 'four' prepared to see the development of a tighter core of states from which they would be excluded within a common policy area.

By limiting the EU to the Petersberg Tasks, with defence remaining the remit of the WEU and NATO, it was not only the post-neutrals who could find support for a crisis-management-competent EU, replete with both civil and military capability. For the British Government, NATO provided for collective defence, and the WEU's Article V was largely irrelevant.[113] And whilst France strongly believed that the retention of an all-European collective defence guarantee was an important element of any future CESDP, it was recognized that this would be a step too far and a decision best postponed if it was not to derail the efforts being swept along by the current, but temporarily pervasive, tide of events. For both London and Paris, keeping the Article V in the WEU and out of the EU might provide a convenient fallback position, retaining future options whilst hoisting a difficult 'elephant' out of the room.

THE KOSOVO FACTOR

On 3 June 1999, the day that the EU Council met in Cologne to discuss a defence role for the EU, a peace deal was struck which brought to an end the NATO air campaign in the FRY. The success of the Alliance in securing a peace may have resulted in initial triumphalism but was quickly challenged by those who questioned both the operation and the outcome.[114] It was clear that the crisis had exposed serious structural flaws in the Alliance relationship that were to influence thinking on both sides of the Atlantic.[115]

Throughout the crisis Washington's leadership had appeared 'erratic', with limited support from the legislature for a US engagement headed by a President facing impeachment.[116] But something new had been happening in Europe: in the face of ethnic cleansing and its humanitarian consequences, domestic opinion across Europe had galvanized around resistance to the behaviours of the old order typified by the Serbian elite.[117] In many ways this grass roots consensus on the need for action to prevent the atrocities being committed in Kosovo was representative of an assertion of the values of a liberal, democratic, 'post-national' and communitarian Europe to a broader geo-political environment. Political agreement on the responsibility to act emerged, not least in the post-neutral states and even in the absence of a clear supporting UN mandate.[118] However, if Kosovo offered an opportunity for Europe to demonstrate its resolve in meeting a 'local' challenge, it served rather to spotlight the humiliating dependency of Europe on its major ally. At the WEU's Bremen meeting, the British Defence Minister had summed up the mood: 'In Kosovo', he said, 'we have all come face to face with the European future, and it is frightening'.[119] Lack of European consensus on the use of ground forces, targeting policy and the timing and nature of negotiations had left many of the important decisions to Washington, whose fear of 'home' casualties had resulted in a decision not to deploy ground forces and to rely on aerial bombing from a 'safe' 15,000 feet, with the consequent negative impact on accuracy and high levels of 'collateral damage'.[120] The US had 'driven' the campaign, its military capabilities in sharp contrast with European limitations.[121] Dominated by US missile and air power, the operation exposed a serious transatlantic capability gap, as it required high-end conventional assets capable of precision and sufficient for prolonged intervention.[122] Over the 78 days of the conflict the Europeans flew only 20% of the air strike sorties, with the US delivering 85% of the munitions and supplying 70% of the aircraft.[123] The US outclassed the Europeans in advanced intelligence, surveillance and communications, and in precision-strike capability, owning the majority of NATO's cruise capability.[124] Militarily dependent in a way that far outstripped its Bosnia experience, Europe's inability to conduct an operation on its own doorstep had worrying implications given Washington's reluctance to put American forces at risk, particularly in cases of unclear US national interest.[125] The limits of the EU's CFSP had been exposed once again. Even where the requirement for action had been broadly acknowledged, national governments proved reluctant to engage in all but the most limited form of collectivity on the basis of national interest convergence, whilst at the same time their lack of credible and committable forces undermined any potential for Europe to establish itself as a serious security actor.

In light of their respective frustrations at the lack of European influence over the Kosovo campaign, the British and French focused their attention on the future development of the EU. Any residual enthusiasm for the WEU had been largely dissipated by its meagre contribution to the resolution of the Kosovo crisis, which had only served to demonstrate its limitations, further undermining any rationale for its continuing existence.[126] Nevertheless, there were some positive signals for those keen to promote a more effective European capability, if only to influence continuing American support. The Europeans had maintained a consistent, if occasionally shaky, front in support of the NATO action, despite some significant disquiet about the operational method and some major collateral bombing errors (not least against the Chinese Embassy). The French and British had offered significant air assets, and the German Luftwaffe had committed their first combat forces since 1945,[127] with bases and logistics support being provided by the Italians and Greeks despite their discomfort with the bombing campaign.[128] And despite the evident limits of Europe's military capabilities, the acceptance of the peace plan drawn up by the EU's envoy Martti Ahtisaari and his Russian co-drafter Viktor Chernomyrdin suggested that Europe had at least a modicum of diplomatic influence.[129] And the peace deal was to see the Europeans at the forefront of the reconstruction and resettlement endeavour. Constituted under the auspices of the UN's Chapter VII, the 50,000 scheduled NATO peacekeepers of the Kosovo Force (KFOR) deployment in support of the UN interim administration for Kosovo (UNIMIK) were to be drawn largely from European forces.[130] From July 1999, with KFOR on the ground, the WEU's contribution was to be through the Satellite Centre, which focused on the development of a Geographic Information System, a sophisticated digital map of the region which was to prove a useful tool in the post-conflict reconstruction work in the area and which was made available to the Geneva International Centre for Humanitarian De-mining in July 1999.[131] If Kosovo had 'exposed the gap between aspiration and reality',[132] the reality for Europe was at the soft end of the military spectrum, cleaning up after the major guests had gone home.

Kosovo proved to be a 'historic catalyst' for the adoption of a plan for construction of a militarily capable EU at the Cologne Summit. The ineffectiveness of the extant arrangements was clearly to no-one's advantage, whichever side of the Atlantic one was on. The structural imbalance of a two-class NATO had been exposed, with the European contribution little more than a 'side-show' until hostilities had come to an end. This growing gap between American and European capability threatened to upend the transatlantic bargain on the perennial, if exacerbated, burden-sharing challenge, whilst the humiliating inability of Europe to 'pull its weight in its own backyard' suggested a European future without influence on allies or foes alike.[133]

PREPARING THE GROUND: COLOGNE AND LUXEMBOURG

At the Cologne meeting of the European Council on 3–4 June 1999, and with the TOA in force (1 May 1999), the member states announced their determination to 'launch a new step in the construction of the European Union'. Approving the German Presidency report on 'Strengthening of the Common European Policy on Security and Defence', the Council embarked the EU on the creation of its own crisis-management capability.[134] With its scope defined by the Petersberg Tasks, this new policy area effectively outlined a division of labour, abrogating hard 'defence' to NATO, which remained 'the foundation of collective defence of its members'. Post-neutral-state rejection of, and French commitment to, a European Article V was to be accommodated by the assurance that the 'policy of the Union shall not prejudice the specific character of the security and defence policy of certain Member States', whilst the 'Article V of the [Modified] Brussels Treaty will in any event be preserved for the Member States party to these Treaties'. The slight, but significant, alteration of wording from the St Malo Declaration did suggest a change in emphasis in the conceived NATO-EU defence relationship, however, as the European Council determined that 'the Union must have the capacity for autonomous action, backed up by credible military forces, the means to decide to use them, and a readiness to do so, in order to respond to international crises *without prejudice to action by NATO*', suggesting a less defined 'right of first refusal' for the Alliance.[135]

Declaring that the EU 'shall play its full role on the international stage', the member states agreed, at Cologne, to give the EU 'the necessary means and capabilities to assume its responsibilities' in the area of security and defence policy. Recognizing the need to avoid unnecessary duplication, Cologne established that, if Europe was indeed to have any autonomous ability, it would require the enhancement of national-, bilateral- and multinational-level capabilities, which in turn required 'the maintenance of a sustained defence effort, the implementation of the necessary adaptations and notably the reinforcement of our capabilities in the field of intelligence, strategic transport, command and control'. The possibility of both autonomous (using only EU assets) and NATO-supported activities was noted: the co-operation arrangements indicated in the Washington Communiqué would be the 'main focus' for those EU operations having recourse to NATO assets. For EU-only actions, it was envisaged that augmented national HQs providing for multinational representation could be used, or those existing command structures within multinational forces such as the Eurocorps. But this was not to be the limit of the aspiration: opening the door for 'tighter' (and, from a US perspective, potentially undesirable and duplicative) command options, Cologne concluded that 'further arrangements to enhance the capacity of European multinational and national forces to respond to crises [sic] situations will be needed'.

Tasked with preparing 'the conditions and measures necessary to achieve these objectives', the EU's General Affairs Council was to define the 'modalities for the inclusion of those functions of the WEU which will be necessary for the EU to fulfil its new responsibilities in the area of the Petersberg tasks'. The integration of the WEU into the EU was rejected in favour of the creation of parallel decision-making structures within the EU's second pillar in order to ensure political control and strategic direction of the new policy area. It was envisaged that the General Affairs Council would be expanded to include Defence Ministers when dealing with CESDP issues, as one dimension of the broader CFSP. A permanent Political and Security Committee (PSC) consisting of national representatives with political and military expertise would steer the CFSP/CESDP, with a Military Committee and Military Staff including a Situation Centre, and supporting bodies such as a Satellite Centre and Institute for Security Studies. Just like the CFSP arrangements before them, the new structures were to be based on intergovernmental decision-making, national authority being ensured through the Council framework and second-pillar decision-making procedures that maintained the Commission and EP 'at the margins' of CFSP/CESDP decision-making.[136] Javier Solana Madariaga, who was to be replaced by the former UK Defence Minister, George Robertson, as NATO's Secretary General in October, was to take up the new post of High Representative for CFSP, under which CESDP would fall, and in order to facilitate the transfer of function, it was envisaged that this post might be combined with that of Secretary General of the WEU.[137] If the WEU was not to be absorbed, it was certainly to be cloned, its organizational assets providing the substance and example for the development of more organic structures within the EU proper. Committed to 'take the necessary decisions' by the end of 2000, the Council foresaw that by that point 'the WEU as an organization would have completed its purpose'.

On the opening day of the Cologne Summit, Cutileiro, speaking at the Transatlantic Forum's European Seminar, acknowledged the 'logic' of the EU taking direct responsibility for what Kosovo had identified as 'today's hardest problems and toughest tasks' associated with crisis management and the Petersberg Tasks. A direct two-way relationship with NATO should be simpler, he assented, and 'should channel stronger, more united European political energies for crisis control because of the bigger political clout the EU enjoys, not least in the eyes of its own members'.[138] But the 'outgoing' Secretary General was also keen to defend his organization and its achievements in the face of this apparent acceptance of its ultimate demise.[139] As a 'facilitating' organization, the WEU had provided a framework, he argued, in which 'better mutual understanding, dialogue and concrete cooperation on questions of European security and defence' had been possible. As to whether the WEU could have 'done even more', his modest organization had not waved 'the WEU flag just for the sake of it', but had sought only to 'add value' where it could.[140] And it had been a pro-active and adaptable organization that had laid the ground for the future development of an EU Security and Defence competence. Not least, it had refocused European attention on crisis-management operations and established the FAWEU designation and the planning, satellite and intelligence support for those operations, along with the instrument for their political control and strategic direction. It had made the 'concept of European operations conducted with NATO assets and capabilities a reality whilst not neglecting the possibility of independent European operations'. Whilst the WEU was not yet ready to 'scupper itself', the transferral of many of its functions to the EU was a 'natural and desirable evolution' and 'a recognition of the work it has [sic] done'. 'Soon', he acknowledged, 'the WEU name will disappear but the assets and capabilities developed by WEU will remain and be further expanded; it is that and that alone which counts'.

In support of the decisions reached in Cologne, the WEU Ministerial meeting in Luxembourg on 22–23 November approved the appointment of Solana as Secretary General of the WEU, replacing Cutileiro, in order to facilitate what increasingly looked like a 'friendly take-over'.[141] Ready to prepare the 'WEU legacy and the inclusion of those functions of WEU which will be deemed necessary by the European Union to fulfil its new responsibilities in the area of crisis-management tasks', the Ministers recognized that the EU was likely to continue to require use of the WEU's operational capabilities in crisis management for some time to come. Hence, the Ministers expressed their intention to strengthen the WEU's assets and capabilities, whilst allowing 'bodies of the Council of the European Union direct access, as required, to the expertise of the Organization's operational structures, including the WEU Secretariat, the Military Staff, the Satellite Centre and the Institute for Security Studies'.[142]

Reaction in Washington to the Cologne commitments on capability development had been largely positive, although alarm had been raised by the implied de-prioritization of NATO as the organization of first choice for the management of future crises.[143] The political approach had been 'alert but relaxed', with officials publicly playing down concerns about the CESDP concept, but making clear to their European allies that there would have to be real military substance to support it. The gap between aspiration and action had been amply evidenced in Yugoslavia, and any decline in US influence without a substantial net gain in a European contribution to Western security appeared a poor bargain to US officials, who perceived the Europeans 'as more likely to mess up than not'.[144] The Military Staff in the Pentagon were clearly sceptical about French motivations and concerned that European efforts might undermine the NATO integrated command structure and fail to lead to significant improvements in capabilities.[145] Talbott, the US Deputy Secretary of State, forewarned the Europeans that the post-Kosovo mood music amongst many US policy-makers was tuned to 'never again', and he believed that, in a future European crisis, a similar US role 'would not be sustainable'. It was time for Europe to pull its weight, but this could not be in competition with the Alliance. Any European defence structure that 'first duplicates the alliance and then competes with the alliance' would be unacceptable.[146] Once again, the Europeans had to find the difficult balance of 'more, but not too much', if they were to satisfy their US ally.

In the months following Cologne, the Europeans, led by the British, had sought to reassure Washington that the CESDP was truly in Alliance interests. In fact, transatlantic relations in the latter part of 1999 had not been altogether cosy: given the 'extraordinary' Senate refusal in October to ratify the Comprehensive Test Ban Treaty despite European exhortations, and with National Missile Defence once again on the agenda, uneasiness about the extent of common interests had resurfaced across the Atlantic. Congressional support for NATO and the ESDI had been secured in early November,[147] but concerns about US influence and non-EU member inclusion had been raised, and the necessity of ensuring NATO prioritization and European capability development rather than 'new institutions outside of the Alliance' had been highlighted.[148] Seeking to supplant the negative 'three Ds' with a more positive approach to the CESDP proposals, the new NATO Secretary General, Lord Robertson, presented his '3Is' to the NATO Assembly: the CESDP would be developed on the basis of 'improvement' of European capability in defence, 'indivisibility' of transatlantic security based on shared values, and 'inclusiveness' and transparency for all allies.[149] But it was clear that European rhetoric and institution-building were not going to be sufficient without a clear, credible and measurable commitment to substantive force capability enhancement.

As part of the approved EU Presidency report on strengthening the CESDP, member states had been advised to 'undertake efforts in line with the conclusions of the ongoing WEU Audit of European defence capabilities', which were presented at the Luxembourg meeting. The Planning Cell audit had been based on an assessment of FAWEU and European forces committed to NATO's planning and review process and that might be made available for the conduct of autonomous European 'Petersberg' operations, as elucidated in the WEU's illustrated profiles and developed by NATO's Combined Joint Planning Staff. Despite the rather optimistic assessment drawn from the audit that 'Europeans, in principle, have the available force levels and resources needed to prepare and implement military operations over the whole range of Petersberg Tasks', it had identified a series of serious shortfalls in capability.[150] The audit concluded that, although EU members were potentially capable of deploying 100,000 men, 500 aircraft and a range of naval and amphibious assets, severe gaps existed in high-intensity combat capacity, stealth technology and precision-strike capabilities, situational analysis, planning, deployability and operational control. The policy document which drew collective conclusions from the audit on the key areas for capacity-building prioritized the shortfall in strategic lift and intelligence as areas for urgent collective action. The qualitative elements of operational effectiveness—availability, deployability, sustainability, survivability and interoperability issues—all required urgent attention, as did the availability of multinational, joint operational and force headquarters, with particular emphasis on Command, Control and Communications (C3).[151]

The Cologne agreements had also spawned a number of bilateral initiatives as member states sought to tackle the capability issues that had arisen from the Council's proposals. The Anglo-Italian Summit held in London in July had resulted in a 'Joint Declaration Launching the European Defence Capabilities Initiative'.[152] This sought to gain support for the setting of 'challenging criteria for European defence capabilities and performance', drawing on the WEU audit and NATO's Defence Co-operation Initiative (DCI) and including a timetable for the achievement of European-wide military capability goals, supported by national capability objectives, and to achieve the widest crisis-management tasks.[153] The proposals also identified the need for some level of harmonization of military requirements, defence structures and procurement if Europe was to make the most of its resources.[154] Concerned that NATO's DCI and the WEU's capabilities audit might 'constitute a US-imposed straightjacket into which national-defence planners would be forced against their will', the French had argued for an EU evaluation of its own force requirements.[155] Nevertheless, the WEU audit was able to provide a 'springboard' for the deliberations on capability requirements to be discussed at the following EU Council in Helsinki in December, and many of the policy paper's recommendations were reflected in the forthcoming Helsinki Force Goals.[156]

Days after the conclusion of the Luxembourg meeting and following talks in London in October, the UK-France Summit of 25 November sought to revitalize their mutual contribution to proceedings, in light of the emerging reality of the European defence condition.[157] The dominance of national structures and practices in defence had resulted in a fragmentation of the European effort, exacerbated by a slow pace of adjustment to post-Cold War security realities. The number of military personnel maintained by NATO's European states numbered around 2 million, almost twice those of the US, but they had struggled to find 40,000 deployable forces for Kosovo.[158] These same states had a combined defence spending of some 60% of the US defence budget, but their bloated Cold War-configured personnel structures consumed three-fifths of their total spending.[159] With planned reductions in French, German and Italian force levels (due in part to post-conscription restructuring), and the recently announced four-year drop in German defence budgets,[160] it had become increasingly evident that in this resource-limited environment it was only through collective action for collective goals that European security and defence aspirations (and US burden-sharing demands) could be met. In a joint statement, the summit called on the forthcoming Helsinki Council to 'take a decisive step forward' in the setting up of the military and political instruments for EU-led operations.[161] Anglo-French proposals included the development of a 50,000–60,000-person European Rapid Reaction Corps (ERRC) with the full range of capabilities to deploy, sustain and command the most demanding of crisis-management operations. The summit also approved the decision announced in Cologne to transform the five-nation Eurocorps into a rapid reaction force available to enhance the EU's crisis-management capability, and there was some 'lobbying' by Eurocorps member states for this to provide the basis for the envisaged ERRC.[162] Offering their national joint operational headquarters (the UK Permanent Joint Headquarters and the French Centre Opérational Inter-armeés) as possible options for command of future EU-led operations, the UK and France also agreed on arrangements for logistics-sharing and the pooling of air, land and sea transport for rapid crisis deployment,[163] provisions to be expanded at the following Franco-German Summit.[164] Seeking to reassure Washington that this was to be a complementary force to NATO, an obligatory nod to NATO's defence primacy was given in the Anglo-French Declaration, which provided that European crisis-management actions would be undertaken only 'where the alliance as a whole is not engaged'.

HELSINKI PUTS THE 'MEAT ON THE BONES'

The decision having been taken by the European Council at Cologne to develop its own crisis-management capability, the pace at which the EU sought to take on those functions from the WEU and establish the capabilities to support them was impressive. By the time of the Helsinki meeting of the European Council on 10–11 December 1999, a consensus had emerged around the British position that, in establishing those political and military mechanisms required for the management and direction of its new crisis-management function, the EU should 'cherry pick' the useful elements of the WEU organization, leaving only the indigestible husk of unresolved issues for the institution to manage.[165]

At Helsinki the Council approved the establishment, by March 2000, of the interim political and military bodies that had been identified at Cologne as necessary to provide the EU with the political and strategic direction for military operations. These would include the interim Political and Security Committee (iPSC) of senior national officials tasked to inform the Council on all aspects of the CFSP and CESDP and to exercise, under Council authority, political control and strategic direction of European operations.[166] An interim Military Committee (iEUMC) of national Chiefs of Defence would provide military advice to the iPSC and direction to the nucleus of a future Military Staff (EUMS), formed in the Council Secretariat with seconded military experts, which in turn would be responsible for the conduct of crisis-management operations, early warning, situation assessment and strategic planning for Petersberg missions including the identification of appropriate multinational and national European forces.[167]

The Anglo-French proposals for a European rapid reaction corps were adopted at Helsinki, and a Headline Goal on military capabilities was established whereby 'co-operating voluntarily in EU-led operations, Member States must be able by 2003, to deploy within 60 days and sustain for at least 1 year, military forces of up to 50,000–60,000 persons capable of the full range of Petersberg tasks'.[168] In fact, the European Rapid Reaction Force (ERRF), as it was to become known, was not to be a standing European Army, or a single capable and deployable force, but rather a catalogue of national forces that might be made available for participation in EU operations. Whilst this did not amount to the ambitious defence convergence recommended by some and in line with other EU policy areas,[169] it did provide a practical approach, on paper at least, to timely defence co-operation in a resource-limited environment. This force concept was to address the shortfalls identified in the WEU's capabilities audit by developing the collective capability necessary for EU-led self-sustaining military action with the necessary command, control, intelligence, communications, logistical and combat support services and structures for the range of Petersberg Tasks.

To fulfil the political commitment to the Headline Goal outlined at Helsinki, the EU's Foreign and Defence Ministers, meeting in the framework of the General Affairs Council on 20 March 2000, approved the strategic and planning assumptions necessary for the elaboration of the policy and planning commitment of member states, including provision for contribution from non-EU European NATO members and EU accession candidates. Given that the 'WEU has already generated a set of illustrative Petersberg mission profiles including scenarios for European-led operation for up to a corps-sized level', the Council agreed that 'this work should be built on for the purposes of elaborating the headline goal'.[170] By July, the interim EUMS, which benefited from the inclusion of personnel experienced in WEU force planning,[171] had established its first draft of a Catalogue of Forces required to meet the Headline Goal, which in turn was to form the basis of the Helsinki Force Catalogue (committed forces) and Helsinki Headline Catalogue (required forces to fulfil the developed scenarios) to be agreed at the November Capabilities Commitment Conference.[172]

Facing bitter domestic Conservative opposition to what was seen as a Europeanization of British policies, of which the Helsinki agreement was yet another striking example, the Blair Government had launched its 'Britain in Europe' initiative in October to try and win domestic favour. Blair had argued that, not only did the EU offer access to a market of 380 million people, but it provided the opportunity to lead through the promotion of British values and the collective international clout that membership ensured. He challenged the 'myth' that there was a choice to be made between Europe and America, arguing that 'we are stronger with the US *because* we are in Europe', offering investment openings to a wider market and able to influence the reform of Europe's economic and political space.[173] And just as there were political and economic 'wins' for Britain in European engagement, the British Government had been at pains to reassure both the House of Commons and the White House that the developing CESDP was in fact a win for the Anglo-American concept of defence.[174] Drawing on the comparative advantages of the EU, defence proper was to remain the remit of NATO, with Europe taking up the military challenge in support of its wider crisis-management tools, to act where the Americans chose not to act, and to enhance its capability as an effective and sharing partner of the Alliance. The CESDP would be intergovernmental in nature, and there would be no European Army in support of the CESDP, which would be developed on the principles of the 3Is, 'reinforcing NATO, not in opposition to it'.[175]

The CESDP concept, as a British initiative, had been given the 'benefit of the doubt' by a wary Washington, but its subsequent design and implementation suggested that Blair may not have been entirely 'up front' over the likely outcome.[176] In a speech days after the Helsinki meeting, Talbott, the US Deputy Secretary of State, unequivocally endorsed the CESDP plan: 'We're not against it, we're not ambivalent, we're not anxious, we're for it. We want to see a Europe that can act effectively through the Alliance or, if NATO is not engaged, on its own. Period, end of debate'.[177] After all, the Europeans were demonstrating their determination to close the transatlantic capability gap, a requirement established at the Washington Summit and for which the DCI had also been designed. Although Talbott suggested that, with its emphasis on capability development, Helsinki represented 'a step—indeed, several steps—in the right direction' it was clear that Washington had become increasingly dissatisfied with the ambitions outlined at Cologne and Helsinki, which suggested a European defence policy with too much autonomy and too little America.[178] In the following months, the US developed what Sloan refers to as a 'yes, but' policy, offering support to the developing CESDP project, but caveated with warnings about the potential damage of any effective decoupling of the transatlantic relationship.[179]

EU-NATO RELATIONS AND THE CHALLENGE OF INSTITUTIONAL PROXIMITY

As the IGC on institutional reform sought consensus on the way forward for European construction in preparation for the December EU Council in Nice, finding agreement on the nature and processes of CESDP development continued to exercise European states. Although the major Atlanticist and Europeanist camps had moved much closer to each other through 1999–2000 in recognition of the mutual benefits of the CESDP, and the post-neutrals had come to embrace the peacekeeping opportunities that a CESDP potentially offered, there was clearly much still to discuss.[180] At the heart of these considerations lay fundamental questions regarding the desired nature of the developing Union, finding form in the discussion of future EU-NATO relations and the 'inclusivity' of CESDP, whilst the potentially 'log-jamming' questions of an Article V commitment for the EU and the parliamentary dimension of European defence were conveniently referred to some later, more propitious moment.

The Helsinki agreement had acknowledged the need to establish the modalities 'for full consultation, co-operation and transparency between the EU and NATO', including the 'appropriate arrangements' to enable 'non-EU European members and other interested States to contribute to EU military crisis-management', although it was noted that this would be 'whilst respecting the Union's decision-making autonomy'. And whilst agreement was reached on arrangements for third-party participation in EU crisis-management operations at the EU Summit at Santa Maria da Feira in June 2000, the questions of EU-NATO relations and European NATO but non-EU access to CESDP remained as irritants in the transatlantic relationship.

After US pressure for a determination on the nature of future EU-NATO procedures had been rejected at Helsinki as premature, given that the EU would not have established its own internal structures, the issue of consultation between the EU and NATO became something of a post-Helsinki problem, with the French holding out against the efforts of its fellow EU members to initiate negotiations. In Washington, the reluctance of EU officials to formalize the EU-NATO consultation procedures looked suspiciously like the French 'reverting to form', seeking to prevent contamination of the EU by the insidious adoption of un-European, US-determined processes.[181] By April 2000, the isolated French agreed to a British plan to establish four EU-NATO working groups to look at the future relationship between the organizations: on military capacity, security, asset transfer and the permanent arrangements for consultation. The first (i)PSC/NAC meeting was held on 19 September, by which time the NATO Secretary General felt able to report that 'NATO-friendly European defence is finally taking shape—and it is taking the right shape'.[182]

But what was clear was that any future relationship between the EU and NATO would, by necessity, be very different from that traditionally between the WEU and the Alliance. The WEU had been established as an 'unequal partner' to NATO, with whom it was committed under its Article IV provisions to 'work in close co-operation' and had established a long history of inter-alliance engagement. The EU had no such commitment, and no tradition or culture of defence co-operation. Its (at least short-term) dependence on access to NATO planning and intelligence, as well as US military capabilities evidently lacking amongst Europe's forces, created practical challenges not least in institutional security standards, complicated in turn by the presence of the post-neutral and non-aligned countries in the EU's second pillar.[183] But more significantly, the EU was an organization with a distinct constituency and a political identity as a serious and independent actor, equipped with a 'tool-bag' of economic and diplomatic resources alongside its own developing military capability, ensuring that it would seek a much more assertive and 'equal' role in any future inter-institutional relationship. The concept of a CESDP suggested something, by nature, distinct from that of the ESDI (with the WEU as its representation), which was still held as a working 'model' by some in the US.[184] The EU was not simply a pillar of the Alliance, but a broader community of collective interest and common policies, legally constructed and politically impelling. The EU's approach to security would draw together the range of military and civilian capabilities,[185] including those 'soft' tools of diplomacy and economic aid managed from outside of the second pillar, in the prevention and management of crisis—and this comprehensive approach would require an exclusive policy-making framework, in which the membership determined the orientation on the basis of common procedures.[186] As the French took over the Presidency of the EU/WEU in July 2000, their enthusiasm for promoting this new European competency was symbolized by the presence of forces from 10 of their European partners at the 14 July Bastille Day parade in Paris.[187] Bolstered by the Eurocorps' assumption of command of KFOR from NATO's Allied Land Forces Central Europe (LANDCENT) headquarters in April, the first multinational European headquarters to be deployed for peacekeeping operations,[188] France at least was clear that a new European defence competence was a reality, to support the economic and political might of the ascending EU. Given the EU's comprehensive capability in support of a common policy interest, the organization appeared destined to become the 'actor of choice' for managing the range of future security challenges, at least in its own neighbourhood.[189]

MEMBERSHIP AND THE QUESTION OF INCLUSIVITY

Central to the challenge of EU-NATO relations was the lack of membership congruence between the organizations and the autonomy of institutional decision-making. The categories of those 'inside' or 'outside' were further complicated by those seeking accession or not, whilst the organizations themselves represented distinct views on the use of force, typified most clearly by the nuclear assumptions of the Alliance in support of its Article 5 collective defence provision, an anathema to the benign crisis-management orientation of the EU's post-neutrals.

The complex task of linking these organizational constituencies had been traditionally assumed by the WEU with its various differentiated memberships. If the WEU was to cease to function, the access of those states holding WEU associate memberships (NATO non-EU) and associate partnerships (the EU and NATO 'waiting room' states) to European defence co-operation mechanisms would be severely affected. The WEU Assembly had consistently insisted that the acquired rights of its associate members and partners must be preserved within the EU framework once it had taken over the WEU's operational functions, but establishing an appropriate mechanism for direct non-EU co-operation in CESDP, whilst respecting the decision-making autonomy of the Union, was problematic.[190] The principle of a single institutional framework for the Union appeared to exclude non-EU European allies or candidate states from full participation in the CESDP area. But variants on that principle had already been accepted with the introduction of 'enhanced co-operation' in areas of EU activity not yet 'ripe' for full inclusion, most notably Monetary Union. Given the potential for log-jamming by the post-neutrals in the intergovernmental area of CESDP, the IGC had revisited earlier Franco-German proposals for extension of some such flexible approach in defence policy and arms co-operation.[191] The WEU itself had represented a form of 'enhanced co-operation', as did the European multinational military formations such as the Eurocorps and EUROMARFOR, but the WEU's acquis, with its broad memberships, was an inclusive form, bringing together all those non-EU allied states and EU candidates that might otherwise be prevented from contributing through the EU's institutions to EU operations.[192]

The major inclusion issue in the development of the CESDP was to be the relationship of the European NATO non-EU powers—the WEU's associate members—to the EU's new policy area. Associate membership of the WEU effectively provisioned full-member-equivalent rights in operations, exercises and planning to which they contributed, participation in discussion on links with the EU, posts in the Planning Cell and a contribution to the budget.[193] The inclusive and consensus-based approach that the Council adopted provided the associate members with a level of influence and engagement that militated against fears of exclusive EU practice and enabled substantive participation in European defence activity through

WEU auspices. At the Washington Summit in April 1999, the allies had attached 'utmost importance to ensuring the fullest possible involvement of non-EU European Allies in EU-led crisis response operations, building on existing consultation arrangements within the WEU',[194] but as the plans for CESDP developed, ambiguity began to creep into the proposals for European non-EU ally engagement.

The Cologne Declaration, which posited the demise of the WEU as the EU took on full responsibility for implementation of its CFSP/CESDP, had recommended that non-EU European allies and partners should be involved with the evolving CESDP 'to the fullest possible extent' and be enabled to 'participate fully and on an equal footing in the EU operations'.[195] Imitating the Washington Communiqué that preceded it, specific reference was made to the fact that European NATO non-EU states' involvement in EU operations should develop 'building on existing consultation arrangements within WEU'. However, this participation was to be 'without prejudice to the principle of the EU's decision-making autonomy, notably the right of the Council to discuss and decide matters of principle and policy', an engagement 'by invitation' formula repeated at Helsinki. The 'tug of war' between those Atlanticists who sought preferential treatment for European NATO non-EU states and the Europeanists who saw the CESDP as an organic part of the larger European project was resolved in part by the consultation arrangements agreed at the Feira Ministerial in June 2000, which established the principle of both a broad and a restricted 'external' engagement with the CESDP.[196] The main forum for non-EU CESDP participation was to be periodic meetings between the EU's PSC and the 15 non-EU European NATO states and EU candidates (15 + 15), but with at least an additional two meetings reserved for the EU and the six non-EU European NATO states (15 + 6), with intensified consultation in times of crisis. Where NATO assets were to be used in operations the 'six' could automatically take part, and the Council could invite them to participate in autonomous (without NATO assets) operations.[197] These arrangements suggested, however, a far more restricted access to defence discussion and action than that provisioned under the WEU arrangements, or in the Assembly's proposals for an EU Consultative Ministerial Council for CESDP, meeting twice yearly at 30 (15 + 15), with full participation rights 'at least equivalent to those they have acquired in the WEU Council as associate members and associate partners'.[198]

The WEU had taken an increasingly 'why not?' rather than 'why?' approach to membership engagement,[199] seeking to develop 'security through participation',[200] and the distinctions between membership categories had dissipated to the extent that most WEU proceedings were open to all, regardless of status. Only full members had voting rights in the Council and carried the Article V guarantee, but much of the business of the organization, including decision-making on operational issues (which all could 'opt in' to with men, machines and/or money) and external relations, was conducted at 28, including all its full, observer, associate member and associate partner states. The 21 states falling into the first three categories and carrying membership in NATO and/or the EU also benefited from inclusion in the joint WEU-EU and WEU-NATO meetings.[201] These various forms of memberships, including the seven NATO and/or EU candidates who held WEU associate partnerships, had prepared the ground for accession to the more complex regulatory system implied by EU membership, and had familiarized states with NATO procedures and the working relationship between NATO and its European pillar, 'promoting habits of cooperation and helping to socialize them into Western and European organizations'.[202] Keen to impress in an environment that linked them to the organizations to which they aspired, the NATO and EU candidate states made full use of their access to the WEU's organs, exercises and operations, its perceived value illustrated by the notably high quality of military and civilian personnel sent in their national delegations.[203]

For many of the CEE states awaiting NATO/EU membership, associate partnership provided a 'comfortable' engagement with European defence, which the development of a more 'Eurocentric' and necessarily exclusive security system was likely to challenge.[204] Poland, the Czech Republic and Hungary had transferred to associate member status in March 1999 upon their admission to NATO, leaving seven associate partners awaiting the next round of accessions.[205] The relationship with the WEU continued to provide some level of reassurance to those states excluded from the first 'wave' of accessions that their security interests remained high on the agenda for the institutions of the evolving security architecture, although this was a position that might be challenged by the WEU's demise in advance of their admission to their desired 'clubs'. For those 'post-neutral' states that were already EU members, observer status in the WEU had been enhanced in an effort to enable them to bring their considerable peacekeeping expertise to bear. Following a decision approved by the European Council in May 1999, all EU states, whatever their WEU status, were permitted to take part in missions for which the EU had recourse to the WEU, with the same planning, decision-making and cost-carrying rights and obligations as full WEU members. They could also designate forces to the WEU (FAWEU), take part in exercises and engage with the work of the Planning Cell.[206] It is notable that as EU members, the WEU observers had the power of veto over EU requests of the WEU, and thus the potential to prevent EU-initiated military action, but had no such power to determine WEU-initiated action taken independently of the EU. The demise of the WEU might close one useful classroom for observer engagement with the culture of defence co-operation, but for the WEU observers, the comprehensive approach to crisis management developing after the Feira European Council offered the preferred option of a common security and defence-lite policy within the EU.

For the three most recent associate members, the challenge of inclusion was a short-term one only, as they were on track for early EU accession. Of the three others, Norway and Iceland had found satisfaction in an 'inter-Nordic understanding' with Sweden and Finland, whereby each would promote the others' status in their respective organizations.[207] But for Turkey, the remaining associate member, the challenge was considered to be far greater, not least given its particular geo-strategic position and its continuing exclusion from the EU, of which its long-time political sparring partner Greece was a member, with Cyprus soon to join. In the WEU, associate member status had, at least initially, offered NATO non-EU states certain privileges over the non-NATO EU neutrals. But now the tables were to be turned: surely, Turkey argued, it could not be right that, as a 'long-standing NATO ally', it might find itself subordinated in European security affairs to those on a faster track to EU membership.[208] Fearful of a loss of influence over European defence activity if the CESDP was to take form within the EU proper, Turkey had insisted on 'case-by-case' decision-making on the provision of NATO assets for EU operations to be included in NATO's new Strategic Concept, exercising its membership right to prevent Alliance support of WEU or EU activities through its veto in the NATO Council.[209] Reminding the Europeans of the lack of 'automaticity' in the provision of NATO assets which would be required for any significant EU operation, the US Ambassador to NATO added his weight to those in Washington and Ankara demanding a 'special status' for Turkey in its security relations with the EU, noting that, should a crisis being dealt with by the EU escalate, Turkey would have a defence commitment to 11 of the EU members.[210] Having been identified as an EU 'candidate' at Helsinki, but with no date set for accession negotiations, Turkey intensified its efforts to preserve the 'rights' accrued from WEU associate membership, which it felt should be transferred to the CESDP provisions should the WEU cease to function as the EU's defence arm.[211] Without that agreement, the CFSP/CESDP was perceived as counter to the basic Turkish requirement of inclusivity. This, in turn, could only limit progress on the CESDP as the concept of 'automatic' provision of NATO assets for EU operations was put on hold awaiting Turkish acceptance.[212]

The WEU's broader co-operation through the Mediterranean Dialogue and its special relations with Russia and Ukraine had been largely overtaken by the various partnership arrangements established by NATO and the EU respectively. Some of the mistrust with which the EUROFOR and EURO-MARFOR multinational FAWEU had been viewed was relieved by Southern Mediterranean states' inclusion as observers on manoeuvres, but the WEU failed to provide a convincing framework for military co-operation. The lack of opportunity for any substantial defence engagement limited the WEU's attractiveness, particularly given that its provisions were largely duplicated in NATO's Mediterranean Dialogue, which had itself been 'shaped in part' by the WEU's example of engagement in the region.[213] Having declared itself ready, from 1998, to supplement the political and security chapter of the EU's Euro-Mediterranean Partnership, as the declared defence arm of the EU and its CFSP, the WEU received no response from its reluctant contractor.[214] By the turn of the decade, as it prepared to hand over its operational role to a newly militarily competent EU, the logic for its continuing presence in the region dissipated.

Throughout the 1990s, the WEU had provided a 'focal point' for the development of partnerships with former Cold War adversaries, preparing the ground not only for eventual NATO and EU accession, but also for constructive and co-operative relationships with unlikely future members.[215] As late as June 1999, an action plan had been agreed for Ambassadorial-level political dialogue with Ukraine, with opportunity for parliamentarian and academic engagement and exchange, practical co-operation including observation of WEU exercises, access for WEU states to Ukrainian training facilities and continuing long-haul air transport and satellite imagery co-operation.[216] But just as the emergence of the EU's CESDP was to make the WEU redundant in the Mediterranean, its relationship with Russia and Ukraine, with whom it had developed effective co-operative partnerships at both a practical (strategic lift) and consultative (defence dialogue) level, were to be subsumed within the provisions of the EU's CFSP/CESDP.

OFF THE IGC AGENDA: DEMOCRACY, DEFENCE AND THE WEU

Whatever the challenges ahead of the EU's CESDP, it had become increasingly clear since Cologne that the WEU's days were numbered. As the interim organs of the new EU policy area breathed into life, the remnants of WEU's raison d'être left but a pale shadow of the WEU's earlier ambitions around which to preserve institutional life. At the Porto meeting of the WEU Council in May 2000, the Ministers had announced that the organization 'stood ready to support, as required, the development of the functions identified by the EU as being necessary to fulfil its new responsibilities in the field of the Petersberg tasks', although they had recognized that this would have 'profound repercussions for WEU as an organisation'.[217] As WEU member states had made known their intention not to renounce the MBT, decisions on the future role of the 'rump' WEU would need to be made. The Permanent Council had established an *ad hoc* Group on Transitional Issues, tasked with carrying out an 'internal reflection' on the challenges of establishing the WEU's legacy. A transition guidance plan for the Military Staff had been approved by September 2000, and a detailed crisis-management continuity plan was in place by October, to be adopted at the WEU's forthcoming Marseille Ministerial, to ensure a smooth transition once the EU's permanent structures were in place.[218] As the arrangements for transition of the WEU's functions to the EU moved apace, two key areas remained largely off the IGC and Nice agendas. The French Presidency had adopted a 'practical approach' to the discussions on ESDP, seeking to avoid the 'institutional quarrels' that had haunted previous efforts at enhancing European defence co-operation.[219] Two central and contentious issues were therefore left for later EU consideration and, consequently, in the lap of the WEU, where they were to become the subjects of 'quiet' reflection largely within the confines of the WEU Assembly.

The first of these issues concerned the parliamentary dimension of European security and defence and, more particularly, the question of scrutiny and accountability of the intergovernmental CFSP/CESDP, as the TEU provided only limited EP oversight of second-pillar activity.[220] If the WEU was to be wound up, there would be 'plenty of scope for the relatively unexamined exercise of executive prerogative' in this crucial area of state interest.[221] Extending the EP's remit into the second pillar was 'red-lined' by the British and others intent on national sovereign control, but the absence of parliamentary scrutiny of CFSP/CESDP did suggest a democratic shortfall that the demise of the WEU Assembly would only exacerbate. This 'dilemma' suggested a reprieve for the WEU Assembly: 'suppressing' it without a successor would suggest a lack of parliamentary significance in the EU, which would likely exacerbate 'existing tensions' between the EP and the Council.[222] But with the creation of a genuine second chamber in the EU 'off the cards', any replacement for the WEU Assembly would need to demonstrate that it provided better 'value for money' as a more effective, efficient and inclusive parliamentary scrutineer.[223]

Following the Assembly's Lisbon 'initiative' of 21 March 2000, in which it had put forward proposals for the future of the parliamentary dimension of European security and defence, agreement had been reached at its Plenary Session in June to transform itself into the 'Assembly of WEU—the interim European Security and Defence Assembly' (ESDA).[224] For as long as the CESDP remained an intergovernmental policy area, the democratic principle of inter-parliamentary oversight, witnessed in the other areas of intergovernmental co-operation (NATO, the Council of Europe and the OSCE), could be satisfied by the WEU Assembly, which could focus its efforts on all areas of the ESDP, as well as the implementation of the MBT Article V and co-operation in armaments (conducted under WEAG and WEAO), which stood outside of the EU. As an interim ESDA it could continue to include representatives from all EU members, candidates and European non-EU NATO members,[225] supported by a Steering Group including the Assembly President, leaders of the 28 national delegations, chairs of national political groups and an EP observer.[226] Subsequent EP reports built on the Lisbon discussions to propose alternative inter-parliamentary arrangements for regular structured discussion of defence issues amongst national foreign and defence committees and relevant European parliamentary committee chairs, along the lines of the EU's Conference of Foreign Affairs Committees; these could replace the WEU Assembly role.[227] With no appetite to address these institutional matters at Nice, the Assembly abandoned hope of including the ESDA concept into a protocol annexed to the TEU. But clearly, if the self-styled ESDA was to function effectively, it would require a Council, representing the interests of all 28, to report to it and to reply to its questions and recommendations, as provisioned between the WEU Council and Assembly. Although the recently established iPSC and WEU Permanent Council representation frequently overlapped, future political exchange between the WEU Assembly and the European Executive might well prove rather more problematic.[228]

The second major issue left largely off the agenda of the EU's IGC was the question of collective defence, with the Assembly reporting that given the 'magnitude of the problem and the absence of consensus among the Fifteen it hardly seems [sic] realistic or prudent to ask now for the matter to be decided' before the Nice meeting.[229] There had been little support for an EP recommendation that the Article V mutual defence clause of the MBT be annexed as an additional protocol to the TEU.[230] The 'crisis-management' focus of the ESDP appeared to have steered the EU away from the course suggested by the Amsterdam provision for a common defence should the European Council so decide. Neither the Cologne nor Helsinki Declarations made reference to the collective defence provision, whilst the Presidency report annexed to the Helsinki Conclusions had affirmed NATO's continuing position as the foundation of collective defence, as well as the preservation of the WEU's Article V. Solana had been emphatic, post-Helsinki, that 'ESDP is *not* about collective defence', something that the presence of the 'neutrals' should confirm.[231] Indeed, even if all EU members had been willing, transferring the WEU's Article V to the EU not only would lack the credibility of a supportable obligation, relying as the WEU had on NATO for implementation, but might offer assumed guarantees to non-NATO members that the allies would not be keen to defend. Nevertheless, the WEU Assembly regretted that, as the WEU was not to be fully integrated into the body of the EU, crisis-management and collective defence responsibilities would be 'exercised separately, by different organisations, on the basis of different treaties' and 'Defence Europe' would not have been achieved.[232] Until such time as a collective defence agreement could be encompassed within the EU framework, many argued that Article V of the MBT would need to be preserved.[233] The renouncing of the WEU's Article V would leave only the weaker-worded NATO guarantee, itself dependent on the continuing engagement of the US in European security, and would represent a backward stride in terms of the European defence commitment desired by, most particularly, the French.[234] However incredible the eviscerated WEU's defence capability might be, the maintenance of its Article V could keep the door ajar for a future EU defence—despite its increasingly apparent delineation from the crisis-management role being embraced within the Union—and could 'hedge the uncertainty' over whether the EU would ever take on the full range of defence responsibilities. And if Article V persisted, so must the Council and Assembly that maintained the relationship with NATO to ensure that the Alliance could carry out the military assistance clause of the Modified Brussels Treaty.[235]

MARSEILLE AND NICE

By the time of their Marseille meeting on 13 November 2000, the WEU Council had gone some way in preparing the WEU's 'departure'.[236] Its member states having accepted the transferral of the WEU's crisis-management responsibilities to the EU, discussions between the two organizations had resulted in agreement 'in principle' on the nature and effect of that transition. In its Marseille Declaration, the WEU Council approved the residual WEU functions and structures necessary to fulfil the commitments of the Brussels Treaty, particularly those arising from Articles V and IX, to which member states reaffirmed their attachment. The WEU suspended the consultation mechanisms established between itself, the EU and NATO respectively, and the WEU's Institute and Satellite Centre were to be transformed into agencies of the EU, whilst its Military Committee and Military Staff would cease to function, in favour of the EU's own structures. The WEU's remaining operational activity in Croatia (WEUDAM) would continue until the end of its mandate, whilst the Albania police mission (MAPE) would be taken over by the EU.[237] Political dialogue with Russia, Ukraine and the Mediterranean states was also to be taken up within the framework of the EU, whilst the Transatlantic Forum would cease to function, its activities to be largely taken up within the EU's 'new' Institute for Security Studies.[238] Only the WEAG and WEAO would continue to conduct their work in the area of arms co-operation for the foreseeable future in the absence of any agreement in the EU context.[239] With provisions to manage its residual Article V and IX functions to be in place by 1 July 2001, the institution was to return to the 'somnolent' existence of its middle years, without operational relevance, but with a parliamentary 'defence consultation' role and holding the collective defence obligation of its members, to be exercised through the capabilities of the Alliance.

At the Nice European Council meeting of 7–9 December 2000, the decisions reached at Cologne, Helsinki and Feira were approved, with the Council agreeing a draft treaty, the new Article 17 of which was to replace that of the TOA relating to a CFSP.[240] Provisions for the permanent structures of the new ESDP (the C having been dropped from the CESDP), including the standing PSC, were laid out in the treaty and in Annex VI of the Presidency Conclusions of the Nice European Council, where the 'Presidency Report on the European Security and Defence Policy' provided much of the detail regarding changes in the ESDP provision.[241] With a 'common defence' for the Union left to a potential future European Council decision, the report emphasized the Union's 'particular characteristic'—its 'capacity to mobilise a vast range of both civilian and military means and instruments, thus giving it an overall crisis-management and conflict-prevention capability in support of the objectives of the Common and Foreign Security Policy'. Excluding the establishment of a European Army, the report acknowledges NATO as the basis of collective defence for its members and identifies the EU's autonomous capacity to make decisions and act in crisis management when

'NATO as a whole is not engaged'. ESDP development was to 'contribute to the vitality of a renewed Transatlantic link' and provide for a 'genuine strategic partnership between the EU and NATO in the management of crises'. The new treaty did, however, note that 'due regard' must be given to the two organizations' decision-making autonomy, suggesting a continuing controversy that the literal vagueness concerning the inter-institutional relationship did not disguise. Equally, in approving non-EU states' access to and engagement with ESDP decision-making and operations on the basis of the Feira provisions, the EU failed to satisfy Turkey and hence secure the EU-NATO arrangements necessary for the release of NATO assets, including planning capabilities, for ESDP operations to which the Presidency Conclusions attached so much importance.[242] Lack of agreement on NATO-EU links persisted at the NAC meeting in Brussels on 14–15 December, because of Turkish dissatisfaction with the participation arrangements, and these issues of inclusiveness and autonomy were to continue to exercise member states and allies for years to come.[243]

For the WEU, whose Marseille Declaration had largely 'predicted' the Nice provisions, the significance of the Nice Treaty was more in what was not said than in what was. Modifying Article 17 of the TEU, Nice removed all references to the WEU's role in implementing EU decisions with defence implications and replaced the specific reference to the WEU as an 'integral part of the development of the Union' with a statement identifying the WEU as simply one possible framework for co-operation.[244] The implication of these omissions was that the WEU would cease to function as the defence arm of the Union: no longer would the EU avail itself of WEU support in strategizing or operationalizing the defence aspects of the CFSP.[245] After the WEU was further cannibalized at Nice, with the EU's adoption of its Satellite Centre and Institute for Security Studies as EU Agencies,[246] it appeared that the Europeans had reached a level of agreement on the form of their CFSP/ESDP that, once made operational, would leave the WEU as merely a 'phantom structure'.[247] Its continuing existence would be based on three remaining functions, the 'left-over' elements as yet unresolved in the EU context. The absence of a defence guarantee from the Nice Treaty provided the WEU with its most pressing role as keeper of the only European common defence commitment outside of NATO. The lack of agreement on parliamentary oversight of the CFSP/ESDP provided purpose for the WEU Assembly as scrutinizer of European defence issues. And the absence of any broad agreement on an EAA at Nice (the new Article offered only the most obtuse reference to EU member-state arms co-operation where they 'deemed appropriate' in support of a progressing defence policy) left the remaining residual WEU task in the form of the continuing work of the WEAG/WEAO.[248] These three functions provided the WEU with a continuing raison d'être, at least until such time as they might be 'resolved' within the EU itself.

The WEU's support to the EU was to be largely through its own dismemberment and the continuance of its 'rump' functions, but its utility as a promoter of the Alliance and as an inter-organizational bridge between NATO and the EU had been largely undone by these developments within the EU's ESDP. With no further operational role and with direct NATO-EU co-operation and dialogue in defence, the WEU's engagement with NATO had declined to that of an interested bystander, with the Assembly retaining an active but largely impotent interest in the management of the Modified Brussels Treaty's Article V.[249] Drawn increasingly into the orbit of the EU, the WEU had lost one of its two traditional roles as its effectiveness as a mechanism for European influence on the Alliance (or the EU's relations with it) declined. NATO members continued to find themselves at odds over the relative weight of member states' influence and dependence, over burden-sharing and common interests and over the role and remit of the Alliance and its relationship with the EU's ESDP, but these challenges were now beyond the WEU's ability to affect.

If those still attached to the WEU had hoped that the organization's selfless dislocation might elicit some nostalgic sympathy for its continuing existence, they must have been sorely disappointed. Support for the organization had largely dissipated, and it seemed that the deconstruction of the WEU was to be a pretty 'brutal' affair. Having been the mainstay of support for the WEU since its inception, the British establishment seemed in favour of hastening a 'clean break' with the WEU and its organs, the House of Commons Defence Select Committee having argued since 2000 that it should be 'wound-up, transferred or floated-off as rapidly as possible, with as little institutional residue as can be achieved'.[250] The WEU Council had agreed to refrain from future meetings at Marseille, and the WEU had immediately begun the shutdown of all of its operational faculties. Its 'political euthanasia' was to be enacted in all but the three secured areas (Article V, Assembly and Arms Cooperation) by July 2001, whilst the organization was to assist where it could in the rapid construction of an effective European defence capability within the EU's second pillar.[251] There was little appetite amongst EU officials, however, for 'learning lessons' from the WEU, which was seen by some as a potential contaminant of the ESDP project. The WEU's perceived operational weakness and subordination to NATO were to undermine the efforts of its staff to transmit the benefits of the organization's extensive knowledge in crisis management and inter-institutional co-operation to the new policy area of the EU, which had determined to adopt a 'best practice' approach without preference for the WEU 'method'. The low level of staff transference from the WEU to the EU was indicative of a certain EU antipathy towards all things WEU.[252]

Despite this institutional resistance, it was clear that the EU might have things to learn from the organization from which it was to inherit many of its new functions, and the 'hand-over' process had effectively begun well before the Marseille and Nice agreements. The two Military Staffs had met informally since the spring of 2000, and the WEU staff's expertise provided continuing support to the immature interim EUMS, the former Director of the WEU Planning Cell being appointed by Solana as its head. The WEU's acquis, its methods and procedures, were to be drawn upon across a range of operationally relevant competencies including operational, command, control and communications (C3) and logistics planning.[253] The WEU's familiarization programme for national military HQs that might be made available for EU autonomous operations had contributed to the necessary inter-military communication and co-operative working practice, whilst the new operational EU would benefit from the experience of the WEU's programme of annual crisis-management exercises which had enabled the development of Standard Operating Procedures for forces co-operating in European crisis-management operations. CMX/CRISEX 2000, which had taken place in February 2000, included civil and military staff from all the WEU nations along with NATO and EU observers and had proved a particularly useful testing ground for the mechanisms of politico-military direction of European operations along with those enabling the potential release of NATO assets for European missions; the last of these exercises took place in June 2001.[254]

The WEU's intelligence-related organs prepared to shut down or pass over to the EU, with the WEU Intelligence Centre passing on its European experience of managing sensitive multinationally sourced politico-military intelligence through the design team for the new EUMS's Intelligence Division. The WEU Situation Centre's experience of joint civil-military co-operation in developing situational awareness proved 'invaluable' in setting the environment for the EU's own SITCEN facility.[255] The WEU's Satellite Centre at Torrejon (Satcen) and its Institute for Security Studies were formally adopted as Agencies of the EU in July 2001 by a joint action of the Council of Ministers, with both institutions developing their competency under the EU umbrella. Satcen was, over time, to increase its imagery data feed from commercial satellite systems and set up access arrangements to government-owned systems such as Hélios II and COSMO-Skymed, widening its support remit to include geographic and imagery intelligence provision to the full range of ESDP civil and military missions, from thematic map provision in the Congo to border-monitoring imagery intelligence in Libya.[256] Equally, the security institute was to make an energetic start as an EU agency: its independence and enthusiasm occasionally put it at odds with Brussels, although its research and analysis were to develop a wide international following.[257] Each of these structures was to develop in relation to its new tasks within the EU, but, equally, each had its origins in the policies, processes and co-operative cultures that had been developed under WEU auspices before their transferral. Whilst the WEU's apparent weaknesses may have made a leper of it for some in the EU, there was no denying that the experience carefully nurtured in the WEU had prepared the ground for the ESDP launch and had an inevitable and significant influence on its early development.

The WEU had, therefore, much to offer to the embryonic ESDP, but Solana had made clear that the aspirations for this new policy area would inevitably create a new set of challenges. The EU had a wide range of potential crisis-management tools at its disposal, but if it was to combine them effectively, and develop a working framework for inter-organizational co-operation, it would require something rather more 'sophisticated' than simply replicating the arrangements in the WEU.[258] Some of these challenges were clearly internal to the organization—the EU's pillar structure threatened institutional coherence in the management of multidimensional security. That the Commission and Council saw themselves potentially at odds over control of the broader CFSP area was something of a dilemma given the dual aspirations of an enhanced international presence and the maintenance of intergovernmentalism in security and defence.[259] And just as these internal difficulties had yet to be addressed, the nature of the future EU-NATO relationship remained unsettled. Concerns regarding decision-making and operational autonomy led to protracted discussions in the EU about future inter-institutional arrangements in the ESDP area.[260]

MAKING IT REAL: FORCE DEVELOPMENT AND THE BERLIN PLUS CHALLENGE

By the time of the NATO Defence Minister Summit of 5 December 2000, in advance of the EU Summit in Nice, the outgoing US Secretary of Defense, William Cohen, had clearly lost his earlier enthusiasm for the CESDP.[261] The French were entirely at odds with Washington's proposals that, to avoid inefficient and wasteful duplication, a consolidated NATO-EU 'European Security and Defence Planning System' should be developed, based on NATO's planning resources at SHAPE.[262] The Europeans should beware, Cohen had warned, of establishing a competing institution that would add nothing to military effectiveness and potentially undermine the transatlantic link, the result of which could be that 'NATO could become a relic'.[263] This had exposed Blair to renewed domestic criticism of his support for the CESDP plans. The Nice Summit had done little to relieve him, as Britain and France found themselves at odds over the French President's calls for an independent operational planning and command capability for European military actions, highlighting a difference in interpretation of the 'autonomy' at the heart of the evolving policy.[264] The French ultimately ceded to the EU-NATO linkage arrangements laid out at Nice and the subsequent NAC Ministerial, which recognized the role of NATO planning systems as integral to the EU's assured access to NATO assets.[265] But Paris rejected calls for a full reintegration of France into NATO, seen by many as a means of enhancing operational effectiveness not only for NATO forces but for the detachable command structures envisioned for European-only operations.[266] The French Government continued to press for more self-sufficient command and planning capabilities for CESDP missions, including the augmentation of national European facilities for mid-level operations.[267]

If Blair had hoped that his European defence Initiative offered the promise of a more progressive transatlantic strategic partnership, the 'bitterly contested' election of President George W. Bush in 2001 foresaw a US more at odds with Europe over a range of issues.[268] Bush had campaigned on the importance of improved US leadership and allied consultation, but the early tone of his Administration suggested that a storm was brewing for transatlantic relations.[269] Bush's political style had much in common with that of the former US President Ronald Reagan, with his 'cowboy-inspired language, his emphasis on religion, and, most important, his deep conservative nationalism': under Bush's leadership a new spirit of righteous Americanism was to prevail.[270] Persisting with many of Clinton's policies, which had been so unpalatable to the Europeans, Bush declared the Kyoto Agreement on global warming dead in March 2001, refused to sign up to the International Criminal Court, withheld dues to the UN (despite agreement on a 22% contribution cap) and was an enthusiastic proponent of Missile Defence.[271] Seeking US approval of the developing ESDP project, the Blair Government continued to promote a 'take' on the Nice agreement, both at home and in the US, that emphasized NATO's decision-making and operational primacy, the crisis-management limits of EU policy and the mutual benefits of an enhanced European capability in support of Alliance interests.[272] This approach appeared to have won favour with the new President, who declared his guarded support for the ESDP following the US-UK Camp David discussions in February 2001, on the basis that 'such a vision would encourage our NATO allies and friends to bolster their defence budgets, perhaps'.[273] Certainly, a more defence-efficient Europe, avoiding costly and unnecessary duplication, capable of carrying out a range of crisis-management tasks and closely linked to a 'first call' NATO, would satisfy, at least in the short term, interests on both sides of the traditional Atlanticist/Europeanist divide. But this was never to be an easy balance. Washington's enthusiasm for the ESDP wavered dramatically even over the first months of the Bush Administration,[274] whilst British support of the February 2001 US attacks on Iraqi air defence installations exposed a deep Atlanticism in UK thinking that threatened to further undermine the Anglo-French motor at the heart of the ESDP initiative.[275]

Nevertheless, in terms of operationalizing the ESDP, significant progress was to be made in the technical aspects of EU-NATO co-operation, with NAC/PSC official meetings initiated in April 2001, practical arrangements for NATO asset-sharing made and military headquarter consultation resulting in steps towards the identification of separable NATO capabilities and planning assets for EU-led operations.[276] At the same time, the Helsinki Headline Goal process, which had been intended as a means to add real substance to the ESDP by determining the military requirements for EU missions and the means by which they might be met, had made real progress.[277] Member states had been quick to offer forces, although this may be seen as a largely symbolic gesture given the non-binding nature of the commitment, which was dependent on case-specific national decisions.[278] As with the WEU's FAWEU before it, these force promises would need to be realized in operations if they were to serve as a credible underpinning for European military responses, particularly in a rapid reaction environment where national dithering would be unconscionable.[279] The development of civilian crisis-management capabilities, initially driven by the post-neutrals, was quickly adopted by the 'Solana circle', who realized the political opportunities for successful and less contentious civil operations. In the rush to develop civilian crisis-management competence, the WEU's experience in civilian missions offered some examples, whilst modified versions of the WEU's illustrative military scenarios and the accompanying lexicon of operational planning were employed by civilian mission planners in developing this new area of competence.[280] By the time of the Laeken Summit in December 2001 the EU Council felt able to announce the operability of the ESDP, its capabilities and structures being such that it might carry out 'some crisis-management operations', whilst the Union would be 'in a position to take on progressively more demanding operations, as the assets and capabilities at its disposal continue to develop'.[281]

The major constraint on further development of the ESDP remained Turkish resistance to any automaticity in the release of NATO assets for EU operations as long as it remained excluded from CFSP/ESDP decision-making. Compromise agreements were reached in Ankara in December 2001, whereby the Turkish veto might be lifted in return for participatory rights in ESDP operations and negative security assurances in the form of written guarantees of non-intervention in the Aegean or Cyprus by EU forces (NATO's own prohibition of inter-allied military conflict also suggested that no EU force could act in Cyprus). As the Ankara Agreement was fiercely negotiated over the following months in the EU, the Greek Government presented their objections to the agreement as essentially a debate about EU decision-making autonomy, whilst the Turkish General Staff, empowered by the gradual disintegration of the Turkish governing coalition during the economic crisis of 2002, rejected any compromise on the Ankara document.[282] With Solana in the negotiating seat, an agreement was eventually reached in December 2002 which included reciprocal negative security assurances between the EU and NATO allies, enhanced non-EU NATO state consultation in the 15 + 6 format and the exclusion of Cyprus and Malta (who were amongst the 10 to conclude EU accession agreements at the forthcoming Copenhagen Council), as non-NATO and non-PfP states, from all arrangements involving NATO assets. Linkage between Turkey's accession prospects and an agreement on what had become known as the Berlin Plus formula (named after the initial WEU-NATO asset-sharing agreements of 1996), seems likely to have been a tipping factor in eventual Turkish acquiescence. In the Presidency Conclusions to the Copenhagen European Council of 12–13 December, Turkey was offered the prospect of accession negotiations 'without delay', if the Commission was able to report to the

Council in December 2004 that Turkey had successfully fulfilled the Copenhagen political criteria.[283] With this commitment on the table, the Berlin Plus arrangements were agreed on the same day by the NATO Council. On 16 December the 'EU-NATO Declaration on ESDP' established a 'strategic partnership' in crisis management between the two organizations, 'founded on shared values, the indivisibility of our security and our determination to tackle the challenges of the new Century'.[284] Recognizing that NATO and the EU were organizations of 'a different nature', the declaration focused on 'partnership' and mutual reinforcement in consultation and development. Permanent arrangements for Berlin Plus were finalized on 11 March 2003, and on 31 March the EU launched its first ever military mission, Operation Concordia, which took over from NATO's operation Allied Harmony in Macedonia. A Berlin Plus arrangement, the operation drew on NATO assets, with DSACEUR as the operational commander running the operation out of the SHAPE, the NATO HQ at Mons. In December 2004 the EU's second Berlin Plus mission was launched, Operation Althea replacing NATO's Stabilization Force in Bosnia, with the majority of the forces simply re-branded as EUFOR and only the war-criminal detection role remaining for the rump NATO mission.[285]

Unfortunately, EU-NATO membership rivalries were to obstruct further development in inter-institutional co-operation, as 'tit for tat' intransigence between Turkey and Cyprus made a mockery of any pretence at interlocking synergy between the Union and the Alliance. In operational terms, the Berlin Plus arrangements were hampered by limitations imposed on the involvement of Cyprus and Malta in NATO-EU security dialogue, and the subsequent insistence by Cyprus that the discussion be constrained largely to the technical aspects of Berlin Plus operations, which resulted in little meaningful dialogue on wider security threats. As the two main protagonists blocked each other's respective NATO and EU access, the future development of the ESDP looked to be severely hampered, if not stymied, by this inter-membership spat.

THE UP AND DOWN YEARS: ESDP AND THE TRANSATLANTIC CHALLENGE

The agreement on Berlin Plus must be seen as something of a high point in NATO-EU relations and took place during a period of extreme 'ups and downs' in transatlantic relations. The terrorist attacks of 11 September 2001 had transformed the focus of US global strategy. With world leaders rushing to offer the US support, NATO's first invocation of its Article 5 was initially rejected by a hyper-power shocked by its own vulnerability and grasped by a desire to bring its own significant power to bear, unhampered by the irritation of allied interests and concerns.[286] A new era of US unilateralism, or at best selective multilateralism, was to be captured by the Secretary of

Defense, Donald Rumsfeld, for whom sentimental adherence to dated alliances was of little advantage in the securing of US interests. From this point, and in tune with the evolving Bush Doctrine of 'benevolent primacy',[287] the US strategic direction dictated that 'it is the mission that defines the alliance and not the alliance that defines the mission'.[288]

Despite the allied show of solidarity through NATO, given the promise of the ESDP, the European reflex to 11 September had been disappointingly, if predictably, national. In the months that followed the attacks, the 'Big Three' European states had irritated the rest of the EU with their initial preference for trilateral discussion of possible national deployments to Afghanistan.[289] Nevertheless, active and largely consistent European support for the US cause in Afghanistan was to result in eventual NATO International Security Assistance Force (ISAF) engagement in August 2003.

However, disagreement over Washington's interventionist intentions in Iraq had flared up in 2002 and led to a serious chilling of transatlantic relations and a further obstacle to ESDP development.[290] The British Prime Minister had largely cast aside his Europeanist enthusiasm, reverting to an unreserved and apparently uncritical Atlanticist position at the head of a faction of largely NATO (and EU) aspirant East European states. His attempt to secure an 'eighteenth' UNSC Resolution, authorizing the military action demanded by Washington in light of the 'evidence' of the Iraqi regime's possession of weapons of mass destruction and suspected Al Qaeda support, met with bitter opposition from his French and German counterparts on the Security Council. Unsightly public squabbling culminated in the most serious crisis in Euro-Atlantic relations since the establishment of NATO as the UK joined the US-led 'coalition of the willing' in what many saw as the illegal invasion of Iraq (launched 19 March 2003), code-named Operation Iraqi Freedom.[291] The hostility of the rhetoric of discontent increasingly coalesced around two distinct visions on the security interests of Europe, one fundamentally Atlanticist and in tune with the emergent US policy orientation, the other Europeanist and defined as much in its opposition to US strategy and method as in reference to a common identity of its own. This division between what Rumsfeld disparagingly referred to as 'old' and 'new' Europe was exacerbated by what appeared to be a policy of European 'disaggregation' on the part of the Americans.[292] But if transatlantic divisions were evident, most striking were the voices of Europe raging against each other, making of Europe a 'sorry figure', incapable of the mature management of internal diversity on which any effective ESDP might rest.[293]

At the Prague Summit of November 2002, NATO's Transformation Agenda was announced, with the new NATO to reflect the US's revised National Security Strategy of January 2002, developed in the light of its new security agenda and dominated by the Global War on Terror. The Prague agreements included a new Capability Commitment, with agreement on the establishment of a NATO Response Force (NRF), a rapid reaction capability of largely European forces, with the critical support assets and levels of interoperability to make it a truly deployable option. As an engine for change, the NRF would test the commitment of the European allies along with the 'future relevance of NATO for America's global security strategy'.[294] Although the NRF was adopted at Prague, many in Europe perceived it as a measure intended to undermine the ERRF, and hence the ESDP, through the establishment of a competing capability drawing on the same national forces.[295] The offer of membership invitations to seven states—the three Baltic states, Slovakia, Slovenia, Romania and Bulgaria—was another US-driven initiative intended to bolster the European security system following 11 September but likely to promote further discontinuity with the EU.[296]

Throughout the travails of the Iraq dispute, the European Convention, which began its work in February 2002 under the Presidency of Giscard d'Estaing, had been conducting a review of the provisions of the EU in the light of its own intended enlargement and the continuing expansion of its competence.[297] A number of bilateral summits had taken place in which the defence aspects of European co-operation had been considered. In January 2003, Franco-German proposals had included calls for a security and defence union, including 'solidarity and common security', 'enhanced cooperation' and an EAA.[298] In February, despite their continuing dispute over Iraq, the British and French had agreed, along with bilateral co-operation on aircraft carrier construction, to link the capability goals for the Union to the most demanding of tasks as a means of progressing the ESDP.[299] But with tensions over Iraq at their height, the Brussels mini Defence Summit of 29 April 2003 was altogether more controversial. Bringing together the anti-Iraq War quartet of Belgium, France, Germany and Luxembourg in exclusive talks aimed at developing a 'hard core of a European military union', the summit proposed the creation of an EU military operational headquarters in Tervuren as a 'nucleus of a collective capability . . . for operational planning and command of EU-led operations without recourse to NATO assets and capabilities'.[300] By September, in an effort to find 'common ground' with his European partners and prevent an unacceptable rift with the US, Blair took the diplomatic risk of endorsing the Franco-German desire for a European 'joint capability to plan and conduct operations without recourse to NATO resources and capabilities', a clear 'red flag' to Washington.[301] Although this must have stuck in Blair's craw and certainly drew him criticism from his American ally, it enabled a compromise to emerge which limited duplication, enhanced co-operation and offered a token autonomy sufficient to satisfy his key European allies. A civil-military cell and NATO liaison arrangements were approved to enhance co-ordination in the extended EUMS in Brussels, and an EU cell was to be established in SHAPE to be augmented for the management of Berlin Plus activities. Most contentiously, a small but augmentable EU operations centre (OpCen), capable of planning and conducting an autonomous small-scale EU operation, was agreed, to be available by 2006.[302]

Symbolically, a step forward had been taken in ESDP independence through a demonstrated internal consensus. But what was significant in this conclusion of what was essentially an operational management issue was that a central transatlantic tension had been muted if not entirely resolved. US acquiescence, bought in part as pay-back for UK support over Iraq, enabled the shifting transatlantic relationship to clear a major hurdle without tearing too many connecting tendons.[303] Blair's role in this transition was central: having given up the WEU, which had traditionally 'taken the strain' in these cross-institutional disputes, the advancement of UK interests required some accommodation of both European and American resolve. Blair later described the UK's 'unique' role: 'call it a bridge, a two lane motorway, a pivot or call it a damn high wire, which is how it often feels'. What it involved was co-joining these tectonic plates without 'subverting our [sic] country either into an American poodle or a European municipality', through the good old British characteristic of 'common sense'.[304]

Despite these challenges, the CFSP/ESDP had made serious strides in the three years following Nice. With agreement on the Berlin Plus formula, and a new EU-NATO Declaration in place, 2003 had seen the launch of a demonstrably operational ESDP. This rapid implementation was evidenced by an impressive 'scoreboard' of deployed operations, including the launch of the EU's first crisis-management operation, the EUPOL police mission in Bosnia; its first military mission, the Berlin Plus Operation Concordia in Macedonia; and its first autonomous military mission, Operation Artemis in the Democratic Republic of the Congo.[305] The EU had begun to occupy a strategic space as a security actor, the nature and vision of which was to be articulated in the European Security Strategy (ESS), launched by the High Representative for the CFSP, in December 2003.

DEFINING STRATEGIC SPACE

The EU had committed itself at Helsinki to developing the necessary assets and capabilities to carry out the full range of conflict prevention and crisis-management activities defined by the Petersberg Tasks.[306] However, there was a considerable lack of consensus on the preferred level of tasking for future ESDP missions, with the French and British at the 'hard' and Sweden at the 'soft' end of the Petersberg spectrum.[307] At the same time, the outlines of the EU's security presence in terms of its geographic scope, and its extent in terms of time and type of likely engagement, remained unclear. Not all EU states shared the same perspective on the role of the ESDP: Denmark took no part in decision-making or actions of the EU with defence implications, and constitutional constraints on some of the post-neutrals precluded them from coercive military activity (including peace enforcement) and bound them to act only with a UNSC mandate.[308]

The developing strategic culture in the EU had been defined in part by the WEU-originated Petersberg Tasks, the adoption of which had framed the EU as essentially a non-aggressive power, its activities determined at the non-coercive and non-offensive end of the mission spectrum. Avoiding overly specific mission definition, not least in order to provide the WEU-esque ambiguity so useful in developing forward enabling consensus, the Petersberg Tasks had been enhanced in the Constitutional Treaty to include 'joint disarmament operations, humanitarian and rescue tasks, military advice and assistance tasks, conflict prevention and peace-keeping tasks, tasks of combat forces in crisis management, including peace-making and post-conflict stabilization. All these tasks may contribute to the fight against terrorism, including by supporting third countries in combating terrorism in their territories'.[309] The realization of the complexity and interconnected-ness of security challenges in the modern era, recognized in the early post-Cold War aspirations for interlocking institutions, required a multifaceted approach to unconventional conflicts which were more often within, rather than between, states and motivated by 'human security' rather than the tra-ditional 'Westphalian' challenges. The EU's adoption of a 'comprehensive approach' to security, a concept given lip-service in some national constitu-encies, was inherent in its CFSP and evolving ESDP, which drew together civil and military tools for positive engagement.

The development of the EU's military capabilities had inevitably contrib-uted to a change in the nature of the organization, from a civilian power to something less than a 'military power'. But it was its approach to security that was to define the EU as something profoundly distinct from and subsequently non-competitive with the NATO alliance. The EU was not an alliance but a *sui generis* power, competent to promote security through attraction, persua-sion and support, rather than through coercion or forcible military action.[310] This identity found expression in Solana's ESS, a document that identified the EU as a 'global actor' with global responsibilities and, in a method reminis-cent of the WEU's Common Reflection of 1995, articulated a collective vision of the EU's place in the world, its goals and interests and the means by which threats to those interests might be managed.[311] In many ways it represented the ethos of the organization, its abiding spirit and a reference point of core assumptions from which future policy and behaviours might be derived. The ESS, in identifying weapons proliferation, state failure, regional conflicts, organized crime and terrorism as key threats, included joint disarmament operations, support for third countries in combating terrorism, and security sector reform as potential missions. And the Strategy determined that the EU should seek a holistic and flexible approach in its security management, including conflict and threat prevention and civilian and humanitarian activ-ity, alongside military operations. The ESDP was not simply another step in the realization of the larger integration project, but a recognition of an existential need emerging from a new world order, adaptation to which was a necessity not only for the EU but, it could be argued, for all security organiza-tions if they were to avoid stagnation and eventual irrelevance.[312]

And if the ESDP was also to be a means of achieving a necessary 'weak' or 'soft' balancing against the US, the declaratory language of this developing policy area would seem to have much for which to thank the WEU, diplomatically coating a greater level of institutional aspiration in a sweetener of outlined transatlantic benefits.[313] In emphasizing the similarity of European and American strategic interests as articulated in the US' post-11 September National Security Strategy, the ESS acknowledged the 'strategic partnership' between the EU and NATO, built upon the framework of permanent arrangements, 'in particular Berlin Plus', and reflecting their 'common determination to tackle the challenges of the new century'.[314]

The WEU and NATO had come to some level of 'understanding' with regards to their respective operational spaces, in terms of both the type and reach of their missions, in part following the competition that led to Sharp Guard, the only example of a NATO-WEU joint operation. The 1999 NATO Strategic Concept had for the first time made reference to Alliance readiness to 'address regional and ethnic conflicts beyond the territory of NATO members', although further references to 'out-of-area' activities had been subdued at European insistence. For many in the US and beyond, NATO's Balkan adventures had been the 'farthest bridge', if not 'the bridge too far', challenging NATO's legitimacy and undermining its protestations of defensiveness: in the interest of the health of the Alliance the floor should be left clear for potential ESDP action beyond Europe and as prescribed by the Petersberg Tasks.[315] Post-Amsterdam, WEU missions, including those directed by the EU, had remained small-scale and at the softer end of the Petersberg spectrum, largely carried out by police officers, and with little relation to the actions with 'defence implications' assumed under the Maastricht Treaty.[316] After the EU had given political direction for WEU-implemented missions in Mostar (police), Croatia (de-mining), Kosovo (satellite intelligence) and Albania (police), it was unsurprising that, as the EU dipped its toe into the operational environment of deployed missions under its ESDP, its first operation was to be at the 'soft' end of potential missions. The experience gained in planning and then conducting the WEU MAPE mission was drawn upon by former MAPE personnel in establishing the EU's own police mission (EUPM) that took over from the UN's International Police Task Force in Bosnia-Herzegovina in January 2003.[317]

With the US' military focus firmly elsewhere post-11 September, the EU had continued the task of 'backfilling', taking on previous NATO deployments in Bosnia and later Kosovo, enabling NATO forces to refocus on the War on Terror.[318] In the decade from 2003, ESDP civil and military operations were to be conducted around the world, both autonomously and with NATO-drawn assets, independently and in support of other organizations, always with a UNSC mandate where required and with varying degrees of success.[319] The Europeans' early interest in Africa as an arena for potential non-competitive WEU military engagement was to find expression in its first small-scale autonomous operation, Operation Artemis in the Democratic Republic of the Congo, although it was in Africa that competition for operational space was later to emerge between NATO and the EU, for example in the case of support to the African Union in Sudan, and in the parallel anti-piracy operations off the Horn of Africa.[320] Disputes over NATO's right to first refusal and competition over operational space would continue to challenge the rhetoric of inter-institutional mutuality and partnership along with the veneer of membership consensus on the role and remit of the EU's developing ESDP.[321] That the WEU had never been used for more 'high-end' missions, including the use of ground forces, had been as much a consequence of its lack of support from national executives and military establishments as of its technical competence. And whilst untested, it had remained a risky and potentially less manageable alternative to national assets. In Operation Artemis and the EU's following military mission in Chad, the Europeans had been prepared to put 'boots on the ground' without practical American support, and whilst these remained fairly small-scale and well-defined missions, they did represent something of a breakthrough for distinctly European military co-operation under EU political auspices.

In response to the altered security environment as reflected in the new tasks outlined in the ESS, a new Headline Goal 2010 was developed in 2004 which focused on qualitative improvements in capabilities, its emphasis being on the interoperability, deployability and sustainability of European forces.[322] Rapidly deployable battlegroups were to provide a new vehicle for force development and were reflective of the small-scale force used to some effect in Operation Artemis. Seen alternatively as a downgrading of European ambitions or a more refined approach to capability development based on upgrading of extant capability, either way it was probably a more realistic aim.[323] A Civilian Headline Goal 2008 was also approved, and in the following years a range of organizational developments were initiated to enhance civilian crisis management, including the establishment of rapidly deployable Civilian Crisis Response Teams, a Civilian Planning and Conduct Capability with a Civilian Operational Commander in the Council Secretariat, and a Crisis Management Planning Directorate.[324] As the EU became increasingly active in the civilian aspects of crisis management, the experience gained from WEU police and civil operations, and the preparatory work of the WEU in the development of a concept for civil-military co-operation (CIMIC), was publicly overlooked in the EU's efforts to establish some distance from what was perceived as its lack-lustre and anachronistic appendage.[325] Nevertheless, the WEU had 'laid the necessary groundwork' for organizational management of this preferred EU mission type.[326]

THE CONSTITUTION

The momentum behind ESDP development within the EU had been secured by the practical realization of operational effect as the EU took on a range of crisis-management tasks from 2003. Having survived the first difficult years, the Convention on the future of the EU was to provide the next opportunity for consolidating and furthering the EU's new policy area, the fulfilment of which could free the WEU from its enforced half-life as the depository of the unachievable in the EU's ESDP context. The Constitutional Treaty, intended to replace the existing treaties on Europe with a single revised and comprehensive text, was signed in Rome with much fanfare by the Heads of State and Government of the 25 EU members on 29 October 2004.[327] It had begun life as a convention 'draft', presented to the European Council in Thessaloniki in June 2003, and the final revised text emerged from extensive high-level negotiation that took place within the IGC that followed. Whilst the key issues of dispute were those related to Commission representation and QMV in the Council, the defence aspects of the text were also 'toned down' during the discussion. Along with provisions for a new Foreign Affairs Ministerial post, the constitution expanded the range of crisis-management tasks and provided for a unique form of enhanced defence co-operation (otherwise excluded from the CFSP/ESDP area) amongst capable and willing states through the 'permanent structured cooperation' scheme.[328] This 'core group' approach was intended to improve military capability through the setting of objectives and benchmarks, a demonstrated commitment and achievement in operational readiness, the pooling and specialization of capabilities and participation in collaborative European equipment programmes. Agreement on this new form of selective co-operation had been reached in September 2003, following French and German reassurances that it would not be exclusive of, or in competition with, NATO and would concentrate on practical capability enhancement, although concerns remained, not least amongst the post-neutral states, that this new 'flexibility' might undermine the cohesiveness of a truly joint approach to CFSP/ESDP development.[329]

But perhaps the most significant departure from earlier ESDP provisions was the introduction of what amounted to a mutual defence clause in the Constitutional Treaty, which could clearly have profound effects for the future 'identity' of the Union and was potentially 'lethal' for the WEU. That agreement had been reached on what appeared to be a revolutionary new commitment for the EU seemed at the very least surprising given traditional resistance from the post-neutrals and the Atlanticist British. The Convention's Defence Working Group had proposed that an 'opt-in' collective defence clause be included in the Convention's proposals, with the 'draft constitution' including a commitment between voluntarily participating states that, should a state come under attack, each 'shall give it aid and assistance by all the means in their power, military or other'.[330] During discussions in the IGC that followed, doubts surfaced about the implications of such a commitment for transatlantic relations and the internal coherence of the Union; the final treaty included an Article 5-like 'mutual assistance' clause, applicable to all, but lacking the clarity of purpose of the originally proposed voluntary provisions.[331] The subsequent Article I-40:7 stated that:

> If a Member State is the victim of armed aggression on its territory, the other Member States shall have towards it an obligation of aid and

assistance by all the means in their power, in accordance with Article 51 of the United Nations Charter. This shall not prejudice the specific character of the security and defence policy of certain Member States. Commitments and cooperation in this area shall be consistent with commitments under the North Atlantic Treaty Organization, which, for those States which are members of it, remains the foundation of their collective defence and the forum for its implementation.

As the first expression of a potential EU mutual defence guarantee, Article 1-40:7 was highly conditional. Adopting the less direct language of 'obligation', the 'specific character' reference offered a 'get out of jail free' card, effectively constituting a voluntary commitment following 'strong resistance' from the four post-neutrals, whilst Atlanticist concerns were to be satisfied by the identification of NATO as 'the foundation' and implementer of allied states' collective defence.[332]

Further to this, Article 1-43 of the Constitutional Treaty laid out the 'solidarity' clause by which 'The Union and its Member States shall act jointly in a spirit of solidarity if a Member State is the object of a terrorist attack or the victim of a natural or man-made disaster. The Union shall mobilize all the instruments at its disposal, including the military resources made available by the Member States'. Together these clauses covered a wide area of mutual assistance and solidarity beyond the limits of collective defence and suggested a broader-based security for which states might require collective means. The generality and lack of contextual precision of these clauses suggested that they were intended rather as enablers than binding obligations, opening up 'possibilities for action' for so inclined states[333] but falling far short of the WEU 'musketeer commitment' (all for one and one for all). Nevertheless, the Dutch were not alone in suggesting during their 2004 Presidency of the WEU that, should the Constitutional Treaty be ratified, the role of the WEU's Article V would be supplanted and the organization should cease to exist.

Governments across Europe were given a 'wake-up call' as the French and then the Dutch provided a resounding 'no' to the Constitution in national referenda in May and June 2005, the political distance of the two constituencies suggesting that there were serious problems with the EU's public identity.[334] As much a reaction to the perceived distance of political elites from their disgruntled citizens, the 'no' votes also reflected fears of an enlarged and unresponsive EU challenging national independence and further removing the people from the polity. With ratification by all states required, the Constitution was 'dead in the water', and in the absence of a 'Plan B', a period of 'reflection' followed as European leaders licked their wounds and considered publicly palatable alternatives to the constitutional method of EU development which might enable necessary institutional reforms. The compromise solution was finally found, following the IGC in the summer of 2007, where agreement was reached on what was largely a re-branding of the provisions of the constitution under a reform treaty, to be signed in Lisbon on 13 December 2007 and coming into force in 2009. In the intervening years, the WEU was to continue to fill the functional gaps left by the limitations of the EU's ESDP provisions at Nice, awaiting their final resolution and its own subsequent and inevitable demise.

THE PARLIAMENTARY DIMENSION: ACCESS AND ACCOUNTABILITY

Following the transferral of the WEU's operational activities to the EU as agreed in 2000, the Assembly had remained as one of the last functioning elements of the WEU, providing as it did a key element of ESDP governance lacking in the EU proper. Its main activities had focused around monitoring of the implications of the MBT's Article V and the necessary co-operation with NATO, on the one hand, and scrutiny of the ESDP and the wider security environment, on the other. But perhaps most significantly, it continued to provide the arena for the inter-parliamentary consensus-building on security and defence issues necessary in this field of intergovernmental co-operation, and the basis for the collective political will required to ensure its effective functioning.[335] The Assembly's institutional solidity in terms of its permanent residence, its specialized staff and its supporting Secretariat, combined with its treaty-based communications with the WEU Council, enabled this continuous inter-parliamentary scrutiny, enquiry, evaluation and dialogue, which in turn contributed to a culture of legitimized co-operation in matters of security and defence for European national governments.[336]

The Nice Treaty had continued the exclusion of the EP from the intergovernmental area of the CFSP and its new ESDP provisions. With no formal powers of scrutiny or approval, the EP's limited engagement with the CFSP/ESDP area was provisioned through the Article 20 of the TEU, whereby the Presidency was directed to 'consult the European Parliament on the main aspects and the basic choices of the common foreign and security policy', to ensure its views were 'duly taken into consideration', and, along with the Commission, to keep it regularly informed of CFSP developments.[337] Nice had also made provision for the EP to make recommendations or ask questions of the Council, which had entered into a non-binding Inter-institutional Agreement in May 1999 to consult annually with the EP on a Council document setting out 'the main aspects and basic choices of the CFSP'.[338] But the Council had no commitment to reply to the 'resolution reports' submitted to it by the EP's Foreign Affairs Committee in response to its own reports.[339] With both the WEU Assembly and EP highly critical of Council and Commission information exchange and consultation on CFSP issues, it was clear that the EU provisions fell far short of the WEU's formal arrangements for parliamentary scrutiny of the work of its Council; the EP lacked the acquis and constituency either to influence its executive or provide the collective voice of the national parliaments ultimately responsible for exercising democratic scrutiny of their governments' security and defence policies.[340]

The WEU Assembly's scrutiny role in relation to the CFSP/ESDP had been enabled in part by the system of double-hatting of national delegations for EU and WEU posts. Foreign and Defence Ministers sat on both the EU and WEU Council, the latter being formally required to report to its Assembly and respond to its written recommendations. The habit of appointing the same national delegates to the WEU's Permanent Council and the EU's PSC also facilitated a level of communication on ESDP activity, not least through the regular Permanent Council engagements with the Assembly Committees. Simultaneously filling the role of Secretary General of the WEU and High Representative for the CFSP, Solana provided the highest level of cross-organizational engagement and a further source of Assembly access to the 'goings on' of the CFSP/ESDP.

Nevertheless, it was clear that in its extant form the WEU Assembly was not fully capable of exercising democratic scrutiny over the ESDP, as its constituency and procedural limitations with regards to the EU proper denied it full access and engagement. The WEU Council had resisted Assembly efforts to work with it to enhance its engagement with the CFSP/ESDP area, arguing that member states did not wish to use the Council to duplicate mechanisms 'by which the EU is striving to develop the ESDP'.[341] In fact, there had been no full Council meetings following the November 2000 Marseille Declaration, its work being conducted largely through written procedure. The Assembly Presidency had, therefore, lost the opportunity to address the 28 Ministers, and no opportunity was offered for committee pre-briefings to inform Ministerial discussions.[342] Continuing to fulfil its formal commitments to the Assembly, the Council's Annual Reports became increasingly uninformative, resulting in the paradoxical situation that the EP, which had little influence over this intergovernmental area of activity, had rather fuller reports on the CFSP and ESDP than did the national parliamentarians of the WEU Assembly, who received a report which became of 'little practical and even less political value'.[343] The Permanent Council continued to meet until May 2002, but often with less than Ambassador-level representation, and after that date meetings were confined largely to its budgetary and administrative working groups. Once again, the Assembly found itself without an active Executive with which to engage, and fearing further marginalization or even extinction, it continued with efforts to sustain an active parliamentary existence, reporting on issues of relevance to the ESDP, seeking linkage with CFSP bodies and making proposals on future inter-parliamentary arrangements.

The Assembly's contribution to the European Convention on the new Europe had been largely in promoting itself as a potential second chamber for the CFSP, more suited to the intergovernmental processes acceptable in defence co-operation, representative of national views and more able to make the connections with NATO than the EP was.[344] The maintenance of the pillar structure that supported national sovereignty and the unanimity rule for the CFSP in the failed Constitution was reflective of the strength of opposition amongst EU members to the deepening of integration in the area of defence. But the question of parliamentary scrutiny over this intergovernmental area had been largely side-stepped by the Constitutional Treaty,[345] which sought institutional streamlining, proposing some minor enhancement of powers for the EP in the area of Foreign Policy and inter-parliamentary conferences to cover the area of security and defence. If a 'double-legislative' was to be avoided, the WEU Assembly had limited appeal, and a possible 'turf war' seemed likely as the EP sought to further enhance its own competence in the CFSP/ESDP area.[346]

The NATO and EU enlargements of 2004, which brought 7 new states into the Alliance and 10 into the EU, had led the WEU Assembly, which had designated itself the 'Interparliamentary European Security and Defence Assembly' in 2003, to challenge the Council on the rights of these accession states to parliamentary representation in the one Assembly able to provide some level of strategic oversight of European security and defence issues. On 28 June 2001, the WEU's Secretary General had announced the Council's decision that, as of January 2002, any further changes to formal WEU membership statuses for non-full members would be unnecessary.[347] Most significantly, as the associate members had been freed from budgetary contributions at the November 2000 Marseille Council meeting, their access to full membership was to be denied, along with that of any future aspiring states. Seeking to (re)establish those rights for accession states that met the differentiated membership criteria as laid down in the Maastricht Treaty and accompanying WEU Declaration of December 1991, the Assembly established a range of new statuses applicable solely to Assembly participation. Alongside the existing full membership, associate membership, and (permanent) observer statuses reserved for pre-2002 participants, provisional rules were established to allow the eight new NATO plus EU membership states (Czech Republic, Estonia, Hungary, Latvia, Lithuania, Poland, Slovak Republic and Slovenia) to become *affiliate members,* the two new NATO but not EU states (Bulgaria and Romania) to become *affiliate associate members* and the two EU but not NATO states (Cyprus and Malta) to become *affiliate permanent observers*. Croatia became an *affiliate associate partner* as an aspirant state, this status replacing the associate partnership (the previous associate partners having moved into one of the new affiliate statuses).[348] An earlier decision had also made provision for a wider European state engagement with Assembly debate, although without the benefit of voting rights, by the establishment of the statuses of 'special guests' (Albania, Bosnia and Herzegovina, Croatia, the former Yugoslav Republic of Macedonia and Serbia-Montenegro) and 'permanent guests' (Russia and Ukraine).[349] This confusing array of memberships was significant in providing the affiliates, who had membership in one or both of the organizations for whom the WEU had a support role, with voting rights in the Assembly's committees[350] and, in the case of affiliate members who had membership of both, in the Assembly's plenary sessions, whilst respecting the Council's decision on the freezing of membership as it applied to Council activity and the guarantees that full membership conferred.[351] These memberships were to be simplified in 2008 under the revised Charter and Rules of Procedure, which further extended full rights in plenary and committee structures to all 27 members of the EU in what was to be renamed the 'European Security and Defence Assembly. The Assembly of the WEU'.[352]

Following the rejection of the Constitutional Treaty, the Assembly had continued with its twice-yearly plenary sessions, bringing together a broad membership of EU, NATO and non-NATO/EU European states to discuss and debate European security and defence issues. Its Committees continued to produce well-regarded reports and recommendations that, once amended and adopted in plenary, received obligatory written Council replies.[353] The Assembly's work in spreading a common European security and defence culture continued to be applauded by national governments,[354] and national parliamentarians meeting in Paris in May 2008 remained highly appreciative of the 'expertise and in-depth political work that were the hallmark of the working committees of the WEU Assembly'.[355] Nevertheless, the findings of the Assembly's 'Contact Group' on national parliamentary engagement with the ESDP (aka the Reinforced Liaison Sub-committee) suggested that parliamentarians often felt 'left on the periphery as regards governments' foreign and defence decisions' although they were 'unaware of any WEU Assembly involvement in that connection'.[356] This failure of the national Assembly delegates to effectively broadcast the work of the organization was to be redressed in part by proposals for strengthening the machinery for consultation and information exchange between the Assembly and national defence committees. Efforts were to be made to enable an Assembly presence at the executive briefings on the CFSP/ESDP provided to the EP's Foreign Affairs Committee and its recently established Subcommittee on Security and Defence, in order to mitigate the lack of any legal consultation require-ment between the EU and the WEU Assembly or national parliaments in these matters.[357] However, the loss of WEU credibility resulting from the initiatives taken post-St Malo provided an unfortunate 'backdrop' for the Assembly's efforts, which 'failed to elicit a satisfactory response' from national parliaments or the media or to create the desired follow-up in terms of launching a process of public debate.[358]

ARMS CO-OPERATION

The military engagements in Kosovo and Afghanistan had highlighted the limitations of European defence capabilities. In much of Europe, large national military forces had been funded at the expense of capital and operational investment, and a system of nationally protected defence indus-tries had been supported on the basis of 'political' (social and technologi-cal) rather than military effectiveness. The nation-based fragmentation of

European arms production had led to inevitable inefficiencies in terms of unit cost, industrial capacity and research and design duplication, making the European defence industry uncompetitive in relation to the increasingly integrated US market.[359] With declining defence budgets and the pace of technological change, if European defence industries were not to lose market share, some level of industrial consolidation was required, involving the rationalization and restructuring of defence industries through mergers and joint ventures and preferably supported by some real co-operation in European procurement policies.[360] For some, the defence rationalization decisions of corporate Europe could well become the 'cement' of European defence integration, the industrial logic behind defence profitability making defence industrial co-operation an integrative driver, ensuring consolidation of the broader defence integration measures that might sustain it.[361]

The WEAG, since its establishment under the WEU in 1992, had been relatively successful in providing a forum for discussion on armaments co-operation, although it had been rather less effective in terms of programme implementation. Its working groups provided for regular discussion and consultation on co-operative opportunities in equipment programmes, research and development, and procedures and economic issues, and its annual Defence Minister and biannual NAD meetings, held at '19' following the accession of six new nations in November 2000, offered a wide engagement for NATO, the EU and 'waiting room' states.[362] The WEAO, established in 1996, shared a legal personality with the WEU, which enabled it to let multinational research contracts; its Research Cell provided administrative support from a field of scientific, engineering and legal experts to state and industry-based project management teams, and assisted in the preparation of contract arrangements for project participants. The WEAO benefited from extensive experience and flexibility in conducting joint research and technology programmes with a range of European research groups, including EUCLID (European Co-operation in the Long Term in Defence), THALES (Technology Arrangements for Laboratories for Defence European Sciences) and SOCRATE (System of Cooperation for Research and Technology in Europe).[363] The attachment to the WEU offered not only the legal basis for WEAO activity, but also the European credentials, whilst maintaining a comfortable distance from the potentially intrusive activities of the EU proper.

In November 2000 in Marseille, the WEAG Defence Ministers, recognizing that the WEU's operational role had come to an end, offered guidelines for a thorough reflection on the future of European arms co-operation. Both the WEAG and WEAO had consistently promoted the concept of an EAA competent to enhance Europe-wide co-operation in arms development and procurement, the WEAO having been created with the aim of developing into such an agency once conditions allowed. An EAA 'Masterplan' had been developed in 1998, and the Ministers had established a Group of National Experts to consider its operational, procedural and legal development. On the basis of their report, and taking into account developments in the ESDP, the Headline Goal and NATO's DCI (and its follow-on, the Prague Capabilities Commitments), agreement was reached in 2002 that the WEAG, 'as the widest forum of European nations', could continue to contribute to maximizing convergence in armaments co-operation issues, whilst additional functions might be found for the WEAO. Passing further consideration of an EAA on to their NADs, the WEAG Ministers endorsed the concept of an 'evolutionary process' towards an EAA once 'appropriate conditions' had been met and a political consensus achieved.[364]

In fact, by 2002 the WEAG had found itself largely overshadowed by the four-nation OCCAR (France, Germany, Italy and the UK) and the 1998 'Letter of Intent' (LoI) group (the OCCAR four plus Spain and Sweden), the members of which were also WEAG/WEAO states.[365] Both OCCAR and LoI offered a 'core club' approach for major EU arms producers keen to promote their trade share in relation to smaller producers. By 2010, these six LoI states were to account for 80% of European industrial capacity and 98% of European defence Research and Development (R&D), with five of these involved in significant joint projects within OCCAR (including the military transport aircraft, the Airbus A400M). It is unsurprising that there was little enthusiasm amongst this group for their investment decisions to be the subject of larger group co-ordination in the WEAG/WEAO framework.[366] This competitive approach was largely supported by the British: the House of Commons Defence Committee considered the OCCAR model as the 'more hopeful way forward' for arms co-operation and had suggested that in the light of the decisions on the WEU taken at Marseille and Nice, if governments felt the need for the continuation of WEAG/WEAO, there was certainly no requirement for 'the WEU umbrella for them to shelter beneath'.[367]

The Constitutional Treaty, in recognition of the work ongoing in the WEAG, had made provision for an intergovernmental EAA to work in the field of defence capabilities development, research, acquisition and armaments. With the Constitution looking increasingly in trouble, and with a defence 'quick win' a useful symbolic boost, the Council Joint Action 2004/551/CFSP of 12 July 2004 unhinged the Agency proposals from the Constitution and approved the establishment of the European Defence Agency (EDA).[368] This Joint Action mandated the EDA 'to support the Member States and the Council in their effort to improve European defence capabilities in the field of crisis management and to sustain the European Security and Defence Policy as it stands now and develops in the future'. It was to fulfil this mission through carrying out four functions: developing defence capabilities, promoting defence research and technology, encouraging armaments co-operation, and creating a competitive European defence equipment market and strengthening the European defence, technological and industrial base.[369] Open to all EU members (Denmark opted out), the EDA also offered special Administrative Arrangements for non-EU allies to co-operate in both discussion and project engagement. This was to be particularly significant for Turkey and Norway, members of the WEAG but not of the EU and hence excluded from full EDA membership.

In view of the intention of the Joint Action that the EDA 'assimilate or incorporate relevant principles and practices of WEAG as appropriate', the WEAG states recognized that European armaments cooperation in the future would be promoted and facilitated within the EU, and that there was 'no longer a need for activities in the framework of the WEAG'.[370] The Defence Ministers held their last meeting in Brussels on 22 November 2004 and the NADs prepared for the final handover of working group activities by 23 May 2005. The WEAO continued to operate until 31 August 2006, by which time its Research Cell had let a total of 138 contracts amounting to in excess of €1b. Of its remaining projects, eight valued collectively at around €67.2m went to national management, whilst 37 projects worth around €193.5m went directly to the EDA.[371]

The EDA was to face a number of challenges, many of which had limited the success of the WEAG/WEAO in the quest to enhance European arms co-operation. The persistence of the EC's strategic industry national protection provisions was something of an obstacle to the construction of a competitive arms market and was of declining practical relevance given the diluted national identity of defence companies, consolidated through joint ventures, acquisitions and legal arrangements.[372] Equally, Commission competence and expertise in industrial and trade policy remained at odds with intergovernmental practice in security and defence questions, although the distinction between civil and military production was increasingly blurred. The EDA was to begin life with a tiny budget (amounting to a total of €23m in 2005), its significance for the future of European defence given lip-service if not the substance that such a core requirement might have warranted.[373] The Agency was a 'promising tool, but still only a tool', suggested the President of the Council of French Defence Companies: everything depended 'on the political will and commitment of the European governments'.[374]

If the WEAG/WEAO arrangement had served its purpose of preparing the ground for the EDA, the loss of these WEU-based arrangements was not without some minuses. The larger EU-inclusive EDA membership was to prove rather more un-wieldy than the WEAG arrangement, and the flexibility of membership, outside of the constraints of EU constituent boundaries, had been lost to some cost. Turkey had found itself snubbed in the rush to follow through on the momentum of an EU decision to draw another aspect of defence within its organizational gambit. Whilst Norway concluded its implementation arrangements for association with the EDA in March 2005, Cyprus denied Turkey approval on the basis of 'political considerations'.[375] Believing itself cheated of its desired administrative arrangement with the EDA, Turkey denied Cyprus the NATO security agreement required for attendance at the EU-NATO Capability Group mechanism designed to promote co-operation in the field of capability development.[376] This exclusion of Cyprus was to further limit the potential for NATO-EU co-operation and any subsequent European benefits, given EU reticence to fully engage without its full membership.[377] Once again, as the WEU shut up yet another of its defence co-operation outposts, the benefits of flexible and inclusive membership structures were only to be truly recognized in their passing.

LISBON FINDS A WAY FOR EUROPEAN DEFENCE

The coming into force of the Lisbon Treaty on 1 December 2009 marked the end of a long process of self-reflection in the EU, the tortuous route to its conclusion resulting in a complex amendment of the Treaties on European Union and Community, whilst adopting much of the substance of the rejected Constitution.[378] The further consolidation of the TEU and of the renamed Treaty on the Functioning of the European Union (TFEU, formerly the TEC) was to put an end to the Union's 'identity crisis', establishing an effective decision-making competence for an enlarged Union by spreading the scope of QMV, whilst emphasizing the role of the state by respecting the principles of subsidiarity and proportionality.[379] In many ways, Lisbon represented the EU's 'arrival' in terms of its security and defence identity, which, having been initiated at Maastricht, had taken the EU from a civilian power making requests, and later 'availing' itself of the subcontracting services of the WEU, to an actor competent to determine and implement common security and defence policies drawing on a range of civilian and military capabilities. Drawing heavily on the work of the buried Constitution, the Lisbon Treaty enhanced the remit of the ESDP well beyond the original Petersberg Tasks, whilst Permanent Structured Cooperation and the legal foundation of the EDA provided for a level of flexible co-operation in defence capability development for willing and military-competent states.[380] The pillar structure was formally rejected (although not the intergovernmental nature of the CFSP area) in favour of a single legal identity for the Union, and a new post of High Representative of the Union for Foreign Affairs and Security Policy was created, double-hatted with that of the Vice-Presidency of the European Commission (TEU Articles 17.7 and 18) to enhance co-ordination across the range of tools available to the EU, including trade and aid, justice and diplomatic means, and supported by a new European External Action Service (TEU Article 27).[381]

It had soon become evident that the Lisbon Treaty had removed the final obstacles to the WEU's departure by the EU's own form of 'smoke and mirrors'. This included a recommendation for parliamentary engagement with the newly named Common Security and Defence Policy (CSDP) that provided only the most rudimentary of access, and the provision of a mutual defence clause so caveated as to be at best highly contestable. Nevertheless, in the spirit of forward movement, following the failure of the Constitutional Treaty, and in the absence of any appetite for significant development in the CSDP area of intergovernmental co-operation, the role of the WEU seemed to have been largely supplanted by the new provisions.[382]

The Lisbon Treaty had acknowledged the importance of national parliamentary involvement in the activities of the Union and had promoted the organizing of inter-parliamentary conferences on specific topics through the auspices of the Conference of Parliamentary Committees for Union Affairs of Parliaments of the European Union (COSAC).[383] 'In particular', these topics might include 'matters of common foreign and security policy, including common security and defence policy'. The new High Representative was to 'regularly consult' with the Parliament and ensure that its views were 'taken into consideration', and the Parliament could ask the Council questions or make recommendations (TEU Article 36), although no provision was made for further written exchange of information between the Council or High Representative and the EP, nor for their informing, consulting or engaging with national parliaments or their collected representatives.

The Assembly's response to the Lisbon Treaty provisions was 'regretful', not least because it was 'even less legible for European citizens' than the failed Constitutional Treaty that had preceded it.[384] The proposed inter-parliamentary conference model appeared to offer neither national nor European parliamentary scrutiny sufficient for the range of CSDP activities envisaged within the Union.[385] Damning in its critique, the Assembly had responded to the initial launch of the treaty in December 2007 by declaring that it considered that the parliamentary provisions on the CFSP/CSDP would ensure that a 'single, coherent and sustainable European foreign policy' was a long way distant and would suffer from 'an embarrassing democratic deficit' which would serve to 'reinforce the idea among European citizens that the European construction process is a mechanism being organized behind their backs by lawyers, diplomats and other authorities who have no real interest in participatory democracy'. Occasional conferences of national and European parliamentary committees would not ensure effective parliamentary scrutiny of the CSDP area, which would lack any permanent system of collective oversight. Indeed, the only way of preventing this alienation of citizens and national parliaments would be for the WEU Assembly to continue its important work.[386]

As to provisions for a common defence for the EU, the post-Lisbon consolidated TEU and TFEU still referred to common defence in an aspirational manner, where the progressive framing of a common Union defence policy 'will lead to a common defence', but only when the European Council unanimously so decides (TEU Article 42.2). This recognized absence of a common defence for the Union helps to situate the adoption in the Lisbon Treaty of the new TEU Article 42.7 'mutual assistance' clause. Reproducing the words of the failed Constitution, Article 42.7 inferred, rather than specified, the possibility of military support and watered down the language of obligation. It retained all the former caveats regarding avoidance of prejudice to the 'specific character' of certain states' security and defence policies and of the need for consistency with NATO commitments (TEU 42.2), with the Alliance remaining the foundation of collective defence for its members (TEU 42.7). Just like the failed Constitution before it, the Lisbon Treaty sought to accommodate a range of diverse sensitivities amongst member states, including those who truly sought a WEU-type Article V, those whose 'neutrality' led them to eschew any collective defence commitment and those for whom NATO had to remain the foundation of their defence.[387] With no evidence that the 'mutual assistance' clause was seen as a practical necessity of the EU's immediate threat environment, it could leave the way clear for a future common defence, add to CDSP credibility and, by selective interpretation of its relevance, rationalize the European defence architecture by enabling the cost-cutting dissolution of the WEU.[388] The limitations of an ambiguous 'mutual assistance' clause that did not necessarily amount to a defence commitment, nor applied equally to all participants, were self-evident and yet appeared to have been conveniently side-stepped.[389]

The reproduced 'solidarity' clause, to be enshrined as Article 222 in the TFEU,[390] offered perhaps the more explicit requirement for joint action by EU member states in assisting each other in the face of a range of security challenges on the continent, including combating terrorism and responding to natural or manmade disasters and emergencies. With the Union's security and defence tasks expanded under the new TEU Article 43 to include those highlighted in the Constitution (joint disarmament operations, military advice and assistance tasks, conflict prevention and post-conflict stabilization—all of which might contribute to the fight against terrorism), the TFEU Article 222 reflected a growing institutional *acceptance* of the complex range of likely security challenges most pressing for the realization of a European security space. If NATO offered traditional collective defence for those who still sought it, the 'mutual defence' clause might provide all that was required, a symbolic collective nod to the aspiration of a minority, signifying little, whilst the 'solidarity' clause had a potential relevance for collective security obligation and action more in tune with the post-Westphalian comprehensive security approach reflected in the ESS and increasingly evident in the 'soft' successes of the emerging CSDP.[391]

END OF THE ROAD FOR THE WEU: THE 2010 DECISION

On 30 March 2010, just before the British General Election, Chris Bryant, the UK's Parliamentary Under Secretary of State for Foreign and Commonwealth Affairs and Minister for Europe, announced the British Government's decision to withdraw from the WEU.[392] The Minister applauded the 'valuable role' played by the organization in promoting 'consultation and co-operation on defence and security matters in Western Europe' and in embedding 'the principle of mutual defence in post-war Europe'. But, he argued, its defence role was 'essentially symbolic' as the Lisbon Treaty continued to make clear in its recognition of NATO as the 'forum and foundation for collective defence of the allies'. As NATO and the US had now 'specifically welcomed' the EU's adoption of the WEU's operational role, the remaining inter-parliamentary function of the WEU's Assembly no longer justified the cost of the organization, which was simply 'no longer relevant to today's European security architecture'.[393]

The motivation behind the British withdrawal from the WEU was variously presented by the Minister (and the Foreign Secretary before him) as cost reduction and institutional rationalization.[394] The Foreign Secretary had argued that the WEU served only to divide the EU membership, the EU having taken on many of the WEU's functions. There was 'no appetite' amongst the 17 non-WEU EU members to join the organization, and any useful reform would require lengthy and potentially unproductive negotiation. If the WEU was no longer required to satisfy the operational requirements of a budding European defence given EU consensus and US support,[395] the residual WEU functions could be either substituted or discarded in the interests of architectural simplicity and coherence. Of the two remaining functions, the British seemed to have accepted the lack of relevance of the WEU's Article V, which the Foreign Secretary seemed to have rather belatedly recognized as being 'overtaken given that all its [WEU's] full members are members of NATO'.[396] His lack of reference to the Lisbon 'mutual assistance' clause suggested that satisfaction with the WEU Article V replacement at Lisbon was hardly a consideration in the British decision to abandon the WEU.

The issue of cross-parliamentary activity and scrutiny of the ESDP did continue to exercise British attention, and it was this area that would be the focus of consultation and discussion during the 12-month notice period required following notification to the Belgium Government of intention to withdraw.[397] Starting with a clean slate and adopting a more 'inclusive' approach, parliamentary scrutiny of the CFSP/CSDP should, the Parliamentary Under Secretary announced, be 'entirely a matter for national Parliaments and co-ordination between them' and an area in which there was 'no reason and no case' for the expansion of the competency of the EP.[398] Acknowledging, in reply to subsequent questions in the House, that many in Europe felt that the 'architecture for examining common security and defence policy in Europe was no longer sufficient', he had laid out his criteria: the Assembly's replacement should be intergovernmental, should involve all EU and non-EU allies and should be 'cost-effective for the British tax payer'. Indeed, he had made clear in his statement that the UK intended to 'use this opportunity to improve the exchange of information and engagement between the EU and NATO'. The WEU Assembly membership structure, he argued, was far too complex, and it was the 'right time to put together a more appropriate structure'. However, when pressed on the means by which Turkey and Norway would be engaged, having lost their associate membership status in the WEU, he seemed to rather shift targets, arguing that 'the most important thing is that we ensure that we have a cost-effective structure'.[399] It appeared that what was sought was essentially an Assembly-lite approach to the serious matter of democratic oversight of the developing European security and defence area, with broad EU/NATO-plus member-state engagement but limited institutional structure. The absence of any concrete proposals for an Assembly replacement at the time of the UK announcement of withdrawal would suggest that enhancing democratic scrutiny was not the driving factor behind the self-declared 'courageous step' taken by the British Government in leading the rush to desert the WEU. The UK had traditionally encouraged practical co-operation in the WEU as a means of containing the EU 'itch' on defence, but the CSDP appeared to have reached its culminating point, posing no further threat to British interests in the maintenance of intergovernmentalism in defence or the primacy of NATO. The WEU was, therefore, no longer required and, being redundant in British eyes, was an unnecessary and disposable cost.[400]

Having taken 'private' soundings from the other WEU member states, the UK was confident of their support, and, by the following day, all 10 had announced their intention to withdraw.[401] The resultant Presidency Statement was delivered without much in the way of public fanfare, which is surprising given that this marked the intended dissolution of such a long-standing arrangement, even if it had ceased to draw the attention of political elites. Noting that 'with the entry into force of the Lisbon Treaty, a new phase in European security and defence begins [sic]', the Statement clearly identifies the EU's new 'mutual assistance' clause as the cause of the WEU's obsolescence, stating:

> Article 42.7 of the Treaty on the European Union now sets out that, if a Member State is the victim of armed aggression on its territory, the other Member States shall have towards it an obligation of aid and assistance by all the means in their power, and states that commitments and cooperation in this area shall be consistent with commitments in NATO, which for its members remains the foundation of their collective defence and the forum for its implementation.
>
> In this context, we remain strongly committed to the principle of mutual defence of article V of the Modified Brussels Treaty.
>
> The WEU has therefore accomplished it historical role. In this light we the States Parties to the Modified Brussels Treaty have collectively decided to terminate the Treaty, thereby effectively closing the organization, and in line with its article XII notify the Treaty's depositary in accordance with national procedures.[402]

The 'substantial' contribution of the WEU Assembly to the 'development of a European culture on security and defence' was also noted in the Presidency Statement. This role should be satisfied in the future 'in accordance with the specific nature of CSDP' through the 'enhancement of interparliamentary dialogue in this field including with candidates for EU accession and other interested parties', for which Protocol 1 on the role of national parliaments in the EU, annexed to the Lisbon Treaty, '*may* provide a basis'.[403] This rather vague reference to future inter-parliamentary dialogue lacked any blueprint for post-Assembly organization of this 'cultural' function. And no mention was made of the role of parliamentary scrutineer of the CSDP area, practiced through the Assembly's treaty-based relationship with the WEU Council, even though it had been limited by its relationship to the executive organs of the CSDP. This was an area ripe for reform if a democratic deficit was not to undermine future national support for collective efforts. Given the Permanent Council's task of 'organising the cessation of WEU activities in accordance with timelines prescribed in the Modified Brussels Treaty preferably by the end of June 2011', any replacement structure would need to be 'up and running' in short order, a challenging proposition given the necessity of 'cultural' familiarity and organizational fit in the absence of any clearly stated consensus on the nature of the task.

With the decision to do away with the Assembly as the last significant remnant of the WEU by June 2011, the necessity to enhance the EU's provision for interparliamentary dialogue on, and scrutiny of, EU security and defence issues became increasingly urgent. The Assembly remained rather more ambitious than the Presidency Statement of termination suggested, in its efforts to prevent an 'institutional void in the area of parliamentary scrutiny of the CSDP'.[404] Arguing for a light but permanent structure, the Assembly Presidency emphasized the legitimate and necessary role of national parliaments in providing democratic scrutiny,[405] establishing a Subcommittee on the Way Ahead to consider options that might satisfy collective requirements of efficiency, effectiveness, inclusion and influence. The Subcommittee put forward proposals for a Steering Committee of Assembly and EP Committee 'heads', under the co-chairmanship of the High Representative and the EU Presidency.[406] This committee would be tasked with determining a 'credible model of interparliamentary scrutiny' which would not 'reduce the role of parliaments to that of mere spectator' and which would build on the WEU Assembly's acquis.[407] Sidelined and in view of the imminent departure of its 'mothership', the Subcommittee continued to draw up proposals for a Standing Interparliamentary Conference on CFSP and CSDP of national and European parliamentarians. But it urged that any deliberations, whilst guided by the Lisbon provisions, follow the 'motto' that the Assembly with its 50 years of experience would wish to pass on to its successors: 'Plan the future by the past'.[408]

The European Affairs Committee of the French Senate had suggested, at the declaration of French withdrawal, that any decision on the Assembly should be 'subject to the creation of a structure bringing together members of Parliament specialising in defence issues of the 27 Member States of the EU'.[409] For the many in the British establishment, fearful of any expansion of EP competence in the event that no other inter-parliamentary arrangements for debate were in place by the time of the WEU Assembly closure, the option of 'doing nothing' appeared closed.[410] By January 2011, the British House of Commons Foreign Affairs, Defence and European Scrutiny Committees had found consensus on a 'conference of committees' model, similar to the informal Conference of Foreign Affairs Committee Chairpersons (COFACC) and the Defence equivalent (CODCC),[411] which would ensure a strong national parliamentary link, with knowledgeable participants, and no costly duplication.[412]

By April 2012 the EU's Conference of Speakers of the European Union Parliaments, which had debated this issue throughout 2011, had reached agreement on the new concept for inter-parliamentary scrutiny of the CSDP in the wake of the WEU Assembly's demise.[413] This would involve the establishment of an Inter-parliamentary Conference for the CFSP and the CSDP, composed of 6 parliamentarians from each EU state's national parliament, along with 16 EP members, with provision for observers (four per state) from the national parliaments of each of the candidate countries and non-EU European NATO members, to meet every six months under the chairmanship of the state holding the rotating Council Presidency, which would also provide the secretariat. The High Representative for Foreign Affairs and Security Policy would be invited to 'set out the outlines and strategies of the common foreign and defence policy of the European Union' at these meetings, the conclusions of which would be reached by consensus and be of a non-binding nature.[414] In replacing the meetings of the COFACC and CODCC it was intended that this new Inter-parliamentary Conference would result in a streamlining of the mechanisms for national parliamentary consultation. Given the limited meeting opportunities, the lack of a permanent 'home' and the discontinuity of secretariat support, it was questionable, however, that this new creation could provide the sort of in-depth, informed and rigorously exercised analysis of European security and defence issues provisioned by the WEU Assembly, or the necessary sighted scrutiny of the CFSP/CSDP. And this would seem to have been made all the more problematic by the creation of the 'quasi-supranational' institutions of the new High Representative and European Action Service that Lisbon had introduced.[415] As the Conference met for the first time in Cyprus on 9–10 September 2012,[416] with a review planned within 18 months, the new approach appeared to offer a less institutionalized arrangement in which parliamentary engagement might well fall short on delivery of both effective scrutiny and cultural depth.[417]

As the WEU was packing up the last of its trunks and preparing to leave the European stage, indicators were suggesting a disappointing start to the post-Lisbon era of EU development and a general decline in the relevance of the CSDP. The demand for European engagements continued to outstrip supply, but the conflicts in Iraq and Afghanistan had dampened any enthusiasm in Europe for future military engagements. The political impetus required to ensure the capabilities to meet declared aspirations for European defence co-operation had been lost, and the EU adopted a 'survival strategy' of largely civil and small-scale CSDP activity unlikely to challenge the external order.[418] The global financial crisis had plunged the world into a recession where austerity politics were likely to dominate government spending plans for years to come, and where European national defence budgets competed with heightened social and welfare expectations in a climate of reduced territorial threat. Distracted by the euro crisis, which threatened the integrity of the whole European project, the CSDP appeared to be stagnating under the weight of the EU's increasing self-doubt.

By the turn of the decade NATO, in contrast, was undergoing something of a revival and preparing for a wider role in the maintenance of international security.[419] Successive summits through the 2000s (Riga 2006, Bucharest 2008, Strasbourg/Kehl 2009) had sought allied political agreement on a range of strategic challenges including the future of the still non-functioning NRF and the global reach of NATO partnerships and interests.[420] The challenge of engaging sufficient and effectively deployable forces for the ISAF mission, combined with the seemingly intransigent nature of the conflict, had severely rocked the Alliance, which was unsure of its territorial or expeditionary priorities. But by the end of 2010, NATO appeared to have emerged from its experiences in Afghanistan with a new confidence, and European satisfaction with the Alliance was at least in part a recognition of continuing dependence on the US for the 'hard-end' military provision for which NATO was the only real player in town.[421] NATO's new Strategic Concept, released at its Lisbon Summit in November 2010, depicted a less Europe-focused organization, capable of both allied defence and intervention and with a much broader range of defence relationships and concerns, including global partners in the coalition against cyber-assault and global-reach terrorism.[422] The new Administration of President Barack Obama in Washington was keen to promote opportunities for global co-operation, including an improved Russia-NATO relationship, with agreements on missile defence and a new strategic arms control treaty.[423] NATO's future seemed secured, if in a form less competitive with the EU, which itself was leaning increasingly towards soft security options. The French had reintegrated into NATO's military structures in 2009 under President Nicolas Sarkosy, indicating to some the end of the driving force behind a common EU security and defence.[424] The Anglo-French Defence Treaty, agreed in the same month as NATO's new Strategic Concept, suggested a return to 'big-player' bilateralism in European defence relationships, driven by national interest and far removed from any pretensions towards a common EU effort.[425]

But perhaps the reality was rather less polarized than suggested by those who foretold the end of the European defence initiative. The management of complex and undefined security challenges required a range of synergistic approaches, perhaps less defined by their political than by their practical advantage. In the essentially national domain of defence, the enhancement of capability, through unilateral, bilateral or multinational co-operation, had potentially positive effects as much at the international as the national level. The impact of declining defence budgets on the pursuit of collective solutions to capability development is contentious, but the bilateralism of the Anglo-French approach, as much as the provision for permanent structured co-operation and the EDA, offered flexible options for capability enhancement unconstrained by the conditionality of more politically ambitious visions for the EU space. The soft end of crisis management, suited to the consensus and tools of the integrated EU, might be both supported by and supportive of a 'gentle' militarism, residing in the intergovernmental half-realm of EU co-operation, with 'real' defence a matter of national or NATO concern. French reintegration into NATO, the provisions of the Lisbon Treaty, recent bilateralism and, of course, the dissolution of the WEU itself all point to a confluence of ideas—an acceptance of limits at the point of the highest achievable consensus. These limits include consensus on the extent of integration in security and defence, where the principle of sovereign authority for military forces had been accepted in the persistence of defence intergovernmentalism. They were reflected in agreement on the acceptable nature of the EU as a *sui generis* power, influencing through attraction and the carefully targeted use of diplomatic and economic tools, and supported by a 'light' collective military option.[426] And they were also recognized in the role of NATO as the core of defence provision for an EU majority, where political as much as military capability defines alliance solidarity and credibility. The decline of institutional pretensions, which had become symbolized by the Atlanticist/Europeanist divide, removed the necessity for an institution that embodied what were often contradictory or competing visions for the management of European security. At the very institutional core of the WEU was the steering principle that European and NATO defence were mutually supportive (or, at least, ought to be). With the WEU's help, it transpired that the two organizations have been able to arrive at that conclusion for themselves.

REFLECTIONS

In the years following the agreements reached at St Malo, the WEU gradually lost its raison d'être. The dual role of the WEU as promoter of both the Alliance and European integration in defence had resulted in its emergence as the interconnecting shaft of a dumbbell-like relationship between the two heavy-weights of European security, NATO and the EU. The WEU's direct relationship with each had facilitated mutual benefits to be realized through, for example, the development of provisions for shared NATO assets for EU-mandated operations carried out under WEU auspices. The Blair Initiative, largely motivated by the embarrassing lack of European strategic and operational influence over the conduct of the Kosovo campaign, removed the cork from the EU defence co-operation bottle, and the alibi of those 'held back' by UK intransigence in their efforts to promote an ESDP. The EU was to realize a CSDP, equipped with the organizational necessities to ensure a working level of operational competence in at least a part of the crisis-management spectrum to which it aspired. The pace of ESDP development was to be facilitated by the cloning or transplantation of organs from the very institution that had nurtured and promoted it. By the turn of the decade, a more direct engagement had been envisaged for the two primary organizations, and whilst this was to prove problematic, the WEU's gradual dismemberment in support of the developing new EU policy denied it further direct influence over either NATO or the Alliance's relationship to the EU. The challenges of true 'defence', the Article V commitment of the Modified Brussels Treaty and the integration of armaments co-operation proved beyond the appetite of the ravenous new security and defence policy area as it emerged in Nice. Along with the sticky problem of parliamentary engagement and oversight, these unpalatable elements were left to the emasculated WEU until such time as a means could be found for their eventual inclusion within the EU proper. The 'constitutional' provisions for the EDA survived the people's rejection of d'Estaing's elite project, and, with the coming into force of the Lisbon Treaty, sufficient diplomatic smoke had been generated to enable the WEU's final departure. As both 'defence' and 'democracy' took a small step forward in the EU with the adoption of the Article 42:7 'mutual assistance' clause and the Inter-parliamentary Conference provisions of Protocol 1, it might well be argued that the demise of the WEU's Article V and Assembly represented an equally small step backwards for Europe, given the limitations of these replacement arrangements. Nevertheless, the WEU had demonstrated that national prerogative in defence was achievable in a co-operative European context, a small but fundamental contribution to the future of the CSDP concept that, without a still unthinkable assault on the core of national sovereignty, could not otherwise have found a foothold in the communitarian body of the EU. The Lisbon formula for defence, and the Nice Treaty that preceded it, represented the victory of intergovernmentalism, which, in building on the functional successes of the WEU, enabled incorporation of this last stronghold of national power into the European body politic in a manner reflective of both community and national interests. In enhancing the remit of the Union through the inter-institutional spill-over of functional competency and a culture permissive of European military co-operation, any spill-back in terms of the introduction of the intergovernmental method had to be weighed against the pragmatic benefits of practical possibility over institutional pretension.

The WEU's achievements in these final years were expressed as much in its departure as in its overt engagements. That its gradual dismemberment was to leave nothing of substance unaccounted for suggests that its legacy was to exist most tellingly in the new structures of the CSDP, re-formed or re-branded from the functional organs of the WEU. There was clearly institutional resistance from within the EU to the contamination of the shiny new

CSDP project by the 'jaded' WEU with its perceived, and for the EU unacceptable, subordination to NATO. Nevertheless, a certain amount of common sense prevailed, not least given the speed of development deemed necessary to demonstrate the workability of this new area of Union competence.

The military structures and processes designed, tested and exercised in the WEU provided examples for the development of an operational CSDP. The WEU's Military Committee, Planning Cell, Situation and Intelligence Centres, and Torejon Satellite Centre were to be remodelled or, in the latter case directly adopted, by the EU. Working concepts would feature in capability planning, including the FAWEU catalogue approach adapted for the Helsinki Force Goals, supported in turn by the WEU's capability audit and its specific illustrative scenarios. The preparation of military personnel advising on, planning for and engaging in multinational European military operations was informed by the experiences of those engaged in the WEU's military structures and operations. WEU crisis-management operations, including the MAPE and Mostar police missions, offered practical experience in civil crisis management, whilst the WEUDAM de-mining mission in Croatia built on earlier WEU maritime operations in Europe and the Gulf to inform future EU mission planning. The EU's first military mission, Operation Concordia in Macedonia, and its subsequent NATO backfill operation, Althea in Bosnia, would have been unthinkable without the years of patient WEU-NATO negotiation and planning that had resulted in the realization of the CJTF concept in the Berlin Plus arrangements and the subsequent availability of NATO assets for EU-led operations.

It is certainly the case that the WEU's operational utility was weakened by the perception amongst member states' officials and military personnel that it lacked the profile and proven credibility to warrant the risk of its deployment in anything but the most limited of crisis-management operations. And it seems likely that EU efforts to avoid being tainted by this perception led to the downplaying of the extent to which the WEU's experience informed the early development of the CSDP.[427] Indeed, the very limitations of the WEU were, in many ways, a catalyst of CSDP development. The WEU had acclimatized EU states to the concept of European defence co-operation and developed many of the essential mechanisms by which this might be facilitated. And finding themselves frustrated by the EU's inability to influence external affairs, the member states were eventually motivated to act. That the EU has subsequently found itself lacking credibility in its own military missions, which have been widely perceived abroad as more about EU flag-flying than the achievement of stated mission objectives, is something that it has shared in common with the WEU and which is, in part, a natural consequence of its immaturity as a militarily competent actor.[428] Its successes have emerged in civil crisis management, an area promoted by the WEU in which the EU has been able to expand its range of missions to include those in the six priority areas defined by the Council and beyond with the conduct of security sector reform and border-management activities.[429] Without the 'avant-garde' work of the WEU, it is unlikely that the ESDP could have made the operational progress that it did in its formative years.[430] The WEU provided an innovative 'laboratory' in which Europeans could develop their own crisis-management approach and was a required staging post for the development of a European security consciousness through which the EU could come to take some responsibility for common security and the defence of mutual values and interests worldwide.

Indeed, it was the WEU that provided, in the defining of the Petersberg Tasks, the initial doctrinal reference for the development of the European concept of crisis management. These tasks were to remain at the core of a broadening CSDP crisis-management spectrum, developed by the EU to reflect a changing post-11 September security environment and the maturing of an EU security identity, as reflected in the 2003 ESS. It is equally the case that throughout its history the WEU had held the beacon for a European 'defence' capability. Whether the replacement of the WEU's Article V with the EU's 'mutual assistance' clause is of any practical significance is questionable, and for the majority of the EU's members this uncertain commitment will be as much reliant on the capabilities of NATO as was the WEU's mutual defence provision that preceded it. The 'solidarity' clause may have more potential for real mutual security co-operation given the nature of likely future security challenges in Europe, and it may indeed have been 'positively foolish' for the EU to persist with the outmoded and unnecessary notion of an EU defence in the Article V sense.[431] As the EU increasingly focuses its CSDP activities at the 'soft end' of the crisis-management spectrum, its operational delineation from NATO may relieve competitive tensions.

Not that the EU's lack of 'hard-end' operational aspiration had absolved European nations from the requirement of maintaining and developing the military capabilities that would make of them effective allies and partners with the US, not least if they wished to continue to benefit from NATO support. To a large part a question of political will, economic pressures on the viability of national defence industries have demanded a level of European armaments co-operation, facilitated in part through the contribution of the WEAG and WEAO, under WEU auspices. Although lacking the level of national and industrial support evidenced in the OCCAR/LoI frameworks, these institutional arrangements had promoted and facilitated a measure of multinational and industrial co-operation in research, design and production, evidenced in the transferral of numerous ongoing co-operative projects to the EU's new EDA at their closure. The challenges to effective collaboration in defence capability development are far from resolved, but the new Agency, and the work of the WEU-based institutions that preceded it, may contribute in turn to a lessening of the perennial Alliance burden-sharing challenge.

The WEU had continued to contribute throughout its final decade to a culture of inclusiveness in European security and defence. It had engaged at a political level with a broad neighbourhood—its differentiated memberships ensuring access to defence debate for those in and out of the primary clubs and preparing the political leadership of a wider Europe for future defence co-operation and engagement. Despite the Council's limited activity post-2000, the Assembly continued to offer opportunity for defence dialogue to a wide membership, with its committee reports scrutinizing, assessing and informing parliamentary and national audiences, supported by the excellent work of the Institute for Security Studies, which was adopted by the EU in 2001. The presence of the EU post-neutrals and the NATO/EU pre-accession 14[432] provided a testing ground for young diplomats, politicians and military personnel. And although the WEU's Mediterranean Dialogue and its special relations with Russia and Ukraine had ceased following the Nice agreement of 2000, access to inter-parliamentary discussions had continued to facilitate a broad exchange of views and helped prepare the ground for the EU and NATO.[433] The flexible and inclusive approach adopted by the WEU had contributed to the development of a European defence culture and was to find reference in the work of the EU's Security and Defence College.[434] The WEU reflected the variable geometries of shifting and aspiring 'club' memberships, and its effectiveness as a meeting place and 'training school' for co-operative defence was facilitated by its low-profile and 'single-issue' focus. One significant challenge for the EU's CSDP remains that it is but one policy area amongst many, with the EU's desire to maintain its political identity making it difficult to include non-EU, and most significantly non-EU NATO, European states in CSDP consultation. Whilst the EU has promoted political discourse with the wider Europe and beyond through its various partner relationships, the proximity of possible engagement of non-EU states to CSDP deliberation and decision-making is restricted well beyond the previous possibilities accorded by WEU association. With Turkey on the outside of the CSDP circle, the 'awkwardness' that persisted in day-to-day EU-NATO co-operation is likely to continue to limit the potential of inter-institutional asset-sharing through the Berlin Plus arrangements.[435]

The WEU Assembly's contribution to spreading and developing a culture of European defence co-operation has been widely recognized, but perhaps more significantly, it persistently sought to ensure that national parliaments maintained a level of collective scrutiny over European defence and security co-operation, both under WEU and EU auspices. Although this role was never fully played out within the EU context because of its lack of institutional access, the WEU Assembly did provide information and analysis of relevant issues through its committee reports, enabling a level of parliamentary scrutiny and popular engagement. It is not clear that, following the abolition of the WEU Parliamentary Assembly in 2011 and the establishment of the new Inter-parliamentary Conference arrangement in the EU, the rigorous information-gathering, analysis and contemplation previously performed through the WEU Assembly mechanisms will be facilitated. With the EP's continuing exclusion from defence, this weakening of inter-parliamentary oversight represents a continuing 'democratic deficit' in the CSDP domain.

Serious challenges remain for the future of the EU and NATO as security providers. For NATO, these include the prioritization of the broad spectrum of its stated commitments and the management of the technology-enhanced capability gap between members, whilst the perennial challenge of burden-sharing continues to raise dark clouds over an operationally weary Alliance. NATO membership had become increasingly and, at least for some, unacceptably two-tiered, one tier specializing in the 'soft' end of humanitarian operations, and in development, peacekeeping and 'talking' tasks, whilst the other was left to conduct the 'hard' combat missions. A new generation of post-Cold War US politicians might well consider abandoning the Alliance, in frustration at the lacking political will and capabilities of their European allies, amply demonstrated by the 2011 operation against the Muammar Gaddafi regime in Libya.[436] For the EU, the evolution of its security and defence culture, in what is predominantly an institution built around a civil consensus, remains a challenge, impacting on the political will, capability enhancement and extra-EU inclusion that could underpin its development as a credible military actor. And unlike the WEU before it, the EU has an institutional presence that raises the risks of even the most uncontroversial of military engagements and precludes the diplomatically constructive ambiguity that might otherwise enable a workable 'consensus'. Consequently, EU CSDP missions remain low-key, short-lived and heavily constrained. Under the Lisbon formula, CSDP decision-making remains essentially within the remit of national governments, despite the increasing role of EU agency in the crisis-management behaviours of the Union. The absence of a permanent structure for inter-parliamentary scrutiny of the CSDP suggests a democratic deficit in the management of this policy area and a potentially weakening omission in terms of parliamentary and popular support. The relationship between the two organizations, NATO and the EU, retains the prickly edge of competitive, if not competing, bodies, with co-operation hampered by the institutional exclusivity that is at once the basis of and the challenge to their continuing relevance. The possibilities for effective asset-sharing, through the Berlin Plus arrangements or potentially their reverse,[437] remain locked in by the seemingly intractable problem of Turkey-Cyprus relations and the limits of non-member inclusion.[438]

With its dual purpose and ambiguous nature, the WEU had once again, throughout the period addressed in this chapter, enabled the highest level of development in European security and defence co-operation within the bounds of a pragmatic convergence of interests. As an expression of the possibilities of a collective European identity in defence, the WEU had enabled accommodation of European interests within the Alliance, as well as a shift in the balance between transatlantic 'partners'. A fermenter of European aspiration in defence, the WEU contained unrealistic EU ambition until such time as a sufficient consensus could emerge in Europe to translate a US-determined ESDI into a European ESDP vision. The agreements reached in Cologne, Helsinki and Nice, supported by the US and the NAC, signified the resolution of the primary tensions that had racked the international institutions of European security since their inception. The rebalancing of NATO through provisions for a European pillar had been accepted, whilst NATO primacy had been assured, at least in the medium term. The development of an intergovernmental crisis-management capability for the EU enabled the assertion of European 'autonomy' whilst supporting the broader transatlantic Alliance on which defence was predicated. And as the WEU was drawn ever closer to a maturing EU, its functional organs and processes enabled the EU's rapid emergence as a fully formed and independent fledgling security actor. As the agreement of limits (at least for the foreseeable future) articulated in the Lisbon Reform Treaty enabled a 'diplomatic' solution to the remaining Article V and inter-parliamentary challenge, the constructive ambiguity of the WEU was no longer required to facilitate a workable compromise for European defence. Clearly areas of contention remained, both within and between the institutions, as the EU settled into a more 'comfortable' post-experimental stage of development, less at odds with a rejuvenated and reformed, outward-focused NATO. The WEU, in facilitating the gradual satisfaction of core concerns, had enabled an acceptable order to emerge and in so doing had effectively served its purpose as a support organization, a promoter of European integration in defence and of alliance between transatlantic allies. Neither the EU nor NATO had further need of a 'nanny', but they had become nevertheless, in some significant part, a product of her upbringing.

NOTES

1. H. Sjursen, 'Missed opportunity or eternal fantasy: the idea of a European security and defence policy', in J. Peterson and H. Sjursen (eds) *A Common Foreign Policy for Europe: Competing Visions of the CFSP*, London: Routledge, 1998, p. 95.
2. G. Lenzi, 'The WEU between NATO and the EU', *Centre for European Integration Studies Discussion Paper*, vol. 4, Bonn: Rheinische Friedrich Wilhelms-Universität, 1998, p. 3.
3. WEU Council of Ministers, *Erfurt Declaration*, 18 November 1997.
4. Anniversary activities included a conference of academics and practitioners in Paris and the production of a number of publications including a Secretariat 'glossy' (*Western European Union: A European Journey*, Brussels: WEU, 1998), an Institute for Security Studies essay collection (G. Lenzi (ed.) *WEU at Fifty*, Paris: WEU ISS, 1998) and a special edition of *Studia Diplomatica* (the journal of the Belgium Royal Institute of International Relations—now Egmont) edited by A. Deighton and E. Remacle, which reflected on 'The Western European Union, 1948–1998: from the Brussels Treaty to the Treaty of Amsterdam', vol. 51, nos. 1–2, 1998.
5. Some in the WEU Assembly argued that Article XII of the Modified Brussels Treaty, which replicated this original Article X provision for withdrawal within one year of a statement of intent being deposited with the Belgian Government, implied that the 50-year period would not be reached until 2004. For

discussion of the two positions see R. A. Wessel, 'The EU as a black widow: devouring the WEU to give birth to a European security and defence policy', in V. Kronenberger (ed.) *The EU and the International Legal Order: Discord or Harmony?* The Hague: T. M. C. Asser Press, 2001, p. 410.

6. G. Lenzi, 'WEU's future: from subcontractor to conveyer belt?' in Lenzi (ed.) *WEU at Fifty,* p. 110.

7. Lenzi, 'The WEU between NATO and the EU', pp. 3–4.

8. W. van Eekelen, *Debating European Security 1945–1998,* The Hague: SDU Publishers, 1998, p. 324.

9. Formed in April 1992 by these two remaining republics of the former Socialist Republic of Yugoslavia, it was to officially drop the name 'Yugoslavia' following their union in February 2003. Serbia and Montenegro both declared their independence in June 2006.

10. See T. Judah, 'Kosovo's road to war', *Survival,* vol. 41, no. 2, summer 1999, pp. 5–18, for a useful background discussion of the crisis.

11. UNSC Resolution 1160 of 31 March 1998 imposed an arms embargo against the FRY, calling for the end of civilian repression and the withdrawal of Serb security forces; the cessation of terrorist acts by the KLA; and negotiations to seek a political solution through enhanced autonomy for Kosovo.

12. The Contact Group comprised representatives from the US, the UK, Germany, France, Italy and Russia.

13. WEU Assembly, rapporteur Mr Baumel, *WEU and Crisis Management in the Balkans,* doc. 1627, 9 November 1998, p. 5.

14. See NATO press release M-NAC-D-1(98)77, 'Statement on Kosovo Issued at the Meeting of the North Atlantic Council in Defence Ministers Session', 11 June 1998, online at http://www.nato.int/docu/pr/1998/index.html.

15. A. H. Cordesman, *The Lessons and Non-lessons of the Air and Missile Campaign in Kosovo,* Westport: Praeger, 2001, p. 11.

16. UNSC Resolution 1199 of 23 September 1998 was a Chapter VII (enforcement) resolution, although Russia, opposed to NATO engagement, questioned whether it was sufficient mandate for military action, rather than a trigger for further consideration.

17. Ambassador Alexander Vershbow's views reported by S. McGinnis, US Embassy, Paris, in his lecture 'Will European security and defense policy strengthen or weaken the transatlantic link?', Cicero Foundation Great Debate seminar, 'The European Security and Defence Identity: a threat to the transatlantic relationship?', Paris, 14 December 2000, online at http://www.cicerofoundation.org/lectures/p4mcginnis.html.

18. See the Labour Party Manifesto, *New Labour: Because Britain Deserves Better,* London: Labour Party, 1997; and Blair's Downing Street address on taking office, 2 May 1997, online at http://www.number10.gov.uk.

19. J. Smith, 'A missed opportunity? New Labour's European policy 1997–2005', *International Affairs,* vol. 81, no. 4, July 2005, p. 703.

20. Prime Minister's statement to the House of Commons, 'European Council (Amsterdam)', House of Commons, *Hansard,* vol. 296, 18 June 1997, cols. 313–6.

21. *The Strategic Defence Review,* Cm 3999, London: The Stationery Office, 1998.The UK defence budget had fallen from a high of 5.3% of the gross domestic product in 1984/5 to 2.5% for 1999/2000, reflecting a post-Cold War 'peace dividend'; the new Labour Government accepted the tight spending measures of the previous Government, with a staged three-year budget reduction assumption in the SDR. 'State of the Defences', *BBC News,* 17 February 2001, online at http://news.bbc.co.uk/news/vote2001/hi/english/main_issues/sections/facts/newsid_1161000/1161166.stm.

22. This 'reshaping' of forces was to include new joint reaction forces, a 3,300 increase in army personnel and a carrier replacement programme. Smart procurement practices were to ensure that equipment was secured 'cheaper, faster and better', whilst innovative public engagement such as the Private Finance Initiative (PFI) and Public Private Partnerships (PPP), underpinned by a new Resource Accounting and Budgeting (RAB) process, would ensure greater efficiencies. See K. Hartley, 'UK defence policy: an economists perspective', 2002, online at http://web.cenet.org.cn/upfile/53075.pdf.

23. 'Modern forces for the modern world', *The Strategic Defence Review*, Cmd. 3999, London: MOD, 8 July 1998. See also C. McInnes, 'Labour's Strategic Defence Review', *International Affairs*, vol. 74, no. 4, October 1998, p. 835.

24. There are no formal records of the Pörtschach Summit discussions, but extracts from the concluding press conference are reprinted in M. Rutten (compiler), 'From St Malo to Nice. European defence: core documents', *Chaillot Paper*, no. 47, Paris: WEU ISS, May 2001, pp. 1–3. Also see references to newsprint reportage of the initiative, much of which pre-dated Blair's Pörtschach 'launch', in parliamentary discussion initiated by C. Blunt MP, 'European Union (defence policy)', House of Commons, *Hansard*, vol. 319, 11 November 1998, col. 283.

25. M. Quinlan, *European Defence Cooperation: Asset or Threat to NATO*, Washington, DC: Woodrow Wilson Center Press, 2001, p. 28, refers to the 'thinking aloud character' of the discussions at Pörtschach.

26. The provisions for the EMU having been established under the Maastricht Treaty, adoption of the single currency represented the third stage, intended for all signatories, once convergence criteria had been met. Denmark and the UK had 'opt-outs' on the third stage. For a brief overview of EMU legislation see 'Towards a single currency: a brief history of EMU' on the EU's website, Europa, last updated 19 July 2011, online at http://europa.eu/legislation_summaries/economic_and_monetary_affairs/introducing_euro_practical_aspects/l25007_en.htm.

27. This spill-over from the economic and monetary to the political and then military spheres has been largely rejected by those who focus on the exogenous nature of the motivations. For example see A. Treacher, 'From civilian power to military actor: the EU's resistible transformation', *European Foreign Affairs Review*, vol. 9, no. 1, spring 2004, p. 50.

28. P. Latawski and M. A. Smith, 'Plus ça change, plus c'est la meme chose. CESDP since 1998: the view from London, Paris and Warsaw', *Journal of European Area Studies*, vol. 10, no. 2, November 2002, p. 213.

29. *The Economist* noted French and German support for the UK 'prodigal son' but suggested that 'British dreams of turning the Franco-German axis into a triangle may be little more than that, while the pound remains in splendid isolation from euro-land'. 'Blair's defence offensive', 12 November 1998, online at http://www.economist.com/node/176061.

30. Blair speaking in the House of Commons following the Helsinki agreements. House of Commons, *Hansard*, vol. 341, 13 December 1999, col. 22.

31. Latawski and Smith, 'Plus ça change', p. 216.

32. P. H. Gordon, 'Their own army? Making European defence work', *Foreign Affairs*, vol. 79, no. 4, July–August 2000, p. 14.

33. The decision-making flow chart for EU-WEU co-operation drawn up for a joint exercise in June 1998 to test the Amsterdam provisions, made public at the WEU Council meeting in Rome in November, identified 25 procedural steps in crisis management, rising to 37–45 if NATO assets were to be utilized. WEU CM (98), 39, 'Modus Operandi of Article J.4.2/Article 17.3 and Flow Chart', 13 November 1998. See M. Jopp, *European Defence Policy: The*

Debate on the Institutional Aspects, Bonn: Institut für Europäische Politik, June–July 1999, p. 4.

34. S. Gordon, 'The United Kingdom: between a rock and a soft place?', in M. A. Smith and G. Timmins (eds) *Uncertain Europe: Building a New European Security Order?,* London: Routledge, 2001, p. 165.

35. S. Hoffmann, 'Towards a common European foreign and security policy?', *Journal of Common Market Studies,* vol. 38, no. 2, June 2000, p. 194.

36. Tony Blair, 'Speech at the Lord Mayor's Banquet', 10 November 1997, online at http://tna.europarchive.org/20050302152644/http://www.strategy-unit. gov.uk/output/Page1070.asp.

37. C. Grant, *Can Britain Lead in Europe?,* London: Centre for European Reform, 1998.

38. For comment see the report by R. Peston and A. Parker, 'UK prepares radical plans for Europe', *Financial Times,* 2 October 1998, p. 1.

39. Grant, *Can Britain Lead in Europe?,* pp. 89 and 48–9.

40. See R. G. Whitman, 'Amsterdam's unfinished business? The Blair Government's initiative and the future of the Western European Union', *Occasional Papers,* no. 7, Paris: WEU ISS, January 1999, p. 7.

41. Robertson's suggested options included EU/WEU merger, merger of some WEU elements with the EU and association of others with NATO, the creation of a more distinct European dimension in NATO and the reinforcement and reinvigoration of the WEU. See *Agence Europe,* no. 7336, 5 November 1998.

42. Cited in S. Duke, 'From Amsterdam to Kosovo: lessons for the future of CFSP', *Eipascope,* no. 2, 1999, p. 11, online at http://www.eipa.eu/files/repository/ eipascope/scop99_2_col.pdf.

43. See R. Hatfield, the MOD Policy Director, to the House of Commons Defence Committee (HCDC), minutes of evidence, 16 February 2000, col. 17, in 'European Security and Defence', Eighth Report, HC 264, Session 1999–2000, May 2000, online at http://www.parliament.the-stationery-office.co.uk/pa/ cm199900/cmselect/cmdfence/264/26402.htm.

44. A. Blair, 'NATO's role in the modern world', remarks to the NAA, Edinburgh, 13 November 1998; also see A. Blair, 'It's time to repay America', *New York Times,* 13 November 1998; and Robertson, 'Defence in Europe', speech to the WEU Assembly in Paris, 1 December 1998, in which he identified the requirement for deployable, sustainable, powerful and flexible European forces, supported by a restructured European defence industrial base and the harmonization of European requirements, online at http://www.chots.mod. ukpolicy/speeches/weu.htm.

45. M. Mathiopoulos and J. Gyarmati, 'St Malo and beyond: towards European defence', *Washington Quarterly,* vol. 22, no. 4, autumn 1999, p. 72.

46. Blunt, 'European Union (defence policy)', col. 286.

47. See M. Harvey, 'Perspectives on the UK's place in the world', Europe Programme Paper 2011/01, London: RIIA, December 2011, p. 8.

48. See R. Dover, 'The Prime Minister and the core Executive: a liberal intergovernmentalist reading of UK defence policy formulation 1997–2000', *British Journal of Politics and International Relations,* vol. 7, no. 4, November 2005, pp. 508–25, for a discussion of the persistence of established core preferences in British policy orientation.

49. J.-Y. Haine, 'An historical perspective', in N. Gnesotto (ed.) *EU Security Policy: The First Five Years (1999–2004),* Paris: EU Institute for Security Studies (EU ISS), 2004, p. 43. Also see A. Blair, 'Shaping a pivotal role for Britain in the world', Lord Mayor's Banquet, Guildhall, London, 22 November 1999.

50. Howorth notes the effect on the Government's thinking of an attitude shift towards European military autonomy amongst a small group of British

Foreign Affairs and Defence officials, themselves part of a wider epistemic community including their French and German counterparts. 'Discourse, ideas, and epistemic communities in European security and defence policy', *West European Politics,* vol. 27, no. 2, March 2004, p. 221.

51. M. Blunden, 'France', in I. Manners and R. G. Whitman (eds) *The Foreign Policies of EU Member States,* Manchester: Manchester University Press, 2000, pp. 20–5.
52. Overall command of the operation, which included French, British, German and Italian contingents, resided with NATO's SACEUR. See Mathiopoulos and Gyarmati, 'St Malo and beyond', p. 67.
53. See Latawski and Smith, 'Plus ça change', p. 220.
54. M. Sutton, *France and the Construction of Europe, 1944 to 2007: The Geopolitical Imperative,* New York: Berghahn, 2011, p. 304.
55. WEU Council of Ministers, *Rome Declaration,* 17 November 1998.
56. See WEU Assembly, rapporteur Mr de Puig (Assembly President), *WEU and European Defence: Beyond Amsterdam,* doc. 1636, 15 March 1999, p. 30.
57. S. Biscop, 'The UK's change of course: a new chance for ESDI', *European Foreign Affairs Review,* vol. 4, no. 2, summer 1999, p. 259.
58. A. Missiroli, 'CFSP, defence and flexibility', *Chaillot Paper,* no. 38, Paris: WEU ISS, February 2000, p. 7, noted that, whilst the French, Germans and British all supported flexibility, 'each meant something different by it'.
59. J. Howorth, 'Britain, France and the European defence initiative', *Survival,* vol. 42, no. 2, summer 2000, p. 34.
60. At the first EU Defence Ministers meeting in November 1998, the desperate requirement for a stronger European presence in dealing with European crises, given the impotence of Europe over Kosovo, had been agreed, providing a permissive context for the Anglo-French consensus.
61. 'UK and France agree military pact', *BBC News,* 4 December 1998, online at http://news.bbc.co.uk/1/hi/uk/228090.stm.
62. Franco-British Summit, *Joint Declaration on European Defence,* St Malo, 4 December 1998.
63. Gordon, 'The United Kingdom: between a rock and a soft place?', p. 164.
64. Howorth, 'Britain, France and the European defence initiative', p. 44, refers to interviews in which he learned that 'under pressure from Washington, the UK discreetly sought to persuade its EU partners to abandon the concept of "autonomy" (and indeed the word) and to replace it with some less robust formula referring simply to "missions in which the US would not be involved"'.
65. *Joint Declaration on European Defence,* St Malo, para. 2.
66. The 'UK-French Letter of Intent on Co-operation in Crisis Management and Operations', reproduced in M. Oakes, *European Defence: From Pörtschach to Helsinki,* Research Paper 00/20, House of Commons Library, 21 February 2000, Annex 1, p. 41, built on earlier agreements on closer bilateral co-operation between services.
67. P. van Ham, 'Europe's common defence policy: implications for the transatlantic relationship', *Security Dialogue,* vol. 31, no. 2, June 2000, p. 217.
68. M. Jopp, 'Germany and the Western European Union', in C. Lankowski and S. Serfaty (eds) 'Europeanizing security? NATO and an integrating Europe', *Research Report,* no. 9, Washington, DC: AICGS (American Institute for Contemporary German Studies), 1999, p. 48.
69. Hoffmann, 'Towards a common European foreign and security policy?', pp. 193–4.
70. Jopp, 'Germany and the Western European Union', p. 35.
71. See Jopp, *European Defence Policy,* p. 10.
72. Biscop, 'The UK's change of course', pp. 250–60.

73. See P. J. Teunissen, 'Strengthening the defence dimension of the EU: an evaluation of concepts, recent initiatives and developments', *European Foreign Affairs Review,* vol. 4, no. 3, autumn 1999, p. 340.
74. WEU, *German Presidency Paper,* Bonn, 24 February 1999, reproduced in Rutten, 'From St Malo to Nice', pp. 14–16.
75. Jopp, *European Defence Policy,* p. 7.
76. Teunissen, 'Strengthening the defence dimension of the EU', p. 342.
77. J. Wright, 'Trusting flexible friends: the dangers of flexibility in NATO and the Western European Union/European Union, *Contemporary Security Policy,* vol. 20, no. 1, April 1999, p. 119.
78. See for example French Defence Minister Alain Richard's speech, 'The security agenda for Europe and North America', at NATO's 50th Anniversary Conference, RUSI, London, 8 March 1999.
79. M. Albright, 'The right balance will secure NATO's future', *Financial Times,* 7 December 1998.
80. J. Howorth, *Security and Defence Policy in the European Union,* Basingstoke: Palgrave Macmillan, 2007, p. 163.
81. Speech by the British Prime Minister, 'NATO, Europe, and our future security', NATO's 50th Anniversary Conference, RUSI, London, 8 March 1999.
82. Address by the US Deputy Secretary, NATO's 50th Anniversary Conference, RUSI, London, 10 March 1999.
83. Luis Maria de Puig at the NATO-WEU first seminar on crisis management in Brussels, February 1999, cited in W. Bradford, *The Western European Union, Yugoslavia, and the (Dis)Integration of the EU, the New Sick Man of Europe,* p. 23, online at http://www.bc.edu/bc_org/avp/law/lwsch/journals/bciclr/24_1/02_TXT.htm.
84. With the Swedes as lead nation, the EU-funded WEUDAM supported the Croatian Mine Action Centre in the areas of 'programme management, planning, project development and geographic information', concluding its work on 30 November 2001. See W. van Eekelen and S. Blockmans, 'European crisis management *avant la lettre*', in S. Blockmans (ed.) *The European Union and Crisis Management: Policy and Legal Aspects,* The Hague: T. M. C. Asser Press, 2008, p. 50.
85. See 'History of WEU', Western European Union website, online at http://www.weu.int/History.htm.
86. See van Eekelen and Blockmans, 'European crisis management *avant la lettre*', p. 49.
87. 'Interim Agreement for Peace and Self-government in Kosovo', Rambouillet, France, 23 February 1999, online at http://jurist.law.pitt.edu/ramb.htm. Note Appendix B: Status of Multi-national Military Implementation Force, which, in providing for complete freedom of movement for NATO forces across the FRY, read more like a 'capitulation' agreement and a significant infringement of sovereignty and was seen by many as (intentionally or otherwise) a cause of the accord's failure. See House of Commons Select Committee on Foreign Affairs, Fourth Report, May 2000, paras. 55–70, online at http://www.publications.parliament.uk/pa/cm199900/cmselect/cmfaff/28/2809.htm.
88. W. Rees, 'The WEU: eliminating the middleman', in M. A. Smith and G. Timmins (eds) *Uncertain Europe: Building a New European Security Order?* London: Routledge, 2001, p. 100.
89. Cited in House of Commons Defence Committee, Third Report, *The European Security and Defence Identity,* 'NATO and the WEU', 13 April 1999, online at http://www.parliament.the-stationery-office.co.uk/pa/cm199899/cmselect/cmdfence/39/3915.htm.

90. Speech by J. Cutileiro, Secretary General of the WEU, during the autumn Session of the WEU Assembly, Paris, 30 November 1998, online at http://www.defense-aerospace.com/article-view/verbatim/16324/speech-by-mr.-jos%C3%A3%C2%A9-cutileiro,-secretary_general-of-the-w.e.u.-(paris,-nov.-30).html.

91. J. Cutileiro, 'NATO and the WEU', NATO's 50th Anniversary Conference, RUSI, London, 10 March 1999.

92. See WEU Council of Ministers, *Erfurt Declaration,* 18 November 1997; and WEU Assembly, rapporteur M. Giannattasio, *The WEU Military Committee,* doc. 1591, 1 December 1997.

93. S. de Spiegeleire, 'The European Security and Defence Identity and NATO: Berlin and beyond', in M. Jopp and H. Ojanen (eds) *European Security Integration: Implications for Non-alignment and Alliances,* Helsinki: Finnish Institute of International Affairs, 1999, p. 82.

94. Members welcomed the agreement reached on the modalities for WEU participation in the NATO defence planning process, including observer-state participation given their potential Petersberg Task contributions, at the WEU Council of Ministers, *Rhodes Declaration,* 12 May 1998.

95. A. J. K. Bailes and G. Messervy-Whiting, 'Death of an institution: the end for Western European Union, a future for European defence?' *Egmont Paper,* no. 46, Gent: Academia Press (for Egmont—the Royal Institute for International Relations, Brussels), May 2011, p. 36, online at http://www.egmontinstitute.be/paperegm/ep46.pdf.

96. De Spiegeleire, 'The European Security and Defence Identity and NATO', p. 90.

97. WEU Assembly, rapporteur Mr Cox, *The NATO Summit and its Implications for Europe,* doc. 1637, 15 March 1999.

98. NAC, *The Alliance's Strategic Concept,* Washington, 24 April 1999, online at http://www.nato.int/cps/en/natolive/official_texts_27433.htm.

99. NAC, 'An alliance for the 21st century', *Washington Summit Communiqué,* Washington, DC, Press Release NAC-S(99)64, 24 April 1999, online at http://www.nato.int/cps/en/natolive/official_texts_27440.htm?selectedLocale=en.

100. *The Alliance's Strategic Concept,* paras. 17–18.

101. *Washington Summit Communiqué,* paras. 8–10.

102. Howorth, *Security and Defence Policy in the European Union,* p. 164.

103. WEU Council of Ministers, *Bremen Declaration,* 10–11 May 1999.

104. The German Defence Minister, Rudolf Scharping, reportedly condemned the WEU at the meeting, arguing that 'today, we have too many institutions and too little substance'. Cited in R. Cohen, 'Dependent on U.S. now, Europe vows defense push', *New York Times,* 12 May 1999.

105. Biscop, 'The UK's change of course', p. 267.

106. See WEU Council of Ministers, *Declaration on the New Associate Members of WEU: The Czech Republic, Hungary and Poland,* Bremen, 10–11 May 1999.

107. 'Blair's defence offensive'.

108. The 'neutrals' had effectively become 'alliance-free states' or 'post-neutrals', the Amsterdam CFSP provisions in relation to the Petersberg Tasks meaning that they no longer met the requirements of strict neutrality. See G. Gustenau, 'Towards a common European policy on security and defence: an Austrian view of the challenges for the "post-neutrals"', *Occasional Paper,* no. 9, Paris: WEU ISS, October 1999, online at http://www.iss.europa.eu/uploads/media/occ009.pdf.

109. D. Phinnemore, 'Austria', in Manners and Whitman (eds) *The Foreign Policies of EU Member States,* p. 215.

110. See, for discussion, D. Keohane, 'Realigning neutrality? Irish defence policy and the EU', *Occasional Paper,* no. 24, Paris: WEU ISS, March 2001.
111. This was to be reflected in the Presidency being tasked by the Cologne Summit to 'elaborate plans for improvement of both joint military and civilian crisis response tools'. M. Merlingen and R. Ostrauskaitė, *European Union Peacebuilding and Policing: Governance and the European Security and Defence Policy,* London: Routledge, 2006, p. 41.
112. Jopp, *European Defence Policy,* p. 14.
113. J. Howorth, 'European integration and defence: the ultimate challenge', *Chaillot Paper,* no. 43, Paris: WEU ISS, November 2000, p. 41.
114. See for example L. Freedman, 'Defence', in A. Seldon (ed.) *The Blair Effect: The Blair Government 1997–2001,* London: Little, Brown, 2001, p. 297, who notes NATO's failure to deter Milošević or, because of the lack of a ground intervention, to impact on ethnic cleansing.
115. Bozo identifies the capability gap, the unequal strategic relationship and the conflict over priorities as the major fault lines exposed by the Kosovo campaign. F. Bozo, 'The effects of Kosovo and the danger of decoupling', in J. Howorth and J. T. S. Keeler (eds) *Defending Europe: The EU, NATO and the Quest for European Autonomy,* Basingstoke: Palgrave, 2003, pp. 61–77.
116. S. Silvestri, 'Atlantic and European defence after Kosovo', *International Spectator,* vol. 34, no. 3, July 1999, p. 14.
117. See E. V. Larson and B. Savych, *Misfortunes of War: Press and Public Reactions to Civilian Deaths in War Time,* Santa Monica, CA: RAND Project Air Force, 2006, online at http://www.dtic.mil/cgi-bin/GetTRDoc?AD=ADA462504.
118. Pond emphasizes the impact of the Kosovo experience on neutrals' thinking when she suggested, in September 1999, that 'old hesitation' about a EU-WEU merger had 'vanished', although this must be understood in the context of the 'defence-lite' terms of the later ESDP provisions. E. Pond, 'Kosovo: catalyst for Europe', *Washington Quarterly,* vol. 22, no. 4, autumn 1999, p. 86.
119. Robertson cited in Cohen 'Dependent on U.S. now, Europe vows defense push'.
120. J. Roper, 'Two cheers for Mr Blair? The political realities of European defence cooperation', *Journal of Common Market Studies,* vol. 38, no. 1, September 2000, p. 8.
121. S. A. Açikimeçe, 'The underlying dynamics of the European Security and Defence Policy', *Perceptions,* vol. 9, no. 1, March–May 2004, p. 120.
122. See D. S. Yost, 'The US-European capabilities gap and the prospects for ESDP', in Howorth and Keeler (eds) *Defending Europe,* pp. 81–106; and P. van Ham, 'Europe's common defence policy', pp. 215–28, for details.
123. P. Truscott, *European Defence: Meeting the Strategic Challenge,* London: Institute for Public Policy Research, 2000, p. 17; and Oakes, *European Defence,* p. 23.
124. Cordesman, *The Lessons and Non-lessons of the Air and Missile Campaign in Kosovo,* p. 25. See the UK Ministry of Defence Report, *Kosovo: Lessons from the Crisis,* Cmd. 4724, London: MOD, June 2000; and the National Audit Office Report, *Kosovo: The Financial Management of Military Operations,* HC 530 Session 1999–2000, London: The Stationary Office, 5 June 2000, which provide examples of the capability shortfalls identified.
125. See Açikimeçe, 'The underlying dynamics of the European Security and Defence Policy', p. 120.
126. See J. Cutiliero, 'Old soldiers never die', *Financial Times,* 12 April 1999, p. 16.
127. Merlingen and Ostrauskaitė identify German support of the NATO bombing campaign as a radical realignment of the German Greens, which turned 'German participation in international peace operations and the construction of

the ESDP into a defining characteristic of its foreign policy'. *European Union Peacebuilding and Policing*, pp. 40–1.

128. C. Grant, *European Defence Post Kosovo?*, Centre for European Reform Working Paper, London: Centre for European Reform, June 1999, p. 2.

129. Grant, *European Defence Post Kosovo?*, p. 3. See M. Weller, 'Negotiating the final status of Kosovo', *Chaillot Paper*, no. 114, Paris: EU ISS, December 2008, pp. 23–4, for details of the 10 June UNSC Resolution 1244 (1999), which provided the basis for the international administration of Kosovo.

130. The Europeans also 'grudgingly' accepted that they would take on the majority of the economic costs (75% over 1999 and 2000) of the Kosovo budget, establishing a Stability Pact for the Balkans to support economic and political regeneration. R. Stefanova, 'Balkan clutter: American and European handling of a powder keg', in H. Gardner and R. Stefanova (eds) *The Transatlantic Agenda: Facing the Challenges of Global Governance*, Aldershot: Ashgate, 2001, pp. 92–3.

131. 'History of the WEU'.

132. J. B. Collester, 'How defence "spilled over" into the CFSP: Western European Union (WEU) and the European Security and Defence Identity', in M. Green Cowles and M. Smith (eds) *The State of the European Union. Volume 5: Risks, Reform, Resistance, and Revival*, Oxford: Oxford University Press, 2000, p. 382.

133. See reference to the Kosovo effect in the speech by the UK Defence Secretary, Geoff Hoon, 'The globalisation of the defence industry: policy implications for NATO and ESDI, the UK's role in European defence', RIIA, London: 29 November 2000.

134. See European Council, 'Declaration on Strengthening the Common European Policy on Security and Defence' (including the Presidency Report), Annex III, *Presidency Conclusions*, Cologne, 3–4 June 1999.

135. St Malo had referred to action 'where the Alliance as a whole is not engaged', an implied precedence which was reintroduced at Helsinki under 'various diplomatic pressures'. Quinlan, *European Defence Cooperation*, pp. 36–7.

136. See Roper, 'Two cheers for Mr Blair?', pp. 20–1.

137. Post St Malo, the post's relevance was to be far greater than initially perceived at Amsterdam, and Solana was a popular choice in that he met the 'French criterion for seniority and pro-activism, the British criterion for user-friendly Atlanticism and the German criterion for Europeanism'. J. Howorth, 'European defence and the changing politics of the European Union: hanging together or hanging separately?' *Journal of Common Market Studies*, vol. 39, no. 4, November 2001, p. 771.

138. J. Cutilero, Transcript of speech at Transatlantic Forum, 3 June 1999.

139. The following citations are from the address by Cutileiro to the WEU Assembly, 'Minutes and Official Reports of Debates', *Proceedings*, vol. II, (Session 45, Part 1), Paris, 14 June 1999.

140. Quinlan, *European Defence Cooperation*, pp. 31–2, notes that the WEU had 'never shaken off an aura of under-achievement, of complex institutional activity poorly reflected in effective output' and had failed to engage 'the personal attention of heads of government, nor had it commanded a sense among them that its shortcomings and disappointments were their own'.

141. A. Missiroli, 'ESDP—how it works', in Gnesotto (ed.) *EU Security Policy*, p. 44. Solana stated, 'The expertise and specialised resources of the WEU have to be put fully at the disposal of the European Union. My own double-hatted appointment as Secretary General of the WEU should assist this process'. Speech to the Institute for European Policy, Berlin, 17 December 1999, cited in Oakes, *European Defence*, p. 29.

142. EU Council of Ministers, *Luxembourg Declaration,* 22–23 November 1999, online at http://www.weu.int/documents/991122luxen.pdf. This co-operation was outlined in the *Declaration on Enhanced Co-operation between the European Union and the Western European Union* annexed to the TOA.

143. J. Kitfield, 'Will Europe ruin NATO?', *Air Force Magazine,* October 2000, p. 61.

144. M. Brenner, 'The United States and the Western European Union', in Lankowski and Serfaty (eds) 'Europeanizing security?', p. 4.

145. S. R. Sloan, 'The United States and European defence', *Chaillot Paper,* no. 39, Paris: WEU ISS, April 2000, p. 26.

146. Talbott speaking at a RUSI seminar in London, cited in R. Cornwell, 'Europe warned not to weaken NATO', *The Independent,* 8 October 1999.

147. House Resolution 59 of 2 November 1999 and Senate Resolution 208 of 8 November 1999.

148. See Sloan, 'The United States and European defence', pp. 26–35.

149. Speech at the 45th Annual Session of the NATO Parliamentary Assembly, Amsterdam, 15 November 1999. See G. Robertson, 'NATO in the new millennium', *NATO Review,* vol. 47, no. 4, winter 1999, pp. 3–7. Those keen to see ESDP as a tool for countering US hegemony and rebalancing transatlantic relations preferred the '3Es' formulation of 'emancipation' from dependency on the US, 'Europeanization' through the development of an integral EU defence entity and 'efficiency' through integrated EU defence resource management. M. J. Brenner, 'Europe's new security vocation', *McNair Paper,* no. 66, Washington, DC: National Defence University, 2002, p. 11.

150. Given that the majority of the declared assets were double-hatted with NATO or pre-deployed in peace support operations, the information and assessment were not altogether realistic. H.-C. Hagman, 'European crisis management and defence: the search for capabilities', *Adelphi Paper,* no. 353, December 2002, pp. 18–20.

151. See WEU Council of Ministers, *Audit of Assets and Capabilities for European Crisis Management Operations: Recommendations for Strengthening European Capabilities for Crisis Management Operations,* Luxembourg, 23 November 1999, online at http://www.weu.int/documents/991122en.pdf.

152. 'Joint Declaration Launching the European Defence Capabilities Initiative', London, 19–20 July 1999, reproduced in Rutten, 'From St Malo to Nice', pp. 46–7.

153. T. C. Salmon and A. J. K. Shepherd, *Towards a European Army: A Military Power in the Making?* London: Reinner, 2003, p. 70.

154. G. Bonvicini, 'European defence: beyond functional convergence: procedures and institutions', *International Spectator,* vol. 34, no. 3, July–September 1999, p. 23.

155. Howorth, 'European integration and defence', p. 39.

156. Hagman, 'European crisis management and defence', p. 20.

157. Howorth, 'European integration and defence', p. 35, notes the significance of this summit as it overcame some of the 'disillusionment' that had crept into the relationship following the 'overblown' expectations of St Malo.

158. Gordon, 'Their own army?', p. 16.

159. Kitfield, 'Will Europe ruin NATO?', p. 62.

160. Truscott, *European Defence,* pp. 39–42.

161. 'Joint Declaration by the British and French Governments on European Defence', Anglo-French Summit, London, 25 November 1999, reproduced in Oakes, *European Defence,* Annex IV, pp. 46–8.

162. See Oakes, *European Defence,* pp. 33–4. J. Dumbrell, *A Special Relationship: Anglo-American Relations from the Cold War to Iraq,* 2nd edn, Hampshire:

Palgrave Macmillan, 2006, p. 236. Franco-German plans for remodelling the Eurocorps as a rapid reaction force for the EU had been first aired at their Toulouse Summit, 28–9 May 1999. Leaking the Anglo-French plans on 14 November, ('Blair backs 30,000 strong Euro army') the *Sunday Times* noted the irony that Downing Street had consistently 'played down' the Franco-German Eurocorps transformation proposals, and cited the Shadow Defence Secretary's reaction to the Anglo-French plan as constituting a 'Euro army by stealth'.

163. M. Evans, 'Britain offers Europe force HQ', *The Times,* 26 November 1999.

164. The European air transport command approved at the Franco-German Summit and designed to manage and co-ordinate European military and civilian airlift capabilities, had to wait another decade to be realized, with agreement reached in 2010 by the Belgians, French, Dutch and Germans. A European airlift co-ordination cell was established in 2001, to gradually transform to include sealift as the Movement Coordination Centre in 2007, with 15 participating states. See S. Wilmers and C. John, 'European Air Transport Command: Transition from ATC to EATC', *European Security and Defence,* vol. 1, April 2011, pp. 35–9.

165. Howorth, 'Britain, France and the European defence initiative', p. 41.

166. The iPSC first convened in March 2000, with these interim arrangements becoming permanently incorporated into the EU structure following the Nice European Council on 7–9 December 2000.

167. The EUMS's remit was not to extend to the exercising of command responsibilities or the development of detailed operational plans, although the French did increasingly depict the EUMS and Military Committee as capable of small-to medium-scale mission planning, depending on the specific challenge.

168. European Council, *Presidency Conclusions,* Helsinki, 10–11 December 1999.

169. See F. Heisbourg 'The EU needs defence convergence criteria', *CER Bulletin,* no. 6, June–July 1999; A. Missiroli, 'European Security and Defence: The case for setting "convergence criteria"', *European Foreign Affairs Review,* vol. 4, no. 4, 1999, pp. 485–500; R. de Wijk, 'Convergence criteria: measuring input or output?', *European Foreign Affairs Review,* vol. 5, no. 3, 2000, pp. 397–417.

170. This 'Food for Thought' paper on the 'Elaboration of the "headline goal"', was first presented at the EU Defence Minister meeting in Sintra, Portugal, on 28 February 2000, along with the 'Toolbox Paper' developed by the EU's Political Committee (PoCo) which addressed 'Military Bodies in the European Union and the Planning and Conduct of EU-led Military Operations', both reproduced in Rutten, 'From St Malo to Nice', pp. 94–107.

171. Bailes and Messervy-Whiting, 'Death of an institution', p. 73.

172. Haine, 'An historical perspective', pp. 45–6.

173. Joint Statement by Blair and the UK Chancellor of the Exchequer Gordon Brown, 'The Conservative enemy has to be defeated: Britain's future is in Europe', *The Independent,* 14 October 1999.

174. S. Croft 'The EU, NATO and Europeanisation: the return of the architectural debate', *European Security,* vol. 9, no. 3, autumn 2000, p. 20, argued that ESDP did not represent a 'change away from NATO and transatlanticism, but towards partnership between Europe's two major institutions . . . It is an idea as much in the interests of NATO as an institution as it is in the interests of the European project'.

175. See House of Commons, *Hansard,* 13 December 1999, vol. 341, cols. 3–6 (Hoon addressing questions on the European Defence Initiative) and col. 21 (the Prime Minister's statement on the Helsinki European Council).

176. Sloan, 'The United States and European defence', p. 18.

177. Talbott also accepted the 3Is in his speech to the NAC, 'The state of the alliance: an American perspective', 15 December 1999, online at http://www.nato.int/docu/speech/1999/s991215c.htm.

178. See for example W. Drozdiak, 'US seems increasingly uncomfortable with EU defense plan', *International Herald Tribune,* 6 March 2000.

179. Sloan, 'The United States and European defence', p. vii.

180. On the national positions of the '15' see Howorth, 'European integration and defence', pp. 44–56.

181. See R. Norton-Taylor, 'US warns EU over joint action on security', *The Guardian,* 23 November 1999.

182. 'NATO's new agenda: more progress than meets the eye', remarks at SACLANT symposium, Reykjavik, Iceland, 6 September 2000, cited in S. R. Sloan, *NATO, the European Union, and the Atlantic Community: The Transatlantic Bargain Challenged,* 2nd edn, Oxford: Rowman and Littlefield, 2005, p. 196.

183. Jopp, *European Defence Policy,* p. 20.

184. The WEU Assembly was later to deplore the fact that no mention was made of the future of the WEU's role in ESDI, which was 'not the same project as ESDP', in subsequent Council documents. WEU Assembly, rapporteur Mr Marshall, *The Implementation of the Common European Security and Defence Policy and the WEU's Future Role—Reply to the Annual Report of the Council,* doc. A/1720, 6 December 2000, p. 2.

185. At Feira, at the insistence of the post-neutral states, agreement had been reached on capability development in the civil aspects of crisis management as a means of balancing the military focus of the evolving ESDP, focusing on the four key areas of police, rule of law, civil administration and civil protection, and providing for the development of a Committee for Civilian Aspects of Crisis-management (CIVCOM). See 'Feira European Council Conclusions', 19–20 June 2000, in Rutten, 'From St Malo to Nice', pp. 120–33.

186. Given the role of the Commission in humanitarian support, conflict prevention and post-conflict reconstruction, some degree of engagement had become an evident necessity, although the British Government was clear on its 'red line' against supranational encroachment into the CFSP/ESDP area. See P. Cornish and G. Edwards, 'Beyond the EU/NATO dichotomy: the beginnings of a European strategic culture', *International Affairs,* vol. 77, no. 3, July 2001, p. 594.

187. French forces were joined by soldiers from eight of its European partners, with British and German fighter aircraft overhead. Kitfield, 'Will Europe ruin NATO?', p. 60.

188. Latawski and Smith, 'Plus ça change', p. 222.

189. See van Ham, 'Europe's common defence policy', p. 221.

190. See for example WEU Assembly, rapporteur Mr Baumel, *WEU after the Washington and Cologne Summits—Reply to the Annual Report of the Council,* doc. 1652, 10 June 1999.

191. See discussion on the Franco-German letter to the pre-Amsterdam IGC, October 1996, in *Agence Europe,* no. 6836, 19 October 1996, pp. 2–3.

192. WEU Assembly, *The Implementation of the Common European Security and Defence Policy,* doc. A/1720, p. 9.

193. Decisions taken at the Rhodes WEU Council of Ministers meeting, 12 May 1998, allowed prospective associate members to take part in discussion on NATO-WEU issues. See WEU Assembly, rapporteurs M. Casan and M. Adamczyk, *The WEU Associate Members and the New European Security Architecture,* doc. A/1690, 5 June 2000.

194. *Washington Summit Communiqué,* para. 9d.

195. *Cologne Declaration,* annex III, para. 3.
196. Howorth, *Security and Defence Policy in the European Union,* pp. 66–7.
197. 'Feira European Council Conclusions', 19–20 June 2000, in Rutten, 'From St Malo to Nice', pp. 120–39.
198. Recommendation 666, doc. 1689, 10 May 2000.
199. M. Wohlfeld, 'Closing the gap: WEU and Central European countries', in Lenzi (ed.) *WEU at Fifty,* p. 89.
200. Van Eekelen and Blockmans, 'European crisis management *avant la lettre*', p. 51.
201. The enhancement of participation rights for all EU member states in Petersberg operations undertaken by WEU, in line with the Amsterdam provisions in the consolidated TEU Article 17.3, was welcomed and further encouraged by Ministers at their Erfurt meeting in November 1997, although some ambiguity remained as to the specific rights of non-EU WEU members and partners in the case of EU-initiated WEU operations.
202. M. J. Baun, *A Wider Europe: The Process and Politics of European Union Enlargement,* Lanham: Rowman and Littlefield, 2000, p. 63.
203. Bailes and Messervy-Whiting, 'Death of an institution', p. 25, note that 'by the mid 2000's, many of the same individuals would be found holding high official, Ambassadorial, or even Ministerial posts (and the military equivalent) in the security apparatus of the nations concerned'.
204. Although keen to accede to the EU, many CEE states had serious misgivings about the ESDP and a keen attachment to Atlanticist principals. Latawski and Smith, 'Plus ça change', p. 225.
205. At the Helsinki European Council it had been suggested that the EU might enlarge as early as 2002, with 12 states (Cyprus, the Czech Republic, Estonia, Hungary, Latvia, Lithuania, Malta, Poland, the Slovak Republic and Slovenia, Bulgaria and Romania) in accession negotiations by February 2000. The first 10 were admitted in 2004 with Romania and Bulgaria awaiting the 2007 intake.
206. 'CFSP: Council Decision of 10 May 1999 concerning the practical arrangements for the participation of all Member States in tasks pursuant to Article 17 (2) of the Treaty on European Union for which the Union avails itself of the WEU', (1999/321/CFSP) *Official Journal* L 123, 13 May 1999, pp. 14–17.
207. A. J. K. Bailes, 'European security from a Nordic perspective: the roles for Finland and Sweden', *Strategic Yearbook 2004,* Stockholm: Swedish National Defence College, 2004, pp. 59–81.
208. H. Kramer, *A Changing Turkey: The Challenge to Europe and the United States,* Washington, DC: Brookings Press, 2000, pp. 217–19. Also see M. B. Ayka, 'Turkey and European Security and Defence Identity/Policy (ESDI/P): a Turkish view', *Journal of Contemporary European Studies,* vol. 13, no. 3, December 2005, pp. 335–59; and S. Tofte, 'Non-EU NATO members and the issue of inclusivity', in Howorth and Keeler (eds) *Defending Europe,* p. 146.
209. Biscop, 'The UK's change of course', pp. 263–4.
210. A. Vershbow, 'The American perspective on ESDI/ESDP', *Perceptions,* vol. 5, no. 3, September–November 2000, pp. 96–107. For discussion see M. Cebeci, 'A delicate process of participation: the question of participation of WEU associate members in decision-making for EU-led Petersberg operations with special reference to Turkey', *Occasional Paper,* no. 10, Paris: WEU ISS, November 1999.
211. Quinlan, *European Defence Cooperation,* p. 46. Also see W. Park, 'Turkey's European Union candidacy: from Luxembourg to Helsinki—to Ankara', *Mediterranean Politics,* vol. 5, no. 3, autumn 2000, pp. 31–53; and the Turkish *Defence White Paper 2000,* part 2, section 1, 'Turkey's viewpoint on NATO,

Western European Union and the European Security and Defence Identity',
which comments on Turkey's desire for full membership of the EU and WEU,
associate membership being a step on the path to full WEU membership.

212. See Turkish Ministry of Foreign Affairs, Press Release following the Helsinki Summit, December 1999, online at http://www.gov.tr/grupb/ba/baa99/December/default.htm#bm09.

213. Bailes and Messervy-Whiting, 'Death of an institution', p. 63. See A. Jacomet, 'Le dialogue Méditerranéen de l'UEO', in M. Ortega (ed.) 'The future of the Euro-Mediterranean security dialogue', *Occasional Paper,* no. 14, Paris: WEU ISS, 2000, pp. 15–19, for details of the WEU's Mediterranean Dialogue activities and the challenges of maintaining the dynamism of its own initiative in the face of EU and NATO engagement in the region.

214. See C. Echeverria, 'Cooperation in peacekeeping among the Euro-Mediterranean armed forces', *Chaillot Paper,* no. 35, Paris: WEU ISS, February 1999, p. 32; and S. Biscop, *Euro-Mediterranean Security: A Search for Partnership,* Aldershot: Ashgate, 2003, p. 52.

215. One British Member of Parliament went so far as to suggest, as late as November 1998, that PfP 'and many other organisations do not have a cat in hell's chance of long-term success unless the WEU is strengthened' M. Hancock, House of Commons, *Hansard,* vol. 319, 11 November 1998, cols. 283–305.

216. *The WEU Today,* Paris: WEU, 2000, p. 19.

217. WEU Council of Ministers, *Porto Declaration,* 16 May 2000.

218. WEU Assembly, *The Implementation of the Common European Security and Defence Policy,* doc. A/1720, pp. 15 and 17.

219. French Defence Minister Richard, cited 16 October 2000 in WEU Assembly, *The Implementation of the Common European Security and Defence Policy,* doc. A/1720, p. 14.

220. See TEU, Title V, Article 21.

221. See HCDC, 'European security and defence', HC 264, col. 81.

222. G. Andréani, 'Why institutions matter', *Survival,* vol. 42, no. 2, summer 2000, p. 88.

223. HCDC, 'European security and defence', HC 264, col. 82.

224. WEU Assembly is used throughout for ease of referencing.

225. S. Hürsoy, *The New Security Concept and German-French Approaches to the European 'Pillar of Defence' 1990–2000,* Marburg: Tectum, 2000, p. 153.

226. The Lisbon Special Session of the Assembly and Standing Committee included the chairs of the Foreign Affairs, European Union Affairs and Defence Committees of national parliaments, as well as representatives from the Russian and European parliaments and NATO's parliamentary assembly. WEU Assembly, *European Security and Defence: The Parliamentary Dimension,* Report of Proceedings, Lisbon, 21 March 2000, online at http://www.docstoc.com/docs/74503512/European-security-and-defence-the-parliamentary-dimension.

227. See Mrs Lalumière's EP draft report of 6 October 2000 and the report of Mr Brok, Chair of the Foreign Affairs Committee of the EP, of 16 October 2000, referenced in WEU Assembly, *The Implementation of the Common European Security and Defence Policy,* doc. A/1720, pp. 15–16.

228. WEU Assembly, *The Implementation of the Common European Security and Defence Policy,* doc. A/1720, pp. 16 and 19.

229. WEU Assembly, rapporteur Mr de Puig, *The Consequences of Including Certain Functions of WEU in the European Union—Reply to the Annual Report of the Council,* doc. A/1689, 5 June 2000.

230. EP, 'Resolution containing the European Parliament's proposals for the Intergovernmental Conference', A5-0086/2000, 13 April 2000, online at http://www.europarl.europa.eu/igc2000/offdoc/offdoc0_0_en.htm.

231. WEU/EU Secretary General Solana, speech at the Institut für Europäische Politik, Berlin, 17 December 1999, cited in Oakes, *European Defence*, p. 37.
232. WEU Assembly, *The Implementation of the Common European Security and Defence Policy,* doc. A/1720, p. 5.
233. See WEU Assembly, rapporteur Mr Marshal, *Security and Defence: The Challenge for Europe after Cologne,* doc. 1662, 19 October 1999.
234. K. Schake, A. Bloch-Lainé and C. Grant, 'Building a European defence capability', *Survival,* vol. 41, no. 1, spring 1999, pp. 33–4.
235. WEU Assembly, *The Implementation of the Common European Security and Defence Policy,* doc. A/1720, p. 3.
236. WEU Council of Ministers, *Marseille Declaration,* 13 November 2000.
237. The WEU MAPE mission concluded at the end of May 2001, the EU having taken over much of the funding of the operation.
238. These provisions were all approved at Nice.
239. The Marseille Declaration noted the extension of the WEAG's membership to 19, including Austria, Finland, Poland, Hungary, the Czech Republic and Sweden as full members.
240. Signed 26 February 2001, and entering into force in February 2003, its key purpose was to deal with the institutional decision-making processes required pre-enlargement. 'Treaty of Nice Amending the Treaty on European Union, the Treaties Establishing the European Communities and Certain Related Acts', *Official Journal* C 80, 10 March 2001.
241. The PSC replaced the PoCo of Directors from national Foreign Ministries which had developed out of the EPC process. For a discussion of the development and role of the PSC see J. Howorth, 'The Political and Security Committee: a case study in supranational inter-governmentalism', *Les Cahiers européens de Sciences Po,* no. 1, Paris: Centre d'études européennes at Sciences Po., 2010. The EUMC and EUMS were not specifically identified in the treaty but appeared in the Presidency Report along with other organizational provisions that it was deemed did not require treaty change, and about which there was some reluctance amongst non-allied EU-states. Missiroli, 'ESDP—how it works', p. 65.
242. European Council, Nice, 7–9 December, *Presidency Conclusions,* Part IV, annex VI, 'Presidency Report on the European Security and Defence Policy', reproduced in Rutten, 'From St Malo to Nice', pp. 172–3.
243. Extracts from the NAC Final Communiqué, Brussels, 14–15 December 2000, reproduced in Rutten, 'From St Malo to Nice', pp. 222–5. Wider political and security dialogue with Russia, Ukraine and other states (including Canada) was envisaged at Nice; ESDP operational participation arrangements for these states had been agreed at the preceding Feira meeting. That Russia was to be offered monthly consultations with the PSC enraged Turkey, for whom two meetings per Presidency were offered in the 15 + 6 format. S. Tofte, 'Non-EU NATO members and the issue of inclusivity', in Howorth and Keeler (eds) *Defending Europe,* p. 147.
244. On Nice see J. W. De Zwann, 'Foreign policy and defence cooperation in the European Union: legal foundations', in Blockmans (ed.) *The European Union and Crisis Management,* pp. 17–36; A. Missiroli (ed.) 'Coherence for security policy: debates—cases—assessments', *Occasional Paper,* no. 27, Paris: WEU ISS, May 2001.
245. S. Duke, 'After the applause stops: Nice's aftermath and the prospects for CESDP', *Eipascope,* no. 1, 2001, pp. 24–6, online at http://www.eipa.eu/files/repository/eipascope/scop2001_1colour.pdf.
246. These agencies would sit under the authority of the EU's Council of Ministers, a status they would formally adopt in January 2002.

247. P. Schmidt, 'The compatibility of security organizations and policies in Europe', in H. Gärtner, A. Hyde-Price and E. Reiter (eds) *Europe's New Security Challenges,* London: Lynne Rienner, 2001, p. 157.

248. See S. Duke, 'CESDP: Nice's overtrumpeted success?', *European Foreign Affairs Review,* vol. 6, no. 2, summer 2001, p. 24, on this 'lost opportunity' at Nice.

249. The lack of reference to NATO in the Marseille Declaration, other than to declare the end of consultation, is an interesting omission given the consistent referencing of the significance of the WEU's dual roles in all previous statements.

250. HCDC, 'European security and defence', HC 264, col. 80.

251. Stef Goris, then President of the WEU Assembly, comments on the WEU's 'brutal collapse' in his foreword to A. Dumoulin, *Union de l'Europe Occidentale: La Déstructuration (1998–2006),* Paris: Éditions Brylant, 2005.

252. Bailes and Messervy-Whiting, 'Death of an institution', p. 47.

253. G. Messervy-Whiting, 'The European Union's nascent Military Staff', *RUSI Journal,* vol. 145, no. 6, December 2000, pp. 21–6.

254. The joint WEU-NATO troop-less exercise in preparation for a WEU-led CJTF operation was conducted on 11–15 June 2001, despite the WEU's transferral of its operational competence to the EU. See Joint WEU/NATO Press Release, 'Western European Union-led Combined Joint Task Force related exercise (Joint Exercise Study 2001)', (2001) 081, 5 June 2001.

255. Bailes and Messervy-Whiting, 'Death of an institution', pp. 73–4. For a discussion of their early development see B. Müller-Wille, 'For our eyes only? Shaping an intelligence community within the EU', *Occasional Paper,* no. 50, Paris: EU ISS, January 2004.

256. See the SatCen homepage for up-to-date review, online at http://www.satcen. europa.eu/.

257. See *The European Union Institute for Security Studies 2002–2006: Five Years for the EU,* Paris: EU-ISS, 2006. In its 20th year, its 10th as an EU agency, the Institute's new Director spoke of his intention 'to be true and pay tribute to its WEU roots' in his vision for its future development. A. Missiroli, 'EUISS 2.0: back to the future', *Analysis,* 20 December 2012, online at http://www. iss.europa.eu/publications/detail/article/euiss-20-back-to-the-future/.

258. Solana, speaking at the first joint meeting of the iPSC and the North Atlantic Permanent Council on 19 September 2000, cited in WEU Assembly, *The Implementation of the Common European Security and Defence Policy,* doc. A/1720, p. 3.

259. A. Deighton, 'The European Security and Defence Policy', *Journal of Common Market Studies,* vol. 40, no. 4, November 2002, pp. 728–30.

260. For details of the NATO-EU interface see J.-V. Haine, 'ESDP and NATO', in Gnesotto (ed.) *EU Security Policy,* pp. 131–44.

261. At the 10 October Defence Ministerial in Birmingham (UK), Cohen had given US support to the CESDP, 'not grudgingly, not with resignation, but with wholehearted conviction', although he emphasized the indivisibility of transatlantic security and saw ESDP as existing 'under the umbrella of NATO itself: separable, but not separate'. See his speech, 'Meeting the challenges to transatlantic security in the 21st century: a way ahead for NATO and the EU', transcribed in M. Oakes, *European Security and Defence Policy,* Research Paper 01/50, House of Commons Library, 2 May 2001, p. 45; and his remarks to the WEU's Transatlantic Forum, Washington, DC, 28 June 2000, online at http://www.useu.be.

262. Yost, 'U.S.-European capabilities gap and the prospects for ESDP', p. 97.

263. A. La Guardia and M. Smith, 'France snubs America over Euro army', *The Telegraph,* 7 December 2000, online at http://www.telegraph.co.uk; and see

discussion in Sloan, *NATO, the European Union, and the Atlantic Community,* pp. 195–6.

264. See G. Jones and A. Evans-Pritchard, 'Chirac angers Blair by backing EU army', *Telegraph,* 8 December 2000; and A. La Guardia and G. Jones, 'Euro army is a threat to NATO, says US', *Telegraph,* 6 December 2000.

265. The Final Communiqué of the NAC Ministerial Meeting of 15 December 2000 laid out a final framework proposal for co-operation, including an enhanced DSACEUR command role for European operations, awaiting Turkish consent.

266. The *ad hoc* operational compromises witnessed in the Kosovo extraction force command arrangements, whereby a French 'lead' officer reported through the AFSOUTH commander to SACEUR, had evident limitations. See Schake et al., 'Building a European defence capability', pp. 35–7.

267. Brenner, 'Europe's new security vocation', p. 48.

268. J. Peterson and M. Pollack, 'Introduction: Europe, America, Bush', in J. Peterson and M. Pollack (eds) *Europe, America, Bush: Transatlantic Relations in the Twenty-first Century,* London: Routledge, 2003, p. 2.

269. I. H. Daalder, 'The United States and Europe: from primacy to partnership?', The Brookings Institution, Washington, DC, 11 June 2001, p. 15, online at http://www.brookings.edu/views/articles/daalder/useuropechapter.pdf.

270. G. Lundestad, *The United States and Western Europe since 1945: From "Empire" by Invitation to Transatlantic Drift,* Oxford: Oxford University Press, 2005, p. 271.

271. Daalder, 'The United States and Europe', pp. 15–19. Hamilton's analysis of the Clinton/Bush approach to the ESDP suggests a 'consistent' but 'shallow' ambivalence, where 'conditional support' reflects an intense (and not well-understood) level of domestic debate. See D Hamilton, 'American perspectives on the European Security and Defence Policy', in J. Pilegaard (ed.) *The Politics of European Security,* Copenhagen: Danish Institute for International Studies, 2004, pp. 143–58. See 'Doubts on both sides of the Atlantic', *The Economist,* vol. 358, issue 8215, 31 March 2001, pp. 45–6, online at http://www.economist.com/node/555350.

272. See Blair's statement to the House on the Nice European Council, House of Commons, *Hansard,* vol. 359, 11 December 2000, col. 349–50.

273. Bush, from transcript of Bush/Blair news conference following their first Camp David meeting, 23 February 2001, cited in Sloan, *NATO, the European Union, and the Atlantic Community,* p. 198. For defence expenditure issues see M. Chalmers, 'The Atlantic burden-sharing debate—widening or fragmenting?', *International Affairs,* vol. 77, no. 3, July 2001, pp. 569–85.

274. See R. E. Hunter, *European Security and Defence Policy: NATO's Companion—or Competitor,* Washington, DC: RAND, 2002, pp. 117–25, on the approach of the new US Administration to the ESDP.

275. J. Burke, K. Ahmed and E. Vulliamy, 'Blair and Bush defy world fury', *The Observer,* 18 February 2001; and R. Norton-Taylor, 'Raid shows Bush-Blair bond on Iraq', *The Guardian,* 19 February 2001.

276. Haine, 'ESDP and NATO', p. 139.

277. For details of the ESDP capability development process see B. Schmitt, 'European capabilities—how many divisions?' in Gnesotto (ed.), *EU Security Policy,* pp. 91–102.

278. Hagman, 'European crisis management and defence', p. 22, notes that the 'Europeans offered more forces to the HFC at the Capabilities Commitment Conference than they had assigned to NATO'.

279. See H.-B. Weisserth, 'The European headline goal: current and future crisis management', in K. von Wogau (ed.) *The Path to European Defence,* Antwerp: Maklu, 2004, pp. 124–6.

280. Kurowska notes that 'traces of this strange origin of civilian missions persist in mandates and planning documents in the form of military terminology such as the concept of operations (CONOPS) and the operational plan (OPLAN)'. X. Kurowska 'The role of ESDP operations', in M. Merlingen and R. Ostrauskaitė (eds) *European Security and Defence Policy: An Implementation Perspective,* London: Routledge, 2008, p. 34.

281. 'Declaration on the Operational Capability of the Common European Security and Defence Policy, Annex II', *Presidency Conclusions,* Laeken European Council, 14–15 December 2001, European Council doc 01/18.

282. On the negotiations and related issues see A. Missiroli, 'EU-NATO co-operation in crisis management: no Turkish delight for ESDP', *Security Dialogue,* vol. 33, no. 1, March 2002, pp. 9–26; and G. Cascone, 'ESDP operations and NATO cooperation, rivalry or muddling through?', in Merlingen and Ostrauskaité (eds) *European Security and Defence Policy,* p. 145.

283. Presidency Conclusions, Copenhagen European Council, 12–13 December 2002, Council of the European Union doc. 15917/02, Brussels, 29 January 2003, para 19.

284. *EU-NATO Declaration on ESDP,* NATO Press Release 142, 16 December 2002.

285. For analysis of the 'success' of Concordia, Althea and other EU military missions see A. Peen Rodt, 'Taking stock of EU military conflict management', *Journal of Contemporary European Research,* vol. 7, no. 1, spring 2011, pp. 41–59.

286. T. Valasek, 'The fight against terrorism: where's NATO?', *World Policy Journal,* vol. 18, no. 4, winter 2001–2, p. 19. NATO's Active Endeavour, a maritime operation in the Mediterranean Sea intended to demonstrate the Alliance's resolve against terrorist activity in the area, was launched in October 2001 and became the first NATO Article 5 operation.

287. The Bush Doctrine was characterized by US moral democratic certitude, the belief in tyrannical evil and the need to counter it with US power, and the requirements of pre-emption in a perilous world. For a thought-provoking discussion see M. T. Owens, 'The Bush Doctrine: the foreign policy of Republican empire', *Orbis,* vol. 53, no. 1, winter 2009, p. 27.

288. See N. Gnessoto, 'Rebuilding', *EU-ISS Newsletter,* 6 April 2003, p. 1.

289. J. Howorth, 'CESDP after 11 September: from short-term confusion to long-term cohesion?', *EUSA Review,* vol. 15, no. 1, winter 2002, p. 1.

290. B. C. Schmidt and M. C. Williams, 'The Bush Doctrine and the Iraq War: neoconservatives versus realists', *Security Studies,* vol. 17, no. 2, April 2008, pp. 191–220, provide insightful analysis of the political forces driving the US intervention. J. Lindley-French, 'Terms of engagement: the paradox of American power and the transatlantic dilemma post-11 September', *Chaillot Paper,* no. 52, Paris: EU ISS, May 2002, suggested that future transatlantic security relations were being called into question by the unilateralism and over-militarism of US policy.

291. See I. Peters, 'ESDP as a transatlantic issue: problems of mutual ambiguity', *International Studies Review,* vol. 6, no. 3, September 2004. p. 393; and S. E. Penska and W. L. Mason, 'EU security cooperation and the transatlantic relationship', *Cooperation and Conflict,* vol. 38, no. 3, September 2003, pp. 255–80.

292. Rumsfeld speaking at a White House press conference in January 2003, where he contrasted the 'old Europe' of Germany and France with a more enlightened or progressive 'new Europe' of largely aspirant CEE states. See 'Plain-speaking Rumsfeld strikes again', *BBC News,* 23 March 2003, online at http://news.bbc.co.uk/2/hi/americas/2843311.stm#sthash.8OaleWBd.dpuf.

293. EU External Affairs Commissioner Chris Patten cited in A. Osborn, 'Dark days for Europe', *The Guardian*, 14 March 2003. For discussion see S. Rohan, 'Of "familiarity" and "contempt": ESDP in the new transatlantic order', in V. Popa (ed.) *New Architecture of Peace*, Timişoara: Central European Academy of Science and Art, 2003, pp. 67–71.

294. Peters, 'ESDP as a transatlantic issue', p. 394.

295. See W. van Eekelen, *From Words to Deeds: The Continuing Debate on European Security*, Brussels and Geneva: Centre for European Policy Studies and Geneva Centre for the Democratic Control of the Armed Forces, 2006, pp. 163–5, on the implications of the NRF for the ESDP.

296. It had been expected that NATO enlargement would slow after the 1999 intake, and the Baltic States saw a 'back door' to NATO through their more likely EU accession. M. Webber, 'NATO enlargement and European defence autonomy', in Howorth and Keeler (eds) *Defending Europe*, pp. 166 and 171.

297. The Convention had been initiated by the December 2001 Laeken Declaration in recognition of the EU's increasing complexity. See R. M. Cutler and A. von Lingen, 'The European Parliament and European Union Security and Defence Policy', *European Security*, vol. 12, no. 2, summer 2003, pp. 1–20, on the EP's influence on the ESDP, including its proposals for the merger of the High Representative and External Relations role.

298. See 'Declaration by the Franco-German Security and Defence Council', Paris, 22 January 2003, in A. Missiroli, *From Copenhagen to Brussels, European Defence: Core Documents,* Paris: EU ISS, 2003, pp. 22–6.

299. See 'Declaration on Strengthening European Cooperation in Security and Defence', Le Touquet, 4 February 2003, in Missiroli, *From Copenhagen to Brussels,* pp. 36–9.

300. 'European Defence Meeting, Tervuren', in Missiroli, *From Copenhagen to Brussels,* pp. 76–80. Also see 'EU military summit: the seven point agreement', *The Guardian*, 29 April 2003.

301. Blair's 'flying visit' to attend the trilateral Berlin Summit of 20 September 2003, at which this agreement was reached, was part of his diplomatic ricocheting over Iraq. See 'Iraq tops agenda at European summit', *BBC News*, 20 September 2003, online at http://news.bbc.co.uk/1/hi/uk_politics/3112860. stm; T. Fuller, 'Summit talk of close European military ties upsets US', *International Herald Tribune*, 17 October 2003.

302. National HQs were to remain the main option for autonomous operations, with the OpCen envisaged as a fall-back position in the absence of a national HQ being identified, particularly for use in civil-military operations. For details of the steps to agreement see van Eekelen, *From Words to Deed*, pp. 162–3.

303. For an insightful collection of papers on the impact of Iraq on transatlantic relations see G. Lindstrom (ed.) *Shift or Rift: Assessing US-EU relations after Iraq*, Paris: EU ISS, 2003.

304. Tony Blair, 'Prime Minister's speech to the Lord Mayor's Banquet', Mansion House, London, 15 November 2004, online at http://tna.europarchive. org/20050302152644/http://www.strategy-unit.gov.uk/output/Page6583.asp.

305. J. Solana, 'The Common Foreign and Security Policy and the European Security and Defence Policy: current status and perspectives', in von Wogau (ed.) *The Path to European Defence*, p. 40.

306. See M. Ortega, 'Beyond Petersberg: missions for the EU military forces', in Gnesotto (ed.) *EU Security Policy*, p. 74.

307. For national perspectives on the Petersberg Tasks see the report *Achieving the Helsinki Headline Goals*, London: Centre for Defence Studies, November 2001.

308. A. Nuutila, 'Missions abroad and complexity of the criminal law frame', AEGIS Research Project, 2012, online at https://sites.google.com/site/arimattinuutila/2012-missions-abroad-and-complexity; and T. Colclough, 'The role of neutrality on Irish defence policy decisions: EU a time for change', *Political Perspectives*, vol. 2, no. 2, 2008, online at http://www.politicalperspectives.org.uk.

309. Constitutional Treaty, Article III-309:1. F. Heisbourg, 'Europe's strategic ambitions: the limits of ambiguity', *Survival*, vol. 42, no. 2, summer 2000, p. 8, noted that the lack of common perception of the Petersberg Tasks, whilst acceptable pre-Helsinki, became increasingly unacceptable as the ESDP took shape.

310. See Howorth, *Security and Defence Policy in the European Union*, pp. 178–206, on the historiography of the debate on the nature of the EU.

311. *A Secure Europe in a Better World, European Security Strategy*, Brussels, 12 December 2003. Also see S. Biscop, *The European Security Strategy: A Global Agenda for Positive Power*, Aldershot: Ashgate, 2005 For concerns regarding a perceived military emphasis in the ESS see R. Whitman, 'Road map for a route march? (De-)civilizing through the EU's security strategy', *European Foreign Affairs Review*, vol. 11, no. 1, spring 2006, pp. 1–15.

312. Deighton acknowledges the importance of 'defining and elaborating a strategic space for the EU as a security actor', both in relation to other international organizations and in accordance with its own requirements of 'institutional coherence, efficiency and legitimacy'. Deighton, 'The European Security and Defence Policy', pp. 719–20.

313. See R. A. Pape, 'Soft balancing against the United States', *International Security*, vol. 30, no. 1, summer 2005, pp. 7–45; S. Walt, *Taming American Power: The Global Response to US Primacy*, New York: Norton, 2005.

314. Solana, *A Secure Europe*, pp. 11–12. *National Security Strategy of the United States of America*, Washington, DC: Office of the President, September 2002. Also see F. Berenskoetter, 'Mapping the mind gap: a comparison of US and European security strategies', *Security Dialogue*, vol. 36, no. 1, March 2005, pp. 71–92.

315. R. E. Hunter, 'External security in the 21st century', in von Wogau (ed.) *The Path to European Defence*, p. 86.

316. Van Eekelen and Blockmans, 'European crisis management *avant la lettre*', p. 51.

317. T. Mühlmann, 'The Police Mission EUPM in Bosnia, 2003–05', in Merlingen and Ostrauskaité (eds) *European Security and Defence Policy*, pp. 43–60; and K. Osland, 'The EU Police Mission in Bosnia and Herzegovina', *International Peacekeeping*, vol. 11, no. 3, autumn 2004, pp. 544–60. The second ESDP police mission in Bosnia, EUPOL Proxima, was launched on 15 December 2003 and, drawing on the experience of EUPM, was the first to be developed from initial concept to deployment. See I. Ionnides, 'EU Police Mission Proxima: testing the "European" approach to building peace', in A. Nowak (ed.) 'Civilian crisis-management the EU way', *Chaillot Paper*, no. 90, Paris: EU ISS, 2006, pp. 69–86.

318. Açikimeşe, 'The underlying dynamics of the European Security and Defence Policy', pp. 130–1.

319. For a regularly updated overview of CSDP missions see 'European Union External Action. Ongoing missions and operations', online at http://www.eeas.europa.eu/csdp/missions-and-operations/.

320. WEU representatives had attended Exercise Gabon 2000 to consider possible EU contributions to peacekeeping in the region in co-operation with the African Union and prepared an evaluation paper in response. WEU Assembly, *The*

Implementation of the Common European Security and Defence Policy, doc. A/1720, p. 6.

321. S. Duke, 'The future of NATO-EU relations: a case of mutual irrelevance through competition?', *Journal of European Integration,* vol. 30, no. 1, March 2008, p. 36.

322. EU states, in various collectives, went on to develop a range of strategic mobility asset co-operation arrangements including the European Air Group, the European Airlift Coordination Centre, the European Sealift Centre, the Movement Coordination Centre Europe (combining the European Airlift and Sealift Centres) and the European Air Transport Command.

323. See Menon, 'Empowering paradise?' p. 233. Van Eekelen refers to the 'picture of leap-frogging organisations', the battlegroups being seen as competition for the NRF, which had challenged the ERRF before it. *From Words to Deeds,* p. 163.

324. On the development of the ESDP's political and administrative governance structures see M. R. Freire, 'The European Security and Defence Policy: history, structures and capabilities', in Merlingen and Ostrauskaité (eds) *European Security and Defence Policy,* pp. 9–24. On civilian crisis-management development see A. Nowak, 'Civilian crisis-management within ESDP', in Nowak (ed.) 'Civilian crisis-management the EU way', pp. 9–37.

325. A WEU CIMIC concept, including Standard Operating Procedures, had been passed to the UN and OSCE in 1999. 'WEU Draft Concept on Civil-Military Cooperation (CIMIC)', WEU Brussels, WEU-DMS 99246, 17 February 1999.

326. Bailes and Messervy-Whiting, 'Death of an institution', p. 62. The WEU antecedents appear to have been largely overlooked in recent studies of the development of the EU's Common Security and Defence Policy (CSDP), the name to be finally adopted for the ESDP area after the coming into force of the Lisbon Treaty in December 2009. See for example M. E. Smith, 'Developing a "comprehensive approach" to international security: institutional learning and the CSDP', in J. Richardson (ed.) *Constructing a Policy-making State? Policy Dynamics in the European Union,* Oxford: Oxford University Press, 2012, chap. 13.

327. The main clauses related to the CFSP/ESDP area may be found in Part 1, Title V, chapter 2, 'Special Provisions', Articles 1–40 (CFSP) and 1–41 (CSDP) of the 'Treaty Establishing a Constitution for Europe', C 310, *EN Official Journal of the European Union,* vol. 47, 16 December 2004, online at http://eur-lex.europa.eu/JOHtml.do?uri=OJ:C:2004:310:SOM:en:HTML.

328. See Article I-41:5 and I-41:6, elaborated on in Article II-312 (on the processes for participation approval) and Protocol 23 (on the criteria for engagement).

329. J. Howorth, 'The Euro-Atlantic security dilemma: France, Britain, and the ESDP', *Journal of Transatlantic Studies,* vol. 3, no. 1, spring 2005, pp. 48–9.

330. The Barnier Report, European Convention Secretariat, Final Report of Working Group VIII on Defence: Michel Barnier, CONV 461/02, Brussels, 16 December 2002; Van Eekelen, *From Words to Deeds,* p. 131; S. Everts and D. Keohane, 'The European Convention and EU foreign policy: learning from failure', *Survival,* vol. 45, no. 3, autumn 2003, p. 173.

331. See A. Missiroli, 'Mind the steps: the Constitutional Treaty and beyond', in Gnesotto (ed.) *EU Security Policy,* pp. 148–9.

332. T. Tiilikainen, *The Mutual Assistance Obligation in the European Union's Treaty of Lisbon,* Helsinki: Ministry for Foreign Affairs of Finland, 2008, pp. 10–12; C. Gourlay and J. Kleymeyer, 'The defence deal in the IGC', *European Security Review,* no. 20, December 2003, pp. 1–3, online at http://isis-europe.eu/sites/default/files/publications-downloads/esr_20.pdf; A. Missiroli, 'The Constitutional Treaty: "enabling text" for foreign policy

and defence', *Analyse,* Paris: EU ISS, 21 October 2004, online at http:// www.iss.europa.eu/fr/publications/detail-page/article/the-constitutional-treaty-enabling-text-for-foreign-policy-and-defence/.

333. A. Missiroli, speaking at the afternoon session, 20 October 2004, cited in WEU Assembly, *Fiftieth Anniversary of the 1954 Paris Agreements,* p. 6.

334. I. Bickerton, 'Dutch find 20 reasons to reject treaty', *Financial Times,* 1 June 2005, online at http://www.ft.com/cms/s/0/032daa64-d2c2-11d9-bead-00000e2511c8.html#axzz2FW4ddyqU.

335. W. van Eeklen, *Able and Willing? Does Europe Have the Means to Stage a Military Operation if It Wants To?,* Conference Proceedings, Brussels: Defensiestudiecentrum, 2004, p. 8.

336. See S.-E. Gavrilescu, 'Parliamentary scrutiny of European Security and Defence Policy: is there anybody in charge?', *Perspectives/Review of International Affairs,* no. 22, July 2004, pp. 75–93; and M. Comelli, 'The democratic accountability of the CSDP and the role of the European Parliament', in E. Greco, N. Pirozzi and S. Silvestri (eds) *EU Crisis Management: Institutions and Capabilities in the Making,* Rome: Instituto Affari Internazionali (IAI Quaderni. English series 19), November 2010, pp. 79–99, online at http:// www.iai.it/pdf/Quaderni/Quaderni_E_19.pdf#page=81.

337. As provided for by the Cologne European Council of June 1999, each six-month rotating Presidency also submitted a report to the European Council setting out progress made during its tenure in ESDP matters. with the EP's Subcommittee on Security and Defence submitting its parliamentary response to this report.

338. The Inter-institutional Agreement of May 2006 enhanced this provision in defining a 'forward-looking Council document' on CFSP that was to be transmitted by 15 June each year and would also include 'an evaluation of the measures launched in the year n-1'. The Council also provided the EP with an annual report on progress on external relations.

339. The EP had made a number of efforts to enhance its influence in the CFSP/ESDP building its relations with NATO's Parliamentary Assembly through delegate attendance at its meetings since 2001 and the holding of joint meetings between their relevant committees.

340. See comments by the Vice-President of the EP, Janusz Onyszkiewicz, in WEU Assembly, *Fiftieth Anniversary of the 1954 Paris Agreements,* p. 6. The TEU's Article 46 exclusion of the CFSP from the jurisdiction of the European Court of Justice amounted to a lack of judicial scrutiny that, together with the parliamentary limitations, suggested a 'considerable democratic deficit of the ESDP'. M. Trybus, *European Union Law and Defence Integration,* Oxford: Hart, 2005, p. 107.

341. WEU Council's reply to Assembly Recommendation 695 on Europe's security and defence policy confronted with international terrorism, 3 December 2001.

342. WEU Assembly, rapporteur Mr Liapis, *The Follow Up to the Nice Decisions on the ESDP and the Completion of the Project for European Defence,* doc. A/1733, 18 June 2001, p. 14.

343. WEU Assembly, rapporteurs M. Hancock and G. Santini, *EU and WEU Council Information on European Security and Defence Policy,* doc. A/2059, 3 December 2009, p. 3.

344. For a summary of the Assembly's contribution and reaction to the Convention's proposals, which it saw as 'wholly unacceptable' in the absence of any clear provision for national parliamentary engagement with the CFSP/ESDP area, see the discussion in WEU Assembly, rapporteur Lord Russell-Johnson, *The WEU Assembly: A Tool for National Parliaments,* doc. A/1950, 20 December 2006, pp. 8–9.

345. H.-G. Pöttering, 'European Union common foreign, security and defence policies: contribution of the European Parliament', in von Wogau (ed.) *The Path
to European Defence*, p. 78.

346. See W. Wagner, 'The democratic legitimacy of the European Security and
Defence Policy', *Occasional Paper*, no. 57, Paris: EU ISS, April 2005, p. 23.

347. See *List of WEU Delegations*, online at http://www.weu.int/Delegations.htm.

348. Decision 27, *The European Security and Defence Policy Following EU and
NATO Enlargement*, adopted 4 June 2004; and Decision 28, *The Implementation of Decision 27: Adoption of a Set of Provisional Rules for the Affiliate
Members and Affiliate Associate Members of the Assembly*, 21 October 2004.
These Decisions were further supplemented in 2005. See WEU Assembly, rapporteur J.-G. Branger, *Implementation of Decision 27 and Order 120: Voting
Rights in Committees for Parliamentary Delegations of Permanent Observer
and Affiliate Permanent Observer Countries* (with annexes), doc. A/1897,
13 June 2005.

349. WEU Assembly, *Decision 26 on the Follow up to Order 118 [3 June 2003] on
Security Policy in an Enlarged Europe*, doc. A/1834, 22 October 2003 and see
Order 119 of the same date.

350. This right was also extended to permanent observers in Order 120, adopted
on 29 November 2004.

351. See comments on the Council's 'denial' of rights by Marcel Glesener, President of the WEU Assembly, *Fiftieth Anniversary of the 1954 Paris Agreements*, p. 3.

352. Order 126 adopted by 4 December 2007, see WEU Assembly, rapporteur
J.-P. Masseret, *The Reform Treaty and Europe's Security and Defence—Reply
to the Annual Report of the Council*, doc. A/1979, 4 December 2007, p. 5.
Members would include all EU states, with full participatory and voting rights
other than over the budget, holding of Presidency and Vice-Presidency and
official language recognition (reserved for the 10). *Associate members* would
be NATO non-EU (Iceland, Norway and Turkey) states, with similar rights
to the new members minus the right to membership of Assembly bureaus.
Partners covered the other European countries (Albania, Armenia, Azerbai-
jan, Bosnia and Herzegovina, Croatia, Georgia, Former Yugoslav Republic
of Macedonia, Moldova, Montenegro, the Russian Federation, Serbia and
Ukraine), which had attendance but not voting rights. *Observers* could also
be invited from other parliaments or inter-parliamentary assemblies at the
discretion of the President. See WEU Assembly, rapporteurs J.-P. Masseret and
H. Daems, *Revision of the Charter and Rules of the Assembly*, doc. A/1999
revised, 6 May 2008, and *Overview*, p. 4, online at http://www.assembly-weu.
eu for Assembly memberships within the four newly defined categories of
members, associates, partners and observers.

353. See WEU Assembly, *The European Defence Debate 1955–2005*, Paris: WEU,
2005, for the Assembly's own narrative of its history.

354. See for example the comments of the French Prime Minister François Fillon
as France prepared to take on the Presidency of the WEU for one year from
January 2008 (and of the EU for six months from July 2008) at the Assembly's
plenary session in December 2007, cited in WEU Assembly, *Strategic Choices
for European Security and Defence*, Press Release no. 7, 2008.

355. See references to the findings of the joint French National Assembly and WEU
Assembly Conference, Palais Bourbon in Paris, 5 May 2008, and rapporteur
Ducarme in WEU Assembly, *Strategic Choices for European Security and
Defence*.

356. WEU Assembly, *The WEU Assembly*, doc. A/1950, p. 12.

357. WEU Assembly, *The WEU Assembly*, doc. A/1950, pp. 10–11.

358. WEU Assembly, rapporteurs J. Greenway and P. Wille, *Interparliamentary Assemblies and External Communications: The Experience of the Committee for Parliamentary and Public Relations*, doc. C/2087, 2 November 2010, p. 3.

359. J. Howorth, 'Foreign and defence policy cooperation', in Peterson and Pollack (eds) *Europe, America, Bush*, p. 17; and K. Schake, *Constructive Duplication: Reducing EU Reliance on US Military Assets*, London: Centre for European Reform Working Paper, 4 January 2002.

360. Mathiopoulos and Gyarmati, 'St Malo and beyond', p. 68. By 2004, the President of the WEU Assembly was warning his fellow parliamentarians of the necessity of greater 'harmonisation of defence needs', without which 'the very survival of Europe's defence industry was threatened'. WEU Assembly, *Fiftieth Anniversary of the 1954 Paris Agreements*, p. 4.

361. See for example Collester, 'How defence "spilled over" into the CFSP', p. 386, who discusses the case of European Aerospace, Defense and Space Company (EADS), formed by German Daimler-Chrysler Aerospace and French Aérospace Matra to become the third largest aerospace company next to Boeing and Lockheed Martin.

362. Austria, the Czech Republic, Finland, Hungary, Poland and Sweden joined Belgium, Denmark, Finland, France, Germany, Greece, Italy, Luxembourg, the Netherlands, Norway, Spain, Turkey and the UK.

363. See WEU Assembly, rapporteur Mr Pitscitello, *Arms Cooperation in Europe: WEAG and EU Activities*, doc. A/1800, 4 December 2002, p. 7.

364. Meeting of the WEAG Defence Ministers, *Rome Declaration*, Rome, 16 May 2002.

365. OCCAR, which had taken on a legal identity in January 2001 that allowed it to agree to contracts and employ staff, expanded to include Belgium (2003) and Spain (2005), with programme contributions from Finland, Sweden, Poland, the Netherlands, Luxembourg and Turkey. The LoI 'Framework Agreement Treaty', signed on 27 July 2000, aimed to establish the political and legal framework necessary to facilitate industrial restructuring and to promote a more competitive and robust European defence technological and industrial base in the global defence market.

366. J.-F. Morel and A. Cameron, 'The EU and defence capabilities: charting the course', in 'European defence capabilities: no adaptability without co-operation', *RUSI Occasional Paper*, March 2010, p. 4, online at http://www.rusi.org/downloads/assets/European_Defence_Capabilities.pdf.

367. HCDC, 'European security and defence', HC 264, col. 78.

368. Trybus, *European Union Law and Defence Integration*, p. 105.

369. See EDA homepage for its mission and recent developments, online at http://www.eda.europa.eu/info-hub/news, and see EDA *Bulletin*, no. 1, December 2005, for an upbeat presentation of its achievements in its first year, online at http://www.eda.europa.eu/docs/documents/Bulletin_1.pdf.

370. 'Closure of WEAG', WEAG website, 30 March 2005, online at http://www.weu.int/weag/.

371. This information has been drawn from the 'Facts and figures' overview, previously on the WEAO website, online at http://www.weao.weu.int/site/index.php.

372. The exclusion of 'arms, munitions and war materials' from competition rules by TEC Article 223, had been retained in the re-numbered Article 296 following the modifications made by the 2007 Amsterdam Treaty. The provision in the post-Amsterdam TEU that 'the progressive framing of a common defence policy will be supported, as Member States consider appropriate, by co-operation between them in the field of armaments' (TEU Article 17.1, TOA J.7.1) had done little to influence behaviours in this regard.

373. J. Mawdsley, 'The gap between rhetoric and reality: weapons acquisition and ESDP', Bonn: Bonn International Centre for Conversion, paper 26, 2002 online at http://www.bicc.de/uploads/tx_bicctools/paper26.pdf.

374. Mr Vigneron in WEU Assembly, *Fiftieth Anniversary of the 1954 Paris Agreements*, (third day) Palais du Luxembourg, 22 October 2004, p. 10.

375. See Turkish Ministry of Foreign Affairs, *The European Union Common Security and Defence Policy (CSDP) and NATO-EU Strategic Cooperation*, online at http://www.mfa.gov.tr/iii_-turkey_s-views-on-current-nato-issues.en.mfa.

376. M. Cebeci, 'NATO-EU co-operation and Turkey', *Turkish Policy Quarterly*, vol. 10, no. 3, fall 2011, p.100.

377. P. Sturm, 'NATO and the EU: cooperation?', *European Security Review*, no. 48, February 2010, online at http://www.isis-europe.eu/sites/default/files/programmes-downloads/2010_artrel_445_eu-nato-capabilities.pdf.

378. The Treaty of Lisbon amending the TEU and the Treaty Establishing the European Community, adopted at the Lisbon Summit, 18–19 October 2007, signed 13 December 2007, and in force 1 December 2009. See J. W. Zwaan, 'Foreign policy and defence cooperation in the European Union: legal foundations', in Blockmans (ed.) *The European Union and Crisis Management*, pp. 28–36 on Lisbon's CFSP/CSDP-related details.

379. See 'Consolidated Versions of the Treaty on European Union and Treaty on Functioning of the European Union Signed on 13 December 2007', *Official Journal of the European Union*, C326, 26 October 2012, pp. 1–390, online at http://eur-lex.europa.eu//legal-content/EN/TXT/?uri=CELEX:12012M/TXT.

380. TEU Article 42:1 on Petersberg Tasks, Article 45 on EDA and Article 46 on Permanent Structured Cooperation. See S. Biscop and J. Coelmont, *Permanent Structured Cooperation for Effective European Armed Forces*, Egmont Security Policy Brief 9, Brussels: Egmont, 2010.

381. As Commission members were forbidden from holding positions in other institutions, little thought appeared to have been given to the WEU, which was to function with only an acting Secretary General, the WEU Secretariat head Arnaud Jacomet, until its final demise.

382. Bailes and Messervy-Whiting, 'Death of an institution', p. 54, suggest that it was the failure of the EU to advance the CSDP beyond the 'Lisbon formula' which gave the UK the confidence to abandon the WEU, which had previously acted as a 'buffer' against any EU competitive or communitarian interests in defence.

383. Created in May 1989 by the Speakers of the Parliaments of the EU member states, COSAC was intended to strengthen the role of national parliaments in relation to EU matters by bringing together their Committees on European Affairs to promote information exchange between the European and national parliaments. Its non-binding contributions may also be submitted to the Council and Commission.

384. WEU Assembly, *The Reform Treaty and Europe's Security and Defence*, doc. A/1979, Recommendation 812, p. 2.

385. Presentation about the Assembly released by the WEU Assembly's Press and Information Office, http://www.assembly-weu.org/en/presentation.

386. WEU Assembly, *The Reform Treaty and Europe's Security and Defence*, doc. A/1979, p. 2.

387. O. Topala, 'How common is CSDP? Solidarity and mutual defence in the Lisbon Treaty', *European Security Review*, International Security Information Service Europe, Brussels, Briefing 4, April 2011, p. 3, online at http://www.isis-europe.eu/sites/default/files/programmes-downloads/2011_artrel_631_esr53-briefing4-solidarity-mutuality.pdf. Also see House of Lords, *European Union*, 10th Report, session 2007–8, for the UK reaction especially in relation

to 'Article V' and the relationship to NATO, online at http://www.publications.parliament.uk/p/ldselect/ldeucom/62/6202.htm.
388. Tiilikainen, *The Mutual Assistance Obligation*, p. 13. J. H. Matlary, *European Union Security Dynamics in the New National Interest*, Basingstoke: Palgrave Macmillan, 2009, pp. 23 and 72–3, argues that it was in the interests of the big states to 'share risk, cost and blame and legitimize the use of force' through the ESDP in this new 'de-territorialized' security environment.
389. The Director of the Council Legal Services had determined that, whilst of the 'utmost symbolic and political importance to the EU', the new clause did not transform the EU into a military alliance, amount to a mutual defence clause nor make any change to the 'respective position of each member state *vis-á-vis* NATO'. J.-C. Prins, *The Constitution for Europe—a Legal Analysis*, Cambridge: Cambridge University Press, 2006, p. 161.
390. In response to the Madrid bombings of 11 March 2004, the European Council had adopted a Common Declaration that largely reproduced the solidarity commitment. See Missiroli, 'Mind the steps', p. 148.
391. For an analysis of the significance of the 'solidarity' clause see S. Myrdal and M. Rhinard, 'The European Union's Solidarity Clause: empty letter or effective tool', *UI Occasional Papers*, no. 2, Stockholm: Swedish Institute of International Affairs, 2010, online at http://www.societalsecurity.eu/uplcads/UIOP%20 2%202010%20Myrdal%20Rhinard%20EU%20Solidarity%20Clause.pdf
392. Written Ministerial Statement, House of Commons, *Hansard*, vol. 508, 30 March 2010, col. 103.
393. Bryant stated that the annual cost to the UK of the Assembly amounted to €2m, although this included the WEU total cost; the Assembly costs amounted to €1.1m per annum and might be considered a relatively small cost for the provision of parliamentary oversight of a major policy area. 'WEU: ten jointly announce dissolution of Western European Union', *European Defence and Diplomacy*, Brussels: Agence Europe SA, 7 April 2010.
394. The FCO encouraged pre-election agreement on WEU withdrawal, given the costs to its budget of what was perceived of as a redundant organization. Bailes and Messervy-Whiting, 'Death of an institution', p. 53.
395. Replacing the two-directional bridge or pivot image of the UK's foreign policy posture with the more multi-relational concept of a 'global hub' (David Miliband, 2008) or 'network' (William Hague, 2010), consecutive Foreign Secretaries appeared to lean increasingly and uncritically US-wise in their foreign policy direction. See Harvey, 'Perspectives on the UK's place in the world', p. 15; and A. Menon, 'Between faith and reason: UK policy towards the US and the EU', *Briefing Paper 03*, London: Chatham House, 2010, p. 2.
396. 'Letter from David Miliband MP, Secretary of State, Foreign and Commonwealth Office, to the Chairman', House of Lords European Union Select Committee, 20 May 2010, online at http://www.parliament.uk/documents/lords-committess/eu-sub-com-c/cwm/CwMSelectDec09-April Ofinal.pdf.
397. The UK Government deposited its 'denunciation' of the Brussels Treaty with the Belgium Government on 7 May 2010, to be recorded as of 30 June 2010 and to take effect exactly one year later. FCO, *The Supplementary List: Treaty Ratifications, Accessions, Withdrawals, Etc.*, Treaty Series no. 20 (2010) no. 1, Cm 7952, October 2010, pp. 122–4.
398. Bryant, Written Ministerial Statement, *Hansard*, 30 March 2010.
399. House of Commons, *Hansard*, vol. 508, 6 April 2010, col. 800.
400. Senior British official, Chatham House, London, May 2011. See 'Letter to the Chair of the House of Commons European Scrutiny Committee from David Lidington MP, Minister for Europe, 15 July 2010', in House of Lords European Union Committee, 7th Report of Session 2010–2011, *Future*

inter-parliamentary scrutiny of EU foreign, defence and security policy, HL Paper 85, London: The Stationary Office, January 2011, Appendix 2, p. 11, where he states that 'one of the prime drivers behind Member State's decision to wind up the WEU was its poor cost-effectiveness'.

401. The Foreign Secretary assured the Committee that his views were shared 'privately' by a majority of WEU member states, who agreed that the WEU should close. Miliband's letter to the Chairman of the House of Lords European Union Select Committee, 20 May 2010.

402. *Statement of the Presidency of the Permanent Council of the WEU on Behalf of the High Contracting Parties to the Modified Brussels Treaty*, Brussels, 31 March 2010.

403. *Statement of the Presidency*, author's italics.

404. See WEU Assembly (Parliamentary and Public Relations Committee reports from the 59th Session), rapporteurs J. Greenway and P. Wille, *Interparliamentary Assemblies and External Communications: The Experience of the Committee for Parliamentary and Public Relations,* doc. C/2087, 3 November 2010, (cited p. 6), and rapporteur M. Karamanali, *Implementing the Lisbon Treaty: Ongoing Debates in the National Parliaments on Monitoring CSDP,* doc. C/2088, 3 November 2010, which offer useful summaries of national concerns regarding future parliamentary oversight of the CFSP/CSDP.

405. Address by the Presidency of the Assembly at the Opening of the 58th Session of the Assembly, Paris, 15 June 2010, transcribed in *European Yearbook,* vol. 58, Leiden: Martinus Nijhoff, 2010.

406. See R. Walter, 'Preserving democracy: parliamentary scrutiny of EU Security and Defence Policy', *RUSI Newsbrief,* vol. 30, no. 3, May 2010, pp. 1–2.

407. WEU Assembly, rapporteurs M. Karamanli and H. Daems, *CSDP Monitoring by National Parliaments and in the European Parliament—Reply to the Annual Report of the Council,* doc. A/2069, 15 June 2010.

408. WEU Assembly, *Interparliamentary Assemblies and External Communications,* doc. C/2087, p. 8.

409. Cited in 'WEU: ten jointly announce dissolution of Western European Union'.

410. See Letter to the Chair of the House of Commons Foreign Affairs Committee (HCFAC) from Mr William Cash MP, Chair of the House of Commons European Scrutiny Committee, 16 December 2010, in House of Lords European Union Committee, 'Future inter-parliamentary scrutiny', p. 13: 'Doing nothing was an option; but, if national parliaments left a vacuum, the European Parliament would move to fill it'.

411. These Conferences had brought together the chairpersons of the national parliamentary committees with the chairs of the relevant committees of the EP.

412. Also see the e-mail to the Chair of the HCFAC from Robert Walter, President of the ESDA, who argued for retention of a small specialist secretariat, a published report to be provided for this new grouping by the High Representative and provision to be made for *ad hoc* committees on specific CFSP issues. Reproduced in HCFAC, 'Future inter-parliamentary scrutiny', p. 12.

413. The concept of an Interparliamentary Conference had been approved at their Brussels meeting in April 2011, with COSAC concurrence, but full agreement on all aspects had not been reached. 'Presidency Conclusions of the Conference of Speakers of the European Union Parliaments, Warsaw, 20–21 April 2012', online at http://isiseurope.files.wordpress.com/2012/04/con clusions_en_fr1.pdf. Also see COSAC, 'Contribution of the XLV COSAC, Budapest, 29–31 May 2011', online at http://www.cosac.eu/documents/ contributions-and-conclusions-of-cosac/.

414. P. Worré, 'Parliamentary scrutiny of CSDP: creation of a new Inter-parliamentary Conference', International Security Information Service, Brussels, 27 April

2012, online at http://isiseurope.wordpress.com/2012/04/27/parliamentary-scrutiny-of-csdp-creation-of-a-new-inter-parliamentary-conference/.

415. Comelli, 'The democratic accountability of the CSDP', p. 94.

416. See 'Conclusions of the Inter-parliamentary Conference for the Common Foreign and Security Policy and the Common Security and Defence Policy, Pafos, 9–10 September 2012', online at http://www.eerstekamer.nl/eu/documenteu/_conclusions_of_the_inter/f=/vj2vlqcybgjc.pdf.

417. For discussion see J. Wouters and K. Raube, 'Europe's Common Security and Defence Policy: the case for inter-parliamentary scrutiny', *Working Paper*, no. 90, Leuven Centre for Global Governance Studies/Institute for International Law, University of Leuven, April 2012, online at http://ghum.kuleuven.be/ggs/publications/working_papers/new_series/wp81–90/wp90.pdf.

418. J. Solana, 'Ten years of European Security and Defence Policy', *ESDP Newsletter*, Special Edition, October 2009, p. 10. See Address by the Presidency of the Assembly at the Opening of the 58th Session of the Assembly, Paris, 15 June 2010, transcribed in *European Yearbook*, vol. 58, p. 160, where he notes that the European External Action Service was still to be set up, the new double-hatted High Representative and the President of the Council were still to 'get to grips with their positions and tasks', and permanent structured co-operation was 'in dire straits'. Battlegroups hadn't been used, Berlin Plus was in disarray, and the EDA had not 'tapped' its potential.

419. Views expressed at Chatham House, International Security Programme Seminar, 'The demise of the Western European Union: lessons for European defence', 10 May 2011. See J. Shea, 'Keeping NATO Relevant', Carnegie Endowment for International Peace, *Policy Outlook*, April 2012, for a good overview of Alliance issues in advance of the Chicago NATO Summit, taking place May 2012.

420. J. Howorth, 'NATO and ESDP: institutional complexities and political realities', *Politique Ètrangère*, vol. 4, 2009, pp. 95–106, online at http://www.cairn.info/revue-politique-etrangere-2009-5-page-95.htm.

421. 'NATO and the EU: a rowless summit', *The Economist*, 20 November 2010, blog online at http://www.economist.com/blogs/charlemagne/2010/11/nato_and_eu.

422. See NATO's new *Strategic Concept for the Defence and Security of the Members of the North Atlantic Treaty Organization—Active Engagement, Modern Defence*, Lisbon: NATO, 19 November 2010. NATO's new mandate included crisis management and co-operative security alongside collective defence, although allied contention over NATO's primary focus remained as nations increasingly took an 'á la carte' approach to engagement. See M. Ducasse and S. Santamato, *The Evolving Relevance of NATO's Article 5, Ten Years after 9/11*, Center for Transatlantic Security Studies, Institute for National Strategic Studies: National Defence University, 8 September 2011.

423. Taking office in 2009, Obama joined his Russian counterpart President Dmitry Medvedev in signing the New START strategic nuclear arms reduction agreement on 8 April 2010, and whilst missile defence was to prove a more divisive issue, the door was opened for discussion on a co-operative arrangement. See S. Pifer, 'New START: Good News for U.S. Security', *Arms Control Today*, Washington, DC: Arms Control Association, May 2010, online at http://www.armscontrol.org/act/2010_05/Pifer; and S. Pifer, *Missile Defense in Europe: Cooperation or Contention?*, Brookings Arms Control and Proliferation Series, no. 8, Washington, DC: Brookings Institute, May 2012, online at http://www.brookings.edu/research/reports/2012/05/08-missile-defense-pifer.

424. For a discussion of the various interpretations of this change in French policy see B. Irondelle and F. Merand, 'France's return to NATO: the death knell for ESDP?', *European Security*, vol. 19, no. 1, March 2010, pp. 29–43.

425. Franco-British Summit Declaration on Security and Defence Cooperation, 2 November 2010. The British Prime Minister, David Cameron, described the deal as a 'practical, hard-headed agreement between two sovereign countries', intended to enhance both joint and independent capability and subsequently the interest of their allies. 'Britain and France sign landmark 50-year defence deal', *The Guardian*, 2 November 2010, online at http://www.guardian.co.uk/politics/2010/nov/02/britain-france.

426. Biscop identifies the range of characterizations of the EU as an agent that consciously seeks to use its power in a distinct manner from the US, with the EU being defined variously as a militarily disinclined 'soft power'; a non-expansive 'civilian power'; a value- and idea-changing 'normative power'; a political, economic or social model exporting 'transformative or structural power'; or a power projection-averse 'tranquil power' or 'puissance tranquille'. 'The ABC of the ESS: ambition, benchmark, culture', in Blockmans (ed.) *The European Union and Crisis Management*, p. 57.

427. Bailes and Messervy-Whiting, 'Death of an institution', p. 69. Messervy-Whiting noted that it was wise 'not to be too open about borrowings from WEU because of the scepticism the WEU triggered in some quarters', cited in rapporteur B. Gomis, *The Demise of the Western European Union: Lessons for European Defence*, London: Chatham House, 10 May 2010, p. 5, online at http://www.chathamhouse.org.uk.

428. K. Bassuener and E. Ferhatović, 'The ESDP in action: the view from the consumer side', in Merlingen and Ostrauskaité, *European Security and Defence Policy*, p. 186.

429. See F. Hoffmeister, 'Inter-pillar coherence in the EU's civilian crisis-management', in Blockmans (ed.) *The European Union and Crisis Management*, pp. 157–80.

430. French Foreign Minister Michel Barnier, speaking at Quai d'Orsay, 21 October 2004, in WEU Assembly, *Fiftieth Anniversary of the 1954 Paris Agreements*, p. 8.

431. Bailes and Messervy-Whiting, 'Death of an institution', p. 81, argue that the MBT notion of a truly 'defence' role for community Europe ran the risk of 'more adversarial relations with neighbours and placing perhaps intolerable strains on its internal consensus, let alone its resource implications'.

432. This includes the post-1997 accession states to NATO (1999, 2004, 2009) and the EU (2004, 2007); the two organizations now have 21 member states in common.

433. A. Dumoulin, 'The activities of WEU', *European Navigator*, for Centre Virtuel de la Connaissance sur l'Europe (CVCE), Luxembourg, December 2009, p. 4, online at http://www.ena.lu/activities_weu-2-35591.

434. Gomis, 'The demise of the Western European Union'.

435. A. Toje, 'The EU, NATO and European defence: a slow train coming', *Occasional Paper*, no. 74, Paris: EU ISS, December 2008, p. 19. S. Ülgen, 'How Turkey wants to reshape NATO', *Europe's World*, June 2011, online at http://carnegieeurope.eu/publications/?fa=44205, provides analysis of the current state of Turkish alliance thinking.

436. Retiring US Defence Secretary Robert Gates cited in I. Traynor, 'US defence chief blasts Europe over NATO', *The Guardian*, 10 June 2011, online at http://www.guardian.co.uk/world/2011/jun/10/nato-dismal-future-pentagon-chief. Also see 'Libya, Europe and the future of NATO: always waiting for the US cavalry', *The Economist*, 10 June 2011, online at http://www.economist.com/blogs/charlemagne/2011/06/libya-europe-and-future-nato; and E. Hallams and B. Schreer, 'Towards a post American Alliance? NATO burden-sharing after Libya', *International Affairs*, vol. 88, no. 2, March 2012, pp. 313–27.

437. Reverse Berlin Plus describes a posited arrangement by which the EU's extensive civil-military resources and planning capability might be drawn on by NATO. Favoured by the US, this concept was rejected by the French and other EU members who feared NATO encroachment into the EU's security sphere. J. Varwick and J. Koops, 'The European Union and NATO—"shrewd interorganizationalism" in the making?', in K. E. Jorgensen (ed.) *The European Union and International Organizations,* London: Routledge, 2009, pp 118–19.

438. For discussion of the continuing challenges see S. J. Smith, 'EU–NATO cooperation: a case of institutional fatigue?', *Journal of European Integration,* vol. 20, no. 2, July 2011, pp. 243–64.

Conclusions

The WEU, an organization with a broad security remit, had a life history that spanned the building of the contemporary European security order from its post-war origins. This study began by asking what the WEU had been intended for, what explained its development and what had been its contribution to the security of Europe. Disparagingly referred to by some as the 'What Earthly Use', the institution suffered consistently from a reputation that underestimated the significance of the role it played in the construction and maintenance of the European security architecture. This through-life examination of the WEU has reappraised its role, from its WU pre-existence derived from the original Brussels Treaty of 1948 to its gradual deconstruction and demise in 2011. Situating the WEU's development in terms of its contribution to the European security order, this study has not simply addressed the dry institutional issues of declarations of intent, organizational structure, function and capabilities. Rather, it has taken a broader approach to understanding the institutional development and role, which places the WEU in the context of the evolving security environment within, and by which, its adaptation was set. As an international organization, the WEU was a product of a complex of cross-cutting factors, most evidently national interests and perspectives, but also organizational trends and structural shifts at the international level. The central contention of this analysis is that the manner in which the WEU evolved and devolved was largely determined by the dominance of two central dynamics in the European security context, to which it was intrinsically connected: the first was the requirements of the transatlantic collective defence alliance, NATO, and the second, the development of a European security dimension within the larger remit of European construction. It was around these two drivers of change that national security preferences jostled and coalesced. As a hybrid organization, formed to support both alliance and integration, WEU development was sensitive to the requirements of each, and, consequently, its history reflects these pressures and provides an indicator of the path of developments in the Alliance and Community context.

It has been the contention of many authors that the WEU was, in some way, caught by the gravitational pull of NATO and the EC/EU as the primary agents of these two constituencies of defence and integration. What this study demonstrates is that the WEU, as a hybrid organization, was not hampered by but rather was animated in response to that 'pull', as states sought to utilize the institution as a means of satisfying their often conflicting interests in these two dynamic processes.

The origins of the WEU's hybrid nature were examined in Chapter 1, with the WU debates demonstrating the prevalence of the two 'big ideas' of collective defence and European integration in the thinking of the original planners. Collective defence was seen as an immediate priority in the post-war period, but low-politics co-operation was also recognized as a means of providing broader-based structural security, most significantly through economic development. Imagined within a single European constituency for co-operation, and with no broad integrative blueprint, these two ideas were seen as complementary elements of a new security order as expressed through the defence and integrative objectives outlined in the 1948 Brussels Treaty of Economic, Social and Cultural Collaboration and Collective Self-Defence. That the ideas became unlinked was largely a product of the structural realities of the time. Europe's inability to provide effectively for its own defence created a fault line between defence and integration, and led to the establishment of a distinct transatlantic defence constituency in the form of the NATO alliance. At the same time, British rejection of the integrative model combined with French fears of untried supranationalism to channel European integrative efforts down the 'low-politics' route provided by the developing EC. Inheriting the WU's dual nature, the WEU acknowledged the dominance of the NATO Alliance and the evolving European Communities as the primary organizations of defence and integration respectively. Pre-destined, therefore, to be a secondary institution, the WEU's core and enduring objective became to support those primary organizations, a continuity of purpose evidenced by the declaratory statements of the WEU over its lifetime.

Judging the WEU's success solely in terms of its own functional development therefore would miss the point that, as the institution evolved and devolved over time, its *ad hoc* adaptations were largely determined by the interests of states in the primary institutions, rather than any self-perpetuating institutional ambitions for the WEU itself.[1] The early transference of its cultural responsibilities to the Council of Europe; its promotion of arms co-operation through its 'rival', the IEPG; and, most evidently, its self-dissection during its final years, leading to its eventual demise, illustrate the essentially supportive nature of this 'ego-free' institution. The WEU consistently ceded functions to more effective players and acted only in a reserve capacity, performing 'first aid' on the other players when required and restricting itself to those activities necessary but unpalatable to the rest of the 'team'.[2]

The significance of the WEU's role as a 'secondary' or support organization should not be underestimated. The maintenance of an effective European security order required the efficient functioning of the primary organizations for defence and integration. That support was required was demonstrated by the manner in which the WEU was utilized throughout its existence to pursue interests which could not be managed directly within the primary organizations but which, if disregarded, threatened the stability of the security system. The WEU served to oil the workings of both alliance relations within NATO and the integrative process in Europe, acting in a support role at times of crisis or stagnation. With a core membership of key European states that, following British entry into the EEC in 1973, were part of both the Alliance and the Community, but excluding the US and the European neutrals, the WEU provided a vehicle for engagement and action that could not be conducted elsewhere. Equipped with a broad security mandate, it facilitated intergovernmental European decision-making on security-related areas including defence, which was excluded from the Communities context and problematic in an alliance dominated by the US. In so doing, it enabled co-operation on security and defence issues that might otherwise compromise consensus in either of the primary organizations.

Both NATO and the evolving Communities suffered from the members' lack of a shared perspective on the requirements of and for alliance and the desired nature and scope of integration. Diverse national interests created tensions between states in their pursuit of their own preferred vision of the nature of these arrangements. Disagreements over US leadership, burden-sharing and perceptions of threat were perennial NATO challenges, whilst disputes over decision-making integration, sectoral expansion into the foreign policy domain and the 'militarization' of civilian-power Europe plagued EC/EU development.

The WEU's contribution to the maintenance and vigour of the Atlantic Alliance took a number of forms, with NATO's stilted, but life-long, engagement with the WEU demonstrating the latter's continuing relevance to Alliance interests. Alliance politics had been dominated by the uneven relationship between the US and its allies, as much as by the common external threat; US hegemony dictated that the needs of NATO were to be prioritized over the development of other institutions. In this light, the WEU might be seen as simply a reflection of the requirements of alliance management, lending support at times of intra-alliance tension or crisis. In 1948 the WU had provided the 'show of commitment' necessary to engage the US in a defence alliance, with NATO adopting many of the largely defunct institution's defence structures. The establishment of the WEU was a reaction to the prevalence of a commonly perceived Soviet threat, and the requirement for a German contribution to the strength of the US-dominated Atlantic Alliance on which European defence was seen to depend. As a means of reassurance for Europeans nervous about West German rearmament, the WEU's new arms control function and UK commitment to continental defence enabled the necessary strengthening of NATO, to which the WEU abdicated the implementation of its mutual defence clause.

In the following decades, recognition of the structural dependency of Europe on the US ensured the essential stability of the NATO alliance. The WEU was to contribute to that stability by providing a non-competitive European 'talking shop' for issues of alliance interest, a pressure valve for airing sporadic tensions and a forum for inclusion of the truculent French following their withdrawal from NATO's integrated military structures in 1966. Tensions within the Alliance grew, however, in the 1980s, resulting from the aspirations of an economically ascendant Europe, the growth of which had been facilitated in no small part by the Atlantic Alliance arrangement. The reactivated WEU was the means by which those aspirations were acknowledged, but without the damage to Alliance interests that might have resulted from the emergence of a more exclusive or rigid arrangement in Europe. Developing its political function as a forum for debate and a mouthpiece in communication with the Alliance, the revitalized WEU was the vehicle by which disaffected Europeans could articulate their common concerns regarding nuclear policy, arms control and an Alliance structure that did not reflect the political realities of the decade. Fearful that ambitions regarding an eventual Community-based defence alternative to NATO might precipitate a premature US withdrawal, Atlanticists also recognized that US domestic support for NATO required a clearly perceived European commitment to a transatlantic defence arrangement that was increasingly regarded as anachronistic. Acknowledging the continuing primacy of the Alliance in defence, the WEU provided the means by which potentially destabilizing European concerns regarding the transatlantic defence relationship could be articulated in a conservative and generally un-presupposing manner, facilitating a necessary, but problematic, readjustment in European influence within the Alliance. The WEU adopted the unenviable task of promoting demonstrable, but non-competitive, European capability enhancement in defence to accompany the European 'voice' in the Alliance, a requirement of a new partnership of costs and benefits. In so doing, it facilitated institutional and cultural change within NATO and contributed to the emergence of a European pillar within the confines of a recognizable, if perhaps less rigid, Alliance structure.

The WEU's subsequent development was very much a part of this process of acceptable Alliance redefinition—where NATO cohesion and effectiveness would depend on the constant rebalancing of its internal mechanisms for allied influence and co-operation. As an expression of a complementary, indeed integral, ESDI within the Alliance, the WEU was to demonstrate the practical operational benefits of a NATO-lite option for the pursuit of out-of-area defence interests. WEU operational possibilities were enhanced through the development of intelligence, planning and asset-sharing arrangements, as a consequence of a NATO-WEU relationship forged over decades of common purpose. As the EU took over the 'defence' mantle from the WEU, it was inheriting a legacy of transatlantic co-operation that, in its self-important rejection of the WEU's diplomatic method, it would do well not to discard.

Also tasked with promoting the 'progressive integration of Europe', the WEU must be seen as an element of the developing dynamic of Europe-building, a process which sought, by constitutional and functional means, to enhance the integration of the states of Europe to form an eventual continental Union which might in time possess the full gamut of supranational powers and attributes. The lack of a consistent and agreed vision for this eventual union did not prevent incremental community-building, as well as some evolutionary integrative leaps. Intended to promote security through the establishment of an interdependent network of common and collective interests, the development of a distinct European security dimension within this wider process had long been an issue of debate. The 1948 Brussels Treaty, as a collective European security commitment, was the first diplomatic move in this direction: the WU, whilst intergovernmental in design, had a broad brief in terms of promoting European co-operation, including in defence. Given the acceptance of NATO predominance in the defence field and the failure of the European Defence Community efforts of the early 1950s, the WEU became the means of accommodating the highest level of defence 'integration' possible in a European context, although US dominance and the Soviet threat ensured that the WEU's defence role quickly lost its political impetus. As European integration found expression in the less contentious areas of low politics, the WEU provided a vehicle for political co-operation and dialogue, facilitating the rapprochement of former wartime adversaries and drawing together national parliamentarians in security and defence dialogue, when it was clearly off the agenda of the evolving Communities. At the same time, in providing a core state forum for discussion of collective integrative interests, it was able to facilitate a political engagement amongst European states that promoted the passage of British entry into the Communities in 1973.

With 'low-politics' integration taking place within the Communities context throughout the following decade, the MBT kept alive the promise of a European collective defence commitment. At the same time, the ceaseless work of the WEU Assembly and its inter-parliamentary committees, active even during the WEU's 'somnolent' years, enabled the gradual development of a culture of collective European discussion of security and defence issues, otherwise consistently excluded from the Communities forum. As Community consensus for an assault on the sovereignty of states in the 'high-politics' area of foreign, security or defence policy was lacking, attention turned to the WEU as a means of exerting some enhanced level of European influence on the external world. And so, from its re-awakening in 1984, the WEU, with its constituency of core European powers, was to perform the security functions that could not be achieved through the Community's EPC process, promoting a European consensus on security necessary for the furtherance of the unification project. As the focus for this effort, the WEU served to separate defence from the evolving integration process, avoiding the negative 'spill-back' that this contentious area of inter-state co-operation might create. The WEU became the core of an emerging European Security and Defence Identity, reflecting the limits of integration and the failure of the Community to meet the security and defence desires of many of its core members. Their unfulfilled aspiration found fruit in the development of an operationally capable WEU, with the first concerted post-war European military action taking place in the Gulf in 1987–8.

With the WEU holding the 'defence' role in trust until such time as a consensus could be reached on a fully competent EU, the Maastricht agreement on a CFSP had opened the way for EU-directed action, under WEU auspices, in police and maritime operations in support of EU policy. Throughout the first decade of the post-Cold War era, the WEU was to provide the practical, doctrinal, experiential and motivational example of both the possibilities and limits of collective European security action. In the absence of an EU member-state agreement on the desirable way forward, the intergovernmental WEU, with its crisis-management and humanitarian task-based orientation, became the proving ground of a European security and defence capability. By piecemeal enhancement of European collective activity in this area, the WEU facilitated an incremental transition of the integrating Europe from a civilian to a militarily competent power. With the 'brakes' finally removed at St Malo, 'defence' was to become the final piece of the European security policy jigsaw, equipped with the structures and commitment required, if not necessarily sufficient, to satisfy the collective security ambitions of the Union. And the WEU had all but fulfilled its purpose: as its organs were variously harvested or cloned over the following years, the relevance of its achievements could not be denied, offering as it did many of the mechanisms through which the new Security and Defence Policy of the EU could be exercised. The final compromise, reached at Lisbon, completed the process of 'assimilation', as the states of the EU found sufficient consensus to commit to an ambiguous mutual 'defence' and a democracy-lite defence scrutiny provision that cleared the way for the WEU's final demise.

That the EU eventually took up the CSDP area, complete with its own military and civil security apparatus, was not determined by the WEU. But this minor organization did enable the gradual development of consensus, supported by practical example, on the scope of a security and defence competence for the EU. Without the compromise developments in European security and defence co-operation facilitated through the WEU over time, it seems unlikely that the EU could have found the internal agreement for its eventual integrative 'leap' into the realm of high politics. That the CSDP remains an essentially intergovernmental arena is reflective of the most profound challenge of the integrative dynamic, the core assault on state sovereignty in defence, which had led to its initial separation from the integrating space, and the subsequent formation of the WEU. The WEU's reserve role was consistently predicated on the expectation that a European security dimension would find its proper place within the broader integration project as it evolved from Communities to Union. That the development of the

EU's security and defence competence will face challenges, many of which were encountered by the WEU before it, is surely inevitable. But with the adoption of a defence role, the torch was finally passed to the EU, and the WEU's task in promotion of that objective was completed.

The history of the WEU, examined in the context of the wider European security environment, demonstrates therefore that it had a significant role to play in supporting both the NATO alliance and the European integration project. It also serves to illuminate how the WEU's development was driven by the dynamic processes at play between alliance and community, where development in one arena impacted on the other, and where the institution-specific interests of states were inevitably complicated by this linkage. Atlanticist/Europeanist perceptions of the desired future construction of the European security space illustrated what appeared to be frequently conflicting objectives. Europeanist dissatisfaction with defence dependency, and aspirations for greater international influence, not least through the eventual development of a European security and defence capability, spurred US resentment of perceived anti-Americanism amongst its 'ungrateful' allies and had the potential to undermine US support for the Alliance. In turn, Atlanticist appeasement of US interests discouraged the promotion of European options for security and defence, where unrealizable pretensions might precipitate a potentially catastrophic American decoupling.

With a foot in both the NATO and EC/EU camps, the hybrid WEU was an institutional representation of the idea that alliance and integrated community need not be competitive or exclusive concepts. Its representation of the mutual benefits of co-operation facilitated a convergence of interests less palatable in the context of the higher-profile organizations. The WEU acted as both a bridge and a buffer between NATO and the EC/EU; its core membership joined the two constituencies and enabled a level of co-operation to emerge without the political challenges of a direct link, which might otherwise present a challenge to institutional principles.[3] For example, US acceptance in the mid 1990s of the CJTF concept of 'separable but not separate' NATO forces releasable for WEU operations, the predecessor of the Berlin Plus agreement on EU access to NATO assets, was predicated on the assumption of WEU subordination and its support as a European pillar of the Alliance. For the EU, on the other hand, the WEU's institutional distance ensured that arrangements for release of NATO military assets did not compromise the EU's status as a major civilian power but offered the realistic possibility of European-led operations under WEU auspices. The WEU equally demonstrated that the Europeanization of security, where it had practical outcomes in terms of enhanced security and defence competence, was not only compatible with, but also desirable from, an Alliance perspective. A representative alliance of common interests would be infinitely stronger than one riven by division and resentment of a US leadership position no longer necessitated by relative power or a commonly accepted existential threat. If the alliance was to remain healthy, a collective European voice, even one that occasionally challenged US positions, was a necessary element. The enhancement of European civil crisis-management competencies, as initially demonstrated by WEU police actions, supported Alliance defence activities, and a more competent Europe would also be a more competent partner, able to take its part of the defence burden, to share tasks where the US chose not to act and to offer real operational support through more efficient use of defence resources. And, just as in 1948–9, the American public, and hence Congress, could not help but be encouraged by Europe's efforts in support of what were, in general, US interests overseas, efforts that visibly demonstrated European political will. Always a difficult line to walk, the WEU's hybrid character as an Alliance-friendly promoter of European integration had enabled it to take the small steps towards the realization of a European CSDP alongside a reinforced and reinvigorated NATO.

As a result of this complex interplay of interests, the WEU's functional development frequently represented both the lowest common denominator and the highest point of compromise between states as they sought to encourage or prevent activity that might promote their interests within the primary institutions. In meeting demands that were both complementary and diverse, the WEU often accommodated apparently irreconcilable images of European security and defence. Hence, its political activity was first promoted by the British to enhance their prospects of EEC membership but was dropped once that ambition had been realized, only to re-emerge in the 1980s in response to increasing transatlantic tensions within the Alliance. The development of the WEU's operational activities in the late 1980s was intended as a means to divert less-favoured NATO 'out-of-area' proposals, and, later, it offered an alternative to the possible integrative direction of the Franco-German defence relationship of the 1990s.

The pursuit of activities in the WEU did not, therefore, necessarily suggest a high level of common motivation or objective, but rather a convergence of interests, where the apparently contradictory aspirations of the Atlanticists and Europeanist found common ground in the actions of this convenient second-best institution. And so, for example, the promotion of the WEU's operational development was a consequence of the convergence of interests of those who sought to enhance the Alliance and those who sought to counter it by the eventual development of a European alternative. By offering some level of co-operation within the WEU, an acceptable compromise could be reached, resulting in incremental change acceptable to all. In this way, the WEU prevented stagnation or regression in the primary organizations, whilst facilitating a staged development of function that was to provide the example for future primary organization development.

The ideational lens through which states perceived their interests in terms of the two dominant security dynamics of defence and integration provided a framework of assumptions regarding the preferred constituency, method and scope of security co-operation which underlay rational self-interest choices. That these preferences were influenced by both domestic political considerations and structural change in the system is evident. However, it has also been noted that the WEU itself contributed to shifting state perceptions as, over its extensive lifetime, it nurtured the dual role of alliance and community promotion that it had been ascribed. As a representation of these twin and common interests, the WEU facilitated the development of a culture of European security and defence co-operation among European elites which was responsive to both alliance and integrative needs and, in turn, influenced state preferences not only regarding the WEU's role but also in their engagement with the primary security organizations themselves. The recognition of shared interest, of mutual sensitivity and common bonds, represented by the compromises sought and achieved within the WEU, contributed to a pragmatic engagement between these two organizations, initiated in Washington in 1999, the continuation of which will be a determining feature of the future security order of Europe.

Clearly, areas of inter-organizational tension remain, in questions of institutional primacy, of political integrity and institutional autonomy, of differentiated roles and commitments and of de-linked memberships and cross-constituency antagonisms. The proximity of the new EU-NATO relationship may be the greatest challenge for these two organizations, now lacking the cushioning effect of the diplomatic WEU in the management of these often highly charged political differences. The WEU provided a convenient vehicle at a distance from the EU and NATO, and consequently from those difficult areas of principle, and this enabled states to utilize it for various national purposes, without the costs of too close an association with either. The low-key nature of the organization, with its broad and inclusive memberships, its extensive security and defence agenda and its mutual engagement with the EU and NATO constituencies, enabled a level of co-operation that the political rigidity of NATO and the EU might well preclude. This rigidity may have both inter- and intra-institutional consequences. The inter-institutional challenges of separate and defined political identities have found expression in the stalled process of sharing assets under Berlin Plus as mutual exclusions prevent effective dialogue and co-operation. Within the EU itself, as the CSDP becomes central to the EU's identity, the potential costs of failure have constrained enthusiasm for action,[4] whilst the increasingly complex and heavy machinery of the post-Lisbon security and defence policy area is some way removed from the inclusive, light and institutionally simple structures of the WEU which it has replaced.[5] That the EU was eventually to find a WEU-esque resolution to the problem of consensus on a 'mutual assistance' clause for the Union is perhaps a reflection of its maturity, and a recognition that institutional robustness, fixed structures and too clear an institutional identity may actually inhibit intergovernmental consensus-making, where national political will is just as, if not more, important as capabilities to securing action.

Practical co-operation in European security and defence has consistently required a level of flexibility and political 'vagueness', where motivation and objective could be variously interpreted. The WEU's real strength lay in its constructive ambiguity, consequent upon its dual support role. Essentially the WEU was a chimera, with states seeking to identify with it in terms of their own preferences for the development of the security structures of Europe. It is true that 'negative' perceptions led at times to a resistance to its use; its somnolent period during the 1970s was a consequence of French resistance to its perceived Atlanticism and the British belief that it had inherently Europeanist pretensions. However, the dual-facing nature of the organization, serving as it did both alliance and community, did enable a convenient convergence of interests to emerge in terms of activity, despite the contradictions in nationally sought objectives. Consequently, both the Europeanist French and Atlanticist British could promote WEU revitalization and development from the 1980s, each choosing to identify with the institution in terms of their stated preferences for the future security order. The subjective lens through which the WEU was perceived enabled the French to identify the WEU as the embryo of a developing European defence identity, a contribution to European integration and a challenge to American hegemony in the Alliance. For the British it would be a means of restricting the widening of the integrative process to include defence by providing an alternative, Alliance-friendly vehicle for intergovernmental European defence co-operation, necessary to ensure a healthy rebalancing of the NATO alliance. That the WEU could be selectively perceived and defined enabled compromise, resulting in the incremental undermining of tensions between various interests as essentially unintended convergence resulted in positive developments for all.

The hybrid nature of the organization and the ambiguity of its position were its positive and enduring characteristics. Its ability to be all things to all people, to bend and adapt to meet interests that were at times inherently conflictual, 'oiled the works' of the broader security framework. On the one hand, the WEU had been the means of managing inter-state diversity in both transatlantic defence and European integration, preventing stagnation in both processes. On the other, it had a significant role in resolving or satisficing the contradictions or tensions that emerged from the relationship between the Atlantic and European processes, for states, between states and between institutions. Acting as a pivot, the WEU joined together the Atlantic and European constituencies of alliance and integration, enabling both to develop and transform without disconnecting one from the other. The WEU's intergovernmental nature, its cross-cutting and inclusive memberships, its fundamental ambiguity and widely cast core functions made it a forum for 'safe' multilateralism. Selective interpretation of its activity, resultant from its ambiguous nature, enabled the highest point of compromise and co-operation in the promotion of European security interests without undermining either of the primary organizations. As a support organization, developed in response to the changing needs of the system, the WEU was an essential contributor to the establishment of the European post-war security order and facilitated the transition of that order to meet the challenges of a new Europe.

NOTES

1. This assumes that what is 'rational' is determined not only by cost-benefit calculations to maximize value but by bargains negotiated between state preferences, determined by complex social and political factors, by the prevalence of core and competing ideas and by the legacy of institutional and policy form.
2. For discussion of the nature of this support role see G. W. Rees, *The Western European Union at the Crossroads: Between Trans-Atlantic Solidarity and European Integration*, Oxford: Westview, 1998, p. 26; and W. van Eekelen, *Debating European Security 1945–1998*, The Hague: SDU Publishers, p. 79.
3. Its inclusive culture was to be exported through its post-Cold War differentiated memberships and partnerships, and these in turn proved a useful preparation ground for the acceding states of the EU and NATO.
4. C. Bickerton, B. Irondelle and A. Menon, 'Security co-operation beyond the nation-state: the EU's Common Security and Defence Policy', *Journal of Common Market Studies*, vol. 49, no. 1, January 2011, pp. 1–21.
5. J. Cutileiro, 'Death of the WEU—how Brussels shot itself in the foot', *Europe's World*, autumn 2011, online at http://www.europesworld.org/2011/10/01/death-of-the-weu-how-brussels-shot-itself-in-the-foot/#.Uz2aelw_0iE.

Index